ANNUAL REVIEW OF IRISH LAW 1996

UNITED KINGDOM
Sweet & Maxwell
London

AUSTRALIA
LBC Information Services
Sydney

CANADA AND USA
Carswell
Toronto • Ontario

NEW ZEALAND
Brooker's
Auckland

SINGAPORE AND MALAYSIA
Thomson Information (S.E. Asia)
Singapore

Annual Review
of Irish Law 1996

Raymond Byrne
B.C.L., LL.M., Barrister-at-Law
Lecturer in Law, Dublin City University

William Binchy
B.A., B.C.L., LL.M., Barrister-at-Law
Regius Professor of Law, Trinity College, Dublin

Round Hall Sweet & Maxwell
1997

Published in 1997 by
Round Hall Sweet & Maxwell
Brehon House, 4 Upper Ormond Quay,
Dublin 7

Typeset by
Gough Typesetting Services, Dublin.

Printed by
Colour Books, Dublin

ISBN 1-85800-080-7

A catalogue record for this book
is available from the British Library.

Table of Contents

Preface

In this tenth volume in the Annual Review series, our purpose continues to be to provide a review of legal developments, judicial and statutory, that occurred in 1996. In terms of case law, this includes those judgments which were delivered in 1996, regardless of whether they have been (or will be) reported and which were circulated up to the date of the preface. Once again, it is a pleasure to thank those who made the task of completing this volume less onerous.

Mr Justice Brian Walsh (who, as we have mentioned in previous volumes, was the originator of the concept of an Annual Review of Irish Law) continues to be most supportive and we remain very grateful for this. Once again, we are in the debt of a number of people for providing access to library facilities. In particular, Ms Peggy McQuinn, of the Office of the Supreme Court, Ms Margaret Byrne and Ms Mary Gaynor, of the Library of the Incorporated Law Society of Ireland, and Mr Johnathon Armstrong, of the King's Inns Library, were as helpful as ever with a number of difficult queries from the authors. And once again, Ms Jennifer Aston, Librarian in the Law Library, Four Courts, was also especially helpful in facilitating access to statutory material which is otherwise very difficult to source.

We would also like to express our heartfelt thanks to the staffs of the Dublin City University and Trinity College libraries for their assistance in the research for this volume. This ninth volume in the Annual Review series also marks a departure from previous years. The authors are delighted to have had the benefit of specialist contributions on Company Law, Communications, Contract Law, Equity and Restitution included in the volume. The authors continue to take final responsibility for the overall text as in the past, but are especially grateful for the contributions of David Tomkin and Adam McAuley in Company Law, Eamon Hall in Communications, Eoin O'Dell in Contract Law and Restitution, Hilary Delany in Equity and Practice and Procedure.

Finally, we are very grateful to Round Hall Sweet & Maxwell and Gilbert Gough, whose professionalism ensures the continued production of this series.

Raymond Byrne and William Binchy,
Dublin

November 1997

Table of Cases

Table of Legislation

Table of Statutory Instruments

Administrative Law

APPROPRIATION

The Appropriation Act 1996 provided as follows. For the year ended 31 December 1996, the amount for supply grants in accordance with the Central Fund (Permanent Provisions) Act 1965 was £11,043,330,000. Under the Public Accounts and Charges Act 1891, the sum for appropriations-in-aid was £1,018,822,499. A shortfall of £2,000 for the year ended December 31, 1994 was also included. The Act also amended section 135B of the Finance Act 1992 in order to extend the period for repayment of amounts in respect of vehicle registration tax in certain cases. The 1996 Act came into effect on its signature by the President on December 20, 1996.

CIVIL SERVICE

Marriage bar   The Civil Service Regulation (Amendment) Act 1996 is a short Act which brings to an end one aspect of the 'marriage bar'. The 1996 Act repealed section 11 of the Civil Service Regulation Act 1956, as amended by section 4 of the Civil Service (Employment of Married Women) Act 1973. Section 11 of the 1956 Act, as amended, had provided for the re-admission to the Civil Service of certain women who retired from it for the purposes of, on or following marriage. The 1996 Act deletes all legislative reference to the 'marriage bar', by which many women civil servants had been required to resign on marriage. Indeed, the marriage bar extended to the wider public service until its repeal on the State's accession to the European Communities in 1973. The Civil Service Regulation (Amendment) Act 1996 (Commencement) Order 1996 (SI. No. 197 of 1996) brought the Act into force on June 25, 1996. On this area, see generally, Curtin, *Employment Equality Law in Ireland* (Round Hall Press, 1990).

COMPTROLLER AND AUDITOR GENERAL

Additional functions   The Comptroller And Auditor General (Section 21) Order 1996 (SI. No. 70 of 1996), made under the Comptroller and Auditor General (Amendment) Act 1993 (1993 Review, 147-50) amended the 1993

Act in order to include County Enterprise Boards within the Comptroller's remit, with effect from March 12, 1996.

DIPLOMATIC RELATIONS

Diplomatic immunity: European Patent Organisation   The European Patent Organisation (Designation and Immunities) Order 1996 (SI No. 392 of 1996) enabled diplomatic immunity to be conferred on the European Patent Organisation and its officials pursuant to the Diplomatic Relations and Immunities Act 1967. The European Patent Organisation was established pursuant to the European Patent Convention, which was implemented by the Patents Act 1992 (1992 Review, 41-6).

Passport and other fees The Diplomatic and Consular Fees (Amendment) Regulations 1996 (SI No. 203 of 1996) further amended the Diplomatic and Consular Fees Regulations 1982, as amended by the Diplomatic and Consular Fees (Amendment) (No. 3) Regulations 1993 (1993 Review, 6). They discontinued lower fees formerly charged for passports processed in October and November of any year as well as the higher fees for 48-page ('full') passports issued for the unexpired period of an existing passport returned for cancellation or endorsement. They also discontinued completely the service of affixing and endorsing the fingerprints of merchant seamen to seamen's identity cards. The 1996 Regulations were made under the Diplomatic and Consular Officers (Provision of Services) Act 1993 (1993 Review, 5-6) and came into effect on August 1, 1996.

DISCLOSURE OF INTERESTS BY PUBLIC OFFICE HOLDERS

The Ethics in Public Office (Designated Positions in Public Bodies) Regulations 1996 (SI No. 57 of 1996), which specifies those offices other than those expressly referred to in the Ethics in Public Office Act 1995 which come within its terms, was referred to in the 1995 Review, 3.

STATE AGENCIES

ACC Bank plc   Section 9 of the Borrowing Powers of Certain Bodies Act 1996 (see below) provides for an increase in the borrowing limit of ACC Bank plc from the level of £1,400 million (set by the ACC Bank Act 1994) to £2,400 million.

Borrowing powers   The Borrowing Powers of Certain Bodies Act 1996 was enacted principally in order to confirm the legal powers of State bodies to engage in capital financing transactions, including finance leases. (See also the increase to the borrowing limit of ACC Bank plc effected by the 1996 Act, discussed above). The 1996 Act came into effect on August 1, 1996: Borrowing Powers of Certain Bodies Act 1996 (Commencement) Order 1996 (SI No. 232 of 1996). It was explained when the legislation was introduced in the Oireachtas that the existing powers of State bodies to borrow funds were set out in the individual pieces of legislation governing them but that questions had been raised concerning their power to engage in certain capital financing transactions related to their borrowing, in particular finance leases, and about the powers of the Minister for Finance to give State guarantees for them. Arising from these concerns, financial institutions had been reluctant to conclude any more of these leases with State bodies until the legal position is clarified.

It was stated that a finance lease is a common form of asset financing where the asset is purchased by a party, other than the lessee, which, by availing of capital allowances and other matters can reduce the cost of financing to the lessee. The lessee in such an arrangement assumes all the risks and rewards of ownership other than legal title to the asset. A number of State bodies had raised finance in recent years by way of finance leases as an alternative to direct borrowing to purchase assets because they were more cost-effective. Since the borrowing powers of State bodies are principally set out in legislation, a statutory amendment was required to confirm their legal powers to engage in the capital financing transactions specified in the 1996 Act. In particular, the 1996 Act aimed to remove any ambiguity in the meaning of the term 'borrowing' in the legislation governing State bodies. In addition, the opportunity was taken, having regard to the continuing evolution of financial markets and instruments, to confer on State bodies the legal authority, subject to the consent of the Minister for Finance after consultation with the Central Bank of Ireland and the Revenue Commissioners, to have recourse in the future to new financial instruments which become commonplace in financial markets.

Commissioners of Public Works   Section 2 of the Commissioners of Public Works (Functions and Powers) Act 1996 provides that it shall be, and be deemed always to have been, a function of the Commissioners:

    (a) to acquire, maintain and dispose of land and interests or rights in or over land, and other property of any kind and interests in such other property, for use by the State, the Commissioners, another State authority or any other person specified by the Minister for Finance,

    (b) to provide for a State authority or a person specified by the Minister such goods and services as may reasonably be required by the authority or person for the purposes of the functions of the authority or person and

(c) to make schemes or other arrangements for the purpose of providing assistance, whether in the form of money, living accommodation, land or other property of any kind, to persons who suffer undue hardship or personal injury or loss of or damage to land or other property by reason of flooding.

Section 3 of the 1996 Act provides that the Commissioners shall have, and be deemed always to have had, power:

(a) to mortgage land or other property of any kind or otherwise charge land or such other property with the payment of money,

(b) to demolish buildings or structures or other works or other property of any kind and

(c) to carry out development, whether on payment or free of charge, as agents for another State authority, a local authority or a health board or any other person.

These provisions should be seen against the background of the difficulties with the Commissioner's powers indicated by the decision in *Howard v. Commissioners of Public Works in Ireland* [1994] 1 I.R. 101 (1993 Review, 430-4). The 1996 Act came into effect on March 6, 1996 on its signature by the President.

Irish Steel   The Irish Steel Limited Act 1996 gave effect in part to the transaction for the sale of the shares in Irish Steel Limited, held by the Minister for Finance, to Ispat Mexicana SA, in effect the privatisation of Irish Steel. The Act enabled the Minister for Enterprise and Employment to fulfil his financial commitments to Irish Steel Ltd/Ispat Mexicana under the agreement for the sale of the shares of Irish Steel Ltd. The Act also provided for the writing off of a loan of £17 million made by the Minister for Finance in 1985 to Irish Steel Ltd. Section 4 provided that £4,617,000 must be lodged in an escrow account in the joint names of the Minister for Enterprise and Employment and Ispat Mexicana. Section 5 enabled the Minister for Enterprise and Employment to make a once off payment to the trustees of the staff pension fund of Irish Steel Ltd in respect of a deficiency identified during the due diligence process leading to the sale to Ispat Mexicana. Section 7 provided for the continuation of guarantees given by the Minister for Enterprise and Employment to ACC Bank plc and to the European Coal and Steel Community in respect of loans to Irish Steel Ltd from those institutions. The guarantees will have to remain in place until the loans are repaid or the loans are prepaid by Ispat Mexicana. Section 9 provided for the repeal of all previous Irish Steel Acts on a date to be appointed by the Minister for Enterprise and Employment by Order. During the passage of the Act, it was estimated that Exchequer costs amount to £37,273,500 which includes the Government loan of £17 million being written off. The Act, apart from section 9, came into effect on April 30 on the President's signature; section 9 came into effect (with the consequent repeal of pre-1996 Irish Steel Acts) on May 30, 1996: Irish Steel Limited Act 1996 (Section 9) Order 1996 (SI No. 153 of 1996).

Teagasc and Environmental Protection Agency   The Johnstown Castle Agricultural College (Amendment) Act 1996 amended the Johnstown Castle Agricultural College (Amendment) Act 1959 to allow Teagasc, the State agricultural research agency, to dispose of part of Johnstown Estate, Wexford, for use for environmental, heritage, amenity or recreational purposes and to lease part of the Estate to the Environmental Protection Agency (established by the Environmental Protection Agency Act 1992 (1992 Review, 529-34).

JUDICIAL REVIEW

Availability for errors within jurisdiction   In *Ryan v. Compensation Tribunal* [1997] 1 I.L.R.M. 194 (H.C.), Costello P. dismissed various challenges to an award of compensation made by the respondent Tribunal. Nonetheless, his judgment is of great importance in drawing attention to the suggestion that errors which do not go to jurisdiction and which do not come within the category of an error on the face of the record may be amenable to judicial review.

The Tribunal in *Ryan* had been established under a non-statutory scheme intended to compensate those women who had either tested positive for or contracted Hepatitis C from the use of human immunoglobulin Anti-D blood products, used to prevent death arising from rhesus negative births. Under the scheme, compensation was to be paid by the State on an *ex gratia* basis. An award by the Tribunal did not involve a waiver of any right of action and a claimant who received an award had a period of one month from receiving notice of the award in which to decide whether to accept or reject it. If accepted, the claimant was, however, required to agree to waive any right of action which she might otherwise have. Claimants under the scheme could be legally represented, the Tribunal could hear oral evidence, expert witnesses could be called, experts could be appointed to advise the Tribunal, awards were to be on the basis of the principles governing the measure of damages in the law of tort, and in calculating an award the Tribunal could take into account any statutory or non-statutory benefits to which the claimant had or would become entitled or had received or would receive as a result of the condition which gave rise to the claimant's claim. No appeal lay from any award of the Tribunal.

The applicant, a married woman in her 40s with 11 children had been diagnosed positive for Hepatitis C, which the Tribunal found had been contracted as a result of an injection of contaminated anti-D in 1978. The Tribunal also found that her prognosis was poor, that her life expectancy had been shortened and that she would remain incapacitated for work. The Tribunal awarded her £25,000 for future loss of earnings, £35,000 for future home help, £5,000 for nursing care and £140,000 in general damages, brining the total to £205,000. The applicant sought judicial review of the Tribunal's decision, particularly that various headings were of such a low level as to amount to an error on the face of the record and to be unreasonable. It was submitted on the behalf of the tribunal that neither grounds of challenge were applicable in this instance.

Costello P. recited the conventional view in judicial review that, in general, only errors of law going to jurisdiction were liable to being quashed on judicial review. Indeed, he stressed that the court was not hearing an appeal from the award of the Tribunal but was being asked to decide whether its decision was reasonable, as defined in the decisions in *The State (Keegan) v. Stardust Victims Compensation Tribunal* [1986] I.R. 642 and *O'Keeffe v. An Bord Pleanála* [1993] 1 I.R. 39 (1991 Review, 16-18). Costello P. pointed out that the Supreme Court had defined "reasonableness" in such a way as to make clear that a tribunal's decision would not be quashed merely because a court disagreed with it; rather the test was whether the impugned decision plainly and unambiguously flew in the face of fundamental reason and common sense. Thus, the court could not interfere with the decision of an administrative decision-making authority merely on the grounds that it was satisfied that on the facts it would have raised different inferences and conclusions or that the case against the decision was much stronger that the case for it. As to the challenge for error on the face of the record, Costello P. accepted, of course, that a decision could be quashed on this ground even where the Tribunal had acted within its jurisdiction, referring to the Supreme Court decision in *Bannon v. Employment Appeals Tribunal* [1993] 1 I.R. 500 (1992 Review, 401-2), where the views expressed in *R v. Northumberland Compensation Appeal Tribunal, ex p. Shaw* [1952] 1 All E.R. 122 were quoted. Costello P. recited the views of Denning L.J. (as he then was) in the *Northumberland* case to the effect that the error must appear on the face of the record and that as regards civil cases, the 'record' included the document which initiated the proceedings, any pleadings and the adjudications, but not the evidence or the reasons, unless the tribunal chose to incorporate them in its adjudication, in which case if those reasons were wrong in law, *certiorari* would lie to quash the decision.

In the *Ryan* case, Costello P. did not accept that the tribunal had erred either on the ground of unreasonableness or by virtue of an error on the face of the record. Without wishing to minimise the detail examination which Costello P. made of each of the applicants' submissions in this respect, it is sufficient for present purposes to note that he found that none had been made out. However, while at one level, Costello P's judgment amounts to the application of accepted principles of judicial review and administrative law, a passage towards the end of his judgment suggests an entirely different approach which it is necessary to quote *in extenso*. Dealing with a particular ground put forward by the applicant concerning an alleged error on the face of the record, Costello P. rejected the suggested argument completely but noted that, even if it had so erred it was not an error on the face of the record. In addition, he added that an error of law could not be a ground for challenging the decision on the ground of unreasonableness since it did not follow that a tribunal which made an error of law thereby flies in the face of fundamental reason and common sense. He added the following important comment:

> But the law relating to *certiorari* has been developing in England and as a result in particular of two cases decided in the House of Lords (*Anisminic Ltd. v. Foreign Compensation Commission* [1969] 2 A.C. 147 and *R v. Hull University Visitor, ex p Page* [1993] A.C. 682) the English courts will now quash the decision of a tribunal which has made any error of law and it is no longer necessary to show that the error was on the face of the record. If, therefore, I had concluded that the tribunal in this case had so erred, I would have relisted the case to hear further submissions as to whether or not I should apply similar principles in this case.

The significance of this passage lies, of course, in the suggestion that all errors of law may be quashed on judicial review. If applied, this would, of course, involve a profound change in administrative law. It would, of course, conflict with the orthodox view expressed by Costello P. in the *Ryan* case itself, namely that judicial review must be distinguished from an appeal on a point of law. Ultimately, the short passage quoted may not ultimately prove particularly significant, but it indicates, at the least, that at least one member of the Irish judiciary is well aware of the developments taking place in this area in different jurisdictions. It remains to be seen whether this clearly *obiter* comment produces any more significant *dicta*.

We also note here that the Tribunal under discussion in the *Ryan* case was established on a statutory basis in 1997 pursuant to the Hepatitis C Compensation Tribunal Act 1997, which we will discuss in the 1997 Review. Other aspects of the Hepatitis C controversy were discussed in *Roe v. Blood Transfusion Service Board and Ors.* [1996] 1 I.L.R.M. 555 (H.C.): see the Constitutional Law chapter, 139, below. See also the Health (Amendment) Act 1996 (discussed in the Health Services chapter, 405, below). A Tribunal of Inquiry into the Hepatitis C controversy was established in 1996. The Report of the Tribunal, published in 1997, will be discussed in the 1997 Review.

Bias In *O'Dwyer v. McDonagh and Ors*, High Court, October 14, 1996, the applicant unsuccessfully sought judicial review of her failure to secure an appointment to a post in Limerick Regional Technical College, where she had been employed for over 20 years. She had been interviewed by a selection panel but another person had been appointed to the post. The applicant was later told by a third party that two members of the selection panel had initially considered the applicant for appointment to the position, but that they had been dissuaded from this by two other members of the panel, allegedly on the basis that the applicant was 'a trouble maker.' The applicant contended that these views had prejudged her prospective candidacy and amounted to bias which vitiated the appointment process. The respondents denied that that there was any basis for the allegations of bias made against the selection board members. On this crucial issue, Barr J. accepted the respondents' version of events, holding that there was no basis for the applicant's allegations. In any event, he held that judicial review did not lie as the selection board was not exercising a judicial or quasi judicial function, nor was it determining legal rights or obligations, thus following the approach of Keane J. in *Rajah v. Royal College of Surgeons in Ireland* [1994] 1 I.R. 384 (HC); [1994] 1 I.L.R.M. 233 (HC) (1993 Review, 17-18). Nonetheless, like Keane J, he went on to discuss the issues raised in the case.

Barr J. held that publication of the reasons of why one or more members of the selection board believed that a particular candidate was unsuitable for a particular post would be gratuitously unfair and would have served no useful purpose. On this aspect of the case, Barr J. accepted that the members of the selection board were entitled to express a view on the applicant's suitability for the post. In particular, he was of the view that members of the selection board who had a long association with the applicant were 'patently' in a better position to appraise her suitability than other members of the selection board. As it had been conceded that these members of the board had acted bona fide, Barr J. concluded that they were entitled, in the best interests of the College, to express views in favour of a particular candidate. Again, in the absence of *mala fides,* he held that the court would not investigate whether the opinions expressed by the board members were well founded, particularly as there was no evidence that the opinions had overborne the will of the other members of the board. On these grounds, Barr J. refused to set aside the decision of the selection board.

Judicial review and discretion In *Coughlan v. Dublin Corporation*, Supreme Court, March 28, 1996 the Supreme Court noted that since the remedies of *mandamus* and *certiorari* were discretionary, there was no case in law or on the facts *requiring* the High Court to engage in such an enquiry. We note in our discussion of the case in the Transport chapter, 631, below, that these latter comments must, of course, be read subject to the well-established case law, including *The State (Vozza) v. Ó Floinn* [1957] I.R. 227, that in certain circumstances *certiorari* will issue *ex debito justitiae*.

Legitimate expectation   In *Abrahamson and Ors v. Law Society of Ireland* [1996] 1 I.R. 403; [1996] 2 I.L.R.M. 481, the applicants, over 800 under-graduate law students in the State's universities successfully argued in the High Court that they should be granted exemptions under the Solicitors Acts 1954 and 1960 (Apprenticeship and Education) Regulations 1991 from the Law Society of Ireland's 'entrance examination' to its professional course, the FE-1 examination. In *Abrahamson*, the applicants argued that they had a legitimate expectation that they would be exempt from FE-1, since at the time they enrolled for their degrees, Reg.15 of the 1991 Regulations provided that they would be granted such an exemption if they had successfully completed the relevant 'core' law subjects in their law degrees set out in Reg.15. The case would not have arisen were it not that, in *Bloomer and Ors v. Incorporated Law Society of Ireland* [1995] 3 I.R. 14 (HC); Supreme Court, February 6, 1996, it had been held that Reg.15 of the 1991 Regulations was invalid for being in breach of Article 6 of the EC Treaty: see the discussion in the Solicitors chapter, 567, below. In the High Court, McCracken J. engaged in a comprehensive analysis of the existing case law on legitimate expectation. He examined in detail the following decisions: *Schmidt v. Secretary of State for Home Affairs* [1969] 2 Ch. 149 (where Lord Denning MR apparently used the phrase for the first time); *R v. Liverpool Corporation, ex p Liverpool Taxi Fleet Operators' Association* [1972] 2 Q.B. 299; *Council of Civil Service Unions v. Minister for the Civil Service* [1985] A.C. 374 (the *GCHQ* case); *Webb v. Ireland* [1988] I.R. 353; [1988] I.L.R.M. 565 (the Derrynaflan Hoard case: see the 1987 Review, 162-4); *Duggan v. An Taoiseach* [1989] I.L.R.M. 710 (1988 Review, 21-4); *Philips v. Medical Council* [1991] 2 I.R. 115 (1990 Review, 277); *Wiley v. Revenue Commissioners* [1994] 2 I.R. 160; [1993] I.L.R.M. 484 (1992 Review, 8-10); *Hempenstall v. Minister for the Environment* [1994] 2 I.R. 20; [1993] I.L.R.M. 318 (1992 Review, 210-11); and *Tara Prospecting Ltd v. Minister for Energy* [1993] I.L.R.M. 771 (1993 Review, 25-28). In the *Abrahamson* case, McCracken J. confessed that he found it 'difficult to reconcile some of these decisions', though he felt that this was to be expected in the context of an evolving concept. Nonetheless, he was prepared to summarise the cases on the basis of the following principles:

(1) It is now well established in our law that the courts will, as a general rule, strive to protect the interests or persons or bodies who have a legitimate expectation that a public body will act in a certain way.

(2) In protecting those interests, the courts will ensure that, where that expectation relates to a procedural matter, the expected procedures will be followed.

(3) Where the legitimate expectation is that a benefit will be secured, the courts will endeavour to obtain that benefit or to compensate the applicant, whether by way of an order of *mandamus*, provided that to do so is lawful.

(4) Where a minister or a public body is given by statute or statutory instrument a discretion or a power to make regulations for the good of the public or of a specific section of the public, the court will not interfere with the exercise of such discretion or power, as to do so would be tantamount to usurping that discretion or power to itself, and would be an undue interference by the court in the affairs of the persons or bodies to whom or to which such discretion or power was given by the legislature.

In the instant case, McCracken J. stated that it was undeniable that representations had been made to the applicants at the start of their third level studies that they would be entitled to an exemption from the FE-1 examination. It was, he felt, reasonable to infer from such representations that the exemption would remain in force for long enough for them to be taken advantage of by first year students. Thus, he concluded that the applicants all had a legitimate expectation that the 1991 Regulations would remain in force and that they would benefit from them. He concluded that the applicants would, in any other situation, have succeeded on this ground, but because Reg.15 of the 1991 Regulations had been declared invalid in the *Bloomer* case, he felt he could not grant any substantive relief. However, while not prepared to grant mandatory relief, he ultimately held that the position of the 800 applicants constituted 'exceptional circumstances' under Reg.30 of the 1991 Regulations and made a declaration to that effect, which required the Law Society to consider exercising its discretion to grant the applicants the exemptions they would have had if Reg.15 had been a valid subsisting statutory provision. As we noted in the Solicitors chapter, 567, below, the Law Society subsequently decided that all law students attending the previously exempted law degrees at the time of the decision in *Abrahamson* were exempt from FE-1, thus restoring the position prior to *Bloomer*, but only for those already studying for law degrees. For students who began their law studies in universities in the Republic from the academic year 1996-97, there is no longer any exemption from FE-1.

The principles concerning legitimate expectation were also applied by Carroll J. in *Navan Tanker Services Ltd v. Meath County Council*, High Court, December 13, 1996, discussed in the Transport chapter, 632, below.

Reasons for decision   In *Manning v. Shackleton* [1994] 1 I.R. 397 (H.C.); [1994] 1 I.L.R.M. 346 (H.C.); [1997] 2 I.L.R.M. 26 (S.C.), the Supreme Court reversed in part the decision of Barron J. in the High Court (1993 Review, 30-

31) in which he had rejected the applicant's claim that the respondent arbitrator should set out the reasons for his decision. The case arose against the background of an arbitration under the Acquisition of Land (Assessment of Compensation) Act 1919, following the compulsory acquisition of some of the applicant's land. In the course of this arbitration, an unconditional offer was made by the County Council which had compulsorily acquired the land of £175,000, exclusive of costs, in full and final settlement of the applicant's claim. On December 12, 1991 the respondent arbitrator made an award of £156,280. As the award did not exceed the offer which had already been made, the applicant was ordered to pay the costs from the date of the offer. The applicant's solicitors subsequently wrote to the respondent requesting that he furnish a written judgment setting out his findings of fact and of law as well as a breakdown of the content of the award, but the respondent declined. On judicial review, Barron J. upheld this approach. While accepting that a person or body required to act judicially may be compelled on judicial review to state such reasons, he concluded that, in the instant case, the applicant had not indicated how he was likely to suffer prejudice or injustice as a result of the failure to state reasons. However, Barron J. remitted the matter to the respondent arbitrator for a determination of whether the award of costs had been correct. This was not appealed by the respondent, but the applicant successfully appealed to the Supreme Court (O'Flaherty, Blayney and Keane JJ.) on the question of setting out the breakdown of the award itself.

Delivering the only judgment in the Supreme Court, Keane J. described the respondent's functions under the Acquisition of Land (Assessment of Compensation) Act 1919 as 'quasi-judicial in nature'. Quoting with approval a passage from the judgment of Finlay C.J. in *The State (Creedon) v. Criminal Injuries Compensation Tribunal* [1988] I.R. 51; [1989] I.L.R.M. 104 (1988 Review, 17-18), he accepted, as Barron J. had in the High Court, that such a person may be obliged in law to give reasons for his decisions. As already indicated, the Supreme Court held, unlike Barron J, that some form of reasons were required in the instant case.

Nonetheless, Keane J. was in substantial agreement with Barron J. in holding that the *Creedon* principles were inapplicable to arbitrations under the 1919 Act. In particular, he pointed out that by virtue of section 3(3) of the 1919 Act, both the applicant and the acquiring County Council were in a position to ensure that they were aware of what precise sum had been awarded by an arbitrator in respect of each of the headings under which the applicant had presented his claim, so that reasons were not in general required. However, Keane J. differed from Barron J. in holding that different considerations applied to an application by one of the parties to the arbitrator, after the publication of an award, to specify the amount awarded in respect of any particular matter the subject of the award. While he accepted that section 3(3) of the 1919 Act could be read as meaning that such an application had to be made during the course of the proceedings, the construction Keane J. favoured was that the application be made as soon as the arbitrator had made the award, or within a reasonable time thereafter. To the extent that the decision of Davitt P. in *Doyle v. Winters,* High Court, January 14, 1953 (cited in Street, *The Law Relating to Local Government,* p.667) was to the contrary, it must be regarded as having been overruled in *Manning* (though the Court did not expressly do so, bearing in mind in particular perhaps that it was unable to find a transcript of the judgment in the case). Keane J. considered that his preferred interpretation was consistent with the test in *Creedon* of 'justice appearing to have been done'. He thus concluded that:

> a claimant or an acquiring local authority [should] be informed of the specific determination arrived at by the arbitrator in respect of each disputed item. To require the arbitrator to do so would not in any sense be to subvert the finality of his award or to encourage litigation: on the contrary, the legislation expressly envisages that he should do so on request and it seemed immaterial, in this context, whether the request is made during the course of the hearing or after the publication of the award.

Finally, the Court also expressed a clear view that the original offer was not an 'unconditional offer' within the meaning of section 5(1) of the 1919 Act, adopting the views expressed in *Fisher v. Great Western Railway Co.* [1911] 1 K.B. 551 and in McDermott and Woulfe, *Compulsory Purchase and Compensation: Law and Practice in Ireland,* p.191 in this respect. Keane J. commented that, although it was unsatisfactory that this was not raised either in the arbitration or in the High Court, the Supreme Court should express a view on it as the matter was, in any event, being remitted to arbitration, and if the Court were to refrain from making a finding on the matter, it would be to permit the arbitration to proceed on a basis which was wrong in law and to permit a procedural argument 'however cogent, to outweigh the requirements of justice.' This view may be contrasted with the more formal approach adopted by the majority of the Court in *Attorney General (Society for the Protection of Unborn Children Ltd.) v. Open Door Counselling Ltd.* [1994 1 I.L.R.M. 256 (1993 Review, 160-5).

Thus, the Court remitted the case to the respondent to enable him to exercise at his option his discretion to direct the payment of costs under section 5(4) of the 1919 Act having regard to the fact that the original offer was not an 'unconditional offer'.

Admiralty

DECLARATION OF OWNERSHIP

In *Bemis v. Owners and all Persons Claiming an Interest in The RMS 'Lusitania'*, High Court, May 14, 1996, the plaintiff instituted proceedings seeking a declaration that he was the sole and exclusive owner of all rights, title and interest in the RMS 'Lusitania', her hull, tackle, appurtenances, engine and apparel. As is well known, the 'Lusitania' had been sunk off the Old Head of Kinsale on May 7, 1915 with huge loss of life and lay since then in Irish territorial waters. At the time of the sinking, the ship was the property of the Cunard Steamship Co, whose insurers had discharged their liability in full, thereby becoming the owners of the ship. In his application, the plaintiff adduced documents of title establishing that title to the ship had devolved on him, and he also referred to judgments of the courts of England and the United States of America upholding his title. The defendants representing the State did not dispute the plaintiff's claim but counterclaimed for a declaration that they were the owners of the cargo on board the ship and the personal effects of the passengers and crew. Barr J. was satisfied that the documents of title adduced established that the plaintiff was the sole and exclusive owner of all rights, title and interest in the RMS 'Lusitania,' her hull, tackle, appurtenances, engines and apparel. The hearing of the counterclaim by the State was adjourned.

OWNERSHIP OF VESSEL AND TONNAGE

In *MFV Girl Cliona; Nederlandse Sheepshypotheekbank NV v. Owners and all Persons Claiming an Interest in MFV Girl Cliona*, Supreme Court, February 14, 1996, the Supreme Court held, *inter alia*, that the tonnage attaching to a registered fishing vessel should not, in the instant case, be separated from the ownership in the vessel itself. The Court also dealt with the right of arrest of a vessel in an admiralty action *in rem*.

The case arose against the background of a claim by the plaintiff bank, commenced as an admiralty action *in rem*, claiming that there were arrears due on a loan agreement and deed of covenant executed in connection with the vessel in question amounting to 1,287,439 Dutch Guilders. Immediately after the issue of the plenary summons, the bank obtained a warrant for the arrest of the vessel pursuant to O.64 of the Rules of the Superior Courts 1986 and the vessel was duly arrested. The defendant contested the figure claimed in respect of the arrears. In the High Court, Barr J. found in favour of the plaintiff bank to the extent of the uncontested amount of the arrears and ordered that the balance of the bank's claim go for plenary hearing. He also ordered that the vessel be sold by public auction, and that the 93.5 tonnes 'fishing quota' granted to the defendants by the Department of the Marine and attaching to the vessel should not pass under the sale. The bank appealed the latter part of Barr J.'s order. The defendant cross-appealed against that part of the order which had found that the arrest of the vessel was valid, arguing that the arrest had been premature on the ground that the loan agreement provided that, where a demand was made for moneys due, the borrower had three days in which to pay. The Supreme Court allowed the bank's appeal and dismissed the defendant's cross-appeal.

As to the bank's application for arrest, the Court held that it was clear from the deed of covenant that the mortgagee's right to possession arose immediately on the principal and interest becoming repayable on demand and there was no question of the bank having to wait three days before moving to get possession of the vessel. In addition, since the proceedings were an admiralty action *in rem* there was no doubt that once the plenary summons had been issued, O.64 of the 1986 Rules entitled the bank to apply for a warrant to arrest the vessel.

Turning to the issue of the tonnage 'fishing quota', the Court drew a distinction between tonnage and any 'quota' attaching to a vessel. It noted that, for a fishing vessel to be authorised to engage in sea fishing pursuant to the Merchant Shipping Acts 1894 to 1992, the vessel must be registered in the register of fishing boats, and a licence must be granted by the Minister for the Marine in relation to the boat. When a fishing vessel was registered in the register, the boat's gross tonnage was entered on the certificate. The Court noted that it was the policy of the Minister to reduce the total tonnage of the Irish fishing fleet, one consequence being the impossibility for the owner of a fishing boat to obtain a licence unless he could have de-registered an existing ship of equal or greater tonnage in the fleet. Thus, a licence would not be granted for a boat which would have the effect of increasing the size of the fleet. If, when the "Girl Cliona" was sold, the defendant was able to retain its tonnage for the purposes of applying it to another vessel, it would not be possible for the purchaser of the "Girl Cliona" to obtain a licence and retain the boat's place within the Irish fleet. If the declaration made in the High Court order remained, the bank's prospects of being able to get a satisfactory price for the vessel would be greatly reduced. The Court concluded that Barr J. had erred in making the declaration that the 93.5 gross tonnage would not pass under the sale of the vessel. Implicit in Barr J.'s declaration was a finding of fact that a 93.5 'fishing quota' had been granted to the ship's owner by the

Department of the Marine. The Supreme Court noted, however, that the claim made by the defendant was, rather, for the beneficial ownership of the tonnage of the vessel and not for any quota. Since there was no evidence to support Barr J.'s finding, the Court set aside this aspect of his order. In addition, the Court concluded that Barr J.'s order had amounted to an intervention by the courts in a matter which was under the control of the Minister for the Marine and should not have been made without the Minister being represented. When the vessel was sold, it would be for the Minister to decide whether to grant a fishing licence to the new owner and his decision should not be pre-empted by any order of the court.

This aspect of the Court's decision did not avail the defendant, however. The Court concluded that ownership of the tonnage formed part of the bank's security. Even if it were possible to separate the ownership of the tonnage from the ownership of the boat, the ownership of the tonnage would clearly be an interest in the boat and thus would have passed under the deed of covenant, which provided that the owner mortgaged and charged in favour of the bank all his "interest present and future in the mortgaged premises". Since the defendant had a beneficial interest in the tonnage of the vessel it passed to the bank under the terms of the mortgage, whether it arose before or after the date of the mortgage.

The Court did not consider it was necessary to decide whether it was theoretically possible to separate the ownership of the tonnage from the ownership of the vessel as, even if it could be done, it was not possible for the defendant, on the facts of the instant case, to assert such ownership. It would, again in theory, have been possible for the defendant to claim the tonnage and thereby to introduce a different ship into the Irish fleet by having the "Girl Cliona" de-registered and withdrawn from the fleet, but it was precluded from doing so by the deed of covenant under which it had been agreed to keep the ship registered.

TIME LIMITS

Extension In *Carleton v. O'Regan* [1997] 1 I.L.R.M. 370 (H.C.), Barr J. declined to extend the two year time limit prescribed by section 46(2) of the Civil Liability Act 1961 for instituting proceedings in negligence involving vessels where the damage is caused to a vessel by the sole or concurrent fault of another vessel. Section 46(3) of the 1961 Act provides that any court having jurisdiction to deal with such proceedings may, subject to any rules of court, extend the two year period to such extent and subject to such conditions as it thinks fit. The plaintiff was the owner of the 'Una Alan' and the defendant the owner of the 'Janora', both being trawlers. In August 1991, when the plaintiff's trawler was tied up, it was struck by the defendant's trawler which was approaching the quay. The defendant did not deny responsibility for the collision. The damage did not affect the seaworthiness of the plaintiff's trawler and it was decided to defer repairs to it until the annual overhaul. Repairs commenced in October 1992 and the defendant's insurers instructed a surveyor to attend the repairs. By letter of November 1992, the insurer wrote to the plaintiff's insurers stating that the repairs were unreasonable in view of the damage involved and the age of the vessel, and that they would dispute quantum if the full cost of the repairs was sought. In August 1993, the plaintiff's insurers faxed a letter to the defendant's insurers stating that the plaintiff had been fully indemnified for the cost of the repairs and that they awaited full details of the plaintiff's claim for loss of fishing. The letter sought an extension of the statutory time limit which was due to expire later that month. The defendant's insurers responded by fax on the same date that it did not accept that there could be any valid claim for the repairs and that it had sought instructions from the defendant with respect to the extension of the time limit. A later fax of September 1993 informed the plaintiff's insurers that it had no instructions to consent to an extension of the time limit. Against that background, as indicated, Barr J. refused to extend the time limit.

He referred to the principles laid down by Sheen J. in a series of authorities, namely, *The 'Myrto'* [1987] 2 Lloyd's Rep. 1, *The 'Gaz Fountain'* [1987] 2 Lloyd's Rep. 151, *The 'Albany' and The 'Marie Josaine'* [1983] 2 Lloyd's Rep. 195, *The 'Seaspeed America'* [1990] 1 Lloyd's Rep. 150 and *The 'Al Tabith' and The 'Alanfushi'* [1993] 2 Lloyd's Rep 214. Barr J. held that the time limit prescribed by section 46(2) of the 1961 Act will not be extended except in special circumstances. Following Sheen J.'s approach, he considered that persons acting for plaintiffs should either issue proceedings or obtain a firm and clear undertaking that the proposed defendants will consent to an extension of the time limit. In considering whether to grant an extension, Barr J. held that the court will consider the length and cause of the delay, whether the delay was beyond the control of the party who was dilatory, whether the proposed defendants contributed to the delay, and whether, if the extension were granted, justice would be done between the parties. In the instant case, he considered that the letter of November 1992 indicated that a serious dispute existed between the parties on quantum. The fact that liability was not in issue did not, in Barr J.'s view, justify the plaintiff's failure to issue a summons within the specified two year period, as it was clear that the dispute on quantum might not be resolved by negotiation. Since no explanation had been given as to the cause of the delay and there was no evidence that the defendant had contributed to the delay he was not prepared to extend the statutory time limit. Finally, nor did he consider that the correspondence between the parties gave rise to any estoppel in favour of the plaintiff, holding that the decisions in *Doran v. Thomas Thompson & Sons Ltd.* [1978] I.R. 223, *Boyce v. McBride* [1987] I.L.R.M. 95 and *Traynor v. Fegan* [1985] I.R. 586 were not applicable to the instant case.

Agriculture

ABATTOIRS

Offal   The Abattoirs (Control of Designated Bovine Offal) Regulations 1996 (SI No. 106 of 1996) made under the Abattoirs Act 1988 (1988 Review, 37-8), control the removal, storage and use of designated bovine offal. They came into effect on April 22, 1996.

ANIMAL DISEASES

BSE: ban on UK bovine products   The European Communities (Importation of Bovine Animals and Products Obtained from Bovine Animals from The United Kingdom) Regulations 1996 (SI No. 87 of 1996) gave effect to a Commission Decision of March 27, 1996, which in effect imposed a world-wide ban on the export of cattle and bovine products from the United Kingdom arising from the incidence of bovine spongiform encephalopathy (BSE) in United Kingdom cattle herds. The Regulations came into effect on March 28, 1996. The European Communities (Importation of Bovine Animals and Products Obtained from Bovine Animals from The United Kingdom) (Amendment) Regulations 1996 (SI No. 210 of 1996) amended SI No. 87 of 1996, above and gave effect to Commission Decision 96/362/EC of June 11, 1996, involving a partial lifting of the ban, at least in so far as bovine semen was concerned. The original March 1996 ban, and the circumstances in which it was partially relaxed in June 1996, was surrounded by enormous political controversy as well as convulsions in the beef trade throughout Europe, in particular because of the link (announced by the UK government in March 1996) between BSE in beef and the increased incidence of a new variant of the equivalent disease in humans, Creutzfeld Jakob Disease. Previously, this disease had been associated with old age only. Creutzfeld Jakob Disease is now a notifiable disease under the Health Act 1947: see the Infectious Diseases (Amendment) Regulations 1996 (SI. No. 384 of 1996), in the Health Services chapter, 409, below. Discussion of the wider political aspects of the BSE controversy, which continued into 1997, is outside the scope of this Review.

BSE: general controls   Associated with the United Kingdom BSE ban and the 'BSE crisis' generally, a number of further restrictions aimed at increasing consumer confidence in beef products were introduced in 1996. The Diseases of Animals (Bovine Spongiform Encephalopathy) Order 1996 (SI No. 271 of 1996), made under the Diseases of Animals Act 1966, amended the Diseases of Animals (Bovine Spongiform Encephalopathy) Order 1989 and introduced a movement permit system for all female animals moving to premises for slaughter or export, with effect from 16 September 1996. The Diseases of Animals (Bovine Spongiform Encephalopathy) (No. 2) Order 1996 (SI No. 278 of 1996) also amended the 1989 Order and revoked the Diseases of Animals (Bovine Spongiform Encephalopathy) (No. 3) Order 1990. It introduced further controls on the purchase of mammalian meat and bone meal. The use of infected bone meal had been regarded as a cause of BSE infection in cattle. The 1996 Order also provided for the appointment of authorised inspectors and conferred additional powers on the Garda Síochána, with effect from October 17, 1996. The Diseases of Animals (Bovine Spongiform Encephalopathy) (No. 3) Order 1996 (SI No. 415 of 1996) introduced labelling requirements for animal and poultry feedingstuffs which contain mammalian meat and bone meal, with effect from January 1, 1997.

Bees The European Communities (Notification of Varroasis in Bees) Regulations 1996 (SI No. 268 of 1996) gave effect to Directive 92/65/EEC. They require beekeepers to notify suspected cases of varroasis in bees. They came into effect on September 3, 1996.

Bovine brucellosis The Brucellosis in Cattle (General Provisions) (Amendment) Order 1996 (SI No. 86 of 1996), made under the Diseases of Animals Act 1966, amended the Brucellosis in Cattle (General Provisions) Order 1991 (1991 Review, 20) and requires the person in charge of a herd of cattle to have them tested for bovine brucellosis within the period specified by the Minister for Agriculture. The 1996 Order came into effect on April 1, 1996.

Bovine TB The Bovine Tuberculosis (Attestation of the State and General Provisions) Order 1996 (SI No. 85 of 1996), made under the Diseases of Animals Act 1966, increased the validity period of the bovine TB pre-movement test and requires the person in charge of a herd to have them tested within the period specified by the Minister for Agriculture, with effect from April 1, 1996. The Bovine Tuberculosis (Attestation of the State and General Provisions) Order 1996 (SI No. 103 of 1996), also made under the 1966 Act, requires herdowners to attach ear tags to bovine animals, replace ineligible or lost tags and sets out the provisions for the issue and supply of ear tags, with effect from April 15, 1996.

Horses The Diseases of Animals (Equine Viral Arteritis) Order 1996 (SI

No. 34 of 1996), also made under the Diseases of Animals Act 1966, lay down certain restrictions on horses in which equine viral arteritis or the virus of that disease exists or is suspected to exist and on semen from such horses, with effect from February 20, 1996.

Poultry: zoonoses   The European Communities (Zoonoses) Regulations 1996 (SI No. 2 of 1996) gave effect to Directive 92/117/EEC. They provide measures to protect against specified zoonoses and to provide information on zoonoses. It also provides for the taking of samples for testing for salmonella and for the slaughter of domestic fowl confirmed as being infected with salmonella. They came into effect on January 8, 1996.

ANIMAL FEEDINGSTUFFS

The European Communities (Feedingstuffs Intended For Particular Nutritional Purposes) Regulations 1996 (SI No. 59 of 1996) gave effect to Directives 93/74/EEC, 94/39/EC, 95/9/EC and 95/10/EC. They sets out requirements for the composition, marketing and labelling of feedingstuffs intended for particular nutritional purposes of animals whose process of assimilation, absorption or metabolism is temporarily or irreversible impaired. They also contain a positive list of intended uses of animal feedingstuffs for particular nutritional purposes. The European Communities (Protein Feedingstuffs) (Amendment) Regulations 1996 (SI No. 186 of 1996) further amended the European Communities (Protein Feedingstuffs) Regulations 1986 and gave effect to Directive 95/33/EC, with effect from June 30, 1996. The European Communities (Feedingstuffs) (Tolerances of Undesirable Substances and Products) (Amendment) Regulations 1996 (SI No. 275 of 1996) further amended the European Communities (Feedingstuffs) (Tolerances of Undesirable Substances and Products) Regulations 1989 and gave effect to Directive 96/6/EC. They amended the maximum permitted levels of aflatoxin B^1 in feedingstuffs for dairy cows. They came into force on September 19, 1996.

ANIMAL REGISTRATION

Bovine animals   The European Communities (Registration of Bovine Animals) Regulations 1996 (SI No. 104 of 1996) gave effect to Directive 92/102/EEC and Regulations (EEC) No. 3508/92 and (EEC) No. 3235/94. They require herdowners to register the births of all cattle within seven days and to keep registers of such births, with effect from April 15, 1996.

Goats, pigs and sheep   The European Communities (Registration Of Holdings And Identification Of Animals) Regulations 1996 (SI No. 1 of 1996) gave effect to Directive 92/102/EEC. They provide for the identification and registration of caprine, ovine and porcine animals and establish a system of registration of holdings on which such animals are held, kept or handled and regulate movement of such animals between holdings. They came into effect on 8 January 1996 for goats and sheep and on March 1, 1996 for pigs. See also the 1994 Review, 13, for earlier Regulations in this area.

ANIMAL REMEDIES

Detailed controls   The extremely lengthy Animal Remedies Regulations 1996 (SI No. 179 of 1996), which run to 61 Regulations and six Schedules, were made under the Animal Remedies Act 1993 (1993 Review, 34-7). The prescribe detailed arrangements for the licensing of animal remedies through the Irish Medicines Board, established by the Irish Medicines Board Act 1995 (1995 Review, 339). They also lay down detailed requirements concerning the manufacture, import, export, sale, supply and administration of animal remedies. Administrative arrangements are provided for in detail, including the fees to be charged, a register of animal remedies, requirements for record keeping and the prosecution of offences. The 1996 Regulations amount to a consolidated and updated regime in this area, and they revoked the following Regulations: the Animal Remedies (Registration of Manufacturers, Importers and Wholesalers) Regulations 1980, the Poisons (Control of Residues in Food of Animal Origin) Regulations 1985 and 1986, the Animal Remedies (Control of Sale) Regulations 1985 and 1986, the European Communities (Veterinary Medicinal Products) Regulations 1986, the Animal Remedies (Prohibition of Certain Sales) Regulations 1991 and Regs. 5 and 7 of the European Communities (Control of Veterinary Medicinal Products and their Residues) Regulations 1990 (the latter Regulations being those at issue in *Meagher v. Minister for Agriculture and Food* [1994] 1 I.R. 329; [1994] 1 I.L.R.M. 1, discussed in the 1993 Review, 299-304). In view of the patent Community origin of much of these pre-1996 Regulations on this topic, it is hardly surprising that the 1996 Regulations give effect to a wide range of European Community obligations, namely Directives 81/851/EEC, 81/852/EEC, 87/20/EEC, 87/22/EEC, 90/676/EEC, 90/677/EEC, 91/412/EEC, 92/18/EEC, 92/74/EEC, 93/40/EEC and 93/41/EEC and the relevant administrative requirements of Regulation (EEC) No. 2377/90 and Regulations (EC) No. 2309/93. The 1996 Regulations came into effect on August 1, 1996.

Prosecution of offences   The decision of the Supreme Court in *Mallon v. Minister For Agriculture and Food* [1996] 1 I.R. 517, discussed in the Constitutional Law chapter, 149-51, below, resulted in the unblocking of several prosecutions alleging infringements of the European Communities (Veterinary Medicinal Products) Regulations 1986, as amended by the European Communities (Control of Androgenic, Gestagenic and Thyrostatic Substances) Regulations 1988 and the European Communities (Control of Veterinary Medicinal Products and their Residues) Regulations 1990. These Regulations had implemented a number of EC Directives banning the use of certain growth promoters. Other challenges to the Regulations had been made in *Meagher v. Minister for Agriculture and Food* [1994] 1 I.R. 329; [1994] 1 I.L.R.M. 1 (1993 Review, 299-304). This area is now regulated by the Animal Remedies Act 1993 (1993 Review, 35-7) and the Animal Remedies Regulations 1996 (SI No. 179 of 1996), discussed immediately above, and the 1996 Regulations have revoked the 1986 and 1990 Regulations discussed in *Mallon*.

ANIMAL WELFARE

Carriage of cattle by sea   The Diseases Of Animals (Carriage Of Cattle By Sea) Order 1996 (SI No. 17 of 1996), made under the Diseases of Animals Act 1966, lays down regulations for the carriage of cattle by sea from the State and provides for inspection and approval of cattle vessels, the loading and care of cattle on vessels, weather conditions and the submission of voyage reports. They came into effect on February 1, 1996.

BOVINE DISEASES LEVY

The Bovine Diseases (Levies) (Amendment) Act 1996 provided for significant changes to the bovine diseases regime. The 1996 Act came fully into effect on 1 July 1996: Bovine Diseases (Levies) (Amendment) Act 1996 (Sections 6 and 7) (Commencement) Order 1996 (SI No. 161 of 1996). Bovine diseases levies were introduced under the Bovine Diseases (Levies) Act 1979 to require the farming community to make a financial contribution to the cost of the disease eradication programmes. The 1979 Act provides for the collection of the levy by the Revenue Commissioners on behalf of the Minister for Agriculture in respect of live exports. During the passage of the 1996 Act, it was explained that on the completion of the Single European Market, Revenue personnel were withdrawn from the export points in January 1993 and alternative administrative arrangements had to be put in place to collect levies on live exports. The amendments to the 1979 Act contained in sections 2 and 3 of the 1996 Act provide for a legal basis for the payment of levies on live exports to the Minister for Agriculture, Food and Forestry rather than to the Revenue Commissioners who had been appointed as agents of the Minister. The 1996 Act also includes a number of other amendments concerning penalties. Section 6 provides that the maximum fines on summary conviction were increased from £500 to £1,500. In addition, section 7 of the 1996 Act also increased the maximum fines in respect of certain offences under sections 48 and 49 of the Diseases of Animals Act 1966. The increases were from £500 to £1,500 in respect of a summary conviction; from £2,000 to £10,000 in respect of a conviction on indictment in respect of certain specified offences and from £1,000 to £5,000 in respect of other indictable offences. These fines had last been increased under section 23 of the Bovine Diseases (Levies) Act 1979. The Bovine Diseases (Levies) Regulations 1996 (SI No. 74 of 1996) prescribed revised rates of disease levy on milk and cattle for slaughter or live export with effect from April 1, 1996.

FOOD PROMOTION BOARD

Board membership   The An Bord Bia (Amendment) Act 1996 amended the An Bord Bia Act 1994 (1994 Review, 15) and thus increased the number of ordinary members of the main Board from 13 to 14 and it increased the number of ordinary members of its meat and livestock subsidiary board and of any other subsidiary boards from 11 to 12. The increases thus effected were intended to ensure that one ordinary member on each board would be appointed on the nomination of an organisation whom the Minister for Agriculture considered to be representative of consumers. The 1996 Act came into effect on July 10, 1996 on its signature by the President.

Levy   The Bord Bia Act 1994 (Levy On Slaughtered Or Exported Livestock) Order 1996 (SI No. 90 of 1996) increased the levy on slaughtered or exported livestock payable under the 1994 Act with effect from 1 April 1996.

KNACKERIES

The European Communities (Knackery) Regulations 1996 (SI No. 396 of 1996) gave effect to Decision No. 95/348/EC. They specify detailed requirements applicable to the licensing and registering of knackery premises and to the collection, treatment and disposal of animal waste to be used as feedstuffs for animals not intended for human consumption. They came into effect on December 31, 1996.

MILK SUPPLY

The Milk (Regulation Of Supply) (Amendment) Act 1996 amended the Milk

(Regulation Of Supply) Acts 1994 (1994 Review, 17) and 1995 (1995 Review, 10) amended the procedures for election to the National Milk Agency and also clarified the arrangements for the transition to the new regime provided for in the 1994 Act. The 1996 Act came into effect on 30 December 1996: Milk (Regulation Of Supply) (Amendment) Act 1996 (Commencement) Order 1996 (SI No. 427 of 1996).

PLANT HEALTH

Cereal seed   The European Communities (Cereal Seed) (Amendment) Regulations 1996 (SI No. 380 of 1996) further amended the European Communities (Cereal Seed) Regulations 1981 by revising the fees for cereal crop inspection and certification of cereal seed required under the Regulations with effect from December 19, 1996.

Fertilisers   The European Communities (Marketing of Fertilisers) Regulations 1996 (SI No. 270 of 1996) further amended the European Communities (Marketing of Fertilisers) Regulations 1978 and gave effect to Directive 96/28/EC. They provide for the marketing of certain nitrogenous and secondary nutrient fertilisers with effect from October 1, 1996.

Fodder plants   The European Communities (Seed of Fodder Plants) (Amendment) Regulations 1996 (SI No. 326 of 1996) prescribed new fees for the certification and testing of fodder plant seed in accordance with the European Communities (Seed of Fodder Plants) Regulations 1981, with effect from October 31, 1996.

Manufacturing standards   The European Communities (Authorization, Placing on the Market, Use and Control of Plant Protection Products) (Amendment) Regulations 1996 (SI No. 159 of 1996) amended the European Communities (Authorization, Placing on the Market, Use and Control of Plant Protection Products) Regulations 1994 (1994 Review, 19) to give effect to Directives 95/35/EC, 95/36/EC and 96/12/EC. They specify the requirements in relation to the fate and behaviour in the environment and impact on non-target species, to be submitted in support of applications for authorisation for marketing and use of plant protection products. They came into effect on July 1, 1996.

Organisms harmful to plants or plant products   The European Communities (Introduction of Organisms Harmful to Plants or Plant Products) (Prohibition) (Amendment) Regulations 1996 (SI No. 54 of 1996), which came into effect on 27 February 1996, implemented Directives 95/65/EC and 95/

66/EC. The European Communities (Introduction of Organisms Harmful to Plants or Plant Products) (Prohibition) (Amendment) (No. 2) Regulations 1995 (SI No. 266 of 1996), which came into effect on 10 September 1996, implemented Directives 96/14/EC and 96/15/EC. Both sets of Regulations involved amendments to the Principal Directive in this area 77/93/EEC. The 1977 Directive was implemented by the European Communities (Introduction of Organisms Harmful to Plants or Plant Products) (Prohibition) 1980. The European Communities (Introduction of Organisms Harmful to Plants and Plant Products) (Prohibition) (Temporary Provisions) Regulations 1996 (SI No. 325 of 1996) gave effect to Commission Decisions 95/506/EC and 96/599/EC. They prohibited the importation of Dutch potatoes which do not meet the standards set down in the 1977 Directive concerning brown rot diseases. They applied from November 5, 1996 to September 30, 1996.

Plant movement   The European Communities (Introduction and Movement of Certain Harmful Organisms, Plants, Plant Products and other Objects for Trial or Scientific Purposes and/or for Work on Variety Selection) Regulations 1996 (SI No. 122 of 1996) gave effect to Directive 95/44/EC. They establish the conditions under which certain harmful organisms, plants or plant products may be introduced or moved in the State for trial or scientific purposes, with effect from May 10, 1996.

Pesticide residues   The European Communities (Pesticide Residues) (Cereals) (Amendment) Regulations 1996 (SI No. 47 of 1996) and the European Communities (Pesticide Residues) (Cereals) (Amendment) (No. 2) Regulations 1996 (SI No. 337 of 1996) amended the European Communities (Pesticide Residues) (Cereals) Regulations 1988 in order to implement Directives 95/39/EC and 96/33/EC, which laid down amended maximum pesticide residue limits for a number of chemical substances in cereals. They came into effect on February 13, 1996 and November 20, 1996, respectively. Similarly, the European Communities (Pesticide Residues) (Products Of Plant Origin, including Fruit and Vegetables) (Amendment) Regulations 1996 (SI No. 316 of 1996) amended the European Communities (Pesticide Residues) (Products Of Plant Origin, including Fruit and Vegetables) Regulations 1994 (1994 Review, 18) to give effect to Directives 95/38/EC and 95/61/EC which laid down amended maximum pesticide residue limits for a number of chemical substances in fruit and vegetables and other products of plant origin. They came into effect on October 1, 1996.

RETIREMENT OF FARMERS

The European Communities (Retirement Of Farmers) Regulations 1996 (SI

No. 150 of 1996) further amended the European Communities (Retirement Of Farmers) Regulations 1974 by increasing the amount of the annuity payable under the Farmers' Retirement Scheme provided for under Directive 72/160/EEC. The annuity for a single person was increased from £2,399 to £2,448 while that for a married person was increased from £3,592 to £3,572 with retrospective effect from May 1, 1996.

TRADE IN ANIMALS, PRODUCTS AND BY-PRODUCTS

Trade in bovine animals and products The European Communities (Trade In Bovine Breeding Animals, their Semen, Ova and Embryos) Regulations 1996 (SI No. 112 of 1996) gave effect to Directives 77/504/EEC, 87/328/EEC, 88/407/EEC, 89/556/EEC, 90/120/EEC, 91/174/EEC, 93/52/EEC, 93/60/EEC and 94/28/EC and Decisions 84/247/EEC, 84/419/EEC, 86/130/EEC, 86/404/EEC, 88/124/EEC, 94/113/EC and 94/515/EC. They lay down the principles relating to the import of bovine animals, their semen, ova or embryos from third countries and creates offences in relation to possession of illegally imported bovine breeding stock. They came into effect on April 23, 1996. The European Communities (Trade In Bovine Breeding Animals, their Semen, Ova and Embryos) (Amendment) Regulations 1996 (SI No. 233 of 1996) amended Reg. 24 of the above Regulations, the effect of which is to permit authorised officers the right of direct entry on premises or lands (other than a private dwelling) without the necessity of a search warrant, with effect from August 1, 1996.

Trade in cattle: United Kingdom The European Communities (Importation Of Cattle from the United Kingdom) Regulations 1996 (SI No. 71 of 1996) gave effect to Directive 90/425/EEC, as amended by 92/118/EEC and revoked the European Communities (Importation of Cattle from the United Kingdom) Regulations 1995 (1995 Review, 15). The effect was to prohibiting the importation of cattle from the United Kingdom except under licence, with effect from March 26, 1996. These Regulations were, however, almost immediately rendered redundant by virtue of the worldwide ban on UK beef associated with the BSE crisis, as introduced by the European Communities (Importation of Bovine Animals and Products Obtained From Bovine Animals from The United Kingdom) Regulations 1996 (SI No. 87 of 1996), discussed above, 17.

Feedingstuffs The European Communities (Additives In Feedingstuffs) (Amendment) Regulations 1996 (SI No. 15 of 1996) amended the European Communities (Additives in Feedingstuffs) Regulations 1989 to give effect to

Directives 95/11/EC, 95/37/EC, 95/55/EC. They concern the assessment of additives in animal nutrition and came into effect on January 24, 1996.

Trade in animals and animal products   The European Communities (Trade in Animals and Animal Semen, Ova and Embryos) Regulations 1996 (SI No. 12 of 1996) gave effect to Directive 92/65/EEC and Decision 95/176/EC. They lay down animal health requirements for animals, semen, ova and embryos not subject to other Community rules (as to which see the 1994 Review, 20-22 and SI No. 112 of 1996, above) and provide for the appointment of authorised officers and their powers and establish offences in the case of contravention of the Regulations. They came into effect on February 1, 1996. Similarly, the European Communities (Trade In Certain Animal Products) Regulations 1996 (SI No. 102 of 1996) gave effect to Decision 96/103/EC, so that the precautionary measures in Directive 92/118/EEC (generally implemented by the European Communities (Trade in Animals and Animal Products) Regulations 1994 (1994 Review, 21-22)) are applicable to other animal products. The 1996 Regulations lay down animal and public health requirement in respect of animal products and provide for the appointment and powers of authorised officers and create offences in case of contravention of the Regulations. They came into effect on April 15, 1996.

WILDLIFE

Wild birds: special protection areas   The European Communities (Conservation of Wild Birds) (Amendment) Regulations 1996 (SI No. 269 of 1996), the European Communities (Conservation of Wild Birds) (Amendment) (No. 2) Regulations 1996 (SI No. 298 of 1996) and the European Communities (Conservation of Wild Birds) (Amendment) (No. 3) Regulations 1996 (SI No. 305 of 1996) amended the Schedule to the European Communities (Conservation of Wild Birds) Regulations 1985 (which had implemented Directive 79/409/EEC) by adding a number of new areas as special protection areas for wildbirds to the existing list and providing that breach of the Regulations is an offence carrying certain penalties.

Aliens, Citizenship and Immigration

ALIENS

'Enter into service' In *Gleeson (Minister for Justice) v. Chi Ho Cheung*, High Court, June 18, 1996, Geoghegan J. held that the prosecution had not made out a case that an offence under the Aliens Order 1946 had occurred. The judgment centred on the meaning of the expression 'enter into the service of' in Article 4 of the 1946 Order, made under the Aliens Act 1935. The factual background was as follows.

In September 1993, the complainant Garda had entered a restaurant in Dublin where he found the defendant working in the kitchen. The defendant had arrived in Ireland from Hong Kong, and had been working for his cousin for the previous two years; he was not in possession of a valid work permit. He was charged under the provisions of Article 4 of the 1946 Order in that he had entered into the service of his cousin in September 1993 otherwise than in accordance with the permit issued to his cousin. When the matter came on for hearing in the District Court, no evidence was submitted relating to the date on which the defendant had commenced employment in the State with his cousin. On a case stated to the High Court, the issue was whether the offence created by the 1946 Order on its proper construction was one that was only committed on the date when service or employment was commenced by an alien, or in the alternative was an offence that was committed on each day that such employment of service continued. Geoghegan J. interpreted it as meaning the former, and he made it clear that a prosecution in the instant case was thus impossible.

The complainant contended that, unless the article was interpreted as effectively creating a continuing offence, there would be a lacuna in the criminal code relating to illegal aliens. But Geoghegan J. held that, as a matter of plain English, it could not be said that the expression 'enter into the service of' could be equated with the expression 'being in the service of' and there was nothing in Article 4 of the 1946 Order to indicate a continuing obligation. He also pointed out the well-established canon that a statutory provision could not be held to create criminal responsibility except by clear unambiguous terms. As to the instant case, he stated that the position could not be rectified by amending the relevant date on the summons, as the proceedings would have been commenced well outside the six month time limit. Finally, he underlined that the plain meaning of the words in Article 4 of the 1946 Order created a 'once and for all offence' committed at the time the employment commenced.

Visa: additional specified States   The Aliens (Amendment) Order 1996 (SI No. 69 of 1996) amended the Aliens Order 1946 so that citizens of Kenya require a transit visa in order to enter the State. The Aliens (Amendment) (No. 2) Order 1996 (SI No. 89 of 1996) amended the Aliens Order 1946 so that citizens of Fiji Mauritius, Tanzania and Zambia require a transit visa in order to enter the State. The Aliens (Amendment) (No. 4) Order 1996 (SI No. 251 of 1996) amended the Aliens Order 1946 so that citizens of Iraq require a transit visa in order to enter the State. The Aliens (Amendment) (No. 5) Order 1996 (SI No. 301 of 1996) provides a complete updated list of the States whose citizens require a transit visa in order to enter the State.

Visa: removal of requirement   The Aliens (Amendment) (No. 3) Order 1996 (SI No. 120) of 1996) further amended the Aliens Order 1946, abolishing the entry visa requirements for nationals of Estonia, Lithuania and Latvia.

CITIZENSHIP

Discretion to refuse naturalisation   In *Mishra v Minister For Justice*, High Court, May 21, 1996, Kelly J. held that, in exercising the statutory discretion to grant a certificate of naturalisation pursuant to the Irish Nationality and Citizenship Acts 1956 and 1986, the Minister for Justice may be guided by a general policy, but that such a policy must not fetter the Minister's discretion in individual cases. The background was as follows.

The applicant was an Indian national. He had qualified as a medical doctor in India and had come to Ireland in 1987 to practice as a medical practitioner. At the time, practitioners who had qualified in a State outside the European Union and who were not Irish citizens obtained temporary registration from the Medical Council pursuant to the Medical Practitioners Act 1978. After five years, full registration was required in order to continue in practise in the State: this in turn required the applicant to obtain Irish citizenship. In 1991 the applicant applied to the respondent Minister for naturalisation pursuant to the Irish Nationality and Citizenship Act 1956. He executed a statutory declaration, stating that he intended to have his usual or principal place of residence in the State after naturalisation. By this time, the applicant had also become a father, and as the child had been born in Ireland it had Irish citizenship. Section 15 of the Irish Nationality and Citizenship Act 1956 (as amended by the Irish Nationality and Citizenship Act 1986) provides as follows:

(1) Upon receipt of an application for a certificate of naturalisation, the Minister [for Justice] may, in his absolute discretion, grant the application, if satisfied that the applicant

(a) is of full age;

(b) is of good character;

(c) has had a period of one year's continuous residence in the State immediately before the date of the application and, during the eight years immediately preceding that date, has had a total residence in the State amounting to four years;

(d) intends in good faith to continue to reside in the State after naturalisation; and

(e) has made, either before a Justice of the District Court, in open Court or in such manner as the Minister, for special reasons, allows, a declaration in the prescribed manner, of fidelity to the nation and loyalty to the State.

(2) The conditions specified in paragraphs (a) to (e) of subsection (1) are referred to in this Act as conditions for naturalisation.'

Section 16 of the 1956 Act (again, as amended by the 1986 Act) provides, *inter alia*, that the Minister may, in his absolute discretion, grant an application for a certificate of naturalisation, even where the conditions for naturalisation set out in section 15 are not complied with 'where the applicant is a parent or guardian acting on behalf of a minor of Irish descent or Irish associations.

Since the applicant's final period of temporary registration under the 1978 Act was due to expire at the end of August 1992, he withdrew his name from the Register of Medical Practitioners with effect from August 3, 1992. In October 1992, the Medical Council amended its rules so as to permit doctors who had qualified outside the European Union to obtain full registration without first obtaining Irish citizenship. By a letter in August 1993, the Minister informed the applicant of her decision to refuse a certificate of naturalisation, without stating the reasons therefor. By a further letter of June 1994, the Minister refused to give such reasons. In July 1994, the applicant was given leave to seek judicial review of the Minister's decision; the relief sought included *certiorari* to quash the Minister's refusal of naturalisation and a declaration that the applicant was entitled to a certificate of naturalisation pursuant to the 1956 Act. In an affidavit filed in the matter, it was averred that the Minister was aware from contact with the Medical Council that some foreign doctors who had acquired Irish citizenship but had not obtained full registration with the Medical Council had left the State shortly after naturalisation and had used their Irish citizenship to gain entry to countries which they could not have entered if they had remained citizens of their country of origin. As a result, it was stated that the general policy of the Minister was not to grant naturalisation to persons who could not be employed in their chosen profession and who were, therefore, likely to leave Ireland subsequent to obtaining Irish citizenship. The affidavit further stated that, since the applicant was legally residing in the State and since he was the father of a dependent Irish citizen, the Minister did not intend to require him to leave the State.

The applicant argued that the Minister's decision was arbitrary and unjust in that it prevented him from supporting an Irish citizen in breach of Articles 40, 41 and 42 of the Constitution, that no reasons had been given for the decision and that the Minister had applied a general policy without adequately considering the individual circumstances of the applicant and his family. Kelly J. quashed the refusal of a certificate of naturalisation and ordered that the Minister consider the applicant's particular circumstances. However, he declined to grant a declaration that the applicant was entitled to a certificate of naturalisation as this would involve a decision on the merits and to trespass on a matter wholly and exclusively for the Minister.

As to the main substance of the decision, Kelly J. held that the Irish Nationality and Citizenship Acts 1956 and 1986 imposed no obligation on the Minister to give reasons for her decision. But, reflecting the case law in recent years in this area, he accepted that an implicit entitlement to reasons may arise in order that a right of appeal might be exercised effectively. There might also be circumstance where, even without a right of appeal, natural justice or fairness required that reasons for a decision be given but Kelly J. did not think it necessary or appropriate to identify these circumstances since the reasons for the ministerial decision had been set out on affidavit and no obstacle had been placed in the way of argument based on these reasons.

He went on to cite with approval the decision of Gannon J. in *Shum v. Ireland* [1986] I.L.R.M. 593 (which in turn flowed from the seminal decision in *East Donegal Co-Op. Ltd. v. Attorney General* [1970] I.R. 317) to the effect that the absolute discretion vested in the Minister must be exercised in accordance with natural or constitutional justice. The dictates of natural or constitutional justice did not, however, require the Minister to give an applicant a hearing or to inform him of the reasons for her decision. Although an applicant might fulfil all the requirements of section 15 of the 1956 Act, Kelly J. emphasised that the Minister might, nonetheless, refuse a certificate of naturalisation on grounds of public policy which had nothing to do with the individual applicant. However, he qualified this broad proposition in some respects. He accepted that while the Minister might exercise her discretion in accordance with a policy or set of rules, he held that the application of such a policy must not fetter the discretion which is conferred by the 1956 Act, or produce a result which was fundamentally at variance with the evidence placed before the Minister by an applicant. In exercising her discretion in the instant case in line with the policy averred to in the affidavit filed in the proceedings, the Minister must have concluded that the applicant would leave Ireland on or subsequent to obtaining Irish citizenship; but the applicant had solemnly declared that it was his intention to have his usual or principal place of residence in the State after naturalisation. Thus, Kelly J. concluded that the application of this general policy, involving the making of an assumption adverse to the applicant's solemnly declared intention concerning his future residence, required, in fundamental fairness, that he at least be given an opportunity to clarify his position. On that basis, Kelly J. in effect remitted the matter to the Minister for further consideration. While not amounting to an order of *mandamus*, the decision placed some limits on the discretion to be exercised, albeit in quite modest terms.

REFUGEE ACT 1996

Background   The Refugee Act 1996 is intended to place on a statutory footing the procedures to be followed in determining whether or not a person should be afforded recognition as a refugee in the State and the consequent status and rights of persons recognised in the State as refugees. At the time of writing the 1996 Act had yet to be brought into force. The background to the 1996 Act is that, since 1956, the State has been a party to the 1951 United Nations Geneva Convention relating to the Status of Refugees and, since 1968 to the 1967 Protocol to the Convention. As to implementation, this was done on a non-statutory basis. While provision was made in the Irish Nationality and Citizenship Act 1986 to facilitate the naturalisation of refugees who applied for Irish citizenship, no other specific statutory provisions dealing with the status of refugees had been made. Administrative procedures for the determination of refugee status in Ireland were drawn up in 1985 in consultation with the United Nations High Commissioner for Refugees. In *Gutrani v Minister for Justice* [1993] 2 I.R. 427 (1992 Review, 22-3, the Supreme Court had held that these arrangements created a legitimate expectation that they would be applied by the Minister in determining refugee status. The 1996 Act provides for a more formal basis on which the obligations arising under the 1951 Convention and 1967 Protocol may be considered. The 1996 Act also enables the State to ratify the Convention, signed in Dublin, which deals with applications for asylum lodged in one of the member states of the European Union. During the passage of the Act, it was stated that the annual cost of implementing the Act would be in the region of £700,000. This would arise from the need for support staff for the Refugee Applications Commissioner and the Refugee Appeal Board envisaged by the Act as well as the use of interpreter services and legal assistance. At the time of writing (July 1997), the main features of the 1996 Act, in particular those concerning the appointment of the Refugee Applications Commissioner and the Refugee Appeal Board, had not been brought into effect. The Refugee Act 1996 (Section 24(1)) (Commencement) Order, 1996 (SI No. 290 of 1996) brought section 24(1) of the 1996 Act (which concerns 'programme refugees', discussed below) into force on October 1, 1996. The Irish Nationality and Citizenship (Fees) Regulations

1996 (SI No. 291 of 1996) waives the payment of fees by persons admitted to
the State as programme refugees, also with effect from October 1, 1996.

Refugees and 'programme refugees'   Refugee is defined in the 1951 Convention and the 1996 Act as a person who 'owing to a well-founded fear of
being persecuted for reasons of race, religion, nationality, membership of a
particular social group or political opinion, is outside the country of his nationality and is unable or, owing to such fear, is unwilling to avail himself of
the protection of that country, or who, not having a nationality and being outside the country of his former habitual residence, is unable or, owing to such
fear, is unwilling to return to it.' For the purposes of the 1996 Act, section 1
provides that 'membership of a particular social group' includes membership
of a trade union and also includes membership of a group of persons whose
defining characteristic is their belonging to the female or the male sex or having a particular sexual orientation.

The 1996 Act also includes provisions dealing with groups of people who
are granted the protection of the State on foot of Government decision. Such
groups are referred to as 'programme refugees'. During the Act's passage in
the Oireachtas, reference was made to groups of people from countries such
as Hungary, Chile, Iran, Vietnam and the former Yugoslavia who have been
admitted to the State for the purposes of temporary protection or resettlement.
Such groups are not necessarily limited to persons who would be deemed to
be refugees under the 1951 Convention or wider international law.

Rights of refugees   Section 3 sets out the rights of persons recognised as
refugees in the State. During the passage of the Act, it was noted that Irish
citizens have rights over and above these refugee rights by virtue of their
citizenship, including the right to vote at elections in the State.

Travel document   Section 4 of the 1996 Act authorises the Minister for Justice to give a travel document (which acts in lieu of a passport for travel purposes in the case of refugees) to a person recognised as a refugee under the
Act. Such a travel document may be refused in the interests of national security or public policy, in accordance with Article 28 of the 1951 Convention.

Prohibition on return of refugee to place of danger   In accordance with
Article 33 of the 1951 Convention, section 5 provides that a person shall not
be expelled from the State or returned to the frontiers of territories where, in
the opinion of the Minister, the life or freedom of the person would be threatened on account of his or her race, religion, nationality, membership of a particular social group or political opinion. The prohibition in the 1996 Act on
what the Convention refers to as *refoulment* goes beyond Article 33 since it
applies to all persons, not merely refugees.

Refugee Applications Commissioner   Section 6 provides for the appointment of a Refugee Applications Commissioner (the Commissioner) who shall be independent in the exercise of his or her functions. The detailed provisions regarding the Commissioner are set out in the First Schedule to the 1996 Act. This provides that the Commissioner shall have had not less than 7 years' experience as a practising barrister or solicitor before his or her appointment and also provides for the appointment by the Minister of staff to assist the Commissioner. Section 7 requires the Commissioner to submit an annual report to the Minister for Justice.

Applications for refugee status   Section 8 deals with applications for declarations for recognition as a refugee. It provides that a person who seeks asylum on arrival at the frontiers of the State must be interviewed by an immigration officer and be informed of the right to apply for a declaration that he or she is a refugee. Where a person is already in the State (whether lawfully or unlawfully) and seeks to be declared a refugee, the person may apply to the Minister for Justice and he or she will be referred to an immigration officer for interview. Section 8(2) requires that an interview shall, where necessary and possible, be conducted with the assistance of an interpreter and that a record of the interview be kept by the immigration officer and a copy furnished to the person interviewed, to the Commissioner and to the United Nations High Commissioner for Refugees (the UNHCR). Section 8(3) provides that a person being interviewed must be informed that he or she is entitled to consult (a) a solicitor and (b) a representative of the UNHCR. Section 8(4) stipulates that, subject to sections 9 and 22, all applications for a declaration must be referred to the Commissioner.

Leave to enter or remain in State   Section 9 provides that a person who has applied for refugee status shall be given leave to enter the State subject to certain conditions. Section 9(1) provides that a person who arrives at the frontiers of the State and who has applied for a declaration that he or she is a refugee shall be given leave to enter the State by an immigration officer subject to the remainder of the section. The immigration officer has no authority to refuse entry to an applicant even if the officer has reservations about his or her bona fides. Section 9(2) provides that a person who is granted leave to enter the State under section 9(1) or a person who is already in the State is entitled to remain in the State while his or her application is being considered. Except in cases where an exclusion or deportation order applies, or an application is withdrawn or deemed to be withdrawn the permission to remain expires only when the entire procedure, including appeals, has been exhausted and the application has been rejected or when, under the Dublin Convention, the application is transferred to another State in the European Union. Section 9(3) provides that a person referred to in section 9(2) shall be given a temporary residence certificate stating his or her name and containing a photograph of the person concerned, specifying the date on which his or her application for a declaration was referred to the Commissioner and stating that, subject to the provisions of the Act, the person shall not be removed from the State before the final determination of his or her application. Under section 9(4) an applicant may not (a) leave or attempt to leave the State without the consent of the Minister or (b) seek or enter employment or carry on any business, trade or profession during the period before the final determination of his or her application for refugee status. Section 9(5) enables an immigration officer, by notice in writing, to require an applicant (a) to reside or remain in particular districts or places in the State, or (b) to report at specified intervals to an immigration officer or member of the Garda Síochána as specified in the notice. Section 9(8) provides that an immigration officer or a member of the Garda Síochána may detain a person where, with reasonable cause, he or she suspects that an applicant (a) poses a threat to national security or public order in the State, (b) has committed a serious non-political crime outside the State, (c) has not made reasonable efforts to establish his or her true identity, (d) intends to leave the State and enter another state without lawful authority, or (e) has, without reasonable cause, destroyed his or her identity or travel documents or is in possession of forged identity documents. Section 9(10) provides that a person detained shall, as soon as practicable, be brought before a judge of the District Court. Section 9(12) provides that the detention provisions shall not apply to a person under 17 years and that where the parents or guardian of a person under 17 years are detained, the immigration officer or member of the Garda Síochána must inform the appropriate Health Board accordingly. Where the Minister for Justice exercises the power under the Aliens Act 1935 to exclude or deport an alien who is a criminal, war criminal or a threat to national security or public order by means of an Order, section 9(15) of the 1996 Act provides that the person who is the subject of the Order is precluded from invoking the terms of the 1996 Act. This clearly retains a great deal of discretion in the hands if the Minister. To confirm this, section 9(16) provides that where a person is refused permission to enter the State under section 19(5), or is not entitled to stay in the State he or she may not make an application for refugee status without the consent of the Minister and any such application already referred to the Commissioner shall be deemed to be withdrawn.

Information to be given to detained persons   Section 10 of the 1996 Act provides that certain information must be given to persons detained under section 9. This includes information that he or she will be brought before a Court to determine if detention is in order, that he or she is entitled to consult a solicitor, to have access to an interpreter and to have notification of the detention sent to the UNHCR and another person.

Investigation of application by Commissioner   Section 11 provides that it shall be the function of the Commissioner to investigate applications and the section also sets out procedures in relation to such investigations. During the passage of the Act in the Oireachtas, it was stated that the procedure envisaged was that an applicant, who may invoke the assistance of a solicitor, will make a written submission to the Commissioner setting out his or her case. The applicant will be interviewed by an officer of the Commissioner, and the Departments of Foreign Affairs and of Justice may be asked to make inquiries regarding the applicant's claim. A copy of all material obtained by the Commissioner will be supplied to the applicant so that he or she can make further submissions. The section also provides, *inter alia*, that, where an application is referred to the Commissioner, the Commissioner shall inform the applicant in writing of the procedures to be observed in the investigation, his or her right to consult a solicitor, his or her entitlement to contact a representative of the Office of the UNHCR, his or her entitlement to make written submissions to the Commissioner, the duty of the applicant to co-operate with the Commissioner and to furnish information relevant to his or her application and the obligation of the applicant to notify the Commissioner of his or her address in the State.

Manifestly unfounded applications   Section 12 provides for the manner in which the Commissioner is to deal with manifestly unfounded applications. It sets out the circumstances which would give rise to a view that an application is manifestly unfounded, for example, where an application does not show on its face any grounds for the contention that the applicant is a refugee. It provides that the Commissioner need not pursue his or her investigations where he or she believes that an application is manifestly unfounded. The applicant must be advised of this by the Commissioner and be given an opportunity to rebut it and an interview with an authorised officer, if requested. If the Commissioner remains of the opinion that the application is manifestly unfounded the Commissioner will recommend that he or she should not be declared a refugee.

Recommendations and reports by Commissioner   Section 13 provides that where the Commissioner has completed an investigation into an application he or she must submit a report, together with his or her recommendation, to the Minister. The applicant and the UNHCR must also be furnished with a copy and the applicant must be notified of his or her right to appeal to the Refugee Appeal Board, discussed below.

Refugee Appeal Board   Section 15 provides for the establishment of a Refugee Appeal Board. to hear and decide appeals under section 16 of the Act. The Appeal Board must be independent in the exercise of its functions. The

Second Schedule to the 1996 Act provides that the Appeal Board shall consist of a chairperson who, before his or her appointment, shall have had not less than ten years' experience as a practising barrister or practising solicitor. It provides for the appointment by the Minister of four other members, one of whom will be an officer of the Minister and one who will be an officer of the Minister for Foreign Affairs. Section 16 provides that an applicant may appeal to the Appeal Board against a recommendation of the Commissioner made under sections 12 or 13. It also obliges the Appeal Board to hold an oral hearing if so requested by the applicant. The Appeal Board must enable the applicant, the Commissioner or an authorised officer to be present at the hearing and to present their case to the Appeal Board in person or through a legal representative and the Appeal Board must also do its utmost to procure an interpreter for the hearing. Hearings are held in private.

Declaration that person is refugee   Section 17 provides that, in general, where a report under section 13 is furnished to the Minister for Justice, he or she shall, if the report includes a recommendation that the applicant should be declared to be a refugee, or if the Appeal Board on appeal so recommend, give to the applicant a statement in writing (referred to in the Act as a declaration) declaring that the person is a refugee. Despite this general obligation, section 17(2) confers on the Minister power to refuse a declaration to a person in the interest of national security or public policy. Where a person has been refused a declaration, the Minister shall send the applicant a notice in writing accordingly and inform him or her that his or her permission to reside in the State has expired and that an order may be made requiring the applicant to leave the State. A copy of the notice will also be sent to the UNHCR and the applicant's solicitor. Section 17(8) provides for the removal from the State of persons who are not refugees or who have no other lawful grounds for being in the State.

Member of family of refugee   Section 18 provides that the Minister for Justice, on application by a refugee and after investigation by the Commissioner, may allow close family relatives or other dependents of the refugee enter the State.

Protection of identity of applicants   Section 19 provides that any material relating to an application which might identify the applicant shall not be made public, except with the applicant's consent.

Prohibition of false information and alteration of identity documents   Section 20 of the 1996 Act deals with offences relating to the giving of false information and the alteration of identity documents.

Dublin Convention   Section 22 deals with the making of orders by the Minister for Justice for the purposes of the Dublin Convention determining the State responsible for examining applications for asylum lodged in one of the Member States of the European Union.

Extradition   Section 25 ensures there is no conflict between the 1996 Act and the provisions of the Extradition Acts 1965 to 1987.

Arts and Culture

NATIONAL PARKS

In *Blascaod Mór Teo v. Minister for the Arts, Culture and the Gaeltacht*, High Court, December 19, 1996, Kelly J. held that the defendant Minister had an implied power pursuant to An Blascaod Mór National Historic Park Act 1989 (1989 Review, 4) to make statutory Regulations under the Act. The case arose against the following background. The 1989 Act provided for the establishment and maintenance on an Blascaod Mór island of a National Historical Park to be managed and developed by the Commissioners of Public Works. Section 4 of the 1989 Act provides that the Commissioners of Public Works may compulsorily acquire land on the island in accordance with the procedures set out in the Schedule to the Act. Paragraph 1 of the Schedule provides that where the Commissioners of Public Works propose to exercise this power, they shall, *inter alia,* give notice of their intention to certain specified persons and publish a notice of their intention in a newspaper circulating in the County of Kerry. Paragraph 1(2) of the Schedule provides that such notices "shall be in the prescribed form", paragraph 4 of the Schedule provides that a vesting order "shall be in the prescribed form" and paragraph 7 of the Schedule provides that "prescribed" means prescribed by regulations made by the Minister for the Gaeltacht. The 1989 Act did not confer an express power on the Minister for the Gaeltacht to make regulations prescribing the form of notices to be used pursuant to paragraph1 of the Schedule or the form of vesting orders to be made pursuant to paragraph 4 of the Schedule. An Blascaod Mór National Historic Park Act 1989 (Forms) Regulations 1990 (1990 Review, 4) prescribe the form of notices and vesting orders to be used pursuant to paragraphs 1 and 4 respectively of the Schedule to the 1989 Act. The 1990 Regulations recite that the regulations are made "in exercise of the powers conferred . . . by paragraphs 1(2) and 4 of the Schedule to the 1989 Act".

The plaintiffs were the owners of land on an Blascaod Mór on whom notices in of an intention to acquire land compulsorily had been served pursuant to paragraph 1 of the Schedule to the 1989 Act. The notices were in the form prescribed by the 1990 Regulations. The plaintiffs instituted proceedings seeking, *inter alia,* a declaration that certain provisions of the 1989 Act were invalid having regard to the provisions of the Constitution and a declaration that the

1990 Regulations and the notices served thereunder were invalid. The issue of whether the 1990 Regulations and the notices were invalid was tried as a preliminary issue. As indicated, Kelly J. held that the Minister had the required power to make the 1990 Regulations.

He held, in accordance with the views expressed in *Attorney General v. Great Eastern Railway Co.* (1885) App. Cas. 473, that the courts may infer a power on the part of a Minister to make regulations under an enactment where, as a matter of statutory interpretation, it appears that the legislature intended to confer such a power on the Minister. He held that this was consistent with the principles concerning the delegation of Regulations-making powers laid down in *Cityview Press Ltd. v. An Chomhairle Oiliúna* [1980] I.R. 381. In the case of the 1989 Act, since paragraph 1 of the Schedule to the Act provided that the notices to be served thereunder should be in the prescribed form and as 'prescribed' was defined in paragraph 7 of the Schedule as meaning prescribed by Regulations made by the Minister for the Gaeltacht, Kelly J. concluded that the Minister had an implied power to make regulations prescribing the form of notices to be used pursuant to paragraph 1 of the Schedule. For other aspects of the proceedings, see *Blascaod Mór Teo v. Commissioners of Public Works in Ireland*, High Court, November 22, 1992 (1992 Review, 139-40).

Commercial Law

Reasons for decision   In *Manning v. Shackleton* [1994] 1 I.R. 397 (H.C.); [1994] 1 I.L.R.M. 346 (H.C.); [1997] 2 I.L.R.M. 26 (S.C.), the Supreme Court reversed in part the decision of Barron J. in the High Court (1993 Review, 30-31) in which he had rejected the applicant's claim that the respondent arbitrator should set out the reasons for his decision: see the discussion in the Administrative Law chapter, 10, above.

Setting aside award: patent error   In *Tobin and Twomey Services Ltd. v. Kerry Foods Ltd. and Kerry Group Plc* [1996] 2 I.L.R.M. 1, the Supreme Court remitted an interim finding of law to an arbitrator for reconsideration under section 36 of the Arbitration Act 1954 where there was an error patent on the face of the decision. The case arose against the background of a contract in which the plaintiff, an electrical contracting company, agreed to carry out works at the defendants' factory in England. During the course of these works, the defendants asked the plaintiff to carry out additional works. A dispute later arose between the parties as to the amount due for the original electrical services contract and the additional works. Having failed to reach agreement, the plaintiff formally invoked the arbitration clause in the electrical services contract. No submission to arbitration *was* signed by either party and no submission was furnished to the arbitrator, but an "Arbitrator's Appointment Form" provided that the arbitrator would deal with disputes which "arose between the parties concerning the method of payment for the whole of the works carried out" at the factory in England. In an interim decision, the arbitrator held that the additional works did not form part of the original electrical services contract and directed that they be excluded from the reference to arbitration. The plaintiff sought to have this set aside. In the High Court, Carroll J. refused the relief sought, but this decision was reversed on appeal to the Supreme Court (Hamilton C.J., O'Flaherty and Blayney JJ.). Delivering the only judgment for the Court, Blayney J. noted that the reference in the arbitrator's appointment form to "the whole of the works" carried out by the plaintiff made it clear that what was submitted to the arbitrator for decision was not just disputes as to the works included in the original electrical services contract, but also the rest of the work carried out. The Court held that the error made by the arbitrator was in concluding that because the additional works did not form part of the subject matter of the electrical services contract, the dispute in respect of those works had not been referred to him for decision. The fact that the defendant claimed that the additional work was the subject of separate contracts was not inconsistent with the clear intention of the parties that disputes in relation to all the works were being submitted to the arbitrator. As no formal submission to arbitration was made, the Court held that what was submitted had to be gathered from the parties' conduct. In this respect, there was no doubt that the dispute as to what was due for the additional works was included in the reference. Blayney J. cited with approval the judgment of O'Hanlon J. in *Portsmouth Arms Hotel Ltd. v. Enniscorthy UDC*, High Court, October 14, 1994 (1995 Review, 20) in concluding that a matter should be remitted to an arbitrator under section 36 of the 1954 Act where, as here, there was an error patent on the face of the interim award.

Setting aside award: reluctance   In *Vogelaar v. Callaghan* [1996] 1 I.R. 88 (H.C.); [1996] 2 I.L.R.M. 226 (H.C.), which was decided shortly after the Supreme Court decision in *Tobin and Twomey Services* above, Barron J. reiterated recent case law to the effect that it is only in rare circumstances that a court should entertain an application to set aside an arbitration award or to have one remitted to the arbitrator for further consideration pursuant to the Arbitration Act 1954. Such applications should only be considered by the court where there was some form of misconduct either by the arbitrator or in the course of the proceedings or in some other way. While Barron J. declined to interfere with the substantive arbitration award in the instant case, he remitted certain elements concerning costs.

The case concerned a building contract between the plaintiff and defendant, in which the defendant agreed to construct a dwelling house. The work carried out was more extensive than anticipated, and the defendant had sought extra money from the plaintiff. The plaintiff refused to pay the sum demanded and offered £20,000 in full and final settlement of all sums claimed. This was rejected by the defendant and the matter was remitted to arbitration. The arbitrator awarded the defendant £13,270, but ordered that the plaintiff pay the defendant's and the arbitrator's costs. The plaintiff had sought the reasons for the award, but had been refused and he then instituted proceedings to set aside the award.

A preliminary point which arose was whether the claim was within the six week time limit specified in the 1954 Act. Although time had, it appeared, run out, Barron J. held that on the facts in the case an extension of the six week time limit was clearly justified. In particular, he noted that the award had been taken up jointly on a date when the six week period had already run, and that it would therefore have been unfair to enforce the time limit as this would have required the issue of proceedings before it could have been known whether or not there was a need to do so.

As to giving reasons, Barron J. noted that, at a preliminary hearing, the arbitrator had indicated that he would not give a reasoned award unless he was specifically asked to do so by one of the parties, and at no time had the plaintiff made any such application. In such circumstances, the plaintiff was precluded from doing so by way of these proceedings. Indeed, he commented that much of the plaintiff's complaint was in reality an effort to appeal the arbitration decision, which amounted to a misunderstanding of the function of the role of the High Court in arbitration. He referred to the Supreme Court's decision in *Keenan v. Shield Insurance Co. Ltd.* [1988] I.R. 89 (see the 1988 Review, 43-6), in which it was made clear that, in general, the courts should not interfere with arbitration awards.

Nonetheless, Barron J. accepted that it was clear that the arbitrator had failed to take into account the offer made by the plaintiff to the defendant when deciding on the costs issue, and to allow the award to stand with the direction as to costs would be to indicate a severe injustice. On this basis, he held that the costs issue fell within a category of cases where remittal should be made. He directed that the remittal should be to make such award as the arbitrator considered proper having regard to the offer made by the plaintiff.

CASUAL TRADING

Forms The Casual Trading Act 1995 (Forms) Regulations 1996 (SI. No. 146 of 1996), made under the Casual Trading Act 1995 (1995 Review, 21-3), prescribe the form for an application for a casual trading licence. They came into effect on June 1, 1996.

COMPETITION

Competition (Amendment) Act 1996 The Competition (Amendment) Act 1996 is discussed separately below, 43-7.

Competition: notification fees The Competition (Notification Fees) Regulations 1996 (SI No. 379 of 1996) specify revised fees to accompany notifications under the Competition Act 1991, with effect from January 1, 1997.

Mergers: notification fees The Mergers or Take-Over (Notification Fees) Regulations 1996 (SI No. 381 of 1996) specify revised fees to accompany notifications under the Mergers, Take-overs and Monopolies (Control) Act 1978, with effect from January 1, 1997.

Prices: magazines The Maximum Prices (Magazines) Order 1996 (SI No. 207 of 1996), made under the Prices Act 1958, re-introduced (for a short time) maximum prices for magazines where the magazines were priced on the cover in sterling. The Order, which provided that the maximum price chargeable was the sterling price increased by 5%, was made against the background of suggestions that retailers were failing to pass on the then strength of the Irish pound on the currency markets. The Order came into effect on July 17, 1996. The Maximum Prices (Magazines) (Revocation) Order 1996 (SI No. 307 of 1996) revoked SI No. 207 of 1996 with effect from October 14, 1996; by this time the Irish pound had returned to below parity with sterling.

Take-over: prohibition and modification　The Proposed Merger or Take-Over Prohibition Order 1996 (SI No. 45 of 1996), made under the Mergers, Take-overs and Monopolies (Control) Act 1978, prohibited the proposed acquisition by Statoil (Ireland) Ltd. of Conoco (Ireland) Ltd. This was modified by the Proposed Merger or Take-Over Prohibition (Amendment) Order 1996 (SI No. 214 of 1996), which prohibited the proposed acquisition unless certain conditions were met. These were subsequently complied with and the acquisition was proceeded with.

COMPETITION (AMENDMENT) ACT 1996

The Competition (Amendment) Act 1996 began its legislative life as the Competition (Amendment) Bill 1994 and was introduced by the then Minister for Enterprise and Employment (Mr Ruairi Quinn) in the Fianna Fáil/Labour Government of 1992 to 1994. On the change of Government in 1994, the Minister in the then Fine Gael/Labour/Democratic Left Government (Mr Richard Bruton) developed a number of substantial modifications prior to its committal to Committee Stage in Dáil Éireann and these were largely incorporated into the Act as passed in 1996. The 1996 Act came into effect on 3 July 1996 on its signature by the President. For comment on the 1996 Act, see Michael Doran, 'The Competition (Amendment) Act 1996 – A New Dawn for Competition Law?' (1996) 14 *ILT* 260.

Public enforcement by Competition Authority　Although the final product differed from that introduced in 1994, nonetheless, the 1996 Act resembled the 1994 Bill in that it provides for the public enforcement of the Competition Act 1991 (see the 1991 Review, 23-6) by the Competition Authority. Both the 1994 Bill provided and the 1996 Act provides that the Minister for Enterprise and Employment may appoint a Director of Competition Enforcement with responsibility for enforcement matters on a day to day basis. But while the original Bill provided and the 1996 Act provides that the Competition Authority could institute civil proceedings under the 1991 Act (civil action being a matter for private action only under the 1991 Act), the 1996 Act has introduced criminal penalties for non-compliance with competition law, which may be prosecuted summarily (but not on indictment) by the Authority.

Criminal offences, penalties and proceedings   Sections 2, 3 and 4 of the 1996 Act constitute elements not to be found in the 1994 Bill as originally published, in that they provide for the 'criminalisation' of anti-competitive actions. Section 2(2)(a) of the 1996 Act provides that an undertaking which enters into, or implements, an agreement, or make or implement a decision, or engage in a concerted practice that would distort competition within the meaning of section 4 of the 1991 Act shall be guilty of an offence. Similarly, section 2(7)(a) of the 1996 Act provides that an undertaking that acts in a manner prohibited by section 5(1) of the 1991 Act, which concerns the abuse of a dominant position, shall be guilty of an offence.

Nonetheless, section 2 also goes on to provide a number of defences in respect of a criminal prosecution for these offences, namely that:

(i)   the defendant did not know, nor could be reasonably expected to have known, that the effect of the agreement, decision or concerted practice concerned, or its dominant position as the case may be, would involve the prevention, restriction or distortion of competition in trade alleged in the proceedings, or

(ii) at all material times a licence or certificate was in force in respect of the agreement, decision or concerted practice concerned and, in the case of a licence, the terms and conditions of the licence were at all material times being complied with; or that, in the case of an alleged dominant position, there was in force an order under section 14 of the 1991 Act.

Section 3 of the 1996 Act sets out the penalties for offences under section 2 of the 1996 Act. On summary conviction, the maximum fine is £1,500, or, in the case of an individual, to such a fine and/or imprisonment for six months. On conviction on indictment, the maximum fine is whichever of the following amounts is the greater, £3,000,000 or 10% of the turnover of the undertaking in the financial year ending in the 12 months prior to the conviction; or, in the case of an individual, to a fine not exceeding whichever of the following amounts is the greater, namely, £3,000,000 or 10% of the turnover of the individual in the financial year ending in the 12 months prior to the conviction and/or imprisonment for two years. Fines imposed for an offence under section 2 brought by the Authority may, on the application of the Authority, be paid to the Authority if the court so orders.

In criminal proceedings for an offence under section 2 of the 1996 Act, section 4 of the 1996 Act authorises the admissibility of opinion evidence from any witness who appears to the court to possess the appropriate qualifications or experience as respects the matter to which his or her evidence relates.

Criminal and civil enforcement by the Authority and 'dawn raids' As indicated above, section 3(6)(a) of the 1996 Act provides, crucially, that summary prosecutions in respect of offences under the 1996 Act may be brought by the Minister or the Authority. Section 7 of the 1996 Act (also reflecting the Bill as originally introduced in 1994) amended section 6 of the 1991 Act and confers a right of action on the Competition Authority for breaches of sections 4 and 5 of the Competition Act 1991. Such actions may be taken on the Authority's own initiative or following complaints made to it from third parties. The extension to the Authority of these powers in the criminal and civil context brought an extra dimension to powers already conferred on it by the Competition Act 1991. Section 21 of the 1991 Act conferred extensive powers of entry, inspection and confiscation on officers of the Authority. Section 11(c) of the 1996 Act extended the scope of these powers to include confiscation of computer discs and other technological records. Although this in itself would be significant, it is the context within which this occurred in the 1996 Act that added greater moment. The 1996 Act ushered in the era of the 'dawn raid' with a view to prosecution or civil action. The first such use of the enhanced powers in the 1991 Act came in early 1997, when the offices of Opel Ireland (also well-known for their sponsorship of the Irish national professional football team) were inspected over a number of days in connection with a pricing strategy known as the 'quibble-free' price deal. The use of the 'dawn raid' brought the Competition Authority into line with the powers conferred on the European Commission in connection with its enforcement of EC competition law: see the European Communities (Rules of Competition) Regulations 1993 (1993 Review, 47).

Studies on Authority's initiative Section 8 of the 1996 Act amended section 11 of the 1991 Act by providing that the Authority may also carry out studies or analyses on its own initiative. The 1991 Act provided that the Competition Authority could carry out studies or analyses only at the request of the Minister for Enterprise and Employment.

Director of Competition Enforcement Section 9 of the 1996 Act amended the Schedule to the 1991 Act by providing that the Minister may appoint a Director of Competition Enforcement who will also be a member of the Competition Authority. The amended Schedule sets out the functions of the Director, who will act in effect as the day-to-day investigator of activities alleged to be in breach of the 1991 or 1996 Acts. The first Director, Patrick Massey, was appointed in October 1996.

Category certificates As envisaged by section 3 of the 1994 Bill, section 5 of the 1996 Act amended section 4 of the 1991 Act and provides that the Competition Authority may certify that a group or category of similar agreements do not contravene section 4 of the 1991. While section 4 of the 1991 Act provided for certificates to be issued by the Authority, there was no provision for category certificates.

Pre-1991 agreements Section 6 of the 1996 Act (again reflecting the Bill as originally introduced in 1994) refers to old agreements, or agreements that were in existence before the 1991 Act came into force. Under the 1991 Act such agreements, having been duly licensed or certified by the Competition Authority, were not afforded protection from damage claims under section 6 of the 1991 Act. Section 6 of the 1996 Act amended section 6(7) of the 1991 Act and confirms that such immunity is afforded during the notification period or until any appeal has been concluded.

Mergers and take-overs generally The 1994 Bill had proposed to remove all merger and take-over agreements from the scope of section 4 of the Competition Act 1991. It will be recalled (1991 Review, 23) that section 4 of the 1991 Act prohibits agreements between undertakings which prevent, restrict or distort competition; since merger or take-over agreements constitute agreements between undertakings, and could in certain cases prevent, restrict or distort competition section 4 of the 1991 Act could clearly apply. The thinking behind the original 1994 Bill had been that since the Mergers, Take-overs and Monopolies (Control) Act 1978 had already a system in place to regulate large scale merger or take-over agreements, there was an unnecessary overlap between the 1978 Act and the 1991 Act. The 1994 Bill had thus proposed the removal of the requirement to notify the Competition Authority under the 1991 of such agreements. It was considered that this would facilitate growth and co-operation between smaller firms, since merger or take-over agreements between them would be excluded from section 4 of the 1991 Act. Ultimately, this was not proceeded with, though other arrangements, in particular the provisions for 'category certificates' under the 1996 Act, will in effect provide comparable relief to that envisaged by the 1994 Bill. A provision on mergers which survived the changes in the enactment process is section 10 of the 1996 Act, which provides that the Minister may prescribe a fee to accompany merger notifications.

Monopolies subject to 1991 Act As envisaged in the 1994 Bill, section 11 of the 1996 Act removes the definition of a monopoly from section 1 of the 1978 Act. The definition was no longer considered useful as it had been replaced by the concept of a dominant position introduced in the 1991 Act. In keeping with this removal, section 16 of the 1996 Act provides that the collective citation for the 1978 Act, as amended by the 1996 Act, is the Mergers and Take-overs (Control) Acts 1978 to 1996, thus clarifying that the 1978 Act concerns mergers and take-overs only.

Parties to agreements Finally, section 12 of the 1996 Act provides that, for the avoidance of doubt, but without prejudice to section 11(a) of the Interpretation Act 1937, references in Part II of the 1991 Act to the parties to an agreement, decision or concerted practice of a kind described in section (1) of the 1991 Act include, and shall be deemed always to have included, references to one or more of the parties to such an agreement, decision or concerted practice. It also provides that such an agreement or decision which a person proposes to conclude or make with one or more other persons may be notified to the Authority under section 7 of the 1991 Act and shall be deemed always to have been capable of being so notified.

CONSUMER PROTECTION

Consumer credit In the 1995 Review, 26-39, we discussed the effect of the Consumer Credit Act 1995. We also discussed there the impact of the following Regulations and Orders of relevance to the 1995 Act: the Consumer Credit Act 1995 (Section 2) Regulations 1996 (SI No. 127 of 1996), the Consumer Credit Act 1995 (Section 36) Regulations 1996 (SI No. 128 of 1996), the Consumer Credit Act 1995 (Section 37) Regulations 1996 (SI No. 129 of 1996), the Consumer Credit Act 1995 (Section 60) Regulations 1996 (SI No. 130 of 1996), the Consumer Credit Act 1995 (Section 86) Regulations 1996 (SI No. 131 of 1996), the Consumer Credit Act 1995 (Section 129) Regulations 1996 (SI No. 132 of 1996), the Consumer Credit Act 1995 (Section 28) Regulations 1996 (SI No. 245 of 1996), the Consumer Credit Act 1995 (Section 60) (No. 2) Regulations 1996 (SI No. 246 of 1996), the Consumer Credit Act 1995 (Section 120) Regulations 1996 (SI No. 247 of 1996), the Consumer Information (Consumer Credit) Order 1987 (Revocation) Order 1996 (SI No. 248 of 1996) and the European Communities (Consumer Credit Act 1995) (Amendment) Regulations 1996 (SI No. 277 of 1996). We did not refer to the Consumer Credit Act 1995 (Section 2) (No. 2) Regulations 1996 (SI No. 369 of 1996), which further supplemented the list of institutions contained in section 2 of the 1995 Act and SI No. 127 of 1996, which are deemed to be credit institutions for the purposes of the 1995 Act. These latter Regulations came into effect on December 3, 1996.

Measurements, metrology and weights The Metrology Act 1996 is discussed separately below, 65.

Misleading advertising: scope and interlocutory relief   In *Dunnes Stores Ltd. v. MANDATE* [1996] 1 I.R. 55 (H.C. & S.C.), the Supreme Court held that the advertisement in issue in the case fell outside the scope of the European Communities (Misleading Advertising) Regulations 1988 (1988 Review, 209 and 1993 Review, 64-6). The Court also held that interlocutory relief was not available under the 1988 Regulations. The plaintiff company operated large retail stores throughout the State and the defendant was a registered trade union representing the majority of the plaintiff's employees. In November 1995, the company learned that the defendant had arranged to place an advertisement in the national press on the following day. The advertisement was headed 'Do they know its Christmas time at all?' and made specific allegations about the company's failure to implement an earlier agreement reached between the parties in the Labour Court. It then went on to explain why the plaintiff's employees had decided to take limited strike action and requested the support of the public. The plaintiff instituted proceedings seeking a declaration that the proposed advertisement was false and misleading within the meaning of the European Communities (Misleading Advertising) Regulations 1988 and an injunction pursuant to the 1988 Regulations restraining the defendant from publishing the advertisement. The plaintiff sought and was granted an interim injunction restraining the publication of the advertisement but was refused an interlocutory injunction in the High Court by Murphy J. While accepting that a fair case had been made out that the advertisement fell within the 1988 Regulations, he concluded that the balance of convenience was against granting interlocutory relief because if the publication were to be prohibited at that stage, the merits of the campaign based on an emotive appeal to financial stringency at Christmas time would be defeated. The plaintiff appealed to the Supreme Court against the refusal of interlocutory relief, and the Court (Hamilton C.J., Blayney and Denham JJ.) dismissed the appeal. It was held that interlocutory relief was not available under the 1988 Regulations and that, in any event, the advertisement fell outside their scope.

Regulation 4(1) of the 1988 Regulations provides that:

> Any person, including the Director may, upon giving notice of the application to any person against whom the order the subject of the application is sought, apply to the High Court for, and may, at the discretion of that Court, be granted, an order prohibiting the publication, or the further publication, of advertising the publication of which is misleading advertising.

Reg. 4(4) provides that where the High Court has made an order under Regulation 4 it may also require publication of its decision in full or in part and in such form as it deems adequate and may also require the publication of a corrective statement. Regulation 4(5) provides that where an application has been made to the Court for an order pursuant to Regulation 4, the Court may order an advertiser to furnish evidence as to the accuracy of any factual claims made in any advertising. Regulation 4(6) provides that in the exercise of its discretion to prohibit advertising, the Court shall take account of all the interests involved and in particular the public interest.

The word 'advertising' is not defined in the 1988 Regulations, but is defined as follows in Article 2(1) of Directive 84/450/EEC (which the 1988 Regulations implemented):

> "Advertising" means the making of a representation in any form in connection with a trade, business, craft or profession in order to promote the supply of goods or services, including immovable property, rights and obligations.

In addition, Article 1 of the 1984 Directive provides:

> The purpose of this directive is to protect consumers, persons carrying on a trade or business or practising a craft or profession and the interest of the public in general against misleading advertising and the unfair consequences thereof.

Delivering the Supreme Court's decision, Blayney J. stated that an order under Regulation 4(1) of the 1988 Regulations prohibiting the publication of misleading advertising is a final and not an interlocutory order. The power given to the court to require publication of its decision in full together with the power to require an advertiser to furnish evidence of the accuracy of any factual claim clearly implies that the Court, on an application for the order, must make a finding as to whether or not the advertising is misleading. Such a finding would not be made on an interlocutory application. In this context, having regard to the fact that the plaintiff's claim was based on the 1988 Regulations, its application for an order prohibiting the publication of the defendant's advertising could only be brought under Regulation 4(1) of the 1988 Regulations.

The Court therefore treated the application as an application for a final order under Regulation 4(1). In this respect, the advertisement which the defendant intended to publish did not promote the supply of goods or services and therefore did not come within the definition of "advertising" in Council Directive 84/450/EEC or within the definition of "misleading advertising" in the 1988 Regulations. The advertisement could not therefore, be the subject of an order under Regulation 4(1) of the 1988 Regulations.

Footwear: labelling The European Communities (Labelling of Footwear) Regulations 1996 (SI No. 63 of 1996) gave effect to Directive 94/11/EC. They require the indication on a label of the main components of footwear either by specific written indications or their corresponding pictograms which must be supplied by manufacturers. The retailer remains responsible for ensuring that footwear bears the required information. The 1996 Regulations apply to most types of footwear, ranging from sandals to thighboots. Certain types of foot-wear are excluded, such as second-hand footwear, or protective footwear cov-ered by the European Communities (Personal Protective Equipment) Regulations 1993 (1993 Review, 480-1). The 1996 Regulations are enforce-able by the Director of Consumer affairs and came into effect on March 23, 1996, with transitional provisions for existing stock up to September 23, 1997.

Price indications   The European Communities (Indication of Prices of Food-stuffs and Non-Food Products) (Amendment) Regulations 1996 (SI No. 124 of 1996) amended the European Communities (Indication of Prices of Food-stuffs and Non-Food Products) Regulations 1993 (1993 Review, 48) to give effect to Directive 95/58/EC. The effect was to extend retrospectively the dead-line for the requirement to indicate the unit price for pre-packaged goods from June 7, 1995 to June 6, 1997. The 1995 date specified in the 1993 Regulations had proved impossible to achieve across the European Union.

Prices: magazines   The Maximum Prices (Magazines) Order 1996 (SI No. 207 of 1996) and the Maximum Prices (Magazines) (Revocation) Order 1996 (SI No. 307 of 1996) are discussed above.

FINANCIAL SERVICES

Banker's duty: irregular endorsements on cheques   In *Shield Life Insur-ance Co Ltd. v. Ulster Bank Ltd*; High Court, December 5, 1995, Costello P. held although a bank is not, in accordance with the Cheques Act 1959, negli-gent by reason only of a failure to concern itself with an irregularity in the endorsement on a cheque, where there were other circumstances, antecedent to or part of the relevant transaction, taken together with the endorsement's irregularity and the failure to concern itself with that irregularity, the bank may be liable for breach of the duty owed to the cheque's true owner.

One of the defendant's bank customers carried on an insurance broker's business linked with the plaintiff. The broker had defrauded the plaintiff com-pany on a number of occasions, two of which were the subject of this litiga-tion. The first concerned a cheque for £30,000 naming the plaintiff as the payee, which was drawn by a woman and given to the broker for transmission to the plaintiff for what she thought was an investment bond which they had issued in her favour. The bond given to her by the broker was, in fact, a for-gery and the plaintiff was unaware of the transaction. The broker had the cheque endorsed with his name and lodged with the defendant for collection. £25,000 of the £30,000 was lodged on his instructions in his 'clients account' and the balance in his 'office account'. On the next day, £23,000 was drawn from the client account by the broker. When the fraud was discovered the following year, the plaintiff's contract with the broker was terminated and the plaintiff later issued a bond to the woman involved in the same terms as that forged by the broker. Before that fraud was discovered, another was in the process of being effected. An individual insurance policy had matured and the proceeds were paid to the individual by a cheque for almost £20,000. The cheque was drawn on the defendant bank and the individual was the payee named on it. The cheque was crossed and the words 'not negotiable' added. The individual arranged with the broker that he would invest £20,000 in an investment bond to be issued by the plaintiff company and the broker delivered to him a forged bond purporting to be issued by the plaintiff. In return, the individual signed the cheque on the reverse side and gave it to the broker with a sum of £172 to make up the £20,000. The broker lodged this cheque with the defendant and on his instructions £2,000 was paid into his office account, £500 was given to the broker in cash and the balance was paid into his client account. Again, the plaintiff later issued a bond to the individual in the same terms as those in the forged bond.

In respect of both frauds, the plaintiff instituted proceedings against the defendant as payee of the cheques claiming to be their true owner and that the bank had wrongly converted them. In the first action, the plaintiff claimed that the bank could only avoid liability by relying on section 4 of the Cheques Act 1959. This provides that where a collecting banker, in good faith and without negligence, received payment for a customer of an instrument or having credited a customer's account with the amount of such an instrument, received payment thereof for himself, and the customer had either no title or a defective title to the instrument, the banker is not liable to the instrument's true owner by reason only of having received payment thereof. In addition, section 4 provides that the banker is not to be treated as having been negligent by reason only of his failure to concern himself with absence of or irregularity in endorsement of an instrument. The defendant submitted that it was more than a collecting agent for the cheques; as it had given value for them by crediting the amount to its customer's account before receiving payment, it was not only a 'holder for value' but also a 'holder in due course' within the meaning of section 29 of the Bills of Exchange Act 1882, and had thus obtained the rights conferred by section 38 of the 1882 Act. As such, even if its customer's title was defective, it held the bill free from those defects and was entitled to enforce payment of it. Thus, the bank claimed that it was the 'true owner' of the cheque, so that no claim for damages for conversion by the payee at common law existed. It also denied that there was any negligence on its part and that it was thereby protected by section 4 of the 1959 Act. Costello P. held against the bank in both claims.

In respect of the first cheque, Costello P. accepted that if value was given by a collecting bank on the transfer of a cheque from a customer, the bank might not merely be an agent for collection but became a "holder for value". He was prepared to assume for the purposes of the case that the bank in the instant case had given value for the cheque. But he pointed out that section 29 of the Bills of Exchange Act 1882 defined 'holder in due course' as a holder who takes the cheque in certain conditions and the bank had first to establish that it was a "holder" of the cheque in accordance with section 2 of the 1882 Act, which defined holder of a bill as "the payee or endorsee of a bill or note who is in possession of it, or the bearer thereof". Costello P. held that the bank was not the "payee" of the cheque (the plaintiff was the payee), nor was it the "endorsee" (the broker had not endorsed it to the bank), nor was it the "bearer" (defined in section 2 as the person in possession of a bill payable to bearer, and the first cheque was not such a cheque).

Costello P. then went on to consider section 2 of the Cheques Act 1959, which deals with a collecting banker who receives an unendorsed cheque for collection on a customer's behalf; he held that section 2 of the 1959 Act only applied when the customer is a "holder" of the cheque. He considered that the bank had never become a 'holder' of the first cheque. In order to constitute the holder of a bill or cheque a holder "in due course", it had to be shown that the bill was "complete and regular on its face". Costello P. noted that this was not the case here as the endorsement was highly irregular since it had not been completed by the payee. Thus, even if the bank were a 'holder" it did not become a "holder in due course" and could not claim any rights under section 38 of the Bills of Exchange Act 1882. The bank had notice of the defect in the broker's title to the cheque as there was no proper endorsement to the broker by the payee, the plaintiff. Thus, the bank could not claim that it was other than an agent for collection of the cheque and it failed to show that the plaintiff was not the true owner of the cheque.

The bank had also submitted that the doctrine of *ex turpi causa non oritur actio* should apply to defeat the plaintiff's claim. Costello P. held that there were no considerations of public policy to justify a refusal of the plaintiff's claim should negligence be established. Distinguishing the circumstances in the instant case from those in *Thackwell v. Barclays Bank plc* [1986] 1 All ER 976, he concluded that the court would not be assisting in the commission of a crime by so doing, as it would not, by awarding damages, be ordering the return of stolen money. Rather, the court's order would in effect compensate the payee of a cheque which had been converted by the collecting bank.

Costello P. went on to state that the plaintiff was entitled to damages for conversion unless the bank could establish that they had taken reasonable care to ensure that their customer's title to the cheque was not defective. All the circumstances surrounding the transaction including past circumstances could be relevant to the question of what facts were sufficient to cause a bank reasonably to suspect that its customer was not the true owner of the cheque. As already indicated, he pointed out that a banker was not to be treated as having been negligent by reason only of a failure to concern himself with an irregularity in the endorsement on a cheque. But there were other circumstances, antecedent to or part of the relevant transaction, which, taken together with the endorsement's irregularity and the failure to concern himself with that irregularity, might be considered by the court on considering whether the banker had been guilty of breach of duty to the cheque's true owner. While each case depended on its own facts, he considered that there could be special circumstances which affected the banker's duty of care to which the banker ought to pay particular regard. Such circumstances could include, as in the instant case, a situation in which a customer maintained two accounts and in which it was clear that the customer was holding money in an account as a trustee. Costello P. noted that the transfers from the client to the office account were not used to pay sums to which the broker was entitled by way of commission; he considered that the size of the transfers and the fact that they were in rounded figures raised an inference that they were not transfers of a percentage of premiums received by the broker. This taken with the evidence of the broker's financial difficulties raised a further inference that it was likely that he was using his clients' money to pay his office expenses and reduce his office account overdraft.

Costello P. accepted that it was common for bankers to accept for collection on their customers' behalf third party cheques which were not endorsed or contained irregular endorsements. However, the nature of the irregularity in this case was important. The payee here had not attempted to endorse the cheque, it was endorsed by the bank's customer, the endorsement was ambiguous, and the customer/broker had asked the bank to pay the cheque's proceeds into his clients account. It could reasonably be inferred, Costello P. considered, that the proceeds did not belong to the broker. Taking into account the inference as to the possible impropriety of the transfers from the customer to the client account, the nature of the endorsement's irregularity and the circumstances surrounding the lodgement, a prudent banker would have made inquiries about the cheque before accepting it for collection. The bank was therefore negligent in the manner it discharged its duty to the plaintiff and the plaintiff's claim for damages for conversion thus succeeded.

Turning to the second cheque, Costello P. held that it was significantly different from the first in that it was crossed with the words "and Co." and marked "not negotiable". The signature on the cheque was ambiguous as it could have been signed by the individual in question as a receipt or he may have intended his signature as an endorsement for the purpose of negotiating it. His evidence in the proceedings was that he had signed the cheque as an endorsement and had given it to the broker together with £172 in payment to the plaintiff of a premium for an investment bond purportedly issued by the plaintiff and handed to him by the broker. Costello P. court approached this aspect of the case on the basis that though this was a not negotiable cheque, it had been endorsed by its payee and given to the broker for delivery to the plaintiff. In those circumstances, section 81 of the Bills of Exchange Act 1882 applied, namely that where a person took a crossed cheque bearing the phrase "not negotiable" he had no title to it. As the broker had no title, the bank obtained no title to the cheque, the "true owner" of the cheque was the plaintiff and the bank owed a duty of care to the plaintiff in relation to it. While the acceptance from a person other than the payee of a crossed cheque without making enquiries was not in itself conclusive evidence of negligence on a banker's part if the payee was defrauded, Costello P. cited with approval the decision in *Crumplin v. London Joint Stock Bank Ltd.* (1914) 109 LT 856 to the effect that this was a matter to be taken into consideration with all the other relevant circumstances when deciding whether the banker was in breach of duty to the true owner. In this respect, the bank had failed to displace the inference of possible impropriety involved in the transfers between the broker's accounts which the evidence in the case if the first cheque had raised. He concluded that a prudent banker should have been mindful of this inference when presented with a non-negotiable cheque for collection by a customer which had an ambiguous signature which might or might not be an attempt to endorse it in his customer's favour. In the circumstances of the transfer of £2,000 to the office account and £500 in cash, a prudent banker would have concerned himself with the propriety of this transaction and have made inquiries before accepting it. Again, he concluded that the bank had failed to establish that it was not negligent.

Costello P. also held that the plaintiff had no reason to suspect fraud at the time the transactions were being effected, and thus there had been no contributory negligence in either case by the plaintiff.

Finally, as to the level of damages, the damages recoverable in respect of the first cheque were the value of that cheque, £30,000. Costello P. held that the sums recoverable by the plaintiff from a third party under a contract entered into between it and the third party could not be set off against those damages. A similar approach was applied to the second cheque.

Credit institutions: supervision   The Supervision of Credit Institutions, Stock Exchange Member Firms and Investment Business Firms Regulations 1996 (SI No. 267 of 1996) gave effect to Directive 95/26/EC. They provide that supervisory bodies of credit institutions, stock exchange member firms and investment business firms shall refuse authorisation to conduct investment business in certain circumstances and impose certain obligations on auditors of such institutions. They came into effect on September 10, 1996. Although the Regulations were made pursuant to section 3 of the European

Communities Act 1972, their title marks a departure from practice hitherto by the omission of the usual 'European Communities' in their title. It is not clear whether this was simply overlooked in their preparation.

Insurance companies: accounts   The European Communities (Insurance Undertakings: Accounts) Regulations 1996 (SI No. 23 of 1996) gave effect to Directive 91/674/EEC. The 1991 Directive and the 1996 Regulations provide for the application of the 4th and 7th Company Law Directives (78/660/EEC and 83/349/EEC) to insurance companies. They require insurance undertakings to prepare and publish annual accounts (balance sheet, profit and loss account and notes) and require those insurance undertakings with subsidiaries or non-insurance holding companies to prepare and publish group accounts, subject to certain exceptions set out in the Regulations. The 1996 Regulations also provide for the preparation of the accounts including their contents, format, valuation of items and information to be included in the notes. They are applicable to accounts drawn up in respect of every financial year beginning on or after January 1, 1995. The 1996 regulations provided for various consequential amendments to the Assurance Companies Act 1909, the Companies Act 1963 and the Companies (Amendment) Act 1986.

Insurance: Switzerland   The European Communities (Swiss Confederation Agreement) Regulations 1996 (SI. No. 25 of 1996) gave effect to Directive 91/371/EEC, which implemented the Agreement between the European Union and Switzerland on direct insurance other than life assurance. The Regulations came into effect on February 8, 1996.

Investment intermediaries: bonding   The Investment Intermediaries Act 1995 (Commencement) (No. 2) Order 1996 (SI No. 28 of 1996) brought the Investment Intermediaries Act 1995 (1995 Review, 41) into force as respects member firms of the Irish Stock Exchange on 1 April 1996 and section 51 of the Act (which deals with the requirement on investment intermediaries to enter into bonding arrangements to protect investors) into force on March 11, 1996 except in respect of certain categories of investment business firms specified in the Order. The Investment Intermediaries Act 1995 (Bonding Of Intermediaries) Regulations 1996 (SI No. 29 of 1996) lay down the detailed information required of investment intermediaries when seeking bonding pursuant to section 51 of the 1995 Act. The Regulations came into effect on March 11, 1996.

INTELLECTUAL PROPERTY

Counterfeit and pirated goods   The European Communities (Counterfeit and Pirated Goods) Regulations 1996 (SI No. 48 of 1996) give effect to the necessary administrative arrangements in order to give full effect to Regulation (EC) No. 3295/94 and Regulation (EC) No. 1367/95. They prohibit the release for free circulation, export, re-export or entry into or within the State of counterfeit and pirated goods. They also lay down a system for applications to the Revenue Commissioners by holders of rights over the original goods being pirated seeking the interception and detention of such goods, requirements for furnishing security to and indemnifying of the Revenue Commissioners against liability arising from such detention and provide that such goods be treated as prohibited goods under the Customs Acts. The Regulations also introduced fines in respect of infringements. They came into effect on February 15, 1996.

Foreign intellectual property protection: WTO States The Copyright (Foreign Countries) Order 1996 (SI No. 36 of 1996) provide for terms of protection for literary, dramatic, musical or artistic works and cinematograph films the authors or makers of which are citizens of, or were first published in, countries of the Berne Union, the Universal Copyright Convention or countries which had ratified the 1993 World Trade Organisation (WTO) Agreement. The Order revoked the Copyright (Foreign Countries) Order 1978 and the Copyright (Foreign Countries) (No. 2) Order 1978. Similarly, the Designs And Trade Marks (International Arrangements) (Amendment) Order 1996 (SI No. 37 of 1996) provided that the provisions of the Industrial and Commercial Property (Protection) Act 1927 and the Trade Marks Act 1963 (the latter since superseded by the Trade Marks Act 1996, discussed below) apply to the foreign states specified in the Schedule to the Order, all of which had ratified the 1993 World Trade Organisation (WTO) Agreement . This Order revoked the Patents, Designs And Trade Marks (International Arrangements) Order 1987. Finally, the Patents (International Arrangements) Order 1996 (SI No. 38 of 1996) declared that section 25 of the Patents Act 1992 (1992 Review, 41-6) shall apply to countries which had ratified the 1993 WTO Agreement. This Order revoked the Patents Act 1964 (Section 93) (Declaration)(Order) 1976. The three Orders came into effect on January 30, 1996. SI No. 37 of 1996 and SI No. 38 of 1996 are discussed below in *Allen & Hanbury Ltd. and Anor v. Controller of Patents, Designs and Trade Marks and Clonmel Healthcare Ltd. (No. 2)* [1997] 1 I.L.R.M. 416 (H.C.).

Passing off: interlocutory injunction In *R. Griggs Group Ltd. and Ors v. Dunnes Stores Ireland Ltd*, High Court, October 4, 1996, McCracken J. declined to grant an interlocutory injunction to the plaintiffs to prevent the defendants from passing off boots which, it was claimed, were similar to the plaintiffs' 'Dr Martens' boots. The plaintiffs were manufactures of footwear and owners of the registered trade mark in 'Dr Martens' boots. The defendant, a large retail outlet which, inter alia, deals in footwear. The plaintiffs claimed that their goods were so distinctive as to be associated in the minds of the public solely with them, but the defendant contended that the features called in aid by the plaintiffs were not unique to the 'Dr Martens' boots. The boots being sold by the defendant had been manufactured by two independent sources in England and Italy but the plaintiffs had not taken any action against the manufacturers.

McCracken J. considered the case law in the area of passing off. Referring to the decision of the House of Lords in *Erven Warnink BV. v. J. Townsend & Sons (Hull) Ltd.* [1979] AC 731, he held that the plaintiffs had no right to protect the design features of their boots unless there was a registered design or the defendants were passing off their goods as those of the plaintiffs. Citing the decision of the Supreme Court in *Adidas Sportchuhfabriken Adi Dassler KA v. Charles O'Neill & Co Ltd.* [1983] I.L.R.M. 12, he noted that the plaintiffs must establish a reputation in the mind of the public and that the public would recognise the combination of features as being unique to the plaintiffs. McCracken J. concluded that the plaintiffs had 'just about done enough' to establish such an arguable case. However, he went on to state that, bearing in mind that the granting of an injunction is an equitable remedy, it seemed inherently inequitable that the proceedings should be brought against a retailer which purchased the goods from two manufacturers while no action was taken against the manufacturers. As to the damage likely to be suffered by the plaintiffs, he held that, in the context of world-wide sales, it was likely to be minimal, whereas the defendant would be deprived of the sales of a complete range of popular footwear, which would be more serious for them. On this basis, he concluded that the balance of convenience lay in favour of refusing an interlocutory injunction. For a similar case, in which an interlocutory injunction was granted, see *Gabicci Plc v. Dunnes Stores Ltd*, High Court, July 31, 1991 (1992 Review, 39-40).

Patent protection: effect of WTO Agreement In *Allen & Hanbury Ltd. and Anor v. Controller of Patents, Designs and Trade Marks and Clonmel Healthcare Ltd. (No. 2)* [1997] 1 I.L.R.M. 416 (H.C.), Carroll J. held that certain provisions of the 1993 World Trade Organisation (WTO) Agreement dealing with Trade Related Aspects of Intellectual Property Rights (the TRIPS Agreement) obliged the Controller of Patents, Designs and Trademarks to refuse the grant of compulsory patent licences pursuant to section 42 of the Patents Act 1964. In *Allen & Hanbury Ltd. and Anor v. Controller of Patents, Designs and Trade Marks and Clonmel Healthcare Ltd*, High Court, February 21, 1996, Carroll J. had decided that the issue concerning the TRIPS Agreement and section 42 of the 1964 Act should be dealt with as a preliminary point of law.

The case arose against the following background. In late 1991 and early

1992, respectively, the second defendant, Clonmel Healthcare, had applied for 'compulsory licences' under section 42 of the 1964 Act to exploit two patents on medicinal products owned by the plaintiff companies. The licences were ultimately granted by the Controller in 1995. The statutory background to the case is rather complex.

Section 42(1) of the Patents Act 1964 provided that where a patent is in force in respect of any invention capable of being used, inter alia, as a medical, surgical or other remedial device, the Controller 'shall' grant a licence under the patent on such terms as he thinks fit where an application is made to him by any interested person, unless it appears there are good reasons for refusing the application having regard to the desirability of encouraging inventors and the growth and development of industry. Such a licence is usually referred to as a compulsory licence. Section 46(3) of the 1964 Act provided, *inter alia*, that no licence shall be given under section 42 which would be at variance with any treaty, convention, arrangement or engagement applying to the State. The Patents Act 1992 (1992 Review, 41-6) came into force on August 1, 1992. While section 5 of the 1992 Act repealed the 1964 Act, the transitional provisions stated that any application for a licence under section 42 of the 1964 Act pending at the commencement of the 1992 Act was to be decided under the provisions of the 1964 Act.

The Agreement on Trade Related Aspects of Intellectual Property Rights (the TRIPS Agreement) is contained in an Annex to the Agreement which established the World Trade Organisation, the WTO Agreement, agreed in Marrakesh, Morocco in December 1993. The first draft of the WTO Agreement, including the draft TRIPS Agreement, had been published on December 20, 1991. The final version of the WTO Agreement, including the TRIPS Agreement, was agreed on 15 December 1993 and signed by the State on 15 April 1994. On 15 November 1994, the Court of Justice of the European Communities, in Opinion No. 1/94, held that the European Union had joint competence with the Member States of the European Union to conclude the WTO Agreement; on the same date the State, together with the European Union and the other Member States of the European Union, deposited instruments of ratification of the WTO Agreement. In December 1994, Council Decision 94/900/EC ratified the WTO Agreement on behalf of the European Union. The WTO Agreement came into force on January 1, 1995.

Article 27(1) of the TRIPS Agreement provides, inter alia, that patents shall be available and patent rights enjoyable 'without discrimination as to the place of invention, the field of technology and whether products are imported or locally produced.' Article 70(6) of TRIPS provides that Article 27 need not be applied by WTO Members where a patent authorisation was granted before the TRIPS Agreement became known to the Member Government. Finally, Article 65(1) of the TRIPS Agreement provides that no WTO Member shall be obliged to apply the provisions of the Agreement before the expiry of one year following the entry into force of the WTO Agreement. This one year transitional period expired on January 1, 1996.

The central issue in the *Allen & Hanburys* case was the plaintiffs' argument that the TRIPS Agreement effectively overrode the 1964 Act. In particular it was argued that the requirement in Article 27 that patents be available 'without discrimination as to . . . the field of technology' was inconsistent with the discriminatory arrangements in section 42 of the 1964 Act which made a special case for medicinal products. It was common case that the TRIPS Agreement was intended to achieve the non-discriminatory effect claimed by the plaintiffs, but a central point of dispute was whether the TRIPS Agreement was part of domestic law and, even if it was, whether it could retrospectively override any entitlements of the second defendant under prior law. The Controller had taken the view that the TRIPS Agreement had no application to the 1964 Act since it had not been enacted into domestic law. In the High Court, Carroll J. reversed.

In the first place, Carroll J. dealt with the application of Article 29.6 of the Constitution, which provides that no international agreement shall be part of the domestic law of the State 'save as may be determined by the Oireachtas.' This was crucial to the meaning of section 46(3) of the 1964 Act which as we have seen provided that no mandatory licence could be granted under section 42 which would be at variance with any treaty or convention applying to the State. Carroll J. held that section 46(3) of the 1964 Act had, in effect, delegated to the Government the power to enter into a treaty with limited effect in domestic law without the need to revert back to the Oireachtas. She went on to hold that the TRIPS Agreement was a treaty or convention applying to the State within the meaning of section 46(3) of the 1964 Act, rejecting the second defendant's argument that section 46 referred to bilateral treaties only. Carroll J. thus concluded that section 46(3) conferred the status of domestic law on the provisions of any treaty which was at variance with the granting of a licence under section 42 of the 1964 Act.

The next issue was whether the TRIPS Agreement could have retrospective effect. Carroll J. held it could though first she rejected a retrospection point raised by the second defendant, which was that, arising from the TRIPS Agreement itself, many of the conventions and agreements in existence prior to TRIPS had become redundant. Indeed, it was pointed out that the Designs and Trade Marks (International Arrangements) (Amendment) Order 1996 (SI No. 37 of 1996) and the Patents (International Arrangements) Order 1996 (SI No. 38 of 1996), had revoked these previous conventions and agreements with effect from January 1996, thus (it was argued) rendering section 46 retrospectively meaningless since the conventions in question had, since January 1996, been removed from the statutory landscape. Carroll J. rejected this argument, pointing out that section 22 of the Interpretation Act 1937 provided that these revocations did not affect any acquired rights. Thus, she concluded:

> If section 46(3) [of the 1964 Act] conferred a right on the plaintiffs not
> to have a compulsory licence granted because this would be in breach of
> a treaty between the State and any convention country, then the revoca-
> tion [of the pre-TRIPS conventions effected by the 1996 Orders] does
> not affect the issue. The proceedings must be continued as if they had
> not been revoked.

This approach is, of course, consistent with the provisions of the Patents Act
1992, which provided that any pending applications be dealt with under the
1964 Act.

The second issue surrounding retrospection, also made by the second defendant, was that section 46(3) of the 1964 Act could not be interpreted as
facilitating summary termination of a property right. Carroll J. also rejected
this. She stated:

> [A]ny right under section 42 [of the 1964 Act] was always subject to the
> infirmity that it could be affected by a [later] treaty and it would be
> necessary for the defendants to look to the transitional provisions of the
> treaty to ascertain their rights.

While this passage has the attraction that it interprets the second defendant's
statutory rights conferred by section 42 of the 1964 Act as being conditional
only, it is ironic that it should come so closely after the portion of her judgment which recognised that the rights the plaintiffs had acquired under section 46 could not be interfered with retrospectively. It may be that this
contradistinction would feature in the Supreme Court, to which the *Allen &
Hanburys* case has been appealed.

Carroll J. went on to deal with the correct interpretation of Article 70(6) of
TRIPS, which prohibited any contrary granting of patent decisions after it had
'become known.' A good deal of discussion focused on whether this should
refer to December 20, 1991, when the first draft of TRIPS was published, or
December 15, 1993, when the final text was agreed. Ultimately, Carroll J.
concluded it was not necessary to decide this point since the Controller's decision in June 1995 had been made after TRIPS had been ratified and thus was
clearly 'known' within the meaning of Article 70(6). As to whether it was
known to the Government, Carroll J. also answered in the affirmative. The
Controller had argued that that his grant of a licence in June 1995 cannot have
been granted by the government since, under section 63 of the Patents Act
1992, he is regarded as 'independent' in the exercise of his functions. However, Carroll J. held that, since section 77(2) of the 1964 Act provided that the
Controller shall act 'under the general superintendence and direction of the
Minister' for Enterprise and Employment, the Controller's decision to grant
the compulsory licences to the second defendant was an authorisation by the

Government within the meaning of Article 70(6) of the TRIPS Agreement. While this conclusion seems to accord with common sense, it leaves open to doubt the precise value of the Controller's independence, unless this is to be interpreted as being free merely of *ultra vires* political pressures.

Finally, Carroll J. dealt with Article 65(1) of the TRIPS Agreement, which provides that no WTO Member shall be obliged to apply the provisions of the Agreement before the expiry of one year following the entry into force of the WTO Agreement, that is, before January 1996. She concluded that Article 65(1) was 'subservient' to the other provisions of the TRIPS Agreement. While she accepted that Article 70(6) amounted to a derogation from Article 27, she noted that Article 70(6) itself ceased to apply at the latest in December 1993. Thus, Article 65 could not apply to the circumstances arising in the instant case because, from December 1993 the Controller could not grant a licence in breach of Article 27.

As already indicated, on the basis of this analysis, Carroll J. concluded that the Controller's decision should be reversed. In view of the obvious importance of the decision, it is not surprising that, as indicated, the decision has been appealed to the Supreme Court. We will deal with the decision of the Supreme Court in a future Review.

Performer protection: foreign country of origin   The Performers' Protection (Foreign Countries) (Amendment) Order 1996 (SI No. 39 of 1996), made under the Performers' Protection Act 1968, amended the Performers' Protection (Foreign Countries) Order 1978 to include countries of the World Trade Organisation. The Order came into effect on January 30, 1996.

Product description: spirit drinks   The European Communities (Definition, Description and Presentation of Spirit Drinks) (Amendment) Regulations 1996 (SI No. 60 of 1996) amended the European Communities (Definition, Description and Presentation of Spirit Drinks) Regulations 1995 and gave effect to Regulation (EC) No. 1267/94. They provide for the protection of the names used to describe certain spirit drinks produced in the United States, as set out in the 1994 (EC) Regulation. The 1996 Regulations came into effect on March 5, 1996.

Trade Marks Act 1996   The Trade Marks Act 1996 is discussed separately below, 68.

Trade mark: removal from register   In *Anheuser-Busch Inc v. Controller of Patents, Designs and Trade Marks (No. 2),* High Court, October 23, 1996, Costello P. granted the plaintiff a declaration under the Trade Marks Act 1963 (since replaced by the Trade Marks Act 1996, discussed below) that a trade mark associated with the well-known brand of beer Budweiser be removed from the Irish register of trade marks on the grounds of non-use. The application had been lodged initially in 1980, but the proceedings took over 17 years to be brought to finality in the High Court.

The applicant, the proprietor in the United States and elsewhere throughout the world of the trade mark in Budweiser, instituted proceedings in many different States concerning the trade marks registered by the Czech company Budweiser Budvar NC, the second respondent, from whom it had bought the rights over Budvar and Budweiser beer. Arising from the difficulty in exporting beer from the former Czechoslovakia during the years of the Communist regime in that State prior to the 1990s, the applicant became the effective sole world-wide seller of Budweiser beer. However, litigation between the companies continued over the years, the second respondent arguing that the purchase of the rights over Budvar was not fully effective. The instant case was one element of this series of proceedings. The central issue in the proceedings was the applicant was unable to obtain registration of its trade mark in Budweiser on the Irish register because of the existence of two trade marks in the name of the second respondent. As indicated, the application to remove these from the register began in 1980. In October 1985, the first respondent refused the application, without stating the grounds. In subsequent judicial review proceedings, the respondent was directed to give reasons for his refusal: *Anheuser-Busch Inc v. Controller of Patents, Designs and Trade Marks* [1987] I.R. 329; [1988] I.L.R.M. 247 (1987 Review, 10-12). The reasons later stated by the respondent were that the only evidence relating to non-use filed by the applicant had not established a prima facie case of non-use. The applicant had stated to the Controller that various investigations and enquiries carried out on its behalf had failed to reveal any instance of use. As already indicated, the applicant successfully appealed against this decision.

The applicant pointed out that, although the second respondent had formally denied the application, it had also specifically referred to the use of the trademark in a number of other countries and the applicant thus argued that the inference could be drawn that it was not being claimed that there had been any use of the trade mark in this State. This proved a critical point with Costello P. He accepted that there was no hard and fast rule as to what was required by way of evidence to establish non-use and that, in the ordinary way, it would not be sufficient for the applicant to make a bald deceleration as to non use and that generally evidence should be given as to what steps were taken to establish this. However, neither was there a hard and fast rule that an applicant who fails to do so will have the case dismissed. In the instant case, the applicant had been entitled to conclude that the second respondent was not alleging that there was any use of its trademark in this State. In that respect, the applicant had established a prima facie case of non-use which became an overwhelming case when all the evidence was considered. As already indicated, Costello P. thus reversed the Controller's decision.

INTERNATIONAL TRADE

Dual-use (civil-military) goods   The European Communities (Control of Exports Of Dual-Use Goods) Regulations 1996 (SI No. 362 of 1996) provide for controls over exports of dual-use goods, that is, goods which have both civil and military uses. They laid down the relevant administrative arrangements, including the requirement that licences for export be obtained from the Department of Trade, the creation of offences and associated penalties, in order to give full effect to Regulation (EC) No. 3381/94, as amended by Regulation (EC) No. 837/95. They came into effect on December 3, 1996. The Control of Exports Order 1996 (SI No. 363 of 1996), made under the Control of Exports Act 1983, contains an updated list of such dual-use goods, replacing the list in the Control of Exports Order 1983 and the Control of Exports Order 1983 (Amendment) Order 1984. The 1996 Order also came into effect on December 10, 1996.

Trade sanctions: breach of statutory duty concerning impounding aircraft   In *Bosphorus Hava Yollari Turizm Ve Ticaret Anonim Sirketi v. Minister for Transport, Energy and Communications and Ors (No. 2)*, High Court, January 22, 1996, Barr J. awarded the plaintiff company damages for the unlawful impounding by the defendant Minister of the applicant company's aircraft. The Minister had acted in purported compliance with the European Communities (Prohibition of Trade with the Federal Republic of Yugoslavia (Serbia and Montenegro)) Regulations 1993. In *Bosphorus Hava Yollari Turizm Ve Ticaret Anonim Sirketi v. Minister for Transport, Energy and Communications and Ors.* [1994] 2 I.L.R.M. 551 (1994 Review, 42-4), Murphy J. had held that the respondent Minister had acted ultra vires the 1993 Regulations.

The case arose against the background of the UN and EC trade sanctions imposed on Serbia and its ally Montenegro in the context of the war in former Yugoslavia which occurred in the early 1990s. The UN Security Council Resolution 820/1993 had been followed by the EC's Council Regulation No. 990/93, which prohibited the export to or the importation from the Federal Republic of Yugoslavia (Serbia and Montenegro) of any commodities or products. The recitals to the Council Regulation noted the adoption of the UN Security Council's Resolution and indeed its terms were reflected in Article 8 of the Regulation itself, which provided that 'all vessels . . . and aircraft in which a majority or controlling interest is held by a person or undertaking in or operating from the Federal Republic of Yugoslavia . . . shall be impounded by the competent authorities of the Member States'. The European Communities (Prohibition of Trade with the Federal Republic of Yugoslavia (Serbia and Montenegro)) Regulations 1993 were made in June 1993 to give effect to the administrative arrangements required to comply fully with the Council Regulation. The respondent Minister was constituted the 'Competent Authority' for the purposes of Article 8 of the Council Regulation.

The applicant was a company incorporated under Turkish law in which all shares were held by Turkish nationals. By a lease agreement made in April 1992, Yugoslav. Airlines (JAT), described as 'the lessor', leased two of its aircraft to the applicant, described as 'the lessee', for a period of 48 months. The lease provided for a monthly rental and a deposit to be paid for each aircraft, and expressly provided that ownership stayed with the lessor but that the lessee had the right to inscribe the aircraft into the Turkish Register of Civil Aviation with notification that the lessor was the owner. Subsequent to delivery, the applicant had complete control of the aircraft and the cabin and flight crew were employees of the applicant. The aircraft were registered with the Turkish Ministry of Transport and Communications General Directorate of Civil Aviation. The relevant certificates identified JAT as the owner of the aircraft and the applicant as the operator. Expert evidence was given that the certificates were conclusive evidence that the aircraft were of Turkish nationality and under the control of the applicant, and that it was possible to register aeroplanes in only one jurisdiction under the Convention on International Civil Aviation. Neither aircraft had returned to Yugoslavia or any of the states of the former Yugoslavia since their delivery to the applicant. One of the aircraft arrived in Dublin in April 1993 for maintenance by the fourth named respondent. The Irish government issued instructions in May 1993 that 'the aircraft was to be stopped'. The respondent Minister then ordered that the aircraft be impounded pursuant to Council Regulation 990/93. The Minister had been advised by the United Nations Sanctions Committee that the aircraft fell within the terms of Resolution 820/1993.

The applicant sought a declaration that the aircraft did not come within the terms of Article 8 of Council Regulation 990/93 and that the first named respondent was not empowered to impound the aircraft. As already indicated, Murphy J. had found in the 1994 decision that the Minister was not empowered to impound the aircraft in question:

> In determining the issue of damages, Barr J. held that the plaintiff was entitled to have the benefit of a Ministerial decision within a reasonable time. He noted that it was common case that the plaintiff was innocent of any involvement in aiding any Serbian organisation in breach of the UN or EC sanctions; in his view, this enhanced the importance of avoiding delay. He therefore concluded that the Minister had failed in his duty to Bosphorus to investigate and decide within a reasonable time whether or not there had been any breach or breaches of Article 1.1(e) of Regulation (EEC) 990/93.

We should note that, while Murphy J. had held in 1994 that the respondent Minister had acted ultra vires the 1993 Regulations, this issue was subsequently referred by the Supreme Court to the Court of Justice pursuant to Article 177 of the EC Treaty. The Court held, in *Bosphorus Hava Yollari Turizm Ve Ticaret Anonim Sirketi v. Minister for Transport, Energy and Communications and Ors (No. 3)*, Court of Justice, 1996, that Article 8 of Regulation (EEC) 990/93 applies to an aircraft which is owned by an undertaking based in or operating from the Federal Republic of Yugoslavia (Serbia and Montenegro), even though the owner leased it for four years to another undertaking, neither based in or operating from that Republic and in which no person or undertaking based in or operating from that Republic has a majority or controlling interest. This, in effect, reversed the decision of Murphy J. in the 1994 decision. On remittal of the case to the Supreme Court, therefore, the Court (Hamilton C.J., O'Flaherty, Blayney, Barrington and Denham JJ.) allowed the appeal against Murphy J's decision, pointing out, as it was required to, that it was bound by the decision of the Court of Justice: *Bosphorus Hava Yollari Turizm Ve Ticaret Anonim Sirketi v. Minister for Transport, Energy and Communications and Ors (No. 4)*, Supreme Court, November 29, 1996. While this clarifies that the Minister may have acted *intra vires* in impounding the aircraft the subject matter of these proceedings, it would not appear to have affected the decision of Barr J, above, that the applicant was entitled to a timely decision by the Minister. In that respect, therefore, the applicant remained entitled to damages for the delay involved. At the time of writing (July 1997), the aircraft remained impounded in Dublin Airport, but it appeared that some finality in the proceedings were within reach.

MEASUREMENTS AND METROLOGY

Metrology Act 1996 The Metrology Act 1996 introduces a new term, metrology (the science of measurement), into what was formerly described as the law of weights and measures. The Act established a re-organised Legal Metrology Service within Forbairt, the State research agency, and consolidated and updated previous legislative provisions on legal metrology. It established the various control procedures necessary to maintain confidence in measurements, specifies the relevant units of measurement, lays down controls for the correct adjustment of instruments, regulates forgery, tampering with or removing of marks and seals, the provides for arrangements for checking weighing equipment and re-states various offences, including those for short measure, misrepresentation and for offences by corporate bodies. Provision for prosecutions, penalties, appeals against seizures and with the transfer of property are also specified. The Act came into effect on May 12, 1997: Metrology Act 1996 (Commencement and Establishment) Order 1997 (SI No. 177 of 1997).

Scope and repeals Section 1 the Act provides, inter alia, that its terms are confined to measurements used for trade, as was the case with pre-1996 legislation in this area. The Act repeals a large deal of such legislation. The 1996 Act retains, with appropriate amendments, the Packaged Goods (Quantity Control) Act 1980, which deals with packaged products.

Legal metrology service   Section 7 of the 1996 Act provides for the establishment within Forbairt of a Legal Metrology Service, for the establishment of the position of and appointment to the post of Director of Legal Metrology through whom the Board will exercise its functions. Section 9 provides for the appointment of inspectors to enforce the Act. Section 10 sets out the powers of inspectors to enter premises, vehicles and vessels for the purposes of inspecting any instruments or goods and to seize them where necessary.

Conformity assessment   Section 14 empowers the Director of Legal Metrology to prescribe the conformity assessment procedures to which instruments intended for use for a prescribed purpose, including instruments intended for public use, will be subjected. It also provides for continued validity of type approvals and verifications valid immediately before the Act came into force in May 1997 and for the optional application of the procedures to instruments not intended for a prescribed use. Section 17 provides for the securing of calibration devices on instruments to prevent unauthorised adjustments. The Director may prescribe specific requirements on sealing or securing of instruments. These requirements should be seen against the background of the general statutory requirements concerning manufacturing standards, now under the general aegis of the National Standards Authority of Ireland.

Units of measurement   Section 18 provides that units of measurement comes within the scope of the 1996 Act and thus replaces the European Communities (Units of Measurement) Regulations 1992 (1992 Review, 46-7), which were revoked when the 1996 Act came into effect. The effect of this is that the international SI or metric system of measurement will largely replace the Imperial measurement system. Section 19 and the Third Schedule to the Act lay down the definitions of Imperial Units in relation to one another and in relation to units of the SI system. Section 20 and the Second Schedule specify the standard reference measures of length, weight and capacity in order that they should be in easily distinguishable denominations, for example, weights are denominated in 1kg, 2kg, 5kg, 10kg, 20kg. This ensures that confusion between any one and the next is minimised.

Offences   Section 23 creates an offence of forgery of conformity marks on instruments and for the sale or use of such instruments. Section 24 creates offences of deliberately rendering an instrument inaccurate, using such an instrument, placing false conformity marks on instruments and for falsely representing an instrument as being type approved. Section 25 creates an offence of removal, defacement, obliteration or breaking of any seal or device applied by an inspector unless done for the purposes of repair or adjustment of the instrument. It places an obligation on the user to have the instrument reverified as soon as practicable after being informed that the seal or tag has been removed.

Public weighing   Section 26 provides that only persons holding a certificate of competency from the Director of Legal Metrology are empowered to attend to a public weighing or measuring on instruments. This service may be provided by local authorities for use by the public, as was the case prior to the 1996 Act. Local authorities may employ persons to attend to any measurements on equipment provided for use by the public. Offences are created if the appointed person fails to carry out the duties of the post. It is also an offence if the person requesting the measurement fails to give his or her correct name and address. Providers of instruments must retain records of measurements for one year.

Sale of solid fuel   Section 27 requires that solid fuel, except peat and wood, shall be sold by weight except where otherwise agreed by the parties to the sale. It also provides that within six months of the coming into effect of the Act (that is, by October 12, 1997), the quantity be displayed on sealed containers/packages of solid fuel and for the issue of a docket on which the quantity is stated in respect of both solid fuel sold loose or in a container.

Short measure and misrepresentation   Section 28 creates an offence of selling or offering for sale by weight, measure or number if the quantity is less than that claimed. Goods packed in accordance with the Packaged Goods (Quantity Control) Act 1980 are excluded. Section 29 provides that misrepresentation as to the quantity of goods is also an offence.

Appeal against seizure   Section 30 provides for an appeal to the District Court against seizure and detention of items under section 10.

Prosecutions   Section 32 provides that summary proceedings for offences may be brought and prosecuted by the Director within 12 months from the date of the offence. The section also establishes that commission by an employee or agent of the accused is sufficient proof of the offence, unless otherwise proven. Section 33 specifies the relevant penalties.

STATISTICS

Population census   The Statistics (Census Of Population) Order 1996 (SI No. 91 of 1996), made under the Statistics Act 1993 (1993 Review, 10), provided for the taking of a census of the population of the State on 28 April 1996. It set out the purpose of the census and the persons by whom the information is to be provided and in respect of whom the information is to be provided.

TRADE MARKS ACT 1996

The Trade Marks Act 1996 replaced and updated the Trade Marks Act 1963. The 1996 Act follows the general structure of the Trade Marks Act 1963, with relevant amendments where appropriate. In addition to providing for a general updating of the law on trade marks, the 1996 Act permitted the registration of 'service trade marks'. It also gave effect to European Community obligations by implementing the provisions of Council Directive 89/104/EEC on the approximation of trade mark laws and Council Regulation (EC) No. 40/94 on the Community trade mark. Finally, the 1996 Act gave effect to the Protocol to the Madrid Agreement concerning the international registration of trade marks, and to certain provisions of the Paris Convention for the protection of Industrial Property. The 1996 Act came into effect on July 1, 1996: Trade Marks Act 1996 (Commencement) Order 1996 (SI No. 198 of 1996).

Registered trade marks   Section 6 of the 1996 Act implements Article 2 of the 1989 Directive and extended the definition of a trade mark to include, inter alia, the shape of goods or of their packaging. The definition also makes it clear that signs which are capable of distinguishing services now fall within the general definition of a trade mark. Subsection (3) also introduces the concept of collective marks. Section 7 of the Act makes it clear that a registered trade mark is a property right.

Grounds for refusal of registration   Section 8 of the 1996 Act gives effect to Article 3 of the 1989 Directive and replaces sections 17 and 18 of the Trade Marks Act 1963. One consequence of section 8 is to abolish the existing division of the Register of Trade Marks into Parts A and B. Trade marks which are devoid of any distinctive character or which consist exclusively of signs or indications which may serve in trade to designate the kind, quality, quantity, intended purpose, value, geographical origin or the time of production of the goods or of rendering of the services, or other characteristics of the goods or services will be precluded from registration unless they can be shown to have before the date of application for registration in fact acquired a distinctive character as a result of use. Section 8(2) also precludes from registration the shape of goods resulting from the nature of the goods themselves or which is necessary to obtain a technical result or which gives substantial value to the goods. Section 8(4) provides that a trade mark may no longer be registered if the application for registration is made in bad faith.

Specially protected emblems   Section 9 of the 1996 Act provides that trade marks consisting of the State emblems of Ireland are precluded from registration unless consent has been given by the appropriate authority for their use. Section 9(2) also precludes from registration a trade mark containing the national flag if the use of the trade mark would be misleading or grossly offensive.

Relative grounds for refusal of registration   Section 10 of the 1996 Act re-enacted the provisions of section 20 of the 1963 Act in that it prohibits the registration of identical and resembling trade marks in the names of different owners. Section 10(2) prevents registration where there is a likelihood of association between the trade mark applied for and an earlier registered trade mark. Section 10(4) also precludes from registration any trade mark whose use in the State is liable to be prevented by virtue of any rule of law protecting unregistered trade marks or by virtue of the law of copyright or registered designs.

Meaning of 'earlier trade mark'   Section 11 of the 1996 Act defines 'earlier trade mark' which would now include a registered trade mark, an international trade mark or a Community trade mark registered under the Community Trade Mark Regulation which has an earlier date of application for registration. Section 12 provides a defence of 'honest concurrent use' in relation to an earlier trade mark.

Rights conferred by registered trade mark   Section 13 of the 1996 Act states that the rights of the proprietor in infringement proceedings have full effect as from the publication of the registration of the trade mark in the Official Journal of Industrial and Commercial Property.

Infringement of registered trade mark   Section 14 of the 1996 Act sets out the acts which amount to infringement. It introduces a fundamental change to the law relating to trade mark infringement in the State in accordance with Article 5 of the 1989 Directive in that for the first time the infringement action is available against those who use an infringing mark in relation to goods or services similar but not necessarily identical to those covered by the infringed registration. The test for infringement is whether there exists a likelihood of confusion on the part of the public including the likelihood of association

with the registered trade mark. Section 13(3) extends the right of infringement
in cases where use of the infringing mark is made in relation to dissimilar
goods or services but where the registered trade mark has a reputation in the
State and where the infringing use would take unfair advantage of or be detrimental to the distinctive character or repute of the registered trade mark.

Limits on effect of registered trade mark   Section 15 of the 1996 Act re-
enacts and extends the provisions of sections 15 and 16 of the Trade Marks
Act 1963.

Exhaustion of rights conferred by registered trade mark   Section 16 of
the 1996 Act gave effect to Article 7 of the 1989 Directive which, in turn, is
based upon established Community jurisprudence and provides that a registered trade mark is not infringed by the use of the trade mark in relation to
goods which have been put on the market in the Community under that trade
mark by the proprietor or with the proprietor's consent. Protection has been
given under section 15(2) to the rights of proprietors where the condition of
the goods has been changed or impaired after they have been put on the market.

Registration subject to disclaimer or limitation   Section 22 of the Trade
Marks Act 1963 empowered the High Court or the Controller to require dis-
claimers of matter common to the trade or otherwise of a non-distinctive character. The new provision in section 17 of the 1996 Act allows an applicant for
registration or a registered proprietor the option of disclaiming any right to the
exclusive use of specified elements in trade marks or to limit their rights to a
specific territory.

Infringement proceedings   Section 18 of the 1996 Act re-stated existing
law but provided that in an action for infringement, the proprietor of a registered trade mark will enjoy the same remedies as are available in respect of the
infringement of any other property right. Section 19 provides for the Court to
make an order requiring the erasure, removal or obliteration of an offending
sign. Where this is not practicable the High Court may make an order to secure the destruction of the infringing goods. Section 20 allows the proprietor
of a registered trade mark to obtain a Court Order for the delivery up to the
proprietor or such person as the Court may direct, of any infringing goods,
material or articles. Section 22 provides that in connection with orders made
under section 20 a period of six years from the date the trade mark was applied
to the infringing goods or material is the time limit applies within which an
application for an order for delivery up must be made. If, during this period of
six years, the registered trade mark proprietor was under a disability or prevented by fraud or concealment from discovering the facts entitling the proprietor to apply for such an order, an application may be made within six years

of the applicant ceasing to be under a disability or being in a position to discover those facts. Section 23 deals with the processing of applications to the Court for an order that goods which have been delivered up under section 20 be destroyed, forfeited or otherwise. Section 24 is a new section, which is intended to prevent vexatious threats of trade mark infringement. A similar provision exists in the case of patents under s53 of the Patents Act 1992. Section 25 of the 1996 Act also confers on the Garda Síochána, on foot of a warrant from the District Court, the power to enter premises and to seize and detain goods which infringe the 1996 Act.

Registered trade mark as object of property   Section 26 specifies the status of a registered trade mark as personal property. Section 27 re-enacts the provisions of section 67 of the Trade Marks Act 1963 and prohibits the registration as joint proprietors of a trade mark of persons who use or propose to use that trade mark independently.

Assignment of registered trade mark   Section 28 replaces the provisions of section 30 of the Trade Marks Act 1963. In particular, it does away with the requirement under section 30(7) of the 1963 Act for publication of notice of an assignment in the Official Journal of a trade mark in use at the date of assignment and assigned without goodwill. Section 28(3) clarifies that assignment of a registered trade mark must be in writing signed by or on behalf of the assignor or, as the case may be, by a personal representative. The requirement is satisfied by bodies corporate by affixing of their seals. Section 28(5) provides that it is now possible to render a registered trade mark, the subject of a charge, in the same way as other personal or moveable properties. Section 28(6) restated the pre-existing law to the effect that an assignment of an unregistered trade mark can only take part in connection with the goodwill of a business.

Registration of transactions affecting registered trade marks   Section 29 replaces sections 33 and 36 of the Trade Marks Act 1963 and provides that all transactions whether by way of assignment or licence or by virtue of security interests must be entered in the Register of Trade Marks. Section 29(3) provides that only registrable transactions are effective against a person acquiring a conflicting interest without notice or a person claiming to be a licensee. Section 29(4) lays down a time limit of six months from the date of the transaction for recording registrable transactions, unless the High Court is satisfied that it was not practicable to do so within the six month period and that an application was made as soon as practicable thereafter. Failure to observe the time limits will result in the new proprietor losing an entitlement to damages or an account to profits in respect of any infringement of the trade mark occurring after the date of the transaction and before recording.

Trust and equities   Section 30 re-enacts the provisions of section 68 of the Trade Marks Act 1963.

Application for registration of trade mark as an object of property   Difficulties had arisen under the 1963 Act as to the recording of assignments and transmission of trade marks which are pending registrations. Section 31 of the 1996 Act allows such assignments and transmissions to be recorded in the same way as those involving registered trade marks. Provision already exists in the analogous situation of patents under section 85 of the Patents Act 1992.

Licensing of registered trade mark   Section 32 replaces the provisions of section 36 of the Trade Marks Act 1963. It simplifies and clarifies the position regarding the licensing of registered trade marks. Section 32(3) states that a licence is not effective unless in writing signed by or on behalf of the grantor, or executed under seal in the case of a body corporate. Section 32(4) states that the provisions of a licence bind the successor in title of the registered proprietor unless the licence otherwise provides. Section 32(5) provides for sub-licensing for the first time.

Exclusive licences   Section 33 defines 'exclusive licence' as a licence authorising the use of a trade mark by the licensee to the exclusion of all other persons including the registered proprietor of the licensed trade mark.

General provisions as to rights of licensees in case of infringement   Section 34 provides that a licensee can call upon the proprietor to institute infringement proceedings failing which the licensee may proceed. However, the licensee may not proceed without the leave of the High Court unless the proprietor is either joined as a plaintiff or added as a defendant. A proprietor who is added as a defendant shall not be liable for any costs in the action unless he takes part in the proceedings.

Exclusive licensee having rights and remedies of assignee   Section 35 makes available to a licensee similar remedies as are available to the registered proprietor.

Exercise of concurrent rights   Section 36 deals with a situation where the registered proprietor and the exclusive licensee have concurrent rights to institute trade mark infringement proceedings and provides that neither may proceed without the leave of the Court unless the other is either joint as a plaintiff or added as a defendant. A person thus joined is not liable to any costs in the action unless that person takes part in the proceedings. Section 36(6) renders the provisions of this section subject to any agreement to the contrary between the exclusive licensee and the proprietor.

Application for registered trade mark   Sections 37 to 39 deal with the requirements of an application for registration of a trade mark. Section 37 provides that goods and services shall be classified for the purposes of the registration of trade marks according to a prescribed system of classification. It appears that the International Classification of goods and services under the Nice agreement of 15 June 1957 as revised will be adhered to. This classifies goods into 34 different classes and services into eight classes.

Priority   Sections 40 and 41 in effect restate existing law with regard to the requirements of the Paris Convention.

Registration procedure   Sections 42 to 46 effectively restate existing law. The examination procedure will continue to involve an official search of earlier trade marks so as to avoid registration of conflicting trade marks in the names of different persons. Publication in the Official Journal of a trade mark application accepted for registration will continue and third parties may oppose the registration or make observations by writing to the Controller. Applicants may at any time withdraw, restrict or amend their applications under section 44 and such changes shall also be published in the Journal.

Duration, renewal and alteration of registered trade mark   Under section 28 of the 1963 Act a trade mark was first registered for a period of seven years and thereafter renewed for successive periods of fourteen years. Section 47 of the 1996 Act now provides that a trade mark shall be registered for ten years and renewable for further ten year periods.

Surrender, revocation and invalidity   Section 50 of the 1996 Act provides for the surrender of a trade mark as against cancellation. The manner and effect of surrender would be dealt with by rules as would the provisions for protecting the interests of other persons having a right in the registered trade mark.

Revocation of registration   Section 51 is in general a re-enactment of section 34 of the Trade Marks Act 1963. However, the concept of bona fide use has now been replaced by the requirement that in order to avoid revocation, the trade mark must be put to genuine use within five years following completion of the registration. The Section provides for revocation on four grounds: failure to make genuine use of the trade mark within five years of registration; a suspension of use for an uninterrupted period of five years without proper reason; the trade mark becoming generic; or that the trade mark has become liable to mislead the public in consequence of the proprietor's use. Section 51(5) provides for revocation to relate only to those goods or services for which grounds for revocation exist.

Grounds for invalidity of registration   Section 52 allows for the registration of a trade mark to be declared invalid on the grounds that such registration is in breach of section 8 of the Act. However, a trade mark may not be declared invalid if, as a result of use, it had acquired a distinctive character subsequent to registration. This section also empowers the Controller to apply to the Court for a declaration of invalidity in the case of fraud.

Effect of acquiescence   Section 53 implements Article 9 of the 1989 Directive and would protect a trade mark against a declaration of invalidity or opposition where the proprietor of an earlier trade mark or right had acquiesced for a continuous period of five years with the use of the registered trade mark.

Collective marks   Section 54 of the 1996 Act introduces a new category of trade mark in that it will now be possible for members of an association which is a proprietor of a trade mark to register it as a collective mark. As distinct from certification trade marks the collective owner may deal in the goods or services whereas a certifying body may not in the case of a certification trade mark.

Certification marks   Section 55 in effect re-enacts the provisions of section 45 of the Trade Marks Act 1963 but simplifies the procedure for obtaining a certification mark. The provisions for granting collective marks and certification marks are set out in the First and Second Schedules respectively of the 1996 Act.

Community trade marks and international matters   When the 1996 Act was being passed in the Oireachtas, it was noted that considerable changes had taken place in the international protection for trade marks since the enactment of the Trade Marks Act 1963. The basic international convention for the protection of industrial property remains the Paris Convention of 1883 which constituted a Union for the Protection of Industrial Property and to which the State adheres. The administrative tasks of the Union are carried out by the World Intellectual Property Organisation (WIPO) which is now an agency of the United Nations. Countries of the Union are entitled separately between themselves to make special agreements for the protection of industrial property as long as these agreements do not contravene the provisions of the Convention. Among such special agreements is the Madrid Agreement entered into by a number of continental European and North African countries and concluded in Madrid on April 14, 1891.

The State is not party to the Madrid Agreement. A protocol to the original Agreement was signed by the State in December 1989 the purpose of which is to enable Irish persons who have applied for registration at the Patents Office to file a single application with the International Office of WIPO in Geneva designating those other contracting countries where registration of a trade mark is required. When thus filed the trade mark will be protected in all countries which have adhered to the Madrid Agreement, unless the mark conflicts with a mark already on the register of a particular country or is otherwise unregistrable under the laws of that country. Separate applications for national registration in the individual countries of the Madrid Agreement are thus unnecessary. The State's adherence to the Protocol will effect considerable savings for industry when protecting their valuable trade marks.

The Community Trade Mark Regulation (EC) No. 40/94 establishes a unitary Community trade mark. This will enable trade mark proprietors to seek one registration for the entire Community rather than rely on separate registrations in the Member States. Registration of marks commenced in 1996. The European Communities (Community Trade Mark) Regulations 1996 (SI No. 10 of 1996) supplement Regulation (EC) No. 40/94 and provide for the payment of a fee in the Patents Office upon lodging an application for a Community Trade Mark. The Regulations came into effect on January 15, 1996, thus predating the 1996 Act.

Part III of the 1996 Act is intended to incorporate the provisions of the Protocol to the Madrid Agreement as part of the domestic trade mark law of the State and to give effect to the Community Trade Mark Regulation. In addition, section 60 enables the Minister to make orders amending the Act if necessary in consequence of any revision or amendment of the Paris Convention. Section 61 introduces in domestic law the protection under the Paris Convention of well-known trade marks (the so-called 'Marque Notoire') regardless of whether the owner carries on business or has any goodwill under the trade mark in the State. The Supreme Court in *C & A Modes v. C & A (Waterford) Ltd.* [1976] I.R. 148 held that it is possible to maintain an action for passing off in the State notwithstanding that the plaintiff does not have a place of business in the State. Section 62 enhances the protection available for the flags, armorial bearings or other emblems of Paris Convention countries.

Administrative provisions Sections 66 to 68 in effect re-enact existing provisions relating to the register under sections 9, 42 and 44 of the 1963 Act. Sections 69 to 75 of the 1996 Act deal with the powers and duties of the Controller covering the power to direct what forms may be used; the provision of information about registered trade marks and applications; the parties to be heard; and the costs and evidence in proceedings before him. They also provide for excluding liability in respect of official acts and require the Controller to report on the execution of the provisions of this Act in his annual report. Section 73 of the Act provides new powers for the Controller to deal with behaviour amounting to contempt of the Patent Office in hearings before the Controller by extending the provisions of section 92 of the Patents Act 1992 to the 1996 Act.

Legal proceedings and appeals Sections 76 to 80 re-enact existing provisions under sections 52, 53, 56 and 57 of the 1963 Act.

Rules and fees Sections 81 and 82 re-enact sections 3 and 4 of the 1963 Act covering the rule-making power of the Minister and the fees to be charged.

Trade mark agents The provisions contained in sections 105 to 109 of the Patents Act 1992 covering patent agents have been substantially followed in sections 83 to 90 of the 1996 Act. Section 91 introduced a new provision and confers a privilege for communications between registered trade mark agents and their clients in the same way as exists for the client/solicitor relationship. The Trade Marks Rules 1996 (SI No. 199 of 1996) prescribe the detailed rules for trade marks and trade mark agents under the 1996 Act and revoke the previous rules applicable under the 1963 Act, the Trade Marks Rules 1963, as amended. The 1996 Rules came into effect on 1 July 1996, the date on which the 1996 Act itself came into force.

Offences Sections 92 to 95 introduce new offences in relation to the fraudulent applications or use of trade marks. Section 92 deals with the growing problem of counterfeiting, a particular problem in connection with designer label clothing. Sections 93 and 94 re-enact sections 63 and 64 of the Act of 1963 respectively. Section 95 enables proceedings for an offence under the 1996 Act to be brought against partnerships and bodies corporate.

Miscellaneous and general Section 96 enables proceedings for an order under section 20 or section 23 of the 1996 Act to be brought in the Circuit Court. Section 97 is intended to give better protection to the State emblems of Ireland. Section 98 provides for the Minister to protect marks abroad which are indicative of Irish origin and re-enacts section 47 of the 1963 Act. Section 99 makes it clear that in any civil proceedings under the Act where the issue of use of a trade mark arises the burden of proving such use shall lie with the proprietor.

Communications

Eamonn G. Hall

It was during the Irish presidency of the European Union, (July–December 1996) that the European Commission Green Paper *Living and Working in the Information Society: People First* (Com (96) 389 final) ('the 1996 Green Paper') was launched. In October 1996, Ireland and the European Commission hosted a colloquium in Dublin Castle on 'People First: Challenges of Living and Working in the European Information Society'. The Green Paper was launched at the Dublin Colloquium.

Europe has been developing a number of strategies to promote the information society . In particular there are two separate but interwoven policies being put into effect. First, there is a determination to strengthen Europe's competitive position in the emerging global information economy. The European communications markets are being deregulated, stimulating competition and innovation with the specific intention of reducing costs and increasing access. Secondly, European policy-makers articulate the thesis that the information society must serve people. The European Commission's White Paper on *Growth, Competitiveness and Employment* (1993) confirmed that information technology was crucial to European competitiveness but also called for an 'economy characterised by solidarity'. The Bangemann Report *European and Global Information Society* (1994) warned of the danger of a two-tier society of have and have-nots in which only part of the population has access to the new technology.

Strengthening economic and social cohesion is a key objective of the European Union. Many will recognise that considerable progress has been made towards convergence in income per head between Member States but disparities between certain regions within the same Member States have tended to widen. The 1996 Green Paper emphasised that information and communication technologies play an important part in supporting regional and local development in promoting integration and empowerment. The key issue is how to maximise the opportunities and minimise the risks of the information and communication technologies.

Concerns have been expressed about the impact of information and communication technologies on cohesion. Many fear that the new technologies will reinforce rather than reduce existing inequalities, leading to a concentration of jobs and production in a few regions. A specific challenge set out in the 1996 Green Paper is the necessity to maximise the potential of telecommunication liberalisation with the development of a new regulatory framework. The issue of universal telecommunication services — a minimum set of services offered at affordable prices — is regarded as an important contribution towards cohesion and an important element in the new regulatory framework. The European Commission has already discussed this issue in a communication on universal service for telecommunications (COM (96) 73).

The challenge to use 'the information society' to strengthen social cohesion and enhance people's ability to participate fully in every aspect of social and economic life, and to make 'the information society' a tool for the creation of an inclusive society was emphasised in the 1996 Green Paper. The information society should be essentially about people and should be used for people and by people to unlock the power of information, not to create new or reinforce existing inequalities between the information rich and the information poor.

The concept of informed democracy is considered as a fundamental aspect of the European model. Real enfranchisement requires access to accurate current information on which to base democratic choices and decisions. For true, inclusive democracy to exist, the entire population must have equal access to information and to make choices effectively and equitably. Accordingly, the policies influencing the laws in relation to regulating the information society must strive to enhance democracy by ensuring equal and public access to the information and communication technology infrastructure, to networked information services and to the skills required to access these services. There is a consciousness among policy-makers that the United States government's national information infrastructure which included an initiative for 'on line government' is an appropriate example of the information and communications technologies that facilitate the creation of new opportunities for greater public participation in an awareness of the political process.

Developments in the law in Ireland in 1996 must be placed in the context of the regulation of the processes of communications by the institutions of the European Union. In the framework of the European Union, Member States have created one single market of 370 million consumers with some 16 million enterprises — the largest economic entity in the world. The European model is built both on competition between enterprises and solidarity between citizens and Member States. Development in statutory regulation in Ireland in relation to communications in 1996 recognised that 'the information society' represented a fundamental change in our time with enormous opportunities for society together with risks for individuals and particular regions.

It would be wrong to give an impression that we are living in an advanced and enlightened society as a direct result of technological change and developments in the law. In a report on the 1996 Dublin Colloquium *People First: Challenges of Living and Working in the European Information Society* published by the Irish Department of Enterprise and Employment with the support of the European Commission (1996), it was stated that only 11% of Europeans have computers and only 3.5% can use the Internet. The challenges are obvious. There are 18 million people unemployed in Europe and these persons already face the risk of poverty and social exclusion. 'The information society' could accentuate these problems. Further, for the vast majority of Europeans there is a growing insecurity about their jobs and their basic standard of living. Many people share a palpable sense of social disintegration and erosion of shared values and a loss of public confidence in leaders and institutions. In this threatening context, there is a necessity to create what may be described as a confidence in progress.

BROADCASTING

Broadcasting Complaints Commission   The seventeenth annual report of the Broadcasting Complaints Commission, a statutory tribunal established pursuant to the Broadcasting Authority Act 1960 as amended by the Broadcasting Authority (Amendment) Act 1976, was published in 1996. A copy of the report, addressed to the Minister for Arts, Culture and the Gaeltacht, is laid before both Houses of the Oireachtas. The chairperson of the Commission is Ms Geri Silke, Barrister.

Three formal decisions of the Commission were published in the 1996 annual report. All three cases related to RTÉ although the jurisdiction of the Broadcasting Complaints Commission was, pursuant to the Radio and Television (Complaints by Members of the Public) Regulations 1992 (S.I. No. 329 of 1992), extended to any sound broadcasting service or any television programme service provided under the Radio and Television Act 1988. These services are sometimes designated as the independent broadcasting services.

In the *Complaint of Fenton Howell* it was alleged that a segment of the Late Late Show on RTÉ 1 dealing with cigarettes under the brand name 'Death' resulted in the promotion of cigarettes and that the matter had been dealt with in a flippant way and had infringed section 18B(1)(b) of the Broadcasting Authority Act 1960 as amended by the Broadcasting Authority (Amendment) Act 1976 which prescribes a degree of objectivity and impartiality. RTÉ in its response acknowledged that advertising for tobacco was prohibited and that RTÉ had introduced its own ban. RTÉ submitted and the Broadcasting Complaints Commission held that the part of the Late Late Show complained about was an item of a 'curio' nature. The programme was fair to all interests concerned in that persons with opposing views were given ample opportunity to air their opinions. The Commission found no breach of the statutory obligations of RTÉ and dismissed the complaint.

In the *Complaint of Stephen O'Byrnes*, a member of the Progressive Democrats, it was submitted by Mr O'Byrnes that RTÉ's decision on the allocation of broadcasting time for the Progressive Democrats in relation to the 1994 European Parliament elections was unfair. RTÉ in its response stated that the issues raised by Mr O'Brynes were far reaching in their implications regarding the interests of persons and parties other than Mr O'Byrnes. RTÉ submitted that the Commission had been established to consider a more limited type of complaint rather than a general complaint. RTÉ argued that this was a complaint about the policy of RTÉ across a whole genre of programming with particular reference to RTÉ's coverage of the European Parliament elections. RTÉ submitted that for the Commission to consider the complaint it would be required to decide whether or not RTÉ's editorial policy was fair.

RTÉ submitted that it was conscious of its obligations of fairness, objectivity and impartiality in relation to news and its treatment of current affairs particularly during election times. To assist RTÉ in this function, an election steering group of senior RTÉ officers had been convened under the chairmanship of the Director General. The steering group adopted a practice when determining the allocation of broadcasting time to registered political parties, of examining the electoral results for the last preceding General Election or the last European Parliament Elections, whichever was the most recent, and to determine the extent of support that each political party had at that election. The steering group consults these results when considering, in a general way, the structure of panels of participants to be involved in RTÉ's radio and television programmes while at the same time being aware of the necessity and duty to afford coverage for smaller parties and independent candidates. RTÉ submitted that it took into account the experience and position of the candidates, the relationship between Government and Opposition parties and the status of outgoing members of the European Parliament.

The Commission held that Mr O'Byrnes' complaint did not come within its jurisdiction. The Commission stated that its jurisdiction was strictly confined to investigating and adjudicating upon limited classes of complaints such as specified items of news, programmes of current affairs, including matters which are either of public controversy or the subject of current public debate, the broadcast of matter which may reasonably be regarded as being likely to promote or incite crime or as tending to undermine the authority of the State or the unreasonable encroaching on the privacy of an individual. The Commission considered that Mr O'Byrnes' complaint related to the policy of RTÉ across a whole genre of programming rather than a complaint on a specific programme. The Commission did not consider that RTÉ was in breach of its obligations under the broadcasting legislation. Accordingly the Commission dismissed the complaint.

Independent Radio and Television Commission Provisions of the Radio and Television Act 1988 were examined by Smyth J. of the High Court in

Radio Limerick One Ltd v. Independent Radio and Television Commission in a judgment delivered on October 14, 1996. In February 1996, the Independent Radio and Television Commission (IRTC) issued Radio Limerick One Ltd with a 14 day notice of termination of its licence for alleged serious and repeated breaches of its broadcasting contract under the Radio and Television Act 1988. Section 14 (4) of the Radio and Television Act 1988, provides as follows:

> (4) Every sound broadcasting contract shall:
>
> > (a) Provide that the Commission may at its discretion suspend or terminate the contract . . .
> > (ii)   If the sound broadcasting contractor has, in the opinion of the Commission, committed serious or repeated breaches of his obligations under the sound broadcasting contract or under this Act.

A contract had been entered into between Radio Limerick One Ltd and the IRTC on August 13, 1989. Smyth J. held that section 14 of the Radio and Television Act 1988 empowering the Commission to terminate a broadcasting contract was clear and unambiguous: the breaches may be serious or repeated. It was contended by Radio Limerick One Ltd that the breaches must be repeated serious breaches. Smyth J. stated that to accept that fundamental submission would be to substitute the word 'and' for 'or' in respect of the breaches conferring the right to terminate the contract. Smyth J. considered that the use of the word 'or' between 'serious' and 'repeated' in section 14(a)(ii) of the 1988 Act clearly indicated that the breaches are to be considered as disjunctive and not conjunctive.

The High Court considered that the IRTC had an abundance of evidence upon which to form the opinion requisite to exercising the discretion conferred upon the IRTC by the 1988 Act. Smyth J. considered that judicial review proceedings cannot be used as an appeal procedure or a chamber to 'second-guess' the Commission. The High Court considered that the IRTC's decision was not based on irrelevant legal considerations or an error of law. Reviewing the evidence as a whole, Smyth J. considered that there was no want of proportionality in the decision of the Commission. Accordingly, he dismissed the application of Radio Limerick One Ltd. Radio Limerick One Ltd appealed to the Supreme Court. The Supreme Court heard the appeal in December 1996 and reserved judgment. Judgment was delivered on January 16, 1997 by the Supreme Court and Keane J. for the Supreme Court upheld the decision of the High Court. The judgment of the Supreme Court will be considered in the 1997 *Annual Review*.

Television licences   The Broadcasting (Receiving Licences) Amendment
Regulations 1996 (S.I. No. 249 of 1996) made by the Minister for Arts, Culture and the Gaeltacht pursuant to the Wireless Telegraphy Act 1926 with the
consent of the Minister for Finance, increased the television licence fee for
monochrome sets from £44 to £52 and the television licence fee for colour
and monochrome sets from £62 to £70.

INTERNATIONAL TREATIES

EUMETSAT Convention   The Dáil on July 4, 1996 approved the terms of
the Amending Protocol to the Convention of the European Organisation for
the Exploitation of Meteorological Satellites, known as EUMETSAT as recommended by the EUMETSAT Council. See 468 *Dáil Debates,* col. 494.

International Telecommunications Union   The terms of the Constitution
and Convention of the International Telecommunications Union (ITU) signed
at Geneva in 1992 and of an amending Instrument signed at Kyoto in 1994
laid before Dáil Éireann on June 17, 1996 were approved by the Dáil on June
26, 1996. See 469, *Dáil Debates*, cols. 1338 and 1339.

The ITU is an inter-governmental organisation, the oldest specialised agency
of the United Nations, within which the public and private sectors co-operate
for the development of telecommunications and the harmonisation of national
telecommunications policies. The ITU adopts international regulations and
treaties governing all terrestrial and outer space uses of the frequency spectrum, as well as the use of the geostationary-satellite orbit and develops standards to ensure the interconnection of telecommunication systems on a
world-wide scale. The ITU is comprised of c.182 Member Administrations.

The 'Constitution' of the ITU is, in effect, an international treaty sub-
scribed to by virtually every nation on earth and thus has considerable significance. The preamble to the 1992 Constitution recognises the sovereign right
of each state to regulate its own processes of telecommunication and notes the
growing importance of telecommunication for the preservation of peace and
the economic and social development of all states. The main purpose of the
Union is to maintain and extend international co-operation between all members of the Union for the improvement and rational use of telecommunications of all kinds, and to harmonise the actions of members in the attainment
of those ends.

Several principles are enshrined in the ITU Constitution which are of some
significance. Article 33 recognises the right of the public to use international
telecommunications services and specifies that the services, and charges shall
be the same for all users in each category without any priority or preference —
a fundamental principle of non-discrimination. In Article 34 members reserve

the right to stop the transmission of any telecommunication messages which may appear dangerous to the security of the state or contrary to its laws, to public order or to decency. In Article 36 members specify that they accept no responsibility towards users of the international telecommunication services particularly as regards claims for damages. In relation to confidentiality, Article 37 specifies that members agree to take all possible measures, compatible with the system of telecommunication used, to ensure the secrecy of international communications. Subject to the provisions of the Constitution concerning the priority of telecommunication relating to safety of life at sea, on land, in the air, or in outer space as well as to epidemiological telecommunications of exceptional urgency of the World Health Organisation, 'government telecommunications messages' are stated to enjoy priority over other telecommunications to the extent practicable upon specific request by the originator.

Article 44 of the ITU Constitution recites the thesis that radio frequencies and the geostationary-satellite orbit are limited natural resources and that they must be used rationally, efficiently and economically so that all countries may have equitable access to both taking into account the special needs of the developing countries and the geographic situation of particular countries. Pursuant to Article 47 of the 1992 ITU Constitution, members agree to take the steps required to prevent the transmission or circulation of false or deceptive distress, urgency, safety or radio identification signals.

LAW REFORM

The Law Reform Commission published its consultation paper *Privacy: Surveillance and the Interception of Communications* in September 1996. The Commission decided to begin its researches into privacy with an examination of privacy in the context of freedom from surveillance and from interception of one's communications. The availability, ease of use and continuous development of sophisticated surveillance and eavesdropping devices made such an examination exceedingly appropriate.

The consultation paper examines technological developments in the context of the deregulation of postal and telecommunications services in an open economy and then proceeds to examine the constitutional basis of the protection of privacy. Civil liability and torts such as trespass, nuisance and defamation which relate to privacy are then examined with a view to considering whether the existing civil law is adequate. The consultation paper considers the power of the State to intercept postal packets and telecommunications and considers the matter in the general context of the State's obligations flowing from membership of the European Union and under the European Convention on Human Rights and the International Covenant on Civil and Political Rights.

In the context of formulating its provisional proposals for reform, the Commission in its paper examines laws and proposals for reform in some other jurisdictions. For example, the Commission considers reports of the Younger and Calcutt Committees in England in the context of invasive surveillance by the media, and notes the positive right to privacy specifically inserted in the French Civil Code.

Among the provisional recommendations with which the Consultation Paper concludes are the creation of new torts of invasion of the privacy of another by means of surveillance and the tort of disclosure or publication of the purport or substance of information or material obtained by means of privacy-invasive surveillance. Other provisional recommendations relate to empowering a court to make a 'privacy order', to restrain persons from invading privacy or disclosing information and the creation of certain offences, including an offence of infringing the integrity of a person by observation, *e.g.* by photography, television broadcast or video recording, without that person's consent, express or implied. The creation of an offence of communicating such recorded observation without consent, an offence of infringing the privacy of a person by listening to or recording by means of an aural device the voice of that person without consent, and an offence of communicating such recording to another without consent are also recommended.

The Law Reform Commission reiterated its recommendation in its *Report on Non-Fatal Offences Against the Person* that an offence of harassment be created. The Commission in the consultation paper encouraged self-regulation in the media.

POSTAL COMMUNICATIONS

Tariffs, terms and conditions of An Post Pursuant to section 70 of the Postal and Telecommunications Services Act 1983, An Post in its Foreign Parcel Post Amendment (No. 31) Scheme 1996 (S.I. No. 299 of 1996) operative from April 1, 1996 increased the fees for parcels sent to destinations outside Ireland. The 1996 Scheme also authorises increases in the fees which may be charged for the insurance service of An Post in relation to parcels. The Inland Post Amendment (No. 55) Scheme 1996 (S.I. No. 300 of 1996) authorised An Post to increase the parcel post rates in the Inland Post Service and to increase fees charged for An Post's EMS Courier Service. The Scheme also empowered An Post to increase the weight limit and introduced a new charging structure for the 24 hour parcel service.

TELECOMMUNICATIONS CARRIER SERVICE

Derogation and liberalisation of telecommunications services Article 90(2) of the EC Treaty provides that undertakings entrusted with the operation of services of general economic interest are to be subject to the rules on competition in so far as the application of such rules does not obstruct the performance in law or in fact of the particular tasks assigned to them. In the telecommunications sector, the application of Article 90(2) has been applied in Directive 90/388/EEC as amended by Directives 96/2/EC and 96/19/EC. Pursuant to these Directives the Commission is authorised to grant on request to a number of Member States the right to maintain during additional time periods certain exclusive rights granted to undertakings to which Member States entrust the provision of a public telecommunications network and telecommunications services, in so far as these measures are necessary to ensure the performance of the particular tasks assigned to the undertakings benefiting from exclusive rights.

On May 15, 1996 the Irish Government requested an additional implementation period until January 1, 2000 regarding the abolition of the exclusive rights granted to Telecom Éireann in relation to the provision of voice telephony and the underlying network infrastructure, instead of January 1, 1998 as provided in Article 2(2) of Directive 90/388/EEC. Similarly the Government requested a derogation until July 1, 1999 regarding the lifting of restrictions on the provision of already liberalised telecommunications services on (a) networks established by a provider of telecommunications services; (b) infrastructures provided by third parties; and (c) the sharing of networks, other facilities and sites, instead of July 1, 1996 as provided for in Article 2(2) of Commission Directive 90/388/EEC. Finally, the Government requested an additional implementation period until January 1, 2000 regarding the direct interconnection of mobile telecommunications networks, instead of immediately as provided in Article 3d of Directive 90/388/EEC.

The EC Commission in a decision of November 27, 1996 (97/114/EEC) considered that pursuant to the general principal of proportionality, any additional implementation period granted must be strictly proportional to what is necessary to achieve the requisite structural adjustment mentioned by the Irish Government.

Having considered and analysed certain comments put forward by interested undertakings, the Commission decided that Ireland may postpone until January 1, 2000 the abolition of the exclusive rights currently granted to Telecom Éireann in relation to the provision of voice telephony and the establishment and provision of public telecommunications networks. Secondly, Ireland was empowered to postpone until January 1, 1999 the lifting of restrictions on the direct interconnection of mobile telecommunications networks with foreign networks subject to certain conditions set out in Article 4 of the Decision. Thirdly, Ireland was authorised to postpone until July 1, 1997 the lifting of restrictions on the provision of already liberalised telecommunication services on (a) networks established by the provider of the telecommunications service, (b) infrastructures provided by third parties, and (c) the sharing of networks, other facilities and sites.

Employment law issues In *McDonnell v. Ireland, the Attorney General, the Minister for Communications and An Post* [1996] 2 I.L.R.M. 222 Carroll J. considered section 45 of the Postal and Telecommunications Services Act 1983. This section relates to the designation of certain civil servants for employment by An Post and Telecom Éireann. The plaintiff had joined the postal service of the State in 1962. In May 1974 he was arrested and charged with membership of the IRA, was convicted by the Special Criminal Court and sentenced to one year's imprisonment. In July 1974 he was informed that he had forfeited his position in the public service as a result of his conviction. Following the case of *Cox .v. Ireland* [1992] 2 I.R. 503 that forfeiture of a position pursuant to a conviction was unconstitutional, Mr McDonnell issued proceedings against Ireland the Attorney General, the Minister for Communications and An Post. An Post claimed that the plaintiff had not been designated by the Minister for employment in An Post pursuant to section 45 of the 1983 Act and further that the plaintiff's claim was barred under the Statute of Limitations 1957. Carroll J. refused the relief sought and held that section 11(2) of the Statute of Limitations 1957 applied to actions for damages for breach of constitutional rights and held that the plaintiff's cause of action arose when he was notified that his position as a civil servant had been forfeited and that An Post was not obliged to employ him under section 45 of the Postal and Telecommunications Services Act 1983 as he had not been designated by the Minister for Communications for employment in An Post.

Establishment of Office of Director of Telecommunications Regulation and sale of shares in Telecom Éireann Significant developments took place in primary legislation during the year under review in relation to the deregulation of telecommunications services. The Telecommunications (Miscellaneous Provisions) Act 1996 (No. 34 of 1996) provided for the establishment of the Office of Director of Telecommunications Regulation ('the Director') and for the transfer to the Director of the functions of the Minister for Transport, Energy and Communications ('the Minister') relating to the regulation of the telecommunications carrier service, radio communications and cable television sectors. The regulation of tariffs for certain telecommunications services and the legislative authority to facilitate the issue and transfer of shares in Telecom Éireann in relation to the sale and issue of equity in that company were also primary purposes of the 1996 Act.

Included in the transfer of powers from the Minister to the Director are powers in relation to the management of the radio frequency spectrum under the Wireless Telegraphy Acts. However, because the radio frequency spectrum is regarded as a finite national resource, section 3 of the 1996 Act provides the Minister will retain a policy role by providing that the Director is obliged to prepare, publish and implement a plan for management of the radio frequency spectrum subject to policy directions issued by the Minister based on good frequency management. The Director is authorised pursuant to s.4 of the Act to make regulations relating to the licensing of wireless telegraphy under section 6 of the Wireless Telegraphy Act 1926. However, regulations shall not be made by the Director other than with the consent of the Minister. Section 4 of the 1996 Act also provides that licences issued by the Director relating to mobile and personal communications must include public service requirements specified and published by the Minister.

To ensure that the Director achieves independence in the exercise of his or her functions, section 6 of the 1996 Act provides for the financing of the costs incurred by the Director in carrying out his or her functions by the imposition of levies on providers of telecommunications services and the retention of licence fees which are payable under the functions transferred to the Director. However, the Director will only be permitted to retain the amounts which are necessary to meet the costs of providing the regulatory services; if there is any surplus, it will be surrendered to the Exchequer.

The Act (section 12) authorised the Director to appoint authorised officers, for the purpose of obtaining information necessary for the exercise of the Director's functions. The section also sets out the powers of authorised officers. An authorised officer is empowered to enter the premises of a provider of telecommunications services, inspect documentation, require persons to provide information relating to the provision of telecommunications services and carry out tests and measurements. Certain penalties in relation to offences for failure to comply with specified requirements are set out in section 13 of the 1996 Act.

The 1996 Act provides for a new method for the regulation of tariffs charged by providers of certain telecommunications services. The services which are subject to regulation are set out in section 7 and are those for which there is no competition in the market concerned and those which are provided by an undertaking which has a dominant position in the market concerned. The legislature considered that price control of services which are not subject to those market conditions was unnecessary. Section 7 of the Act provides that the Minister may make an order specifying an overall limit, called a price cap, on the annual percentage change in charges that can be imposed for a specified group of telecommunications services designated as a 'basket of telecommunications services' provided by the relevant undertaking.

Section 7 of the 1996 Act provided that a price cap order may be reviewed by the Director after two years on the initiative of the Minister. The Director may modify the order on the basis of such review. Five years after the making of the price cap order by the Minister, the Director may modify the order on his or her own initiative. Before modifying an order made by the Minister, the Director is obliged to inform each provider of telecommunications services concerned of the intention to make the order, inform the provider of the right to make representations on the terms of the proposed order and take into consideration any such representations made within two months of the notification of the Director's intention to make an order.

The restrictions relating to the issue and transfer of shares in Telecom Éireann as set out in the Postal and Telecommunications Services Act 1983 restricting the issue of shares to the Minister for Finance, the Minister for Transport, Energy and Communications and the subscribers to the company's memorandum of association were removed by section 8 of the 1996 Act. This section enabled what has been termed a 'strategic alliance' to be concluded. During 1996 the Government agreed to the sale of shares in Telecom Éireann to a consortium comprising PTT Telecom BV of the Netherlands (KPN) and Telia AB (Publ) of Sweden. The consortium acquired a 20% stake in Telecom Éireann with an option to purchase a further 15% over a three year period. Section 8 of the 1996 Act also provides for employee shareholding in Telecom Éireann by enabling the company to issue and the Minister to transfer shares for the purpose of employee shareholding schemes.

The Worker Participation (State Enterprises) Acts 1977 and 1988 in relation to Telecom Éireann were modified by section 10 of the 1996 Act by providing that the number of employee directors to be appointed under those Acts was not to exceed one third of the number that the Minister was otherwise entitled to appoint under the articles of association of the company. The purpose of this provision was to accommodate the appointment of directors to the board of Telecom Éireann by the KPN/Telia consortium.

The Worker Participation (State Enterprises) Order, 1996 (S.I. No. 405 of 1996) made by the Minister for Enterprise and Employment pursuant to the Worker Participation (State Enterprises) Acts, 1977 and 1988 provided that the number of directors of Telecom Éireann is to be twelve and the appropriate number of what may be described as employee directors was to be two. This Order revoked the provisions of the Worker Participation (State Enterprises) Order, 1988 in so far as it related to Telecom Éireann. Subsequently, the Telecommunications (Miscellaneous Provisions) Act 1996 (Expiration of Terms of Office) Order 1996 (S.I. No. 409 of 1996) provided that the terms of office of two of the employee directors would expire. However, under section 10 of the Telecommunications (Miscellaneous Provisions) Act 1996 provision was made for 'alternate directors'. Pursuant to section 10(9) of the 1996 Act a person appointed by the Minister as 'an alternate director' may attend and participate in meetings of the directors of Telecom Éireann but shall not vote except when the director to whom she or she is an alternate is not present.

Mobile services The European Communities (Mobile and Personal Communications) Regulations, 1996 (S.I. No. 123 of 1996) represent a further significant development in the deregulation of telecommunications carrier services. The regulations were made pursuant to section 3 of the European Communities Act 1972 for the purpose of giving effect to Commission Directive No. 90/388/EEC of June 28, 1990 and Commission Directive 96/2/EC of January 16, 1996. Directive 90/388/EEC provided for the abolition of special or exclusive rights granted by Member States in respect of the provision of telecommunications services — subject to certain exceptions. However, that Directive did not apply to mobile services. Commission Directive 96/2/EC of January 16, 1996 amended Directive 90/388/EEC specifically in the context of mobile telecommunications services.

The EC Commission in the Directives referred to above considered that restrictions on the number of undertakings authorised to provide mobile and personal communications services pursuant to exclusive rights constituted restrictions which would be incompatible with Article 90 of the Treaty establishing the European Community in conjunction with Article 59, if such limitation could not be justified under specific Treaty provisions or the essential requirements doctrine. This was so because such exclusive rights may prevent other undertakings from supplying the services concerned to and from other Member States. Commission Directive 96/2/EC liberalised the market for mobile and personal communications. Section 87 of the Postal and Telecommunications Services Act 1983 granted the exclusive privilege to Telecom Éireann of offering, providing and maintaining telecommunications services for transmitting, receiving, collecting and delivering telecommunications messages within the State up to a connection point in the premises of a subscriber for any such service subject to certain exceptions.

Regulation 3 of the 1996 Regulations provide that section 87 of the 1983 Act was to be construed as not applying to mobile and personal communications services or mobile or personal communications systems. Accordingly, the exclusive privilege of Telecom Éireann in relation to mobile communications services ceased on May 16, 1996, the date the Regulations came into force.

The 1996 Regulations also amended section 111 of the Postal and Telecommunication Services Act 1983 in the context of licensing of telecommunications services. The Regulations stipulate that a person shall not provide mobile and personal communications services or mobile and personal communications systems otherwise than in accordance with a licence granted by the Minister for Transport, Energy and Communications ('the Minister'). The Minister is specifically authorised in the amended section 111 of the 1983 Act to provide in a licence for mobile services, conditions authorising the suspension or revocation of the licence in certain circumstances. The Regulations acknowledge the applicability of the principles of constitutional and natural justice by providing that where, the Minister proposes to refuse to grant a mobile licence or to revoke or suspend or amend a term or condition of a licence, the Minister must notify the applicant for the licence, or the holder, and give reasons and take into account any representations made. There is a right of appeal to the High Court against the decision of the Minister provided that the decision is not simply to amend a term or condition of the licence concerned. The High Court may confirm the decision or direct the Minister as appropriate to refrain from granting, revoking or suspending the licence concerned. The Minister must comply with the direction and shall not implement the decision unless and until it is appropriate to do so having regard to the outcome of the proceedings.

In the 1996 Regulations, an authorised officer is empowered where he or she reasonably suspects that an offence has been committed on or at any premises or other place, to enter the premises and there to make such inspections, tests and measurements of apparatus found in the premises. The person in charge of a premises or place entered by an authorised officer and a person found on such premises is obliged to furnish to the officers such information as he or she may reasonably require for the purposes set out in the amended section 111 of the Postal and Telecommunications Services Act 1983. Such person shall not hinder or obstruct the officer in the performance of his or her functions. The amended section 111 of the 1983 Act also provides that a person who contravenes any provision of the section shall be guilty of an offence and shall be liable on summary conviction to a fine not exceeding £1,000 or to imprisonment for a term not exceeding 12 months or both.

The amended section 111 of the 1983 Act specifically authorised the Minister to grant a licence to ESat Digifone Ltd, the successful applicant selected by the Minister pursuant to a competition held in 1995 to provide within the State a public pan-European cellular digital land-based mobile telecommunications system (GSM) in competition with the State-owned provider Eircell Ltd, a subsidiary of Telecom Éireann. Specifically, in the 1996 Regulations, the Minister was authorised to grant a licence to Eircell Ltd in respect of the mobile and personal communications services and the mobile and personal communications systems provided by Eircell Ltd, immediately before the commencement of the Regulations.

The 1996 Regulations stipulate that operators of mobile communications systems shall be entitled to interconnect their systems with the public telecommunications network of Telecom Éireann and shall be entitled to have access to such number of points of interconnection as are necessary for the purposes of their systems. The conditions for such interconnection are to be determined on the basis of objective criteria and must be transparent, non-discriminatory and compatible with the principle of proportionality. Parties to an interconnection agreement are to furnish a copy to the Minister. The Regulations provide that if the operator of a mobile telecommunications system and Telecom Éireann are unable to agree upon the conditions of a proposed interconnection agreement, the Minister may by notice in writing specify the conditions subject to which the interconnection concerned shall be effected and the parties are obliged to comply with those conditions.

Oireachtas telephone allowance   The Oireachtas (Allowances to Members) (Constituency Telephone Allowance) Regulations 1996 (S.I. No. 413 of 1996) provide for the payment of an unvouched annual constituency telephone allowance to Oireachtas members. The annual allowance for Dáil Deputies is £2,000; for Senators it is specified at £1,000 and an additional £1,000 is payable to the chairpersons of Oireachtas Committees and Dáil Party Whips.

The 1996 Regulations replaced the previous arrangements whereby members of the Oireachtas were paid a contribution of 75% of the vouched cost of telephone calls from designated telephone numbers in their homes or constituency offices — where the constituency offices were not located in Leinster House.

Premium rate telephone services   The first report of the regulator of premium rate services (RegTel) was published in 1996. A premium rate telephone service is a telephone service in respect of which part of the telephone charge paid or payable by a telephone customer is shared between the telecommunications network operator and the provider of information or other provider of services over the telephone. See the Telecommunications (Premium Rate Telephone Service) Scheme, 1995 (S.I. 194 of 1995). Pursuant to the 1995 Scheme a service provider must comply at all times with any code of practice published by the regulator of premium rate telephone services. A code of practice was published in the 1996 Annual Report. The regulator is, in effect, a single member company limited by shares whose objects are the supervision of the content and promotional material relating to premium rate telephone services for the protection of the public, the setting of standards relating to such content and promotion, the monitoring of these services so as to ensure that they comply with the standards, and the investigation of complaints.

In relation to the exercise of those functions, a specific contract was entered into between Telecom Éireann and the regulator company ('RegTel') under which Telecom Éireann agreed to act upon the direction of the regulator on the barring of access to any premium rate telephone service in certain circumstances. Under parallel agreements between the network operator (Telecom Éireann) and each service provider, it was agreed that the service provider and Telecom Éireann would make an equal contribution to the funding of the office of the regulator and that the service provider's contribution to such funding would be deducted from payments due under such agreements and paid over to the regulator.

The 1996 Report of RegTel confirmed that a number of complaints had been received by the regulator in particular in relation to what may be termed sex chat lines. The 1996 Report confirmed that on a regular basis telephone numbers which were advertised in various publications were telephoned by the office of the regulator to ensure that the code of practice was being observed. Any apparent breaches were taken up with the service provider who was asked to reply within a certain period. The report noted that dating services, provided a useful facility for persons of all ages but these services must not be allowed to be tarnished by the few service providers for purposes which might not only breach an agreed code of practice but might infringe the criminal law. The 1996 report stipulated that only by monitoring some services frequently and all services occasionally could the public be assured that regulation was fulfilling the need for which it was established. The report noted that the proliferation of international 'sex' and 'chat lines' was a cause of grave concern world-wide. The report noted that similar regulators elsewhere in Europe emphasised that it was their aim that the regulatory system within each country should equally apply to incoming premium rate service calls wherever they originate.

Judge Mary Kotsonouris, as the de facto regulator, noted in the 1996 report that she was in favour of statutory authority which would lead to the present 'quasi voluntary basis' for the regulation of premium rate services being more clearly defined. This was raised in the context of general consumer protection. The report considered that the lack of regulation on the Internet was greatly deplored by many people because of perceived harmful affects not least of which was described as 'image pornography'. Fears were expressed that the Internet afforded easy cover to the dissemination of racial and class hatreds. The report noted that where the Internet was accessed by premium rate numbers then such provision of services was within the sphere of regulation of RegTel but that did not extend to general access by way of modem.

Price cap on telecommunication services provided by Telecom Éireann The Telecommunications Tariff Regulation Order 1996 (S.I. 393 of 1996) provided a framework for future changes in Telecom Éireann's telecommunications tariffs. Previously Telecom Éireann's tariffs were regulated under section 90 of the Postal and Telecommunications Services Act 1983 which required the consent of the Minister for Transport, Energy and Communications ('the Minister') for price increases. The 1996 Order regulates defined services provided by Telecom Éireann for which it is considered there is no competition and for which Telecom Éireann is considered to hold a dominant position in the relevant market . These services include the provision of telephone exchange lines, the provisions of Integrated Services Digital Network (ISDN) lines, local dialled calls, international dialled calls, operator calls, directory enquiry and payphone calls. The order places a price cap on Telecom Éireann's tariffs such that there will be an overall downward movement in tariffs which should be at least equal to the annual percentage change in the consumer price index less 6%. However, the 1996 Order provides that within this overall cap, Telecom Éireann will have flexibility to adjust tariffs although each individual telecommunications service within the basket cannot increase by more than the annual percentage change in the consumer price index plus 2%. In addition, increases in tariffs will be further restricted by the requirement that the average bill of the low volume user cannot increase by more than the annual percentage change in the consumer price index. The price cap is to apply on an annual basis and commenced on January 1, 1997.

Social welfare insurance and contribution by Telecom Éireann employees Pursuant to the Social Welfare (Consolidated Contributions and Insurability) (Amendment) Regulations 1996 (S.I. No. 416 of 1996) the Minister for Social Welfare, pursuant to section 12 of the Social Welfare Act 1996, provided that the modified social insurance status of employees of Telecom Éireann would be maintained following the sale and issue of equity in Telecom Éireann to the consortium comprising PTT Telecom BV of the Netherlands and Telia AB (Publ) of Sweden.

Telecommunications schemes of Telecom Éireann Pursuant to section 90 of the Postal and Telecommunications Services Act 1983, Telecom Éireann in its Telecommunications (Amendment) Scheme 1996, (S.I. No. 65 of 1996) reduced certain telecommunications charges and effected certain other modifications to the Telecommunications Scheme 1994 (S.I. No. 177 of 1994). The Telecommunications (Amendment) (No. 2) Scheme 1996 (S.I. No. 406 of 1996) made by Telecom Éireann pursuant to section 90 of the 1983 Act empowered Telecom Éireann to reduce further certain telecommunications charges and provided for the introduction of a prepaid chargecard service and effected certain other modification to the Telecommunications Scheme 1994.

VIDEO RECORDINGS

The Video Recordings Act 1989 (Supply Certificate and Labelling) (Amendment) Regulations 1996 (S.I. No. 407 of 1996) provided for changes in relation to the labels and labelling of video recordings. The changes to video classifications are: (a) substitution of the words 'under parental guidance' for the words 'in the company of a responsible adult' in the classification 'fit for viewing generally but in the case of a child under 12 years, only in the company of a responsible adult'; and (b) introduction of an additional classification of 'fit for viewing by persons aged 12 years or more'. Because of these changes, two new symbols are prescribed by the 1996 Regulations for use on classification labels.

PUBLICATIONS

Among the articles and publications on communications law in Ireland in 1996 were the following: D. Byrne, 'Information Technology Matters', 27 *Law Lib* 189-92 (1996); J. Casey, 'Planning and Telecommunications Masts: Some Recent Issues' 3, *I.P.E. L.J*, 3-10 (1996); F. Hackett, 'The Changing Face of Telecommunications in Ireland', 7 *ULR*, 230-233. E.G. Hall, 'Telephone Assault'. (Nuisance Telephone Calls) 90 *G.LS.I.* 359-60 (1996), E.G. Hall, 'Aspects of the Legal and Regulatory Regimes in Telecommunications in the United Kingdom and Ireland' in C. Scott and O. Audeoud (editors), *The Future of EC Telecommunications Law*, Bundesanzeiger, Academy of European Law in Trier, (1996). E.G. Hall, 'Utopia Beckons or are Barbarians at the Gate; Emerging Legal Issues on the Internet' a paper presented to a Conference on *The Internet Emerging Legal Issues*, Law School, Trinity College, Dublin, March 6, 1996. P. Lambert, 'Cues, Cameras and Courtroom Actors: Resisting the Temptation of Courtroom Television Cameras', 14 *I.L.T.* 13-17 (1996); E O'Dell, 'Copyright and Databases, Irish and European Dimensions', a paper presented to a Conference on the Internet: Emerging Legal Issues, Law School, Trinity College, Dublin, March 6, 1996.

Company Law

Dr David Tomkin and Adam McAuley

Piercing the corporate veil *Allied Irish Coal v. Powell Duffryn International Fuels Ltd* [1997] 1 I.L.R.M. 306. When may two or more companies in a group be regarded as a single economic entity?

In this case, Allied Irish Coal Ltd (Allied) purchased coal from Powell Duffryn International Fuels Ltd (Powell). A dispute arose. Allied claimed that Powell breached their contract by failing to supply coal. These proceedings were instituted in 1984. A statement of claim was not delivered until 1990. Powell was a wholly owned subsidiary: Powell Duffryn International Fuels plc ('the plc').

In 1995, Allied found out that the plc proposed to sell off Powell, the subsidiary company. Allied believed that the plc was doing this to distance itself from its subsidiary. Allied brought an application to join the plc as a co-defendant to the existing proceedings.

Allied argued that the court should grant its application to join the plc as co-defendant, as the plc and the defendant were a single economic entity. The main factor prompting this argument was that the defendant had no substantial resources of its own. The subsidiary was controlled by the plc in every aspect of its business. It operated as a department of the plc. Allied argued that there is a basic principle of company law that where justice demands it, the court may regard two or more companies as a single economic entity. Allied therefore claimed that the sum due on foot of the contract with Powell was payable by the plc.

In reply, the plc admitted that Powell was one of its subsidiaries, but averred the plc was a separate legal entity with its own board. It prepared its own accounts. The identification of Powell and the plc was exclusively in respect of group accounts. This did not turn the companies into a single economic entity.

The plc further denied that it intended to sell its shareholding in the subsidiary. Instead, it said that it was proposed merely to sell off some of the subsidiary's assets.

In the High Court, Laffoy J. stated that it was inappropriate to attempt to resolve conflicts of evidence where the evidence in question was given exclusively as affidavit evidence. The correct approach is to accept the plaintiff's version of the disputed facts, and to inquire whether legal principles applied to these facts make out a stateable case. Laffoy J. held that if the plaintiff had made out a stateable case, the court would then allow the plc to be joined as a co-defendant.

Laffoy J. examined the legal principle upon which Allied's arguments hinged. Allied argued that Costello J. decided in *Power Supermarkets Ltd v. Crumlin Investments Ltd*, High Court, June 22, 1981, that a court could treat two or more related companies' businesses as a single economic entity where the justice of the case required it. Laffoy J.'s difficulty lay not so much with the correctness of this dictum, but whether in this instant case, the facts existed to allow its application.

Here, Laffoy J. decided that Allied was attempting to use the principle in *Power Supermarkets* to render the plc's assets available to answer the subsidiary's liability. Laffoy J. decided that the principle in *Power Supermarkets* was not intended to be used in circumstances such as these. Allied's claim was fundamentally at variance with the principle of separate corporate legal personality and limited liability laid down in *Saloman v. Saloman* [1897] A.C. 22.

What does a court require before it lifts the corporate veil? In *Power Supermarkets*, Costello J. referred to the 'justice of the case' as if it were a critical defining factor. However, obviously, the term is too broad to provide any clear prospective indication of when it may be applicable. In this case, Laffoy J. found that the sole motive for raising the question of an exemption was that the defendant was not a good mark, but the holding company was.

Southern Milling Ltd v. Kantoher Food Products Ltd & Carton Brothers Ltd High Court, April 26, concerned another attempt to lift the corporate veil, this time on different grounds. Southern Milling Ltd (Southern) had a supply contract with Kantoher Food Products Ltd (Kantoher). Kantoher went into liquidation owing Southern £292,215. The liquidator of Kantoher paid 25p in the pound to Southern. This left an outstanding sum of £162,183. The allegation was that Carton Brothers Ltd (Carton Brothers) had wrongfully procured the refusal by Kantoher to pay sums Kantoher owed to Southern. Carton Brothers induced Kantoher to breach the contract through Mr Carton. Mr Carton was a shareholder of Carton Brothers, and the *de facto* managing director of Kantoher. The allegation was that though Carton Brothers and Kantoher were separate companies, there had been a conspiracy, and therefore the veil should be lifted, so that Carton Brothers should be liable to Southern.

In the High Court, Geoghegan J. reviewed the connection between Kantoher and Carton Brothers. The relationship was complex. It involved three different companies. Effectively, Carton Brothers controlled Kantoher. Carton Brothers was run by the Carton family. Mr Carton had become the *de facto* managing director of Kantoher.

Geoghegan J. found as a matter of fact that though Kantoher's decision to refuse payment to Southern was attributable to Mr Carton, this fact did not mean that Carton Brothers could be held liable in tort. The decision not to pay, or to delay payment was a managerial decision made within Kantoher. Even if the motive of Mr Carton related in whole or in part to a potential liability of Carton Brothers, this was not *per se* wrong. Geoghegan J. held that Mr Carton should be permitted to have regard to his family interest. It would be unwarranted and wholly artificial to suggest that in some way or other such motivation constituted inducement of breach of contract by Carton Brothers.

Southern relied upon the Supreme Court's decision in *Taylor v. Smyth* [1991] 1 I.R. 142. In *Taylor*, the Supreme Court decided that an agreement causing injury to a person by unlawful means is an actionable conspiracy notwithstanding that the conspiracy may be between an individual, and a limited liability company under that individual's control. Southern's argument was that Mr Carton's double interest of itself constituted the conspiracy: but Geoghegan J. decided that further evidence was necessary, and accordingly he dismissed Southern's action.

Shares vested in a personal representative *Arulchelvan v. Wright*, High Court, February 7, 1996 concerned a dispute about whether two extraordinary general meetings of two private companies were quorate.

The shares in the first company (RHL) were all beneficially owned by MW. MW held 50% of the shares in his own name. MW's sister, LW, held 49% in trust for him.

The shares in the second company (HSL) were held 50% by MW, and 50% by LW.

MW died in 1992. Probate was granted to two of the three executors: the deceased's sister (LW) and a third person, FH. The grant of probate was not noted on the register of members of the company, nor had the personal representatives procured their registration as members in their own name.

LW and FH appear to have been concerned to become directors of both companies. Accordingly, they sought to convene and hold EGMs of the two companies.

Were these meetings quorate or not? At both meetings, only one shareholder properly entered in the register of members was present: LW. The company's memorandum and articles provided for a quorum of two. LW argued that the quorum requirement was satisfied, as she had invited her solicitor to be present, and appointed him her proxy. The claim was that she and her solicitor-proxy constituted a quorum. She also argued that she possessed an extra entitlement to be present, as she was one of the personal representatives of her brother and by that fact, was entitled to be present. This argument was also advanced by the other personal representative, FH in respect of FH's shareholding in the other company RHL.

A solicitor who acted for the widow and for another director (RA) was also present at both EGMS. This solicitor denied that the meeting was quorate, an obvious point, which one would think was incapable of contradiction, and one which turned out to be quite correct. However, LW and FH pressed on, and passed certain resolutions co-opting themselves to the board of directors.

This case was brought by the widow and RA. They sought two declarations. First, that neither EGM was a quorate meeting. Second, any resolution passed at either meeting was invalid and of no effect, including the appointment of any director.

In the High Court, Carroll J. outlined the net issue – whether there was a quorum at either meeting and whether the business of the meeting was properly transacted. Carroll J. examined the definition of a member in section 31 of the Companies Act 1963. This section states that membership is dependent on entry on the register of members. This includes where a personal representative wishes to exercise any right conferred by membership in relation to meetings of the company. Carroll J. found the companies' regulations clear. The right to attend, speak and vote at a meeting is conferred only by membership. In this case, neither LW or FH been registered as members in respect of the shares of MW which passed to them as personal representatives. They could not therefore be counted as forming part of the quorum at the two meetings in question, in that capacity. The net result was that there was only one registered shareholder present, LW. One person does not constitute a quorum for an EGM such as this. Carroll J. did recognise that there were exceptions: such as under section 135, or where one person holds all of a class of shares. Carroll J. held that no business was transacted at either meeting. She granted the declarations sought by the plaintiffs.

The case does not answer the interesting point as to whether a person who is registered as the owner of two parcels of shares, one in his or her own name, and the other as personal representative, may defeat the quorum requirements in a Table A company by giving a proxy to another person in respect of one of the parcels of shares. This could very well happen in a company such as the second company, where MW and LW own 100% of the shares, and MW dies and LW is both the sole residual member and is registered as the personal representative of the other deceased shareholder. No obvious substantive objection appears to LW appointing a proxy in respect of some of her shares, and thus convening and holding a quorate EGM. However, if this is done, the presence of other members' interests, or other persons' interests might introduce other considerations. It might be that though a meeting where LW appointed a proxy in respect of one parcel of shares might be *validly constituted*, the business transacted could nevertheless become actionable under section 205 or 213 as constituting some substantive disregard of member's interests, or oppressive conduct. This is a nice paradigm of the distinction between valid form, and substantive injustice.

The Admissibility of an Inspector's report under section 22 of the Companies Act 1990   *Countyglen plc v. Carway* High Court, February 20, 1996.

When an inspector has reported on a company, and there is subsequent litigation, what use may be made of the inspector's report? Is it conclusive evidence of the facts in the report? What is the definition of 'facts'?

In 1994, the Minister for Enterprise and Employment appointed Frank Clarke SC as an inspector under the provisions of section 22 of the Companies Act 1990. The warrant required him to investigate the affairs of Countyglen plc, specifying in particular, two transactions, the Lawrence/Wyndham and Orbitron transactions. The Inspector completed and delivered his interim and final report. The High Court ordered that the final report was to be published and circulated, except for one appendix.

As a result of the findings contained in the report, three civil actions were instituted.

The first action, the main action, was a claim by Countyglen plc that the defendants (the members of the Carway family and others) were guilty of deceit, fraud, conspiracy to defraud and/or in breach of section 60 of the Companies Act 1963 in connection with the two transactions. Countyglen claimed that a sum of £1,144,948 was illegally removed during these transactions, and sought its return. Countyglen plc obtained uncontested judgment against *some* of the defendants. The *other* defendants, who were all members of the Carway family, disputed Countyglen's claims, and resisted the action.

In the second and third actions, Countyglen plc claimed that a bank and firm of solicitors had acted negligently in carrying out their respective functions in effecting these two transactions. The company sought damages for these breaches of duty.

A preliminary matter arose for consideration. Countyglen plc sought to tender in evidence the inspector's interim and final reports in accordance with section 22 of the 1990 Act in all the actions. Section 22 provides that a copy of a report of an inspector appointed under the Act shall be admissible in any civil proceedings. Section 22 specifies that the facts set out in the report shall be admissible without further proof, unless evidence to the contrary is shown, and that the opinion of the inspector shall be admissible in relation to any matter contained in the report. Countyglen plc wished to rely on the facts set out in the reports as proof of its claims in all three actions. However, it intimated that it did not intend to rely upon the opinions of the Inspector.

The penalties therefore raised as a preliminary matter the question of the construction of section 22 and the interpretation of an inspector's report '[as] admissible in any civil proceedings as evidence . . . (a) of the facts set out therein without further proof unless the contrary is shown'.

Countyglen argued that once a section 22 report is admitted in evidence, the facts set out in the report are accorded the status of evidence. If these facts are unfavourable to a party in the proceedings, the evidential burden then shifts to such party to disprove these facts. The term 'facts' has a broad meaning within section 22. It includes statements of uncontested fact, findings of primary fact and factual inferences.

The Carway family argued that Countyglen's interpretation of section 22 introduced into our system of justice the 'alien inquisitorial system'. Such a result would infringe the constitutional requirement in Article 34.1 that justice shall be administered in Courts established by law by judges appointed in the manner provided by the Constitution. Countyglen's interpretation breached each of the Carway family member's constitutional guarantee of fair procedures. In particular, each would be denied the right to confront and cross-examine persons giving evidence against him or her. The Carway family admitted that some account had to be taken of the facts set out in the report, however the report's findings of fact were insufficient to be *prima facie* evidence at the trial. The facts in the report could be relied on in *ex parte* applications and in interlocutory applications. The Carway family argued that the meaning attached to the word 'facts' was not as broad as that put forward by Countyglen. 'Facts', they argued, could include any finding of fact, but did not include any description contained in the report of what people said were facts, nor did it include any inferences. They suggested, in the alternative, that were the court to interpret 'facts' as not limited to findings of fact, the entire report would have to be admitted, together with any transcripts of oral testimony or interviews on which the report was based.

Counsel for the bank and solicitors advanced a third interpretation of section 22. They agreed that Countyglen's interpretation violated their clients' constitutional guarantees of fair procedures. The bank and solicitors argued that the word 'fact' had an even narrower definition. 'Facts' could only be findings of primary facts clearly expressed as such. Facts did not include *inter alia* all the material which witnesses had averred was fact, nor inferences from fact, nor conclusions nor opinions. If a dispute arises as to whether a particular matter is or is not a finding of primary fact, this must be decided against the person who seeks to use the report. The bank also argued that for the purposes of section 22 a report included all of the report even that part which a court had held should not be published.

In the High Court, Laffoy J. held herself unable to find any relevant Irish or UK statute law or case law which could assist in interpreting section 22.

Laffoy J. applied two canons of construction in her interpretation of section 22. First, she held that the primary and literal approach to the construction of the statute is appropriate when balancing rights and powers under the Constitution. Second, the presumption of constitutionality applies to the Companies Act 1990. Thus, if there exist two possible reasonable interpretations of an Act or section, one unconstitutional, the other constitutional, it must be presumed that the legislature intended only the constitutional construction. However, the court, when using the presumption of constitutionality, should not substitute for the existing legislative provision, a provision made by the judge himself. The courts would then be performing the constitutional function of the Oireachtas to legislate.

Laffoy J, applying these canons of construction, queried whether any of the interpretations put forward by the parties were 'reasonably open'. She found that Countyglen's interpretation was reasonably open and was the most obvious interpretation of the intention of the legislature. The Carway interpretation (that the legislature merely intended that *some* account must be taken of the facts set out in the report) was not reasonably open no matter how far the language was stretched.

On the other hand, counsel for the bank and the solicitors' firm combined the purposive approach and the presumption of constitutionality. The latter requires that where two or more constructions are reasonably open, and one is constitutional and the other unconstitutional, it must be presumed that the Oireachtas intended the constitutional reading.

The bank and solicitors argued that the purpose behind section 22 was to change the rule against hearsay, which automatically precluded the use of an inspector's report in civil proceedings. The bank and solicitors argued that the section went no further than this. Further, it was argued that when one applies the 'double construction' rule of interpretation derived from *East Donegal Co-operative Society v. Attorney General* [1970] I.R. 317, there must be read into section 22 the implication that the admission of the report in evidence does not breach the constitutional guarantees of fair procedures. Laffoy J. accepted that in a section 22 application, no court should infringe the constitutional right of a party to fair procedures. However, Laffoy J. asserted that the bank's and the solicitors' interpretation was an attempt to dictate what constituted the constitutional guarantee of fair procedures, by seeking to apply the principle of proportionality outlined by Costello P. in *Heaney v. Ireland* [1994] 2 I.L.R.M. 420 at 431. Laffoy J. could find nothing in the wording of the section to suggest that the legislature intended that section 22 had to pass a proportionality test.

Laffoy J. believed that the legislature's intention behind this section is clear. A copy of an inspector's report is admissible as evidence of the facts set out in the report. The bank and solicitor sought to re-define the section as one which provides that everything in the report is admissible as evidence about the party against whom it is being used. This suggestion was rejected by Laffoy J, on the grounds that such an interpretation was not reasonably open.

Laffoy J. then considered what interpretation should be given to the word 'facts' in section 22. Laffoy J. sought guidance as to the definition of this term, by considering how the term 'facts' is defined for the purpose of the application of the appellate jurisdiction of the Supreme Court. In *VC v. JM and GM* [1987] I.R. 510 the Supreme Court divided facts into two types. First, there are primary or basic facts. These are determinations of fact depending upon the assessment by the judge of the credibility or quality of the witnesses. It is for this reason that an oral hearing takes place. As the primary facts are based on the view of the trial judge, the appellate court is very reluctant to interfere with the judge's findings. Second, there are secondary or inferred facts. These are facts which do not follow directly from an assessment or evaluation of the credibility of witnesses or the weight to be attached to their evidence, but derive from inferences drawn from primary facts. The inferences of secondary facts are found by a process of deduction from the facts found or admitted. As secondary facts are based on deductions, an appellate court is more willing to interfere with these.

Bearing these interpretations in mind, Laffoy J. applied a literal interpretation to section 22 and restricted 'facts' to basic or primary facts, not to secondary facts. Laffoy J. believed that the words 'without further proof' indicated that the legislature intended that facts should be proved by witnesses in the ordinary way. Hence deductions or inferences do not acquire the status of proven facts under section 22. Laffoy J. approved of the bank and solicitor's construction that 'facts' in section 22 means only findings of primary fact clearly expressed as such. Laffoy J. therefore held that the interim and final reports were admissible. All findings of primary fact clearly expressed as such in the reports had the status of proven facts, unless disproved. However, Laffoy J. stated that facts admitted by virtue of section 22 do not have any special status or probative force.

Laffoy J. held that an 'inspector's report' under section 22 meant the report received by the court, including any part omitted from circulation or publication. In applying section 22, the court had to have regard to the constitutional right of every party to fair procedures. Laffoy J. accepted that the embargo on the publication of the appendix might give rise to difficulties in the three actions. Laffoy J. decided that such difficulties would have to be addressed only as they arose. Laffoy J. decided that the 'report' does not include any transcripts or interviews taken by the inspector.

None of the parties challenged the constitutionality of section 22. The defendants claimed that Laffoy J.'s interpretation was constitutionally flawed. Laffoy J. refused to hold that this method of constitutional challenge was permissible. Laffoy J. held that if a question arose about the section's constitutionality, it was necessary to make a direct claim that the *section* was unconstitutional. A similar situation had arisen in *Hegarty v. O'Loughran* [1990] 1 I.R. 148. In that case, the Supreme Court rejected an argument that its construction of a statutory provision was constitutionally flawed. Finlay C.J. refused to consider the constitutionality of the provision unless and until a full and proper challenge was brought by a person affected by it. Laffoy J. endorsed and adopted Finlay C.J.'s approach.

Laffoy J.'s holding is clearly correct, that section 22 permits the use of primary findings of fact in the inspector's report, but not inferences and deductions therefrom. Were a court of law to adopt more than just the facts of an inspector's report, the court would be acting unconstitutionally in two ways.

First, the court would necessarily be eschewing part of its judicial function prescribed by the Constitution. Second, there would be a violation of the constitutional right of fair procedures of the parties to the case. This is why, when a court allows the introduction of facts from the inspector's reports, this is done only on the basis that the facts contained in the inspector's report are disputable, and may be rebutted in any subsequent court proceedings by the introduction of evidence for that purpose.

Grounds for petitioning for court protection   In *Re Butler's Engineering Ltd* High Court, March 1, Keane J. examined what interests the examinership legislation is designed to protect, and what a petitioner must show in order to establish that there are grounds for the appointment of an examiner.

In this case, three petitions were presented in respect of three associated companies. Two of the companies were engaged in manufacturing and erecting structural steel works. The third company beneficially owned the entire issued share capital of the other two.

For some time, the group had been in financial difficulties. In 1988, the company had invested £13 million in new factory premises, plant and machinery. This had been done in the hope of increasing the business of the group. However, the cost of the factory and plant had run over budget. The group had a dispute with their primary supplier, British Steel. Eventually in 1993, British Steel stopped supplying the group. The group turned to a new supplier, Preussag Stahl AG (Preussag). This German company was more a retailer than wholesaler; its charges were accordingly higher. All these misfortunes took place at a time of general recession, when the building trade fell to a new low.

By 1994, the financial difficulties of the group were acute. It negotiated new arrangements with its banks. It also commenced negotiations with the Revenue Commissioners. During this time some new construction contracts came the group's way. By October 1995, the group's financial position had not improved. The group employed a firm of accountants to find new investors. The companies suffered a further blow when the chairman and founder died on December 28, 1995.

On February 19, 1996 the ICC Bank, to whom the companies in the group were indebted, appointed a receiver over the companies' assets. On February 21, a creditor sought court protection for the companies, on an *ex parte* basis.

The original statement of affairs presented in the petition stated that the liabilities of the company exceeded the assets by £1.86 million. A subsequent statement showed the deficiency as £15.6 million. Keane J. found that the audited accounts for the period ending March 31, 1994 showed a trading loss for that period of over £0.5 million. The auditors had been unable to certify the accounts as showing a true and fair view. The initial report of the accountants employed to find new investors stated that the information concerning the companies' financial position was 'very limited'.

At the hearing of the petition, the receiver opposed the appointment of an examiner. The receiver informed the court that the bank was owed in excess of £4.6 million. Another secured creditor, Irish Intercontinental Bank, was owed £1.2 million. A secured trading creditor was owed £1 million. All these creditors opposed the petition. However the petition was supported by five trading creditors, who were owed £404,866 in total.

In the High Court, Keane J. considered when may a company be placed under court protection. In *Re Atlantic Magnetics Ltd* [1993] 2 I.R. 561, Lardner J. had distinguished between three situations which may face a court in an application to place a company under court protection. First, where the evidence shows that there is no practical possibility of the company's survival. Second, where the evidence shows a strong possibility of corporate survival, given the requisite adjustments. Third, where the situation is not clear-cut in either direction, and where there is a conflict of evidence regarding the company's affairs. Lardner J. said that the court faced with the third situation should ask whether the evidence leads to the conclusion that in all the circumstances, it appears worthwhile to order an investigation by the examiner into the company's affairs, to ascertain whether it can survive. Lardner J. said there should be 'some reasonable prospect' of the company's survival. In the Supreme Court, Finlay C.J. agreed in general terms with Lardner J.'s test. However, Finlay C.J. qualified his approbation. He held that the court should look for 'some prospect' of survival, rather than for some 'reasonable' prospect. Finlay C.J. rejected the 'real prospect of survival' test contained in the English legislation. Finlay C.J. said that the court should be very slow to appoint an examiner, when there is no identifiable possibility of survival.

McCarthy J. also expressed reservations about Lardner J.'s definition, pointing out that it was difficult for a court to come to any conclusion, until the examiner had presented his initial report. McCarthy J. discussed the policy of the Act. It was designed to afford a breathing space for the company at the expense of some of its creditors. The Supreme Court, in *Re Holidair* [1994] 1 I.L.R.M. 483 approved of both Finlay C.J. and McCarthy J.'s criteria in *Re Atlantic Magnetics Ltd* [1993] 2 I.R. 561.

Keane J. in *Re Butler's Engineering* agreed with Finlay C.J. that the jurisdiction of the court to appoint an examiner is not limited to cases where the company will certainly survive. Keane J. held that the terms of section 2 conferred a wide discretion on the court. Keane J. explained that although the court has jurisdiction to appoint an examiner where it will not necessarily facilitate the survival of the company, the court should be slow to make the order unless there is an 'identifiable possibility' of survival. The court is bound to exercise its discretion having regard to the particular circumstances of each case. It must do so judicially, and in accordance with strict criteria laid down by the Supreme Court in *Re Atlantic Magnetics Ltd* and *Re Holidair*.

Keane J. examined the majority opinions in *Re Atlantic Magnetics Ltd.* Keane J. stated that Finlay C.J. affirmed Lardner J.'s test except that he required that the word *'reasonable'* be deleted from the phrase *'some reasonable prospect of survival'*. McCarthy J., on the other hand, required that the entire phrase *'some reasonable prospect of survival'* should be omitted. Keane J. said that McCarthy J.'s decision could not be regarded as part of the majority judgment of the court.

Keane J. considered what constituted the threshold of Finlay CJ's test. It will be remembered that Finlay C.J. said that there had to be some prospect of survival. However, later in his judgment, Finlay C.J. noted that a court should be extremely hesitant in appointing an examiner where there is *'no identifiable prospect of survival'*. Keane J. questioned whether the test of 'no identifiable prospect of survival' imposes a lower threshold than 'some prospect of survival'? Keane J.'s answer is not clear, but appears to incline towards the affirmative. Keane J.'s approach is that *jurisdiction* to appoint arises if 'there is at least a possibility' that the company will survive, if an examiner is appointed. According to Keane J, Finlay C.J.'s test is of more significance in cases where there is a conflict of evidence.

Keane J. adverted to the purpose underlying the examinership legislation, namely to protect the company, and as result, its shareholders, employees and creditors. However, Keane J. noted that a court considering the appointment of an examiner should bear in mind the drastic abridgement of creditors' rights such a course may bring about. Even the three weeks' breathing space may have serious consequences for creditors, particularly so, when the control of the company remains in the hands of those whose management may have led to or contributed to its insolvency. Keane J. stressed that the onus is on those presenting the examinership petition to show that there is at least an *identifiable* prospect of the company's survival as a going concern if an examiner is appointed. This onus was not met by any bald assertion that the company will survive.

Keane J. then sought to discover whether the petitioner in this case had demonstrated that there was an identifiable prospect of survival of the *Butler Engineering* group. Keane J. found that the initial requirements of section 2(1) had been met. The company was grossly insolvent. This was not disputed. The main reason for this was the dispute with British Steel, and the high cost of steel obtained from Preussag. Keane J. said that there was no scintilla of evidence before the court that anything had been done to find a supplier whose prices were cheaper. The contracts which the petitioner hoped could rescue the company from its plight were incapable of fulfilment unless the company could find another supplier. In fact, Preusagg, the current supplier, opposed this petition. In the absence of identification of a supplier, the only way the company could be saved would be by new investment.

Keane J. examined the petition's averments about the possibility of outside investment; the information about this was sparse in the extreme. Keane J. also held that a petitioner must clearly set out the company's financial position. This can only be objectively demonstrated where proper books of account have been kept.The petitioners had failed to evidence that such records had been kept. Finally, Keane J. noted that the petition was not supported by all the directors, and though this fact was not conclusive, it did not inspire Keane J.'s confidence. For these reasons, he dismissed the petition.

Two points should be made. The first is one of principle. The second is pragmatic.

First, the definition of a test regarding the appointment of an examiner will always give rise both to debate about the underlying policy reasons behind the legislation. These have been judicially recognised as to provide a breathing space for the company, and to protect employment: see Costello J. in *Selukwe* (see 1992 Annual Review 93–94). Keane J, in this case, points out that despite these two policy considerations, courts should still be aware of the rights and interests of creditors. Doubtless these policy considerations are fundamental to the reason why the legislation was introduced. There is a danger that giving undue weight to one or other of the policy considerations may lead to judicial legislation.

Second, we make the more pragmatic point that an examinership petition is presented without any truly independent evidence to support it. The court must rely on the accuracy of the petition and its supporting affidavits. Indeed, the purpose of the first report of the examiner must be in part to confirm the truth or otherwise of the averments in the petition and supporting affidavits.

This obviously leaves open potential abuse. Clearly, Keane J. is correct to suggest that no bald assertion in the petition, that the company could be rendered profitable is sufficient, and also, the presentation of inadequate, or uncertified accounts is unsatisfactory. But from the point of view of legal advisers, the question is, how firm must the accountant's proposals be, before the advice is given to lodge a petition? Must the petitioner show that there should be concrete plans available as to what reorganisation may be implemented if the examinership is granted? This is perhaps something that should happen after the examinership is in place: see the excellent discussion in I. Lynch, J. Marshall, R. O'Ferrall, *Corporate Insolvency & Rescue* (Butterworths, Dublin 1996), chapters 10 and 11. Obviously, there may be cases where there is some fundamental impediment which is apparent to the court at petition stage, and the court will seek some guidance from the petitioner as to how this fundamental flaw will be overcome. Indeed just such an apparent flaw occurred in this case. However, in most insolvency situations, the difficulties will not be so much a single fundamental problem, but a variety of commercial and accounting difficulties which will need consideration and contextualisation by an expert insolvency practitioner, rather than judicial appraisal on the hearing of a petition on affidavit.

Keane J.'s approach was endorsed by Budd J. in *In re Westport Property Construction Company Ltd,* September 13.

Restraining a winding up petition *Truck and Machinery Sales Ltd v. Marubeni Komatsu Ltd* [1996] 1 I.R. 12. The Companies Acts 1963-1990 provide that if a creditor is owed £1000, such a creditor may present a petition to wind up the debtor company. The amount due must be specific, certain and indisputable, otherwise the petition will be disallowed, and the petitioner will be required to sue for debt in the ordinary way. The courts have refused to allow the winding up jurisdiction to become a forum for resolving disputed debts.

Problems arise in practice. First of all, there are creditors who are certainly owed a sum greater than £1000 by the company, but there is some dispute about the exact sum. This case suggests an attractively simple solution. It holds that the petitioner should sue for so much as is clearly undisputed and indisputable, which must be over £1000. If there is any balance due and owing to the creditor, the creditor should initiate proceedings for that balance, and/or claim in the winding up in respect of the balance.

Truck and Machinery Sales Ltd (TMS) was set up in order to *inter alia* buy and sell trucks, machinery and plant in Ireland and abroad. In 1992, the company's markets in Europe were poor. The company identified a market in the United Arab Emirates. The company purchased second hand equipment from the defendant, a Japanese export company at a cost of £2.9 million sterling. This sum was to be paid under a Credit Sale Agreement. The agreement required TMS to pay Marubeni Komatsu Ltd (MKL) on or before October 31, 1992. This agreement contained a reservation of title clause under which MKL retained title of the goods until payment.

The goods in question made their way to Dubai in the UAE. Problem arose on their arrival. A United Arab Emirates company, Galadari Trucks and Heavy Equipment Ltd, claimed that it had the right to be the sole distributor of this equipment in the UAE. MKL argued that this distribution contract only related to new and not to second hand machinery. However, the authorities in Dubai agreed with the United Arab Emirates company. TMS was prohibited from moving the goods from Dubai's duty free zone. It could not sell them.

TMS commenced negotiations concerning its indebtedness to MKL under the credit sale agreement. MKL agreed that TMS could transport some of its equipment to Holland. This was sold at auction, and the proceeds went some way to reducing TMS's indebtedness. In addition, TMS was allowed to return trucks to MKL. These negotiations reduced TMS's indebtedness to MKL by over £1 million sterling. However, MKL instructed a firm of solicitors to obtain the remaining £2.35 million sterling owed under the credit sale agreement. The solicitors served TMS with a 21 day demand letter in accordance section 214 of the Companies Act 1963. If TMS failed to pay the remaining sum within 21 days, MKL's solicitors would petition the High Court to have the company wound up pursuant to sections 213 and 214 of the Companies Acts 1963-90.

TMS sought an injunction prohibiting the presentation of MKL's petition and/or an injunction restraining its advertisement. TMS claimed that MKL were estopped from petitioning for a winding up, as MKL had agreed not to bring such proceedings. On the 23 December 1993, MKL had allegedly entered into an agreement not to proceed further with legal action against TMS for the recovery of the sums in question. This agreement was evidence in a fax sent by the sales director of MKL. In the fax, the sales director said that it was not the intention of MKL to proceed further with legal action, provided MKL received a part payment of '£750,000 – £1 million'. MKL was willing to wait for the balance until the remaining equipment was sold through alternative channels. Alternatively, if the sale proceeds did not clear the outstanding debt, MKL agreed to await the outcome of legal proceedings in Dubai. TMS claimed that the presentation of this petition by MKL was in breach of this agreement.

MKL disputed TMS's claim. The sales director claimed that he had sent the fax to the TMS's bank in order to facilitate the release of moneys from the bank. The fax was not intended to constitute a waiver to the payment of the debt. MKL pointed to matters which arose subsequent to the fax and were inconsistent with TMS's claim. TMS arranged for the auction of the remaining equipment in Amsterdam. It had arranged for the transfer of the sum into one of MKL's bank accounts. A cheque for £500,000 was sent. It was returned marked 'payment stopped'. MKL had entered into further discussions and correspondence with TMS in an attempt to secure payment for the outstanding sums. MKL believed that these events were inconsistent with TMS's claim that the balance of the debt had been waived.

In the High Court, Keane J. said that it was clear that where a company in good faith and on substantial grounds disputes *any* liability in respect of the alleged debt, a court will either dismiss a winding up petition, or will restrain the future presenting of such a petition. *Mann v. Goldstein* [1968] 2 All E.R. 769 decided that the courts will not allow a winding up petition to be used to enforce payment of a debt which is *bona fide* disputed. This dictum was subsequently approved by the Court of Appeal in *Stonegate Securities Ltd v. Gregory* [1980] 1 All E.R. 241. The *rationes* of these decisions were approved of by O'Hanlon J. in *Re Pageboy Couriers Ltd* [1983] I.L.R.M. 511.

Keane J. considered the meaning of the phrase 'any liability' in this context. In *Re Tweeds Garages Ltd* [1962] 1 All E.R. 121, the English High Court decided that where a company admits its indebtedness to the creditor for a sum exceeding £1,000, but disputes the balance even on substantial grounds, the creditor should not normally be restrained form presenting a petition. This principle was approved of by the Court of Appeal in *Taylor's Industrial Flooring Ltd v. M & H Plant Hire (Manchester) Ltd* (1990) B.C.L.C. 21.

Keane J. noted the latest Irish case in this area: *Clandown v. Davis* [1994] 2 I.L.R.M. 536: see 1994 Annual Review at 69. In *Clandown*, a former employee claimed that she was owed in excess of £50,000. She attempted to use her claim to ground a petition to liquidate the company. The company learnt of this. It sought an injunction restraining her from advertising the petition. In the High Court, Morris J. stated that he believed that the company did owe the employee money, but was unable to quantify this sum. For this reason, Morris J. held that a petition could not be used to enforce payment of a debt which is *bona fide* disputed. Morris J. therefore granted the injunction. Keane J. interpreted Morris J.'s decision as holding that a court could restrain a petition where part only of the debt was disputed. However, Keane J. noted that Morris J. had not been referred to *Re Tweeds Garage Ltd* [1962] 1 All E.R. 121, nor to *Taylor's Industrial Flooring Ltd v. M & H Plant Hire (Manchester) Ltd* [1990] B.C.L.C. 21.

Keane J. drew attention to his *ex tempore* judgment in *Patrick Butterly and Sons Ltd v. Top Security Ltd* of September 27, 1995. In *Butterly*, Keane J. applying the principle in *Re Tweeds Garages Ltd.* held that where a company admits its indebtedness to a creditor for a sum exceeding £1,000 but disputes the balance, even on substantial grounds, that creditor should not normally be restrained from presenting the petition. Keane J. was not persuaded to adopt a different approach in this case.

Keane J. considered what principles a court should apply, when faced with an application for an interlocutory injunction of a winding up petition. Keane J. approved of the approach of Buckley L.J. in *Bryanston Finance Ltd v. De Vries (No. 2)* [1976] 1 Ch. 63. In *Bryanston Finance*, Buckley L.J. held that when considering an application to restrain a winding up petition, the court should apply the principles used in a *quia timet* injunction when restraining the commencement of winding up proceedings. The right to present a petition for a winding up of a company is a right conferred by statute. A petitioner should not be restrained from exercising it, except on clear and persuasive grounds. Buckley L.J. found that greater harm was caused to a petitioner when restraining a petition, than to a company when the petition was allowed to proceed.

Keane J. recognised that an attempt to restrain a petition is usually interlocutory in nature. However, Keane J. decided that a court considering an application to restrain a petition should not apply the principles established in *Campus Oil Ltd v. Minister for Industry and Energy (No. 2)* [1983] I.R. 88 when deciding whether to grant or withhold interlocutory injunctive relief. In an application for an interlocutory injunction, the court is being asked to restrain conduct which it is alleged is violating the plaintiff's rights. A court must be satisfied as to the following three issues where interlocutory injunctions are sought. First, that there is fair question to be tried. Second, that damages will not be an adequate remedy. Third, that the balance of convenience (including the desirability of preserving the *status quo* pending the determination of the action) points to the granting of the injunction. These factors were not relevant in an application to restrain a winding up petition, which prevents a person from exercising his right of access to the courts.

Keane J. found that the courts could interfere with a petitioner's right of access to the courts. Keane J. approved of Buckley L.J.'s requirement in *Bryanston Finance* that the company must show that the presentation of the petition constitutes at least a *prima facie* abuse of process. Keane J. believed that the constitutional right of access to the court should not be interfered with, unless in exceptional circumstances. This principle was applicable to the presentation of a petition for the winding-up of a company by a person with the appropriate *locus standi*. The High Court has power to restrain a petition, but this power should only be exercised where *prima facie* the presentation of the petition constitutes an abuse of process. Keane J. held that the burden of proof is on the company to establish that the petition constitutes an abuse of process. Relying on *Coulson Sanderson & Ward v. Ward* [1986] 2 B.C.C. 99, Keane J. explained that in many cases a company will establish a *prima facie* case by showing that the petition is bound to fail, or at least that there is a suitable alternative remedy.

Keane J. stated that it was clear that where the would-be petitioner is a contingent or prospective creditor, the court being asked to restrain the petition is not concerned with whether the creditor will be able to meet the requirements of section 215(c). This section requires that a contingent or prospective creditor must give security for costs and satisfy the court that a *prima facie* case for the winding-up subsists, before the court shall give a hearing to a winding-up petition. Keane J. agreed with Goulding J.'s interpretation of this statutory requirement in *Holt Southy Ltd v. Catnic Components Ltd* [1978] 2 All E.R. 276. Goulding J. held where it is shown that the petitioner is a creditor or contingent creditor, it is for the court which hears the petition to determine whether the statutory requirements for the granting of the relief sought in the petition have been met.

Keane J. considered that the fact of a company's insolvency was not a ground for allowing a petition to proceed where it had been shown that the petition constituted an abuse of process. Keane J. said that the company's solvency or insolvency was an important factor for a court to consider when exercising the court's equitable discretion in granting or withholding injunctive relief. A court considering such an application must do so, particularly with the interests of the creditors in mind. Keane J. found support for this in the Australian case *Kinsela v. Russell Kinsela Properties Ltd (In Liquidation)* [1986] 4 N.S.W.L.R. 722. In this Australian case, the court decided that when a company is insolvent, due consideration should be given to the interests of the creditors. Keane J. pointed out that this principle had been expressly approved by both the Irish High and Supreme Courts in *Re Frederick Inns Ltd*

[1991] I.L.R.M. 582; [1994] 1 I.L.R.M. 387.

Keane J. expressed sympathy with TMS's position. Keane J. recognised that its insolvency had arisen primarily through no fault of its own. MKL recognised this, and adopted a patient and understanding attitude. However, Keane J. stated that the only question was whether TMS was entitled to an injunction restraining MKL from presenting a petition for the winding up of TMS. Keane J. was satisfied that the injunction should be granted.

TMS had failed to establish a *prima facie* case that the presentation of the petition constituted an abuse of process. Keane J. found that if the one fax upon which TMS relied had been read in isolation it might be said to afford grounds on which TMS might dispute the debt claimed in the statutory demand. However, reading all the correspondence, Keane J. found that MKL at no stage waived the balance of the purchase price due to it. Keane J. found that TMS was left under no illusion that it was being waived. In fact, TMS had tendered a cheque. This was wholly inconsistent with any such belief. Keane J. was satisfied that TMS had failed to demonstrate that the petition, if presented, was bound to fail. Keane J. held that at this stage, there was no alternative remedy available to MKL.

Keane J. questioned whether TMS was insolvent or not. Keane J. said that there was sufficient evidence of the TMS's insolvency to refuse the injunctive relief sought.

Keane J. considered the company's claim. First, TMS argued that MKL should be restrained from presenting its petition, as it had agreed with TMS not to proceed. MKL argued that there was no consideration to support the alleged agreement. Keane J. stated that it was settled law since the decision of the House of Lords in *Foakes v. Beer* (1888) 9 App. Cas. 605 that a promise to pay part of a debt is not good consideration in law. This principle had been applied in similar circumstances in *Re Selectmove* [1995] 2 All E.R. 531. In this case, the company argued that it had come to an arrangement with the UK revenue as to the payment of arrears. The UK revenue subsequently presented a petition to wind up the company. The English Court of Appeal followed *Foakes v. Beer* (1888) 9 App. Cas. 605 and rejected the argument that a promise to pay a sum which the debtor was already bound by law to pay to the promisee could afford any consideration to support the contract. Keane J. decided to follow this approach. It could be traced to *Pinnel's* case (1602) 5 Co. Rep. 117a. Keane J. said that even if he were to accept that the fax created the agreement alleged by TMS, the agreement was legally unenforceable in accordance with the Court of Appeal's decision in *Re Selectmove*.

TMS argued in the alternative that the principle of promissory estoppel was applicable, and MKL was estopped from presenting a petition. Again, MKL argued that the necessary conditions do not exist to give rise to an estoppel. According to Keane J, the principle of 'promissory estoppel' first appeared in English law in *Hughes v. Metropolitan Railway Company* (1877)

2 App. Cas. 439 and was given renewed life by *Central London Property Trust Ltd v. High Trees House Ltd* [1947] K.B. 130. Promissory estoppel arises where parties to an agreement enter into a course of negotiations which has the effect of leading one of the parties to believe either that the strict rights arising under the contract will not be enforced or will be kept in suspense. Having regard to the dealings between the parties, a court may decide that it is inequitable for a party to rely strictly upon his or her rights. Keane J. found that the negotiations between the parties was such that it could not have left any reasonable person under the impression that MKL were waiving their entitlement to the balance of the debt. On the contrary, Keane J. stated that MKL had made continuous requests for payment of the account, and TMS had put forward proposals in response. Keane J. held that to estop MKL from taking legal proceedings to enforce their rights would be a negation of equity.

Three points arise for consideration from this case.

First, clients should now be advised to present a petition for that part of the debt which is indisputable, and which is over £1000, and either sue or prove in the liquidation for the balance.

Second, Keane J. points out that section 213 is so framed as to accord the High Court a discretion as to whether it will order a liquidation. Thus, a petitioner who can prove his or her debt is *prima facie* entitled to place the company in liquidation. Keane J. states that the courts will interfere where the petition is shown to be an abuse of process. Keane J. gives two examples of what constitutes an abuse of process in this context which he derives from *Coulson Sanderson & Ward v. Ward* [1986] 2 B.C.C. 99. One is where the petitioner's cause is demonstrated to be hopeless. Obviously this is an abuse of process. Two is where a petitioner may have an alternative remedy. This is more controversial. Why should the petitioner be inhibited from exercising his legal claim, merely because he has another route? Keane J. is suggesting that a creditor who has not been paid, and who can prove his debt, may be denied the winding up petition, if the court thinks that the creditor should employ some alternative to the winding up procedure. What alternatives exist in practice? As the law now stands, a corporate tenant who for no good reason refuses to pay rent, will enjoy two or three years in uninterrupted possession of the premises, by the time the courts have snailed their way to judgment in favour of the innocent landlord.

Third, Keane J. relied upon the decision in *Re Frederick Inns Ltd* as authority for the proposition that in considering a winding up application, the court is entitled to approach the company's position with the interests of the general body of creditors particularly in mind. This should be contrasted with McCracken J.'s dicta in the next case, *Re Genport*. In *Re Genport* McCracken J. held himself entitled to have regard to the interests of the general body of creditors in mind, when considering a winding up petition. McCracken J. relied for this not on case law, but on the authority of section 309 of the

Companies Act 1963.

Under section 309, the creditors whose interests are being considered by the court must be present or represented before the court, and presumably the court must restrict itself to the representations made to it by such creditors. However, what Keane J. is advocating is a judicial approach which takes into account the interests of the general body of creditors, presumably whether represented or not. This case was appealed to the Supreme Court which upheld Keane J.'s decision.

Restraining a winding-up petition *In re Genport Ltd*, High Court, November 21, concerned a petition for the winding up of a company. The petition arose from complex disputes between a tenant and a landlord.

Genport was and is a tenant of substantial premises, Sachs Hotel. The landlord sought to forfeit the lease as a consequence of various breaches of covenant by Genport. Genport instituted proceedings against the landlord. The parties came to a settlement, and the proceedings were withdrawn. However, a subsequent dispute arose, relating to alterations to the settlement agreement after it had been signed. Genport reinstituted the proceedings not only against the landlord, but against one of the landlord's employees. In the High Court, Murphy J. dismissed Genport's action. He awarded the landlord's employee two-thirds of her costs as against Genport. Genport sought and obtained a stay of 14 days on the High Court order. Genport lodged an appeal against the award to the Supreme Court and sought a further stay on the High Court order from the Supreme Court. The Supreme Court refused to grant a stay on the High Court order. So, following taxation, the landlord's employee was owed £52,363.88.

The employee served a 21 day demand letter pursuant to section 214 of the Companies Act 1963 for £52,363.88, plus a further £21,000 in interest. The employee was not paid. She presented a petition to wind up Genport. The petition was adjourned on a number of occasions. In addition, there currently exist other proceedings between Genport and its landlord.

In the High Court, McCracken J. stated that the petitioner had proved that Genport was unable to pay its debts and the court was entitled to wind up the company pursuant to section 213. However, section 213 is not mandatory. The court hearing a winding up petition retains a discretion to grant or refuse the order. Relying upon McCarthy J.'s judgment *In re Bula* [1990] 1 I.R. 440, McCracken J. held that the petitioner was *prima facie* entitled to her winding up order, unless Genport could show that the petition was for an ulterior purpose, though not necessarily an improper one. If the company was able to show that it was for an ulterior purpose, the burden of proof shifts back to the petitioner. McCracken J. examined three of Genport's claims, to see if there existed an ulterior purpose behind this petition.

First, Genport argued that the petition was financed by the company's landlord, in order to bring to an end the remaining legal proceedings between the landlord and the tenant. McCracken J. stated that this allegation of itself was not sufficient to establish an ulterior purpose to the petition. A large creditor of a company has a perfectly proper commercial interest in preventing a company dissipating assets in litigation. McCracken J. pointed out that it may well be in the interests of the creditors in many cases that a winding up order be made to prevent a highly litigious company from spending all its assets on what may be doubtful litigation.

Second, McCracken J. found that this petition would result in the forfeiture of the lease and the loss of goodwill in the company's hotel restaurant and night-club business. This would greatly benefit the landlord. In addition, if the lease was forfeited there would be no assets to pay the other creditors. McCracken J. held section 309 entitled the court to have regard to the views of the trade creditors with regard to the petition. All four trade creditors opposed the petition. They wished the company to continue trading.

Finally, McCracken J. noted that there existed partly heard litigation between the company and its landlord. McCracken J. believed that it would be difficult for a liquidator to take up such an action, as the action had reached a late stage. Indeed, the liquidator might decide that the litigation was pointless as the principal asset had gone.

McCracken J. stated that neither factor taken on its own was sufficiently strong to dismiss or stay the petition. However, there was an ulterior, though not necessarily an improper, motive behind the petition. This, coupled with the fact that a winding up may not be of benefit to ordinary creditors, swayed the balance in favour of the company. McCracken J. decided not to dismiss the petition, but stayed it pending the outcome of the ongoing litigation.

Two points should be made about this judgment.

First, it affirms the principle that a petitioner cannot claim that he is entitled as of right to an order to wind up the company. The petitioner makes his claim. The Supreme Court in *Re Bula Ltd* [1990] 1 I.R. 440 at 448, Keane J. in *Truck & Machinery Sales Ltd*, and McCracken J., in this case, hold that a petitioner is *prima facie* entitled to the granting of a winding up petition. However, it is not a foregone conclusion. The company may reply by alleging that the petition has been brought for an ulterior purpose (such as was alleged in this case). Then, assuming the company has demonstrated the ulterior purpose, then the burden of proof shifts back to the petitioner. What the petitioner must prove or disprove is not clear. Is it that the ulterior purpose is not *improper*? Or is it merely that the company has to refute the existence of an ulterior motive? The practical application of this dictum is unclear.

McCracken J. endorsed the Supreme Court's dictum that an ulterior purpose may be sufficient to shift the burden back on the petitioner. However, though this may prove an enticing vista for the academic rambler, in a hard-nosed commercial context, the critical issue is whether the petitioner's claim is or is not improper, and whether the impropriety is, or will become manifest.

This raises a second point: when will a court refuse a petition on the grounds that though the petitioner's claim is perfectly justifiable, the other creditors do not want the company to be wound up? The determination of the petition to wind up a company is not the conventional plaintiff/defendant action. The winding up procedure, which requires the advertisement of the petition, allows for all creditors who so wish, to be heard. For this reason, the legislation envisages some broader judicial activity; namely the consideration not merely of the petitioner's and company's interests, but all those legitimate interests which are represented before the court. Section 309(1) should be considered in this regard, since it allows the court to ascertain the wishes of creditors and contributories before, deciding whether to grant or refuse a petition.

Keeping proper books of account   *In re Mantruck Services Ltd: Mehigan v. Duignan* [1997] 1 I.L.R.M. 171. In 1988, a company was established with two shareholders. One of these shareholders, JD, was a director. JD's wife was the other director. On July 2, 1993, the creditors resolved to wind the company up voluntarily and to appoint a liquidator. An employee of the liquidator visited the company's premises and collected all documents, records and books of the company that he found.

On July 29, 1993, the voluntary liquidation was converted into a court liquidation. On examining the material supplied by the creditor's liquidator, the official liquidator formed the opinion that there were 'significant and extensive' omissions in the company's records. As a consequence, there was great uncertainty as to the assets and liabilities of the company and this greatly impeded the winding up. On application by the liquidator, the High Court made an order, *inter alia,* requiring the two directors to hand over all the books and documents. However, the order was primarily directed at JD. JD's only response was the production of two invoices.

During the next two years, the liquidator was in regular contact with JD in a vain attempt to obtain documents he believed were still in JD's possession. JD told the liquidator that proper books and records had been maintained and the voluntary liquidator's employee had collected all these from the company's premises.

Finally, the liquidator brought proceedings under section 150 and section 204 of the Companies Act 1990 against JD. The High Court ordered that JD be examined on oath by the Master of the High Court. During this examination, JD informed the Master that purchases, sales and receipts of the company were written up into a temporary record book. The information was than taken from this book and then transferred to computer disc. The invoices and temporary record book were then destroyed. In 1992, the VAT Inspector learnt of this practice and informed the company that it should keep manual records. This was done thereafter.

The High Court applications under section 150 and section 204 began on June 18, 1996. During the hearing, the director informed the court that there might be certain books, papers and records either at the company's premises or at the director's farm. The director was ordered to deliver these books, papers, and records to the liquidator. The hearing was adjourned until July 16, 1996. At the resumed hearing, the liquidator informed the court that he had received 29 computer discs and 5 red Cathedral books from the director. These books comprised a sales book, a purchases book and two cash books and a wages book. The liquidator explained to the court that the discs were unusable, and the data inaccessible. The five books still contained significant omissions. The liquidator outlined the various time periods and matters that related to these omissions. He stated that he was still unable to ascertain the position of the company and its assets and liabilities. This was attributable to the failure of the company to keep proper books and records. The liquidator estimated that 80% of his time and that of his staff was spent trying to overcome the deficiencies in the books and records of the company. The liquidator informed the court that JD had not been in any way co-operative. The liquidator was therefore unable to wind up the company. However, various other witnesses testified as to the existence or non-existence of manual records.

In the High Court, Shanley J. pointed out that before any liability could be imposed upon an officer of the company under section 204 of the Companies Act 1990 the following matters had to be proved in evidence.

First, the company in question must be in the process of being wound up.

Second, the company must be unable to pay its debts.

Third, the court had to be satisfied that the company was in contravention of section 202 of the Companies Act 1990, by failing to keep proper books of account. This meant that the court had to be satisfied that the company had committed a criminal offence. Section 202 clearly lays out what records a company must 'keep'. Shanley J. interpreted 'keep' as imposing upon the company a continuous positive obligation to create and maintain books and records in a specified manner. A company is not the mere passive custodian of the books and records.

Fourth, the contravention by the company of section 202 must:

(a) contribute to the inability of the company to pay its debts;
(b) result in substantial uncertainty as to the assets and liabilities of the company; or,
(c) substantially impede the orderly winding up of the company.

Fifth, an officer or former officer must knowingly and wilfully authorise or permit the contravention by the company of section 202 or be convicted under sections 194, 197 or 242 in relation to a statement concerning the keeping of proper books of account.

Shanley J. stated that the definition of 'officer' was very wide. It includes directors of a company, the auditor of the company, and any person convicted of providing false information under the Companies Acts. Section 204 was sufficiently wide to include a shareholder who is an officer in default. Shanley J. held that if these five conditions were satisfied, the Court could impose unlimited liability on the officer in question for the debts of the company.

Shanley J. pointed out that section 204 does not require a direct causal relation between a section 202 contravention and liability under section 204. Such a connection may well not exist. In such a case, Shanley J. opined that it would be clearly unjustifiable in principle to impose full liability upon the officers of the company.

In other cases, there may be a direct link between the section 202 offence and the liabilities of the company. In such case there is no injustice in imposing liability on the officers for these debts.

Shanley J. stated that there can be differing forms of contravention of section 202. Some contraventions can arise as a result of a simple failure to record the requisite information, whilst other contraventions may involve a deliberate intention to evade tax. Shanley J. held that a court exercising its discretion under section 204 should not view both of these contraventions in the same light. The court would clearly impose greater liability on those officers who tried to evade tax.

The court could impose personal liability on officers of the company where the contravention of section 202 did *not* in itself caused loss to the company. The contravention had substantially impeded the orderly winding up of the company, or resulted in substantial uncertainty as to its assets and liabilities, that would be sufficient to allow the court to impose personal liability. Shanley J. held that the court would again have regard to the circumstances surrounding the contravention of section 204. He stated that the court's discretion had to be exercised in a careful and proportionate manner. If a court exercised its discretion in a disproportionate manner, this would amount to an unjust attack on the personal rights of the officer.

Shanley J. gave some guidance on how this discretion was to be exercised.

First, he stated that the presumption of constitutionality required that the judge should exercise his discretion in a constitutional fashion. Shanley J. approved of Murphy J.'s dictum in *O'Keeffe v. Ferris* [1993] 3 I.R. 165. In *O'Keeffe v. Ferris*, Murphy J. considered how a judge should exercise his discretion for imposing liability upon directors who are found to have recklessly or fraudulently traded. Murphy J. held that the judge should ensure that the burden imposed upon the director is commensurate with the loss suffered by the company.

Second, Shanley J. reviewed the interpretation that a New Zealand court gave to the equivalent section 202 and 204 statutory provisions in the New Zealand Companies Acts. In *Maloc Construction Ltd (In Liquidation) v.*

Chadwick & Others [1986] 3 N.Z.C.L.C. 99, 794, Tompkins J. suggested that
there were three relevant factors in exercising this statutory discretion:

> (a) there must be a causal relationship between the contravention of sec-
> tion 202, the officer's contribution to the contravention and the conse-
> quent losses;
> (b) the court would see whether the officer was in some way blamewor-
> thy. The more culpable the officer, the greater his personal liability; and,
> (c) the court had to consider whether debts were being incurred when
> the contravention took place.

Applying the *ratio* of these two cases to the section 204 discretion, Shanley J.
held that the court had to ask itself two questions:

> (i) to what extent did the contravention of section 202 result in financial
> loss to the company?
> (ii) If it did result in financial loss, were such losses reasonably foresee-
> able by the officer as a result of the contravention?

Shanley J. held that, save in exceptional cases, liability should not be imposed
for contravention not resulting in loss, or for losses not reasonably foreseeable as a result of the contravention. He stated further that no higher degree of
probability of a contravention of section 202 is required, than in any other
civil matter.

Shanley J. reverted to the facts of the case before him. He listed the six
specific deficiencies in the books and the time periods to which these deficiencies related. Shanley J. rejected the director's claim that the information
could be retrieved from the computer discs. This assertion was based on a
conversation that the director had with a software engineer. This engineer was
never called to give evidence. Shanley J. accepted that without the information allegedly encrypted in the discs, the liquidator could not ascertain the
financial position of the company, nor what the company's assets and liabilities, as there were no manual debtors' or creditors' ledgers. Shanley J. was
concerned with the accuracy of the director's version of events as it related to
the five missing red Cathedral books.

Shanley J. concluded that the deficiencies in the company's books and
records were such that it was impossible to determine the financial position of
the company with any accuracy nor to audit the company.

Shanley J. held that the company was in contravention of section 202.
Shanley J. was satisfied that the company, having contravened the section,
was unable to pay its debts at the date of its winding up. As a consequence of
this contravention, there was a great deal of uncertainty as to the assets and
liabilities of the company, and, in addition, substantially impeded the orderly

winding up of the company. The director was an officer of the company who he found had knowingly and wilfully authorised and permitted the section 202 contravention. The director was unable to avail of any of the defences of section 204.

Shanley J. held that it was impossible to separate the liabilities as a result of the breaches of section 202, prior to the winding-up of the company. However, he decided that the time and cost involved in overcoming the deficiencies in the books by the liquidator was reasonably foreseeable by the director. Shanley J. ordered that the director should be personally liable to the company for a sum equivalent to the liquidator's fee in overcoming the deficiencies in the books: £91,239.80. In addition, Shanley J. imposed a five year restriction on the director, according to the provisions of section 150.

This judgment contains the first Irish judicial amplification concerning the duty to maintain proper books and accounts. Shanley J.'s judgment is important for at least five reasons.

First, Shanley J.'s judgment stresses that the primary responsibility for keeping proper books and records falls on the company. If the company is in breach of this liability, the officers will be liable upon the company's conviction. In this context, the term 'officer' is significant. The primary persons fixed with liability will be the *directors*. But the statute uses the term 'officer', and this specifically includes 'auditor'. Thus, there is a case for saying that where the directors involve the auditors of the company in keeping books and records or preparing accounts at any stage anterior to certification of the accounts, the auditors may not be able to evade liability for figures which essentially they have helped to produce.

Second, Shanley J. points out how the duty must be fulfilled: that is to say, officers must not merely act as passive custodians, but rather the books and records must be in a particular form with specified contents. The recording must be on a timely and consistent basis, must enable the financial position of the company to be determined with reasonable accuracy, and shall contain records of all sums received and expended by the company. Though all this is doubtless inherent in the 1986 Act Shanley J.'s judgment, which deals with the consequences of breach of the statute, throws the matter into sharp relief.

Third, the judgment points out that in order to hold an officer civilly liable for the failure to maintain proper books and records, it is not necessary to establish a clear link between the imperfect records and a specific corporate debt or liability. This seems reasonable, as where the books and records are substantially deficient, it will be by definition impossible to re-create a full picture. Certain inferences from deficiencies may of course be justified, but that is a different matter. In this case, there is obvious justice in the finding that the defaulting director should be liable to the company for the liquidator's fees incurred in attempting to remedy the accounting defects. It may serve as a warning to others.

Fourth, the imposition of liability by a judge must be effected in accordance with the requirements of the Constitution: that is to say that liability will be tied in to the degree of blameworthiness of the officer. If a trial judge imposes liability in excess of the blameworthiness, then the officer may bring a challenge for infringement of his constitutional rights.

Fifth, one wonders whether there are any proposals for hard empirical research into whether these sections are actually effective, not merely in raising the standard of record keeping, but also, in preventing the abuse of limited liability?

Restriction of directors   *Carway v. Attorney General* [1997] 1 I.L.R.M. 110. Section 149 of the Companies Acts lays down in what circumstances the High Court may restrict a company director. First, the court may exercise its power of restriction, when it has been proved that the company is unable to pay its debts, within the meaning of section 214 of the Companies Act 1963, either at the commencement of, or during the course of the liquidation. Second, the court has jurisdiction to restrict a director, where the liquidator certifies at any time during the liquidation that the company is unable to pay its debts, within the meaning of section 214 of the Companies Act 1963.

In this case, the liquidator certified that the company was unable to pay its debts. During the course of the restriction proceedings, the directors sought to challenge the constitutionality of this power of certification. The High Court adjourned the proceedings in order to have the constitutionality issue tried as a preliminary matter.

The directors claimed that this power of certification was unconstitutional, as there was no means of disputing the assertion in the liquidator's certificate that the company was insolvent. The section created an irrebuttable presumption of insolvency contrary to the principles laid down in *Maher v. Attorney General* [1973] I.R. 140 and *The State (McEldowney) v. Kelleher* [1983] I.R. 289. The directors argued that the liquidator's certificate is a justiciable issue which cannot be removed from the High Court's jurisdiction. Indeed the directors went further. They claimed that the section was not warranted. The liquidator could prove the company's insolvency in court by reference to the company's books and documents. Alternatively, even if the directors were entitled to mount a challenge to the certificate, practically speaking, they would be deprived of access to the necessary evidence. All the books and documents were in the possession of the liquidator and therefore, so the argument ran, unavailable to the directors. The directors pointed out that there was also a possibility that during a liquidation a company could *become* solvent. Finally, the directors argued that a section 150 order interferes with the constitutional right to earn a livelihood and a breach of a section 150 order carries with it criminal sanctions.

The Attorney General argued that the certificate is only a preliminary step.

There is nothing to prevent directors from producing evidence to prove that the company is not insolvent. The Attorney General drew attention to the wording of section 104 of the Companies Act 1963, which clearly establishes an irrebuttable presumption that the certificate of the registrar of companies shall be conclusive. Section 149(1)(b), he pointed out, does not contain similar wording.

In the High Court, Carroll J. referred to the statutory provisions under consideration in the cases of *Maher v. Attorney General* [1973] I.R. 140 and *The State (McEldowney) v. Kelleher* [1983] I.R. 289. In both cases, the court decided that the wording or the effect of the relevant provisions was to deprive the courts of their constitutional adjudicatory duty on criminal matters. Carroll J. found that section 149 made no provision for the liquidator's certificate to be conclusive. The purpose of section 149 is to identify companies and persons for the purposes of bringing restriction proceedings. Carroll J. was unable to find anything which would support the contention that the certificate should be irrebuttable. The certificate merely sets in motion the restriction proceedings. Carroll J. considered that the principle enunciated in *Re Haughey* [1971] I.R. 217 was applicable. In that case, the Supreme Court held that the certificate of the committee of Public Accounts of Dáil Éireann was a preliminary step to the commencement of a full trial of a criminal offence in the High Court. Likewise, a liquidator's certificate under section 149 is a preliminary step. There is nothing to prevent a director challenging the insolvency of the company or adducing any evidence in order to satisfy the court that the director in question acted honestly and responsibly. Carroll J. held that there is nothing in the section which warrants the interpretation that the certificate is to be conclusive evidence of the insolvency of the company. Carroll J. stated that a director who needs access to the books of the company to prepare his answer to a section 150 application can always apply to court if he is obstructed by the liquidator. Carroll J. held that it did not matter that all the company's debts are paid in full. All the section requires to trigger off Chapter 1 of Part VII, is that the company should be unable to pay its debts either at the commencement or during the course of the liquidation. Finally, the fact that a section 150 order affects a person's ability to earn a livelihood or that criminal sanctions flow from a breach of section 150 were not grounds for declaring that subsection unconstitutional.

This judgment gives liquidators some indication of how the certification procedure should be used, and therefore may ensure its more frequent use. Carroll J.'s judgment also gives some practical guidance as to how a director can challenge the certificate.

Restriction of directors in a company in receivership   *In Re Cavan Crystal Group Ltd (in receivership)* High Court, April 26. The Companies Acts, 1963-1990 provide for the disqualification and restriction of directors of insolvent companies. Some of the most recent cases in this area are the subject of analysis in the Company Law chapter in the 1995 Annual Review, see pages 79-85.

Though the procedure for such disqualification and restriction is well understood in the context of insolvent liquidations, section 154 applies the disqualification and restriction procedures to insolvent *receiverships*.

This case concerned a restriction application brought by the receiver of the Cavan Crystal Group Ltd. This company experienced financial difficulties in the 1990s. Additional capital was then raised. The investment obtained was insufficient to fund the running of the company. During 1992, these problems became more acute. The VAT, PAYE and PRSI returns of the company were irregular. The company went into examinership during 1995. A receiver and manager was subsequently appointed. The receiver brought these restriction proceedings against the managing director, the company secretary, and five other directors of the company. The receiver claimed that the managing director, the secretary and the other directors either permitted, condoned or falsified tax returns.

In the High Court, Murphy J. stated that Chapter 1 of Part VII applied equally to companies in receivership as to those in liquidation. The only prerequisite is that the company is insolvent. Murphy J. had no doubt that Cavan Crystal Group Ltd was insolvent.

Murphy J. stated that it was well accepted that section 150 is mandatory. The court must place a five year restriction on the director, unless a director discharges the onus of proof squarely imposed upon him of satisfying the court 'as to any of the matters specified in subsection 2'. This lists the three statutory defences available to a restriction order. The first defence is available where a director proves to the court that he has acted 'honestly and responsibly' in relation to the conduct of the affairs of the company. The other two defence are available to those who are directors solely by reason of their nomination as such either by a financial institution or a venture capital company prescribed by the Minister for Enterprise and Employment. Once a defence is proved, no restriction can be placed on the director concerned.

Murphy J. then examined the respective position of the officers of the company. One of the directors was not caught by section 150. This director had resigned more than 12 months prior to the commencement of the receivership. Section 149(2) of the Companies Act 1990 grant such directors exemption from restriction proceedings. The fact of his resignation was not noted in the company file in the Companies Office. All of the other parties were admittedly directors of the company at the relevant period. The board of the company included two directors nominated by a financial institution and a joint venture capital company. These two directors claimed that for this reason, they were respectively entitled to an exemption. Murphy J. found that the director nominated by the venture capital company was not entitled to the exemption. The venture capital company in question had not been prescribed by the Minister for Enterprise and Employment. The receiver and manager argued that section 150(2) requires that a nominated director must *in addition* prove that he acted honestly and responsibly in relation to the conduct of the affairs of the company to obtain a defence to a restriction order. Murphy J. held that though the defences were related to each other, they were alternatives, and not to be read cumulatively. However, Murphy J. noted that each of the provisions which afforded defences for directors nominated by financial institutions, commenced with a proviso that they should be read 'subject' to the honest and responsible defence.

Murphy J. then turned to the receiver and manager's claim that the relevant officers had permitted, condoned or falsified the tax returns in 1992. Neither the managing director nor the company secretary argued that the statutory restrictions should not apply to them. Murphy J. stated that if the other directors had allowed, condoned or falsified the company's accounts, this would constitute 'irresponsible conduct' for the purposes of section 150. In their defence, the other directors argued that these highly irregular activities had been undertaken solely to keep the company afloat and not for any personal gain.

Murphy J. had to decide whether the remaining directors had permitted these irregularities and what was their response on learning of these irregularities. The directors were able to show that they only became aware of the irregularities in July 1994. In September 1994, the board commissioned a report to review, *inter alia*, the management and stewardship of the company. The report was critical of the board's operation. The directors were able to prove that they attended monthly board meetings during 1994. At these meetings, monthly management accounts were presented by the managing director. According to Murphy J.'s analysis of the minutes of these monthly meetings, the directors showed interest and concern. It was irrelevant that an expert with the benefit of hindsight might have advocated a better approach. Murphy J. added finally that the non-nominated directors had made large personal investments in the company that had to be written off. Murphy J. was satisfied that all the directors had acted honestly and responsibly and no restriction orders should be made. Each party had to bear his own costs.

Preferential creditors in a liquidation *In re H. Williams (Tallaght) Ltd* High Court, October 7. This company went into receivership in 1987. The receiver was appointed by the holders of a debenture secured by a floating charge. In accordance with section 98(1) of the Companies Act 1963, the receiver treated the Revenue Commissioners as preferential creditors with respect to the PAYE and PRSI owed by the company. The receiver paid the debenture holders in full and the company ceased to be in receivership.

In 1991, the company went into liquidation. The Revenue Commissioners claimed that they were preferential creditors under section 285 of the Companies Act 1963, in respect of a corporate tax liability. The liquidator rejected their claim for two reasons. First, he argued that if one read section 98 in conjunction with section 285, a creditor was precluded from having a preferential claim in a receivership and a preferential claim in a subsequent liquidation. Second, if the Revenue Commissioners were entitled to their 'double' preference, their claim was statute barred.

In the High Court, Geoghegan J. rejected the liquidator's first argument, finding it clearly unsustainable. Geoghegan J. examined the relationship between section 98 and section 285. Section 98 requires the receiver to accord preferential status to certain debts specified in section 285. This was the only link between the two sections. There was nothing in section 98 which suggested that a preferential creditor was precluded from being paid his preferential debt in a receivership and then claiming for different debts as a preferential creditor in a subsequent liquidation. The situation could well arise where a company would go into receivership on foot of a debenture secured by a floating charge. The receiver may succeed in paying in full the debenture holder after discharging the preferential debts. The company may well then go into liquidation years afterwards. Nothing would then prevent a creditor such as the Revenue Commissioners claiming in the subsequent liquidation in respect of debts due to them; certainly not that they had been paid other sums due to them in the past.

The liquidator's argument rested on a reading – or misreading – of *United Bars Ltd v. Revenue Commissioners* [1991] 1 I.R. 396. Geoghegan J. found that the liquidator was taking the *United Bars Ltd* case out of context. In the *United Bars Ltd*, Murphy J. expressed the view that the only purpose of section 98 should be to equate the rights of preferential creditors in a receivership with those in liquidation. The section was not designed to improve upon these rights. Geoghegan J. pointed out that in *United Bars Ltd* Murphy J. had to decide whether assets realised by a receiver on foot of a fixed charge as distinct from a floating charge were to be used for the purposes of discharging preferential creditors. Relying on English authority, Murphy J. decided that the assets realised on foot of a fixed charge were to be used for the purpose of discharging preferential creditors. However, Murphy J. accepted that there were arguments both ways. One strong point in favour of the view taken by the English courts was that in a liquidation, preferential creditors have no right to preferential payment out of the assets the subject matter of a *fixed* charge. Their only recourse is to the assets the subject matter of a *floating* charge. Murphy J. doubted whether it could have been intended that preferential creditors claiming under section 98 could be held to be in a better position; that is to say, entitled to the same priority out of assets realised from a fixed charge. Geoghegan J. explained this was the context in which equality came into play in the *United Bars Ltd* case, but had no relevance to the arguments in this case. Geoghegan held that the Revenue Commissioner's claim was well founded.

The liquidator's second argument was that the Revenue Commissioners' claim was statute-barred. Under section 285(14), a creditor has six months from the time the liquidation is advertised in the newspaper to apply to a liquidator seeking payment of his debts. Unlike section 134 of the Companies Act 1990, there was no discretion given to the court to extend this time period. Geoghegan J. found that the Revenue Commissioners applied after the six months had expired and were therefore statute barred.

Companies Act 1990 (Uncertificated Securities) Regulations 1996 (SI No. 68 of 1996) These technical regulations are hugely important in practice. They will no doubt raise certain questions about the legal entitlement of those entered into a computer system as a member of a company, about issues such as transfer of securities, and about questions of computer records as evidence.

The aim of these regulations is to provide for the paperless transfer of securities in a company, including shares and debentures, by computer transaction. Such transactions are effected, the regulations inform us, by the somewhat spectral process of issuing 'dematerialised instructions'.

Instead of a share certificate, the buyer obtains an 'uncertificated unit'.

The record is one which is computer-entered and computer-maintained, so Chapter II of the regulations amplify the provisions for transfer, recording and registration of such units.

Chapter III provides for the approval or recognition of an operator, and the delegation of Ministerial responsibility for the running of this system to a designated body, e.g. a Stock Exchange.

Chapter IV contains certain anti-abuse provisions, and asserts the conclusiveness of the information recorded in the system.

Chapter V deals with the application of section 204(1) of the 1963 Act and notices thereunder to those holding uncertificated units of a security.

Chapter VI and the schedules covers detail such as evidence of system entries, and operator rules.

Some of the principal alterations to company secretarial practice are as follows:

(i) special arrangements are required with the Revenue Commissioners in order to ensure that tax is collected and paid on uncertificated securities;

(ii) a company which is a participating issuer must differentiate the number of shares or equivalent each member holds in uncertificated and certificated form, and the statutory instrument specifies what entries must be made in the register of members;

(iii) provision is made for membership of the company in respect of uncertificated shares or equivalent;

(iv) restrictions are placed on the amendment of those designated as holders of uncertificated shares or equivalent;

(v) regulations govern notices of meetings to those registered as holders of uncertificated shares or equivalent;

(vi) regulations governing the issue of a transfer of title to uncertificated units of a security on a register of securities.

The regulations contain a provision that a participating issuer may refuse to register a transfer of title where the proposed transferee is a minor; it is thought that no similar provision exists under Irish law in the context of manual transfers and therefore one questions upon what basis this restriction may be justified as constitutional.

Competition (Amendment) Act 1996   This Act has been comprehensively annotated by Mary Catherine Lucey (1996) ICLSA 19. Section 2 of the 1996 Act makes certain types of anti-competitive activity a crime. This may sound alarm bells in some quarters, but Hutchinson (Commercial Law Practitioner – March 1997 p. 47-53) provides some reassurance. He states that 'the Minister for Enterprise and Employment, the sponsor of the 1996 Act has admitted . . . that it will be extremely difficult to convict anyone of an offence under the competition laws'.

The proscribed activity involves 'agreements, decisions, and concerted practices', failure to comply with a licence issued under section 4(2) of the Competition Act 1991; 'abuse of a dominant position' as defined in section 5(1) of the 1991 Act and breaches of any order made under section 14 of the Competition Act 1991.

The present authors mention this section because by definition, the crime is one committed by an 'undertaking'. This is defined in the Competition Act 1991 as a person being an individual or . . . a body corporate . . . engaged for gain in the production, supply or distribution of goods or the provision of a service'. Hence, practitioners may need to apprise their clients who may possibly be at risk that the penalty of breach of this Act will affect the liability of directors officers and managers. Close supervision of employees and others is required.

Section 3 provides that directors, officers and managers may be liable in criminal law for the commission by the undertaking of such crimes. Further, section 6 provides that directors, managers and officers may be personally liable in respect of the anti-competitive activities of the undertakings. There is an exclusion for professional advisers provided that such persons are not acting as shadow directors.

The Act provides certain defences. First, that the undertaking complied with the terms of the licence or order. Second, that the undertaking 'did not know, nor in all the circumstances of the case could the defendant be reasonably expected to know' that the effect would be to prevent, restrict or distort competition or that the Act would constitute abuse of a dominant position. Lucey points out that the burden of proof is a contentious issue, and she discusses various contributions to the Dáil Debates. Hutchinson in his article, discusses whether or not the sections create crimes of strict liability or intent, and inclines to the former view. Hutchinson points out that upon one reading of the statute as ultimately passed, it is at least possible that an undertaking may be convicted of contravention of the Act even if the management of the undertaking issued express instructions to all employees forbidding them to enter into anti-competitive agreements: *Re Supply of Ready Mixed Concrete (No. 2)* [1995] 1 A.C. 456.

Proceeds of Crime Act 1996   This Act accords the High Court jurisdiction to deal with property of a value not less than £10,000 which is the proceeds of crime. The Act provides that an interim, interlocutory or a disposal order may be made over such property. The Act envisages that such property might find its way into ownership by a company. A company for this purpose is one which may be wound up under the Companies Acts, 1963-1990.

Where a company is in possession of the proceeds of crime, a problem will arise where the company is placed in liquidation. At that stage, a question will arise as to the ownership or entitlement of the property. The *bona fide* creditors of the company will have claims, so will those statutorily entitled under this act to the proceeds of crime.

Section 13 differentiates between property which has been made the subject of a court order before the company has been placed into liquidation, and an order which has been made after the company has been placed in liquidation. In the former case, a liquidator or a provisional liquidator is precluded from dealing with the property the proceeds of crime. In the latter case, the court is precluded from making any order over the property, where such an order will inhibit the liquidator from discharging his functions to the company's creditors or from paying expenses properly incurred.

The time when a company is considered for this Act to be in liquidation is obviously critical. This is defined in section 13(2) as the 'relevant time'. The relevant time is computed as follows:

(a) [w]here no order has been made to wind up the company, the time of the passing of the resolution for the voluntary winding up of the company;

(b) where an order has been made to wind up the company, and before presentation of a petition to wind up, a resolution to wind up has been passed, the time of the passing of the resolution to wind up; or

(c) in any other case, where an order has been made to wind up the company, the time that the order was made.

Obviously, whereas this information will not be part and parcel of every routine liquidation, in cases where it might or does apply, liquidators and those acting for them must be aware of this legislation. It is therefore of some importance to insolvency practitioners.

Conflicts of Law

ADOPTION

Under the Adoption Act 1991, recognition under Irish law is afforded to certain foreign adoptions: see the 1991 Review 52. In order to be recognised the foreign adoption must have 'essentially' the same legal effect as respects the termination and creation of parental rights and duties with respect to the child in the place where it was effected as an adoption effected by an adoption order' in Irish law: section 1(2) of the 1991 Act. In *B. and B. v. An Bórd Uchtála* [1997] 1 I.L.R.M. 15, the Supreme Court, affirming Flood J., held that adoptions under the law of the People's Republic of China fulfilled this requirement.

Under Irish law, an adoption involves essentially the irrevocable transfer of parental rights and duties from the natural parents to the adoptive parents. Under Chinese law, an adoption may be terminated with the agreement of the adoptive parents and the person who placed out the child for adoption. The child's consent must also be obtained where he or she has already reached the age of ten. The adoption must be terminated on the demand of the person who placed out the child for adoption, where the adopter fails to perform the duty of caring for the adoptee or commits maltreatment, abandonment, or other acts of encroachment upon the lawful rights of the minor adopted child': Article 25 of the Adoption Law of December 29, 1991.

In the instant case, Irish couples wishing to adopt three Chinese children were informed by An Bórd Uchtála that it considered that an adoption effected under the Chinese law was fundamentally different in its nature and effect from an adoption order under Irish law, on account of the fact that it could be terminated by agreement between the parties. In *certiorari* proceedings taken by these couples, the Supreme Court, affirming Flood J., rejected this interpretation.

Murphy J. (Hamilton C.J., O'Flaherty, Blayney and Barrington JJ. concurring) laid emphasis on the fact that Chinese law had unequivocally provided that the rights and duties in the relationship between the adopted child and his or her natural parents should terminate with the establishment of the adoptive relationship. This was as comprehensive a termination as was effected by adoption orders made under section 9 of the Adoption Act 1952. It had not been suggested in the Chinese legislation that the possibility of consensual termination of the adoptive relationship arose from any residual parental right: '[t]he termination of such rights is comprehensive and unequivocal.' The possibility that the adoptive relationship might be terminated by external events or even by the agreement of the parties did not, in Murphy J.'s opinion, deprive the relationship of the fundamental character in that behalf m[ight] be unknown or unacceptable in different jurisdictions.' He speculated that it was the likelihood of such variations within different jurisdictions which influenced the Oireachtas in focusing attention on particular conditions or incidents specified in the definition in section (b), so as to ensure that the relationship characterised as an adoption in the foreign legal system possessed all the features that Irish law regarded as 'essential and a condition precedent to granting domestic recognition to a "foreign adoption."

In *McC. and McD. v. Eastern Health Board* [1997] 1 I.L.R.M. 349, the Supreme Court held that the requirement, specified by section 8 (1) of the Adoption Act 1991, that the health board carry out an assessment on would-be adopters ordinarily resident in its functional area 'as soon as practicable' should be determined by a reference of the circumstances of the particular health board rather than by making a comparison with the practices of other health boards, which might have superior resources and more suitably qualified and experienced personnel. In the instant case, the delays were the result of the considerable increase in the number of applications in relation to foreign adoptions in the functional area of the Eastern Health Board, the imposition of new statutory responsibilities in the area of child care on the Board (cf. the 1991 Review, 52) and the shortage generally of qualified and experienced personnel capable of carrying out the necessary assessment under section 8(1).

CONTRACT

The Supreme Court, in *Fraser v. Buckle* [1996] 2 I.L.R.M. 34, affirmed Costello J. in holding that heir-location contacts are contrary to both Irish public policy and public policy in English law, which was the proper law of the contracts in the instant case. The only difference in emphasis between the High Court and the Supreme Court was that Costello J. regarded the issue of *Irish* public policy as predominant, whereas the Supreme Court placed emphasis on *English* public policy.

O'Flaherty J. (Hamilton C.J. and Barrington J. concurring) considered that he should put the issue of the proper law of the contact 'in the vanguard' of his decision rather than assign it, as Costello J. had done, the subsidiary position. He appeared to regard this as a matter of logical sequence. This is scarcely the case. There is nothing out of order in an Irish court holding, without prejudice to what the proper law maybe, Irish public policy trumps it. Indeed this is one of the few areas in private international law where conventional connecting factors give way to the predominant policies of the forum.

In the context of the particular problem of the enforceability of heir-locator contracts, there are particular difficulties in an Irish court's coming to any confident conclusion as to the present state of English law. O'Flaherty J. himself acknowledged that,

> [w]hile one would always approach the enterprise of discovering other people's laws with due deference, when the law in question seems to be in a state of flux, one must, in addition, regard it a risky business.

He admitted that Lord Mustill in *Giles v. Thompson* [1994] 1 A.C. 142, at 153 had 'presag[ed] a very restricted future role for maintenance and champerty', but considered that, in spite of their 'apparent relegation' it was the position that heir-locator contracts stood condemned by the decision of *Rees v. De Bernardy* [1896] 2 Ch. 437 and the decision had 'not been disapproved of to date.'

It has to be said that Costello J.'s emphasis on Irish public policy seems preferable. Only an Irish court can speak with ultimate authority on this issue whereas all Irish assessment of English law is capable of being revealed as mistaken at any moment by the contingency of the English legal process.

O'Flaherty J. appeared to consider that what is characterised as a finding of fact by the trial judge on the questions of English law should be given 'great respect' by the appellate court; *sed quaere*. As Cairns J. observed in *Parkasho v. Singh* [1968] P. 233, at 250, foreign law is 'a question of fact of a particular kind.' The truth of the matter is that the court must engage in a process of legal, rather than factual analysis. Before *Fraser v. Buckle*, the Supreme Court (as presently constituted and in it earlier manifestation) had shown no similar deference to the trial court. *McNamara v. Owners of the S.S. Hatteras* [1933] I.R. 675 is a prime example.

DOMICILE

In *M.O'G. v. R. O'G.*, High Court, May 16, 1996, Lavan J. had to determine whether a divorce obtained in England in 1981 should be recognised under the principles set out by the Supreme Court in *W. v. W.* [1993] 2 IR 476: see the 1992 Review, 115-26. The parties, both Irish, married in 1967. They went to England the following year. The husband was employed in a factory and as a building worker. The parties separated in 1974. In 1980 the wife commenced divorce proceedings; a decree absolute was made in December 1981. In the meantime the parties had become reconciled. They returned to Ireland to live in the husband's family home, which had been given to the husband many years previously. The parties' relationship after their return to Ireland was unhappy and the wife in 1995 applied for certain reliefs not specified in Lavan J.'s judgment) under the Judicial Separation and Family Law Reform Act 1989. The husband raised the preliminary objections that the parties were no longer married to each other.

The Circuit Court judge held in favour of the husband. Lavan J. reversed. He was not satisfied that sufficient evidence had been adduced to show that the wife had abandoned her Irish domicile of origin. While living in England, the applicant had intended to return to live in Ireland when the family's financial situation so permitted. The fact that she had asserted an English domicile in her divorce petition did not affect the issue as she had not been properly advised as to the meaning of that concept.

Lavan J's holding seems well justified by the facts stated in his judgment. The parties' connection with England, while of reasonably long duration, lacked the intensity that would warrant a finding of an acquisition by either of them of an English domicile of choice.

JURISDICTION

Tort   The special jurisdictional ground relating to tort is set out in article 5(3) of the Brussels Convention of 1968:

> A person domiciled in a contracting state may in another contracting state be sued in matters relating to tort, delict or quasi-delict in the courts for the place where the harmful event occurred.

In *Handelswekerij G.J. Bier BV v. Mines de Potasse d'Alsace* (Case 21/76) [1976] E.C.R. 1735, the Court of Justice interpreted the expression 'the place where the harmful event occurred' as giving the plaintiff the option to commence proceedings *either* at the place where the damage occurred *or* at the place of the event giving rise to it.

In *Casey t/a Casey International Plant Sales and Hire v. Ingersoll-Rand Sales Co. Ltd.*, [1996] 2 I.L.R.M. 456, the plaintiff took proceedings in Ireland for negligent misstatement against a U.S. company with a place of business in England and Wales. He claimed that the defendant had agreed to sell him a piling rig of 1991 vintage but had in fact sold a 1989 model which did not comply with agreed specifications. He contended that the agreement had been made partly in writing and partly orally. His difficulty was in showing that any aspect of the alleged tort had taken place in Ireland. Although he was an Irish citizen domiciled in Ireland and maintained a business premises and residence when the State, that premises was only a 'representative ' office; he had a business address in the United Arab Emirates and none of the representations before the making of the contract by him in Ireland. Accordingly, Shanley J. found, even if the defendant had made a series of negligent mis-statements in the lead up to the contract and was in breach of its duty of care to the plaintiff, the plaintiff had not, on the affidavit, satisfied him that he breach of that duty had occurred in Ireland. Shanley J. accordingly made an order striking out the plaintiff's claim for want of jurisdiction.

It might perhaps be thought that, even if the plaintiff's principal place of business was abroad, the financial damage that he allegedly sustained permeated to Ireland, where he had the strongest of personal connections (domicile, nationality and a residence) and clear business connections (the 'representative' office in Dublin). It seems that Shanley J. was willing to accept that such an overflow was indeed possible; he rejected it, however, on the basis that, 'if the pecuniary damage had in fact occurred in this jurisdiction, the plaintiff should not have had any difficulty in satisfying the court of this fact on affidavit.'

Prior proceedings In *Fox v. Taher*, High Court, January 24, 1996, Costello J. addressed the issue of whether proceedings in the Irish courts should have to concede priority to proceedings in relation to the same issue which had earlier been initiated in the English courts. The defendants, invoking Article 21 of the Brussels Convention, sought to have the Irish court decline jurisdiction or, at least, stay the proceedings. Kinlen J. had already deemed service good within the jurisdiction.

Costello J. considered it 'perfectly clear' that he could not decline jurisdiction until he had first set aside Kinlen J.'s judgment:

> If the court sets aside the judgment it can then consider whether or not it should decline jurisdiction. But the jurisdiction of the court is now spent in relation to the plaintiff's claim. The court has, in fact, exercised its jurisdiction and given judgment for the plaintiff, and what remains is the question of staying execution of the judgment.

Jurisdiction Order 11, r. 8 of the Rules of the Superior Courts 1986 provides in respect of service out of the jurisdiction, that, where the defendant is not, or is not known or believed to be, a citizen of Ireland, notice of the summons and not the summons itself, is to be served on the defendant. In *Short v. Ireland* High Court, March 30, 1995 (1994 No. 175IP.), O'Hanlon J. observed that:

> ... this is a requirement involved in the comity of nations which should be observed meticulously although the progress toward European Union has brought about the change in procedure involved in cases falling

under r. 11A in respect o which service out of the jurisdiction can be affected without having first to seek leave of the court.

The reason why only notice, of the summons is to be served is essentially one of deference to the principle of sovereignty in the international context. Thus in *Cookney v. Anderson* (1863) 1 D.G.J. & S 365, Lord Westbury stated that

> [t]he right of administering justice is the attribute of sovereignty; and all persons within the dominions of a sovereign or within his allegiance and under his protection. If therefore one sovereign causes process to be served in the territory of another and summons a foreign sovereign to his court of justice, it is in fact an invasion of sovereignty, and would be unjustifiable, unless done with consent; which is assumed to be the fact, if it be done in a case where a foreign judgment would, by international law, be accepted as binding.

In *O'Connor v. Commercial General and Marine Ltd and Omne Re S.A. t/a Omne Gulf Insurance Co.*, [1996] 2 I.L.R.M. 291, the plaintiff had admittedly served the summons, rather than notice therefor, upon the second-named defendant, who was a limited liability company incorporated in Belgium, with its place of business there. He sought to justify this omission by arguing, first, that notwithstanding O. 11, r. 8, which went back to the British regime. He noted that in England the distinction between service of the writ and notice therefore had been abolished, but saw no reason on that account to depart from the requirements of the Irish rule:

> While consideration might be given to the desirability of making an alteration of the summons so as to conform to the English form, while it retains its existing form the practice in England is of no relevance.

CHILD ABDUCTION

In *In re E.S. (a minor); A.S. v. E.H. and M.H.*, High Court, May 8, 1996, Budd J. declined to strike out an application by the father of an infant for the return to England of his child, who had been taken to Ireland by his maternal grandmother and aunt on the death of his mother. The kernel of the defendants' argument was that Article 12 of the Luxembourg Convention makes it clear that, in cases where a child is removed when there is no prior enforceable decision relating to his or her custody, the provision of the Convention apply to any subsequent decision 'relating to the custody of the child and declaring the removal to be unlawful'. The father had initiated proceedings in England in which he had been awarded custody but there had been no judicial declaration that the removal of his child had been unlawful. The proceedings in England were still ongoing, the defendants having sought an adjournment.

In Budd J.'s view, the English court would make the necessary declaration if requested to do so. He considered that the defendants had thwarted the making of the necessary declaration by seeking an adjournment. He emphasised the principle of the comity of the courts. Since the matter would be dealt with by the English court within a week, he considered that the proceedings should not be struck out.

FOREIGN JUDGMENT

In *Petronelli v. Collins*, High Court, July 19, 1996, Costello J. considered, but did not have to determine an important issue relating to the principle that a foreign judgment will not be enforced if it has been obtained by fraud. If the defendant asserts that the judgment was thus obtained by fraud and that issue has been investigated and rejected by the foreign court, should the Irish court be bound by that finding or should it make its own assessment of the matter? The English courts continue to favour the latter approach (cf. *Jet Holding Inc. v. Patel* [1989] 2 All E.R. 648), but courts in the United States, Canada and Australia prefer the former approach (cf., e.g., *Kelley v. Findlay* [1991] N.S.W.L.R. 464.

In the instant case, the boxer Stephen Collins sought to resist the enforcement of a default judgment obtained against him in Massachussetts on the basis of fraud. He had initiated a claim alleging 'fraud on the court' in the United States with respect to the judgment.

Costello J. stayed an earlier judgment, obtained in Ireland by the plaintiffs, enforcing the Massachussetts judgment. He decided that if the sum awarded by the Massachussetts judgment was lodged in court, the earlier Irish judgment would be set aside and liberty given to the defendant to enter an appearance and file an affidavit to resist the application for summary judgment.

LAW REFORM

1996 marked the final year of ten years' service with the Law Reform of four of the Commissioners: John Buckley, William Duncan, Maureen Gaffney and Simon O'Leary. Their period of tenure was remarkably productive: thirty reports and ten consultation papers were published. The President of the Commission, Mr. Justice Anthony Hederman, remained in office at the end of the year.

In 1996, the Commission published three reports: the *Report on Family*

Courts (LRC 52 – 1996), which we analyse in the Family Law Chapter below, 365, the *Report on Sentencing* (LRC 53 – 1996), and the *Report on Personal Injuries: Periodic Payments and Structured Settlements* (LRC 54 – 1996). The Commission also published a *Consultation Paper on Privacy: Surveillance and the Interception of Communications*, which we consider, also in the Torts Chapter, below, 604.

A significant volume of legislation implements several earlier recommendations of the Commission. The Powers of Attorney Act 1996 introduces a system of enduring powers of attorney, recommended by the Commission in its *Report on Land Law and Conveyancing Law: (2) Enduring Powers of Attorney* (LRC 31 – 1989), analysed in the 1989 Review, 316. The Domestic Violence Act 1996, which we analyse in the Family Law Chapter below, 358-67, reflects some of the recommendations relating to the power of Health Boards to apply for barring and protection orders contained in the Commission's *Report on Child Sexual Abuse* (LRC 32 – 1990): see the 1990 Review, 246-53.

The Commission's recommendations in its Report on the *Confiscation of the Proceeds of Crime* (LRC 35 – 1991) (noted in the 1991 Review, 132) are given substantial effect by the Proceeds of Crime Act 1996: see below, 234, section 14 of the *Criminal Assets Bureau Act 1996* and section 1 of the Disclosure of Certain Information for Taxation and Other Purposes Act 1996.

FAMILY COURTS

There has been an international debate for over forty years on the subject of family courts. Much of the discussion has been symptomatic of wider philosophical concerns: the desire to place less, or no, emphasis on the matrimonial "fault", the perception of marital disharmony as a symptom of a pathology in the international relationship and the notion of the judge as a benevolent inquisitor, handing out authoritative prescriptions for the best interests of the spouses and the children. The early models of family courts therefore emphasised a strong intrusive role for the judges, with a focus on the totality of the spouses' relationship as a proper subject for scientific analysis.

This view of the family court was consistent with the philosophy of the English Law Commission in 1966, which recommended a "no-fault" divorce jurisdiction based on a judicial investigation on whether the marriage had irretrievably broken down. Once 'irretrievable breakdown' became a ground for divorce in 1969, the perceptions changed because it became obvious very quickly that a system of divorce which is based on irretrievable breakdown of marriage actually is one that provides for divorce by consent and by unilateral repudiation.

In truth, with a divorce jurisdiction that allows for unilateral repudiation there is nothing really left for the judge to decide in determining whether the marriage has 'irretrievably broken down'. If one spouse says that, so far as he or she is concerned, the marriage is over, the denial by the other spouse will carry no weight. The judge may have to make sure that any minimum period of 'living apart' has been established, but there is no judicial role in examining the nature of the parties' matrimonial relationship and in coming up with authoritative scientific prescriptions. A modern 'no fault' divorce regime is entirely hostile with such intrusion and lays strong emphasis on non-judicial strategies, epitomised by mediation.

The apotheosis of the contemporary divorce philosophy is that courts should have no role in the curtailing the autonomy of the individual in the pursuit of his or her life plans. One may find the odd statutory provisions requiring a court to have regard to the welfare of collateral victims – most obviously children – but no mature legal system takes them seriously. Once divorce based on unilateral repudiation is accepted, there is no credible judicial attempt in any country to modify that jurisdiction on the basis of the damage caused to others.

It is against this background that the Law Reform Commission published its *Report on Family Courts* (LRC 52 – 1996) in March 1996, when the referendum introducing divorce was still under a judicial cloud of uncertainty.

The Commission proposes the establishment of a system of Regional Family Courts, operating as a division of the Circuit Court, in about fifteen regional centres. These courts would be presided over by judges nominated to serve for a period of at least one year and assigned on the basis of their suitability to deal with family law matters.

The jurisdiction of the Regional Family Court would be comprehensive and include all emergency remedies under the Child Care Act 1991 (cf. the 1991 Review, 232) and the Domestic Violence Act 1996 (below, 358), for example. The District Courts' jurisdiction in family law matters would be limited to the making of emergency orders and interim orders 'especially in situations of emergency': para. 4.43.

The Commission proposes that each Regional Family Court should have attached to it a Family Court Information Centre, with responsibility for providing to the parties information relating to available alternatives to litigation. Parties involved in proceedings for judicial separation would be required to attend the Centre to receive this information; parties involved in other family litigation would be given the opportunity to do so.

The Commission places a strong emphasis on mediation and recommends the development of a mediation service in conjunction with the Regional Family Courts. It proposes that mediated agreements should normally be reviewed by the parties' respectful legal advisers. The courts should have a power of review, supplemented by a power of variation, in relation to agreements concerning maintenance and property, on the basis of newly discovered facts or a change in the economic circumstances of the parties.

The Commission proposes that the court should have power to appoint an independent legal representative for a child in family proceedings where this appears necessary in the child's interests. Such a need might arise where the extent of hostility between the parents is severe, involving frequent resort to litigation, or where mental illness or child abuse is in issue.

The Commission takes the position in relation to proceedings which involve an active dispute between the parties that, save in two very specific and limited respects, the adversarial tradition should continue to hold sway. This is because of the need to respect the requirements of a fair hearing, adhering to the principles of constitutional and natural justice. The two new exceptions it proposes are, first, extension of the judicial power to procure a report on any question affecting the welfare of the infant in guardianship proceedings so that it applies to *any* proceeding in which the welfare of a dependent child is relevant and, secondly, the establishment of a discretionary judicial power to procure a financial report from an accountant or other qualified independent person in proceedings involving maintenance or other financial orders or property orders.

Whilst opposed to compulsory training for family court judges, the Commission favours the taking of measures, as a matter of urgency, to enable the judiciary to organise judicial studies on a systematic basis, with a management board, chaired by the Chief Justice (or nominee), comprising a majority of judges, backed by adequate financial and administrative support. It recommends also that specialist courses on family law should be made availing to practicing lawyers, with, downstream, the possibility of certification attaching to their successful completion.

Constitutional Law

ADMINISTRATION OF JUSTICE

In *Roe v. Blood Transfusion Service Board and Ors.* [1996] 1 I.L.R.M. 555, Laffoy J. held that the requirement in Article 34.1 of the Constitution that justice be administered in public precluded the plaintiff from using a pseudonym in pursuing her claim against the defendants. The plaintiff had instituted proceedings in what became a *cause celebre* during 1996 and into 1997. She was one of thousands of women who, during the late 1970s and early 1980s, had been given Human Immunoglobulin-Anti-D (in order to prevent death in rhesus negative births) which had been infected with the hepatitis C virus. In the proceedings, she claimed that the infected blood product, which had caused her to sustain severe personal injuries, in particular liver damage, had come to be given to her by reason of the defendants' negligence and other tortious actions. In the instant application, she pleaded that for the purposes of the proceedings she had adopted the name 'Bridget M. Roe' and that her address was care of her solicitors at their address. A number of the defendants (though not the third defendant, the National Drugs Advisory Board, now the Irish Medicines Board) pleaded that the plaintiff was not entitled to adopt this name or any assumed name. The plaintiff averred that she wished to use an alias in order to protect her privacy. It was claimed that the protection of her privacy was not merely a matter of preventing embarrassment, but was a matter of preventing real injustice to her. Her solicitor averred that from her experience of dealing with this case and a large number of similar cases, persons who were known in the community to carry the Hepatitis C virus were subjected to invidious discrimination and were socially ostracised. It was also pointed out that her real name and address had been disclosed to the defendants. It was acknowledged by the plaintiff that the trial of the action would have to be held in public and she would have to give oral testimony in open court. It was also accepted that her case did not fall within the provisions of section 45 of the Courts (Supplemental Provisions) Act 1961, which permits hearings otherwise than in public in certain named instances. However, it was submitted that Article 34 of the Constitution was not an impediment to the granting of the relief sought as she was not seeking a hearing other than in public.

She had urged by counsel for the plaintiff to follow the practice adopted by courts of the United States of America which have allowed plaintiffs under certain special circumstances to use fictitious names. Counsel had relied on the decision of the US Federal District Court in *Doe v Deschamps,* 64 F. 2d. 652 (1974) and of the Federal Court of Appeals, 5th Circuit, in *Southern Methodist University Association of Women Law Students v. Wynne,* 599 F. 2d. 707 (1979).

As indicated, Laffoy J. refused the relief sought by the plaintiff. In this respect, she relied strongly on the views expressed by Walsh J. in *In re R. Ltd..* [1989] I.R. 126; [1989] I.L.R.M. 757 (1989 Review, 55-8). She also relied on the views expressed by Hamilton P. (as he then was) in an *ex tempore* judgment in *Claimant v. Board of St. James' Hospital,* High Court, May 10, 1989. In that case, the plaintiffs were haemophiliacs who alleged that they had been infected by the HIV virus as a result of blood products which were supplied to them or approved for supply to them. The application was for liberty to issue a plenary summons and serve a statement of claim against the intended defendants without disclosing the name and address of the plaintiff. It was acknowledged by counsel for the applicants that the hearing of the intended actions would have to be in public and that interlocutory applications in connection with the intended action would have to be heard in public. Laffoy J. quoted with approval the following passage from the judgment of Hamilton P. refusing the application:

> As I say, Article 34 of the Constitution is quite specific, it is mandatory. It says that justice shall be administered in public and, having regard to the statement of the Chief Justice and Walsh J. [in *In re R. Ltd.*] that proceedings, including pleadings, affidavits, exhibits, as well as oral testimony [*sic*], I can find nothing in the law or in any of the Rules of Courts which would permit me to accede to this application. . . .

In dismissing the application in the *Roe* case, Laffoy J. commented:

> The plaintiff's stated objective in seeking to prosecute these proceedings under a fictitious name is to keep her identity out of the public domain. In my view, in the context of the underlying rationale of Article 34.1, the public disclosure of the true identities of parties to civil litigation is essential if justice is to be administered in public. In a situation in which the true identity of a plaintiff in a civil action is known to the parties to the action and to the court but is concealed from the public, members of the general public cannot see for themselves that justice is done.

It is to be regretted that the Court's rejection of the plaintiff's application did not deal in greater detail with the basis on which the United States courts had accepted that an alias or pseudonym could be used. It will be recalled that, in *In re R. Ltd.,* Walsh J. had cited with approval United States authority, in particular the judgment of Black J. in *In re Oliver*, 333 U.S. 257 (1948), in coming to his conclusion that, in the circumstances of the *R.* case, the proceedings should be held in public. It would have seemed appropriate, therefore, to have discussed in more detail the reasons why the American precedents cited had held that the use of pseudonyms did not infringe the United States Constitution, particularly as this issue had not been debated in *In re R. Ltd.*. Indeed, it is difficult to see the connection between a hearing to which the public has access and the need to use real names. It was not suggested that the various legislative restrictions on access by the public were, in themselves, constitutionally infirm, since Article 34.1 expressly envisages barring public access in cases prescribed by law. A less severe restriction on publicity for court proceedings should hardly, therefore, be regarded as being *ex facie* unacceptable under Article 34.1, as would seemed to be assumed both by Hamilton P. (as he then was) and by Laffoy J. In addition, it is almost inconceivable that counsel or the Court were unaware of the other litigation initiated by haemophiliacs who, as in the *Claimant* case, had contracted HIV/AIDS arising from the use of infected Factor VIII blood products, and who were allowed to proceed in the Irish courts using pseudonyms, after an *ex tempore* order had been made in the Supreme Court (albeit made on consent). For later proceedings involving that litigation, see *Doe v. Armour Pharmaceutical Co Inc* [1994] 1 I.L.R.M. 416 (1994 Review, 91-4). It is notable that all the defendants in the *Doe* case were private sector corporations; no State bodies were involved. It might have been supposed that private sector entities would have been less amenable to a rights-based privacy argument than State institutions who, after all, are the creation of and the servants of the citizens of the State. Nor was any reference made in the *Roe* case to the use, for example, of video link evidence in certain criminal trials, which has been upheld in *Donnelly v. Ireland*, High Court, December 3, 1996 (see the Criminal Law chapter, 261, below). The views expressed in *Roe* might conceivably place in doubt the use of protective screens to hide witnesses from members of a public gallery. It is to be hoped that, on another occasion, the decision in *Roe* will be subjected to further scrutiny and that the right to privacy adumbrated in that case will receive greater acknowledgement.

As indicated, the instant case became a cause celebre during 1996 and 1997. Arising from Laffoy J.'s judgment, the case proceeded using the plaintiff's real name: see *McCole v. Blood Transfusion Service Board and Ors.*, High Court, June 11, 1996 (Practice and Procedure chapter, 488, below). The *McCole* case was ultimately settled in 1996, but a Tribunal of Inquiry into the Hepatitis-C controversy and some aspects of the *McCole* case was later established in 1996. The Report of the Tribunal, published in 1997, will be discussed in the 1997 Review. In addition, a non-statutory Compensation Tribunal had also been established to deal on an *ex gratia* basis with compensation claims by those women who had contracted Hepatitis-C: see *Ryan v. Compen-*

sation Tribunal [1997] 1 I.L.R.M. 194 (H.C.), discussed in the Administrative Law chapter, 5, above. The Tribunal was established on a statutory basis in 1997 pursuant to the Hepatitis C Compensation Tribunal Act 1997, which we will discuss in the 1997 Review. See also the Health (Amendment) Act 1996 (discussed in the Health Services chapter, 405, below) which was enacted to make available medical and counselling services without charge to persons who had contracted hepatitis C directly or indirectly from the use of Human Immunoglobulin-Anti-D.

HIGH COURT

Exclusive jurisdiction to determine constitutionality In *Director of Public Prosecutions v. Dougan* [1997] 1 I.L.R.M. 550 (H.C.), *sub nom. The People v. Dougan* [1996] 1 I.R. 544 (H.C.), Geoghegan J. confirmed that a District Court judge is precluded by Article 34.3.2° of the Constitution from using the case stated procedure to challenge the constitutional validity of a statutory provision. See the discussion in the Practice and Procedure chapter, 468, below.

JUDICIAL INDEPENDENCE

Pension arrangements In *McMenamin v. Ireland* [1994] 2 I.L.R.M. 151 (H.C.); [1997] 2 I.L.R.M. 177 (S.C.), the Supreme Court upheld the findings of Geoghegan J. in the High Court (1994 Review, 115-7) that there were certain deficiencies in the pensions arrangements made for judges of the District Court, though it declined to grant any formal relief. The case arose against the following background.

Paragraph 8 of the Schedule to the Courts (Supplemental Provisions) Act 1961 provides that a judge of the District Court who, having reached the age of 65, vacates his office after at least 20 years' service shall be granted a pension for life of two-thirds of his remuneration at the time of such vacation of office. Section 2 of the Courts of Justice and Court Officers (Superannuation) Act 1961 applies to any person appointed as a judge of the Supreme Court, High Court, Circuit Court or District Court. Section 2(2) of that Act provides that on the grant of a pension to any person to whom the section applies, there shall be granted to that person a gratuity equal to one and one-half times the yearly amount of the pension as reduced under section 2(5). Section 2(3) provides that if a judge of the Supreme Court, High Court, Circuit Court or District Court dies while in office after having served as such for five years or more, there shall be granted to his personal representative a gratuity equal to the yearly amount of his salary. Section 2(5) provides that the pension payable to a person to whom section 2 applies shall be reduced by one-fourth. The applicant had been appointed as a judge of the District Court on March 1, 1983 and was due to retire on February 4, 1997. The applicant claimed that given the disparity between the benefits received by way of gratuity and the proportion by which the pension was reduced by section 2(5), the scheme had been irrational from its inception, or alternatively had become irrational as a result of changes in economic circumstances since its enactment. It was also argued that the scheme was invalid having regard to Article 40.1 of the Constitution in that Circuit Court judges qualified for a full pension after 15 years' service, while 20 years' service was required in the case of District Court judges.

Geoghegan J. granted a declaration that the State, in permitting a gross inequality to arise as between the reduction in the pension of District Court judges and the cost of lump sum gratuities intended to be met by such reduction, was in breach of its constitutional duty to secure pension rights for district judges which were not irrational or wholly inequitable. The defendants appealed to the Supreme Court, but the Court (Hamilton C.J., O'Flaherty, Blayney, Denham and Barrington JJ.) unanimously concurred with Geoghegan J. that a gross inequality had been permitted to develop.

The Court accepted that the operation of the Courts of Justice and Court Officers (Superannuation) Act 1961 had led to an injustice for the applicant and other judges of the District Court in that the reduction of 25% of their pension entitlement was not being compensated for by the payment of the retirement gratuity payable to them.

As to the appropriate remedial response, Hamilton C.J. (who delivered one of the leading judgments, with which Denham and Barrington JJ. concurred) quoted the following propositions in his own judgment in *McKenna v. An Taoiseach (No.2)* [1995] 2 I.R. 1; [1996] 1 I.L.R.M. 81 (1995 Review, 138):

> 1. The courts have no power, either express or implied, to supervise or interfere with the exercise by the Government of its executive functions provided that it acts within the restraints imposed by the Constitution on the exercise of such powers.
> 2. If, however, the Government acts otherwise than in accordance with the provisions of the Constitution and in clear disregard thereof, the courts are not only entitled but obliged to intervene.
> 3. The courts are only entitled to intervene if the circumstances are such as to amount to a clear disregard by the Government of the powers and duties conferred on it by the Constitution.

Having regard to the respect which each of the organs of government must pay to each other, I am satisfied that where it was alleged that either the Oireachtas or the Government has acted other than in accordance with the provisions of the Constitution, such fact must be clearly established.

Applying these principles to the instant case, Hamilton C.J. accepted that in the context of Article 35.5 of the Constitution which provided that the remuneration of judge was not to be reduced during the continuance in office of a judge, remuneration undoubtedly included pension entitlements. He also accepted that the situation with regard to judicial pensions had changed radically since 1961, and the reduction of 25% of a judge's pension was sufficient to fund a gratuity of 1.9 times the judges pension and not 1.5 times the pension as was provided for by the 1961 Act. The Chief Justice went on to conclude that the failure to reduce the reduction to 22% or the failure to increase the gratuity to 1.9 times the annual pension both amounted to a reduction or diminution of the pension entitlement of the applicant, in breach of Article 35.5. However, he stated that the manner in which the situation was to be remedied was a matter for the Oireachtas, and it was not open for the Court to interfere with the manner in which the situation was dealt with by the Oireachtas unless the Oireachtas failed to have regard to its constitutional obligations. Thus, he considered that the Court should not to make a declaration giving effect to its views, because having regard to the traditional separation of powers, he was satisfied that once the Government was made aware of the Court's views, it would take the necessary steps to have the matter remedied in accordance with law and in accordance with its constitutional obligations. On this basis, the Court did not uphold the declaration made in the High Court.

In a concurring judgment Blayney J. (with whom Denham and Barrington JJ. also agreed) also rejected the applicant's cross-appeal concerning the finding in the High Court that there had been no breach of the equality guarantee in Article 40.1. The applicant had argued that the pension arrangements for District Court judges were markedly different from their colleagues in the Circuit Court. But Blayney J. held that, in making out a case of unfair discrimination, one must ensure that one was comparing like with like. He cited the oft-quoted views of Ó Dálaigh C.J. in *The State (Hartley) v. Governor of Mountjoy* Prison, Supreme Court, December 21, 1967 to the effect that a diversity of arrangements did not effect discrimination between citizens in their legal rights. On this basis, he found that no ground for challenging the 1961 Act under Article 40.1 had been made out. Finally, we should noted two aspects of the remaining judgment, delivered by O'Flaherty J. (with whom Barrington J. concurred). He reviewed in some detail the development of the jurisdiction of the District Court since its establishment under the Courts of Justice Act 1924 (and indeed, its pre-1924 origins, citing Kotsonouris, *Retreat from Revolution* (Irish Academic Press, 1994)) and its importance as the 'fulcrum of our judicial system.' His summary might prove to be a useful introduction for students of the law. O'Flaherty J. also accepted that the Court was acting correctly in declining to make any declaratory orders in the case, and that the authorities might have been postponed taking any remedial action until the Court had given its decision. He finished his judgment by stating, pointedly: 'That has now been done and the time for decision has arrived.' At the time of writing (July 1997), no amending legislation has been introduced.

LIBERTY

Third party application In *Gallagher v. Director of Central Mental Hospital*, High Court, July 9, 1996, Geoghegan J. rejected an application in which a third party sought to be joined in an inquiry under Article 40.4.2°. The applicant, Mr Gallagher, had been tried for the murder of two women and had been found guilty but insane, and was subsequently detained in the Central Mental Hospital. In previous proceedings, *Application of Gallagher* [1991] 1 I.R. 31; [1991] I.L.R.M. 339 (1990 Review, 164-6), the Supreme Court held that where a person is found guilty but insane of murder, the release of the person is solely a matter for the Executive to determine. The applicant's instant application under Article 40.4.2° sought his release from custody, arguing that there was no justification for his further detention. The third party, seeking to be joined in the inquiry was the uncle and brother-in-law of the two victims of the applicant. He averred that he had a genuine apprehension that the applicant's release would pose a danger to his own life and the lives of other relatives and people in his locality. He averred that the applicant had threatened him on a number of occasions and had attempted to kill him. Both the applicant and respondent (representing the State) opposed the motion that the third party be joined to the proceedings. Geoghegan J. agreed. While he accepted that, in principle at least, it might be open to argument that a third party be given a hearing in some instances in the interests of fair procedures, this was not such a case. In particular, he noted that the respondent in the instant case was opposing the applicant's application for immediate release; since this was the only issue before the Court, there was no conflict of interest between Mr Maguire and the respondent and thus no need for additional representation. He also noted that, subject to one minor exception it had never been a feature of our jurisprudence that a victim, and still less an alleged potential victim, should be given a hearing in the criminal process. He considered that such representation could dangerously compromise the necessary independence and detachment of the Court and jury. On this basis, he refused the relief sought. In *Gallagher v. Director of Central Mental Hospital (No.2)*, High Court, September 6, 1996, the High Court subsequently dismissed the applicant's application for his release: see the Criminal Law chapter, 246, below.

OIREACHTAS

Allowances to members　The Oireachtas (Miscellaneous Provisions) and Ministerial and Parliamentary Offices (Amendment) Act 1996 made a number of significant changes to the regime for allowances for Oireachtas members. Changes to the regime under the Oireachtas (Allowances to Members) Act 1962 for attendance at Oireachtas Committee meetings were made, while certain limits were imposed on secretarial and telephone allowances. More significantly, the 1996 Act amended the Ministerial and Parliamentary Offices Act 1938 by providing for the first time of payments for expenses incurred by the parliamentary leader of any registered political party in Dáil Éireann. A sliding scale applies where the leader has the following number of party colleagues: less then five; between five and 10; between 10 and 60; over 60. This replaces the system whereby only the Leader of the Opposition, that is of the largest opposition party, was paid an allowance. Although the Act was passed on December 20, 1996, section 7 provided that it was deemed to have come into effect on January 1, 1996.

Delegation of statutory powers　In *Lovett v. Minister For Education* [1997] 1 I.L.R.M. 89, Kelly J. held to be unconstitutional an element of the Secondary Teachers Superannuation (Amendment) Scheme 1935, a statutory Scheme made under the Teachers Superannuation Act 1928 on the basis that it failed to comply with the test laid down by O'Higgins C.J. in *Cityview Press Ltd. v. An Chomhairle Oiliúna* [1980] I.R. 381, namely that it was more than a mere giving effect to the principles and policies of, or filling in of details in, the 1928 Act as laid down by the Oireachtas. The case is discussed in the Education chapter, 284, below.

Voting and physical disability　The Electoral (Amendment) Act 1996 amended the Electoral Act 1992 (1992 Review, 141-4) in order to facilitate access to polling stations for electors with physical disability in particular. Section 2 of the 1996 Act amended section 28 of the Electoral Act 1992, by requiring each local authority to endeavour to appoint as polling places only such areas as would allow the returning officer to provide at each polling place at least one polling station which is accessible to wheelchair users. Section 3 of the 1996 Act also amended section 94 of the 1992 Act by providing that Electoral Regulations to be made by the Minister for the Environment may include arrangements intended to facilitate voters with visual impairments to mark their ballot papers without assistance. Such arrangement may include provision for ballot papers in Braille at some time in the future. Indeed, the next local government elections may be used as a 'trial' basis for such an arrangement, and the 1996 Act also amended the Local Elections Regulations 1995 (1995 Review, 368) with this in mind. Finally, the 1996 Act also amended section 17 of the 1992 Act with a view to amending the arrangements for postal voting for persons unable to attend a polling station by reason of the severity of their physical disability. The 1996 Act came into effect on December 25, 1996, on its signature by the President.

Voting refusal: negligence and defamation   In *Graham v. Ireland and Ors*, High Court, May 1, 1996, Morris J. declined to allow a combined negligence and defamation action go to a jury in the following circumstances. The plaintiff had been refused a vote when he attended to vote at his polling station in the 1987 General Election. The plaintiff's father had earlier presented himself to vote in the morning of the General Election and the presiding officer had mistakenly furnished him with a ballot paper believing he was entitled to vote at that polling station. The plaintiff's name and corresponding number on the electoral roll had then been marked to indicate that he had voted.

When the plaintiff arrived to vote, the returning officer indicated to him that he did not have a vote and refused to allow him to vote. The plaintiff claimed damages for defamation or in the alternative damages for breach of constitutional right to vote at a general election which arose due to the negligence of the servants or agents of the Minister for the Environment. As indicated, Morris J. withdrew the case from the jury on the grounds that the words complained of were not capable of a defamatory meaning. He went on to dismiss the plaintiff's claim in respect of negligence, on the basis that the decision reached by the presiding officer had been incorrect but it was a judgment she made based on valid grounds and in accordance with the discretion vested in her by the Department of the Environment. In that respect, he concluded that this did not amount to negligence.

PROPERTY RIGHTS

In *Lovett v. Minister For Education* [1997] 1 I.L.R.M. 89, Kelly J. held that an element of the Secondary Teachers Superannuation (Amendment) Scheme 1935, a statutory Scheme made under the Teachers Superannuation Act 1928 failed the proportionality test adumbrated by the Supreme Court in *Cox v. Ireland* [1992] 2 I.R. 503 (1991 Review, 105-7). While expressing his views on this aspect of the case, Kelly J. did not grant a declaration as to the constitutionality since it had already been struck down on other grounds. See the discussion of the case in the Education chapter, 284, below.

RELIGION

In *Campaign to Separate Church and State Ltd. v. Minister for Education*

[1996] 2 I.L.R.M. 241, Costello P. held that the provision of money by the State from public funds for the purpose of enabling the management boards of Community Schools to pay the salaries of chaplains, employed by such boards in accordance with the terms of their respective trust deeds, did not constitute the endowment of religion by the State within the meaning of Article 44.2.2° of the Constitution.

Article 44.2.2° provides: 'The State guarantees not to endow any religion.' Article 42.4 provides:

> The State shall provide for free primary education and shall endeavour to supplement and give reasonable aid to private and corporate educational initiative, and, when the public good requires it, provide other educational facilities or institutions with due regard, however, for the rights of parents, especially in the matter of religious and moral formation.

Community schools, that is, denominational post-primary schools, are established and managed in accordance with a standard private deed of trust developed by the Department of Education, but without statutory authority apart from the annual Appropriation Act (see the Administrative Law chapter, 1) which authorises the disbursement of public moneys for the purposes of community schools. The board of management of each such school is required to ensure that there is religious worship and instruction for the pupils of the school except for pupils whose parents request in writing that their child be withdrawn from religious worship or religious instruction. The respondent Minister pays from public funds the school's teachers of religion or religious instruction.

In addition, clause 11 of the standard trust deed for a community school directs the school's board of management to appoint a chaplain nominated by the competent religious authority who shall be employed outside the normal quota of teachers allocated by the Department, and directs that the appointee be a full-time member of the school staff and that he should be paid a salary equivalent to that of a teacher in the school. The respondent Minister issued guidelines for the exercise of the pastoral role by chaplains appointed to Roman Catholic community schools. Those guidelines expanded on the following headings: personal contact with individual students, class contact, religious worship, and the maintenance of a lively interest in recreational, cultural and apostolic activities.

The plaintiff company was formed so as to promote the aims of citizens who wished to effect a separation of every Church from the State in all matters pertaining to finance, education, health and welfare of citizens. The plaintiff did not object to the salaries of teachers of religion in community schools being paid from the public purse, but they opposed the payment of the salaries of chaplains appointed to such schools from that source. However, it did not oppose the payment of the salaries of chaplains in hospitals or the Defence Forces from that source. The plaintiff issued a plenary summons in which it sought a declaration that the payment of the salaries of community school chaplains from the public purse contravened the prohibition contained in Article 44.2.2° of the Constitution. As indicated, Costello P. dismissed the claims.

Costello P. noted that, in Article 42.1 of the Constitution, the State guarantees the right and duty of parents to provide for the religious education of their children, while Article 42.4 declares that the State shall provide, when the public good requires it, other educational facilities or institutions with due regard for the rights of parents, especially in the matter of religious and moral formation. He held that the provisions in the trust deeds for the appointment and payment of chaplains in community schools as well as teachers of religion there constituted a recognition of parental rights in regard to the religious and moral formation of children. Consequently, the grant of State financial aid for the purpose of protecting such parental rights did not constitute the endowment of religion within the meaning of Article 44.2.2°.

SEVERABILITY

In *Mallon v. Minister For Agriculture and Food* [1996] 1 I.R. 517 (S.C.), the Supreme Court dealt with another aspect of the challenges to Regulations made by the respondent Minister to implement EC Directives prohibiting the use of hormone growth promoters in animals. A previous decision in this area, *Meagher v. Minister for Agriculture and Food* [1994] 1 I.R. 329; [1994] 1 I.L.R.M. 1, was discussed in the 1993 Review, 299-304. In *Mallon*, eight summonses had been issued against the applicant alleging infringements of the European Communities (Veterinary Medicinal Products) Regulations 1986, as amended by the European Communities (Control of Androgenic, Gestagenic and Thyrostatic Substances) Regulations 1988 and the European Communities (Control of Veterinary Medicinal Products and their Residues) Regulations 1990. Seven of the summonses alleged infringements of regulation 4(1) of the 1988 Regulations, while the eighth alleged infringement of regulation 13 of the 1988 Regulations. Regulation 32(6) of the 1988 Regulations had provided for a penalty of a fine not exceeding £1,000 and/or imprisonment of a term not exceeding one year. Regulation 3(3) of the 1990 Regulations purported to amend that provision by leaving the maximum fine at £15,000 but increasing the maximum term of imprisonment to two years. Regulation 11(1) of the 1990 Regulations also provided for a maximum term of imprisonment of two years for any contravention of the 1990 Regulations.

The applicant obtained leave to bring to bring judicial review challenging the 1988 and 1990 Regulations, seeking prohibition of the prosecutions against him and an order of *certiorari* quashing in their entirety the 1988 and 1990 Regulations. In particular, he contended that the 1990 Regulations were unconstitutional in that they provided for the punishment of a minor offence by imprisonment for up to two years, contrary to Article 38 of the Constitution. In the High Court, it was held that regulations 3(3) and 11(1) of the 1990 Regulations were unconstitutional; but that since regulation (3) was invalid, it could not have repealed the penalties provided for in the 1988 Regulations which thus remained in force, unamended. As for regulation 11(1) of the 1990 Regulations, the High Court was satisfied that the invalidity of the provision arose only from the last words of the paragraph, which provided for a two year term of imprisonment, and that if those words were severed the remainder of the paragraph was valid, thus leaving in place the penalty of £15,000. In this respect, the High Court purported to follow the views expressed on severability in *Maher v. Attorney General* [1973] I.R. 140 and *Desmond v. Glackin (No. 2)* [1992] 2 I.R. 67 (1992 Review, 74-80). The High Court ordered that the prosecutions against the applicant could proceed on the basis that regulation 32(6) of the 1988 Regulations had not been repealed and was valid, and that regulation 11(1) of the 1990 Regulations was to be read as if the provision allowing for two years imprisonment had been deleted therefrom.

The applicant appealed to the Supreme Court, which allowed his appeal, at least in part. The Court held that regulation 3(3) of the 1990 Regulations was *void ab initio* and never had the force of law and was thus incapable of amending regulation 32(6) of the 1988 Regulations. The trial judge had thus been correct in his view that the prosecutions against the applicant could proceed on the basis that the 1988 Regulations remained in full force and unamended. On this point, therefore, the applicant's appeal was dismissed.

However, the Supreme Court differed from the High Court on the severability point. It held that it was clear from the decision in *Maher v. Attorney General* that severability of a statute was only permissible if the remainder of an Act or Regulation could be held to stand independently and legally operable as representing the will of the legislature and that what remained was not so inextricably bound up with the part held invalid that it could not survive independently as representing the will of the legislature. In enacting the 1990 Regulations, the Court considered that it had been the intention of the Minister to create an offence and that such offence was to be regarded as of such a serious nature as to render a person who contravened the Regulations liable not only to a fine of £1,000 but to a prison term of up to two years. It had clearly not been the Minister's intention, the Court felt, that the punishment for such an offence would be limited to a fine not exceeding £1,000, and that consequently the deletion of the words 'imprisonment for a term not exceeding two years or both' was not in accordance with such legislative intent. The trial judge had thus erred in law in allowing the Regulation to stand with these words excised, and consequently the Supreme Court held that the applicant was entitled to a declaration that regulation 11(1) was unconstitutional.

As seven of the summonses against the applicant related to offences contrary to regulation 11(1) of the 1990 Regulations, and as no penalty was now provided for a breach of those Regulations, the Court granted the applicant an order prohibiting any further hearing of any prosecutions brought against him pursuant to the 1990 Regulations. However, as indicated, the prosecution concerning the 1988 Regulations was allowed to proceed. Indeed, we may note here that the *Mallon* case led to a number of successful prosecutions under the 1988 Regulations later in 1996 and into 1997, all of which had been stayed pending the outcome in the case.

TRIAL OF OFFENCES

In *Kavanagh v. Government of Ireland and Ors.* [1996] 1 I.L.R.M. 133 (H.C.); [1997] 1 I.L.R.M. 321 (S.C.), the Supreme Court (affirming Laffoy J. in the High Court) dismissed a constitutional challenge to the validity of the establishment of the special criminal court. The background to the case was as follows.

Article 38.3 of the Constitution provides that '[s]pecial courts may be established by law for the trial of offences in cases where it may be determined in accordance with such law that the ordinary courts are inadequate to secure the effective administration of justice, and the preservation of public peace and order' and that '[t]he constitution, powers, jurisdiction and procedure of such special courts shall be prescribed by law.' The relevant law enacted in accordance with Article 38.3 is Part V of the Offences Against the State Act 1939. Section 35 of the 1939 Act provides that Part V. shall come into force (and special criminal courts may thus be established) where the Government makes and publishes a proclamation declaring that it 'is satisfied that the ordinary courts are inadequate to secure the effective administration of justice and the preservation of public peace and order'. This is clearly based on the formula in Article 38.3 of the Constitution. Part V of the 1939 Act also provides for the matters referred to in Article 38.3, the composition of and detailed procedures to be followed by special criminal courts. A significant feature of the 1939 Act is that it is possible to have cases transferred from the ordinary criminal courts, that is, the District Court, the Circuit Court and the High Court. This can be effected in one of two ways. First, section 36 of the 1939 Act provides that certain lists of offences may be specified by the Government by statutory Order as offences which the ordinary courts are to be deemed inadequate within the terms of Article 38.3 of the Constitution. These offences are referred to as 'scheduled offences' and are transferred automatically to the special criminal courts. The current list of scheduled offences is contained in the Offences against the State (Scheduled Offences) Order 1972.

Second, where an offence is not a scheduled offence, section 46 of the 1939 Act provides that an individual trial may be transferred to a special criminal court where the Director of Public Prosecutions issues a certificate under section 47 stating that in his opinion the ordinary courts are inadequate to secure the effective administration of justice and the preservation of public peace and order. Once such a certificate is issued the case must be transferred by the ordinary court to a special criminal court.

In May 1972, the Government had made a proclamation under section 35(2) of the Offences Against the State Act 1939 in which it was declared that the ordinary courts were inadequate to secure the effective administration of justice and the preservation of public peace and order and, as a result, a Special Criminal Court was established. In 1994, the applicant was arrested and charged with a number of offences, including false imprisonment, robbery and possession of a firearm. Not all these offences were scheduled offences and, in respect of these, the Director of Public Prosecutions certified, pursuant to section 47(2) of the 1939 Act that, he was of the opinion that the ordinary courts were inadequate to secure the effective administration of justice and the preservation of public peace and order. The applicant was accordingly brought before the Special Criminal Court and charged with all the offences, including those which were non-scheduled. The applicant subsequently sought judicial review of the Director's decision under section 47 of the 1939 Act.

The applicant had initially argued that section 35 of the 1939 Act was unconstitutional, but this ground was not pursued. He argued, *inter alia*, that the Special Criminal Court had been established in 1972 to counter the threat to the State posed by the conflict in Northern Ireland and that it was never intended that the court be used to try "ordinary" crime; that, once invoked, the Government had a duty to keep the 1972 decision under review and to revoke it once it was satisfied that the ordinary courts were adequate to secure the effective administration of justice; and that if either of these grounds succeeded, the certificate issued by the Director was invalid. The applicant also relied on what he referred to as a representation alleged to have been made by the Attorney General to the Human Rights Committee of the General Assembly of the United Nations in October 1993 to the effect that the Special Criminal Court had been established to deal with the situation in Northern Ireland.

As already indicated, Laffoy J. dismissed the application and, on appeal, the Supreme Court (Hamilton C.J., O'Flaherty, Blayney, Barrington and Keane JJ.) affirmed this and dismissed the appeal. Since there was no direct challenge to the constitutionality of section 35 of the 1939 Act, the Court was not required to deliver one judgment only. Both Barrington and Keane JJ. delivered judgments with which the other members of the Court agreed.

Barrington J. noted that it was clear from Article 38.3 of the Constitution that special courts could be established "by law" and that the power to decide whether such courts should be established was vested in the legislature in which was also invested (by Article 15.2) the sole and exclusive power for making laws for the State. He added, in an important passage:

> The question of whether the ordinary courts are or are not adequate to secure the effective administration of justice and the preservation of public peace and order is primarily a political question, and, for that reason, is left to the legislature and the executive.

The applicant had argued that, in deciding whether to make a proclamation under section 35(2) of the 1939 Act, the Government was acting judicially in the sense that it was adjudicating upon the rights of any particular citizen because it had to be 'satisfied' that a certain situation existed. Citing the judgment of Gavan Duffy J. in *The State (Burke) v. Lennon* [1940] I.R. 139 (on which the applicant had relied), Barrington J. rejected this argument, stating that many decisions made by Ministers remained outside the judicial or quasi-judicial realm even where the Minister exercises a statutory power requiring the Minister to be 'satisfied' that a particular state of affairs existed. In the instant case, he considered that, in issuing a proclamation under section 35 of the 1939 Act, the Government was making a political judgement on the adequacy of the ordinary courts to secure the effective administration of justice and the preservation of public peace and order, and he felt that it was natural that such a political decision should be primarily subject to political control.

Barrington J. went on to consider the argument that Part V. of the 1939 Act was confined to 'subversive' crime and did not extend to 'ordinary' crime. Barrington J. noted that the framers of the 1939 Act and of the 1972 proclamation considered it impractical or undesirable to draw a rigid distinction between subversive and ordinary crime. For that reason, he felt, the Government had the power under section 36 of the 1939 Act to declare offences of any particular class or kind to be scheduled offences. For the same reason the Director was empowered by section 47(2) of the 1939 Act to certify that the ordinary courts were inadequate in relation to the trial of a person charged with a non-scheduled offence. He quoted with approval the views of Walsh J. in *The People v. Quilligan and O'Reilly* [1986] I.R. 495, in which he had pointed out that, by contrast with the other provisions of the 1939 Act, Part V of the 1939 Act was in the nature of 'temporary emergency legislation', and dealt with the adequacy of the courts either generally or in relation to a specific kind of crime, not confined to any rigid categorisation. It thus availed the applicant nothing to submit that the offences in respect of which he had been charged were not of a subversive nature, because the issue involved was, in Barrington J.'s view, not the nature of the offences but the adequacy, in the opinion of the Government or the Director, of the ordinary courts to deal with them.

As to whether the Government was under an obligation to keep the 1972 proclamation under review, Barrington J. accepted that there was some merit in this argument. He recited the applicant's arguments that the situation in Northern Ireland had altered since 1972, that majority jury verdicts had been introduced by the Criminal Justice Act 1984 (thereby reducing the risk of jury intimidation), that the volume of cases coming before the Special criminal Court had fallen off dramatically and that the applicant had himself been tried on previous occasions before a jury court and that nobody had suggested that the ordinary courts had been inadequate on those occasions. And while he stated that the respondents' affidavits on their review of the situation were 'not very informative', Barrington J. accepted that it was nonetheless clear that the Government had the situation under review and that it was their present opinion that it was necessary to maintain the Special Criminal Court. In these circumstances, he was prepared to accept that the 1972 proclamation retained the presumption of constitutionality and withstood the challenge in the instant case.

Finally, Barrington J. turned to the statement by the Attorney General to the United Nations. He doubted whether the Attorney's address constituted a representation. It was, in his view, a general description of the need which required the establishment of the Special Criminal Court and there was nothing in it which in any way inhibited the Director from exercising the powers conferred on him by the 1939 Act.

In a concurring judgment, Keane J. agreed that there was no evidence in this case of any abuse which would justify the Court in interfering with the validity of the exercise of any of the powers conferred by the 1939 Act. He added, however, that save in the exceptional circumstances of war and national emergency envisaged by Article 28.3 of the Constitution, 'the courts at all times retain their jurisdiction to intervene so as to ensure that the exercise of these drastic powers to abridge the citizens' rights is not abused by the arm of government to which they have been entrusted.' Thus, although the Court rejected the applicant's case, it reiterated its view that judicial review remains as an important method of correcting misuse of power. Indeed, one might add that, even where the emergency power conferred by Article 28.3 of the Constitution is concerned, the decision of the Court in *In re the Emergency Powers Bill 1976* [1977] I.R. 159 indicates that review may even extend (if only in terms of procedural protections) to check the use of such power.

Video link evidence   In *Donnelly v. Ireland*, High Court, December 3, 1996, Costello P. rejected the plaintiff's constitutional challenge to section 13 of the Criminal Evidence Act 1992 (1992 Review, 262-4), by which evidence may be given in certain criminal trials by way of video link. The defendant had been charged with sexual assault and had been informed one week before his trial that section 13 of the 1992 Act would be used for the evidence to be given by the complainant. It was accepted that the reason behind the enactment of section 13 was that young persons under the age of 17 were likely to be traumatised by the experience of giving evidence in court and that its purpose was to minimise this trauma. The complainant being under 17 years of age, section 13 provides that the trial judge is required to assume that the giving of evidence in the normal manner would be likely to lead to trauma in the witness and that only if there is good reason should permission to give video link evidence be refused. If an accused objected to the procedure, he had to show the trial judge that there existed "good reasons" why section 13 should not operate. The section did not require the trial judge to examine each young witness to see whether they would be traumatised. The trial judge ruled that, in the instant case, the section 13 procedure was appropriate. The defendant was convicted The central feature of his challenge to the constitutionality of section 13 of the 1992 Act was that it restricted his 'right to confront' witnesses or his right to fair procedures in that it was based on an assumption that a witness under 17 would be traumatised if required to give evidence in court in the presence of the accused.

As already indicated, Costello P. dismissed the claim, as indeed Kinlen J. had done in *White v. Ireland* [1995] 2 I.R. 268, to which Costello P. referred in his judgment. Costello P. noted that the "right to confront" witnesses in United States law was a right which, unlike the Irish Constitution, was expressly contained in the Sixth Amendment to Federal Constitution and had been the subject of considerable judicial examination.

He referred to Article 38 of the Constitution of Ireland, which provides that no person should be tried on any criminal charge save in due course of law, and that the leading decision *The State (Healy) v. Donoghue* [1976] I.R. 325 had interpreted it to mean that an accused had a right to be adequately informed of the nature and substance of the accusation, to have the matter tried in his presence by an impartial and independent court or arbitrator, to hear and test by examination the evidence against him, to be allowed to give or call evidence in his defence, and to be heard in argument or submissions before judgment is given. Costello P. accepted that If the constitutional guarantee of fair procedures was breached by statute, it would be unconstitutional. He held that if section 13 of the 1992 Act breached that guarantee, there could be no question of balancing Article 38.1 against other constitutional rights or interests (such as the interest if the community to see those accused of crime brought to justice) and the section would have to be condemned.

Costello P. considered that, in his trial, the defendant had had the benefit of all the procedures outlined in the *Healy* case as being necessary to constitute a fair trial. Referring with approval to the decision of Kinlen J. in *White*, Costello P. held that the absence of a physical confrontation was fair to the accused and that a criminal trial in modern times did not become unfair if there was not such confrontation. He noted that the jury would see the witness at all times, and the absence of a physical confrontation between the witness and the accused would have no significant effect on the ability of a false accuser to mislead a jury. As a corollary to this finding that section 13 did not infringe a defendant's constitutional right to fair procedures, Costello P. held that it followed that the right to a physical confrontation by an accused of his or her accusers was not a constitutionally protected right and that he was not required to consider whether the section had impermissibly restricted the exercise of a protected right. The effectiveness of the constitutional right to cross-examine was not adversely affected even when it took place when the witness was not in the physical presence of the accused. Finally, Costello P. referred to the origins of the 1992 Act in proposals emanating from the Law Reform Commission (1992 Review, 262). He noted that once it was established that there was no unfairness involved in allowing evidence to be given in the absence of a physical confrontation, the Oireachtas had been free to adopt proposals from the Commission as to the circumstances in which the procedures would be permitted or to enact legislation so as to require the trial judge to decide on a case-by-case basis whether video link evidence was permissible.

Contract Law

Eoin O'Dell, School of Law, Trinity College Dublin

BREACH OF CONTRACT

In *Clarke v. Kilternan Motor Co.* (High Court, December 10, 1996) the parties had concluded an oral agreement that the plaintiff would run the defendant's filling station and shop, retain a commission, and pay the remaining proceeds over to the defendant. The defendant claimed that there had been a subsequent oral variation, but McCracken J. did "not think that the plaintiff agreed to it in any real sense of that word, or that there was an sufficient meeting of minds to vary the terms of the original agreement" (p. 4). The plaintiff suffered financial difficultes, and operated a bank account in which he kept for his own use for several days the proceeds due to the defendant. The parties had two inconclusive meetings, one quite heated, after which they held a stocktake, and the plaintiff returned the keys of the premises to the defendants. Nevertheless, the plaintiff claimed that the agreement had been wrongfully terminated by the defendant, and that he was entitled to six months minimum reasonable notice. There were also amounts due to both parties at that date, including proceeds due to the defendant under the contract which the plaintiff had retained and subsequently spent. McCracken J. held that either the agreement was in fact terminated by the plaintiff, whose financial difficulties were such that it was impossible for him to continue, or, the defendant would have been entitled to terminate without notice for the plaintiff's operation of the bank account in breach of contract. On this latter point, he held that "it was clearly a fundamental condition of the agreement" that the plaintiff would pay the proceeds to the defendant. The operation of the bank account had "the effect of delaying the payment to the defendants for several days, while the plaintiff had the use of the money during that time, and in my view was a fundamental breach of the agreement between the parties, which would have justified an immediate termination by the defendant". (p. 8). He also calculated the amounts due each way and gave judgment for the difference. Accordingly, although he held that a term providing for reasonable notice of termination could be implied into the contract, (discussed in the Implied Terms section, below, pp. 195-200), McCracken J. did not have to consider what would have constituted reasonable notice in the circumstances.

CONDITIONAL CONTRACTS

Where a contract makes completion subject to certain matters being completed not later than a specified date or such later date as the parties may agree, the parties may agree such later date orally and not necessarily in writing. In agreeing a date orally, they were not varying the agreement, but merely performing it. Keane J. (Hamilton C.J. and O'Flaherty J. concurring) so held, *ex tempore*, in *Duggan v. AIB Finance* (Supreme Court, November 19, 1996). Pursuant to a scheme which required the consent of the Minister for Finance, the business of a third party was to be tranferred to the respondent bank; as a consequence, a debt owed by the appellant to the third party had, by contract in writing, been assigned to the respondent, conditional upon the Minister's approval and other matters being completed not later than a specified date or such later date as the parties may agree. In an action to enforce the debt, the High Court had found in favour of the respondent bank, and, for the above reasons, Keane J. dismissed appeal. In so doing, he also observed that "an equitable assignment of a chose in action . . . requires no particular formalities" (approving *Brandt's v. Dunlop Rubber Co.* [1905] A.C. 454), but observed that the relevant assignment had nevertheless been in writing. For these reasons, the debt had been validly assigned, and the appellant was properly held liable upon it.

CONSIDERATION

Past Consideration   The issue of consideration was briefly before the Supreme Court in *First National Commercial Bank v. Anglin* [1996] 1 I.R. 75 (*aff'g* High Court, unreported, February 20, 1996, Costello J., *ex tempore*) in which the defendant sought (unsuccessfully) to resist the enforcement of a guarantee on the grounds that it was unsupported by consideration, any relevant consideration being past.

In the 1995 Review, 184-96, it was argued that the essence of consideration is that each party to a contract gives and receives something: a bargained-for exchange. In this scenario, it may be said in respect of each party's giving, that the party giving suffers a detriment and the other party gains a corresponding benefit; or, in respect of each party's receipt, that the party receiving gains a benefit and the other party suffers a corresponding detriment. So, in the situation of a sale of goods for a price, there is 'something for something': the seller suffers the detriment of giving over the goods and the buyer gains the benefit of getting them, while the seller gains the benefit of the receipt of the price and the buyer suffers the detriment of paying it. If the paradigm is 'something in return for something', then it follows that where a contract seems to provide for 'something for nothing', it does not provide for consideration and is consequently unenforceable. Thus, let something be done by P, for which D later promises to pay; "it is clear that the service was not performed as the price of the promise. The notion of bargain involves that the promises (or the promise and the act in a unilateral contract) should be given, each in return for the other. . . ." (Atiyah, *An Introduction to the Law of Contract* (5th ed., Clarendon Press, Oxford, 1995), p. 123). Since D already has the benefit of P's performance, his promise is not given in return for the performance; in effect, P would get something for nothing; thus, from the perspective of D's promise, the consideration to support it was past, and P cannot enforce it.

For example, in *Provincial Bank of Ireland v. O'Donnell* (1933) 67 I.L.T.R. 142; [1934] N.I. 33 (NI CA) (cited with approval in *Riordan v. Carroll* [1996] 2 I.L.R.M. 263, 273 *per* Kinlen J; see the 1995 Review, 183) the defendant wife gave a guarantee to the plaintiff bank in consideration of "advances heretofore made . . ." by the bank to her husband. The bank sought to enforce the guarantee against the wife, but, from the perspective of this agreement, the bank having already given the advances had given only a past consideration, and the guarantee was unenforceable.

Thus, essence of the rule against past consideration is that if P has performed, and D had later promised to pay, P cannot enforce D's promise. However, if P had performed as a consequence of D implicitly promising to pay, the later express promise is simply an express articulation of this prior implicit but unarticulated promise. On this analysis, P's performance was in return for D's unarticulated but implicit promise to pay, and from the perspective of this promise, the consideration is good. In other words, the situation is in fact the pardigmatic 'something for something': a performance in return for the promise to pay.

The best way to prove this prior implicit promise is by a request from D to perform, since the promise to pay for performance can easily be discovered in that request, as in the leading cases of *Lampleigh v. Braithwait* (1615) Hob. 105; 80 E.R. 255 and *Pao On v. Lau Yiu Long* [1980] A.C. 614; [1979] 3 All ER 65. In *Pao On*, P agreed with a third party (T) to sell shares in one company in return for shares in another company, and further agreed with T not to sell 60% of the shares received for at least a year in return for an indemnity from T on the share price. However, this indemnity was cancelled. D (T's owners) then agreed with P that they, D, would indemnify P if the share price fell, in consideration of P having entered into the main sale agreement with the T. As in *Provincial Bank of Ireland v. O'Donnell*, from the perspective of this second agreement, P, having already entered into the main sale agreement, would seem to have given only a past consideration; so that the contract of indemnity would have been unenforeceable. P nevertheless sued upon it, and D predictably argued that the consideration was past. Lord Scarman for the Privy Council held otherwise: D had requested P not to sell 60% of the shares for a year, in return for which P would be indemnified for any loss arising out of holding the shares. When the initial indemnity was cancelled, and the later indemnity agreement put in place, there was in effect an initial request by D coupled with an implicit promise to pay, D's later promise was merely the later articulation of this implicit promise, and from the perspective of this initial implicit promise, the consideration was not past but contemporary.

Furthermore, if it is correct to explain the principle in *Pao On* and *Lampleigh* as turning upon an unarticulated but nonetheless real promise prior to the performance, of which the subsequent promise is merely the articulation, then, although a request is probably the best way to show this prior unarticulated promise, in principle, anything which goes to show a prior unarticulated but nonetheless real promise to pay for the performance should be sufficient.

A situation which at first blush seems very similar to *Provincial Bank of Ireland v. O'Donnell* arose in *First National Commercial Bank v. Anglin*. The plaintiff bank made a loan to a company; the defendant executed a guarantee in respect of that loan in favour of the plaintiffs, who issued a summary summons to enforce it; the Master transferred the case to the judge's list, and in the High Court, (unreported, February 20, 1996) Costello J. in an *ex tempore* granted summary judgment in favour of the plaintiff. On appeal, Murphy J. (Hamilton C.J. and Denham J. concurring) affirmed. (On the summary nature of the proceedings, see our Practice and Procedure chapter, 493, below). In the appeal, it was argued that if the loan had been made in February 1989, but the guarantee had not been executed until September 1989, "it followed that the Guarantee was void as having been given for a past consideration" ([1996] 1 I.R. 75, 78). However, Murphy J. had "no doubt but that the Guarantee was executed by Mr Agnlin not on, but before, the 1st of February" ([1996] 1 I.R. 75, 81). Thus, there was "no question whatever of that document having been executed subsequent to the 1st of February 1989 and certainly not as late as September of that year." (*ibid*). Since there was no credible evidence for what the defendant had sought to assert, a probable defence had not been established on the facts, and the summary judgment was affirmed.

However, Murphy J. did go on to examine briefly the substantive point of law raised on the appeal, to the effect that the execution of the guarantee subsequent to the draw-down of the loan constituted past consideration. Had the circumstances in *Anglin* simply been as the defendant-appellant had contended, then, by analogy with *O'Donnell*, the guarantee, given subsequent to the loan and merely in consideration for it, would have been given for a past consideration, and thus for no valid consideration, and would therefore have been void and unenforceable. However, Murphy J. found that, in "the first place, the loan was made expressly and unequivocally on terms that the Guarantee would be given by Mr Anglin . . . as he recognises and, secondly, the Guarantee in its terms extends to present as well as future indebtedness of the Principal Debtor." ([1996] 1 I.R. 75, 81). Whether or not the second reason is sufficient in the light of *O'Donnell*, the first is determinative: if the contract expressly stated that the loan was given in return for both the debtor's liability to pay and the guarantee, then a later execution of the guarantee is merely the fulfilling of a valid contractual obligation undertaken for a consideration which was contemporary and not past; in other words, it is the pardigmatic 'something for something': a performance by the plaintiff bank in return for the defendant's express promise of a guarantee. Thus, there was consideration for the guarantee.

It will thus be seen that there can be problems with whether a guarantor or surety has received consideration in return for the guarantee or security. In practice, as we have just seen, in "the case of a guarantee for existing debts, the lending of the money in the past is generally insufficient since it constitutes 'past consideration'. [Therefore, t]he consideration relied upon in practice commonly takes the form of the lender, at the request of the surety, forebearing to sue the principal debtor for a period (often only one day) and/or making or continuing advances or otherwise giving credit or affording banking facilities for as long as the bank may think fit to the principal debtor". (Mee (1995) 46 *N.I.L.Q.* 147, 159 referring to *Chitty on Contracts* (26th ed, Sweet & Maxwell, London, 1989) vol. II, pp. 1349-1352; (see now 27th ed, (1994), vol II, pp. 1313-1315, and supplement (1996), p. 343); however, where such a consideration is not expressed, "though this might easily have been done" Andrews L.J. in *O'Donnell* felt "unable to put a forced construction upon words which [were] in no way ambiguous merely to make the guarantee binding" (1933) 67 I.L.T.R. 142, 143; [1934] N.I. 33, 44). Of course, since forebearance to sue is good consideration, the bank undertaking to forebear to sue for a day gives good consideration for the guarantee.

The alternative consideration, the promise to make further advances or supply other credit or banking facilities, seems very common; for example, it was the form of consideration given the bank to the surety wife who secured the banks previous advances to her husband in *Bank of Novia Scotia v. Hogan* (Supreme Court, 6 November 1996; affirming High Court, December 21, 1992; see at p. 2 of the judgment of Keane J. in the High Court. This case is discussed in detail in the Undue Influence section, below, 219-27). Though common, this type of consideration is rather problematic. For example, in *O'Donnell*, the bank secured the guarantee in consideration of "advances heretofore made or that might hereafter be made", and not only did the first half of this fail for past consideration, but the second half also failed as embodying only an illusory consideration. This may be an extreme example, but it is indicative of the care which has to be taken in respect of guarantees sought after the principal loan has been granted. In the event, on the facts of *Anglin*, past consideration was not made out and illusory consideration did not arise, but they are nonetheless traps for unwary banks.

Consideration and the part payment of a debt   The issue of consideration also arose in *Truck and Machinery Sales v. Marubeni Komatsu* [1996] 1 I.R. 12 where Keane J. was faced with the question of whether and when, in principle, part payment of an existing debt can constitute consideration for a contract. As outlined above, the essence of consideration is that each party to a contract gives and receives something, a bargained-for exchange, in which the paradigm is 'something in return for something'; from which it follows that where a contract seems to provide for 'something for nothing', it does not provide for consideration and is consequently unenforceable. Thus, where a contract already provides for a given price for a given performance, an agreement to accept a lesser price for that same performance is unenforceable for want of consideration: given that the price is already due, the reduction in the amount owed is 'something for nothing', unsupported by consideration, and thus unenforceable. This rule, that part payment of an existing debt does not discharge that debt and is no consideration for an agreement that the debt is discharged, is usually taken to have been established by *Pinnel's Case* (1602) 5 Co. Rep. 117a; 77 E.R. 237 and confirmed by the House of Lords in *Foakes v. Beer* (1884) 9 App. Cas. 605 (over a powerful dissent from Lord Blackburne). However, to this rule, there are some recognised exceptions; so that part payment early, or in a different place, or by some new means, or in a composition with creditors, can constitute consideration. In all such cases, there is again a something for something: the additional matters are in return for the promise to forgive the debt (see also Lyall, *Land Law in Ireland* (Oak Tree Press, Dublin, 1994), p. 117 for a further interesting exception).

These matters were extensively analysed in the 1995 Review, 186-96, in the context of the decision of the Court of Appeal in *Williams v. Roffey* [1991] 1 Q.B. 1; [1990] 1 All E.R. 512, where it was held that although the performance an existing duty will usually not constitute consideration for a promise so to perform, if the promisee derives a practical benefit from such performance, that benefit can constitute consideration for such a promise. Although the case has been welcomed as demonstrating a "flexible approach to consideration in a commercial context" (*European Consulting v. Refco* (April 12, 1995, Queen's Bench, Mance J.); see the 1995 Review, 186 with references, and Meyer-Rochow (1997) 71 *A.L.J.* 532), both aspects of this holding are entirely consistent with the approach to consideration as paradigmatically 'something for something' (and paradigmatically not 'something for nothing') set out above. Thus, where a contract already provides for a given performance for a given price, an agreement merely to perform that same performance for a higher price is unenforceable: given that the performance is already due, the increase in price is 'something for nothing', unsupported by consideration, and thus unenforceable. However, if the background circumstances have changed, then the receipt of the original performance in the new circumstances is a practical benefit, a 'something different', and there is again a 'something for something'. In the 1995 Review, 188, it was argued that this is the key to *Williams v. Roffey*. It was further argued, first, that a similar notion of practical benefit is to be found in Irish law in the judgment of Murphy J. in *In re PMPA Garage (Longmile) Ltd (No. 1)* [1992] 1 I.R. 315, and second, that "[v]ery often it will be of practical benefit to a trade creditor to receive a part-payment in satisfaction of the full amount, especially where payment is early, or in a different place, or by some new means, or in a composition with creditors; thus, the recognised exceptions to *Foakes v. Beer* can be seen simply as examples of the recognition of practical benefit in the context of part-payment prior to *Williams v. Roffey*. . . . In all cases, it is of the essence of the second agreement that the creditor is in fact getting 'something different'. Thus, where part-payment results in the debtor getting 'something for nothing', there is no consideration, (*Foakes v. Beer*), but where the creditor in fact gets a practical benefit (a 'something different') then there is good consideration (*Williams v. Roffey*). On this analysis, . . . the latter case does not amount to the death-knell for the former; it merely rationally explains the existing exceptions to the former. . . . Consequently, then, the notion of 'practical benefit' has an important role to play in the context of consideration for part payment of a debt. Furthermore, adherence to precedent (the rule in *Pinnel's Case* and *Foakes v. Beer*) should not preclude its application because the exceptions to that rule are best understood as examples of such a practical benefit. " (1995 Review, 193-4).

Thus, in *Re Selectmove* [1995] 1 W.L.R. 474; [1995] 2 All E.R. 533 (C.A.), where a company owed a debt to the Revenue, the Court of Appeal considered that, whilst a subsequenlty agreed repayment schedule might have constituted a "practical benefit" within the *Williams v. Roffey* understanding of that notion, the decision of the House of Lords in *Foakes v. Beer* rendered it "impossible" find consideration for what in fact amounted to a part payment of a debt. On the approach urged in the 1995 Review and outlined above, however, this conflict disappears; there is no inconsistency between *Pinnel's Case* and *Williams v. Roffey*, and it is not necessary to feel constrained by the former into the non-application of the latter.

On the other hand, if *Foakes v. Beer* is understood to preclude a finding of 'practical benefit' in the context of the part payment of a debt, then the Court of Appeal in *Re Selectmove* was constrained by the doctrine of precedent to arrive at the conclusion it did. However, in the New South Wales case of *Musumeci v. Winadell* (1994) 34 N.S.W.L.R. 723, Santow J. did not feel bound by the chains of precedent to follow *Foakes v. Beer*, and preferred instead to follow *Williams v. Roffey*. It was pointed out in the 1995 Review that there seemed until then to have been no post-1961 (mistyped as 1963 on p. 194 of the 1995 Review) – and thus binding – example of the application of *Foakes v. Beer* in an Irish court. Had matters remained so, – and if the reconciliation between *Foakes v. Beer* and *Williams v. Roffey* advanced above were not accepted – then the type of considerations of precedent which constrained the Court of Appeal in *Re Selectmove* would still not have prevented an Irish court reaching a result similar to *Musumeci v. Winadell* in an appropriate case. However, the context of the discussion in the 1995 Review was the acceptance of the rule in *Pinnel's Case* and *Foakes v. Beer* by Kinlen J. in *Riordan v. Carroll* [1996] 2 I.L.R.M. 263, a case of a simple waiver of rent, a reduction of a debt without consideration, and properly held unenforceable (*Pinnel's Case, Foakes v. Beer*). It was submitted that "[t]here was nothing on the facts to suggest that the lessors or the plaintiff-assignees received any practical benefit from the waiver; in fact, quite the contrary. Thus, there was nothing upon which to ground an argument based upon *Williams v. Roffey*, or *PMPA*; and nothing in the facts or the holding in *Riordan v. Carroll* precludes an Irish court applying them to reach a result such as that in *Musumeci v. Winadell* . . .", 1995 Review, 195. This conclusion must now be revisited and may need to be revised in the light of the decision of Keane J. in *Truck and Machinery Sales v. Marubeni Komatsu* [1996] 1 I.R. 12.

A company, intending to sell machinery in Dubai, purchased it from the creditor, but then ran into difficulties in Dubai and were unable to sell it on. St£ 2.3m of the purchase price remained due to the creditor. To the company's consequent difficulties, the creditor adopted a "patient and understanding attitude" ([1996] 1 I.R. 12, 30), but when it could wait no longer, the creditor presented a petition seeking to wind up the company. In this action, the company in turn sought to prevent the presentation of the petition, *inter alia* on the ground that there was an agreement between the parties that the debt had been waived. (On the principles underlying the company's application, see the Company Law chapter, above, 107-113; Canniffe (1997) *C.L.P.* 30; McCann (1996) *Bar. Rev.* 6). Keane J. dismissed the application; and his decision was upheld *ex tempore* on appeal March 13, 1996 (see reporter's note: [1996] 1 I.R. 12, 31). As to whether there was such an agreement, the creditor had sent a fax to a bank with which the company were in discussion in which the creditor said that it had told the company that "provided a part payment of approximately 0.75 to 1.0 million pounds is paid to us promptly, we would wait for the balance . . .". Though in isolation this might have appeared to constitute an agreement to waive the debt, Keane J. held that "when one reads the entire correspondence, it becomes clear beyond argument that [the creditor] at no stage waived the balance of the purchase price due to it." ([1996] 1 I.R. 12, 30).

Furthermore, the question of whether any such agreement would have been enforceable was fully argued before him, and Keane J. continued that "even if I were satisfied as a matter of fact that [such an agreement existed] . . . it would seem clearly unenforceable in the light of the legal principles to which I have referred." (*id.*). Those legal principles were the decisions in *Pinnel's Case* and *Foakes v. Beer*, and, since, it had not been urged upon him that he should depart from those cases, he was, accordingly, satisfied that he should adopt the approach taken by the Court of Appeal in *In re Selectmove* ([1996] 1 I.R. 12, 29). In the first place, as has been argued above, the application of *Pinnel's Case* and *Foakes v. Beer* does not preclude a finding of consideration based upon practical benefit to enforce a promise to waive part of an existing debt. In the second, even if it does, since it was not urged upon Keane J. that he should depart from *Foakes v. Beer*, his approval of *Re Selectmove* was, strictly speaking, unnecessary; and a re-consideration of the issue, in the context of a full appraisal of the status of *Foakes v. Beer* in Irish law, is still possible; in which case, *Musumeci v. Winadell* provides support for the view that in jurisdictions in which *Foakes v. Beer* is not directly binding, there can be good reasons to depart from it so as to allow for such a finding of consideration.

If, for either of the above two reasons, Keane J. had sought on the facts for a 'practical benefit' to the creditor as consideration received for the alleged promise to waive the existing debt, it is submitted that he would have found none. In *Williams v. Roffey*, the builder had obtained many practical benefits from the continuance of contract: he avoided penalties under his headcontract, he obtained the carpenter's continued performance in circumstrances where otherwise he would not have and thus also avoided the trouble and expense of obtaining a substitute, he obtained a generally more orderly and efficient performance of the contract, and avoided substantial penalties under his headcontract. In *Anangel v. Ishikawajima-Harima (No 2)* [1990] 2 Lloyd's Rep. 526, the ship-builder obtained the practical benefit of completing a sale to a key customer in a difficult market in order to encourage their other reluctant customers to follow suit ([1990] 2 Lloyd's Rep. 526, 544). And in *Musumeci v. Winadell*, a landlord who received part payment thereby improved his cash flow, creating immediate benefits. Thus, the benefits tend to flow from improved cash flow consequent upon the fact of payment. On the other hand, there is no such improvement in market position or cash flow to be found on the facts of *Re Selectmove*, where it is difficult to see how the Revenue would have obtained a practical benefit on the facts from part payment. Although part payment or instalment payments by debtors are often of practical benefit to creditors, they will not invariably be so: if there is no practical benefit, then *Foakes v. Beer* applies; but if there is such a practical benefit, then the situation is within one of the exceptions. On the facts of *Truck and Machinery Sales v. Marubeni Komatsu*, first, the creditor does not seem to have been in cash flow or market difficulties where the part payment would have constituted a practical benefit; second, no relevant part payment had in fact been made, so that those benefits could not have accrued; and, third, there would seem to have been no benefits accruing to the creditor from the mere fact of company's promise to make the part payment. There being no benefit to the creditor, the facts come properly within the *Foakes v. Beer* rule, rather than *Williams v. Roffey.*

In sum, then, whilst it is well settled that the part payment of a debt provides no consideration for a promise not to enforce that debt (*Pinnel's Case,
Foakes v. Beer*), if there is something more on the facts (such as payment in
advance, or in a different place, or by some new means, or in a composition
with creditors) it is also well settled that there is in such circumstances good
consideration. If such matters are described as practical benefits, then *Williams
v. Roffey* explains why there is good consideration in such circumstances. The
question then becomes whether there is simply a promise to waive a debt
(which *Pinnel's Case* properly holds confers no benefit and thus does not
constitute consideration) or whether the part-payment confers a practical benefit upon the promisor (in which case it will constitute good consideration).
Thus, there is no conflict between *Pinnel's Case* and *Williams v. Roffey.* It is
submitted, therefore, that the Court of Appeal in *Re Selectmove* and Keane J.
following them in *Truck and Machinery Sales v. Marubeni Komatsu* ought
not to have preceived one. However, on the facts of the both such cases, there
was no practical benefit, and thus no consideration; so the decision would not
have been different had the practical benefit approach been applied.

Nevertheless, since, as pointed out above, the decision of Keane J. need
not be seen as the last word in an Irish court on this topic, it is to be hoped that
if the matter is once again to be litigated, an Irish court will consider whether
the circumstances of part-payment amount to a practical benefit to the promisor, and can therefore constitute good consideration, rather than feel constrained
by received misunderstanding of precedent not to do so.

Estoppel   Since the decsion of Denning J. in *Central London Property Trust
v. High Trees House* [1947] K.B. 130, in which he disinterred the judgment of
Lord Cairns in *Hughes v. Metropolitan Railway Co* (1877) 2 App. Cas. 439
and deployed it as the basis of a doctrine by which a person who has foreseeably
relied to his detriment upon the promise of another may be allowed to prevent
that other from going back upon that promise, it has been accepted that if a
person promises to waive a debt, and the debtor foreseeably detrimentally
relies upon that promise, the promisor may be estopped from denying that
promised waiver. Such were the facts of *High Trees* itself, where a landlord,
promising to require only half-rent for the duration of the war, was not allowed to go back on that promise; but, once the war was over, the terms of the
promise had been spent, and he was once again free to charge full rent. Thus,
where consideration fails, estoppel is often reached for as an alternative reason to enforce a promise. It was thus in *Riordan v. Carroll* (above); and it has
been argued that the doctrine would provide a more appropriate basis for the
decision in *Williams v. Roffey* (see the 1995 Review, 195). Almost predictably,
therefore, the applicant in also *Truck and Machinery Sales v. Marubeni
Komatsu* sought to rely on *High Trees.* Keane J. cited it as authority for the

proposition that "where parties to a contract enter into a course of negotiations which has the effect of leading one of those parties to suppose that strict rights arising under the contract will not be enforced, or will be kept in suspense, the person who might otherwise have enforced those rights will not be allowed to enforce them where it would be inequitable having regard to the dealings which have taken place between the parties" ([1996] 1 I.R. 12, 29) and pointed out that "a not dissimilar approach was adopted by the Supreme Court in *Webb v. Ireland* [1988] I.R. 353" (*id.*, for an analysis of the modern status of promissory estoppel in Irish law in the light; *inter alia*, of *Webb*, see O'Dell (1992) 14 *DULJ* (*ns*) 123; cf Coughlan (1993) 15 *D.U.L.J.* (*n.s.*) 188). However, as with a similar plea in *Riordan v. Carroll*, the estoppel argument failed on the facts: it could not be said that "the course of negotiations between the parties was such that it could have left any reasonable person under the impression that [the creditor was] waiving ... [its] entitlement to the balance of the debt. On the contrary, the correspondence indicates that the repeated requests from [the creditor] for payment of its account were met with a succession of proposals from [the company] which, for the most part, were never implemented by the latter. To hold, at this stage, that [the creditor] should be estopped from taking legal proceedings to enforce its right would, in the light of the correspondence, be a negation of equity." ([1996] 1 I.R. 12, 30-31). *D&C Builders v. Rees* [1966] 2 Q.B. 617 is often presented as an example of inequity on the part of a plaintiff rendering it inequitable for the plaintiff to rely on the equitable doctrine of promissory estoppel; this aspect of the decision of Keane J. in *Truck and Machinery Sales v. Marubeni Komatsu* supplies another.

DEFENCES

Contributory negligence Contributory negligence is often seen to reduce liability in the tort of negligence. However, it can also reduce liability in contract (sections 2 and 34(1) of the Civil Liability Act, 1961; *Lyons v. Thomas* [1986] I.R. 666 (H.C., Murphy J.). This would seem to be sufficient to meet claims for negligent misstatement in tort and for damages in contract under the terms of section 45(1) of the Sale of Goods and Supply of Services 1980. In England, where there is no equivalent extension of the principle of contributory negligence in the Law Reform (Contributory Negligence) Act, 1945 beyond tort (see section 4 of the 1945 Act), it has however been held that a claim under section 2(1) of the Misrepresentation Act, 1967 – which is in the same terms as section 45(1) of the Irish 1980 Act – is nevertheless susceptible to a (partial) defence of contibutory negligence (*Gran Gelato v. Richcliff* [1992] Ch 560, 572-575). In light of such considerations, in *O'Donnell v. Truck and Machinery Sales* (High Court, June 7, 1996) (discussed in the Implied Terms section, below, 199) Moriarty J. held that the defendant's liability in damages for negligent misrepresentation in tort, and under the terms of section 45 of the 1980 Act in contract, could "in principle" (p. 13) be reduced by the plaintiffs' contributory negligence, though he continued that he "would readily accept that in many commercial cases involving representations or contractual terms it may be deemed inappropriate".

He had found that O'Donnell were liable for such misrepresentations in relation to the sale of Volvo L150 mechanical shovels to TMS; TMS had requested that they be fitted with larger tyres, and one of O'Donnell's misrepresentations consisted in his failure to give an adequate warning about the unsuitability of these larger tyres. On the question whether TMS were guilty of contributory negligence in requesting the larger tyres, Moriarty J. held that since TMS "insisted on a relatively radical departure from the then standard specification for . . . commercial reasons, in the knowledge that it must to some degree impact negatively upon performance, albeit not to the extent of general sluggishness . . . some appropriate discounting on a basis of contributory negligence will be required" (p. 14) and was in fact awarded (pp. 18-19).

The National Lottery   It was only a matter of time before the new national pastime, the National Lottery, generated litigation; the only surprise is that the first reported decision comes ten years after the National Lottery Act, 1986 installed the Lottery in the national psyche. That decision is *Carroll v. An Post National Lottery Company* [1996] 1 I.R. 443 (analysed further in this chapter in the sections on Exclusion Clauses (immediately below), Implied Terms (197-99), and Offer and Acceptance (208-10). In *Carroll*, if Costello P. had found that the failure by a vendor to process a tendered playslip amounted to a breach of contract by the Lottery company, he indicated (*obiter*) that, as the "plaintiff was bound by the term of the contract which incorporated the rule requiring examination of the ticket by a player after its receipt (Rule 4(5)(a)) and as this rule was breached" a slight degree of contributory neglience would have been established, amounting to 10% of the relevant liability. ([1996] 1 I.R. 443, 465-466).

EXCLUSION   CLAUSES

Incorporation   A contract may contain terms set out on its face, or it may incorporate a clause or clauses by reference to other documents. For example, in *Sweeney v. Mulcahy* [1993] I.L.R.M. 289, an architect, in respect of work to be done in 1984, had sent the plaintiff a copy of Royal Institute of Architects of Ireland Conditions of Engagement; in 1987, the same architect offered to carry out other work subject to the RIAI conditions. O'Hanlon J. held that "the agreement between the plaintiff and the defendant must be regarded as incorporating the RIAI Conditions . . . as this was expressly put forward by the defendant at the outset as the basis upon which she was prepared to act as architect in the matter . . ." ([1993] I.L.R.M. 289, 291). However, the cirsumstances are often more disputed – and thus scrutinised with more care by the courts – when the clause which it is sought to incorporate is one which excludes the liability of one party for injury or loss caused to the other. In such circumstances, "[i]f the exemption clause is set out, or referred to, in a document which is simply handed by one party to the other . . . it will be incorporated into the contract only if reasonable notice of its existence is given to the party adversely affected by it. . . . The party relying on the exemption clause need not show that he actually brought it to the notice of the other party, but only that he took reasonable steps to do so. The test is whether the former party took such steps – not whether the latter should, in the exercise of reasonable caution, have discovered or read the clause." (Treitel, *The Law of Contract* (Sweet & Maxwell, London, 9th ed, 1995), p. 198).

Many of the early leading cases on this involve plaintiffs suing railway companies. In such cases, railway tickets often had printed on their face an instruction like "See Back". On the back, there was often a statement to the effect that the ticket was issued subject to the conditions set out in the company's timetables or bye-laws; these conditions almost invariably contained exclusion clauses. If the plaintiff had read such conditions and then bought a ticket, he would of course be taken to have agreed to contract on the basis of such conditions. The difficulties began where a plaintiff had not read the conditions, and the question was whether the defendant railway company could nevertheless rely on any exclusion clauses contained in such conditions. In the early days of the railways in Ireland and England, it was held that the railway companies could rely on such clauses, first, because the plaintiff had the means to read the timetable or bye-law and thus had constructive notice (as in the early Irish case of *Johnson v. Great Souther and Western Railway Co* (1874) I.R. 9 C.L. 108), and then, in a change of focus from the position of the plaintiff to the actions of the defendant, because the steps taken by the defendant to bring the clause to the attention of the plaintiff were reasonable in the circumstances, as in the early and leading English case of *Parker v. South East Railway* (1877) 2 C.P.D. 416. In that case, the plaintiffs had deposited his bag at the defendant's cloak room, and received a ticket the front of which contained *inter alia* the words "see back" and the back of which contained an exclusion clause. The bag was lost or stolen, the plaintiff sued, and the defendant sought to rely on the exclusion clause. Mellish L.J. held that "if in the course of making a contract one party delivers to another a paper containing writing, and the party receiving the paper *knows* that the paper contains conditions which the party delivering it intends to constitute the contract, I have no doubt that the party receiving the paper does, by receiving and keeping it, assent to the conditions contained in it, although he does not read, and does not know what they are". ((1877) 2 C.P.D. 416, 421, *per* Mellish L.J. (emphasis added)). As to whether the "party receiving the paper" in fact *"knows* that the paper contains conditions", Mellish L.J. went on to hold that if what the railway company "do is sufficient to inform people in general that the ticket contains conditions", if what they do, in other words, is "reasonable notice that the writing contained conditions" (p. 423) such a party will be taken to have so known. Consequently, in what has become the classical statement of the relevant principles, Mellish L.J. summarised the relevant law in a series of directions for a jury:

> if the person receiving the ticket did not see or know that there was writing on the ticket, he is not bound by those conditions; . . .

> if he knew there was writing, and knew or believed that the writing contained conditions, then he is bound by those conditions . . .

> if he knew there was writing on the ticket, but did not know or believe that the writing contained conditions, nevertheless he would be bound if the delivering of the ticket to him in such a manner that he could see there was writing upon it, was, in the opinion of the jury, reasonable notice that the writing contained conditions. (423).

On this analysis, whether the plaintiff is bound by the exclusion clause turns on whether he knew of its existence, which itself turns on first, whether he knew there was writing on the ticket, and second, whether the defendant had taken reasonable steps to bring to the attention of the plaintiff that the writing contained or referred to conditions such as the exclusion clause. In *Parker*, the requirement that the plaintiff know that there was writing on the ticket was important, since at the time, such a tickets was regarded "'as a mere voucher for the reciept of the package deposited, and a means of identifying him as the owner when he sought to reclaim it' and in that sense not containing any special condition to which his attention was to be drawn". (*Thompson v. London Midland & Scottish Railway* [1930] 1 K.B. 41, 49-50 *per* Lord Hanworth M.R.). Thus, where writing on a ticket or receipt was not usual, for a plaintiff to be bound by such writing, he must have known of it; but, once he knows of it, (even, it seems, if the plaintiff was aware only in a vague and general way that the ticket is issued subject to some conditions, as in *Taggant v. Northern Counties Railway* (1897) 31 I.L.T. 404n (Palles C.B.)) he is bound by any conditions of which he was aware or in respect of which the defendant had taken reasonable steps to bring to his attention.

Where writing on tickets and receipts was the exception, it was necessary that there be a finding of suh specific knowledge; but according as such writing became practically universal, courts almost came to regard it as a matter of general knowledge that there would be such writing, and the cases turned instead simply on whether the defendant had taken reasonable steps to ensure that the fact that the writing contained conditions including exclusion clauses had been brought to the attention of the plaintiff. If Mellish L.J. in *Parker* provided a classical offer and acceptance analysis for the case in which the plaintiff did not have such general knowledge, the later decision of Swift J. in *Nunan v. Southern Rly Co* [1923] 2 KB 703 provided a similar analysis for the case in which the plaintiff did possess such general knowledge: "where a contract is made by the delivery . . . of a document in a common form stating the terms upon which the person delivering it will enter into the proposed contract, such a form constitutes the offer of the party who tenders it, and if the form is accepted without objection . . . [the acceptor] is as a general rule bound by its contents and his act amounts to an acceptance whether he reads the document or otherwise informs himself of its contents or not, and the conditions contained in the document are binding upon him" (47; approved in *Thompson v. London Midland & Scottish Railway* [1930] 1 K.B. 41, 47 *per* Lord Hanworth M.R.; see also *ibid.,* p. 51).

The position which emerges from the ticket cases – which seemed to have come to assume assume that a plaintiff is aware, as a matter of general knowledge, that tickets and receipts contain writing, – is that if the actions of the defendant in seeking to bring the clause to the attention of the plaintiff are reasonable, the clause will be effective. A particularly striking example of this is supplied by *Thompson v. London Midland & Scottish Railway* [1930] 1 K.B. 41, a niece and her father as agents for an illiterate aunt bought her a railway ticket. The ticket said "Excursion. For conditions see back"; the back referred on to the conditions in the company's timetables which contained an exclusion clause; and the Court of Appeal held that such steps constituted reasonable notice to the agents and thus to the aunt. Indeed, for them, it was the only question to be decided (see, e.g. at p. 52 *per* Lawrence L.J.; at p. 54 *per* Sankey L.J.). To similar effect on the question of reasonable notice are the decisions of the Supreme Court in *Early v. Great Southern Railway* [1940] I.R. 409 (*cp* the earlier *Stewart v. London and NW Rly Co* (1864) 33 L.J. (Ex.) 199) and Davitt P. in *Shea v. Great Southern Railway* [1944] Ir. Jur. Rep. 26. Of course, if the steps taken by the defendant are not reasonable, (as in *Ryan v. Great Southern & Western Railway* (1898) 32 I.L.T.R. 108, where the conditions could not have been learned without special enquiry) then the plaintiff will not be held to have notice of the terms and will not be bound by them.

The National Lottery has introduced many new kinds of tickets, playslips, cards and so on, many of which contain or refer to exclusion clauses. Whether the exclusion clauses referrred to on a playslip were properly incorporated was the key issue in the judgment of Costello P. in *Carroll v. An Post National Lottery Company* [1996] 1 I.R. 443, which in many ways provides a moden example of the railway ticket cases discussed above. The plaintiff handed four Lotto playslips to a vendor, who processed three, one twice. He failed to process the fourth, which the plaintiff claimed contained the numbers which won the relevant Lotto draw. He claimed that this amounted, first, to negligence for which the Lottery company were vicariously liable, and, second, to a breach of contract by the Lottery company itself. On the plaintiff's claim in tort, Costello P. held that the vendor was an independent contractor for whose negligence the Lottery company was not vicariously liable. On the plaintiff's claim in contract, Costello P. held that no term, express or implied, had been breached. Had one been, the defendant claimed that the exclusion clauses in the contract provided them with a complete defence, and "as the parties may [have] wish[ed] to have [a] decision on all the issues that have been raised" Costello P. considered "whether or not the defendant company can rely on the exemption clauses . . ." ([1996] 1 I.R. 443, 459). Strictly speaking, therefore, Costello P.'s conclusions on this issue are *obiter*, but it arose as follows. On the front of the playslip, at the bottom, and printed in red in block captials, was the direction to the player: "See Instructions On Reverse Side". On the reverse side, under the heading "Rules and Regulations" it was provided that:

> tickets may not be sold to persons under the age of 18. The National Lottery, its agents or contractors, shall not be responsible for lost or stolen tickets. Players acknoledge that Lotto Agents are acting on their behalf in entering plays into the National Lottery computer system. The National Lottery accepts no responsibility for tickets cancelled in error or where the apparent numbers on a ticket disagree with the numbers on file at the central computer for that ticket.

Immediately following it, in bold type, it was provided that:

> By playing the game, a player agrees to abide by the National Lottery Rules and Regulations in effect at the time the play is made. A summary of these rules is available for inspection at your local Lotto Agent.

Those rules and regulations (as authorised by the Minister for Finance pursuant to the terms of section 28 of the National Lottery Act, 1986) in turn provided that:

> The National Lottery shall not in any circumstances be liable to a player for any acts or ommissions by the Lotto agents. (Rule 4(3)(f))

Applying the rules of offer and acceptance (below, 208-10) Costello P. held that the terms of the contract were "contained on the reverse side of the playslip", that the clause in bold type "incorporated into their contract all terms of the rules authorised by the Minister", so that the "two exemption clauses . . . Rule 4(3)(f) of the incorporated rules and [the] 'playslip exemption' printed on the reverse of the playslip, are part of the parties' contractual terms" ([1996] 1 I.R. 443, 454). Thus, he found as a fact:

> that the plaintiff knew there were rules printed on the reverse side of the playslip and that he did not read them. This finding means that . . . the plaintiff is bound by them (see *Parker v. South Eastern Railway* (1877) 2 CPD 416, 423) and they are enforceable terms of the parties' contract. And this applies both to the term printed on the reverse side of the playslip by which a player accepted that the Lotto agents acted on their behalf in entering plays into the National Lottery computer system and also to the Rule 4(3)(f) incorporated into the contract by the term on the reverse side (see *Thompson v. London Midland and Scotish Railway Co* [1930] 1 K.B. 41). This means that, in principle, . . . [these terms] had contractual effect . . . and will be enforced by the courts. ([1996] 1 I.R. 443, 461; cp 456).

Costello P. qualified this in two ways:

> [First.] When it is generally known that tickets and other documents which contain documents are not read by those to whom they are given there is an implied understanding that there is no condition included in them which is unreasonable to the knowledge of the party tendering them . . . So, if it can be shown in this case that either of the exemption clauses on whic the defendant relies was unreasonable the plaintiff is not bound by it. [Second,] if the condition relied on by the party tendering the document is particularly onerous or unusual that party must show that it has been fairly and reasonably brought to the other party's attention. ([1996] 1 I.R. 443, 461; citing, for the second qualification, *Spurling v. Bradshaw* [1956] 3 All E.R. 121; *Thornton v. Shoe Lane Parking* [1971] 2 Q.B. 163; *Interfoto Picture Library v. Stilletto Visual Programmes* [1989] Q.B. 433).

There is much here to conjure with. For example, though the ticket cases proceed from a position that the the plaintiff must have known at least that there was writing on the relevant ticket, the fact that the existence of such writing on such tickets is almost a matter of common knowledge has meant that in many of the more recent analyses, courts and commentators have proceeded directly to the question whether the actions of the defendant were reasonable in bringing any conditions in the writing to the attention of the plaintiff. However, for Costello P. in *Carroll*, the "fact that the plaintiff knew there were rules printed on the reverse side of the playslip . . . *means* that . . . the plaintiff is bound by them" (emphasis added, citing *Parker v. South Eastern Railway* (1877) 2 C.P.D. 416, 423); here, Costello P. has gone back to first principles and reaffirmed that the knowledge of the plaintiff is the base from which further analysis proceeds. Building upon *Parker*, many subsequent authorities establish the proposition that, where a plaintiff has not read the terms and conditions before entering into the contract, the defendant must have taken reasonable steps to bring the terms to the notice of the plaintiff before the plaintiff is bound by them. *Carroll* draws attention once more to the logically prior proposition that a plaintiff who knows that there are rules or conditions printed on the reverse side of a ticket or playslip is bound by them, whether or not the defendant took reasonable steps to bring them to his attention. In this respect, his decision provides a welcome and crucial reminder of this important matter. However, since the existence of such rules on such playslips is a matter of common knowledge, Costello P. could have reached the same conclusion on the basis of Swift J's analysis in *Nunan*. Indeed, – and notwithstanding the examples given in the judgment of Mellish L.J. in *Parker*, – it is now difficult to conceive of circumstances in which a plaintiff could successfully plead that he was not aware (whether as a matter of specific or of general knowldge) that a ticket did not contain some writing.

The terms in which Costello P. chose to express the first of his two qualifications above are, however, not free from difficulty. In the ticket cases, the courts required that reasonable steps be taken by the railway companies to bring conditions to the notice of the passanger; in the modern development of the ticket cases approved by Costello P., the courts required that onerous or unusual terms be specifically brought to the attention of the other party. In both such situations, a court is not striking down the clause because of its substance but because the process by which it was sought to be incorporated was not sufficient to bring it to the attention of the other party. In other words, the court is not so much concerned with the reasonableness or the substantive fairness of the term as with the reasonableness of the procedure by which the term became part of the contract (on the distinction between procedural and substantive unfairness, see, e.g., Leff "Unconscionability and the Code: The Emperor's New Clause" 117 *U.Pal. Rev.* 485 (1967); for an application of the distinction, see, e.g., *Hart v. O'Connor* [1985] A.C. 1000, 1018 *per* Lord Brightman; for various critiques of Leff's conception, see Craswell 60 *UChiLRev* 1 (1993); Epstein 18 *Journal of Law and Economics* 293 (1975); Schwartz 63 *Virginia L.Rev.* 1053 (1977)). Sometimes, statute adds a requirement of substantive fairness to one of procedural fairness; for example, section 40(1) of the Sale of Goods and Supply of Services Act, 1980, provides that ". . . any term of a contract implied by virture of section 39 may be negatived or varied by an express term . . . except that where the recipient of the service deals as a consumer it must be shown that the express term is fair and reasonable and has been specifically brought to his attention." The express statutory requirement that, in certain circumstances, an exclusion clause be fair and reasonable, is a requirement of susbstantive fairness, additional to the requirement of procedural fairness that the clause be brought specifically to the consumer's attention. Absent such express statutory examples, the focus of the common law's protection is not on the substantive fairness of the term but upon the procedural fairness of the process by which it became a term of the contract.

On the other hand, there are some faint traces of substantive fairness in both *Parker* and *Thompson*. Thus, in the former, Bramwell L.J. was of the view that there should be "an implied understanding that there is no condition unreasonable to the knowledge of the party tendering the document and not insisting on its being read" ((1877) 2 C.P.D. 416, 428), a view approved in the latter by Lord Hanworth MR ([1930] 1 K.B. 41, 50) and Lawrence L.J. ([1930] 1 K.B. 41, 53). Neverthekess, it is clear that Bramwell L.J.'s *dictum* is predicated not upon the unreasonableness of the term *per se*, but upon the failure of the party tendering it to insist upon it being read. In other words, the *dictum* requires that the unreasonable term be struck down, not because it was unreasonable, but because it was not brought to the attention of the other party. In this respect, therefore, it is no more than a precursor to Lord Denning's judgments in *Spurling* and *Thornton*, (and Bingham L.J.'s judgment in *Interfoto* folloing them) and is still consistent with notions of procedural rather than of substantive unfairness. Indeed, in *Carroll*, Costello P. specifically approved this line of authority (in his second qualification above), and, applying it, held that neither exclusion clause was particularly onerous or unusual, so that defendant Lottery company was "not required to give special notice of these particular terms to the purchasers" ([1996] 1 I.R. 445, 465).

Nevertheless, in *Carroll*, referring, it seems, to Bramwell L.J.'s *dictum* above, Costello P. also held that "if it can be shown in this case that either of the exemption clauses on which the defendant relies was unreasonable the plaintiff is not bound by it." To hold that if a clause is unreasonable, the other party is not bound by it, is to focus on the substantive fairness or reasonableness of the term rather than upon the reasonableness of the procedure by which the term became part of the contract. That Costello P. understood this to mean that an unreasonable exclusion clause is not binding seems to be borne out by his enquiry into whether the clauses were reasonable ([1996] 1 I.R. 443, 464), his conclusion that they were, and his view that his conclusions on the common law "*also* means that . . . there had been compliance with section 40 of the Act of 1980" ([1996] 1 I.R. 443, 465; emphasis added). This could only be so if, in Costello P.'s opinion, the common law analysis which he derived from the ticket cases contained a focus upon the substantive fairness of the terms, as the statutory analysis expressly requires.

Lord Denning, in another of his innovations – that, as a matter of law, an exclusion clause could not exclude liability for a fundamental breach – made an attempt in this area to move from the traditional focus upon procedural fairness to a focus instead upon the substantive fairness or reasonableness of the term itself. This radical approach sat uncomfortably with the orthodox common law focus upon procedural fairness, until, in England, the Unfair Contract Terms Act 1977 gave the courts a more general power to police the substantive fairness of certain contractual terms, supplemented now by the statutory instrument (S.I. No. 3159 of 1994) implementing the *Unfair Contract Terms Directive*, and they felt able to abandon Lord Denning's approach in favour of the statutory regime. Whether Irish law has or should have likewise abandoned that approach is unclear and is the focus of the analysis in the1995 Review. For present purposes, it is sufficient to note that if Costello P. is properly to be taken as having said, in *Carroll*, that an unreasonable exclusion clause is not binding, then he seems to have gone even further than Lord Denning's doctrine of fundamental breach. This is not to say that such a development is unwelcome – indeed, there is much to be said for the development of doctrine of substantive fairness (see, e.g., Smith "In Defence of Substantive Fairness" (1996) 112 *L.Q.R.* 138, where, however, the analysis focusses on harmful abnormal prices as the index of substantive unfairness) – it is merely to point out that, not only is it *obiter*, but the ticket cases from which Costello P. purported to derive this development do not support it.

In any event, it is clear from Costello P.'s judgment that, whether one applied a test focussed upon whether the defendant had taken reasonable steps to bring the terms to the notice of the plaintiff (the traditional test), or a test focussed upon whether the terms were reasonable (as Costello P. seems to have done), the defendant Lottery Company could rely on the conditions on the reverse of the playslip. First, as to whether the defendant had taken such reasonable steps, Costello P. held that they had "done what was reasonably necessary to bring to the notice of the purchasers of Lotto tickets the exempting term relating to the status of the agent printed on the back of the playslip by drawing the attention of purchasers to 'instructions' on the rear of the playslip and by printing the exempting term in such a way as to make it readily accessible to, and understandable by, readers of the matter printed on the reverse side of the playslip." ([1996] 1 I.R. 445, 465). He had earlier, in a passage set out above, held that the exclusion clause comprised in Rule 4(3)(f) referred to but not set out on the playslip was also incorporated ([1996] 1 I.R. 443, 461; cp 456), approving *Thompson*. Indeed, given that Costello P. had no difficulty in finding that reference on the reverse of a playslip to a set of rules – set by and available from the Minister, but only a summary of which was available from the vendor – was sufficient notice, it may be questioned whether Treitel's speculation that "it seems probable that the steps taken [in *Thompson*] to incorporate the clause would not now be regarded as sufficient" (Treitel, p. 199) accurately reflects the position in Ireland. On the other hand, in *Ryan v. Great*

Southern & Western Railway (1898) 32 I.L.T.R. 108, where the conditions could not have been learned without special enquiry, Gisbon J. held that the "defendants failed to do what was reasonably sufficient to give the plaintiff notice of the restriction of liability" ((1898) 32 I.L.T.R. 108, 108); *quaere* whether the availability from the vendor of merely a summary of the rules, coupled with the need to enquire of the Lottery company or of the Minister for a full set of the rules, might not amount to such "special enquiry"? Furthermore, it would not be difficult for a clause in terms similar to Rule 4(3)(f), excluding any liability of Lottery company for any acts or ommissions by the vendor, to be added to the reverse of the playslip in the paragraph containing the agency exemption; perhaps, therefore, it would not be difficult to hold that this incorporation by reference does not amount to the taking of reasonable steps.

Second, as to whether the exclusion clauses were reasonable, Costello P. held that Rule 4(3)(f) exempting the Lottery company from vicarious liability for the negligence of vendors is "merely declaratory of the existing legal position, and is therefore reasonable." ([1996] 1 I.R. 445, 464). He further held that the term relating to agency printed on the reverse of the playslip "must be construed as meaning that the Lotto agent is acting s the *company's* agent (not the *player's* agent) when receiving playslips and entering them into the terminal. . . . [This] draws attention and gives effect to the rule by which the company is not liable for the agent's negligence. . . . [It] is declaratory of the existing legal position . . . [because] it gives recognition to the legal relationship arising from the rules authorised by the Minister." (*Id.*) Furthermore, both exemptions were reasonable protection from fraud, as "the absence of a protective exemption clause might make the whole National Lottery unworkable" (*Id.*) However, whilst the need to protect itself from fraud might make *some* exclusion clause reasonable, it does not necessarily make *every* exclusion clause reasonable; whether a particular clause is in fact reasonable would depend on the proper interpretation of its terms; and that interpretation would be informed by the standard rules for the interpretation of exclusion clauses, in particular, the *contra proferentem* rule. Thus, although the absence of an exclusion clause might make the Lottery unworkable, it is up to the Lottery company to draft with special care a clause which achieves that end, even when, consistently with the *contra proferentem* rule, the clause is read strictly against the interests of the Lottery company; it is not for a court to supply a broad interpretation to the clause to achieve an end which eluded those who drafted the clause. Thus, on the question of whether the need to protect itself from fraud justified the Lottery company inserting an exclusion, Costello P.'s analysis was incomplete; but, in the light of his finding that the clauses were declaratory of the general law, this is not fatal to his conclusion that the exclusion clauses were reasonable.

Of course, as we have seen, section 40 of the 1980 Act makes such an enquiry necessary if a term has been implied by section 39 and the contract seeks to exclude liability for its breach. In *Carroll*, Costello P. held that contract between the plaintiff-player and the defendant-Lottery company was not one for the supply of a service, and so the section 39 and the section 40 enquiry did not arise; but he went on to hold that if it were a contract for the supply of a service, "the exemption printed on the playslip to the effect that the Lotto agent at the time was the player's agent was brought to the plaintiff's attention and as required by section 40 the implied term on which the plaintiff relies had been lawfully negatived in this case". ([1996] 1 I.R. 445, 459). Returning to that point in the aftermath of his conclusion that the exclusion clauses were reasonable at common law, Costello P. held that this "also means that . . . there had been compliance with section 40 of the Act of 1980 in that the term was fair and reasonable and had been specifically brought to the plaintiff's attention." ([1996] 1 I.R. 445, 465).

Finally, the question whether exclusion clauses form part of a contract is only half the battle; there must also be an enquiry as to whether the clauses are sufficiently precisely drafted to exclude the particular breach, and in this interpretation exercise, the clauses are construed strictly *contra proferentem*. Though the plaintiff submitted that the clauses were not free from doubt so that the *contra proferentem* rule was applicable; in particular, the plaintiff submitted that since the playslip exclusion clause contained an acknowledgement that the Lotto vendor was acting on behalf of the player in "entering plays into the National Lottery computer system", and the act of negligence ocurred "when the playslip was not being entered into the computer system" the exemption clause does not apply. ([1996] 1 I.R. 445, 460). Costello P. does not seem anywhere to have provided a direct reply to this submission, but even if this clause does not protect the defendant Lottery company, the other exclusion clause contained in Rule 4(3)(f) that the "National Lottery shall not in any circumstances be liable to a player for any acts or ommissions by the Lotto agents" would seem, on even the strictest *contra proferentem* reading, capable of excluding the Lottery company's liability to the plaintiff.

In the end, therefore, this aspect of *Carroll v. An Post National Lottery Co* came to this: whether the contract between the plaintiff and the defendant contain a clause or clauses which successfully exclude any liability which the defendant may bear towards to the plaintiff; and, though *obiter*, Costello P. held that it did.

GOOD FAITH

The principle of good faith has recetly begun to find a place in the sun in the common law (see e.g. O'Connor, *Good Faith in English Law* (Dartmouth, 1990) and Beatson and Friedmann (eds.), *Good Faith and Fault in Contract*

Law (Clarendon Press, Oxford, 1995). This development has been especially marked in Australia; thus, in an important judgment in *Renard Constructions v. Minister for Public Works* (1992) 26 N.S.W.L.R. 234 (N.S.W. C.A.) 263-268; (1992) 33 Con. L.R. 72, 107-113, Priestly JA, building upon a paper by Lord Steyn (since published as "The Role of Good Faith and Fair Dealing in Contract Law: A Hair-Shirt Philosophy ?" (1991) Denning L.J. 131), derived a principle of good faith as a matter of Australian law.

The main modern attempt in England to develop and deploy a common law principle of good faith is to be found in the judgment of Bingham L.J. in the Court of Appeal in *Interfoto Picture Library v. Stilletto Visual Programmes* [1989] Q.B. 433 rationalising the requirement that onerous conditions be specifically brought to a contracting party's attention on that basis (on which issue, see now generally Harrison, *Good Fatih in Sales* (Sweet & Maxwell, London, 1997) esp chapters 2 and 18). Though the House of Lords seems, in the later case of *Walford v. Miles* [1992] 2 A.C. 128 (HL), to have treated a principle of good faith in negotiation as inconsistent with the common law, Colombo "Good Faith: The Law and Morality" (1993) Denning L.J. 23 argues that the ethic of individualism, upon which objections to good faith reasoning in the common law are founded, does not in fact preclude some limitations upon economic ruthlessness, allowing the choice in favour of a principle of good faith to be sqaurely faced. Again, Bingham LJ's approach in *Interfoto* also underlies the Unfair Contract Terms Directive (see the 1995 Review, 197-201), and there is now a substantial body of academic literature on the contours of the emerging principle of good faith in English law (see e.g. Brownsword (1994) 7 *JCL* 197; Brownsword (1996) 49(2) *C.L.P.* 11). There some are important traces of an incohate good faith principle in Irish law. Thus, in *Hickey v. Roches Stores (No. 1)* [1993] *Restitution Law Review* 196 (14 July 1976) Finlay P. held that a party who makes a profit from a bad faith breach of contract must make restitution of that profit to the innocent party. And in the 1993 Review, it was argued that the expansive Irish judicial deployment of the principle of good faith in insurance cases was such as to make it "clear that if the Irish judiciary were to discover a duty of good faith elsewhere or more generally in the law of contract, they would be able to deal with its complexities".

Another appreciable trace of good faith in the judgment of Costello P. in *Carroll v. An Post National Lottery Co.* [1996] 1 I.R. 445 seems to bring the development of such a generalised principle ever closer. In *Carroll*, the plaintiff had sued the Lottery company for a breach of contract, comprised in the failure of the vendor to process a playslip, and the defendant had sought to rely on certain exclusion clauses (immediately above). Approving the approach of Bingham L.J. in *Interfoto*, Costello P. explained, *obiter*, that whilst the refusal of the courts to permit a party to rely on unfair or onerous clauses was based on the principles of consent underlying the law of contract generally, it

was also based on "the application of the concept of fair dealing in the particular circumstances" ([1996] 1 I.R. 445, 463). Indeed, in *Carroll*, Costello P.
held, *obiter* in respect of the rules to be derived from the antecedent ticket
cases that "if it can be shown in this case that either of the exemption clauses
on which the defendant relies was unreasonable the plaintiff is not bound by
it" ([1996] 1 I.R. 443, 461). It was submitted above that this focus on the
substantive fairness of the term is not justified by the authorities relied upon
by Costello P.; but if it is nonetheless accepted, then, as an example of how
Irish law is prepared to test the fairness of the terms of the contract, it may also
be presented as another infiltration of good faith notions into Irish law. Given
that the decision of Bingham L.J. was one of the matters relied upon by Lord
Steyn in his paper (*supra*) and by Priestly J.A. in *Renard* in their spelling out
of a common law principle of good faith, the decision of Costello P. in *Carroll*
may be another important straw suggesting that the wind in Ireland is beginning to blow in favour of a principle of good faith, as it seems strongly now to
do in Australia.

ILLEGALITY

Evolving flexibility   The 1993 Review (184-189) and the 1995 Review (204-
9) contained analyses of increasing judicial flexibility – under the guise of the
'public conscience' test – when faced with a plea that a claim fails for illegality. Perhaps an example of such flexibility, though not in that guise, is to be
found in *Vogelaar v. Callaghan*   [1996] 1 I.R. 88 (see Simons (1996) *Bar
Review* 68). The parties had entered into a building contract containing terms
designed to underpay VAT. A dispute arose, which was referred to arbitration,
and the arbiter awarded the builder £ 13,270.10 inclusive of VAT. On an application to set aside the award (on which see, generally, Simons (1997) 15
I.L.T. (n.s.) 74) Barron J. acknowledged that the "courts will not stand over an
illegal contract" but continued that "the arbitrator has made it clear that he did
not regard the contract as being one to defraud the Revenue in respect of VAT.
There is no reason for seeking to upset that decision upon the grounds that it
could not have been come to. The arbitrator heard the evidence and was in a
proper position to ascertain the truth". ([1996] 1 I.R. 88, 93; [1996] 2 I.L.R.M.
226, 231).

   Barron J. has in the past taken a much less tolerant attitude to contracts to
defraud the Revenue (see, e.g., *Hayden v. Quinn* [1994] E.L.R. 45; on which
see Barry (1994) 12 *I.L.T. (ns)* 32, and the 1993 Review, pp. 188-189, 379,
where *Hayden* is criticised as a step back to the days before the evolving
judicial flexibility to illegality as a consequence of the public conscience test)
and the courts in general have not been slow to refuse to entertain contractual

or restitutionary claims arising out of building contracts tainted by illegality (see, e.g., *Taylor v. Bhail* [1996] C.L.C. 377; on which see Rose (1996) 112 *LQR* 545). It would not therefore have been difficult for Barron J. to hold that the contract was void for illegality, thereby posing the question whether the arbitration clause could survive (see, e.g. *Harbour Insurance v. Kansa General* [1993] Q.B. 701 where that question was answered in the affirmative: see pp. 708-709 *per* Ralph Gibson L.J., 715-717 *per* Leggatt L.J., 722-726 *per* Hoffmann L.J., and, at first instance: [1992] 1 Lloyd's Rep 81, 93 *per* Steyn J.). Of course, the general trend is for the courts to hold that an arbitration clause in a contract terminated by a supervening event may survive (*Heyman v. Darwins* [1942] A.C. 356 (H.L.); *Parkarran v. M&P Construction* [1996] 1 I.R. 83; cf. *Superwood v. Sun Alliance* [1995] 3 I.R. 303, 377-381 *per* Blayney J., criticised in the 1995 Review, 231-2). Such decisions are often seen as evidence of strong policy of judicial support of the arbitration process; and whilst they deal with terminated valid contracts, it may be that decisions like *Harbour Insurance* and *dicta* like that of Barron J. above, allowing the issue of whether the contract is void for illegality to go to the arbitrator, simply illustrate that such a policy may be sufficiently strong to allow such matters as the prior validity of the contract to be referred to arbitration: for example, in *Harbour Insurance*, Hoffmann L.J. was of the view that it "is necessary to bear in mind the owerful commercial reasons for upholding arbitration clauses unless it is clear that this would offend the policy of the illegality rule" ([1993] Q.B. 701, 724).

On the other hand, the essential point in *Heyman* is that in a contract which is terminated, certain clauses can continue to bind the parties; and it may be questioned whether the same logic can apply to a contract void *ab initio* (compare Mustill and Boyd *Commercial Arbitration* (2nd ed, Butterworths, London, 1989), p. 113). In such a case, there being no contract in the first place, there is no binding arbitration clause, and thus no jurisdiction for the arbitrator. Nevertheless, by allowing the issue to be adjudicated upon, the decision of Barron J. in *Vogelaar* – like the decision of the Court of Appeal in *Harbour Assurance* – may be indicative of a softening of judicial hostility to illegality, since, in its strictest form, the maxim *ex turpi causa non oritur actio* would necessarily render a contract void and – on the analysis immediately above – preclude any adjudication upon a dispute arising from it. By allowing an arbitrator to address that question, the implication is that the alleged illegality need not automatically have the effect of rendering the contract void.

An more express example of such flexibility is to be found in the judgment of Keane J. in *Carrigaline Community Television Broadcasting v. Minister for Transport* [1997] 1 I.L.R.M. 241. In the context of pleas based upon equitable principles such as laches and the maxim that he who comes to equity must come with clean hands ([1997] 1 I.L.R.M. 241, 292-293), Keane J. observed that there "is also a legal principle of more general appliction, which has been invoked in these proceedings, *ex turpi causa non oritur actio*. This maxim recognises the reluctance of courts to allow thoe who have themselves repudiated the law to invoke the law when it seems expedient to them to do so". ([1997] 1 I.L.R.M. 241, 293). Note first that Keane J. described a judicial *"reluctance"*, not a judicial refusal. In applying the equitable principles, Keane J. was prepared to grant some relief to the plaintiff, notwithstanding "significant delay" and "circumstances which render it arguably inequitable to grant the relief in the present case" ([1997] 1 I.L.R.M. 241, 299) since he was prepared to "have regard to the serious injustice that would result to the plaintiffs if they were refused relief in the circumstances where, as I have found, they have been unjustifiably deprived by the Minister of their constitutional right to a fair and impartial assessment of their application." ([1997] 1 I.L.R.M. 241, 300). And, in a similarly flexible application of the maxim *ex turpi causa non oritur actio*, although the plaintiffs' rebroadcasting activities were in breach of the law, Keane J. held that:

> A court required to uphold the law cannot condone or excuse that conduct. Nor should it seek to punish the offender by depriving him of his constitutional rights. . . . The salutory *ex turpi causa* maxim and the equitable principle that he who comes to equity must come with clean hands retain their ancient vigour in the law. But they should not be allowed to work a greater injustice by depriving citizens of the right to natural justice and fair procedures. ([1997] 1 I.L.R.M. 241, 300)

If this approach to *ex turpi causa* holds good in the context of contracts, and there is every reason why it should, then, rather than simply holding that a claim fails *in limine* because the contract is tainted by illegality, a court will consider whether dismissing a plaintiff's claim would work a greater injustice than entertaining a cliam tainted by illegality. This is precisely the enquiry mandated by the public conscience test, and it is submitted that this decision of Keane J. ought to be seen as another Irish example of its application.

Contracts prejudical to the constitutionally protected special position of marriage Public policy, rendering contracts unenforceable, is at best a vague and amorphous conept, at worst a dangerous and destabilising legal doctrine. Indeed, in *Fender v. St John Mildmay* [1938] A.C. 1, Lord Atkin, after a thorough citation of authorities counselling caution in the use of such public policy, stated that "the doctrine should only be invoked in clear cases in which the harm to the public is substantially incontestable, and does not depend on the idiosyncratic inferences of a few judicial minds. In popular language . . . the contract should be given the benefit of the doubt". ([1938] A.C. 1, 12). Even more trenchantly, Lord Wright in the same case expressly disavowed the proposition that "a judge has peculiar powers in a question of public policy in acting upon his individual views of predilection and can on these grounds refuse to enforce a contract . . .". ([1938] A.C. 1, 40).

On the other hand, the common law has always regarded with suspicion contracts tending to encourage immorality, so that, for example, a payment "to a mistress for past or future habitation . . . [is given] for no consideration that law recognise[s]" (*Banque Belge pour l'Etranger v. Hambrouck* [1921] 1 KB 321 *per* Scrutton L.J.); though it now seems that where a promise by a man to pay money to a woman with whom he had "illicitly cohabited in the past is not contrary to public policy since it does not *promote* immorality. It is simply void because the consideration for it is past, and it will be valid if made in a deed". (Treitel, pp. 402-403). Furthermore, in this context, courts in other jurisdictions have been prepared to take a flexible, evolving view of immorality (e.g. Clark, *Contract Law in Ireland* (3rd ed, Sweet & Maxwell, London, 1992), pp. 298-230). Such a flexible view of whether a contract in fact is contrary to public policy is reflexive on this prior issue of the flexibility on the issue of whether, although the contract is contrary to public policy, it would nevertheless be enforced, seen in the public conscience test referred to above.

The common law has always regarded with equal suspicion contracts prejudicial to the institution of marriage. Thus, "a contract between husband and wife, made *during cohabitation*, for a future as distinguished from a present separation, is void" (*McMahon v. McMahon* [1913] 1 I.R. 428, 434 *per* Palles C.B., emphasis in original). Further, "an agreement in an ante-nuptial settlement . . . by which the husband makes provision for the wife in the event of their ceasing to cohabit, is void by reason of its being opposed to public policy". ([1913] 1 I.R. 428, 446 *per* Holmes L.J.). The Court of Appeal did accept, however, that an agreement between a *separated* couple dealing with separation was not contrary to public policy (see e.g. [1913] 1 I.R. 428, 447 *per* Holmes L.J.; 440-441 *per* Palles C.B. following, on this point, *Wilson v. Wilson* (1848) 1 H.L.C. 538, and followed in *Courtney v. Courtney* [1923] 2 I.R. 31, in turn followed in *K v. K* (High Court, February 12, 1988, MacKenzie J.); see also *Hyman v. Hyman* [1929] A.C. 601, 625 *per* Lord Atkin; and *Fender v. St John-Mildmay* [1938] A.C. 1, 18-21 *per* Lord Atkin; 43-44 *per* Lord Wright). In *McMahon* itself, the relevant contract, between separated parties seeking to become reconciled to one another again, was intended to regulate any future separation. The Court of Appeal held that such a contract encouraged the parties to reconcile, and, since "arrival at an agreement for a reconciliation is a matter which the law ought to encourage" ([1913] 1 I.R. 428, 444 *per* Palles C.B.; cp. at 447 *per* Holmes L.J.) the contract tended "more to reconciliation and future cohabitation . . . than to future separation" (*id*), the contract was not, therefore, contrary to public policy.

The effect of Article 41 of the Constitution upon these two heads of public policy seems to have attracted little analysis, but it seems clear that it has also generated a third, related but distinct, head of public policy, and may therefore be the fount for other such heads. As to that head generated by Article 41, before the amendment of section 3 subsection 2 of that article, the constitutional prohibition upon divorce it contained gave rise to a public policy leaning heavily against divorce. In particular, courts looked with disfavour upon applications to court which were consequent upon divorce proceedings. Thus, in *Mayo-Perrott v. Mayo-Perrott* [1958] I.R. 336, the Supreme Court denied an application for the costs of a foreign divorce, Kingsmill-Moore J. holding that it could not "be doubted that the public policy of this country, as reflected in the Constitution, does not favour divorce a vinculo and though the law may recognise the change of status effected by it as an accomplished fact, it would fail to carry out public policy if, by a decree of its own Courts, it gave assistance to the process of divorce by entertaining a suit for the costs of such proceedings."([1958] I.R. 336, 350). Again, in *Dalton v. Dalton* ([1982] I.L.R.M. 418), on an application to have made a rule of court a separation agreement which contained a clause by which the parties agreed "to obtain a Decree of Divorce a Vinculo . . .", O'Hanlon J. held that "considerations of public policy require that the Court shall not lend its support to an agreement providing for the obtaining of a divorce a vinculo by a husband and wife . . .". ([1981] I.L.R.M. 418, 419). The removal of the prohibition upon divorce, and its replacement with a constititutional right to divorce, must have spelt the demise of this particular head of public policy. The lesson to be drawn, though, is that the Constitution in general, and Article 41 in particular, can generate heads of public policy capable of precluding a court's aid in enforcing contracts. However, in this context, clarity of analysis requires that each of these three heads of public policy (those which render void, first, contracts prejudicial to the institution of marriage, second, contracts tending to promote immorality, and, third, contracts contrary to any special public policy generated by Article 41) be kept clearly separate.

An illustration of just such constitutional potency seems to have been provided by the decision of Kelly J. in *Ennis v. Butterly* [1996] 1 I.R. 426; [1997] 1 I.L.R.M. 28. The parties had separated from their respective spouses, and were involved in a relationship between 1984 and 1995, during most of which time they lived together as a family. The plaintiff claimed that she and the defendant had entered into an agreeement to marry and an agreement to cohabit as a couple until the marriage was possible, and sought damages for the defendant's breach of this contract. "In consideration of that agreement, the plaintiff discontinued her business and lived as a full-time housewife and homemaker". ([1996] 1 I.R. 426, 435; [1997] 1 I.L.R.M. 28, 36). The defendant applied to have the claim struck out.

As to the first agreement, Kelly J. held that section 2 of the Family Law Act, 1981 "which abolished the action for breach of promise of marriage . . . is fatal to [that] claim . . . Indeed, even before the enactment of the Act of 1981,

at common law it had been held in England that a promise by a married person
to marry one who knew that person was already married was unenforceable as
being against public policy . . .". ([1996] 1 I.R. 426, 436; [1997] 1 I.L.R.M.
28, 36). As to the second, Kelly J. held that "the contract contended for here is
unenforceable as a matter of public policy. . . . it is clearly an attempt to enforce a contract the consideration for which is wifely services being rendered
on the part of a mistress. Such contracts were always regarded as illegal and
unenforceable and remain so." ([1996] 1 I.R. 426, 439; [1997] 1 I.L.R.M. 28,
39). Thus, since the contract was contrary to public policy, the claim for breach
would necessarily fail, and Kelly J. struck out that claim. However, the plaintiff also made a claim in tort in misrepresentation, but since Kelly J. could not
conclude that that claim must inevitably fail, he refused to strike that out, and
allowed it to proceed, but only in so far as it did not arise out of, or amount to
the indirect enforcement of, the unenforceable contract. The issues arising
from this case are also discussed in the Practice and Procedure chapter, below,
487. The analysis here is confined to the public policy issues, upon which
there seem to be two distinct holdings in Kelly J's judgment. For him, public
policy rendered necessarily unenforceable, first, a promise by a married person to marry one who knew that person was already married, and, second, an
agreement by two separated people to live together as a family pending possible marriage.

As to the first, rendering unenforceable a promise to marry by a person
already married, it does not appear from his judgment either that it was argued
to him or that he considered that that public policy may have evolved beyond
what was to be found in the cases which he cited, namely *Spiers v. Hunt* [1908]
1 K.B. 720, *Wilson v. Carnley* [1908] 1 K.B.729, and *Siveyer v. Allison* [1935]
2 K.B. 403. However, on a later issue, Kelly J. himself carried out just such
an exercise: in response to an argument based on public policy embodied in
an English case decided in 1846, Kelly J. observed that "[w]hatever may have
been the public policy in England in 1846 . . . this case must be decided upon
the public policy of this State". ([1996] 1 I.R. 426, 438; [1997] 1 I.L.R.M. 28,
38). In *Spiers v. Hunt*, a man promised to marry another woman upon the
death of his wife, but the promise was held illegal as tending to break up a
marriage, to encourage immorality and even lead to the crime of bigamy. In
Siveyer v. Allison, (followed on this point in *Siveyer v. Allison*) a man's promise to marry another woman because he believed himself entitled to have his
marriage annulled was likewise unenforceable. With respect, if the promise is
to marry when the spouse is dead, none of these reasons holds; and if the
promise is to marry upon annullment, the marriage has never in law existed,
and again none of these reasons holds. These cases received very short shrift
at the hands of the majority in *Fender v. St John Mildmay* [1938] A.C. 1 (see
e.g. at pp. 15-16 *per* Lord Atkin; at pp. 46-50 *per* Lord Wright); Lord Atkin
nevertheless accepted that "there is real substance in the objection that such a

promise tends to produce conduct which violates the solemn obligations of married life" (*id*, p. 16). With respect, whilst that may hold in respect of a valid marriage (as in *Spiers v. Hunt*), it can have no relevance to a situation where the marriage was void (as it was thought to have been in *Wilson v. Carnley*). Instead, it is suggested that the key element of these cases should be understood to be the fact that the promisee knew that there was no prospect that the promisor, because already married and thus required to be loyal to another, could carry out the promise. In the light of the major change effected to the social and legal landscape by the progressive liberalisation of divorce in England (see, e.g., Eeekelar. *Regulating Divorce* (Oxford, 1991); Stone *Road to Divorce. England 1530-1987* (Oxford, 1995)) it would not have been surprising if the public policy inherent in those three cases were to have been revised. Under the more liberal divorce regime now obtaining, the promisor would be in a position to obtain a divorce and then marry the promisee; in which case, the disability under which the promisor acted in the above cases – the lack of prospect, to the knowledge of the promisee, that the promisor, because already married, could carry out the promise, – is removed, and, on their logic, there would no longer be a bar to the enforcement of the promise.

For example, the House of Lords in *Fender v. St John Mildmay* [1938] A.C. 1 held that where a man had already obtained a decree *nisi* of divorce, and was awaiting the decree absolute, and in that interim made promises to marry, such promises were not contrary to public policy, and he could properly be held liable for their breach. Though authority prior to *Fender* suggested that a promise by a party seeking a divorce would not be enforceable (*Skipp v. Kelly* (1926) 42 T.L.R. 258, in which the divorce was described as "pending" (259) and in which the point seems to have been assumed rather than decided) the logic of Lord Atkin in *Fender* seems to apply to allow the enforceability of such agreements (though cf per Lord Thankerton at [1938] A.C. 1, 23). The abolition of the action for breach of promise to marry by section 1 of the Law Reform (Miscellaneous Provisions) Act 1970 in England meant that this issue has not been directly litigated. However, section 2 of the Act (cp section 5 of Ireland's Family Law Act 1980) contemplates some issues where the agreement is relevant, and in *Shaw v. Fitzgearld* [1992] 1 FLR 357, an already married man who promised to marry the woman upon divorce from his wife was successfully sued under section 2. In other words, public policy did not now lean against such a contract, and, since it could be relied upon in an action on foot of section 2, presumably, it would therefore have been enforceable in the absence of section 1. Thus, it seems that the three cases upon which Kelly J. relied probably no longer represent good law in England; consequently, the availability of divorce at English law has worked a change in this aspect of public policy, so that it does not now automatically render unenforceable a promise by one who is married to marry another.

As to whether Irish law has also made a similar move, for so long as marriage was constitutionally indissoluble, there would seem to be little space for such an evolution. On the other hand, both parties to *Ennis v. Butterly* were legally separated; in this respect, their duties in respect of their existing marriage were very similar to those of the husband in *Fender* between the decrees *nisi* and absolute: if his promise to marry has no impact upon his existing matrimonial obligations or upon the public interest (see [1938] A.C. 1, 16-17, 21 *per* Lord Atkin), neither should the respondent's promise in *Ennis*. Indeed, in *Fender*, Lord Atkin gave the following example: "If a respectable man whose wife has fled with the lodger leaving the children in his charge engages himself to another respectable person to marry her as soon as he is free, no public interests suffer. In my opinion they benefit, Similarly, in the converse case of a wife whose husband is living with another woman of whose child he is the father." Though reflecting a little of its time, nonetheless, this passage clearly illustrates that, as a matter of common law, a promise to marry by persons in the circumstances of those party to *Ennis v. Butterly* would not have been contrary to English public policy. Since that reasoning is predicated upon the non-existence in reality of the promisor's obligations to his or her formal spouse, and since that is the consequence of a judicial separation as a matter of Irish law, that logic would seem to be equally applicable at Irish law, notwithstanding the former terms of Article 41.3.2°.

However, as a matter of Irish law, marriage is no longer constitutionally indissoluble. Judgment was given in *Ennis v. Butterly* on July 26, 1996; more than seven months before, by referendum held on November 24, 1995, a majority of the People voted to amend the Constitution to provide for the introduction of a divorce jurisdiction, and, after the Supreme Court dismissed the challenge to the referendum in *Hanafin v. Ireland* (Supreme Court, June 12, 1996) the resulting amendment was enacted by the Fifteenth Amendment of the Constitution Act 1996. In *R.C. v. CC* [1997] 1 I.L.R.M. 401 Barron J. confirmed that the section thereby added in effect created a constitutional right to divorce. The exercise of that right is now regulated by the terms of the Family Law (Divorce) Act, 1996, which was signed by the President on November 27, 1996 and came into force on February 27, 1997 (on which, see generally, Walls and Bergin *The Law of Divorce in Ireland* (Jordans, Bristol, 1997), and the Family Law chapter, below, 352). However much the logic in *Wilson v. Carnley* [1908] 1 K.B. 729, *Spiers v. Hunt* [1908] 1 K.B. 720 and *Siveyer v. Allison* [1935] 2 K.B. 403 might have been applicable as a matter of Irish law prior to this amendment to the Constitution, on the date upon which Kelly J. gave judgment, the constitutional basis upon which Kelly J. purported to rely had been radically altered by the recognition of a constitutional right to divorce; the relevant public policy must likewise have altered, and yet the judgment of Kelly J. is bereft of discussion of this point. It is at least arguable that this consequential shift in the focus of public policy had swept away the logic underlying *Wilson*, *Spiers* and *Hunt*, and laid the groundwork for the acceptance of *Fender* in Irish law.

Consequently, at Irish law, there should no longer be any justification for regarding as different the positions of unmarried and married promisors, since both could be in a position to fulfill the terms of the promise. Thus, if a batchelor who promised to marry a woman would have been liable for his breach of that promise, a man on the point of imminent divorce who promised to marry a woman would equally have been liable. However, any such argument has, in any event, been rendered moot by the terms of section 2 of the Family Law Act, 1981 in Ireland (and of section 1 of the Law Reform (Miscellaneous Provisions) Act 1970 in England), which abolished the action for breach of promise to marry, and the decision of Kelly J. on this point is sustainable on that ground. Nevertheless, the point is still of importance, since it illustrates the need for caution in matters of evolving public policy, in particular, that matters which were contrary to public policy in a byegone age may no longer be so.

As to the second aspect of public policy relied upon by Kelly J., rendering unenforceable an agreement by two separated people to live together as a family pending possible marriage, an argument similar to the above may also be possible, and, in this context, such an argument would be crucial, given that there is no statutory enactment determinative of the issue. Kelly J. began by observing that in England no obligation arose as a matter of law by which the defendant in this case would be obliged to support the plaintiff, and held that the law in Ireland "is no different and, if anything, would lean more strongly against such a concept having regard to the special position of marriage under the Constitution." ([1996] 1 I.R. 426, 438; [1997] 1 I.L.R.M. 28, 38). True this may be, but, with respect, it is irrelevant to the plaintiff's claim: she did not claim that an obligation on the defendant to support her arose as a matter of law, rather she claimed instead that by contract he voluntarily agreed to do so. It is of the essence of a contract that one agrees to assume obligations towards the other party or parties to the contract that would not otherwise arise. The mere fact that the law does not oblige the contractor to discharge the obligation is nothing to point, except in so far as its absence may provide the very reason why the contract, any contract, is entered into in the first place! Thus, the absence of an obligation arising by operation of law upon the defendant is irrelevant to the question whether he agreed to assume such an obligation, and to the question directly at issue in the case of whether the law ought to enforce such a contract. (Therefore, the dicussion of such an obligation imposed by the law upon one of the former cohabitees to make payments similar to maintenance to the other, desribed (*quaere*, perjoratively ?) as "palimony" was entirely irrelevant to the matter in hand, and was therefore *obiter.* Furthermore, if the discussion below as the proper understanding of Article 41 is correct, then Kelly J.'s *obiter* conclusions on this issue are, as shown below, insecure at best).

That matter to one side, the *ratio* of Kelly J.'s decision is to be found in his analysis of the question whether an agreement by two separated people to live together as a family pending possible marriage is contrary to public policy. That was to be found:

> in the first instance in the Constitution and, in particular, Article 41 thereof. In that Article, the State recognises the family as the natural primary and fundamental unit group of society and as a moral institution possessing inalienable and imprescriptible right antecedent and superior to all positive law. The State pledges itsef to guard with special care the institution of marriage, on which the family is founded and to protect it against attack. . . . Given the special place of marriage and the family under Irish law, it appears to me that the public policy of this state ordains that non-marital cohabitation does not and cannot have the same constitutional status as marriage. Moreover, the State has pledged to guard with special care the institution of marriage. But does this mean that agreements, the consideration for which is cohabitation, are incapable of being enforced ? In my view it does since otherwise the pledge on the part of the State, of which this Court is one organ, to guard with special care the institution of marriage would be much diluted. To permit an express cohabitation contract . . . to be enforced would be to give it a similar status in law as a marriage contract. It did not have such a status prior to the coming into effect of the Constitution, rather such contracts were regarded as illegal and unenforceable as a matter of public policy. Far from enhancing the position at law of such contracts the Constitution requires marriage to be guarded with special care. In my view, this reinforces the existing common law doctrines concerning the non-enforceability of cohabitation contracts. I am therefore of opinion that, as a matter of public policy, such agreements cannot be enforced. ([1996] 1 I.R. 426, 438-439; [1997] 1 I.L.R.M. 28, 38-39).

In this passage, Kelly J. seems to have deployed three distinct aspects of public policy: two at common law which render unenforceable, first, contracts tending to promote immorality, and, second, contracts prejudicial to the institution of marriage, and a third derived from the constitution which seems to be a stronger version of the second. As pointed out above, they are analytically distinct heads of public policy, treated separately in the books (e.g. Clark, p. 298 (immorality), p. 325 (marriage)). Each such matter, to the extent that it figures in the decision of Kelly J. in *Ennis v. Butterly* will therefore be analysed separately.

As to the first such aspect of public policy, that a cohabitation contract is void for tending to promote immoratility, though at one time the law regarded a promise between a man and woman to live together without being married as immoral (e.g. *Fender v. St John Mildmay* [1938] A.C. 1, 42 *per* Lord Wright; and see generally Poulter (1974) 124 *NLJ* 999 and 1034), it is submitted that public policy has evolved well beyond a point where it would today have such an effect. For example, Clark (p. 298) quotes Sable J. in *Andrews v. Parker* [1973] Qd. R. 93, 104:

Are the actions of people today to be judged in the light of the standards of the last century ? As counsel for the plaintiff said, cases discussing what was then by community standards sexual immorality appear to have been decided in the days when for the sake of decency the legs of tables wore drapes . . . I do not accept that immoral today means precisely what it did in the days of *Pearse v. Brooks* [(1866) 1 Ex 213 in which the owner could not sue for damage to a carriage hired by a prostitute for her work]. I am, I believe, entitled to look at the word under modern social standards.

Following this, an agreement between cohabiting partners that one would buy the other's interest in the house if the relationship failed, was enforced in the New South Wales case of *Seidler v. Schallhofer* [1982] 2 N.S.W.L.R. 80, (see Clark, p. 299). Indeed, in *Fender v. St John Mildmay*, on an application to enforce a promise to marry made by a man after he had obtained a decree *nisi* of divorce, but before it was made absolute, Lord Atkin dismissed "with some indignation the idea that public policy is involved on the ground that such promises tend to immorality"([1938] A.C. 1, 17).

If the fact that a legal or equitable right derived from cohabitation meant that it was against public policy for the courts to lend their aid in the enforcement of those rights, it would mean, for example, that the courts would not only refuse to enforce such contracts, but also refuse to give effect to property rights arising from resulting or constructive trusts as between the parties to such a relationship, since that relationship would be the basis upon which the trust would be raised. However, in *Tinsley v. Milligan* [1994] 1 A.C. 340 (H.L.), the parties were cohabiting lesbians, the plaintiff sought a resulting trust, and it was nowhere objected that since the relationship which gave rise to the trust was immoral, public policy would for that reason preclude the courts from hearing the application (which was in the event successful). If the courts will give effect to such property rights, there is no reason why they should not also give effect to contractual ones arising from such a relationship. Thus, Treitel concludes that the "traditional common law approach to immoral contracts is progressively being abandonded in cases concerning the arrangements between person who live together in a common household as husband and wife without being married. . . . [illustrations of this suggest] that the old common law rule governing immoral contracts will in future be confined to meretricious relationships. Where domestic arrangements between parties to the present group of stable relationships satisfy the requirement of contractual intention, they should not be struck down on grounds of public policy." (Treitel, p. 404; cp Pawlowski (1996) 146 *N.L.J.* 1125; see generally, Barton, *Cohabi-*

tation Contracts (Aldershot, 1985); Oliver, *Cohabitation. The Legal Implications* (Bicester, 1987); Lush, *Cohabitation and Co-Ownership Precedents* (Jordans, Bristol, 1995): there is a definite easing of the auhtors' perceptions of the role of public policy in invalidating such contracts over the period covered by these books). In other words, cohabitiation in a stable relationship is not for that reason to be regarded as meretricious; something more is required.

The 1996 Census shows that more than 31,00 family units consist of cohabiting couples; indeed, since many of the people involved are aged over 30, the census concludes that cohabitation is a permanent union rather than just a precursor to marriage (see the *Irish Times*, July 26, 1997, p. 5). In many respects, Irish law seems already to have accommodated itself to this important social reality. For example, in *W. O'R. v. E.H.* [1996] 2 I.R. 248, (see the Family Law chapter, below, 368) Murphy J. observed that "[f]or better or for worse, it is clearly the fact that long term relationships having many of the characteristics of a family based on marriage have become commonplace. Relationships which would have been the cause of grave concern a generation ago are now widely accepted." ([1996] 2 I.R. 248, 286). Consequently, Hamilton C.J. held, *inter alia*, that "where the children are born as a result of a stable and established relationship and nurtured at the commencement of life by father and mother in a *de facto* family as opposed to a constitutional family, then the father, on application to the Court under section 6A of the Guardianship of Infants Act 1964 [to be appointed guardian of such children], has extensive rights of interest and concern." ([1996] 2 I.R. 248, 269-270). Such judicial acceptance of the social reality of non-marital *de facto* long term relationships, such judicial acceptance of the social reality of cohabitation as an alternative to marriage, signals strongly that there is now no justification for Irish law in condemning such relationships as immoral and thus condemning contracts between partners to such relationships as contrary to public policy. (On similar social and legal evolutions in this context, see, generally, Eekelaar and Katz (eds.), *Marriage and Cohabitation in Contemporary Societies* (Butterworths, London, 1980)).

It is submitted, therefore, that far from contemplating, in Kelly J.'s words, "*existing* common law doctrines concerning the non-enforceability of cohabitation contracts" (emphasis added) the common law (unencumbered by constitutional considerations) does in fact contemplate the enforceability of cohabitation agreements. On this approach, the agreement in *Ennis v. Butterly* would not be regarded as meretricious simply because of the cohabitation. Thus, here, as in the context of the discussion above of the policy rendering unenforceable a promise to marry by a person already married, public policy has been evolving to point where matters which were contrary to public policy in a byegone age are so no longer, and had Kelly J. considered such evolution, his decision on this aspect of public policy could, and it is submitted, should, have gone the other way. However, there are also in the above extract strong elements of the public policy rendering unenforceable contracts prejudicial to the institution of marriage.

Turning, then, to this aspect of public policy, the key to Kelly J.'s reasoning is his view that to "permit an express cohabitation contract . . . to be enforced would be to give it a similar status in law as a marriage contract" which cannot be done, since this would "much dilute[]" the constitutional "pledge on the part of the State, of which this Court is one organ, to guard with special care the institution of marriage." Although the context of these remarks was as to the enforceability of an agreement by two separated people to live together as a family pending possible marriage, this analysis is clearly intended to apply to any cohabitation contract, and thus to an agreement by two separated people simply to live together, or indeed, an agreement by two unmarried people to live together. Further, his analysis seems apt to catch not just an agreement between such people to live together, but also any agreement made by such people in that context, such as an agreement relating to property, or to payments equivalent to maintenance in the event of the relationship breaking down. If Kelly J.'s reasoning from the special constitutional protection of marriage holds, then Irish public policy does properly render such contracts unenforceable.

It is submitted, however, that Kelly J.'s reasoning does not hold. For example, if it were based simply upon the common law public policy against contracts prejudicial to the institution of marriage, it would be vulnerable to the objections set out above that such a policy has undergone an evolution in parallel with social developments. Crucially Kelly J.'s reasoning sidesteps this and relies instead and exclusively upon the special constitutional protection of marriage secured by Article 41.

As a threshold issue, whilst it is true that before its amendment, Article 41 could be said to describe a coherent philosophy of a society the fundamental unit group of which is the family founded upon indissoluble marraige, nonetheless, the subsequent amendment of Article 41.3.2° to allow for a constitutional right to divorce has at least substantially altered that philosphy. Indeed, it may be queried whether, in the aftermath of the amendment, Article 41 really contains a unitary and coherent intelligbile public policy.

More generally, and absent *Ennis v. Butterly*, the effect of Article 41 seems to be that if the State were to secure to married couples or families some rights benefits entitlements or protections it was not extending to couples or familes not founded upon marriage, such an action would be constitutionally permissibe; but it would not require that securing such rights benefits entitlements or protections to couples or familes not founded upon marriage be deemed unconstitutional. For example, in *WO'R v. EH* (above) although the majority of the court held that such interests are materially different from the constitutional rights flowing from Article 41 which would accrue to a natural father married to the child's mother, the Supreme Court did not see the existence of such Article 41 rights as necessarily excluding the extensive rights of interest and concern which a natural father has for his child. Thus, whilst the law cannot provide a more favourable tax regime to cohabiting couples than to married couples (*Murphy v. AG* [1982] I.R. 241), and Article 41 does not require that cohabiting couples be subject to same tax or social welfare regimes as marred couples (e.g. *Lowth v. Minister for Social Welfare* [1994] 1 I.L.R.M. 378, see the 1993 Review, p. 523), the conventional understanding of that article (for example by analogy with *W. O'R. v. E.H.*) would not preclude a similar tax or social welfare regime being applied to both married and cohabiting couples.

On the other hand, to reason that anything that gives to a relationship "a similar status in law as a marriage" is contrary to the constitution, as Kelly J. seems to have done in *Ennis v. Butterly*, would amount to holding that the law is constitutionally not allowed to treat a cohabiting couple on the same basis as a married couple. In other words, the conventional constitutional position that it is permissible not to treat them the same becomes transmuted into one in which it is required that they be treated differently. This seems to countenance a constitutional mandate to discriminate against cohabiting couples. Quite clearly, this is inconsistent with the established approach to Article 41 outlined in the previous paragraph, and ought therefore to be rejected. Thus, it is simply not the case that anything that gives to a relationship "a similar status in law as a marriage" is contrary to the constitution. If it were, on a very practical level, it would have disturbing implications for vast areas of relatively settled legal and equitable doctrine, to say nothing of the type of statutory entitlements referred to in the previous paragraph.

For example, if Kelly J.'s reasoning were to survive, then, to the extent that the law already provides that cohabiting couples have the same treatment as married couples, such provision, on Kelly J.'s logic, seems to be constitutionally questionable. Take the example of the application of trust doctrines to a family home (see e.g., Delany, pp. 153-165 (resulting trusts), 215-216 (constructive trusts); Duncan and Scully, pp. 264–288, paras 10.007–10.049; Mee (1992) 14 *DULJ* (*ns*) 19). Such doctrines have been applied not only to matrimonial property, but also to property in stable non-marital relationships. Indeed, as Delany points out, such equitable doctrines "apply equally to cohabitees, and it is in relation to this category of persons that any future developments in this area are likely to take place, given that the position of spouses will probably continue to be increasingly governed by legislation." (p. 155). If Kelly J.'s understanding of constitutional policy is correct, this seems to render constitutionally suspect – at the very least – the application of such doctrines beyond the matrimonial context. Ineed, for a cohabitee, who could otherwise establish a resulting or constructive trust to be robbed of such proprietary interests in this way seems grossly harsh and unfair. Again, the doctrine of undue influence by a third party (see below, 219-27, with references) is of particular application to the situation of a husband exercising undue influence over his wife to have her secure a loan from a bank; and Kelly J's reasoning may impact upon this doctrine in two ways. First, it would render constitutionally suspect the application of this doctrine to cohabitees; again, a grossly harsh and unfair result. Second, one understanding of the doctrine (the "special equity" strategy) provided protection simply because the surety was a wife, but it was suggested in the 1993 Review that such a strategy would be considered unconstitutional, and it seems to have been rejected by the Supreme Court in *Bank of Nova Scotia v. Hogan* (below, 222-7). However, Kelly J's understanding of constitutional policy seems, on the contrary, to make such a doctrine constitutionally required. On the other hand, in the absence of such an understanding, the fact that a spouse can rely on the equitable doctrines of resulting and constructive trusts, and of undue influence would not preclude a cohabitee likewise from relying upon those doctrines. (Similarly, and *pace* Kelly J. above, the fact that a spouse can, as a matter of law, claim maintenance upon separation or divorce, need not of itself preclude the development of a similar claim for cohabitees. Certainly, Article 41 might not require such an obligation, but it does not preclude, in an appropriate case, the generation of a similar entitlement by deploying an appropriate doctrine of law or equity (whether that doctrine is a development of an existing one, or is entirely novel, and whether or not it is characterised as "palimony")).

Of course, as Kelly J. himself pointed out, the existence of these equitable doctrines cannot determine the content of constitutional policy ([1996] 1 I.R. 426, 439-440; [1997] 1 I.L.R.M. 28, 39). It is not clear, however, whether Kelly J. himself crossed that line in seeming to use his understanding of the common law rules on the enforceability of cohabitation agreements to support his view that such agreements were contrary to the constitution and thus to public policy. Furthermore, although such doctrines do not directly determine the content of constitutional policy, they or similar doctrines are symptomatic of a more general development in the law also to be seen in the evolution of notions of public policy sketched above and may be taken as examples of the direction of the law, of society, of social policy, indeed of contemporary morality; and these matters in turn form the backdrop to an evoluvative interpretation of the constitution. Constitutional norms would almost certainly have required Kelly J's understanding of public policy in 1937. However, Bunreacht na hÉireann is not to be interpreted as a static document but as an instrument evolving in parallel with social evolution. Thus, for example, Walsh J., writing extra-judicially, has stated that "the meaning of a provision of the Constitution . . . can be construed in the context of constantly changing times . . . It always speaks in the present tense." (O'Reilly and Redmond, *Cases and Materials on the Irish Constitution* (Dublin, 1980), p. xi). Murphy J. in the Supreme Court in *W. O'R. v. E.H.* [1996] 2 I.R. 248 (above) was prepared to accept the social reality of cohabitation in the interpretation of the Constitution; Kelly J. in the High Court in *Ennis v. Butterly* should have done likewise. Had he done so, it is submitted that he ought to have concluded that constitutional policy, interpreted in the light of the social reality of cohabitation, would not preclude a court from enforcing a contract entered into between a cohabiting couple.

Finally it is not made clear in the judgment whether the constitution is being used to remould and reinforce the existing common law policy or is being used to generate a further head of public policy; but, in either case, such principles of constitutional interpretation likewise permit the courts to have regard to the social fact of the acceptance and acceptability of cohabitation.

It is therefore clear that the logic of Kelly J.'s decision in *Ennis v. Butterly* – to the effect that that anything that gives to a relationship "a similar status in law as a marriage" is contrary to the constitution – is inconsistent with established principles of constitutional law and interpretation, and has disturbing implications for much common law and equitable doctrine: it cannot be right, and ought not to be followed. However, the fact that the logic of Kelly J.'s main *ratio* falls does not of itself mean that the decision also falls, since it may be supportable on other grounds; in particular, if the action was no more than one seeking damages for breach of a promise to marry (when free to do so), then section 2 of the Family Law Act 1981, by abolishing the action for damage for breach of promise to marry, would seem to present, as Kelly J. found, an insuperable obstacle to the plaintiff's claim. But an action to enforce, or to seek damages for breach of, another agreement, for example, in relation to the distribution of property, which would fail under Kelly J.'s understanding of constitutional policy, would, if that understanding were to fall, be maintainable. This is as it ought to be.

IMPLIED TERMS

Terms may be implied into contracts either as a matter of fact (because the term was, or would be presumed to have been, intended by the parties) or as a matter of law. In the latter case, if the term is implied by the common law, it happens because certain terms are required by the nature of the contract itself (see, e.g., *Liverpool City Co v. Irwin* [1977] A.C. 239); a term may also be implied by statute, for example, by the Sale of Goods and Supply of Services Act, 1980.

Terms implied in fact   An example of terms implied as a matter of fact is supplied by *Clarke v. Kilternan Motor Co.* (High Court, December 10, 1996). We have already seen above that in this case, the parties to an agreement had fallen out; the plaintiff claimed that the agreement had been wrongfully terminated by the defendant, and that he was entitled to six months minimum rea-

sonable notice. McCracken J. held that either the plaintiff had himself terminated the agreement or that his breaches of contract allowed the defendant to
terminate without notice. However, McCracken J. had accepted that:

> There undoubtedly was a legally binding agreement between the parties
> which unfortunately was not reduced to writing. I am satisfied that the
> agreement did not provide for any specific form of termination, but that
> it would be implied into the agreement that either party could determine
> it on reasonable notice. It is also implied that either party could termi-
> nate the agreement without notice if there were a fundamental breach by
> the other party. (p. 7)

This seems to be consistent with the same judge's approach in *Carna Foods
v. Eagle Star Insurance Co.* [1995] 1 I.R. 526; [1995] 2 I.L.R.M. 474 (see the
1995 Review, 210) in which he held that neither of the standard tests for the
implication in fact of terms was satisfied, and thus supplies support for the
view that in this case, the terms implied as to determination on reasonable
notice are terms implied in fact. On the particular issue, in *Royal Trust Company of Canada v. Kelly* (High Court, February 27, 1989) Barron J. (having
held that "a party to a contract cannot voluntarily create conditions which will
prevent performance of that contract" (at p. 13)) held that "it is an implied
term of every contract of employment other than for a fixed period that it can
be terminated upon reasonable notice" (p. 14; *cp Walsh v. Dublin Health Authority* (1964) 98 I.L.T.R. 82 (Budd J.); *Carvill v. Irish Industrial Bank* [1968]
I.R. 325, (SCt) 342-343 *per* O'Keeffe J.). On the other hand, in the contemporary *NEHB v. Grehan* [1989] I.R. 422 Costello J. held that in an employment
contract with a specific termination clause, the implication of an additional
term allowing termination on reasonable notice was thereby excluded by the
actual or presumed intentions of the parties. Again, since the justification for
such implication resides in the presumed intentions of the parties, if their intentions are quite clearly that the contract should run indefinitely, then there is
no room for the implication of a term allowing unilateral termination on reasonable notice (see Clark, p. 122; *cp Walsh* (1964) 98 I.L.T.R. 82, 86-87 *per*
Budd J.).

It would seem, therefore, that if a contract of employment is silent on termination, a term allowing for termination upon reasonable notice will readily
be implied; but if the contract contains detailed provisions dealing with termination, or if it is clearly for a fixed term or for indefinite duration, a further
term allowing for termination upon reasonable notice will not so readily be
implied (see, generally, Forde *Employment Law* (Round Hall, Dublin, 1992),
pp. 160-163). This approach has not been confined to contracts of employment. Thus, contracts "of agency are also terminable upon giving reasonable
notice" (Clark, p. 121; citing *Ward v. Spivak* [1957] I.R. 40). It would seem to

be likewise with distribution agreements, at least at common law (*Irish Welding v. Philips Electrical* (High Court, October 8, 1976, Finlay P.) and the position does not seem to have been altered by relevant EU block exemptions (e.g., Regulation 1983/83) or Competition Authority category licences (e.g., C.A. Dec. No. 144; November 5, 1993)).

There being in *Clarke v. Kilternan Motor Co.* neither a term as to the termination of the contract between the parties nor a term fixing the duration of the contract, then, by analogy with these cases, there would seem to be no impediment to the implication of a term that the contract would have been terminable upon reasonable notice.

Lotto and implied terms   When the inevitable happened, and the National Lottery finally generated litigation in the form of *Carroll v. An Post National Lottery Company* [1996] 1 I.R. 443, the decision of Costello P. provided an example of a plaintiff seeking the implication of a term into a contract both as a term implied in fact and as on implied by the Sale of Goods and Supply of Services Act, 1980. The plaintiff claimed that the failure by a vendor to process a tendered playslip amounted to a breach of contract by the defendant Lottery company. By an application of the rules of offer and acceptance (considered below, 208-10) Costello P. held that a contract had arisen between the plaintiff and the Lottery company, the terms of which were "contained on the reverse side of the playslip" ([1996] 1 I.R. 443, 454). The plaintiff argued that there was also implied into the contract a term that "the counterhand would use reasonable skill and care in entering his [the plaintiff's] plays into the Lotto draw". ([1996] 1 I.R. 443, 459). Costello P. rejected this claim:

> The Act of 1986 provides that the National Lottery is to be held in accordance with rules approved by the Minister for Finance (s. 28) and the rules so approved have an express condition that the National Lottery shall not in any circumstances be liable to a player for any acts or omissions by the Lotto agents (Rule 4(3)(f)). The court cannot properly imply into the parties' contract a term which not only is not contained in the rules but which would be directly contrary to an express term in the rules as approved by the Minister. Secondly the court will only imply a term in a contract if it is necessary to do so in order to give effect to the intention of the parties. In this case the defendant company quite clearly expressed its intention that it would not be liable for the negligence of its Lotto agents and so the court cannot imply a term which is contrary to the clear intention of one of the parties. ([1996] 1 I.R. 443, 459).

We have already seen that if a contract has a termination provisions, a court will not readily imply a term providing an alternative or contrary termination procedure; thus, in *Tradax v. Irish Grain Board*, Henchy J. would not countenance "the introduction of the implied term . . . [which] would run counter to [an] express term". ([1984] I.R. 1, 17; note, however, the range of opinions expressed in *Johnstone v. Bloomsbury Health Authority* [1991] 2 All E.R. 293 (C.A.)). The approach of Costello P. here, in refusing to imply a term in the face of an express contrary term, is entirely consistent with this orthodoxy. Indeed, the second reason which he gives is usually given as the justification for this position. But there may be a little more to it than that. As the Supreme Court made clear in *Tradax*, terms are implied into a contract for two related but separate reasons. First, it may have been the intention of the parties that the term be included, but for them, it was "so obvious that it [went] without saying; so that, if while the parties making their bargain, an officious bystander were to suggest some express provision for it in the agreement, they would testily suppress him with a common 'Oh, of course'." (*Shirlaw v. Southern Foundries* [1939] 2 K.B. 206, 227 *per* MacKinnon L.J.; *affd* [1940] A.C. 701). Second, the courts presume that the parties intend that their contract will in fact be operable, and so will imply terms into it necessary to give it effect, thus a term may be implied "from the presumed intention of the parties with the object of giving the transaction such efficacy as both parties must have intended that at all events it should have." (*The Moorcock* (1889) 14 P.D. 64, 68 *per* Bowen L.J.). Clearly, if the parties had directed their minds to an issue and included a term expressly dealing with it, then there is no basis upon which it can be said that a contrary term was so obvious that it went without saying, and therefore no basis upon which to imply such a term for that reason. Thus, on the first test for the implication of terms, Costello P.'s reasoning holds. On the second, if the contract is plainly unworkable, to give it business efficacy and make it workable, as the parties are presumed to have intended, a necessary term will be implied; if that implied term has to override an express term to ensure that the contract is workable, that would seem to be justified by the presumed intention of the parties. There may thus be circumstances in which it is possible and justifiable for a court to imply a term into a contract contrary to the expressed intentions of the parties. However, on the facts of *Carroll*, the contract between the player and the Lottery company was not plainly unworkable, and thus there again is no basis on this test for the implication of a term.

The plaintiff also claimed that the contract was for the supply of a service, that by section 39 of the 1980 Act there was implied into that contract a term that the supply "will supply the service with skill, care and diligence", and that this term was breached on the facts. However, Costello P. had described the contract as one "by which the defendant company sells lottery tickets to members of the public who have agreed to purchase them in accordance with the authorised rules"; therefore he did "not consider that the defendant company has contracted to deliver a service to those seeking lottery tickets – the contract is to sell a ticket which confers rights and obligations on the parties to the contract". ([1996] 1 I.R. 443, 454). Thus, "there was no term implied into the parties' contract by virtue of [section 39 of] the 1980 Act." ([1996] 1 I.R. 443, 459). Indeed, it is pointed out below (208-10) that if Costello P. had been prepared to find that the Lottery company had offered to supply a service, it may be that the offer had not validly been accepted and no contract would anyhow have arisen. However, Costello P. went on to hold (*obiter*) that even if there had been a breach of contract, liability was successfully excluded by the terms printed on the playslip (see above, 197).

Terms implied by law A further, perhaps more orthodox, example of terms implied as a matter of law by the 1980 Act is supplied by the decision of Moriarty J. in *O'Donnell v. Truck and Machinery Sales* (High Court, June 7, 1996). Here, O'Donnell had supplied Volvo L150 and L180 mechanical shovels to TMS, and had sued TMS for the outstanding purchase price plus interest on two L180s; Costello P. (High Court, November 21, 1995) held for O'Donnell on this issue. TMS had counterclaimed, *inter alia*, that the L150s so sold were in breach of the terms implied into the contracts of sale by sections 14(2) and 14(4) of the Sale of Goods Act, 1893 as amended by section 10 of the Sale of Goods and Supply of Services Act, 1980; that counterclaim was the subject matter of the decision of Moriarty J., who held that

on no realistic appraisal of appropriately proven defects in the L150s supplied can it be said that they were not of merchantable quality or reasonably fit for the purpose for which [they were] required. . . . it seems to me, construing the evidence in totality, . . . that given such factors as the relative prices obtained on resale in varying circumstances, the overall hire records, durability and income generated in favour of [O'Donnell] by those shovels which became part of the hire fleet, the relative incidents of repairs required and the apparent evaluation of the L150s in Ireland and other marketplaces by other purchasers and users[,] that neither term has been shown to be infringed. (p. 8)

This seems to have been the first occasion upon which the terms of section 14 of the 1893 Act have been the subject of a written Superior Court judgment since their amendement by section 10 of the 1980 Act (cp. Clark, p. 166; Gill (1987) 5 *ILT* (*ns*) 57; and see, generally, Bell, *The Modern Law of Personal Property in England and Ireland* (Butterworths, London, 1989), pp. 277-282; the leading Irish case on the section prior to amendment was *Wallis v. Russell* [1902] 2 I.R. 585; see also *McCullough Sales v. Chetham Timber* [1985] I.L.R.M. 217n (February 1, 1983; Doyle J.)). There is little more detail on such matters in the judgment than appears from the extract just quoted, and it is not clear however what the effect of such factors is to be. For example, as to "relative prices obtained on resale", it has been held in *Harlingdon v. Hull* that "the question whether goods are reasonably fit for resale cannot depend on whether they can or cannot be resold without making a loss" ([1990] 1 All

E.R. 737, 745 *per* Nourse L.J.; cp. p. 753 *per* Slade L.J.; cf. pp. 749-750 *per* Stuart Smith L.J. dissenting) even though one of the uses for the painting in question was that it could be resold, and the fact that it turned out to be an almost worthless fake made a loss on the resale inevitable. It may be that Moriarty J. is taking the contrary view; the context of his remark seems to suggest this. On the other hand, the import of "durability" and "the relative incidents of repairs required" are clear: if the goods are not durable (expressly required by section 14(3), and meaning that the goods "must remain in a merchantable state for some reasonable period following the sale . . ." (Forde, *Commercial Law in Ireland* (Butterworths, Dublin, 1990), p. 50)) or if relatively frequent repairs are required, then goods are not of merchanatble quality. The factors outlined in the above extract from Moriarty J's judgment constitute a useful exposition of the matters which may be taken into account in determining whether there has been a breach of the terms implied by section 14 that that goods be generally of merchantable quality and thus fit for the purposes for which they are meant (section 14(2)) or be fit for specific disclosed purposes (section 14(4); on which see now *Slater v. Finning* [1996] 3 WLR 190 (HL)).

MISREPRESENTATION

Definition   A misrepresentation is a false statement of fact. In principle, silence will not usually constitute a misrepresentation, because silence is ambiguous, and as such cannot be understood as making a clear statement. However, if the circumstances give rise to a duty of disclosure, silence in such circumstances is no longer ambiguous and amounts to a representation that there is nothing to disclose. A duty of disclosure will arise, for example, if that which is unsaid negates that which is said; or if that which was said, though true at the time, is made false by events. In both cases, the incomplete disclosure creates just as incorrect an impression as an outright falsity and thereby constitutes a misrepresentation. A good example is provided by another aspect of the decision of Moriarty J. in *O'Donnell v. Truck and Machinery Sales* (High Court, June 7, 1996) (immediately above). Moriarty J. found that TMS had bought Volvo L150 mechanical shovels on foot of misrepresentations by O'Donnell that they were "equal to, and in some ways superior to" the relevant market leader (the Caterpillar 966), though he was in possession of and familiar with literature to the effect that the L150 was not the Caterpillar 966's equal. Further, O'Donnell knew that TMS intended to hire the shovels out for quarrying and was aware that Volvo were at an advanced state of development of a product more suited than the existing L150s for quarrying, but did not so inform TMS. Again, TMS requested that the tyres on the L150s be replaced with larger tyres, which O'Donnell did, but gave "no serious or adequate warning" that the larger tyres were unsuitable. Moriarty J. held O'Donnell liable both for the untruths and for the incomplete disclosures; in particular, he held that O'Donnell's knowledge of the development of an alternative model "ought to have been . . . conveyed to" TMS (p. 11), and he seems likewise to have required that an adequate warning as to unsuitability of the larger tyres be given to TMS (p. 12).

Remedies Where a misrepresentation has induced a contract, a plaintiff who has thereby suffered loss may have a remedy in tort or in contract. As to remedies in contract, the primary remedy is rescission of the contract, to put the parties back in the position they would have been in had the contract never been made. As to remedies in tort, if the misrepresentation which induced the plaintiff to enter into the contract was fradulent or negligent, then there are grounds for an action in tort on the basis of the fraud or negligence. The action for fraud or deceit is founded upon *Derry v. Peek* (1889) 14 App Cas 337 (approved in *Superwood v. Sun Alliance* [1995] 3 I.R. 303, 327-328 *per* Denham J.) and the calculation of damages in such a situation is governed by *Smith New Court Securities v. Scrimgeour Vickers* [1997] A.C. 249; [1996] 4 All E.R. 769 (H.L.), at pp. 777-779 *per* Lord Browne-Wilkinson; cp. at pp. 791-793 *per* Lord Steyn) that the plaintiff is entitled to be compensated for all the loss – including consequential loss – caused by the misrepresentation, whether or not it was foreseeable. The action for negligence derived is derived from *Hedley Byrne v. Heller* [1964] A.C. 465 and *Esso v. Mardon* [1976] 2 All E.R. 5 and the calculation of damages is governed by the ordinary principles of negligence, compensating the plaintiff for all foreseeable losses so as to put him in the position he would have been had the tort not occurred. (On the differences between the fraud measure and the negligence measure, see *Banque Bruxelles Lambert SA v. Eagle Star Insurance* [1997] A.C. 191, 215-216 *per* Lord Hoffmann).

There is no remedy in tort at common law for innocent misrepresentation, but if that innocent misrepresentation induced a plaintiff to enter a loss-making contract, then section 45(1) of the Sale of Goods and Supply of Services Act, 1980 provides the plaintiff with a remedy in damages:

> Where a person has entered into a contract after a misrepresentation has been made to him by another party thereto and as a result thereof he has suffered loss, then, if the person making the representation would be liable to damages in respect thereof had the misrepresentation been made fraudulently, that person shall be so liable notwithstanding that the misrepresentation was not made fraudulently, unless he proves that he had reasonable ground to believe and did believe up to the time the contract was made that the facts represented were true.

The remedy is available to a plaintiff as though the other party were fraudulent, even though not, unless the other party reasonably believed his representation. The courts in England have adopted a narrow view of what constitutes such a reasonable belief (*Howard Marine v. Ogden* [1978] 2 All E.R. 1134; Brownsword (1978) 41 *MLR* 735) thus preserving a relatively wide power to award damages. As to the measure of damages, in *Royscot Trust v. Rogerson* [1991] 2 QB 297 (see Hooley (1991) 107 *LQR* 547) the leading English case on section 2(1) of Misrepresentation Act 1967, which is in the same terms as section 45(1), it was held that on the true construction of that section: first, that damages under that section were intended to put the plaintiff in the position he would have been had he never entered the contract (ie, the tort measue; as opposed to the contract measure, by which he would have been put in the position he would have been had the misrepresentation been true); and second the relevant tort measure was the measure for fraudulent misrepresentation rather than for negligence at common law, so that a plaintiff would be entitled to recover all losses suffered by it flowing from the misrepresentation, which includes unforeseeable losses "provided that they were not otherwise too remote" (*Royscot Trust v. Rogerson* [1991] 2 Q.B. 297, 307)

In *O'Donnell v. Truck and Machinery Sales* the misrepresentations gave rise to liability both on the basis of the common law relating to negligent misrepresentation in tort and on the basis of the statutory remedy provided by section 45(1) of the 1980 Act. Moriarty J. found that O'Donnell was "[p]atently" under a duty of care in relation to the representations he made to TMS, which were "instrumental" in persuading TMS to purchase the shovels, which were clearly either untrue or incomplete, and hence constituted actionable mispresentations.

> . . . whilst differences in the measure of damages appropriate to negligent misrepresentation and statutory misrepresentation may arise, it is clear that what is applicable is such a sum of money as should suffice to place [TMS, the misrepresentees] into the position they would have been in had the relevant misrepresentations been true. (pp. 14-15).

Fourth, at common law, the negligence measure of damages is such amount as would put the plaintiff in the position he would have been had the tort not occurred; in the context of misrepresentation, this means putting the plaintiff in the position he would have been had there been no negligent misrepresentation by compensating him for those losses which were caused by the misrepresentation. Quaere whether this is different from putting him in the position he would have been had the misrepresentation been true ? In any event, the actual calculation of such damages caused Moriarty J. great difficulty, given that the figures claimed by TMS seem to have been "spuriously inflated to a high degree" (p. 17) but he nevertheless strove to "quantify a sum that is fair and appropriate" (p. 18) and, on a claim initially cast as "exceeding three quarters of a million pounds" (p. 15), in the event awarded £ 151,200.

With respect, it makes a great deal of difference whether a plaintiff has claimed at common law or under the statute. First, at common law, it is clear from *Banque Bruxelles* and *Smith New Court Securities* that a plaintiff who claims for fraudulent misrepresentation at common law is entitled to a greater measure of damages than one who claims for negligent misrepresentation. (*Downs v. Chappell* [1997] 1 W.L.R. 426, where Hobhouse L.J. had sought to equate the two measures, was doubted by Hoffmann in *Banque Bruxelles* and disapproved by Lord Browne-Wilkinson in *Smith New Court Securities*). Second, for so long as *Royscot Trust* is accepted, a plaintiff who sues on foot of section 45(1) of the 1980 Act (or section 2(1) of the English 1967 Act) gets the fraud measure of damages, not the negligence measure. Third, that section "was designed to establish liability in damages for negligent misrepresentation" (Hooley (1991) 107 *L.Q.R.* 547, 550); and from the previous proposition, it follows that a plaintiff pleading negligent misrepresentation on foot of the statute would nevertheless be entitled to the fraud measure of damages; even though the same plaintiff pleading negligent misrepresention at common law would only be entitled to the negligence measure of damages. Such matters may have mattered little, but as the English authorities illustrate, there are many circumstances in which they can matter a great deal.

MISTAKE

Recent authority has confirmed that when the parties to a contract share a common mistake, if it is sufficiently fundamental, relating to the essential basis upon which the parties contract, the common law will consider the contract void; if it is not so fundamental, but still serious or material, equity may consider the contract voidable and liable to be set aside. (e.g., *Associated Japanese Bank v. Crédit du Nord* [1988] 3 All ER 902; *O'Neill v. Ryan (No 3)* [1991] I.L.R.M. 674; [1992] 1 I.R. 166 (Costello J.); *aff'd* [1992] 1 I.R. 193 (S Ct)). The decision of the Court of Appeal in *Huddersfield Banking Co v. Lister* [1895] 2 Ch. 273 is often presented as a strong illustration of a wide application of the equitable jurisdiction (*e.g.* Cheshire, Fifoot and Furmston, *The Law of Contract* (13th ed, Butterworths, London, 1996), pp. 247-248; Clark, pp. 207-208), and that decision has recently been cited with apparent approval of that point in *Cue Club v. Navaro* (Supreme Court, October 23, 1996).

In *Huddersfield Banking Co v. Lister*, a bank which held a mortgage over a mill and fixtures agreed with the liquidator of the mill that certain looms in the mill were not fixtures, and therefore consented to a court order for the sale of the looms by the liquidator. However, it later transpired that the looms had been attached to the mill and therefore constituted fixtures at the date of the mortgage and had thereafter been wrongfully detached. At first instance, Vaughan Williams J. held that he could "set aside the order . . . upon any ground which would justify [him[in setting aside an agreement" (276) so that "if a party has been induced by a mistake common to both parties to consent to a decree or order, the Court has power to relieve him . . .". (277). On appeal, the Court of Appeal upheld. Lindley L.J. held that such a consent order could be set aside "upon any grounds which invalidate the agreement [which] it expresses in a more formal way" (280); and that one such ground, made out here on the facts, was mistake (280-281); Lopes L.J. concurred; and Kay L.J. held "that, both on principle and on authority, when once the Court finds that an agreement has been come to between parties who were under *a common mistake of material fact*, the Court may set it aside, and the Court has ample jurisdiction to set aside the order founded upon the agreement". (284, emphasis added).

Huddersfield Banking v. Lister, along with the decision of the House of Lords on appeal from Ireland in *Cooper v. Phibbs* (1867) L.R. 2 H.L. 149, is a crucial plank in the reasoning of Denning L.J. in *Solle v. Butcher* [1950] 1 K.B. 671, 694, where he championed a wide equitable jurisdiction to set aside contracts concluded on tbe basis of a material common mistake. He repeated these views many times (e.g. in *Leaf v. International Galleries* [1953] 1 QB 646; *Rose v. Pim* [1953] 2 Q.B. 450; *Oscar Chess v. Williams* [1957] 1 W.L.R. 370; *Magee v. Pennine Insurance* [1969] 2 Q.B. 507) and they have since been accepted by other judges, not only in those cases, but also in *Grist v. Bailey* [1967] Ch. 532 (Goff J.); *Laurence v. Lexcourt Holdings* [1978] 2 All E.R. 819 (Brian Dillon Q.C.) and *Associated Japanese Bank v. Crédit du Nord* [1988] 3 All E.R. 902 (Steyn J.). Thus, in   *O'Neill v. Ryan (No 3)* [1991] I.L.R.M. 674; [1992] 1 I.R. 166 Costello J., following *Solle v. Buthcer*, held that "the court may in the exercise of equitable jurisdiction set aside an agreement", which observation was made in the course of a judgment on mistake which the Supreme Court approved as "a significant contribution to our jurisprudence on this aspect of of contract law" [1992] 1 I.R. 193, 196 *per* O'Flaherty J. Thus, it seems that as a matter of Irish law, a "court may . . . also set aside a contract on the ground of a shared common mistake even though it is not avoided by that mistake" (Farrell, *Irish Law of Specific Performance* (Butterworths, Dublin, 1994), p. 271, para 9.69).

On the other hand, it has been argued with much force that neither *Hudderfsield Banking* nor (in particular) *Cooper v. Phibbs* bear the meaning which Lord Denning sought to attribute to them in *Solle v. Butcher* (see, *e.g.*, respectively, Slade (1954) 70 *L.Q.R.* 385, 405; Matthews (1989) 105 *L.Q.R.* 599; Cartwright (1987) 103 *L.Q.R.* 594), and therefore, that equity does not and ought not recognise a jurisdiction to set aside contracts on the grounds of common mistake (*e.g.* Meagher, Gummow and Lehane *Equity: Doctrines and Remedies* (3rd ed, Butterworths, Sydney, 1992), pp. 374-379, paras 1417-1426). Nevertheless, the balance of the argument now seems to be with Goff and Jones' observation that, whilst it is probably still open to courts of final appeal such as the House of Lords (or in Ireland, the Supreme Court) "to conclude that there is no independent doctrine of mistake in equity . . . it would be regrettable if [such a court] did so, for equity's intervention has given the courts a balanced and flexible power to grant relief from the consequences of relief.The trend of the present authorities suggests that, despite the relative novelty and uncertatiny of Lord Denning's formulation of the equitable doctrine, the courts are ready to accept the exitence of an independent equitable jurisdiction to set aside a contract for mistake." (*The Law of Restitution* (4th ed, Sweet & Maxwell, London, 1993), pp. 216-217). Furthermore, the Irish writing on this subject seems unanimously to support this view. In addition to Clark and Farrell (referred to above) both Keane, *Equity and the Law of Trusts in the Republic of Ireland* (Butterworths, London, 1988), pp. 259-264 paras 17.09-17.15 and Delany, *Equity and the Law of Trusts in Ireland* (Round Hall Sweet & Maxwell, Dublin 1996), pp. 474-477 accept the existence of the equitable jurisdiction, the former concluding that "[d]espite the reservations expressed as to the correctness of [Lord Denning's decisions] . . . the courts should possess a jurisdiction in equity (even if it owes more to Lord Denning's penchant for innovation than strict precedent to set aside a contract into which the parties have entered under a shared misapprehension as to a fundamental matter[] . . ." (p. 262, para 17.13); and *O'Neill v. Ryan* (*supra*) provides Irish judicial approval of this approach.

As we have seen, this equitable jurisdiction is founded, in part, upon *Huddersfield Banking v. Lister*, which was approved (without reference to the above controversy) by the Supreme Court in *Cue Club v. Navaro* (Supreme Court, October 23, 1996). The plaintiffs held a lease from the defendants, owed them arrears of rent, and had consented to a judgment in the Circuit Court in respect of the arrears. The defendants subsequently sought to forfeit the lease, and the plaintiffs applied to the High Court for relief against the forfeiture, and also sought an order setting aside the judgment of the Circuit Court on the ground that the consent to the order was vitiated by a common mistake on the grounds that the amount of rent outstanding had been miscalculated. Barron J. (March 11, 1996) struck out the plaintiffs' application, and the plaintiffs appealed. In the Supreme Court, Murphy J. (Hamilton CJ., Barrington J. concurring), held that the claim for relief against forfeiture was bound to fail and was properly struck out but the claim for recovery of rent overpaid on the basis of the mistaken consent to judgment, (though "unlikely in the extreme . . . [to] succeed" (p. 11)) was allowed to proceed "but only so far as it relates to ascertaining the amount of rent properly due and the recovery of any possible overpayment" (p. 16). In this regard, Murphy J. referred (at p. 11) with apparent approval to the views of Kay L.J. in *Huddersfield Banking v. Lister*, set out above, that a court of equity can set aside a contract concluded on the basis of a material common mistake, and can go on to set aside a consent judgment entered on the basis of such a contract. This would therefore seem to constitute some futher degree of Supreme Court approval of the equitable jurisdction consistent with the balance of the above argument, and thus, with *O'Neill v. Ryan,* may be taken as another recent authority confirming that when the parties to a contract share a common mistake, if it is serious or material, equity may consider the contract voidable and liable to be set aside (subject, of course, to the standard equitable bars to rescission, and to any terms which may be imposed).

OFFER AND ACCEPTANCE

Contracts of sale in shops, and contracts with all the world   "Contractual obligations derive from agreement made between two or more parties under which one promises or undertakes with the other the performance of some action. Ordinarily the existence of agreement presupposes an offer by one party to perform the action on certain terms and the acceptance of that offer by the other."*Tansey v. College of Occupational Therapists* [1995] 2 I.L.R.M. 601, 615 *per* Murphy J. In the context of contracts concluded in a shop, it is generally thought that a customer by presenting selected items at the till makes an offer to buy them, which the shopkeeper then accepts. Thus, where goods are displayed in a shop with a price and/or other terms, that display is not usually taken to constitute an offer to sell, but instead an invitation to treat, *Minister for Industry and Commerce v. Pim* [1966] I.R. 154 (Davitt P.); in such a situation, "the contract is not completed until, the customer having indicated the articles which he needs, the shopkeeper, or someone on his behalf, accepts the offer" *Pharmaceutical Society of Great Britain v. Boots Cash Chemists Ltd* [1953] 1 Q.B. 401, 406 *per* Somervell L.J.

Of course, though also justifiable as a matter of convenience, such a rule is usually justified on the basis that it represents the presumed intention of the shop owner that the displays in the shop constitute invitations to treat and not offers. However, something which would ordinarily be taken to constitute an invitation to treat, may have been intended as an offer, and if that intention is clear, then, of couse, it will be regarded as an offer capable of acceptance. For example, in the great case of *Carlill v. Carbolic Smoke Ball Co* [1893] 1 Q.B. 256, the Court of Appeal held that although advertisments are usually not intended to be offers, the advertisment in the case was so clearly and seriously meant that it in fact did constitute an offer; for Bowen L.J.: ". . . it was intended to be understood by the public as an offer which was to acted upon". Thus, "a notice in a shop window stating that 'We will beat an TV . . . price by £ 20 on the spot' has been described as 'a continuing offer'." (Treitel, p. 13, citing *R v.Warwickshire CC ex. p Johnson* [1993] A.C. 583, 588).

Take the example of a Lotto ticket sold in a shop. In the usual course of events, a ticket is purchased by the player filling in a playslip and handing it to a vendor, who processes it through a Lotto machine which prints the ticket; the vendor then hands over the ticket in return for the price. At least three analyses of the situation from the perspective of the rules of offer and acceptance seem possible. First, if the analysis in *Boots* and *Pim* were to be applied, when the playslip is tendered, the player offers, on the terms on the playslip, to buy a Lotto ticket; the vendor accepts the offer by processing the playslip. Second, if, by analogy with *Carlill* and *Johnson*, it was intended by the vendor that the playslip constitute an offer – and this intention was clear from the terms on the playslip – then the tender by the player constitutes the acceptance of the offer. In either case, a contract is then concluded between the player and the vendor, and its terms are the terms on the playslip. It is, however, simply a contract for the purchase and sale of a lottery ticket. There may in turn be a contract between the vendor and the Lottery company which runs the Lotto game; but the relevant contract upon which the player can sue and be sued is the contract with the vendor, and unless that contract provides otherwise, there is on this analysis no contract between the player and the Lottery company. If there is no contract between the player and company, the company cannot be liable to the player for breach of contract.

The third possibility arises by analogy with another aspect of *Carlill*, in which the manufacturer of the carbolic smoke ball, by means of an advertisment in a newspaper, made an offer to all the world that they would pay £ 100 to anyone who bought and used the smokeball but did not have their influenza cured. For Bowen L.J., the advertisment was "an offer made to all the world; and why should not an offer be made to all the world which is to ripen into a contract with anybody who comes forward and performs the condition ? . . . although the offer is made to the world, the contract is made with that limited portion of the public who some forward and perform the condition on the faith of the advertisment", and this approach was approved and followed by Murphy J. in *Tansey*. Thus, in *Carlill* itself, the offer in the advertisment was accepted by Mrs Carlill when she bought and used the smokeball, and when it did not cure her influenza, the manufacturer was liable in contract for the £100. By analogy, the playslip could constitute an offer by the Lottery company that if, in accordance with the terms contained on the playslip, a ticket were purchased from a vendor which contained the numbers in the draw, then the Lottery company would pay the ticket holder a prize. That offer would in turn be accepted by the player purchasing a ticket from a vendor. Not only would there be a contract between the player and the vendor (on either of the above two bases) but a further contract would then also be concluded between the player and the Lottery company, upon the terms contained on the playslip.

In *Carroll v. An Post National Lottery Company* [1996] 1 I.R. 443 (discussed above), faced with just this question of the proper contractual analysis of the purchase of a Lotto ticket, Costello P. held that

> a contractual relationship arises between a player who obtains a ticket
> and defendant company who is holding the lottery. The payslip . . . con-
> stitutes an offer by which the defendant company offers to sell lottery
> tickets to members of the public who complete the payslips in accord-
> ance with the prescribed rules. This offer is accepted when the member
> of the public completes the playslip in accordance with the rules and
> tenders it to the Lotto agent together with the price prescribed by the
> rules appropriate for the number of 'plays' he or she has completed. The
> terms of the parties' contract are contained on the reverse side of the
> playslip. . . . The contract between players and the defendant is a con-
> tract by which the defendant company sells lottery tickets to members of
> the public who have agreed to purchase them in accordance with the
> authorised rules. ([1996] 1 I.R. 443, 454).

In effect, therefore, and without considering the relationship between the player
and the vendor discussed in the first two analyses outlined above, Costello P.
favoured an analysis along the lines of the third, by which the Lottery company makes an offer to all the world on each its playslips, which offer is accepted by a player when a playslip is tendered. (*Quaere* whether the same
reasoning would have generated a contract in *Madden v. The Turf Club* [1997]
2 I.L.R.M. 148. In *Carroll*, the plaintiff handed four Lotto playslips to a vendor (the Lotto agent), who processed three, one twice, but failed to process
the fourth, which the plaintiff claimed contained the numbers which won the
relevant Lotto draw.

According to Costello P., the relevant contract – by which the Lottery company sells tickets to members of the public who have agreed to purchase them
in accordance with the rules – was concluded when the player tendered the
playslips to the vendor. At least two important consequences flow from this
analysis: first, each playslip constitutes a separate offer, independently accepted by each tender resulting in a ticket, so that for each playslip there is a
separate contract. Second, if there is, upon tender of the playslip, a contract to
sell a ticket, if a ticket is not sold in accordance with the playslips tendered,
then there would seem to be a *prima facie* a breach of contract. It follows from
this second point that, here, the failure on the part of the vendor to process the
fourth playslip and sell the resulting ticket would have constituted a breach of
contract by the company: the relevant breach of contract consists in the mere
failure to process the playslip. In the case itself, Costello P. considered that if
there had been a breach of a term that the vendor would exercise due skill care
and diligence, liability would nevertheless have been excluded by the terms of
the contract; it follows that any liability for a mere failure to process the playslip
would also have successfully been met with the exclusion clauses (above,

197-99).

In the alternative, Costello P. could have found that the terms of the Lottery company's offer, accepted by the player's tender of the playslip, was not so much an offer to sell a ticket as an offer to give a prize to winning tickets, or, perhaps, an offer to hold a draw and give a prize to winning tickets. This would have amounted to characterising the contract as one for the supply of a service, which he rejected ([1996] 1 I.R. 443, 454, 458-459). Had he so accepted, then he would have had to consider whether the player had in fact successfully accepted this offer. Clearly, when an offer is made to all the world, the putative acceptor must actually perform the conditions laid down in the offer for that performance to constitute acceptance of the offer. If, for example, Mrs Carlill, intending to buy the defendant's smokeball, instead purchased a different influenza remedy, she would not have satisfied the terms of the defendant's offer, and would not therefore have contracted with them. If she had requested the smokeball from the vendor, she may have an action in breach of contract against that vendor; but by not fulfilling the terms of the defendant's offer, she would not have concluded a contract with them. It is here that the terms of the Lottery company's offer become crucial. At least two alternatives suggest themselves.

First, if, on the facts of *Carroll*, the relevant offer by the Lottery company is to give a prize to winning tickets, then, since the plaintiff had not in fact purchased a ticket with the relevant numbers on it, he had not fulfilled the terms of the offer, and had not therefore concluded a contract with the Lottery company. The player may also have made a contract with the vendor (along the lines of the first and second analyses outlined above) and may therefore have an action in breach of contract against that vendor; but by not fulfilling the terms of the Lottery company's offer, he would not have concluded a contract with them. Unlike in the case itself, the acceptance would not be constituted by the player's tender of the playslip but by the purchase of the ticket, and if that purchase had not happened, as in this hypothetical, the player would not have fulfilled the terms of the offer and thereby accepted it, and no contract in relation to the prize would have arisen in the first place as between the plaintiff-player and the defendant-Lottery company for the breach of which the defendant could be liable. By denying the existence of a contract, this approach excludes contractual liability by the Lottery company to the player; in the event, however, Costello P. reached a similar conclusion by finding that there was a contract between the parties but that, either no term was implied of which the defendant was in breach, or, that the terms of the contract successfully excluded any liability that may have accrued to the defendant. (There is at least one significant difference between this approach and that actually taken by Costello P.: if the defendant were in breach of a duty of care in tort owed to the plaintiff – unlikely if *Madden v. The Turf Club* (Supreme Court, February 17, 1997, analysed in next year's Review) is correct – then the defendant could have relied on the relevant exclusion clauses to exclude this liability only if there were a contract between them, which there would not have been on the approach discussed here, though there was on that taken by Costello P. Even then, Costello P.'s interpretation of the exclusion clauses as not "exempt[ing] the defendant company from liability for the negligence of own servants and employees" [1996] 1 I.R. 443, 465, it may be that the exemption clauses would not be sufficient to exclude liability for the breach of such a duty of care).

Second, if, however, the relevant offer by the Lottery company is to hold a draw and give a prize to winning tickets, then the relevant acceptance could either be the purchase of a ticket (as in the analysis immediately above) or the tender of the playslip (as in the case itself). If it is the former, then, the above analysis demonstrates that no contract arises between the parties; if the latter, then, as in the case itself, a contract does arise. It would then be a contract to supply a service into which section 39 of the 1980 Act would imply a term (above, 197-99) but, for the breach of which, liability would have been validly excluded (above, 199).

In any event, whatever the proper analysis of offer and acceptance here is, the facts of *Carroll* provide, in the context of the significant social phenomenon that is the National Lottery, a fascinating real-life example of that beast beloved of text-books and contract exams, the contract with all the world.

Communication of offers and acceptances; and prescribed modes of such communication   Logic and principle dictate a general rule that the offer or acceptance must be communicated to the other party in the negotiations. This principle is at the heart of the great case of *Carlill v. Carbolic Smokeball Company* [1893] 1 Q.B. 256, in which Bowen L.J. held that "an acceptance of an offer ought to be notified to the person who makes the offer, in order that the two minds may come together" and Lindley L.J. held that "when an offer is made, it is necessary in order to make a binding contract, not only that it should be accepted, but that the acceptance should be notified". It is also at the heart of the decision of Murphy J. in *Tansey v. College of Occupational Therapists* [1995] 2 I.L.R.M. 601.

Whether there was such a communication was an issue which was addressed by Murphy J. in *Kennedy and ors v. AIB plc and AIB Finance Ltd* (High Court, 18 May 1995). Murphy J., after detailing the facts, held that essentially, the plaintiff's claim was laid in contract; they contended that "on three occasions the Defendants . . . agreed to provide [loan] facilities . . . On the balance of probabilities, I am not satisfied that [the agents] made the statements or representations alleged by the Plaintiffs. Accordingly, the claim in contract must fail." This claim is analysed in the 1995 Review, 217. Alternative claims in negligence and for breach of a bank's duty of confidentiality also failed. The plaintiffs appealed (Supreme Court, 29 October 1996) and Hamilton C.J. (O'Flaherty and Denham JJ. concurring) dismissed the appeal. On the contract point, Hamilton C.J. sustained Murphy J.'s findings of fact, and dismissed the appeal (pp. 21-23; 31-33; 40-41).

The same issue was also addressed by Blayney J. (Hamilton C.J., Barrington J. concurring) in the Supreme Court *Embourg v. Tyler* (March 5, 1996); he held that since "the defendant never communicated to the plaintiffs an acceptance of the plaintiffs' offer to purchase, no contract ever came into existence and so there is no contract of which the plaintiffs could claim specific performance" (p. 19). There was on the facts the further wrinkle that the parties had prescribed a mode for that communication: the plaintiffs, by letter, indicated a willingness to sell certain property; the letter concluded with the sentence, *inter alia*, that "neither our negotiations to date, nor this letter, can form part of, nor create, any binding contract between the parties, which must await the formal execution of the appropriate legal documentation by both sides". The defendants, by letter, indicated a willingness to purchase the property; this letter stated, *inter alia*, that "no binding contract is to be deemed to exist until such time as a contract has herein has been executed by all parties". Further correspondence between the parties contained similar statements. Although the plaintiffs had exectued the contract, the defendants, (on officer of one of whom had signed it) had not returned it, and Murphy J. held that this did not amount to the execution of the contract; as the defendants' acceptance of the plaintiffs' offer was not in the presribed terms, no contract had come into existence (pp. 18-19): in "the absence of a communicated acceptance no contract ever came into existence". *Embourg v. Tyler* therefore provides a good example of the general principle that where "an offer states that it can only be accepted in a certain way, the offeror is not, in general, bound unless acceptance is made in that way. Thus if the offeror asks for the acceptance to be sent to a particular place an acceptance sent elsewhere will not bind him, nor, if he asks for an acceptance in writing, will be one bound by one that is oral." (Treitel, p. 29, footnotes omitted).

The case also contains *dicta* on the process adopted by the parties and their solicitors in this case. First, although the procedure of the exchange of contracts is a common feature of English rather than Irish conveyancing practice, Blayney J. (referring to the discussion of *Eccles v. Bryant* [1948] 1 Ch. 93 in the judgment of Keane J. in *Mulhall v. Haren* [1981] I.R. 364, 377-378) considered that "the Court [wa]s not being asked to decide in the abstract if the English practice should be followed. The issue is whether in the light of the negotiations between the parties, and their conduct, it was their intention that it should be." (p. 22). Second, whilst the letters between the parties were headed "subject to contract", the effect of that phrase, – now seemingly settled in the earlier Supreme Court judgment in *Boyle v. Lee* [1992] 1 I.R. 555; [1992] I.L.R.M. 65 (on which see the 1991 Review, 112-13, 125-27; and Dwyer

" 'Subject to Contract' – A Controversy Resolved ?" (1993) 3 *ISLR* 16) – was again on these facts to establish that the parties' intention was that an enforceable contract would not come into existence except by an exchange of written contracts (p. 23). However, he concluded that it "does not follow that whenever there is a sale subject to contract no binding contract comes into existence until contracts have been exchanged. Each case must be decided on its own facts." (p. 26). This should not be seen as an unfortunate prelude of a return to the controversy settled in *Boyle*, but rather as a signal that, although the effect of the phrase 'subject to contract' is that no contract can come into existence based upon correspondence in which that phrase was used, it does not follow that an exchange of written contracts will be necessary for such a contract to come into existence. In principle, all that is necessary is that there be an offer and an acceptance, which may be expressed in correspondence without the term, or which may be by means of an exchange of written contract, or by any other means amounting to an offer and acceptance.

PRINCIPLES OF INTERPRETATION

The *contra proferentem* rule   If a party to a contract chooses "to adopt ambiguous words it seems to me good sense, as well as established law, that those words should be interpreted in the sense which is adverse to the persons who chose and introduced them. . . ." (*In re Sweeney and Kennedy Arbitration* [1950] I.R. 85, 98 *per* Kingsmill-Moore J.). Though this rule is especially striclty applied in the context of exclusion clauses and (*Lynch v. Lynch* [1996] 1 I.L.R.M. 311 provides a good example), it is nonetheless of general application across the entire of the law of contract, and formed the basis of the decision of Keane J. in the Supreme Court in *Cuffe v. CIE and An Post* (Supreme Court, 22 October 1996).

An employee of CIE was injured lifting a mail-bag at Thurles railway station, and recovered in negligence at common law from his employer, CIE. In turn, CIE sought an indemnity from An Post on foot of a contract which provided, *inter alia,* that CIE would indemnify An Post "from and against all actions suits claims or demands arising under the Workmen's Compensation Acts 1934 to 1955 or any statutory reenactment or modification thereof in respect of any personal injury by accident to any guard or servant of [CIE] while in charge of mails . . .". The claim for the indemnity succeeded in the High Court but failed in the Supreme Court. The net issue was whether the indemnity was confined to statutory actions or extended to common law actions.

Keane J. (Hamilton C.J. and Blayney JJ. concurring) held that "[a]s with any other contract, the court is essentially concerned with ascertaining the intention of the parties" (p. 4), rejected an interpretation advanced on behalf of An Post which "would, in effect, . . . rewrite an important provision of the contract" (p. 5), and pointed out (pp. 5-6):

> that this provision was clearly inserted for the benefit of the Minister [the notional employer of CIE employees]. It may be, indeed, that the entire document emanated from the Minister, as the copy produced to us would suggest, but even if the *contra proferentem* rule did not apply to the document, it was undoubtedly for the Minister to ensure that the provision had the extended meaning which his successors now seek to attach to it and they cannot complain if an ambiguously worded provision – if such it is – inserted for their benefit is read against them rather than in their favour. The words of Kingsmill Moore J. in *Roscommon Co Co v. Waldron* [1963] I.R. 407, 419 seem to me to be entirely applicable to this situation:

If the council desired the clause to have a meaning so favourable to it, so onerous to the contractor, and so exceptional in an indemnity it was the business of the Council to make such meaning clear beyond dubiety.

Thus, the words of the clause, inserted by the Minister, envisaged an indemnity to him only in respect of statutory actions. A *contra proferentem* reading confined the clause to that meaning.

REMEDIES FOR BREACH OF CONTRACT

An interesting remedy, for breach by a lessor of a duty to insure leased goods, arose in the course of the judgment of O'Flaherty J. in *Homan v. Kiernan and Lombard & Ulster Banking* (Supreme Court, November 22, 1996; see Dignam (1997) *Bar Review* 403). Section 118 of the Road Traffic Act, 1961 provides that where "a person . . . uses a mechanically propelled vehicle with the consent of the owner of the owner the user shall . . . be deemed to use the vehicle as the servant of the owner but only in so far as the user acts in accordance with such consent". To the extent that a user is liable in negligence for an accident involving such a vehicle, section 118 operates to make the owner vicariously liable. In *Homan v. Kiernan and Lombard & Ulster Banking*, Lombard had leased a truck to Kiernan; Homan had been injured in a collision with the truck. *Prima facie*, Lombard, as owner of the truck could be vicariously liable to Homan. However, although the lease required Kiernan to insure, Kiernan had failed to do so, and the question was whether the failure to adhere to the terms of the lease rendered Lombard's consent void. Flood J. (High Court, July 19, 1996) so held; but on appeal (Supreme Court, November 22, 1996) O'Flaherty J. (Barrington and Murphy JJ. concurring) held, for policy reasons, that the failure to insure "did not vitiate the consent that Kiernan had undoubtedly had been given to drive this vehicle by Lombard" (p. 10).

During the course of his judgment, O'Flaherty J. observed that if "there is a breach of that obligation [on Kiernan to insure] then the owner [Lombard] may insure and recover the costs thereof from the lessee forthwith." (p. 7). This remedy would seem to be an alternative to the standard remedies provided by the law for breach of contract. It is not uncommon in leases of real property for the tenant to undertake to insure the demised premises (e.g. Wylie, *Irish Land Law* (2nd ed., Professional Books, Abingdon, 1986), pp. 815-816, para. 17.050) and in such circumstances if the tenant fails to insure, the it seems that landlord may do so and, if reasonable, recover such amount from the tenant (*Sepes Establishment v. KSK Enterprises* [1993] 2 I.R. 225; [1993] I.L.R.M. 46 (H.C., O'Hanlon J.); Supreme Court, May 21, 1996: here, the lessor undertook to pay 20% of the cost of insuring the premises, the lessee 80%; the lessor procured the insurance, it was held that the premium was not unreasonable and that the lessor was entitled to recover the lessee's 80%). O'Flaherty J. here plainly seems to allow the extension of this principle from leases of real property to leases of personal property, and, if justified, has extended the range of remedies available for such breaches of contract.

Damages   An interesting approach to the calculation of damages for breach of a contract to sell property was taken by Costello P. in *Commerical Fleet Truck Rental v. The Mayer Co.* (High Court, October 11, 1996). The plaintiffs had exercised an option to purchase property they were leasing from the defendants, but difficulties had arisen. In the present action, the plaintiff purchasers were granted an order of specific performance against the defendants who had in breach of contract failed to complete. During the currency of the dispute (contained largely in fitful correspondence between the parties' solicitors) and the litigation, the plaintiffs had remained a tenant of the defendant paying rent according to the lease, and before Costello P. they sought to set off the rent so paid against the outstanding purchase price, on the grounds that such payment of rent would have been avoided had the sale not been prevented by the defendants' breach of contract. Costello P., however, held that the measure of the plaintiffs' loss flowing from the defendants' breach of contract "is the difference between the rent actually paid [in the relevant period] and the sums it would have to have paid to service the loan to purchase the premises" which damages would then be set off against the balance of the purchase price outstanding.

RISK ALLOCATION BY CONTRACT

Where the parties to a contract adopt terms *inter se* to distribute the risks of performance, in principle, the courts should respect this allocation. A strong form of this principle is to be found in the decision of O'Flaherty J. in the Supreme Court in *McCann and Cummins v. Brinks Allied and Ulster Bank* (Supreme Court, November 4, 1996). Here, the plaintiffs were security men employed by Brinks Allied. They were injured in a holdup during a cash delivery to the bank, and sued both Brinks and the bank. Their claim against Brinks succeeded in full on the basis that Brinks had failed to provide a safe system of work; but Morris J. refused to make the bank liable essentially on the grounds that the risk here had been cast upon Brinks by the contract between Brinks and the bank (High Court, May 12, 1995; see the 1995 Review, 232-4). On appeal, O'Flaherty J. (Blayney and Murphy JJ. concurring) expressly adopted this approach.

Brinks argued that the bank was also liable to the plaintiffs in tort, but O'Flaherty J. held that what subsisted between Brinks and the bank was "a contractual relationship between two commercial organisations. The bank engaged Brinks to carry out what was undoubtedly a hazardous activitiy and for which they would be responsible for providing for the safety of their own employees. It would be wrong to infer from the relationship between the parties that the bank, nonetheless, was to be held in a position of owing a duty of care to the Brinks employees". (p. 8). Thus, O'Flaherty J. concluded that "the legal solution to the problem posed is to say that the parties reached an agreement that the risk would lie with Brinks to make sure that the cash was delivered safely . . . In this case the contract was a circumstance which prevented any duty of care arising on the part of the bank *vis-á-vis* the Brinks' employees. It is, therefore, a preventative factor, rather than an intervening one, which negatives the existence of a duty of care here." (pp. 9-10).

The tort elements of the argument are analysed in the Tort chapter, below, pp. 000-000; for present purposes it is sufficient to observe that, so far as the law of contract is concerned, the essence of the case is that the parties' allocation of any risk ought to be respected. In the 1995 Review, 234, it was suggested that this result was "entirely consistent" with a line of authorities in which it has been held that, if A contracts to have B do some work, and B has the benefit of an exclusion clause in the contract, and B hires C to do the work, C may also the benefit of the exclusion clause, even though C is not a party to the contract between A and B (e.g. *Elder, Dempster v. Paterson, Zochonis* [1924] A.C. 522; *The Mahkutai* [1996] 3 All E.R. 502 (H.L.); *cp London Drugs v. Kuehne & Nagel International* (1992) 97 D.L.R. (4th) 261 (S.C.C.)). It should, however, be noted, that in such circumstances, the court is not denying that C owes A a duty of care, it is merely stating that though a duty of care arises, the exclusion clause provides C with a defence. O'Flaherty

J. in *McCann* expressly went further, denying that C owed A any duty of care, and it may be questioned whether the alloaction of risks as between two parties to a contract (here A and B) should require the denial of a duty of care by one of those parties (A) to a third party (C) who is not a party to a contract. In *McCann*, there was a contract between A and B, in which the risks of performance are cast upon B. If B performs and suffers loss, as between A and B that is a loss for which B has agreed that A is not to be responsible; he himself is to bear it, and he cannot look to A for compensation. If, instead, B has C perform, and C is injured, again, as between A and B that is a loss for which B has agreed that A is not to be responsible; again B has to bear it. This does not seem to require that A is not liable to C; instead, it seems to require that B indemnify A in respect of any liability which A may have to C; and if the express terms of the contract cast the risk upon B but do not expressly require such an indemnity, then an implied term that B will so indemnify A should not be far to seek.

On the facts of *McCann*, the employee-plaintiffs, C, had already recovered from their employer, B, and the question in the Supreme Court was whether A was also liable to C, so that B could treat A as a concurrent wrongdoer. In other words, the question was whether *as between A and B*, A could be made liable to C; and the contractual allocation of risks as between A and B required that the question be answered in the negative. On the particular facts of the case, since B had already been found liable to C, it did not particularly matter whether respect for the contractual allocation of risks as between A and B was to be achieved by denying any liablility (for example in tort) by A to C (as O'Flaherty J. did), or by requiring that B idemnify A in respect of any liability to C; since in either case B would be fully liable to C. But in some circumstances, it could matter considerably; for example, let the contract between A and B be the same, but C has chosen only to sue A. Here, whether C's claim against A entirely disappears, or whether A is liable to C but has an indemnity from B, becomes of great practical importance. On O'Flaherty J's approach, C is owed no duty of care, and C must lose. On the other hand, if A owes a duty of care to C but recovers an indemnity from B, then C need not lose. In either case, A is not out of pocket, which is the intent of the contract between A and B and the aim of O'Flaherty J's judgment. In both cases, the position of A is the same, but in the former, the result is unjust to C, whereas in the latter it is not. Consquently, the latter approach, by which B would indemnify A for any liability to C, ought to be preferred.

Two further considerations justify this conclusion. First, O'Flaherty J's reasoning in *McCann* destabalizes the law of tort; this is addressed below in the tort chapter, 577-9. Second, O'Flaherty J's reasoning in *McCann* also destabalizes the law of contract: it is a cardinal principle of the law of contract that a person who is not a party to a contract cannot acquire rights and liabilities under that contract. Though riven with exceptions, this doctrine of privity is still central to the law of contract. On the facts of *McCann*, the risks as between A and B were allocated by a contract between A and B. C was not a party to the agreement between A and B, and could not thus be bound by it. Therefore, an agreement between A and B cannot exclude A's liability to C. It is true that there are many exceptions to the doctrine of privity, and that it has been the subject of many cogent judicial and academic attacks (see, for example, the 1995 Review, 234). It is also true that the exemption clause cases above represent one of those exception. But even if the doctrine of privity were held not to apply here, or the common law were to abandon the doctrine of privity so that the principle were accepted that a person not a party to a contract could in principle obtain rights and liabilities under that contract, it would still be necessary to determine whether in a case such as this, C should obtain, from the contract between A and B, an inability to sue A; nothing in the case suggests that O'Flaherty J. undertook such an analysis, and nothing in principle requires such an outcome. Thus, from the perspective of the Law of Contract, the approach of O'Flaherty J. is antithetical to the principle of privity, and his decision should not be seen as a *sub silentio* departure from it.

In conclusion, therefore, while the approach of Morris and O'Flaherty JJ. is to be welcomed for their deference to contractual allocation of risk, this principle does not require O'Flaherty J's denial of a duty of care in tort between the bank and the plaintiffs, and would have been better served by the implication of a term to the effect that if the bank were to be liable to the plaintiffs, Brinks would indemnify the bank for such liability. In that way, the principle of contractual allocation of risk would be subserved, but the structures of the law of tort and the law of contract would not be destabilized.

SPECIFIC PERFORMANCE

A relatively straightfoward claim for specific performance presented itself to Costello P. in *Commerical Fleet Truck Rental v. The Mayer Co.* (High Court, October 11, 1996) (above) and he granted the decree. The plaintiff company held from the defendant both a lease of factory premises, and a licence to use – in common with three other tenants – an adjoining yard for business purposes to use "with or without vehicles . . . for all purposes incidental to the use of the demised premises". The lease granted the tenant an option to purchase a 999 lease in the property on the terms of the Law Society's contract for sale, and an irrevocable 999 year licence over the yard "for the same purpose" as the former licence. The plaintiff purported to exercise these options, and the parties agreed that the under the resulting conveyance, the defendant would convey the fee simple rather than a 999 year lease in the premises. Though the defendants disputed it, Costello P. also found that the defendants agreed to convey not to the plaintiff company but to its two directors (p. 14), and that since the licence was appurtenant to the lease, it would have been assignable with the lease, and was thus not personal to the plaintiff but assignable to and exerisable by the directors (pp. 16-17). In any event, the defendants agreement to convey to the directors "implied an agreement that the license would also be granted to them". (p. 17).

Some time after the exercise of the option, the defendant's solicitor wrote to the plaintiff's solicitor with a draft contract of sale (containing various special conditions) but referring to the yard as a car park shared with the other tenants and the defendants in which the plaintiffs could have four spaces. The plaintiff's solicitor replied, disputing as too narrow, and inconsitent with the licence and option, the definition of the yard as a car park, but enclosed a deposit in respect of the purchase and an amended draft contract of sale from which two of the special conditions had been deleted, and which named the plaintiff company's directors as purchasers. Seven months later, the defendant's solicitor replied with a draft licence on their earlier terms and an amended draft contract naming as purchasers the plaintiff and not its directors. The following month, the defendants served a notice to complete upon the plaintiffs; there followed acrimonious correspondence, and, in this action. the plaintiffs sought specific performance of a contract of sale of the premises and a licence over the yard on the terms set forth in the option, as varied by agreement to provide for conveyance of the freehold rather than a 999 year lease.

Costello P. held that the "plaintiffs are clearly entitled to have that contract specifically enforced if the defendant resiles from it. That is what in my opinion the defendant has done . . . [when he] refused to grant a licence in accordance with" (pp. 11-12) the terms of the original licence, for business use with the other tenants, rather than as a car park shared not only with the other tenants but also with the defendants. Thus, the defendant company was "contractually bound to grant a licence in the form granted in the option agreement, namely a licence to use the yard in common with the owners of the three adjoining factory units, but not in common with the defendant company as well". (p. 13) As to the terms of the contract of sale, the "parties had agreed that the sale would be subject to the conditions in the Law Society's draft contract. No condition similar to Special Condition 4 [one of the two conditions which had been inserted by the defendant but disputed by the plaintiff] was contained in it and the plaintiffs cannot be required to agree to it." (p. 15). Presumably, though Costello P. does not say so, the same reasoning would have applied to exclude the other disputed special condition, but, because the parties had agreed other special conditions, they would have been included. In the event, therefore, Costello P. ordered specific performance of a contract for the sale of the fee simple in the factory premises to the directors, including a licence to use the adjoining yard for business purposes.

UNDUE INFLUENCE

A bank makes a loan to a borrower, upon foot of a security provided by a surety. When the borrower defaults, and the plaintiff bank (P) seeks to enforce the security, the defendant surety (D) may seek to resist on the ground that the borrower (T, a third party to the contract between P and D) by means of undue influence, coerced the surety to grant the security to the bank. There are at least seven possible analyses of such a situation (see the 1993 Review, 194-209 and the 1995 Review, 235-9; note that apart from the seven positions outlined below, section 3 of the Family Home Protection Act, 1976 may also be relevant; see *id* analysing *Bank of Ireland v. Smyth* [1993] 2 I.R. 102; [1993] I.L.R.M. 790 (H.C.); [1996] 1 I.L.R.M. 241 (S.C.)).

First, since the enforceability of the contract against D is based upon D's consent, the simple fact of T's coercion vitiating D's consent to the contract should be sufficient to allow D to avoid the contract with P (the "coercion *simpliciter* " strategy). Second, if T were an agent for P, since the acts of the agent are the acts of the principal, if T has coerced D, in law it is as if P had coerced D, and D can avoid the contract (the "agency" strategy). Third, the contract between P and D may be said to be unenforceable because, and only when, P actually knew of T's undue influence: on this view, it is not enough that P have constructive notice of T's undue influence (the "actual knowledge" strategy). Fourth, since T's exercise of undue influence is an equitable wrong which gives the party coerced, D, an equity to set aside the contract, if P has notice of T's undue influence, then D can avoid the contract (the "notice" strategy). Fifth, the contract between P and D may be said to be unenforceable because of P's complicity or culpability in T's equitable fraud on D (and the basis of that complicity is P's notice of T's equitable fraud), (the "equitable fraud" strategy). Sixth, a court could simply hold that in all the circumstances of the case, T's coercion made it "unconscionable" for P to enforce the contract as against D, or the transaction was "improvident" for D (the "unconscionability" strategy) – (a recent important application of this doctrine is provided by *Crédit Lyonnais v. Burch* [1997] 1 All E.R. 144; [1997] 1 F.L.R. 11; [1996] 5 Bank L.R. 233; (1996) 146 *N.L.J.* 1421 (C.A.), on which see Hooley and O'Sulllivan [1997] *L.M.C.L.Q.* 17 (critical of the decision); Chen-Wishart [1997] *C.L.J.* 60 (approving of it, and seeing in unconscionability a general justification for the undue influence jurisdiction in equity). Seventh, if T and D are husband and wife, and if vulnerable wives possess a special equity as against creditors such as P to whom they offer security for debts of their husbands, then D may be able to avoid the contract with P (the "special equity" strategy).

The analysis in the 1993 and 1995 Reviews concluded in favour of the first, coercion *simpliciter*, strategy on the ground that it is entirely sound in principle. As to the alternatives: either a court enforces a contract plainly procured by objectionable means, or spuriously finds that T is an agent for P (if using the "agency" strategy), or that P knew of T's undue influence (if using the "actual knowledge" strategy), or that P had notice of T's undue influence (if using the "notice" or "equitable fraud" strategies). The unconscionability strategy allows the court to render objectionable contracts unenforceable, but if that result is achieved as a consequence simply of the fact of the (actual or presumed) undue influence, saying that the transaction is thereby unconscionable or improvident adds nothing of substance to the analysis and is not therefore necessary. As to the "special equity" strategy, it is probably unconstitutional having regard to the emerging constitutional doctrine of spousal equality, and, if not, should anyhow be rejected as adding as little to the analysis as characterising the transaction as unconscionable. The agency, actual knowledge, notice, equitable fraud, unconscionability and special equity strategies being unsatisfactory, the law should reject them and adopt the coercion *simpliciter* strategy. A similar conclusion seems to have been reached by Delany: "[p]erhaps the best approach is that if there is no wrongdoing on a husband's part, then a financial institution should not be penalised, even if it has failed to take any steps to ensure that the wife understands the transaction and has received independent legal advice. However, where a husband has been engaged in conduct amounting to the exercise of undue influence, the bank can only enforce the gurantee provided it has taken the steps just referred to." (*Equity and the Law of Trusts in Ireland* (Round Hall Sweet & Maxwell, 1996), pp. 489-490). For Delany, then, the simple fact of the undue influence would have the effect of invalidating the transaction, unless the undue influence were cured. Such an approach would have the merit of laying down clear guidelines which would protect any surety wife in need of protection, and allow a bank to be sure that any transaction entered into after such steps would be valid, without having recourse to unsatisfactory metaphysical debates about matters such as the quality of the bank's notice.

English law has committed itself to the notice strategy; the matter has been unequivocally settled by the speech of Lord Browne-Wilkinson in the House of Lords in *Barclays Bank v. O'Brien* [1994] 1 A.C. 180, though it is arguable that the authorities supported that position even before his Lordship's decision (see *e.g.*, Chin, "Undue Influence and Third Parties" (1992) 5 *J.C.L.* 108; *cp* Gardner "A Confused Wife's Equity" (1982) 2 *O.J.L.S.* 130, 134). However, before the decision of Murphy J. (O'Flaherty and Blayney JJ. concurring) in the Supreme Court in this year's *Bank of Novia Scotia v. Hogan* (unreported, November 6, 1996) the matter had not been judicially settled in Ireland, though five occasions for such a resolution had presented themselves to the courts.

The first opportunity seems to to have been *Provincial Bank of Ireland v. McKeever* [1941] I.R. 471. Trustees (T) advised beneficiaries (D) to secure an overdraft with the bank (P) by way of mortgages, thereby extinguishing the trustees' personal liability on the overdraft. In an action by the bank against the beneficiaries to enforce the mortgages, Black J. held, first, that a presumption of undue influence arose as between the trustees and beneficiaries (T and D) (480-481); second, that it arose "not ony against [T], but also against [P], if that party is aware of the circumstances which give rise to the equity against [T]" (482); third, that since P was in fact aware of the circumstances, it would not be able to enforce the mortgages if the presumption were not rebutted; and fourth, that the presumption was rebuttable (484), and − although D had not received independent advice (486) − had nonetheless been rebutted. Whilst it is clear that Black J.'s predicating of D's equity to set the mortgage aside upon P's "awareness" of the circumstances probably represented a judicial rejection of the "coercion *simpliciter*" stragegy, and the "agency" strategy (in particular, because Black J. held that it was unnecessary that P "should 'claim under'" T (482)) and probably of the "unconscionability" strategy, the requirement of "awareness" was ambiguous as between the "actual knowledge" and "notice" strategies (*dicta* at p. 483 speak of P "knowing" of the circumstances, whereas *dicta* at p. 484 refer to P having "taken with notice"), and may even have been sufficiently wide to encompass rationalisation as an example of the "equitable fraud" strategy; and by the very nature of the facts, the case said nothing as to the status of the wife's "special equity" strategy. The earlier *McMackin v. Hibernian Bank* [1905] I.R. 296 − contemplating the law protecing children not yet emancipated from their parents' influence "not by curtailing their capacity to deal with others, but by biding the consciences of those who deal with them . . . [when] the Court is jealous in its investigation of cases of the kind" ([1905] I.R. 296, 304-305 *per* Barton J.) seems to contain the seeds of quite a different "special equity", though in the end liability seems to have attached because the creditor had "full knowledge and full notice of all the circumstances that gave rise to the equity" (306), in which case, the decision is similar to *McKeever*. In any event, though the matter was raised, and some important clarification resulted, it could hardly have been said that either *McMackin v. Hibernian Bank* or *Provincial Bank of Ireland v. McKeever* had unequivocally settled it.

Second, in *Gregg v. Kidd* [1956] I.R. 183, although undue influence was pleaded against the recipient, "the evidence was mainly directed to establishing that influence had been obtained and exercised over [D] by . . . [T]. There is no doubt in my mind that if it be shown that this deed was obtained by the undue influence of [T] . . . this deed cannot stand" ([1956] I.R. 183, 195 *per* Budd J.). Although Budd J. later found that P "knew all about [T's] efforts . . . he was perfectly aware of [T's] influence over [D] and perfectly willing to accept the benefit of its exercise on his behalf" ([1956] I.R. 183, 200), in his statement of relevant principle, it was enough for him that T had unduly influenced D to confer the benefit upon P; which seems to be a rather straightforward assumption and application of the coercion *simpliciter* strategy.

Furthermore, Budd J. declined a request to decide the case on the basis of the unconscionability strategy (205-206), though in terms which recognised the general utility of that doctrine and did not reject it in principle on the facts. This, coupled with the absence of a discussion on this point of either *McMackin* or *McKeever*, or of the knowledge and notice strategies as matters of principle, probably means that the matter cannot be regarded as having been settled by *Gregg v. Kidd* either.

Third, the matter did not properly arise for discussion in the earlier proceedings of *Bank of Ireland v. Smyth* (see the discussion 1993 Review, pp. 202-208; Mee (1996) 14 *I.L.T.* (*ns*) 188 (part 1), 209 (part 2); and Sanfey (1996) 3 *C.L.P.* 31), since, in the end, the case resolved itself into a question of the proper interpretation of the Family Home Protection Act, 1976. A similar fate befell the fourth opportunity: this year's *AIB v. Finnegan* [1996] 1 I.L.R.M. 401. Here AIB, (the Bank) made a loan, secured by way of mortgage, to Mr Finnegan to purchase a family home. At the office of Mr Finnegan's solicitors, Mrs Finnegan signed a form under section 3 of the Family Home Protection Act, 1976 to the effect that she consented to that transaction. When the Bank sought possession on foot of the mortgage, she resisted, claiming that she did not understand the nature of the document which she had signed; but the Bank contended that it was a bona fide purchaser protected by section 3(3) of the Act. In the High Court (July 11, 1995), Carroll J. held that the Bank was entitled to its order for possession: "This is a case where the bank had no knowledge of any claim by Mrs Finnegan. It dealt with her entirely through her husband's solicitor, and its going too far to say that a bank must deal directly with the spouse, and cannot rely on normal conveyancing practice between solicitors. . . . [The Bank] is in the position of a *bona fide* purchaser for value without notice . . .". An appeal to the Supreme Court was allowed. Since section 3(4) provides that "if any question arises in any proceedings as to whether a conveyance is valid . . . the burden of proving that validity shall be on the person alleging it". Thus, "[h]ere, the bank is alleging the mortgage is valid by reason of section 3(3) and accordingly the burden of proving that validity rests on the bank." A full plenary hearing in the High Court was ordered, but the case seems to have been settled before the plenary hearing came on, and before, therefore, a resolution of the issue was possible.

The fifth opportunity was presented by the litigation in *Bank of Novia Scotia v. Hogan*. In the High Court (December 21, 1992), Keane J. was faced with a plea, based upon *Chaplin v. Brammall* [1907] 1 K.B. 233 and *Turnbull v. Duvall* [1902] A.C. 429 to the effect that Mrs Hogan was someone "who required genuinely independent advice before she entered into a transaction which, from her point of view, was of no direct benefit." (p. 12). Taking the plea first on its merits, Keane J. held that Mrs Hogan had, in the event received independent legal advice (p. 13). Though *Turnbull* has come to be seen as the genesis of the "agency" approach, it and *Chaplin* were relied upon in *Yerkey v. Jones* to generate, in favour of a surety wife, a "special equity" which sounds extraordinarily similar to the plea on behalf of the wife before Keane J. However, the learned judge understood it simply as a "suggestion that a wife is always presumed to be acting under the influence of her husband in such circumstances" (p. 12) and held that such a presumption "is not borne out by other authorities" (*ibid*). Beyond this, however, the judgment of Keane J. provided little guidance on the question of which approach to the question of the enforceability by the bank of the surety wife's security would be adopted.

The matter seems to have been resolved on appeal in that case: Murphy J. distinguished *Smyth*, rejected the special equity strategy, and adopted the notice stragegy (though without reference to the ambiguity in *McKeever* or the alternative position adopted in *Gregg v. Kidd*) placing Irish law on the same footing as English law on this point – indeed, Scots law, which had earlier adopted the "actual knowledge" strategy (*Mumford v. Bank of Scotland* 1994 S.L.T. 1288), has been placed on a similar footing following the acceptance of *O'Brien* by the House of Lords on appeal from Scotland in *Smith v. Bank of Scotland* (House of Lords, unreported, 12 June 1997). In *Hogan*, Mrs Hogan, having received indepedent legal advice, deposited with the bank title deeds to her property as an unlimited security upon her husband's indebtedness. Applying the notice strategy, Murphy J. found that Mr Hogan had not exercised undue influence over Mrs Hogan, but held that he done so and had an equity in her favour arisen of which the bank had notice, then the solicitor's independent legal advice to Mrs Hogan would have afforded a defence to the bank; he also found as a fact that the bank had not exercised any undue influence over Mrs Hogan; he therefore concluded that the bank's security over Mrs Hogan's property was valid and enforceable (the case is also analysed in detail in our Equity chapter, below, 297). Murphy J. distinguished *Bank of Ireland v. Smyth* on the grounds that "cases turning on the adequacy of a consent required and alleged to have been given under [s.3 of] the Family Home Protection Act, 1976 are distinguishable from those in which it is alleged that a spouse in dealing with his or her own property did, or may have, acted under undue influence" (pp. 10-11), so that the "crucial distinction is that Mrs Hogan was dealing with property of which she was the owner whereas Mrs Smyth was being asked to give and purported to give her consent under section 3 of the Family Home Protection Act 1976 to a mortgage of the family home by her husband." (p. 10; compare the similar conclusion in the 1993 Review, 202-208). Furthermore, Murphy J. rejected the "special equity" strategy on the grounds that he did not find it "satisfying as a matter of legal logic or fully acceptable as an analysis of the rights or capabilities of women generally and married women in particular" (p. 13). This chill is but one example of the frosty reception now being accorded to this doctrine in the common law world generally (see the 1993 Review, 200-201; the 1995 Review, 235-9; and Williams, "Equitable Principles for the Protection of Vulnerable Guarantors:

Is the Principle of *Yerkey v. Jones* Still Needed ?" (1994) 8 *JCL* 67). These red herrings once exposed, the way was clear for Murphy J. to determine the proper legal analysis of the situation sketched at the outset of this section and which presented itself for resolution in *Hogan*.

At the outset of his analysis on this point, Murphy J. approved the traditional views which he derived from the speech of Lord Browne-Wilkinson in *O'Brien*, that "(i) as between the innocent party and the alleged wrongdoer the burden of proving the exercise of undue influence falls on the inncoent party. (ii) There are, however, recognised categories of relationship within which there is apresumption that the alleged wrongdoer has abused his position so that the onus is on him to prove that such was not the case. (iii) The decision in *Bank of Montreal v. Stuart* [1911] A.C. 120 determined that the relationship between husband and wife did not as a matter of law raise a presumption of undue influence by a husband over his wife." (p. 12) It is understandable that the speech of Lord Browne-Wilkinson having in this regard provided so reliable a road-map, Murphy J. chose to be guided by it again in adopting and applying to the facts of *Hogan* the notice strategy outlined in *O'Brien*. It is, perhaps, to be regretted that the other strategies and earlier Irish authorities outlined above seem not to have been before him, if only because a more complete knowledge of the options available would render more secure the coclusion reached.

Rather more unfortunate, however, is the central role which the notion of independent legal advice seems to play in the case; Murphy J. tells us that "the greater part of the argument before this court (and much of the judgment of the learned trial judge) related to the sufficiency of the advice given" (p. 7) by the solicitor on the grounds that his firm acted for the bank in other matters, and that the advice was unsatisfactory and given in the bank in the presence of the officials at a time when Mrs. Hogan was effectively committed to the transaction. "It was argued that independent legal advice should be given privately and in good time, so that a client could, without undue embarrassment, withdrawn from a transaction if that was to be the outcome of the advice given to her. or to him" (p. 8). As to the independence of the advice, in the High Court, Keane J. had held although the solicitors who had acted for the husband and wife in this case had "acted for the bank from time to time, they did not act for them in relation to these transactions." (at p. 5 of his judgment). As to the quality of the advice, Keane J. found that the solicitor present with the wife (and husband and manager) in the bank had explained to Mrs Hogan that she was under no obligation to make the deposit but that if she did so, the Bank would be entitled to sell the property in the event of a default by her husband (at pp. 6-9). Consequently, he held that the bank was not in breach of any fiduciary duties which it may have owed to Mr Hogan (p. 10). Similarly, in the Supreme Court, Murphy J. held that the "availability of appropriate indepedent legal advice to Mrs Hogan would afford the Bank a defence on a claim by her in respect of an equity to set aside the transaction if such equity had existed" (pp. 15-16) though, since Mr Hogan had not exercised undue influence upon her, Mrs Hogan had no such equity. It was argued in the 1993 Review, 195-196 and again in the 1995 Review, 236, that the presence of independent advice is at best an unreliable guide. There may be no such advice, and yet the contract could be voluntary; or, there may be independent advice, and yet the undue influence could be so strong that such advice would be ineffective or ignored. In either such case, a search simply for independent advice would reach a different conclusion to an analysis of whether there was in truth a voluntary consent. Consequently, independent advice is not some talismanic cure for coercion; it may be an important factor to be taken into account, but it should not be used a proxy for an analysis as to whether a spouse's consent was a valid one. (Similar views are expressed by Barton J. in *McMakin v. Hibernian Bank* [1905] I.R. 296, 304-305, by Budd J. in *Gregg v. Kidd* [1956] I.R. 183,196-197, in which the advice from the solicitor may not have been independent and was certainly inadequate to enable the plaintiff to understand what he was doing (204-205), and by Black J. in *Provincial Bank of Ireland v. McKeever* [1941] I.R. 471, 484-481, in which there was no indepedent legal advice, but the presumption was nevertheless rebutted on the facts). Thus, if Mr Hogan had in fact exercised such undue influence upon Mrs Hogan, then the few short sentences from her solicitor at the bank may very well not have had any impact at all in removing the effect of such undue influence and rendering her consent a real one.

Though the effect of the decision of Murphy J. in *Hogan* can be shortly stated (*Smyth* distinguished; *Yerkey* rejected; *O'Brien* in the House adopted), there occur in the course of his judgment both a passage which is not as clear as it might be, and a question which Murphy J. seemed to leave open. The problematic passage occurs during Murphy J.'s treatment of the special equity strategy. Having referred to certain aspects of the speech of Lord Browne-Wilkinson in the House of Lords in *Barclay's Bank v. O'Brien*, Murphy J. continued that:

> notwithstandng the fact that the relationship of husband and wife has been held not to raise a presumption of undue influence some special status does appear to have been accorded to wives in a variety of decided cases. Scott L.J. [in the Court of Appeal in *Barclay's Bank v. Brien* [1993] Q.B. 109] referred to married women being treated by the law *"more tenderly"* than others and in the Australian case of *Yerkey v. Jones* (1939) 63 C.L.R. 649 Dixon J. referred to *"the invalidating tendency"* applied by the Courts in relation to transactions between a husband and a wife. The consequence appears to be that whilst the matrimonial relationship as such does not give rise to a presumption of undue influence it may be possible to identify circumstances in a particular case which

would more readily raise that presumption in favour of a wife than any outside party. I confess that I do not find the conclusions of the House of Lords in this regard satisfying as a matter of legal logic or fully acceptable as an analysis of the rights or capabilities of women generally and married women in particular. (at pp. 12-13; emphasis in original).

Clearly the tenor of the last sentence is to reject the invalidating tendency as inappropriate to the capabilities of women, but the reference to the "conclusions of the House of Lords" is puzzling. Even more so is his later comment that, the "House of Lords went on to apply the *'invalidating tendency'* and *'tender treatment'* principles to the facts of the *Barclays Bank* case . . .". However, in *Barclays Bank v. O'Brien*, it was Scott L.J. in the Court of Appeal who advocated the invalidating tendency / special equity approach; in the House of Lords, Lord Browne-Wilkinson, far from applying it to the facts, *rejected* it as unjustified in principle, inconsistent with established law on the presumption of undue influence, unsupported by authority (apart from *Yerkey v. Jones*), and unnecessary if the notice strategy is properly applied ([1994] 1 A.C. 180, 195). On his Lordship's approach in the House of Lords, if D's consent to the contract of security with P was procured by T by the exercise of equitable fraud, an equity arose in D's favour, and if P had notice of that equity, P could not enforce the security as against D. He gave undue influence and misrepresentation as examples of this equitable fraud: invalidating tendencies and special equities are nowhere to be seen in this analysis. Consequently, it seems that the House of Lords, unlike the Court of Appeal, far from adopting *Yerkey v. Jones*, in fact advocted a position on this point broadly similar to the sentiments of Murphy J. in the last sentence above. It is thererfore submitted that Murphy J. must be taken as rejecting on this point, not the conclusions of the House of Lords, but those of the Court of Appeal.

Finally, as to the question which Murphy J. seemed to leave open, towards the end of his judgment, he assumed, "without deciding, that married women in this jurisdiction may in certain circumstances enjoy as against their husbands a presumption that undue influence was excercised", allowed "that those circumstances existed in the present case" and held that "the fatal flaw in Mrs Hogan's case is that no undue influence was exercised by her husband and that she has no equity against him to have the transaction set aside and, that being so, she has no prior equity on which she can rely in order to defeat the Bank's claim". (p. 15). Cearly, what Murphy J. had in mind in the passage is the orthodox analysis of undue influence, and not the *Yerkey v. Jones* principle, as it seems that he had already rejected that princple, which anyhow turns not on the bank's notice of the husband's undue influence over the wife but upon a duty upon the bank to treat with special tenderness the surety wife by ensuring that she is at least independently advised, whether or not there was any actual or presumed undue influence, and, if there was, whether or not the bank had notice of it. As to that question of whether married women may enjoy as against their husbands a presumption that undue influence was excercised, the orthodox analysis of undue influence already supplies an answer.

On the principles adopted by Costello J. in *O'Flanagan v. Ray-Ger* (1963-1993) Ir. Co. Law Rep. 289 (April 28, 1983), equity will give relief against undue influence actually exercised, and, in relationships where one party has great influence over the other, and there is a significant risk that this party will take advantage of this influence and coerce or victimise the other party into a contract, equity will raise a presumption that the stronger party obtained that benefit by virtue of the exercise of undue influence. In the context of the relationship between a banker and a customer, whislt in principle, a banker may be found to have exercised actual undue influence over the customer, there is no presumption of undue influence in the banker-customer relationship, though the particular facts of a particular relationship may raise the presumption. Thus, in *Lloyd's Bank v. Bundy* [1975] Q.B. 326, an old man, surety for his son's debts, relied entirely on his bank manager; the Court of Appeal held that the circumstances raised a presumption of undue influence on the part of the bank manager; whereas, in *Nat West v. Morgan* [1985] A.C. 686, the relationship between surety wife and the bank manager did not go beyond ordinary business relationship into one of reliance; thus there were no circumstances to raise the presumption; likewise in *Hogan* (to the same effet; see Keane J. in the High Court (at pp. 14-15) expressly following *Morgan*; Murphy J. on appeal (p. 16)). Similarly, in the husband-wife relationship: in principle, if a husband has actually coerced his wife, then she can plead actual undue against him; and, although, as Murphy J. himself made clear earlier his judgment in *Hogan*, the husband-wife relationship does not automatically raise the presumption, nonetheless, the individual circumstances of any given marital relationship can give rise to such a presumption. Thus, there was no question for Murphy J. to leave open. In the end, however, if, as seems likely, *Hogan* has had the effect of clarifying the law on undue influence by a third party, then it is the most significant of this year's decisions on the Law of Contract.

Criminal Law

A series of four Acts enacted by or presented to the Oireachtas within days of each other in late June and early July 1996 aimed to provide a more effective legislative basis on which to enforce existing legislation concerning organised crime, in particular drug trafficking. The Acts in question were: the Disclosure of Certain Information for Taxation and Other Purposes Act 1996 (232, below), the Criminal Justice (Drug Trafficking) Act 1996 (241, below), the Proceeds of Crime Act 1996 (233, below) and the Criminal Assets Bureau Act 1996 (234, below). The legislative activity may be seen against the immediate background of the murder of investigative journalist Veronica Guerin on the outskirts of Dublin in June 1996. It was accepted that her murder, which resulted in widespread revulsion, was most likely to have been organised by members of a criminal gang or gangs operating in Ireland whose activities had been highlighted in a series of newspaper articles written by Veronica Guerin. We discuss these legislative provisions in turn. One other significant change was the Sixteenth Amendment to the Constitution Act 1996, enacted on foot of the approval by referendum in November 1996 of restrictions on the granting of bail.

ASSAULT

Jurisdiction of District Court: title to land involved   In *Curtis v. Brennan*, High Court, May 23, 1996, Moriarty J. considered whether the respondent judge of the District Court continued to have jurisdiction in an assault case in which the parties had been involved in a dispute over the ownership of land. He held that section 46 of the Offences against the Person Act 1861, which provides for ouster of the District Court's jurisdiction where a question as to title arose in an assault, did not apply where, as here, the alleged question of title to lands did not go to the heart of the matter to such an extent that an adjudication on the criminal summons or charge would fundamentally depend on such question of title. He referred to *R. v. French* [1902] 1 K.B. 637 in this context. He thus concluded that the respondent retained jurisdiction.

BAIL

Estreatment   In *Director of Public Prosecutions v. Martin and Callinan*,

High Court, May 23, 1996, Flood J. estreated bail where independent sureties were found wholly in dereliction of duty. The first and second respondents had been approved as independent sureties in two separate sums of £20,000 in respect of three accused persons who had been granted bail by the High Court. The conditions attaching to the bail included that the accused resided with the respondents and report to the local Garda station. The three accused failed to appear for trial. One was later re-arrested and returned to the jurisdiction. The Director applied to have the surety of each respondent estreated. Flood J. granted the application in so far as the non-appearance was related to dereliction. Applying the decision in *The State (Tynan) v. Sweeney* [1965] I.R. 444, he noted that the court had a discretion under the Fines (Ireland) Act 1851 to forfeit a recognisance and was empowered to take into account the means by which the defaulting surety has discharged his obligations. He held that the second respondent was wholly in dereliction of his duty and took no interest whatsoever in the movements or activities of one of the accused. As to the first respondent, Flood J. found he was fully aware that two of the accused were about to abscond and he took no active steps to advise the Gardaí in time. However, since the failure of the third accused (who had been subsequently re-arrested) to appear for trial was due to the act of a third party, exercising his judicial discretion, Flood J. declined to estreat the recognisance associated with him.

Refusal of bail if person likely to commit offence on bail   The Sixteenth Amendment of the Constitution Act 1996, enacted on foot of a referendum held in November 1996, provided for an additional sub-section to be added to Article 40.4 of the Constitution, the provision which deals with deprivation of personal liberty. Article 40.4.7° of the Constitution, inserted by the Sixteenth Amendment Act states:

> Provision may be made by law for the refusal of bail by a court to a person charged with a serious offence where it is reasonably considered necessary to prevent the commission of a serious offence by that person.

The effect of the new Article 40.4.7° is that legislation could be enacted providing for the refusal of bail on the basis that a person charged with a 'serious offence' (a novel term introduced into the Constitution by the 1996 amendment) may be likely to commit an offence if granted bail. Such a ground was held impermissible by the Supreme Court in its landmark ruling *The People v. O'Callaghan* [1966] I.R. 501, which it confirmed in its decision in *Ryan v. Director of Public Prosecutions* [1989] I.R. 399; [1989] I.L.R.M. 333 (1988 Review, 144-7). The reversing of the *O'Callaghan* decision (which was attempted in conventional precedental terms in the *Ryan* case) has been on the political agenda for a number of years. The November 1996 referendum was held against the background of virtually unanimous political support for its terms, a unanimity which may be connected with the murder of journalist Veronica Guerin referred to at the outset of this chapter. Nonetheless, the restriction effected by the 1996 amendment on granting of bail, and the consequent increase in the numbers who are likely to be remanded in custody pending trial, had been widely criticised both prior to and during the referendum campaign. Among the many articles on the matter may be mentioned Paul O'Mahony's 'The Proposed Bail Referendum: An Unholy Grail?' (1995) 13 *I.L.T.* 234; see also his collection of essays *Criminal Chaos: Seven Crises in Irish Criminal Justice* (Round Hall Sweet & Maxwell, 1997).

The legislation envisaged by Article 40.4.7° has now been acted as the Bail Act 1997, and we will its terms in the 1997 Review. A particular aspect of the 1997 Act requiring analysis is the extent to which it provides an exhaustive list of the terms 'serious offence' within the meaning of Article 40.4.7°. The 1997 Act also provides for a number of important reforms in bail procedure unconnected with the 1996 referendum. For an example of the application of the *O'Callaghan* principles, in which bail was refused to four applicants, see the judgment of Kelly J. in *Hegarty and Ors. v. Director of Public Prosecutions*, High Court, November 29, 1996. While Kelly J. accepted that, under the pre-1997 criteria the right to bail could only be displaced in circumstances where there was evidence sufficient to satisfy the court, that there was a reasonable possibility that an applicant would interfere with witnesses pending the full hearing or would not turn up for trial, he concluded that in the case of the four applicants there was sufficient evidence before the court in the case to justify such refusal. The charges involved in the applications included possession of explosives and false imprisonment. It is notable that Kelly J. refused bail in circumstances where he accepted that he could not take account of whether the applicants might be likely to commit further crimes if granted bail. That factor may now, of course, be taken into account under the Bail Act 1997, though in the *Hegarty* case the absence of that entitlement did not preclude the refusal of bail.

CHILDREN

Reformatory school: whether Roman Catholic   In *Director of Public Prosecutions (Houlihan) v. Gencer and Minister for Education* [1997] 1 I.L.R.M. 57, the Supreme Court (Hamilton CJ., Blayney, Denham, Barrington and Keane JJ.) held that, where a reformatory school has the services of a Roman Catholic chaplain and requires Roman Catholic detainees to attend Mass at the weekends and where the only religious representative on the board of management is a nominee of the Roman Catholic Archbishop of Dublin, the absence of a particular form of structured religious instruction does not mean that the school is not "conducted in accordance with the doctrines" of the Roman Catholic Church within the meaning of section 133(18) of the Children Act 1908.

Section 57 of the Children Act 1908 (as amended by the Children Act 1941) provides that where a youthful offender between the ages of 12 and 17 is convicted of an offence punishable in the case of an adult with penal servitude or imprisonment, the court may order that he be sent to a certified reformatory school. Section 45 of the Children Act 1908, as adapted by the Children Act 1908 (Adaptation) Order 1928, provides for the certification by the Minister for Education of any reformatory or industrial school as fit for the reception of youthful offenders pursuant to the 1908 Act. Section 66 of the Children Act 1908 (as adapted by the 1928 Order) provides that the court 'shall endeavour to ascertain the religious persuasion to which the offender or child belongs, and the detention order shall, where practicable, specify the religious persuasion to which the offender or child appears to belong and a school conducted in accordance with that persuasion shall, where practicable, be selected.' Section 133 of the Children Act 1908 modifies the Act in its application to Ireland and provides that 'a youthful offender or child who appears to belong to the Roman Catholic Church shall not be ordered to be sent, removed, or transferred to any school save to a certified school conducted in accordance with the doctrines of that church'.

Two reformatory schools, Trinity House Reformatory School and Oberstown Reformatory School, have been certified by the Minister for Education pursuant to section 45 of the 1908 Act. These schools share a campus with Oberstown Girls Centre. At the time of the instant case, there were 75 pupils in the three schools and one full-time Roman Catholic chaplain who celebrated Mass in Trinity House every weekend. Attendance was compulsory for Roman Catholic detainees. The curriculum makes no specific provision for religious instruction. Trinity House is governed by a board of management appointed by the Minister of whom one is a nominee of the Roman Catholic Archbishop of Dublin. The respondent was a child within the meaning of the 1908 Act. He was convicted of burglary in the Children's Court (the District Court). The District Court judge was of the view that neither Trinity House Reformatory School nor Oberstown Reformatory School were "conducted in accordance with the doctrines" of the Roman Catholic church within the meaning of s. 133(18) of the 1908 Act and, accordingly, that he could not send the respondent to either institution. On a case stated to the High Court it was held that it was open to the District Court judge to consider that the matters referred to were not a sufficient compliance with section 133(18) of the 1908 Act and that there was evidence to support his finding that neither institution was conducted in accordance with the doctrines of the Roman Catholic Church. The Minister appealed to the Supreme Court, and the Court reversed the High Court decision

Delivering the only judgment for the Supreme Court, Keane J. considered

that all the facts before the District Court judge indicated that both institutions
were intended to cater exclusively for detainees of the Roman Catholic faith.
In circumstances where such a certified school has the services of a Roman
Catholic Chaplain, where attendance at Mass at the weekends is compulsory
for all Roman Catholic detainees and where the only religious representative
on the board of management is a nominee of the Roman Catholic Archbishop
of Dublin, he considered that it could not reasonably be said that the absence
of a particular form of structured religious instruction deprived the school of
the character of one "conducted in accordance with the doctrines" of the Roman Catholic Church within the meaning of section 133(18) of the 1908 Act.

CONFISCATION OF PROCEEDS OF CRIME

Use of information held by Revenue authorities   The Disclosure of Certain Information for Taxation and Other Purposes Act 1996 was one of the
series of legislative measures referred to at the beginning of the Chapter enacted to provide a more effective basis on which to tackle organised criminal
activity. The Act amended the Criminal Justice Act 1994 (1994 Review, 174-
5) and other legislation in order to facilitate a freer flow of information from
the Revenue Commissioners to the Garda Síochána in certain cases. The Act
came into effect on July 30, 1996 on its signature by the President. In essence,
the Act was aimed at ensuring that the type of approach made famous in the
United States in the 1930s in the investigation of Chicago-based criminal gangs
(such as those headed by Al Capone) could be adopted in the State. The main
features of the Act are as follows. Section 2 amended section 32 of the Criminal Justice Act 1994 by providing that the Revenue Commissioners may give
information relating to a person to a Chief Superintendent of the Garda Síochána
or to the head of any body established to identify the assets of crime, to deprive or deny criminals of the benefits of such assets, and to pursue subsequent investigations leading to proceedings. This envisaged the Criminal Assets
Bureau, established by the Criminal Assets Bureau Act 1996 (discussed below, 234). To release information, the Revenue Commissioners must have
reasonable grounds for suspecting that the information relates to a person who
has derived profits from unlawful activity and that the information will assist
in a relevant investigation. A relevant investigation means an investigation
into drug trafficking or money laundering or offences other than drug trafficking. Section 3 amended section 57 of the Criminal Justice Act 1994 in order to
permit information reported to the Garda Síochána to be used not only in an
investigation into an offence under sections 31 or 32 of the 1994 Act (which
concern money laundering) but any other offence. Such a use was envisaged
in Article 6 of Directive 91/308/EEC, the Directive whose principal provisions were implemented in the 1994 Act. Section 5 of the 1996 Act amended

section 184 of the Income Tax Act 1967 and provides for the making of an assessment to income tax in the absence of a return or in circumstances where the inspector has received information as to the insufficiency of any statement received from a person. It also provides that the source of any Garda information used is not to be revealed except with the permission of a Chief Superintendent. Section 12 of the 1996 Act provides for anonymity for Revenue officials involved in any body, such as the Criminal Assets Bureau, whose functions are discussed below, 234.

Confiscation of proceeds of crime   The Proceeds of Crime Act 1996 was another of the series of legislative measures referred to at the beginning of the Chapter enacted to provide a more effective basis on which to tackle organised criminal activity. It began its legislative life as a Private Member's Bill, the Organised Crime (Restraint and Disposal of Illicit Assets) Bill 1996, introduced by John O'Donoghue T.D. While the Act differs in a number of respects from the Bill, its essential elements remained in place, namely, the conferring on the High Court of the power to order that the proceeds of crime be preserved (or confiscated) and, ultimately, disposed of by the State. The 1996 Act came into effect on August 4, 1996 on its signature by the President.

Interim preservation order   Section 2(1) of the 1996 Act provides:

> Where it is shown to the satisfaction of the Court on application to it *ex parte* in that behalf by a member [of the Garda Síochána or an authorised officer [of the Revenue Commissioners]—
> (a) that a person is in possession or control of—
>   (i) specified property and that the property constitutes, directly or indirectly, proceeds of crime, or
>   (ii) specified property that was acquired, in whole or in part, with or in connection with property that, directly or indirectly, constitutes proceeds of crime,
> and
> (b) that the value of the property or, as the case may be, the total value of the property referred to in both subparagraphs (i) and (ii), of paragraph (a) is not less than £10,000,
>
> the Court may make an order ("an interim order") prohibiting the person or any other specified person or any other person having notice of the order from disposing of or otherwise dealing with the whole or, if appropriate, a specified part of the property or diminishing its value during the period of 21 days from the date of the making of the order.

The *ex parte* nature of such application indicates the extreme nature of the powers being granted to the High Court under the 1996 Act. This is mitigated somewhat by the limited duration of the interim order made. The constitutional validity of such orders may be tested by reference to the principles established in *Clancy v. Ireland* [1988] I.R. 326; [1989] I.R. 670 (1988 Review, 127-30), in which the High Court upheld the validity of comparable, though not identical, provisions contained in the Offences against the State (Amendment) Act 1985

Interlocutory preservation order Section 3 of the 1996 Act contains comparable provisions, based on both parties involved in a dispute over the criminal nature of the proceeds, referred to as an interlocutory order. Rather like an interlocutory injunction, section 3 provides that an interlocutory order shall continue in force until the determination of an application for a disposal order in relation to the property concerned.

Disposal order Section 4 of the 1996 Act provides that where an interlocutory order has been in force for not less than seven years in relation to specified property, the High Court, on application to it in that behalf may make a 'disposal order' directing that the whole or, if appropriate, a specified part of the property be transferred, subject to such terms and conditions as the Court may specify, to the Minister for Justice or to such other person as the Court may determine. The Court shall make a disposal order in relation to any property the subject of an application unless it is shown to its satisfaction that that particular property does not constitute, directly or indirectly, proceeds of crime and was not acquired, in whole or in part, with or in connection with property that, directly or indirectly, constitutes proceeds of crime. Section 4(4) makes explicit that a disposal order shall operate to deprive the respondent in such an application of his or her rights (if any) in or to the property to which it relates and, upon the making of the order, the property shall stand transferred to the Minister or other person to whom it relates.

Consequential provisions The 1996 Act also contains other important consequential provisions, including power to appoint receivers to property and the application of its provisions to companies and to those declared bankrupt.

CRIMINAL ASSETS BUREAU

The Criminal Assets Bureau Act 1996 was another of the series of legislative measures referred to at the beginning of the Chapter enacted to provide a more effective basis on which to tackle organised criminal activity. The Act established the eponymous Bureau on a statutory basis; it had been organised on an administrative basis earlier in 1996. The Act came into effect on October 11, 1996 on the President's signature but the Bureau was formally established on October 15, 1996: Criminal Assets Bureau Act 1996 (Establishment Day) Order 1996 (SI No.310 of 1996).

Functions of Bureau   Section 4 of the Act requires the Bureau to identify criminal assets or suspected criminal assets, wherever situated, and to take appropriate steps under the law to deprive the holders of such assets of their use or benefit, including preparatory work in connection with proceedings. This should be seen in conjunction with the Disclosure of Certain Information for Taxation and Other Purposes Act 1996, discussed above, 232, and the Proceeds of Crime Act 1996, discussed above, 233, both of which may be used by the Bureau for the purposes of ensuring the confiscation of criminal assets. Section 5 provides that the Bureau will operate through its officers, who will be members of the Garda Síochána, officers of the Revenue Commissioners and officers of the Minister for Social Welfare. The Bureau will, by use of the powers vested in those persons, take all necessary actions under relevant legislation to apply the law to the proceeds of criminal activity or suspected criminal activity and the assets derived from such activities. The Bureau will also investigate and determine claims in respect of social welfare benefit made by any person engaged in criminal activity. Provision is made to allow the Minister for Social Welfare to transfer a case from his or her Department to the Bureau where there are reasonable grounds to believe that an investigation of that case in the normal way may result in intimidation of the staff of the Department. Co-operation with foreign jurisdictions is also provided for. The Bureau is thus an inter-disciplinary entity with powers of investigation not unlike the United States Federal Bureau of Investigation. While the remit of the Irish Bureau is less extensive, nonetheless its establishment represents a significant change in the arrangements for the investigation of criminal matters.

Personnel   Section 7 provides for the appointment of a Chief Superintendent of the Garda Síochána as the Chief Bureau Officer and where necessary for the appointment of an Acting Chief Bureau Officer. Such appointments shall be made by the Commissioner of the Garda Síochána to whom the Chief Bureau Officer reports. The Chief Bureau Officer, who will also be a bureau officer, will be responsible for the management, control and administration of the Bureau. Section 8 provides for the appointment of bureau officers, that they will be appointed from members of the Garda Síochána, officers of the Revenue Commissioners or officers of the Minister for Social Welfare. Their powers and duties will be those which he or she had in their respective roles prior to appointment to the Bureau. Section 9 makes provision for the staff for the Bureau, which include the Bureau Legal Officer who will be appointed by the Minister for Justice with the consent of the Attorney General and the Minister for Finance, and who will report directly to the Chief Bureau Officer. The presence of a Legal Officer indicates the extent to which the Bureau involves a move towards a unified prosecution regime, though the functions of the Director of Public Prosecutions are not affected by the 1996 Act. To that extent, therefore, the Bureau is not an Irish equivalent of the British Crown Prosecution Service (CPS).

Anonymity for officers Section 10 provides for anonymity for persons who are bureau officers or staff of the Bureau, in particular non-Garda officers of the Bureau. Section 11 makes it an offence to identify by publication a person who, being or having been a Revenue or Social Welfare officer, is or was a bureau officer or a member of the staff of the Bureau. It also makes it an offence to identify by publication a member of the family of any Bureau officer. This section does not apply to the Chief Bureau Officer, the Acting Chief Bureau Officer or the Bureau Legal Officer.

Search warrants Section 14 makes provision for a search warrant to be issued to a Garda bureau officer either by a judge of the District Court or where necessary by a member of the Garda Síochána not below the rank of superintendent.

CRIMINAL INJURIES COMPENSATION

Reasons for decisions In *Gavin v. Criminal Injuries Compensation Tribunal*, High Court, February 9, 1996, Carroll J. granted the applicant judicial review of a decision of the respondent Tribunal, and confirmed that an applicant for criminal injuries compensation should be made aware of the general and broad terms of the grounds on which he had failed. The applicant had suffered severe injuries when he had attempted to prevent his care from being stolen in February 1984. The applicant lodged a claim with the Tribunal in respect of his injuries and was awarded and accepted over £2,000 in September 1985 in respect of special damages. Subsequently, the crime became something of a *cause celebre*, because the applicant had identified two persons as having been involved in the theft, but having been convicted twice, their convictions were ultimately quashed: see *The People v. Meleady and Grogan*, Supreme Court, March 4, 1997, which we will discuss in the 1997 Review. Arising from the substantial publicity which the case attracted the applicant became the victim of a concerted campaign of intimidation. His car and company car were damaged outside his home in November 1984, and he suffered a number of verbal and written threats and obscene letters. He brought five fresh applications, the first in respect of the November 1984 incident, for which he claimed mental injuries, the other four were claims for mental stress. He alleged that since the incidents he had suffered loss of concentration, suffered from a post-traumatic stress disorder, had developed alcohol dependency, had lost his job and had been obliged to sell his home. As regards special damages, these were quantified at over £500,000 for loss of earnings (past and future), but did not include any claim for pain and suffering (the Tribunal has been precluded since 1986 from awarding general damages for pain and suffering). The Tribunal dealt with all five applications together. It decided that the applicant had suffered serious psychological injury as a result of the campaign of intimidation against him, and awarded him £100,000 to cover all aspects of the various applications. The applicant sought an explanation as to why his claim for £500,000 had not been granted, but the Tribunal declined to give reasons. During the judicial review proceedings, the Tribunal's secretary averred that the respondent had not been satisfied that the entirety of the personal injuries and consequential loss and damage of which the applicant had complained was directly attributable to the incidents set out in his applications. As indicated, Carroll J. quashed the Tribunal's award and appeared to lean strongly in favour of the applicant's substantive claim.

She began by reiterating that, in *The State (Creedon) v. Criminal Injuries Compensation Tribunal* [1988] I.R. 51; [1989] I.L.R.M. 104 (1988 Review, 17-18), the Supreme Court had held that the requirement that justice should appear to be done necessitated that an unsuccessful applicant before the Tribunal should be made aware in general and broad terms of the grounds on which he had failed. Carroll J. considered that it was not acceptable for the Tribunal's secretary to purport to say what the Tribunal had thought and what its reasons were, particularly having regard to the long history of trauma and delay which the applicant had suffered. She went on to hold that the Tribunal's decision failed the test of reasonableness laid down in *The State (Keegan) v. Stardust Victims Compensation Tribunal* and *O'Keeffe v. An Bórd Pleanála* [1993] 1 I.R. 39; [1992] I.L.R.M. 237 (1991 Review, 16-18). She considered that it flew in the face of reason to reduce the full claim for no apparent reason and that the applicant was thus entitled to succeed on this ground alone and to an order of *certiorari* and *mandamus*.

In addition, Carroll J. felt she should comment on a number of other reasons put forward in the Tribunal Secretary's affidavit in case they should be relied on when the respondent came to reconsider the matter. In particular, the Tribunal's secretary had averred that it considered that the applicant's difficulties had been caused by a number of different factors including the original theft of his car. Carroll J. held that When the Tribunal came to reconsider the matter, it would have to decide whether the post-traumatic stress disorder would have occurred in any event following the original theft if the campaign of intimidation had not taken place. If the answer was no then the applicant should have been dealt with as someone who had been psychologically damaged but who was symptom free. She considered that there was evidence that the onset of the symptoms of the stress disorder followed after the commencement of the campaign of intimidation. Finally, she dealt with the Tribunal's averment that the applicant had failed to show that his various employment difficulties were directly attributable "solely" to the incidents complained of. Carroll J. noted that there was no mention in the Scheme of Compensation for Injuries Criminally Inflicted, under which the Tribunal had been established, which stated that the injury, loss and damage must be solely attributable to a crime of violence. If the Tribunal found that the applicant's injury was directly attributable in whole or in part to the events complained of, he was entitled to compensation without reduction, save only if the Tribunal were to find that the original crime partially caused the injuries in the sense of being a *causa causans*. In that case, citing *Orr v. Criminal Injuries Compensation Board, ex p. Ince* [1973] 3 All E.R. 808, Carroll J. held that the proportion attributable to that could be reduced. On this basis, Carroll J. remitted the matter to the Tribunal, but her comments, particularly since they were not strictly necessary to her decision, appeared to lean in the applicant's favour in most respects.

DELAY

Execution of warrant   In *Dunne v. Director of Public Prosecutions*, High Court, June 6, 1996, Carney J. held that there had been no unreasonable delay in executing a warrant for the applicant's arrest on charges of assault in the following circumstances. Within two weeks of the warrant being issued, the Gardaí had sought to execute it by calling to the applicant's family home. The Garda was told that the applicant no longer lived there and a search of the premises satisfied the Garda of this. The Garda had told the applicant's father that the applicant could contact him at the Garda station to resolve the matter, but the applicant made no communication with the Gardaí on foot of this. There was a further visit to the applicant's family home some weeks later, which also proved fruitless. It was not for another two years that the applicant was seen by the Garda in question appearing in Court. Within a further two weeks, the Garda executed the warrant for the applicant's arrest. On judicial review, the applicant claimed that he had been living at home for the two year period during which the warrant remained unexecuted and that he had appeared before the District Court during the currency of the warrant on at least 25 occasions. As indicated, Carney J. declined to grant the applicant the order of prohibition sought.

Carney J. accepted that a warrant was a command to arrest rather than merely an authority or permission to arrest and it was clear that if the Gardaí 'sat on a warrant' and waited for the person to gratuitously fall into their laps, they could be held culpable, as in *The State (Flynn) v. Governor of Mountjoy Prison*, High Court, May 6, 1987 (1987 Review, 121-2). However, in the instant case he considered that there had been two reasonably prompt efforts to execute the warrant at the applicant's only known residence and that any further visits would have been pointless. In those circumstances, he held that there had been no unreasonable delay.

Fraud In *Gibbs v. President of the Dublin Circuit Criminal Court*, High Court, May 16, 1996, Kelly J. granted an order of prohibition arising from delay in the context of a relatively simple prosecution for fraud. He accepted that the court must have regard to the level of complexity of the charges and must also bear in mind the importance of the presumption of innocence and the right to silence. In doing so, he applied the relevant principles arising from the leading case *The State (O'Connell) v. Fawsitt* [1986] I.R. 362, as applied in *Director of Public Prosecutions v. Byrne* [1994] 2 I.R. 236 (1993 Review, 223-6), *Cahalane v. Murphy* [1994] 2 I.R. 262 (1994 Review, 171-2) and *Hogan v. President of Circuit Court* [1994] 2 I.R. 513 (1994 Review, 173).

In *Gibbs*, the Gardaí had received a complaint in 1987 against the applicant, in which it had been alleged that he had promised the complainant to invest a sum of money in an investment without risk, that he had persuaded the complainant to endorse a cheque for £75,000 in the applicant's favour, that he had subsequently provided documentation, purportedly signed by a third party on behalf of a Cypriot investment company to support the fact of investment of the money, but had then failed to make the promised payments which ought to have been made under the investment. The first Garda in charge of the investigation interviewed the third party whose name had appeared on the supporting documentation and had made a number of calls to the applicant's house but had failed to contact him. The next Garda in charge also visited the applicant's house and, having failed to make contact, caused his name to be circulated through Garda channels in 1989, thereby indicating he was wanted for questioning. A third Garda took up responsibility for the investigation in 1991 and eventually made contact with the applicant's wife at his address. She denied receiving the notes left by the Gardaí on previous occasions and stated that her husband no longer lived there but had moved abroad. In February 1992 the Gardaí made contact with the applicant in a Social Welfare Services office in County Dublin. At this point the applicant claimed he had not been aware that the Gardaí were looking for him. It was later shown in evidence that the applicant had attended at the Social Welfare Services offices on a weekly basis from 1989. An interview was arranged by the applicant's solicitor in July 1992, during which he handed over a list of a number of people who could prove his innocence in the whole affair because, he claimed, they had been defrauded by the third party who had signed the supporting documentation and. A request was made to the applicant's solicitor to allow the Gardaí access to his bank accounts and to indicate whether he was prepared to make a cautioned statement. In October 1992 his solicitor was contacted again and a second interview was arranged for December 1992. At this meeting the applicant handed over photocopies of one of his bank account pass books but refused to allow access to the account. A court order was then obtained to examine the account and copies of the cheques issued for withdrawal from the account were supplied to the Gardaí in March 1993. In July 1993 an investigation file was forwarded to the office of the Director of Public Prosecution, who directed that further information be obtained and this was furnished to the Director in October 1993. Having briefed counsel and received his advices, the book of evidence was ready for service in January 1994 and a warrant to arrest the applicant was issued in March 1994. In October 1994, the applicant was returned for trial.

As indicated from this chronology, the lapse of time between the original complaint being made and the application for the warrant was well in excess of six years. The applicant submitted that the delay which had occurred had been so excessive as to raise an inference that the risk of an unfair trial had been established and that an actual prejudice could be established arising from the delay. As to prejudice, he noted that he no longer had the receipt of the money which he had given to the third party who had signed the letter from the Cypriot finance company. In addition he asserted that he would be prejudiced in a trial by the absence of this third party and the absence of the people he had named as having been defrauded by the third party who, he claimed, could exonerate him. Finally, he also claimed that he was so ill in 1994 that he was unfit to face charges at that time and that his mental health had declined over the previous eight years. As indicated, Kelly J. granted the order of prohibition sought.

He commented that it was difficult to accept that the case had been prosecuted with the appropriate degree of vigour. In particular, they had failed to make contact with the applicant during the time he was reporting weekly to the relevant Social Welfare Services office. Had the investigation been pursued with the appropriate vigour, contact would have been made with the applicant long before the date it was actually achieved. In addition, the period between the initial contact with the applicant in 1992 and his eventual arrest in 1994 was, in Kelly J.'s view, excessive. He also opined that, from an examination of the book of evidence, the case could not be regarded as complex and this was a factor which the court was entitled to take into account when considering the delay which had occurred. In all the circumstances, Kelly J. was satisfied that the delay which had taken place was by its length, unjust and unfair and was of a type which required the court to intervene. In addition, he concluded that some element of actual prejudice also arose. On this basis, he granted the relief sought.

Summary prosecution The principles laid down by the Supreme Court in *Director of Public Prosecutions v. Byrne* [1994] 2 I.L.R.M. 91 (1993 Review,

223-6) were discussed in *National Authority for Occupational Safety and Health v. O'K Tools Hire and Sales Ltd*, High Court, July 11, 1996 (see the Safety and Health chapter, 542, below).

DRUG TRAFFICKING

The Criminal Justice (Drug Trafficking) Act 1996 was the fourth of the series of legislative measures referred to at the beginning of the Chapter enacted to provide a more effective basis on which to tackle organised criminal activity. It provided for increased police powers of detention in drug trafficking cases, the issue of search warrants by members of the Garda Síochána not below the rank of superintendent in such cases and attendance of, and participation by, customs officers in the questioning of persons detained by the Garda Síochána in connection with drug trafficking offences. The Act came into effect on September 9, 1996: Criminal Justice (Drug Trafficking) Act 1996 (Commencement) Order 1996 (SI No. 257 of 1996).

Drug trafficking defined Section 1 of the 1996 Act provides that 'drug trafficking offence' has the same meaning as in section 3(1) of the Criminal Justice Act 1994 (1994 Review, 174-5), namely: an offence under any Regulations made under section 5 of the Misuse of Drugs Act 1977 involving the manufacture, production, preparation, importation, exportation, supply, offering to supply, distribution or transportation of a controlled drug; offences under section 15 of the 1977 Act, that is, possession of a controlled drug for unlawful sale or supply; offences under section 20 of the 1977 Act, that is, assisting in or inducing the commission outside the State of an offence punishable under a law corresponding to that contained in the 1977 Act; an offence under the Customs Acts in connection with the importation or exportation of a controlled drug or in connection with the fraudulent evasion of any prohibition, restriction or obligation in relation to such importation or exportation; offences under sections 31 of the 1994 Act in relation to the proceeds of drug trafficking; offences under sections 33 and 34 of the 1994 Act concerning drug trafficking offences at sea; and aiding, abetting, counselling or procuring the commission of any of these offences or attempting or conspiring to commit any such offence or inciting another person to do so.

Arrest and detention for seven days Section 2 of the 1996 Act provides that a person who is suspected of a drug trafficking offence may be arrested and detained by a member of the Garda Síochána and taken to a Garda station. Where the member believes that the arrested person has concealed a controlled drug in his or her body that person may be detained in a place which is designated by the Minister for Justice under section 2(7) of the 1996 Act.

Section 2 goes on to specify that the period of detention may extend, under certain conditions, to up to seven days. The initial period of detention is for up to 6 hours. This period may be extended for a further period of up to 18 hours and subsequently for a further period of up to 24 hours on the direction of a chief superintendent who, on each occasion that the extension is granted, has reasonable grounds for believing that the further period of detention is necessary for the proper investigation of the offence. The chief superintendent's directions may be given orally or in writing and if given orally it must be recorded in writing as soon as practicable. This period of up to 48 hours detention is thus a matter for the police authorities and is thus comparable to that contained in section 30 of the Offences against the State Act 1939. Any further extensions may only be granted on foot of a judicial order. Section 2(2) provides that a judge of the District Court is empowered to issue a warrant extending the period of detention for up to a further 72 hours and for a final period of up to a further 48 hours upon an application by a member of the Garda Síochána not below the rank of chief superintendent who has, at the time of each application, reasonable grounds for believing that the further detention is necessary for the proper investigation of the offence. The judge's power to authorise these periods of detention will be exercised only where he or she is satisfied that the detention is necessary for the proper investigation of the offence and that the investigation is being conducted diligently and expeditiously. The detained person must be brought before the court on each occasion and will be given the opportunity to make submissions or call evidence on his or her behalf. The intervention of the judicial power after a period of 48 hours would appear to have been influenced by the decisions of the European Court of Human Rights in *Brogan v. United Kingdom* (1989) 11 E.H.R.R. 117 and *Brannigan v. United Kingdom* (decision of May 26, 1993), in which the Court held that detention beyond a period of four days without judicial intervention was contrary to Article 5 of the Convention on Human Rights and Fundamental Freedoms, unless justified by exceptional circumstances necessitating a derogation from the Convention. Indeed, since the 1996 Act is not legislation enacted pursuant to Article 28.3.3° of the Constitution, it would thus be unlikely to be regarded as being in conformity with the Constitution without the judicial intervention envisaged by the 1996 Act. At the time of issuing a warrant for the further detention of a person the judge may order that the person be brought before the court again at any time or times during the period of detention and if the judge is not satisfied at that time that the detention is justified he shall order the immediate release of the person. Section 2(5) provides that the maximum period for which a person can be detained under the section is 168 hours. Finally, section 2(6) provides that the Offences against the State Act 1939 and the Criminal Justice Act 1984, which contain provisions for arrest and detention without warrant, will not be affected by the operation of the detention provisions under the 1996 Act.

Forensic samples   Section 3 provides that the powers contained in the Criminal Justice (Forensic Evidence) Act 1990 (1990 Review, 206) for the taking of bodily samples will apply to persons detained under this 1996 Act.

Re-arrest   Section 4(1) of the 1996 Act prohibits the re-arrest for the same suspected offence of a person who has been released without being charged, except when authorised by a judge who is satisfied on information supplied on oath by a Garda not below the rank of superintendent that further information has come to the knowledge of the Gardaí since the person's release. Where a person has been re-arrested on the authority of a judge the periods of detention permitted under section 2 are modified so that the re-arrested person may be detained initially for 6 hours which can be extended by 18 hours on the authority of a chief superintendent. Thereafter the detention period may be extended for periods up to 24 hours, 72 hours and 48 hours under warrants issued by a judge in accordance with the procedures laid down in section 2 as modified. A person re-arrested under a warrant issued by a judge for an offence which is not a drug trafficking offence will be dealt with under section 4 of the Criminal Justice Act 1984.

Rights of detained persons   Section 5 applies various provisions of the Criminal Justice Act 1984 to persons detained under the 1996 Act. These include those relating to: the release of a person when there are no longer reasonable grounds for suspecting him or her; the requirement that a person be charged when there is evidence to do so, subject to exceptions; the provision of medical attention; access to a solicitor and notification of detention; the powers of the Gardaí in relation to detained persons; and the destruction of records where a detained person is not prosecuted or where he or she is acquitted.

Officers of customs and excise   Section 6 provides that the Minister for Justice may, following consultation with the Minister for Finance, make Regulations providing for the attendance of, and participation by, an officer of customs and excise in the questioning of a person detained under section 2 of the 1996 Act or section 4 of the Criminal Justice Act 1984 where the offence is one of drug trafficking.

Inferences from failure to account   Section 7 of the 1996 Act (which was not contained in the Bill as originally published) provides that inferences may be drawn at trial from the failure of a person to mention certain facts. Modelled on sections 18 and 19 of the Criminal Justice Act 1984, the use of such provisions may be explained by the decision in *Rock v. Ireland*, High Court, November 10, 1995 (1995 Review, 243) that those such provisions may withstand constitutional scrutiny.

Search warrants Section 8 amends section 26 of the Misuse of Drugs Act 1977, which empowered judges of the District Court to issue search warrants, by conferring these powers on members of the Garda Síochána not below the rank of superintendent. The power will be exercised by the Gardaí in circumstances where particular urgency arises and where it is necessary for the investigation of a drug trafficking offence. This power is subject to the further proviso that the warrant will cease to have effect after 24 hours. Section 9 of the Act inserted a new section 13A into the Public Dance Halls Act 1935, empowering the Gardaí to enter a dance hall to ensure that no drug trafficking offence under the Criminal Justice Act 1994 is being committed.

Duration of certain provisions Section 11 provides that sections 2, 3, 4, 5 and 6 will cease to operate after 12 months from the date of commencement of the Act (that is, will cease with effect from September 9, 1997) unless a resolution is passed by both Houses of the Oireachtas resolving that one or some or all of them shall continue in operation. A resolution continuing these sections in force was passed by the Oireachtas in 1997.

Money laundering The connected provisions concerning drug trafficking in the Criminal Justice Act 1994 (1994 Review, 174-5) are discussed in the more general context of money laundering, 249, below.

EVIDENCE

The case law and legislation relevant to evidentiary matters are discussed in the Evidence chapter, 307, below.

EXTRADITION

Appearance in court after extradition no bar to renvoi In *Lloyd v. Hogan* [1996] 2 I.L.R.M. 313 (H.C.), the applicant had been convicted at Belfast Crown Court of assault with intent to rob and sentenced to two years and six months. In 1995 he had been granted temporary release but failed to return to prison. In September 1995 a warrant was issued for his arrest and in the relevant Garda authorities authorised the execution of the warrant in the State pursuant to the Extradition Act 1965. In October 1995 the applicant was arrested on foot of this warrant. In November 1995 an order was made by the respondent judge of the District Court to extradite him. The applicant sought an order of *certiorari* quashing this decision. Kelly J. refused the application. The applicant had argued that since section 43(3) of the 1965 Act states that the purpose of the arrest is to 'enable' the arrested person to be taken to a place where he is to undergo imprisonment, the fact that a judicial intervention, namely an appearance before a Magistrates Court in Northern Ireland, is to take place is inconsistent with what is contemplated by the 1965 Act. Kelly J. rejected this argument. He held that the indorsement by the Garda authorities of the extradition warrant was *intra vires* the 1965 Act and the arrest on foot of the warrant was also valid. As there had been no suggestion of any form of conscious or deliberate violation of the applicant's rights nor abuse of the process of the court, Kelly J. concluded that even if there was a defect in the warrant which was endorsed under section 43 of the 1965 Act, the detention on foot of that was clearly spent by the time complaint was made to the High Court. On these grounds, he dismissed the application.

Convention countries The Extradition (European Convention on the Suppression of Terrorism) Act 1987 (Designation of Convention Countries) (Amendment) Order 1996 provided that the European Convention on the Suppression of Terrorism (which was implemented by the 1987 Act: see 1987 Review, 130) applies to the Czech Republic, Malta, Poland and Slovakia in addition to those States specified in the Extradition (European Convention on the Suppression of Terrorism) Act 1987 (Designation of Convention Countries) (Amendment) Order 1989 (1989 Review, 164).

Constitutional rights: requirement to protect In *Brien v. King*, High Court, July 5, 1996, Barr J. confirmed that, when hearing an application for an extradition order, the duty of a District Court judge is not restricted to an enquiry as to whether the requirements laid down by the Extradition Act 1965 have been complied with. Referring to the decision of the Supreme Court in *Ellis v. O'Dea* [1989] I.R. 531; [1990] I.L.R.M. 87 (1989 Review, 160-3), Barr J. held that the judge also has a duty to protect the constitutional rights of the person against whom extradition has been sought.

Form of provisional request In *Smithers v. Governor Of Mountjoy Prison*, High Court, May 3, 1996, Kelly J. held that once a provisional request for extradition, in that case for fraud committed in the United States, contained a statement demonstrating an intention on the part of the requesting State to send a request for extradition, the requirements of section 27 of the Extradition Act 1965 and the relevant Extradition Treaty would be deemed to have been complied with. He held that it was not, therefore, necessary to reproduce the precise formula of words specified in section 27 of the 1965 Act.

Oppressive to extradite In *Kwok Ming Wan v. Conroy*, High Court, November 17, 1996, Smyth J. declined to order the applicant's extradition having regard to his family and business circumstances. The applicant, who had been born in Hong Kong was charged in England in 1986 with unlawfully wounding and causing grievous bodily harm. He absconded during the trial and came to Ireland where he later married, had four children and established a business. He was convicted in his absence. The English authorities were not aware of his whereabouts until November 1994; the Irish authorities were aware of the applicant but were not aware that he was wanted in England. In March and May 1994, the applicant gave false information to the Irish authorities and concealed the offence. Extradition proceedings were commenced in late 1994 and the applicant sought an order under section 50 of the Extradition Act 1965 directing his release by reason of the lapse of time since the commission of the offence and conviction. Smyth J. held that the applicant' family circumstances were to be borne in mind and, in the instant case, there were exceptional circumstances and his conduct was consistent with a free man putting down roots. On this basis only, he directed the applicant's release.

INSANITY

Recommendations of advisory committee   In *Gallagher v. Director of Central Mental Hospital (No.2)*, High Court, September 6, 1996, the High Court dismissed the applicant's application for his release under Article 40.4.2° of the Constitution. The applicant had been tried for the murder of two women and had been found guilty but insane, and was subsequently detained in the Central Mental Hospital. In *Application of Gallagher* [1991] 1 I.R. 31; [1991] I.L.R.M. 339 (1990 Review, 164-6), the Supreme Court held that where a person is found guilty but insane of murder, the release of the person is solely a matter for the Executive to determine. Subsequently, the Minister for Justice established a non-statutory Advisory Committee to advise on the question of the applicant's release. The applicant applied in April 1996 under Article 40.4.2° seeking his release from custody, arguing that there was no justification for his further detention on the ground that that was not suffering from any mental illness. In response, the Minister, acting on the Advisory Committee's recommendations, wrote to the applicant indicating that she proposed a programme of limited outings from the Central Mental Hospital, in which the applicant was detained. The medical evidence before the Minister indicated that, although the applicant was suffering from a personality disorder he was neither mentally ill (in the legal sense) nor imminently dangerous and that it was safe to release him on a phased and limited basis.

As indicated, the High Court dismissed the application for an order directing the applicant's immediate release. The Court reiterated the view in *Application of Gallagher* [1991] 1 I.R. 31; [1991] I.L.R.M. 339 (1990 Review, 164-6) that the issue of release is solely a matter for the Executive to determine, but that a failure on the part of the Executive to behave quasi-judicially or to use fair and constitutional procedures could be subject to review.

In the instant case, the Court accepted that the Minister had, albeit with some delay, broadly accepted the Advisory Committee's recommendation even though she was not obliged to do so. The Court indicated that the applicant was entitled to a timely decision on his request for release and that a decision ought to have been arrived at by the Minister in her quasi-judicial role. While there had been a failure in this respect, the delay involved did not justify an order for the applicant's immediate release under Article 40; such a delay would have to be gross and of a magnitude far in excess of what was involved in the instant case. Indeed, the Court added that complaints of this nature and seriousness were more appropriate for judicial review than the *habeas corpus* type application under Article 40.4.

Ultimately, the Court accepted that the decision communicated to the applicant in the wake of his instant application could not be regarded as unreasonable or irrational. While her decision might be described as minimalist, the Court concluded that it could not be said to be disproportionate in the legal sense. On this basis, the Court dismissed the application. For another issue raised in the application, see *Gallagher v. Director of Central Mental Hospital*, High Court, July 9, 1996, discussed in the Constitutional Law chapter, 145, above.

LARCENY

Fraudulent conversion In *The People v. Traynor*, Court of Criminal Appeal, October 16, 1996, the Court held that, to sustain a charge that an accused fraudulently converted moneys to his own use, it was necessary to adduce evidence that the accused dishonestly took the moneys or applied them to some purpose of his own. In the instant case, the Court quashed the defendant's conviction for fraudulent conversion. The Court held that there was no evidence on which the jury could find that the defendant had converted any money to his own use. While he had received two cheques, the Court held that there was no evidence as to what happened to the moneys after the defendant had lodged the first to his company's bank account and had given the second to his business associate believing it would be lodged to the account. To sustain a charge that the defendant had fraudulently converted the moneys to his own use, it was necessary to adduce evidence that he dishonestly took the moneys or applied them to some purpose of his own. There was no such evidence and the only evidence was that the person to whom the cheques had been made out was not paid. There could have been a number of reasons for this and it fell short of establishing the offence charged. A charge of forgery in the case was upheld.

LEGAL AID

Fees   The Criminal Justice (Legal Aid) (Amendment) Regulations 1996 (SI No. 311 of 1996), made under the Criminal Justice (Legal Aid) Act 1962, provided for the payment of a fee of £350 to solicitors who are assigned to exceptional cases in the District and Circuit Courts. The determination of whether a case is exceptional is for the Department of Justice after consulting the Chief State Solicitor. The Regulations applied retrospectively from June 1, 1993.

MISCARRIAGE OF JUSTICE

Newly discovered evidence   In *The People v. Gannon*, Supreme Court, December 17, 1996, discussed below, 255, the Supreme Court considered whether documents uncovered after the defendant's trial constituted a newly discovered fact which showed a miscarriage of justice within the meaning of section 2 of the Criminal Procedure Act 1993 (1993 Review, 211).

MISUSE OF DRUGS

Drug trafficking   The Criminal Justice (Drug Trafficking) Act 1996 is discussed above, 241.

Search and detention power   In *Farrelly v. Devally*, High Court, July 19, 1996, members of the Garda Síochána were monitoring the movements of known drug addicts when they observed the applicant stopping his car nearby. They approached him and informed him that he was being detained for the purposes of a search under the Misuse of Drugs Acts 1977 to 1984, and that he and his car would be brought to a Garda Station for this purpose. The applicant then assaulted the Gardaí. He was later charged with and convicted of unlawfully obstructing a Garda by refusing to allow himself to be searched, contrary to section 21(4) of the Misuse of Drugs Act 1977 and of unlawfully assaulting Gardaí in the due execution of their duty contrary to section 12 of the Prevention of Crimes Act 1871. The applicant sought judicial review on the grounds that the Gardaí had no authority to remove him or his vehicle to a Garda Station under section 23 of the Misuse of Drugs Act 1977 (as amended by section 12 of the Misuse of Drugs Act 1984) unless he had failed to comply with a request to accompany them to the Garda Station and to take the vehicle with him. Since no such request had been made, he argued that he had been entitled to resist the Gardaí. Morris J. disagreed.

Section 23 of the Misuse of Drugs Act 1977 (as amended by section 12 of the Misuse of Drugs Act 1984) provides that a member of the Garda Síochána who with reasonable cause suspects that a person is in possession of a controlled drug may without warrant, search such person and any vehicle in which he suspects that such drug may be found. It also provides that a member of the Garda Síochána may require such person to accompany him to a Garda Station for the purpose of being searched and may also require him to take the vehicle to a place which the member considers suitable for such search. Morris J. accepted that the powers conferred by the 1977 and 1984 Act constituted a significant interference with the liberty of the citizen and that, accordingly, the courts required strict compliance with their provisions, citing O'Hanlon J.'s judgment in *Director of Public Prosecutions v. Rooney* [1992] 2 I.R. 7 (1992 Review, 304) in support. Thus, if the Gardaí had attempted to bring the applicant and his vehicle to the Garda station without first complying with the requirements of section 23 of the 1977 Act, they would have been acting without lawful authority. But, in informing him that they intended to bring him to the Garda Station before first requiring him to accompany them, albeit without subsequently attempting to bring him to the Garda Station in view of the intervening assaults, they had not acted unlawfully. Thus, the defendant's conviction was upheld.

MONEY LAUNDERING

Drug trafficking at sea and international co-operation   The Criminal Justice Act 1994 (Commencement) Order 1996 (SI No. 333 of 1996) brought Part V (sections 33-37, dealing with drug trafficking offences at sea) and Part VII (sections 46-56, dealing with international co-operation) of the Criminal Justice Act 1994 (1994 Review, 174-5) into force on November 15, 1996.

External confiscation orders   The Criminal Justice Act 1994 (Section 46(6)) Regulations 1996 (SI No. 343 of 1996) provide for the necessary adjustments required concerning the provisions of the Criminal Justice Act 1994 (1994 Review, 174-5) dealing with confiscation orders in order to accommodate those provisions to the making of external confiscation orders under section 46 of the 1994 Act, that is, orders for the confiscation of assets held outside the State. The Regulations came into effect on December 3, 1996. The Criminal Justice Act 1994 (Section 46(1)) Order 1996 (SI No. 344 of 1996) lists those States in respect of whom the High Court may make an external confiscation order pursuant to section 46 of the 1994 Act. The Order also came into effect on December 3, 1996.

External forfeiture orders   The Criminal Justice Act 1994 (Section 47(1)) Order 1996 (SI No.342 of 1996) lists those States in respect of whom the High

Court may make a forfeiture order pursuant to section 47 of the Criminal Justice Act 1994 (1994 Review, 174-5). The Order came into effect on December 3, 1996.

Seizure of money　The Criminal Justice Act 1994 (Section 44) Regulations, 1996 (SI No. 167 of 1996), made under the Criminal Justice Act 1994 (1994 Review, 174-5) prescribe the sum of £5,000 as the minimum sum for the purposes of the power of the Garda Síochána to seize money under section 38 of the 1994 Act. The Regulations came into effect on June 14, 1996.

Search for material outside State　The Criminal Justice Act 1994 (Section 55(1)) Order 1996 (SI No. 341 of 1996) lists those States in respect of whom the Gardaí may apply to the Irish courts for a search warrant to pursue money laundering outside the State pursuant to section 55 of the Criminal Justice Act 1994 (1994 Review, 174-5). The Order came into effect on December 3, 1996.

MURDER

Natural and probable consequences　In *The People v. Hull*, Court of Criminal Appeal, July 8, 1996, the Court upheld as correct the various directions of the trial judge (Carroll J.) to the jury concerning the charge of murder against the defendant, on which he was found guilty. The evidence was that the defendant had shot the victim through a closed door; the defendant had pleaded guilty to manslaughter, but this plea had not been accepted. The Court held that the learned trial judge had dealt adequately with the question asked by the jury about 'natural and probable consequences'. In instructing the jury to acquit the defendant if the firing was accidental, the trial judge had, in the Court's view, correctly directed them that, if they took this view, it meant that the presumption that the applicant intended to cause death or serious injury had been rebutted and so he was entitled to be acquitted. On this area, see also *The People v. Douglas* [1985] I.L.R.M. 25, which concerned shooting with intent to commit murder.

OFFENCES AGAINST THE PERSON

Grievous bodily harm: *mens rea*　In *The People v. McBride* [1996] 1 I.R. 312; [1997] 1 I.L.R.M. 233, the Court of Criminal Appeal quashed convictions for offences including grievous bodily harm imposed on the defendant and directed a retrial. The Court focused on the need to ensure that *mens rea* had been established.

The defendant had been convicted in the Circuit Criminal Court on three separate counts arising from the same incident: causing grievous bodily harm with intent, contrary to section 18 of the Offences Against the Person Act 1861; unlawfully and maliciously inflicting grievous bodily harm, contrary to section 20 of the 1861 Act; and assault occasioning actual bodily harm, contrary to section 47 of the 1861 Act. The grounds of appeal concerned errors or omissions in the trial judge's charge and concentrated on the way on which the trial judge dealt with the question of intention in regard to each of the counts.

Dealing with the first count, the Court of Criminal Appeal considered that part of the manner in which the trial judge dealt with the question of intention was erroneous. The defendant had said in his inculpatory statement that his mind had gone blank when he hit the victim and the Court held that this statement was clearly relevant to the question of whether he had the necessary intent at the time he committed the assault. It was not correct to dismiss it, as the trial judge had done, as something which was not a defence to the charge, but was something which the jury had to consider in the context of whether the defendant had the appropriate intent or not. The Court added that the jury should have been told that while there was a presumption that the defendant intended the natural and probable consequences of his act, this could be rebutted and that one of the things that they had to consider was whether the prosecution had satisfied them beyond reasonable doubt that the presumption had not been rebutted and in considering that they had to take into account what the defendant had said in his statement.

As to the second count, the trial judge had said that the difference between counts 1 and 2 was that 'the intent is not required to be proved in the second count'. The Court of Criminal Appeal noted that this could have been interpreted to mean that the particular intent specified in count 1 was not required, or that it was not necessary to have any intent at all. The trial judge had also stated that as the act had to be done maliciously, it had to be a deliberate act of inflicting grievous bodily harm. On this, the Court stated that this would indicate that the grievous bodily harm must have been intended and so there must have been an intent to cause it. However, the Court considered that the trial judge had also added, in an apparently contradictory manner, that even if there were not evidence that the grievous bodily harm was caused intentionally, the jury could convict. If this was the sense in which the jury had construed the direction, the Court considered that this clearly amounted to a misdirection. Indeed, the Court considered that what the trial judge had said in relation to count 3 indicated that, on count 2, no mental element was necessary. Since this was clearly not correct, the verdict could not stand.

Turning to count 3, the trial judge had said: 'again, you don't have to be satisfied there was an intention'. The Court of Criminal Appeal noted that this, in effect, ruled out any requirement for *mens rea* because if there was no intention there was no *mens rea*, which the Court noted (perhaps unintentionally) was a necessary ingredient of every crime. Focusing on the specific offence of 'assault occasioning actual bodily harm', the Court stated that there must be an intention on the part of an accused to apply force to the body of the victim and it was incorrect for the trial judge to direct the jury that they did not have to be satisfied that there was an intention. For further discussion of the *mens rea* requirements under the 1861 Act, see Una Ní Raifeartaigh's comments, (1996) 6 *Irish Criminal Law Journal* 143-4.

PROCEDURE

Disclosure of information by prosecution   Three decisions in 1996 dealt with the duty imposed on the prosecution to disclose information to the defence. In the first of these, *The People v. Kelly*, Court of Criminal Appeal, March 4, 1996, the defendant had been convicted in the Circuit Court with possession of a controlled drug for the purpose of supplying it to another, contrary to sections 3 and 15 of the Misuse of Drugs Act 1977. An issue concerning directions by the trial judge to the jury is dealt with separately below, 258. The prosecution case was that the defendant had been observed meeting a passenger at Dublin Airport, that they drove to a hotel, that this passenger went into the hotel, came out with a plastic bag and handed it to the defendant. The bag contained 1kg of cocaine. The defendant claimed that he had been asked to collect the passenger from the airport by a third party who had stayed with him in Dublin before he had picked up the passenger, that he had never touched the bag and that he thought it contained money for the third party. During his cross-examination at trial, it was put to the defendant that the third party whom the defendant said had stayed with him and asked him to collect the passenger from the airport had been stopped less than a week before the pick up date in Roscommon driving a blue Mercedes car. On appeal to the Court of Criminal Appeal (Blayney, Carroll and Morris JJ.), the defendant argued that this line of cross-examination had been directed at establishing that the third party had a Mercedes car available to him on the date in question and was thus directed at undermining the defendant's argument that he had been asked to collect the person from the airport. The Court rejected this suggestion and concluded that it had instead been directed at establishing that the third party was not in Dublin on that date and to suggest that the defendant's evidence that the third party had stayed with him in Dublin at that time was not to be believed. The Court pointed out that the first time the prosecution was aware that the third party was supposed to have stayed with the defendant was when the defendant had given this evidence during his trial and it would not have been possible that prior notice of the evidence could have been given to the defence. The defendant had also argued that the manner in which the prosecution had conducted its fingerprinting had breached fair procedures; in particular, that it should have made available to the defence all records created during fingerprinting. The Court also rejected this point. It pointed out that the prosecution's fingerprint expert had only found smudges on the bag containing the cocaine, which he indicated at the trial had no evidential value. The smudges were thus of no assistance either to the prosecution or defence.

While the Court thus dismissed the defendant's arguments concerning disclosure, it accepted as a general principle that there was an obligation on the prosecution to make such material available if it existed. Of some interest is that the Court accepted the principles to that effect laid down by the English Court of Appeal (Criminal Division) in *R. v. Ward (Judith)* [1993] 1 W.L.R. 619, one of the well-known miscarriage of justice cases of recent years. The Court of Criminal Appeal pointed out, however, that such material had to exist to be disclosed and, in the instant case, the fingerprint expert did not have any record of his examination and so there was no relevant material in regard to it which ought to have been disclosed to the defence. The Court noted that the bag was at all times available for examination to the defence and the defence expert did not carry out any tests on it. Thus, there was no basis on which it could be alleged that there was a failure on the part of the prosecution to make available relevant material. The detailed principles set out in the *Ward* case, above, are discussed by Una Ní Raifeartaigh in her comments on the *Kelly* case, (1996) 6 I.C.L.J. 124, at 128-9.

In the second judgment on disclosure, *The People v. Flannery*, High Court (Central Criminal Court), June 25, 1996, Barr J., as presiding judge in the defendant's trial for murder, directed the jury to enter a not guilty verdict after it emerged that the prosecution had failed to disclose material information to the defence. Indeed, so serious did he consider the breach in this case that he ordered that the defendant not be prosecuted again on the charge.

The case involved a series of failures to disclose relevant information. The first such difficulty centred on whether the alleged murder victim was, in fact, dead. After the book of evidence had been served in the case, the Gardaí had furnished the defendant's solicitor with 24 statements obtained from witnesses who averred they had seen the alleged murder victim after the date he had been reported missing. It seemed that none of these statements had been furnished to the prosecution. But the key element of non-disclosure centred on the key prosecution witness, a nephew of the defendant's, who testified that the defendant had admitted to the nephew that he had murdered the person in question and had, in his (the uncle's) flat, requested the nephew to dig up the body of the alleged murder victim. Under cross-examination, the nephew admitted that he had a drink and drugs problem which necessitated treatment in a detoxification unit but stated that his drug taking was limited to alcohol, marijuana and a form of valium. The prosecution conceded that the credibility of the prosecution case depended on the credibility of the nephew's evidence.

It also emerged for the first time during cross-examination that the nephew had told a number of friends about what had happened in his uncle's flat soon after the event. The officer in charge of the investigation had been aware of this and had taken statements from two friends of the nephew about what he had told them. These statements had not bee furnished to the prosecution and were disclosed for the first time after the nephew's cross-examination during trial. The accounts by the nephew's friends differed significantly from the nephew's testimony. At this stage, Barr J. was then assured by the Gardaí that there were no other relevant documents in their possession. However, when the trial resumed, more relevant documents emerged, one of which was a report from a juvenile liaison officer to the investigating Gardaí of an interview with a fellow patient of the nephew's. The fellow patient appeared to indicate that the nephew had taken an hallucinatory drug before the critical incident in the defendant's flat and that this may have induced him to have seen the head of the alleged murder victim. No attempt had been made to interview this potential witness and the report from the juvenile liaison officer was filed away. The Gardaí gave evidence to Barr J. that they understood that this witness was not prepared to make a formal statement but were unable to offer an explanation as to why they had come to that conclusion. A final piece of information also emerged: the nephew indicated that he had been coached by a police officer as to how he might deal with cross-examination.

The Gardaí accepted that all of the documents referred to were relevant but claimed that officers in the investigation team, through admitted gross incompetence and negligence, had erroneously filed them away in a manner that they had been completely overlooked. Barr J. did not accept the Garda explanations and he concluded that there had been a conscious and deliberate policy, probably orchestrated by the officer in charge of the investigation and at least one other member of his team, to subvert the course of justice in this trial.

Nor did Barr J. accept that an experienced Garda would fail to appreciate the far-reaching significance of the documents in question or would fail to appreciate that he had a duty to furnish them to the prosecution and, in turn, to the defence. He felt that his conclusions were fortified, firstly, by the failure to interview the witness described in the juvenile liaison officer's report and, second, by the evidence given by the nephew that he had been coached.

He concluded that the Garda investigating team had resorted to a policy aimed at depriving the defendant of his constitutional right to a fair trial. He rejected the suggestion of continuing with the present trial after an appropriate adjournment as the trial had been so tainted that it could not have satisfactorily retrieved. As indicated, he went on to state that the defendant could not be assured of his constitutional right to a fair trial if a new trial was directed to take place at a later date. Barr J. referred to the revelations in the case as a grievous wrong which were so serious as to stigmatise the entire prosecution to such an extent that significant doubt had to remain that the defendant might never have had the benefit of a fair trial. Indeed, he expressed 'significant doubt' as to whether full disclosure had been made by the Gardaí even at this stage and he considered that the coaching could not be undone.

In effect, Barr J. granted an order of prohibition by placing a permanent bar on the defendant being charged in the future. It is not surprising that the strong condemnatory language used by Barr J. in his judgment attracted a great deal of media coverage to the case at the time (its tone and the fact that a reasoned judgment was delivered both being themselves unusual in the Central Criminal Court): see *The Irish Times*, June 26, 1996. See also *The People v. Scannell*, Court of Criminal Appeal, June 18, 1996.

In the third decision on disclosure, *The People v. Gannon*, Supreme Court, December 17, 1996, the Supreme Court declined to interfere with a conviction for rape where new evidence had been uncovered. The case against the defendant depended entirely on visual identification. The rape had not been reported for six weeks and the defendant had not been identified for a further three weeks. During the trial the complainant was not challenged on the description she had given of her assailant. Over five years after the trial, in August 1993 two documents which had not been produced by the State during the trial came to the attention of the defence. These were: notes taken by the first person to whom the rape had been reported; and a report prepared by a Garda based on these notes. Both documents contained descriptions of the assailant. The defendant argued that these documents constituted a newly discovered fact which showed a miscarriage of justice within the meaning of section 2 of the Criminal Procedure Act 1993 (1993 Review, 211). The Criminal Court of Appeal held that the likelihood was that the documents would not have been availed of and that the information in them added nothing new to the case. The Court certified that the case involved a point of law of exceptional public importance. The Supreme Court ultimately dismissed the appeal.

The Court held that, in determining whether a newly discovered fact has rendered a conviction unsafe and unsatisfactory it is required to carry out an objective evaluation of the newly discovered fact with a view to determining whether the conviction at issue was unsafe and unsatisfactory and the court cannot have regard solely to the course taken by the defence at the trial. Applying this test, the Court held that here was nothing in the description contained in the notes and report which could have assisted the defendant in any way, because when the descriptions were compared the discrepancies appeared to be minimal. The Court accepted the test in the English decision *R v. Kulasingham and Sivilingham*, Court of Appeal (Criminal Division), May 27, 1994 that non-disclosure of evidence which would probably affect the manner in which the defence might meet the case could lead to a quashing of a conviction, but the facts in this case do not support such a conclusion.

For previous discussion of disclosure, see *Murphy v. Director of Public Prosecutions* [1989] I.L.R.M. 71 (1988 Review, 172), *The People v. Marsh, Irish Times,* November 21, 1989 (1989 Review, 177) and *The People v. Marsh,* Irish Times, 28 February 1991 (1991 Review, 166, which also refers to an unusual retort from the Director of Public Prosecutions). See also Paul O'Connor's article (1989) 7 I.L.T. 158 and Una Ní Raifeartaigh's comments on the *Kelly* case, already referred to, (1996) 6 *Irish Criminal Law Journal* 124, at 128-9.

Discovery of documents: whether available   In *The People v. Flynn and Keely* [1996] 1 I.L.R.M. 317, Judge Moriarty (now Moriarty J.) held that discovery was not available in the ordinary manner in a criminal trial. He accepted that a literal interpretation of O.31, r.29 of the Rules of the Superior Courts 1986 might lead to the conclusion that it applied to criminal proceedings. Nonetheless, he considered that the arrangements contained in O.31 of the 1986 Rules were inapplicable to a criminal trial, particularly because there was lacking the mutuality inherent in seeking discovery between parties. While rejecting the application for discovery by the defendants in this case, Judge Moriarty (as he then was) noted that, if it were to emerge that there had been a failure to supply the defendants with relevant information, this might become highly significant in the trial itself. In this respect, he was alluding to the duty on the prosecution to disclose information to the defence, which was adumbrated with such strength by Barr J. in *The People v. Flannery*, High Court (Central Criminal Court), June 25, 1996, discussed above.

Judge's direction to jury to acquit: whether within jurisdiction   In *Director of Public Prosecutions v. Kelly* [1997] 1 I.L.R.M. 497 (H.C.), Laffoy J. held that the respondent trial judge had erred in directing the acquittal of a person where a prosecution witness had not appeared to give evidence. The charges involved alleged offences under the Offences against the Person Act 1861 and the Criminal Law (Rape) (Amendment) Act 1990. Prior to the trial date, it emerged that a doctor who had examined the complainant would be unavailable to testify at the trial. The trial was re-listed for hearing. It subsequently transpired that the doctor would be unavailable at the adjourned date, and the defendant had applied for an order of prohibition in respect of the trial. That application was not proceeded with on the basis of a written commitment that the doctor would attend the trial. At the next adjourned date, it emerged that the doctor would not be available to give evidence.

The respondent trial judge expressed the view that the trial should not proceed without the presence of the doctor. The defendant wished to proceed with the trial, but when the doctor failed to attend, the trial judge directed the empanelled jury to acquit the defendant. No evidence had been heard by the respondent or the jury at any stage. The Director sought judicial review of the respondent's decision, seeking an order of *certiorari* quashing it and an order remitting the case to the Circuit Court pursuant to O.84, r.26(4) of the Rules of the Superior Courts 1986. Although Laffoy J. held that the respondent had acted *ultra vires*, she declined to remit the case.

She framed the case as involving the issue as to the respondent's role in ensuring that the defendant would not be deprived of a trial in due course of law, as required by Article 38.1 of the Constitution, had the case proceeded in the absence of the doctor. She commented:

> I have no doubt that, in a criminal trial on indictment, a trial judge has no jurisdiction to direct the jury to find the accused person not guilty where the prosecution has not been allowed to open its case or to adduce any evidence. While no authority was cited in support of this proposition, it seems to me that a conclusion to the contrary would be so fundamentally at variance with principle as to be wholly unsustainable.

While not expressing to ground this in any authority, Laffoy J. felt that it did find some support in the case law on delay deriving from *The State (O'Connell) v. Fawsitt* [1986] I.R. 362 (see the 1993 Review, 223-6 and 1994 Review, 171-4), in that the appropriate remedy in delay as well as in cases such as the present was for the accused person to be given an opportunity to seek an order of prohibition from the High Court. Thus, she concluded that the trial judge had exceeded his jurisdiction in purporting to direct the jury to acquit the defendant in the instant case.

Laffoy J. declined, however, to grant the remedies sought by the Director. Citing without further elaboration the decision of the Supreme Court in *The State (Tynan) v. Keane* [1968] I.R. 348, she concluded that if she granted the reliefs sought and the matter was remitted to the Circuit Criminal Court, the defendant 'could not plead *autrefois acquit,* his acquittal being based on an adjudication which was in excess of jurisdiction, which was no adjudication at all.' While this is an area fraught with difficulty, it might be argued that, since the jury had been empanelled in the instant case, the plea of *autrefois acquit* might very well have been available. See the discussion in the 1992 Review, 268-70, of the Supreme Court's decision in *Sweeney v. Brophy* [1993] 2 I.R. 202 (HC & SC); [1992] I.L.R.M. 479 (H.C.); [1993] I.L.R.M. 449 (S.C.). Nonetheless, although the decision in *Sweeney* was not cited by Laffoy J., she applied another aspect of its holding, namely, that since *certiorari* is a discretionary remedy and the power to remit under O.84, r.26(4) of the 1986 Rules was also discretionary, the Court should take into account the potential for prejudice if the matter were remitted, including the impact of any delay which would be inherent in any remittal. In the instant case, Laffoy J. held that the absence of the doctor from the retrial and the time gap between the alleged offences and any retrial, likely to be over four years, both militated against remittal. This approach is entirely consistent with the approach taken in *Sweeney*.

Judge's directions to jury: whether oppressive In *The People v. Kelly*, Court of Criminal Appeal, 4 March 1996, the Court dealt, *inter alia*, with the extent to which it would interfere with the manner in which a trial judge gave directions to a jury. An issue concerning the duty of disclosure by the prosecution is dealt with separately above, 252. As already indicated from that discussion, the defendant had been convicted in the Circuit Court with possession of a controlled drug for the purpose of supplying it to another, contrary to sections 3 and 15 of the Misuse of Drugs Act 1977. He submitted that the trial judge had put excessive pressure on the jury to bring in a verdict after they had informed him that they were unable to agree. The jury had retired to consider their verdict at 12.14 p.m. and were brought back at 1.30 p.m. when they informed the court that they had not reached a verdict. Their deliberations resumed at 2.34 p.m. and they were brought back again at 4 p.m. when they again replied in the negative to the question whether they had reached a unanimous verdict. The trial judge then instructed them that they could bring in a majority verdict. The jury returned at 5.06 p.m. when the foreman informed the court that no verdict had been reached. A conversation in general terms then took place between the trial judge and the foreman as to how long the jury should spend trying to reach a verdict. The jury retired at 5.10 p.m. and returned with a majority verdict at 6.34 p.m. The defendant alleged that the trial judge had extracted the verdict from the jury and that the jury should have been discharged at 5.06 p.m. The Court of Criminal Appeal refused the application for leave to appeal against conviction. On this point, the Court held that, generally, unless a judge gave directions or exercised his discretion in a way that was oppressive to a jury, an appeal court should not interfere with the judge's discretion. In the instant case the Court considered that the manner in which the trial judge exercised his discretion was in no way oppressive to the jury and this was clear from the dialogue between the judge and the jury foreman when the jury returned to the court at 5.06 p.m. No pressure whatever was put on the jury, the foreman asked if they could have more time and the judge made it clear that if they could not agree they should come back to him. This approach is in line with the views expressed in *The People v. Doran* (1987) 3 Frewen 125 (1987 Review, 142).

Withdrawal of summary and institution of trial on indictment In *Kelly v. Director Of Public Prosecutions*, Supreme Court, June 28, 1996, the Supreme Court held that the Director may withdraw summary proceedings and institute proceedings by way of indictment where there has been no adjudication on any issue in the summary proceedings and the accused has not been put in jeopardy.

Summonses charging the applicant with dangerous driving contrary to section 53 of the Road Traffic Act 1961, as amended, had been issued in the wake of a traffic accident in which a person had died. The application for the issue of the summonses had not been made within the six month time limit in section 10(4) of the Petty Sessions (Ireland) Act 1851. The summonses were listed for hearing on a date in February 1993 but, on the Director's application, were adjourned to a date in May 1993. Prior to that date, the applicant was arrested and charged with dangerous driving causing death contrary to section 53 of the Road Traffic Act 1961, as amended. At the hearing of the District Court summonses in May 1993, the charge of dangerous driving was struck out on the Director's application and the remaining summonses were adjourned. The Chief State Solicitor subsequently informed the applicant's solicitors by letter that all of the summonses were being withdrawn at the Director's direction. The book of evidence in respect of the charge of dangerous driving causing death was served on the applicant The applicant sought an order of prohibition in respect of the trial on the grounds that the prosecution was an attempt to circumvent the failure of the Director to apply for the issue of the District Court summons within the time permitted by s. 10(4) of the Petty Sessions (Ireland) Act 1851. The claim was dismissed in the High Court, and this conclusion was upheld on appeal to the Supreme Court.

The Court held that the instant case did not fall into the circumstances in *Attorney General (Ó Maonaigh) v. Fitzgerald* [1964] I.R. 458, in which it was held that an acquittal on a summary charge of dangerous driving is a bar to a subsequent charge on indictment of dangerous driving. Since, in the instant case the summary proceedings had not been determined, the Director was not estopped from prosecuting the applicant on indictment. Thus, until an accused has been convicted or acquitted, the State was entitled to reconsider a decision to proceed by way of summary trial and opt for trial on indictment. Having regard, however, to the decision of Finlay P. (as he then was) in *The State (O'Callaghan) v. Ó hUadhaigh* [1977] I.R. 42 (which concerned the application of fair procedures in the use of the *nolle prosequi*), the Supreme Court added that the Director's powers may not be exercised in such a way as to constitute an abuse of the right of an accused to a fair trial. Since there had been no adjudication on any issue in the instant case and the applicant had not been in jeopardy by virtue of the summary proceedings, there was no injustice to him in the withdrawal of the summary proceedings and the institution of proceedings by way of indictment.

Alternative verdicts: grievous bodily harm In *The People v. McBride* [1996] 1 I.R. 312; [1997] 1 I.L.R.M. 233, discussed above in the context of *mens rea*, the Court of Criminal Appeal quashed convictions for offences including grievous bodily harm imposed on the defendant and directed a retrial. The defendant had been convicted in the Circuit Criminal Court on three separate counts arising from the same incident: causing grievous bodily harm with intent, contrary to section 18 of the Offences Against the Person Act 1861; unlawfully and maliciously inflicting grievous bodily harm, contrary to section 20 of the 1861 Act; and assault occasioning actual bodily harm, contrary to section 47 of the 1861 Act. The Court of Criminal Appeal held that the jury did not understand what was meant by there being alternative counts since they had convicted the defendant on all three. They should have been directed by the trial judge that as the three counts were alternative counts in descending order of seriousness, they should start by considering count 1 and only proceed to count 2 if they found the defendant not guilty on count 1 and so on and should not bring in any verdict on counts 2 and 3 if they had found him guilty on count 1.

Amendment of summons   In *Ó Síochain v. Coy*, Supreme Court, January 19, 1996, the Supreme Court held that the conviction of the applicant in the District Court in his absence on a charge that he had driven a car without insurance, after the Court had amended the summons stating the charge, did not invalidate the conviction where the applicant's absence was deliberate. The trial had initially been adjourned when the applicant failed to appear in the District Court on the day named in the summons which had been served on him. The summons alleged that he had driven a motor car in a public place without an approved policy of insurance having been issued in respect of such driving, contrary to the relevant provisions of the Road Traffic Act 1961, as amended. The summons described the car as bearing the registration number 969 MIW. Notice of the adjournment was served on the applicant. At the adjourned hearing, the applicant did not appear but a friend attended on his instructions and took a careful note of the evidence in relation to the registration details of the car. The prosecution successfully applied to the respondent judge for an amendment of the summons pursuant to Rule 88 of the District Court Rules 1948 by the substitution of 969 MIU (being the correct registration letters and numbers) for 969 MIW. The applicant applied to the High Court for an order of *certiorari* quashing his conviction, which was dismissed by Keane J. and this was affirmed by the Supreme Court. The Court held that since the applicant had notice of the resumed hearing of the charge, the respondent judge had jurisdiction to make the amendment requested by the prosecution pursuant to the 1948 Rules; nor did the Court consider that there had been any breach of the requirement of fair procedures at the trial of the applicant. The applicant had also sought to introduce complaints of perjury and contempt of court on the part of the prosecuting Gardaí. The Supreme Court held that these were not relevant to a judicial review.

Book of evidence   In *Director Of Public Prosecutions v. McMenamin*, High Court, March 23, 1996, Barron J. confirmed that the 'book of evidence' served on an accused under the Criminal Procedure Act 1967 need only include statements by those whom the State intends to call as witnesses at the trial. The Director had instituted charges involving assault occasioning actual bodily harm and the accused had opted for trial on indictment. The book of evidence was served on the accused, and copies of statements of evidence of other witnesses it was not intended to call at trial were also served on him. The respondent judge of the District Court was of the view that these statements should have been included in the book of evidence and adjourned the matter to enable the Director to furnish a fresh book of evidence. The Director declined to do so and he was refused a return for trial by the respondent who also made an order refusing informations. The Director sought an order of *certiorari* to quash this order and an order of *mandamus* directing the respondent to consider as adequate the book of evidence furnished by the Director. Barron J. granted the relief sought.

He held that section 6 of the Criminal Procedure Act 1967 requires only that the book of evidence include statements by those whom it is intended to call as witnesses at the trial. By seeking to have the evidence of other persons put in the book of evidence, the defence had, in Barron J.'s view, been seeking to force the prosecution to call such persons as witnesses at the trial; the defence was not entitled to do this. Barron J. concluded by stating that, unless these witnesses had made depositions in accordance with section 7 of the 1967 Act, their statements were not matters of evidence before the respondent judge.

Return for trial to specific court In *Ward v. Judge Of Longford District Court and Ors*, High Court, May 17, 1996, Kelly J. held that in exercising the power in section 45 of the Offences Against the State Act 1939 to direct that an accused person be returned for trial in a specific court, the Director of Public Prosecutions is not administering justice nor is he in any way interfering with the independence of the judiciary. He also rejected various challenges made to the preliminary examination procedure under the Criminal Procedure Act 1967. In particular, Kelly J. rejected the submission that the procedure under the 1967 Act involved a person being returned for trial without any evidence of an offence being established. Kelly J. pointed out that section 8 of the Criminal Procedure Act 1967 required a judge to be of the opinion that there was a sufficient case to put an accused on trial for the offence with which he had been charged. In addition, citing *Costello v. Director of Public Prosecutions* [1984] I.R. 346, he held that the applicant did not have the right to question whether he had a case to answer decided by a grand jury, and he concluded that there was nothing unconstitutional about the method by which a preliminary investigation is conducted.

Video link evidence In *Donnelly v. Ireland*, High Court, December 3, 1996,

Costello P. rejected the plaintiff's constitutional challenge to section 13 of the Criminal Evidence Act 1992 (1992 Review, 262-4), by which evidence may be given in certain criminal trials by way of video link. See the discussion in the Constitutional Law chapter, 154, above.

ROAD TRAFFIC

Custody Regulations not complied with   In *Director of Public Prosecutions (Lenihan) v. McGuire*, High Court, July 31, 1996, Kelly J. held that non-compliance with the requirement in the Criminal Justice Act 1984 (Treatment of Persons in Custody in Garda Síochána Stations) Regulations 1987 that the name of the member in charge be entered into the station diary could not, in itself, lead to the dismissal of a charge under section 49 of the Road Traffic Act 1961. Citing O'Hanlon J.'s decision in *Director of Public Prosecutions v. Spratt* [1995] 1 I.R. 585 (1995 Review, 244), Kelly J. concluded that there must be a causal link between failure to comply with the 1987 Regulations and whatever prejudice is alleged to have been suffered by an accused as a result thereof.

Disqualification for refusal to supply sample   In *Director of Public Prosecutions v. Dougan* [1997] 1 I.L.R.M. 550 (H.C.), *sub nom. The People v. Dougan* [1996] 1 I.R. 544 (H.C.), the defendant had been charged, *inter alia*, with refusing to comply with the request of a medical practitioner to provide a sample of blood or urine, contrary to section 13(3) of the Road Traffic Act 1994 (1994 Review, 219). The District Court judge hearing the case raised the question whether the penalties applicable took the offence outside the range of minor offences triable summarily under Article 38.5 of the Constitution. Geoghegan J. declined to address the issue directly on case stated, though he indicated that the 1994 Act might be able to withstand constitutional challenge: see the discussion in the Practice and Procedure chapter, 468, below.

Driving without insurance: shifting of burden   In *Stokes v. O'Donnell and Ors.* [1996] 2 I.L.R.M. 538 (H.C.), Laffoy J. applied the presumption in section 56(4) of the Road Traffic Act 1961, which provides that where a demand has been made and a person has refused or failed to produce a certificate of insurance, it shall be presumed until the contrary is shown that the vehicle was being used in contravention of the section. The applicant had been charged with driving without insurance under section 56 of the 1961 Act. At the trial, the prosecuting Garda gave evidence that the applicant had produced a certificate of insurance but a representative of the insurance company involved also gave evidence that the certificate was not a policy of his insurance company. The applicant was convicted by the respondent judge of the District Court.

The applicant unsuccessfully sought to review his conviction on the grounds that there was no evidence upon which the presumption in section 56(4) of the 1961 Act could be applied. Laffoy J. considered that, although the Garda did not testify in explicit terms that the applicant had failed, following demand, to produce a certificate of insurance within the meaning of section 56, there was evidence on which the District Court could conclude that the presumption had been raised and that the evidential burden then passed to the applicant. Distinguishing the instant case from the circumstances in *Director of Public Prosecutions v. O'Donoghue* [1991] 1 I.R. 448 (1991 Review, 172-3) and *McNally v. Martin* [1995] 1 I.L.R.M. 350 (1994 Review, 7-8) Laffoy J. concluded that in determining that the applicant had a case to answer the respondent judge had acted within jurisdiction and as the applicant had not rebutted the presumption, the conviction was also within jurisdiction.

Refusal to supply blood or urine sample: 'refuses' and 'fails' In *Director of Public Prosecutions v. Doyle* [1997] 1 I.L.R.M. 379 (H.C.), Geoghegan J. held that the purpose of section 13 of the Road Traffic (Amendment) Act 1978 is to require a sample of blood or urine that is capable of being tested and that it did not create two offences by using the words 'refuses' and 'fails.' Section 13 of the 1978 Act provides that, where a person has been arrested under the Act, an offence is committed where the person 'refuses or fails' to permit a designated registered medical practitioner to take a blood specimen or to provide a urine specimen. The defendant had been charged with failing to comply with a request under section 13 of the 1978 Act. The defendant argued that she was entitled to an acquittal because, although the evidence might have established a "refusal", it did not establish a "failure". Geoghegan J., on a case stated, declined to accede to this argument. He considered that the words "fail or refuse" had been used in section 13 of the 1978 Act to avoid all possible loopholes and strained interpretations of the section. When read as a whole, he concluded that the purpose of the section was to ensure that either a blood or a urine sample would be provided in such a form that was testable. In the instant case, the defendant had flatly refused to permit any sample to be taken, and that constituted not merely a refusal but also a failure. He also pointed out that the offence consisted of non-compliance with the requirement and that could take the form of an express refusal in which case there was both a refusal and a failure or it could take the form of non compliance notwithstanding that the defendant had agreed to comply with the requirement, in which case the more appropriate word in the summons would be failure.

SEARCH AND SEIZURE

Extraordinary excusing circumstances principle not applicable   In *Director of Public Prosecutions v. Delaney and Ors.* [1996] 1 I.L.R.M. 536 (H.C.) and *Freeman v. Director of Public Prosecutions*, High Court, November 18, 1996, Morris and Carney JJ. confirmed, respectively, that the principle by which confessions obtained in breach of constitutional rights may be admissible in 'extraordinary excusing circumstances' does not apply to obtaining other forms of evidence. Nonetheless, in both cases, convictions were upheld notwithstanding breaches of the constitutional right to the inviolability of the dwelling.

In *Delaney*, the issue arose against a background where Gardaí had been called to a scene in which a large group of people were attempting, in effect, to burn the flat inside which the defendants had barricaded themselves. The object of the proposed burning appeared to be to remove the defendants from the area on a permanent basis. When the Gardaí arrived, they believed that the defendants were in imminent physical danger and were also aware that there were a number of children and their mother in the premises at the time. They decided to enter the premises in those circumstances. The flat was owned by one of the defendants and he had refused to allow the Gardaí enter. The defendants were later charged with a number of offences, including assault and obstructing the Gardaí in the exercise of their duties. At the conclusion of the prosecution case, the issue arose in *Delaney* whether the Gardaí were entitled to enter the premises. On a case stated, Morris J. held that it was possible to justify the entry, even accepting that the flat's owner had not consented to the entry. The prosecution had cited in support of the entry power the concept of 'extraordinary excusing circumstances' first adumbrated by the Supreme Court in *The People v. O'Brien* [1965] I.R. 142. Morris J. pointed out that, in *The People v. Shaw* [1982] I.R. 1, it had been clearly held that the principles in the *O'Brien* case were confined to the admissibility of confessions obtained in breach of constitutional rights and that they were not applicable to other situations, such as the instant case where an entry of dwelling within the meaning of Article 40.5 of the Constitution was at issue. In the absence of this principle being applicable, the Gardaí then argued that there was a statutory power of entry justifying the action they had taken in the instant case, but Morris J. held that there was no such power of entry in the instant case. However, he gave some hope to the prosecution when he examined a final aspect of the case. While he accepted that the owner of the flat had not given consent to entry, he indicated that the mother and the children who were in the flat may have given an implied consent to enter, citing the judgment of O'Flaherty J. in *Director of Public Prosecutions v. Forbes* [1993] I.L.R.M. 817 (1993 Review, 248-9), though accepting that his (Morris J.'s) views as to what constituted implied consent was rather extensive. Morris J. attempted to bolster his views by referring to another element of the decision in *The People v. Shaw* [1982] I.R. 1, above, namely that where two constitutional rights are in conflict - in the instant case, the inviolability of the dwelling and the right to life of the mother and her children - the Gardaí were entitled to make a judgment as to how to achieve a balance between these rights, having regard to the greater weight to be attached to the right to life of the mother and her children. Remitting the case to the District Court, he concluded that it was a matter for the trial judge to determine whether there was a justification for the entry of the flat in the instant case. Without anticipating that decision, he strongly indicated that, if the trial judge so decided, there was, in his view, 'satisfactory evidence for so doing.' Thus, although Morris J. rejected the application of the 'extraordinary excusing circumstances' principle, the outcome is not much different, though the basis for this was that the right to life of the mother and children took priority over the right of the defendants: such a scenario is unlikely to be present in all cases. For some detailed criticism of the use by Morris J. of the *O'Brien* and *Shaw* cases, see Una Ní Raifeartaigh's comments, (1996) 6 *I.C.L.J.* 130-31.

In the second case in which the issue arose, *Freeman v. Director of Public Prosecutions*, High Court, November 18, 1996, there was no 'competing' rights invokved, but nonetheless a *prima facie* breach of Article 40.5 did not prevent a conviction. In this case, the Gardaí had observed the applicant, along with two other men, unloading goods from a white van into the applicant's house. As the Gardaí approached, they were seen by the men who ran into the house slamming the door behind them. The Gardaí, having identified themselves to the occupants, opened the door with the key, which was still in the lock, and entered the premises. Inside they found a number of items and pursued the men outside, where they arrested the applicant under the Larceny Act 1916 for handling stolen goods. The applicant was then taken to a Garda station where he was detained under section 4 of the Criminal Justice Act 1984 for the purpose of investigating the offence. A search warrant was obtained subsequent to the arrest and the search recovered shoes which forensic analysis indicated had been in contact with the floor of the shop from which the items had been stolen. A search of the van revealed other stolen items. The applicant was convicted of handling stolen goods under the 1916 Act and also failing to account for his movements under section 16 of the Criminal Justice Act 1984. Section 41 of the Larceny Act 1916 provides that any person found committing any offence under the Act may be immediately apprehended without a warrant, by any person, and forthwith taken together with the property before a justice of the peace. On a case stated, Carney J. held that the entry of the applicant's house was in breach of Article 40.5 of the Constitution and that his subsequent arrest under section 4 of the 1984 Act was invalid. Unlike the *Delaney* case, above, there were no balancing of rights to be done in the instant case, but as indicated Carney J. upheld the conviction for handling stolen goods.

Carney J. held that section 41(1) of the Larceny Act 1916 was wide enough to permit a valid legal arrest on private property even in circumstances where the Gardaí involved may be trespassers. Referring to the principles in *Director of Public Prosecutions v. McCreesh* [1992] 2 I.R. 239 (1990 Review, 131-2), he accepted that it provided for the arrest without warrant of any person committing an offence under the 1916 Act and therefore must implicitly authorise the entry onto private property where that was necessary to effect such an arrest.

The question, therefore, was whether there was sufficient authority to justify the interference with the right to the inviolability of the dwelling which, Carney J. noted, Article 40.5 of the Constitution had elevated in clear and unqualified terms. In the instant case, he held that the applicant's arrest had not been authorised by section 41 of the 1916 Act since it had breached Article 40.5. Citing with approval Morris J.'s judgment in *Director of Public Prosecutions v. Delaney and Ors.* [1996] 1 I.L.R.M. 536 (H.C.), above, Carney J. held that the principle which allowed for the admissibility of unconstitutionally obtained evidence in extraordinary excusing circumstances was concerned only with the admissibility of evidence and it did not flow as a corollary that the Director was entitled to breach constitutional rights in extraordinary excusing circumstances. On this basis, he held that the charge against the applicant of failing to account for his movements under section 16 of the 1984 Act could not be supported as his initial arrest under the 1984 Act was tainted with the entry of the dwelling in breach of Article 40.5.

Despite this finding, Carney J. upheld the conviction for handling stolen goods under the 1916 Act. It had been argued that, in the instant case, there was a need to prevent the imminent destruction of vital evidence. Carney J. was not prepared to attribute too wide a scope to the notion of imminent destruction of evidence as that could undermine the rationale of a rule if it was to be invoked in circumstances where well meaning haste on the part of the Gardaí could lead to unconstitutional acts. Nonetheless, as the Gardaí had come upon the applicant in what Carney J. described as *flagrante delicto* (perhaps 'red handed' might have been a more apt description for a charge of handling stolen property) and there was no time to obtain a search warrant, he concluded that there was material on which the District Court could exercise its discretion to admit the evidence, in accordance with the principles laid down in *The People v. Lawless* (1985) 3 Frewen 30. In those circumstances, he concluded that the District Court had been correct in convicting the applicant of the charge of handling stolen goods. It remains to be seen whether this approach, which on its face seems difficult to reconcile with Carney J.'s initial view on the breach of Article 40.5, would survive an appeal to the Supreme Court. In the absence of the balancing of rights in the *Delaney* case, above, it is difficult to justify the conclusion that the conviction in the instant case is consistent with the 'elevated' status of Article 40.5 to which Carney J. referred in his judgment.

SEARCH WARRANT

Belief based on informer In *Director of Public Prosecutions v. Sweeney*, High Court, March 26, 1996, Morris J. held that it was not necessary that a Chief Superintendent be in direct receipt of eye witness evidence in order to form the necessary belief for the issuing of a search warrant under section 29(1) of the Offences against the State Act 1939. In the instant case, the defendant had been charged with possession of counterfeit or 'pirate' videos, contrary to the Copyright Act 1963, as amended by the Copyright (Amendment) Act 1987. The principal evidence consisted of material obtained following a search of the defendant's premises pursuant to a search warrant issued by a Chief Superintendent under the 1939 Act. The warrant had been issued basis of information which had been given to the Chief Superintendent, and at the time he issued the warrant, he had reasonable grounds for believing that evidence relating to a scheduled offence under the 1939 Act would be found there. At the defendant's trial in the District Court, the District Court judge found the warrant to be invalid on the basis, *inter alia*, that it was based on hearsay evidence, on information from a source within an illegal organisation and that the Superintendent acted without jurisdiction in issuing the said warrant because he had no information before him which would have enabled him to be satisfied that there were reasonable grounds for such suspicion. Accordingly, he dismissed all the summonses against the defendant. On a case stated, Morris J. held that the District Court judge had erred.

The defendant had relied on the decision in *Byrne v. Gray* [1988] I.R. 31 (1987 Review, 86), but Morris J. considered that there was a fundamental distinction to be drawn between the facts in *Byrne* and those in the instant case. In *Sweeney*, he held, the Chief Superintendent had been kept closely in touch with the information he had been given, and as a result of what he had been told, he had formed his own view. Morris J. noted that the District Court judge had found that his belief had been reasonable. The Superintendent had thus not been relying on someone else's opinion, but had formed his own opinion. He concluded that to require that a Chief Superintendent was entitled to form the necessary belief only on the receipt of direct evidence from an eye witness would, in Morris J.'s view, be to make section 29(1) of the 1939 Act inoperable. As to the fact that the evidence came from an informer, Morris J. held that it was for the Chief Superintendent's function to evaluate such evidence, and if having done so he formed the belief that the necessary evidence was to be found on the defendant's premises, he was entitled to issue the warrant. On this basis, as indicated, Morris J. concluded that the judge had erred in law and he remitted the case to the District Court.

SENTENCING

Concurrent or consecutive   In *The People v. B. (T.)*, Court of Criminal Appeal, 6 November 1996, the Court of Criminal Appeal upheld the imposition of consecutive sentences against the following background. The defendant had pleaded guilty in the Circuit Court to 16 counts of indecent assault and 16 counts of sexual assault against his daughter, and two counts of sexual assault against another girl. The trial judge imposed sentences of four years imprisonment in respect of two of the counts of indecent assault involving the defendant's daughter and ordered the sentences to run consecutively. In imposing sentence the judge referred to the fact that the maximum sentence for indecent assault (the subject matter of earlier counts) was 10 years but for sexual assault (the later counts) was five years. In imposing sentence he said that he was taking into account the other charges to which the defendant had pleaded guilty. On appeal against the severity of the sentences, the Court of Criminal Appeal declined to interfere with the sentences imposed.

The Court accepted that it was a matter exclusively for the prosecution to decide whether charges of aggravated sexual assault and attempted rape should have been preferred against the defendant. Since the prosecution had elected to charge the defendant solely with indecent assault and sexual assault the Court noted that the trial judge had correctly approached the imposition of sentence without regard to the more serious charges which the defendant would have faced had a different decision been taken. The Court stated that, having regard to the gravity of the offences, the maximum sentence of five years in respect of each count would have been appropriate were it not for the plea of guilty, and that the reduction in the sentence to four years gave sufficient weight to that plea.

The Court identified the essential issue as whether the trial judge erred in principle in imposing consecutive sentences. The Court stated that the jurisdiction of the courts to impose concurrent or consecutive sentences where a person had been convicted of more than one offence was a common law jurisdiction. It accepted the general view, as expressed by the English Court of Appeal in *R v. Lawrence* (1989) 11 Cr. App. R.(S.) 580, that concurrent sentences should be imposed for offences arising out of one incident or transaction, although there were exceptional cases where the sentencing tribunal might depart from the usual practice. The Court also accepted that the 'totality principle' applied in English courts, where a court should consider the total sentence in relation to the totality of the offending and in relation to sentence levels for other crimes had been endorsed in this jurisdiction by McCarthy J. in *The People v. Healy* [1990] 1 I.R. 388 (1989 Review, 183-4) (to which might also be added the view of the Court itself in *The People v. Farrell*, Court of Criminal Appeal, July 23, 1990 (1990 Review, 245-6)).

In the instant case, the Court considered that it was clear that the offences in respect of which the defendant had pleaded guilty did not arise out of the same incident or transaction but were committed at intervals over a lengthy period of years; it had clearly been within the discretion of the trial judge to impose consecutive sentences if he thought that appropriate; and in applying the totality principle the resulting sentence of eight years could not be regarded as unjust, having regard to the gravity of the offences and the serious consequences for the complainant. On this basis, the Court dismissed the application for leave to appeal.

Dangerous driving causing death: leniency In *The People v. Connolly*, Court of Criminal Appeal, November 25, 1996, the Court declined to interfere with a sentence on the grounds of undue leniency. The defendant had been sentenced to three years' imprisonment for dangerous driving causing death to two people. The sentence was reviewed after five months and the balance suspended. The trial judge accepted evidence regarding the defendant's good conduct after the offence. The Director of Public Prosecutions appealed to the Court of Criminal Appeal under section 2 of the Criminal Justice Act 1993 (1993 Review, 255) on the ground that the suspension of the sentence amounted to undue leniency. As indicated, the appeal was unsuccessful. The Court held that the trial judge was not entitled to take into account the behaviour of the applicant in prison since the time that the sentence was imposed, but the crucial question was whether the trial judge had kept a balance between the particular circumstances of the commission of the offence and the relevant personal circumstances of the person sentenced, as indicated in its decision in *The People v. Byrne, sub nom Director of Public Prosecutions v. Byrne* [1995] 1 I.L.R.M. 279 (1994 Review, 224-6). In this respect, the Court considered that the trial judge should have regard to the principle of proportionality and that he had done so. In conclusion, the Court held that although there was 'no doubt' that the decision to suspend the balance of the sentence was lenient, the Court was not satisfied that it amounted to 'undue leniency' within the meaning of the 1993 Act.

Delay in trial In *The People v. J.(T.)*, Court of Criminal Appeal, November 6, 1996, the Court of Criminal Appeal reduced to six months a sentence of five years (the last 18 months being suspended) imposed on the defendant in the Circuit Court after he had pleaded guilty to indecent assault, the trial judge taking into account several other offences. The offences occurred between the years 1980 and 1984 when the complainant was in her early teenage years, but only came to light in 1995 when she made a detailed statement to the Gardaí. During the trial the complainant stated that she could not understand why the accused had been charged with indecent assault only and not with rape. The Court of Criminal Appeal pointed out that at the time the offences to which the defendant pleaded guilty were committed, the offence of "indecent assault" extended to all forms of non-consensual sexual activity which did not amount to rape or buggery. Where a girl was under the age of 17 at the time of commission of the alleged offences, consent was no defence. The maximum sentence under the Criminal Law (Rape) Act 1981 for indecent assault was 10 years imprisonment. The Criminal Law (Rape) (Amendment) Act 1990 substituted for the offence of indecent assault the offences of "sexual assault" and "aggravated sexual assault". The maximum sentence for sexual assault is five years imprisonment and for aggravated sexual assault is life imprisonment. The Court of Criminal Appeal pointed out that, had a jury been satisfied beyond reasonable doubt that the defendant had committed the various acts detailed in the complainant's statement without her consent, he could have been convicted of rape, buggery, unlawful carnal knowledge of a girl under the age of 17 and, possibly, of a girl under the age of 15, all of which, excepting the third, would 'have attracted a maximum sentence of life imprisonment. Nonetheless, in this case, the prosecution had preferred charges of indecent assault only against the defendant and it would have been inappropriate, the Court stated, for it to speculate as to the reasons which led the prosecution not to prefer charges of a more serious nature against him. It was enough to say that the case had to be approached on the basis that the defendant had never been charged with such offences and had never admitted that he was guilty of the acts of rape, buggery and oral intercourse detailed in the complainant's statement.

The court was, however, satisfied that the trial judge had been correct in treating this as a case which came with the more serious category of cases within the offence of "indecent assault". The real question was whether he gave sufficient weight to the mitigating factors relied upon by the defendant, namely, the consequences for the defendant, a person of previous good character, and the fact that the offences had occurred 13 years before the trial. The Court accepted that there were obvious reasons why such a long time could elapse before the alleged conduct was reported in cases such as this. Citing the decision in *G. v. Director of Public Prosecutions* [1994] 1 I.R. 374 (1994 Review, 174), the Court noted that this was why a different test had been adopted in deciding whether the trial of an accused charged with what may be described as child sexual abuse should be prohibited for violation of the constitutional right to an expeditious trial from the test applicable in other cases. That did not mean, the Court added, that if and when the accused was ultimately convicted the court could or should disregard the length of time which had elapsed since the offences were committed.

The Court stated that the lapse of time could be relevant in determining to what extent the accused was likely to re-offend and whether the accused's rehabilitation had already been achieved having regard to the accused's conduct in the interval. In the instant case, the offending conduct had come to an end 10 years before the trial, he had not offended in any respect since, and was married and in steady employment. All the evidence pointed to the offences having been incidents in the defendant's past which he deeply regretted and had not been repeated. The lapse of time was also significant concerning the different climate of opinion which prevailed in current times in respect of offences of this nature. Significantly, the Court admitted and accepted that, if the defendant had been prosecuted in the early 1980s, he would have received a significantly less severe sentence of imprisonment. In this respect, the court was satisfied that the criminal justice system could not be indifferent to the fact that an accused would probably have received a more lenient sentence had he not been deprived of what would otherwise have been his constitutional right to an expeditious trial. Taking this into account, the Court concluded that the trial judge was in error in giving insufficient weight to all of these factors and, as already indicated, it substituted a sentence of six months for that imposed in the Circuit Court. It is important to bear in mind the historical context in which this decision was made: the sentence imposed in the instant case could not be regarded as setting a 'tariff' for delayed child sexual abuse cases. Of particular relevance in this context was that the offences had occurred at a time when, the Court frankly admitted, the general awareness within the community of the problem of child sexual abused was low and that this extended to the sentencing regime likely to have been applied by the judiciary at that time. Although the Court did not cite any decisions in support of this, it must be assumed that this concurs with the experience of practitioners in this area. In that sense, the decision in the case reflects the reality that many such cases currently coming before the courts should not be considered with the benefit of hindsight. Where cases arise in the future, however, it must be assumed that the 'tariff' will be increased in line, at least to some extent, with contemporary knowledge and mores in society.

Discrepancy between co-accused In *The People v. Johnston*, Court of Criminal Appeal, July 1, 1996, the Court confirmed that the fact that a co-accused may have been dealt with too leniently is not a basis on which a sentence should be varied. The defendant had been charged with a number of others on charges of, *inter alia*, murder, robbery and possession of firearms with intent to endanger life. The charges arose out of an attempted bank robbery and subsequent homicide. The defendant had pleaded guilty to the robbery and firearms charges, for which he received sentences up to 12 years, but not guilty on the murder charge. He was found guilty of manslaughter on the latter charge and sentenced to life imprisonment, later reduced to 15 years on appeal to the Court of Criminal Appeal. It later emerged that, at that appeal, the Court of Criminal Appeal had been under the impression that none of the defendant's co-accused had been found guilty of manslaughter and had drawn a distinction between the defendant's and their sentences on that basis. It later transpired that one of them had pleaded guilty to manslaughter and been sentenced to four years. The defendant than applied to the Court of Criminal Appeal for review of his sentence pursuant to section 2 of the Criminal Procedure Act 1993 (1993 Review, 211) on the basis that that misunderstanding on the first appeal constituted a newly discovered fact within the meaning of section 2 of the 1993 Act. The Court agreed to hear the application for review under the 1993 Act, but affirmed the sentences imposed on the defendant on all counts. As indicated, the Court held that, even if a co-accused has been dealt with too leniently is not a basis on which the defendant's sentence should be varied, approving the approach taken in *Application of Poyning* [1972] I.R. 402. Taking account of the defendant's previous convictions, the Court concluded that the sentences imposed were appropriate in the circumstances.

Forgery   In *The People v. Malocco*, Court of Criminal Appeal, 23 May 1996, the Court declined to interfere with a sentence of five years penal servitude imposed on the defendant, who had been found guilty in the Circuit Criminal Court on six counts of forging documents and uttering forged documents. The defendant had been a partner in a firm of solicitors who acted for a group of newspapers in connection with libel claims. It was claimed that the applicant had obtained funds from this group for the purpose of either compromising or making lodgements in respect of specific proceedings but that the funds were never applied for those purposes. In the application for leave to appeal, the defendant unsuccessfully raised a number of evidential points, discussed in the Evidence chapter, 321, below. Nor did the Court of Criminal Appeal accept that the sentence imposed was excessively severe. The Court did not detect any error in principle in the approach adopted by the trial judge and was satisfied that no ground had been established for interfering with the sentence imposed.

Guilty plea   In the 1995 Review, 257, we noted that in *The People v. D.(J.)*, High Court, April 27, 1995 and *The People v. R.(J.)*, High Court, December 5, 1995 Carney J. had held that, where an accused had made a full confession and had pleaded guilty to the offence of rape, the imposition of the maximum sentence was precluded and the court was confined to imposing such a determinate sentence as would take full account of all the factors for and against the accused. In *The People v. Bambrick* [1996] 1 I.R. 265 (H.C.), Carney J. reaffirmed the approach he had taken in the two earlier decisions, in the context of a plea of guilty to manslaughter involving the homicide of two women.

The deaths involved the use by the defendant of bondage on both victims. Carney J. was of the view that the killing of the defendant's second victim with the knowledge of what he had done to the first victim satisfied him that the defendant had a propensity to re-offend. Given that he was liable because of his age to be sexually active on release with remission from any determinate sentence, Carney J. would have preferred to protect the community and the defendant from himself by imposing the maximum sentence of life imprisonment with the possibility of release only after a substantial punitive period had expired and where the Minister for Justice's expert advisors would be satisfied that he no longer posed a danger or threat to the community and women in particular. However, as indicated, he felt precluded from so doing.

In the instant case, the details of the crimes were only known through the defendant's confession. Carney J. also noted that the Director had accepted the defendant's plea of guilty to manslaughter and he was therefore entitled to a sentence which was in reality less than that which he would have received had he been convicted of murder. In this context, Carney J. expressly stated that it would be judicially dishonest to impose a sentence of 30 years, for example, and say that it was a lesser sentence than life imprisonment. He stated that he would only impose a sentence within known and existing guidelines. On this basis, he imposed a sentence of 15 years on the first count and 18 years on the second, the sentences to run concurrently. We reiterate here the doubts expressed in the 1995 Review, 258, as to whether Carney J.'s approach in which the maximum sentence is always precluded where a plea of guilty has been entered is, in fact, required by the existing sentencing jurisprudence. We would add, however, that the honesty in sentencing policy expressed by Carney J. is to be welcomed, in particular his comments in *Bambrick* on the reality of imposing a long determinate sentence of 30 years as opposed to a life sentence.

Partly suspended sentence: effect on remission   In *O'Brien v. Governor of Limerick Prison*, High Court, July 31, 1996; Supreme Court, February 13, 1997, the Supreme Court, reversing Geoghegan J., held that where a sentence of imprisonment has been suspended in part, remission may be earned by a prisoner on the part which has not been suspended rather than the whole of his sentence. The impact of the decision on the imposition of partly suspended sentences is discussed in the Prisons chapter, 498, below.

SEXUAL OFFENCES

Extra-territorial jurisdiction: child sex tourism   The Sexual Offences (Jurisdiction) Act 1996, which began its legislative life as the Sexual Offences (Jurisdiction) Bill 1995, a Private Members Bill introduced by Eoin Ryan T.D. and John O'Donoghue T.D., aims to extend the criminal law to criminal acts involving children committed outside the State by citizens ordinarily resident in the State. In that respect, it seeks to impose criminal sanctions both on those who organise 'child sex tourism' and also on those, in particular paedophiles, who engage in acts abroad with children which would be criminal under the laws of this State if committed in the State. The Act came into effect on December 19, 1996 on its signature by the President.

Section 1 of the Act defines 'a child' as a person under the age of 17 for the purposes of the Act. Section 2(1) of the Act, its central provision, states:

> Where a person, being a citizen of the State or being ordinarily resident in the State, does an act, in a place other than the State ('the place'), against or involving a child which—
> (a) constitutes an offence under the law of the place, and
> (b) if done within the State, would constitute an offence under, or referred to in, an enactment specified in the *Schedule* to this Act,
>
> he or she shall be guilty of the second-mentioned offence.

The Schedule to the 1996 Act lists the following enactments:

1. Section 1 of the Criminal Law Amendment Act 1935.
2. Section 2 of the Criminal Law Amendment Act 1935.
3. Section 2 of the Criminal Law (Rape) Act 1981.
4. Section 2 of the Criminal Law (Rape) (Amendment) Act 1990.
5. Section 3 of the Criminal Law (Rape) (Amendment) Act 1990.
6. Section 4 of the Criminal Law (Rape) (Amendment) Act 1990.
7. Section 3 of the Criminal Law (Sexual Offences) Act 1993.
8. Section 4 of the Criminal Law (Sexual Offences) Act 1993.
9. Section 5 of the Criminal Law (Sexual Offences) Act 1993.

Section 2 of the 1996 Act also provides that it is an offence for any person to engage in an attempt to commit such offences or to aid or abet their commission. Section 3 of the Act provides that it is an offence for any person who, in the State, makes an arrangement to transport a person to a place in or outside the State or who authorises the making of such an arrangement for or on behalf of another person, knowingly for the purpose of enabling that person or any other person to commit an offence, which is an offence by virtue of section 2(1) of the Act. Finally, section 4 provides that it is an offence for a person to publish information which is intended to or, having regard to all the circumstances, is likely to promote, advocate or incite the commission of an offence, which is an offence by virtue of section 2(1) of the Act. The Act also contains supplemental provisions, including those which provide for the rule against double jeopardy in respect of a person who has been convicted in a court of a State in which the offence was committed.

Rape: consent   In *The People v. McDonagh (M.)* [1996] 1 I.R. 565; [1996] 2 I.L.R.M. 468, the Supreme Court considered the interpretation of section 2 of the Criminal Law (Rape) Act 1981, which deals with consent. Section 2 of the 1981 Act provides:

(1) A man commits rape if:
    (a) he has unlawful sexual intercourse with a woman who at the time of the intercourse does not consent to it, and
    (b) at that time he knows that she does not consent to the intercourse or he is reckless as to whether she does or does not consent to it,
and references to rape in this Act and any other enactment shall be construed accordingly.

(2) It is hereby declared that if at a trial for a rape offence the jury has to consider whether a man believed that a woman was consenting to sexual intercourse, the presence or absence of reasonable grounds for such a belief is a matter to which the jury is to have regard, in conjunction with any other relevant matters, in considering whether he so believed.

In *McDonagh*, the Court confirmed recent case law to the effect that it is not necessary that the trial judge should refer to and explain to the jury the provisions of section 2(2) in every rape trial in which the fact of sexual intercourse was admitted and in which the defence that the complainant consented to the intercourse is raised. The Court also engaged in an historical analysis of the origins of section 2(2) of the 1981 Act, including its parliamentary origins.

The background to the case was, briefly, as follows. The defendants had been tried and convicted of the rape of a woman. At their trial, they denied the complainant's version of events and claimed that she had consented to sexual intercourse in return for payment. It was clear that the jury rejected their version of events. Their conviction was affirmed by the Court of Criminal Appeal, but the Court certified that the case involved a point of law of exceptional public importance within the meaning of section 94 of the Courts of Justice Act 1924. As indicated, the Supreme Court (Hamilton CJ., Costello P., Denham, Barrington and Murphy JJ.) affirmed.

Delivering the only judgment in the Supreme Court, Costello P. first strongly supported reference to the parliamentary history of legislation as a means of statutory interpretation. He stated:

It has long been established that a court may, as an aid to the construction of a statute or one of its provisions, consider the legislative history, a terms which includes the legislative antecedents of the provisions under construction as well as pre-parliamentary material and parliamentary material relating to it.

He asserted that, in construing section 2 of the 1981 Act, the Court should not confine itself to the text of the Act even where, as here, the text appeared to be unambiguous. Citing the Supreme Court's decision in *Bourke v. Attorney General* [1972] I.R. 36 (which concerned the interpretation of the Extradition Act 1965 by reference to the European Convention on Extradition and the *travaux preparatoires* on which it was based), he stated that the Court should reject the exclusionary rule, which would forbid reference to such external sources, contended for by the defendants. Indeed, he suggested that the Court should have regard to any aspect of the enactment's legislative history which may be of assistance. He expressly approved the views of the United States Federal Supreme Court in *United States v. American Trucking Association,* 310 U.S. 534 (1940) where the Court stated that where an aid to construction is available, there was no 'rule of law' which would forbid its use.

It is hardly surprising that Costello P. should take this approach, since he had pioneered the use of parliamentary debates as a means of interpretation in *Wavin Pipes Ltd. v. Hepworth Iron Co Ltd.* [1982] 8 F.S.R. 32. Nonetheless, it seems an overstatement to suggest that such an approach is long-established, since it is certainly the case that many judges have declined to take this approach: see *Conaty v. Tipperary (NR) County Council* (1987) 7 *I.L.T.* 22 (1989 Review, 406) and Byrne and McCutcheon, *The Irish Legal System* (3rd ed., Butterworths, 1996), pp.540-1. Nonetheless, the unanimous view of the Supreme Court in the *McDonagh* case, as expressed by Costello P, and the support to be found for this approach in, for example, the decision of the House of Lords in *Pepper v. Hart* [1993] A.C. 591 (curiously, not cited by Costello P.) must surely confirm the ascendancy for this view.

Costello P. had also drawn attention to another aspect of the relevance parliamentary materials when he stated:

> Irish statutes frequently and for very good reasons adopt with or without amendment the provisions of statutes enacted by the United Kingdom parliament dealing with the same topic and so the legislative history of Irish statutes may very well include the legislative history of the corresponding enactment of the United Kingdom parliament.

This frank admission of the origins of much post-1922 Irish legislative output was particularly important in the context of section 2 of the 1981 Act, as Costello P. pointed out. He noted that section 2 of the 1981 Act replicated section 1 of the British Sexual Offences (Amendment) Act 1976. He also noted that the British 1976 Act was enacted in the wake of the decision of the House of Lords in *R. v. Morgan* [1976] A.C. 182 in which it was held that the crime of rape consisted in having sexual intercourse with a woman with intent to do so without her consent or with indifference as to whether or not she consented and that it could not be committed if that essential *mens rea* was absent. Accordingly, if an accused in fact believed that the woman had consented, whether or not that belief was based on reasonable grounds, he could not be guilty of rape. Costello P. pointed out that, because of the resultant controversy which arose and in particular because the speeches of the Law Lords had been interpreted by some commentators as meaning that if an accused gave evidence that he believed that the complainant was consenting he must be acquitted, an advisory committee had been established, which concluded that the *Morgan* decision had been right in principle and recommended its codification by statute, which was later enshrined in section 1(2) of the British 1976 Act. Costello P. cited the leading textbook Smith and Hogan, *Criminal Law*, 7th ed., p.451 for this summary of the legislative history of the British 1976 Act. He then pointed out that section 2 of the 1981 Act were identical to those in the 1976 Act.

He then turned to the suggestion by the defendants that a trial judge is required to explain the provisions of section 2(2) of the 1981 Act in every case. As indicated, he rejected this submission and pointed out that it had been rejected by English authority which had examined the British 1976 Act and that the English approach had already been applied by the Court of Criminal Appeal here. He referred to the decisions in *The People v. Gaffey (No. 2)*, Court of Criminal Appeal, May 10, 1991 (1991 Review, 183), *The People v. F.*, Court of Criminal Appeal, May 27, 1993 (1993 Review, 266), *The People v. Rock (J.)*, Court of Criminal Appeal, July 29, 1993 (1993 Review, 267) and *The People v. Creighton* [1994] 1 I.L.R.M. 551, in which the Court had quoted with approval the views expressed by the Court of Appeal (Criminal Division) in *R v. Taylor* (1984) 80 Cr. App. Rep. 327. To this list, Costello P. added a number of other English decisions to the same effect. Costello P. commented, in a passage which encapsulates the decision in *McDonagh* (emphasis in original):

> In every criminal trial the trial judge is required to determine what are the issues to be considered by the jury in the light of the evidence and the manner in which the case on behalf of the accused has been presented. This judicial function will involve the trial judge determining in some cases whether, *inter alia*, an issue arises as to whether the accused mistakenly believed that the complainant had consented to the intercourse which admittedly took place. The trial judge may *incorrectly* conclude that no issue under subs.(2) [of the 1981 Act] arises (in which case the jury's verdict may be set aside) but the *possibility of error* in the exercise of a judicial function does not mean that it is one which the law prohibits.
>
> I must conclude, therefore, on an analysis of the section that it is not necessary that the trial judge should refer to and explain to the jury the provisions of s. 2(2) [of the 1981 Act] in every rape trial in which the

fact of sexual intercourse is admitted and in which the defence that the complainant consented to the intercourse is raised.

As to whether a reference to section 2(2) of the 1981 Act was required in the instant case, Costello P. quoted with approval the following summary of the issues made by the Court of Criminal Appeal:

> This was not a case in which a jury had to consider whether a man believed that a woman was consenting to sexual intercourse; no such case was made. It was not a question of belief; it was a question of fact — did the prosecutrix look for sex with the McDonaghs and did she offer it for the sum of £30 to all concerned.

Commenting that this summary of the issue which arose in the case was succinct, accurate and in accordance with what transpired at the trial, Costello P. concluded that there was no need in the instant case for the trial judge to have referred the jury to section 2(2) of the 1981 Act. On this basis, the Supreme Court upheld the defendants' convictions and affirmed the decision of the Court of Criminal Appeal.

SPECIAL CRIMINAL COURTS

In *Kavanagh v. Government of Ireland and Ors.* [1996] 1 I.L.R.M. 133 (H.C.); [1997] 1 I.L.R.M. 321 (S.C.), the Supreme Court (affirming Laffoy J. in the High Court) dismissed a constitutional challenge to the validity of the establishment of the special criminal court. The case is discussed in the Constitutional Law chapter, 151, above.

STRICT LIABILITY OFFENCES

We noted in the 1994 Review, 228-31 that, in *Maguire v. Shannon Regional Fisheries Board* [1994] 2 I.L.R.M. 253 and *Shannon Regional Fisheries Board v. Cavan County Council*, High Court, December 21, 1994; Supreme Court, July 30, 1996, Lynch and Murphy JJ., respectively had held (while judges of the High Court) that offences under section 171 of the Fisheries (Consolidation) Act 1959, as amended, concerning water pollution constituted offences of strict liability in respect of which it was not necessary to establish *mens rea*. In the latter case, *Shannon Regional Fisheries Board v. Cavan County Council*, the Supreme Court (Blayney, and O'Flaherty JJ., Keane J. dissenting) affirmed the views expressed in the High Court.

The circumstances were that the defendant was a local authority required by statute to receive public sewage and the offences related to discharges from sewage treatment works operated by the defendant in its capacity as sanitary authority. The sewage treatment works had been constructed in 1951 and were designed to cater for a population of 700 persons. As a result of population increase and the improved domestic sanitary facilities in the area, as well as the increase in the per capita of population volume of effluent requiring treatment since 1951, the sewage treatment works had become inadequate for their purpose. The defendant Council had made efforts to up-grade or replace the existing works but the capital needed for such projects were only available to a local authority from the Department of Environment. Section 171(1) of the 1959 Act provides *inter alia*:

> Any person who . . . throws, empties, permits or causes to fall into any waters any deleterious matter . . . shall, unless such act is done under and in accordance with a licence granted by the Minister under this section, be guilty of an offence under this section. . . .

In the trial of the prosecution brought by the Fisheries Board, the District Court judge concluded that the defendant Council had taken all reasonable care to prevent the entry of deleterious matter into the areas in question. However, on a case stated to the High Court, Murphy J., as already indicated, approved the decision of Lynch J. in *Maguire v. Shannon Regional Fisheries Board* [1994] 2 I.L.R.M. 253, above, and held that the offence created by section 171(1)(b) of the 1959 Act, as amended, was one of strict liability in which *mens rea,* negligence and/or knowledge were not essential ingredients. In the Supreme Court, the majority (Blayney and O'Flaherty JJ.) held that an offence under section 171 of the 1959 Act had been clearly established on the facts as the Council had deliberately discharged imperfectly treated sewage from the water treatment plant. They added that even if it were accepted that the Council had no option but to discharge deleterious matter into the watercourses this did not constitute a defence to the charge. In that respect, they approved the views expressed by Lord Wilberforce in *Alphacell Ltd. v. Woodward* [1972] A.C. 824. Dissenting, Keane J. argued that the law should recognise that there is an intermediate range of offences, of which an offence under section 171(1) of the 1959 Act was one, in which, while full proof of *mens rea* is not required and the proof of the prohibited act *prima facie* imports the commission of the offence, the defendant may avoid liability by proving that it took reasonable care, as here. This suggestion, supported by compendious reference to authority, may yet prove influential in future cases. But while the majority view prevails, prosecutions in such cases cannot be successfully met with a plea of lack of resources. In that context, the approach suggested by Murphy J. in the High Court in the instant case (1994 Review, 230-1), in which he advocated the wide use of the Probation of Offenders Act 1907, would appear to provide some respite, albeit in mitigation only.

Defence Forces

DISCIPLINE

Court-martial: impact of preliminary investigation   In *Scariff v. Taylor*
[1996] 1 I.R. 242; [1996] 2 I.L.R.M. 278, the Supreme Court held that the
prohibition against an accused soldier being legally represented at the preliminary investigation of a charge made against him by his commanding officer, or when the Army authorities take a summary of the evidence prior to
his court-martial, does not infringe the soldier's right to fair procedures. The
applicant, a soldier in the Defence Forces, was accused of being involved in
an incident in which the nose of a fellow soldier was broken. The applicant's
commanding officer held an informal investigation into the incident as required by rule 6(1) of the Rules of Procedure (Defence Forces) 1954. On that
occasion no counsel or representative was allowed to appear for the applicant
or for the prosecution since such representation is prohibited by rule 6(1). The
applicant's commanding officer remanded the applicant for trial by limited
court-martial and directed that a summary of the evidence be taken. That summary was taken on oath on another occasion and again no counsel or representative was allowed to appear on behalf of the applicant since such
representation is prohibited by rule 12 of the 1954 Rules. On both occasions
the applicant was allowed to give evidence, to call witnesses and to cross-
examine witnesses who gave evidence in support of the allegations made against
him. The Convening Authority settled the charge to be made against the applicant, namely, the commission of a civil offence contrary to section 169 of the
Defence Act 1954, being assault occasioning actual bodily harm contrary to
section 47 of the Offences Against the Person Act 1861. The court-martial
decided that it had jurisdiction to proceed with the trial of the applicant and
the applicant was represented by solicitor and counsel. The applicant pleaded
not guilty to the charge and, in such circumstances, the summary of the evidence taken at the initial enquiry directed by the commanding officer is not
placed before the court-martial.

The applicant sought an order of *certiorari* quashing the decision of the
commanding officer not to dismiss the complaint made against the applicant,
the decision which convened the court-martial, and the decision of that court
to proceed with the trial of the applicant on the said charge. The applicant
contended that the procedures under the 1954 Rules infringed his constitutional right to fair procedures. In the High Court, Carroll J. dismissed the

application (High Court, July 26, 1994), and this was confirmed on appeal by the Supreme High Court. The Court considered that special considerations were applicable where the courts were asked to review the procedures that had been applied in the course of enforcing discipline within the Defence Forces. It held that in the instant case, there had been no breach of the requirements of fair procedures by depriving the applicant of an opportunity to be represented by professional advisers either (a) at the initial investigation of the charge made against him or (b) when the authorities took the summary of the relevant evidence, since the applicant was not in jeopardy at those stages. Nor was there any reason to assume that the court-martial would conduct the trial otherwise than in accordance with the demands of fair procedures and of constitutional justice. Finally, the Court noted that, in circumstances such as occurred here where the defendant pleaded guilty, there was no likelihood that any statement made by the applicant during the initial investigation or the taking of such summary would be adduced in evidence before the court-martial.

Court martial: 'trial within a trial'   In *Finn and Mulraney v. Convening Authority*, Courts-Martial Appeal Court, June 11, 1996, the Court held that the procedure to be employed at courts-martial as to the admissibility of inculpatory statements should, with one point of difference, be that adopted in civilian trials, the Special Criminal Court being a comparable court. Thus, the Court held that a court-martial should first decide whether the statement should be admitted in evidence as being truly voluntary and, if so, should allow the accused to make submissions as to whether the content of the statements are true. The Court referred, *inter alia*, to the decisions of the Supreme Court in *The People v. Conroy* [1986] I.R. 460; [1988] I.L.R.M. 4 and *The People v. Quilligan and O'Reilly* [1993] 2 I.R. 305 (1992 Review, 271) in this context. Because this had not occurred in the instant case, the Court directed a re-hearing of the charges against the applicants. The Court also provided some guidance for the future by suggesting that the method to be adopted should be as already indicated with the exception that it should not be necessary to traverse again matters that have to do exclusively with the admissibility issue.

Legal effect of preliminary investigation   In *Dunford v. Minister For Defence*, High Court, December 15, 1996 Laffoy J held that a preliminary investigation conducted under the Rules of Procedure (Defence Forces) 1954 does not constitute a determination of a charge. The decision is consistent with that in the *Scariff* case, above. The applicant in *Dunford*, a soldier in the Defence Forces, was charged with having made a false accusation against a fellow soldier, knowing the same to be false, contrary to section 141 of the Defence Act 1954. The applicant's commanding officer held an informal preliminary enquiry into the circumstances of the charge; in accordance with rule 6 of the

1954 Rules. As already indicated in the summary of the *Scariff* case, the applicant was not permitted to be legally represented at that enquiry. At the conclusion of the preliminary investigation, the officer is required to ask the accused soldier whether he consented to a summary trial on that charge or wished to be tried by court-martial, and to inform the soldier of the probable penalty which would be imposed in the event of a conviction after a summary trial. If the soldier so consents, he may be tried summarily by his commanding officer on the charge. In the instant case, the applicant's commanding officer, having decided that the charge should not be dismissed, informed the applicant of the probable penalty on conviction after a summary trial and put the applicant to his election and he chose to be tried by court-martial. The applicant was remanded for trial by court-martial. He applied for an order of *certiorari* quashing the order of his commanding officer 'convicting the applicant of making a false statement' As indicated, Laffoy J. dismissed the application. She held that the applicant's claim was based on the false premise that he had been tried on the charge and convicted by his commanding officer. Citing with approval the judgment of Carroll J in *Scariff v. Taylor* (which we have seen was subsequently upheld by the Supreme Court), Laffoy J. considered that the commanding officer's involvement in formulating and preferring the charge, in conducting the preliminary enquiry, and in remanding the applicant for trial by court-martial, could not be challenged on the ground of bias or partiality since they did not constitute determinations on the charges brought. Nor did she consider that the requirements of fair procedures demanded legal representation for the applicant at the preliminary enquiry into the charge made against him. Again, this is now supported by the views expressed in the Supreme Court in *Scariff*, above. Finally, Laffoy J. held that the applicant's complaint that a statement of his had been procured by duress imposed by the military police was a matter for the court-martial, if the complaint was raised in that court.

REPATRIATION

In *Lee v. Minister for Defence and Ors.*, High Court, June 19, 1996, Barron J. held that there is no requirement that an inquiry as to whether a member of the Defence Forces should be repatriated on medical grounds be conducted judicially, even where the incident giving rise to the inquiry has also been the subject of disciplinary proceedings.

The applicant, the security officer of an Irish battalion in Lebanon, carried out a security check while under the influence of alcohol, during which he brandished his pistol and accused soldiers on duty of failing to man their post properly. Disciplinary proceedings against him were commenced and he was also directed to see the Battalion Medical Officer. After an informal meeting, the Medical Officer concluded that the applicant should be repatriated on medical grounds. The applicant's commanding officer took the view that the repatriation on medical grounds should be postponed until the conclusion of the disciplinary proceedings. The applicant did not put forward any evidence to the disciplinary hearing; he was found guilty of two offences under section 168 of the Defence Act 1954, and was sentenced to a reprimand. The formal assessment of the applicant by the Medical Officer took place shortly afterwards, and it was recommended that the applicant be repatriated on medical grounds as he was emotionally immature especially in his dealing with stress. Having been repatriated, the applicant applied for an order of *certiorari* seeking to quash the disciplinary convictions and the decision to repatriate him on medical grounds. He argued that the decision to repatriate him had, in effect, been made before the disciplinary hearing and that, if he had known, it would have been open to him to argue that he had brandished his pistol to demonstrate the consequences of lapses of security and not as a result of stress or in order to threaten.

As indicated, Barron J. refused the relief sought. He accepted that, while the disciplinary proceedings were required to be conducted judicially, the medical inquiry resulting in the applicant's repatriation on medical grounds was not. The applicant's superiors were not obliged to inform him that he would be repatriated if he did not challenge the facts as presented to the disciplinary hearing, if such was the case. On this basis, he concluded that appropriate procedures had been followed.

Education

RECOGNITION OF QUALIFICATIONS

Professional qualifications   The European Communities (Second General System for the Recognition of Professional Education And Training) Regulations 1996 (SI No. 135 of 1996) gave effect to Directives 92/51/EEC, 94/38/EC and 95/43/EC with effect from May 21, 1996. They introduced a general system for the recognition of professional education and training of the professions specified in the Regulations (including, for example, the legal and medical professions). The reference in the title to a 'second general system' indicates that the 1996 Regulations supplement a previous recognition system provided for by Directive 89/84/EEC, which was implemented by the European Communities (General System for the Recognition of Higher Education Diplomas) Regulations 1991 (1991 Review, 187). The 1996 Regulations are much more wide-ranging in scope.

SECONDARY SCHOOLS

Salaries for religious chaplains   In *Campaign To Separate Church And State Ltd. v. Minister for Education* [1996] 2 I.L.R.M. 241, Costello P. held that the provision of money by the State from public funds for the purpose of enabling the management boards of Community Schools to pay the salaries of chaplains, employed by such boards in accordance with the terms of their respective trust deeds, did not constitute the endowment of religion by the State within the meaning of Article 44.2.2° of the Constitution. The decision is discussed in the Constitutional Law chapter, 147, above.

Superannuation: forfeiture on conviction   In *Lovett v. Minister for Education* [1997] 1 I.L.R.M. 89, Kelly J. held to be unconstitutional an element of the Secondary Teachers Superannuation (Amendment) Scheme 1935, a statutory Scheme made under the Teachers Superannuation Act 1928. The case arose against the following background.

The applicant had been suspended as principal of a community school following the discovery of irregularities in its finances. For some time prior to the suspension, the applicant had been absent from work on grounds of ill health and, following the suspension he notified the respondent Minister that he wished to apply for early retirement. The Minister made a number of *ex gratia* payments to the applicant in lieu of remuneration from the date of his suspension. The applicant was later charged with offences of dishonesty and, having pleaded guilty to three charges, was sent forward to the Circuit Court for sentencing. The applicant then applied to the Minister for early retirement on the grounds of disability and was informed that in view of his guilty plea all *ex gratia* payments would cease immediately. Sentencing had been adjourned on a number of occasions as the Court had indicated it would not impose sentence until the applicant's pension position was clarified. The applicant was informed by letter that his application for early retirement on grounds of disability had been approved and that a payment on account in respect of his pension would issue. As the pension position now appeared to be dealt with, the Circuit Court proceeded to impose a sentence of two years imprisonment. Subsequently, the Minister informed the applicant by letter that, in accordance with para.8(1) of the 1935 statutory superannuation Scheme, his pension was automatically forfeited on the basis that he had been sentenced to a term of imprisonment exceeding 12 months. The applicant then issued proceedings claiming, *inter alia,* that paragraph 8(1) of the 1935 Scheme was *ultra vires*. As indicated, Kelly J. acceded to this argument.

He referred to section 2 of the Teachers Superannuation Act 1928, which empowers the Minister to prepare a scheme with the object of providing pensions and gratuities for any particular class or classes of teachers and to carry the scheme into execution. Section 3 of the Act sets out the provisions which may be contained in the scheme, including provisions relating to the administration of the fund and payment of pensions and gratuities to specified persons. The Secondary Teachers Superannuation (Amendment) Scheme 1935 (amending the Secondary Teachers Superannuation Scheme 1929) was purportedly made under these provisions of the 1928 Act. Kelly J. accepted that section 3 of the 1928 Act was permissive as to what could be contained in such a scheme but did not amount to an exhaustive list of the provisions which could be so contained.

Kelly J went on to consider whether the 1935 Scheme complied with the test laid down by O'Higgins C.J. in *Cityview Press Ltd. v. An Chomhairle Oiliúna* [1980] I.R. 381, namely whether it was more than a mere giving effect to the principles and policies of, or filling in of details in, the 1928 Act as laid down by the Oireachtas. He concluded that paragraph 8(1) of the 1935 Scheme went far beyond the policies contained in the 1928 Act. He noted that the Act had as its object the formulation and carrying out of schemes for the provision of pensions for former teachers, but had nothing to do with deterring the commission of serious crimes, whether by teachers or retired teachers. He held that the forfeiture provision in paragraph 8(1) of the 1935 Scheme could not be regarded as the mere filling in or completion of a detail by the Minister.

Kelly J. also went on to deal with a constitutional issue raised by the applicant, namely whether his right to a pension constituted a property right which was protected by the Constitution. Kelly J. noted that paragraph 8(1) of the 1935 Scheme applied across the entire range of the criminal law. Since it was not confined to crimes relating to the occupation or office of the retiree, it could also apply to a large number of crimes of widely varying seriousness. While he accepted that the Minister had an interest in deterring crime in general, this did not justify singling out retired teachers with these special measures. Thus, para.8(1) also failed the proportionality test adumbrated by the Supreme Court in *Cox v. Ireland* [1992] 2 I.R. 503 (1991 Review, 105-7). In view of this and the fact that para.8(1) was mandatory in its operation, Kelly J. held that the provisions did not protect the applicant's constitutional rights as far as practicable, as required by Article 40.3 of the Constitution. While expressing his views on this aspect of the of case, Kelly J. decided that he would, in accordance with established principles of judicial self-restraint (see *Kelly's The Irish Constitution*, 3rd ed, p.449) not grant a declaration as to the constitutionality since it had already been struck down on the *ultra vires* ground.

UNIVERSITIES

Retirement at 65   In *Eogan v. University College Dublin* [1996] 1 I.R. 390; [1996] 2 I.L.R.M. 302 (H.C.), Shanley J. refused to disturb a decision of the respondent University College's governing body that the applicant not be continued in office on his reaching 65 years of age. The applicant, a distinguished academic in archaeology, had joined University College Dublin as a lecturer in 1965. In 1979 he had been appointed a Professor of Archaeology. The statutory background to the case was that Statute I of the University College, made pursuant to the Irish Universities Act 1908, provides that each professor shall continue in office until aged 65 then for a further five years provided this is recommended by the Governing Body. The Governing Body had made a policy decision on November 24, 1987 to introduce a retirement age of 65 years. The applicant had objected to this decision by letter dated June 6, 1989. In September 1995, the applicant reached 65 years of age. By letter dated June 28, 1995, he was informed that the Governing Body of University College Dublin had decided not to recommend his continuance in office as Professor. The applicant sought judicial review of the decision, on the ground that when he joined the University College it was represented to him that he would continue in office until aged 70. As indicated, Shanley J. refused the relief sought.

As to whether judicial review lay, Shanley J. answered in the affirmative. He cited with approval the decisions in *Re Malone's Application* [1988] N.I.

67, *Beirne v. Garda Commissioner* [1993] I.L.R.M. 1 (1992 Review, 392-3) and *Geoghegan v. Institute of Chartered Accountants in Ireland* [1995] 3 I.R. 86 (1995 Review, 132). He noted that the applicant's appointment and the decision not to continue him in office derived from the powers contained in Statute I, Chapter XIV of the University College, which had been made pursuant to the Irish Universities Act 1908. Thus both decisions were in substance made pursuant to statute and thus amenable to judicial review. However, as to the substance of the applicant's claim, he concluded that there were rational grounds for the early retirement scheme and, as the applicant was offered and availed of every opportunity to comment on the scheme, he was not entitled to an order for judicial review. On this basis, the application was dismissed.

VOCATIONAL EDUCATION

Additional grants   The Vocational Education (Grants For Annual Schemes Of Committees) Regulations 1996 (SI No. 428 of 1996), made under the Vocational Education Act 1930, lay down the payment of additional and supplemental and special grants to VECs in the financial year commencing on January 1, 1996.

Electricity and Energy

MINERAL EXPLORATION

Applications for licences and fees   The Minerals Development (Application Fees for Certain State Mining Licenses) Regulations 1996 (SI No.259 of 1995) revised the fees for applying for mining licences. The 1996 Regulations came into effect on September 1, 1996.

PETROLEUM

Whitegate offtake   The Fuels (Petroleum Oils) (Amendment) Order 1996 (SI No.73 of 1996), made under the Fuels (Control of Supplies) Act 1971, amended the Fuels (Petroleum Oils) Order 1983, which requires petroleum fuel importers to purchase a proportion of their products from the State-owned Irish National Petroleum Corporation Ltd's refinery in Whitegate, Cork (1994 Review, 240). The Order enabled the introduction of road loading charges in respect of petroleum required to be purchased from Whitegate. The Fuels (Petroleum Oils) (Amendment) (No. 2) Order 1996 (SI No.404 of 1996) reduced from 35% to 20% the percentage of petroleum which importers must acquire from Whitegate under the 1983 Order, with effect from January 1, 1997. The Petroleum Oils (Regulation or Control of Acquisition, Supply, Distribution or Marketing) (Continuance) Order 1996 (SI No.358 of 1996) continued through 1997 the regime outlined in the 1983 Order, as amended.

Equity

Hilary Delany, Law School, Trinity College, Dublin

TRUSTS

Constructive Trusts   As Barron J. stated in the recent decision of *Murray v. Murray* High Court, December, 15 1995: 'It is I think quite clear that the law will impose a constructive trust in all circumstances where it would be unjust and unconscionable not to do so.' This idea was explored in considerable detail by Budd J. in *Dublin Corporation v. Ancient Guild of Incorporated Brick and Stone Layers and Allied Trades Union,* High Court, March 6, 1996, although it should be noted that when the case came before the Supreme Court (see [1996] 2 I.L.R.M. 547), the decision was reversed and the court did not find it necessary to explore the constructive trust issue. However, the decision of Budd J. provides a most comprehensive and useful commentary on the circumstances in which a constructive trust will arise whenever 'justice and good conscience' require it.

The plaintiff corporation issued a compulsory purchase order which affected a hall owned by the defendants. An arbitrator made an award on the basis of the cost of reinstatement of the building and the defendants then substantially demolished the premises making reinstatement impractical. The plaintiff sought a declaration that the union held the sum awarded in trust for the reconstruction of the building and a mandatory injunction requiring the money to be applied for this purpose, or in the alternative, sought repayment of a sum which represented the difference between the figure awarded and that which would have represented the market value of the premises if reinstatement had not been envisaged. [Budd J. proceeded to examine the plaintiff's claim for restitution of part of the award on the basis of unjust enrichment. However, he also considered whether the sum awarded by the arbitrator was impressed with a trust for the plaintiff's benefit. Budd J. rejected the contention that a resulting trust arose as he was satisfied that it was the intention of the corporation that the defendants should take the sum awarded beneficially.

In relation to the possibility of a constructive trust arising, the defend sought to argue that no such trust could be inferred as monies held on a constructive trust at the outset could not subsequen pressed with such a trust at the behest of the donor on account which occurred after the giving of the money. However, Budd J. pointed to Denning M.R.'s statement in *Hussey v. Palmer* [1972] 3 All E.R. 744 to the effect that the trust may arise 'later on, as the circumstances require'. Budd J. identified two types of constructive trust, one which arises where there is a fiduciary relationship and the other which arises because of the particular circumstances in which a person holds property. While this latter form of constructive trust has been described as arising 'whenever justice and good conscience require it', Budd J. commented that the Irish courts have been cautious about adopting such a nebulous touchstone as 'justice and good conscience'. He referred to *Chase Manhattan Bank NA v. Israel British Bank (London) Ltd* [1981] Ch. 105 and to the decision of Carroll J. in *Re Irish Shipping Ltd* [1986] I.L.R.M. 518 in which, he said, the learned judge had used the device of a constructive trust in an equitable way to ensure that a rightful owner recovered a sum of money mistakenly credited to another. Budd J. said that in the case before him, the corporation had given extra money to the defendants for the express purpose of reinstatement of the building, an option which had been rendered impractical, and accordingly this sum had been paid over on a mistaken assumption as to the purpose to which it was to be applied. While counsel for the defendants argued that the plaintiff no longer had any right to determine the use to which the fund should be put once it had been awarded, Budd J. was satisfied that it was unconscionable for the defendants to take the additional money when there was no intention to carry out the reinstatement. He stated that traditional doctrines of equity permit the imposition of a constructive trust to prevent a person from asserting or exercising a legal right in circumstances where this would amount to unconscionable conduct. In the view of Budd J. 'a system of rules has been evolved which, on the whole, is both practical and just but which cannot claim scientific precision as a whole.' Accordingly he held that the extra money was paid to the defendant under a mistaken assumption and said that while the case was on the outer margins of the circumstances in which the law will imply a constructive trust, it seemed to him that there was strong justification for holding that a constructive trust had arisen. In reaching this conclusion, Budd J. said that he relied in particular on the application of the concept of a constructive trust by Carroll J. in *Re Irish Shipping Ltd* and by Costello J. in *HKN Invest Oy v. Incotrade PVT Ltd* [1993] 3 I.R. 152 as indicative of how flexibly the concept has been applied in this jurisdiction.

On appeal to the Supreme Court, the defendants argued that by virtue of the doctrine of *res judicata*, the finality of the arbitration award could not be attacked and submitted that they had not at any stage represented that the hall would be reinstated. The Supreme Court allowed the defendants' appeal and held that the award was final and binding on both parties. Keane J. accepted that in certain circumstances a person can be obliged to effect restitution where it would be unjust to retain the property but held that the doctrine of *res judicata* could not be significantly abridged by the invocation of the concept of unjust enrichment.

Nevertheless, the judgment of Budd J. is important as it shows a further willingness on the part of the judiciary in this jurisdiction to impose a constructive trust 'to satisfy the demands of justice and good conscience'. Whether such a development is to be welcomed is in some respects questionable; Budd J. himself commented that the system of rules which has evolved 'cannot claim scientific precision as a whole'. It is submitted that while such precision is not necessary or indeed desirable in this area of the law, some element of principle and consistency is required. What should be avoided in any event is the scenario adverted to by Professor Maudsley in relation to earlier English decisions and quoted in the decision of Budd J. that 'it is possible to read into recent decisions a rule that in cases in which the plaintiff ought to win, but there is no legal doctrine or authority to support him, a constructive trust in his favour will do the trick'.

Removal of trustees   It is well established that the court has an inherent jurisdiction to remove trustees from their office where they have acted dishonestly or incompetently or even where their conduct is deliberately obstructive. This point was confirmed by Murnaghan J. in *Arnott v. Arnott* (1924) 58 I.L.T.R. 145 where he stated that while the jurisdiction of the court was usually resorted to when a trustee has mismanaged a trust or has been proved dishonest or incompetent, the guiding principle to which all others must be subordinate was the welfare of the beneficiaries. This point has recently been stressed again by Barron J. in *Spencer v. Kinsella* [1996] 2 I.L.R.M. 401 in a judgment which although it ultimately failed to resolve some of the problems faced by the plaintiffs, did provide useful guidance in relation to the circumstances in which a trustee may be removed from his office.

Showgrounds in Gorey were vested in trustees on trust so that they might be used as a sports ground, park or pleasure ground subject to conditions as to payment or otherwise to be prescribed by the trustees. In recent years the grounds had been used by a local football club and coursing club and the land had also been used for the grazing of sheep. Complaints against the trustees were made by the football club which had spent money on the repair and maintenance of the grounds, and it was alleged that they were neglecting their duties and that the grounds were being allowed to fall into a state of disrepair. The plaintiffs sought the removal of the trustees on the grounds that they had persistently refused to act when called on to do so. They were supported in their claims by one of the defendants but the remaining trustees submitted that they had at all times acted in a *bona fide* manner and argued that the exercise of their powers should not be interfered with by the court unless they had acted *mala fide*, capriciously or outside the terms of the trust. Barron J. accepted that the existing situation could not be allowed to continue and said that a reorganisation must take place, either with or without the assistance of the court. While he acknowledged that it was difficult to find local people who had no affiliation with any organisation seeking to use the grounds, he stated that 'in all cases of trust, it is a truism to say that no trustee should allow his interest to conflict with his duty'. In his view some of the trustees were too closely identified with the interests of users of the club to be regarded as truly impartial. Barron J. referred to the *Arnott* case and said that a trust is set up for the welfare of beneficiaries and before determining whether or not any trustee should be removed it is necessary to determine whether his continuation in office will be detrimental to such welfare. He concluded that the welfare of the beneficiaries was being affected by the difficulties which had been brought to the court's attention and said that in view of the existing conflict of interest some of the trustees who found themselves in such a position of conflict should step down and allow a general reorganisation to take place. Barron J. stated that what was required was the appointment of trustees who were as far as possible impartial as between the various users of the grounds. However, he decided not to exercise the powers of the court at that time and to adjourn the matter for six months to enable the administration of the trust to be placed on a proper footing. The decision of Barron J. is currently under appeal to the Supreme Court and it seems likely that the matter will not be resolved without further court intervention. However, Barron J.'s judgment is useful in that it stresses that the overriding principle to which the court must have regard in exercising its power to remove trustees is the welfare of the beneficiaries. Clearly the court can act where although there has been no breach of trust or actual misconduct, the conflict of interest existing amongst the trustees is such that the trust can no longer function effectively. This point had already been made in the judgment of Chatterton V.C. in *Moore v. McGlynn* [1894] 1 I.R. 74 in which the defendant trustee was discharged from further performance of his duties where he had set up a rival business in competition to that of which he was trustee for the benefit of the family of his deceased brother.

From a practical perspective conflict of interest can be as damaging to the welfare of the beneficiaries of a trust as actual misconduct and by placing the interests of the beneficiaries at the forefront of the matters to which the court should have regard, the decision of Barron J. should ensure that sufficient attention is given to this point. His pragmatic approach is to be welcomed and it is submitted that while it is important that trustees seek to work together to resolve their differences it is also crucial that the court retains a power to intervene where the welfare of the beneficiaries is not being adequately protected.

EQUITABLE REMEDIES

Interlocutory injunctions It was suggested by Lord Cairns in *Doherty v. Allman* (1878) 3 App. Cas. 709 that where an injunction is sought to secure the enforcement of a negative contractual obligation it should issue almost as a matter of course. However, it has been said that this statement is 'the starting point, not a summation of equity's attitude to negative stipulations' (see Meagher, Gummow and Lehane *Equity Doctrines and Remedies* (3rd ed., 1992) p.568 and more recent authority in England would suggest that the principle must be applied in the light of the surrounding circumstances of each case (see *Shaw v. Applegate* [1977] 1 W.L.R. 970, 975 *per* Buckley L.J.). While it was accepted by the Supreme Court in *Dublin Port and Docks Board v. Britannia Dredging Co. Ltd* [1968] I.R. 136 that the so called principle in *Doherty v. Allman* should apply where was a 'plain and uncontested breach of a clear covenant,' the viewpoint was doubted by Keane J. in *TMG Group Ltd v. Al Babtain Trading and Contracting Co.* [1982] I.L.R.M. 343 where he stated that he did not think that Ó Dálaigh C.J. in the *Britannia* case 'was laying down any general principle that, in all cases where the plaintiff establishes a *prima facie* case of a breach of a negative stipulation in a contract, the court could disregard any question of the balance of convenience as between the parties.' (See also the approach of McCarthy J. in *Irish Shell Ltd v. Elm Motors Ltd* [1984] I.R. 200.)

This question has recently been addressed again by the Supreme Court in *Premier Dairies Ltd v. Doyle* [1996] 1 I.L.R.M. 363. In a judgment delivered on September 29, 1995, Kinlen J. held that the defendants, who had entered into distribution agreements with the plaintiff to deliver its products, should be held to the terms of the negative covenant contained in the agreements preventing them from competing with the plaintiff and found that the decision of the Supreme Court in *Dublin Port and Docks Board v. Britannia Dredging Co. Ltd* governed the case. However, the defendants appealed against this order arguing, *inter alia*, that the clause in question was contrary to sections 4 and 5 of the Competition Act 1991. O'Flaherty J. dismissed the appeal but it is interesting to note the comment which he made about the *Doherty v. Allman/ Britannia Dredging* principle. He was satisfied that if there had been no other factors in the case he would have held that it came 'four square within the *Britannia Dredging* decision'. However, O'Flaherty J. was satisfied that as there was scope for an argument to be made as to the applicability of the Competition Act 1991 which he described as 'a rather complex piece of legislation which, so far, has not been judicially mined to any extent', it was not in his view appropriate to apply the *Britannia Dredging* principle to the case. O'Flaherty J. accordingly went on to consider whether there was a fair case to be tried, which he was satisfied that there was, and to consider where the balance of convenience lay. While he disagreed with Kinlen J. about the applicability of the *Britannia Dredging* principle, O'Flaherty J. was satisfied that the former's conclusion that the balance of convenience favoured the plaintiffs was correct and for this reason affirmed his decision to grant the interlocutory relief sought. On balance the comments of McCarthy J. in *Irish Shell Ltd v. Elm Motors Ltd* [1984] I.R. 200 namely that save in the most exceptional circumstances, the determination of an application for an inter-locutory injunction lies solely on a consideration of the questions of whether a fair case has been made out and where the balance of convenience lies, would seem the most appropriate response to the question of whether the courts should continue to apply the *Doherty v. Allman/Britannia Dredging* principle.

Mandatory interlocutory injunctions   Recent case law would suggest that where a mandatory interlocutory injunction is sought, the plaintiff must estab-lish a strong and clear case 'so that the court can feel a degree of assurance that at a trial of the action a similar injunction would be granted' (*per* Denham J. in *Boyhan v. Beef Tribunal* [1992] I.L.R.M. 545, 556. See also *Boyle v. An Post* [1992] E.L.R. 65). However, the judgment of Carroll J. in *A. & N. Phar-macy Ltd v. United Drug Wholesale Ltd* [1996] 2 I.L.R.M. 42 suggests that less rigourous standards may be applied in such cases.

The plaintiff, which was a newly established pharmacy, sought a manda-tory interlocutory injunction compelling the defendant, a wholesaler in its area, to supply it with non generic pharmaceutical products. As a result of the re-fusal of the defendant and other major wholesalers to supply the plaintiff, it had been forced to import products from abroad at anti-competitive prices. Carroll J. was satisfied that there was a serious issue to be tried and that the balance of convenience favoured the plaintiff. It was likely that damages would not be an adequate remedy because the plaintiff would be forced out of busi-ness if it could not obtain the supplies it required. Carroll J. accordingly granted a mandatory injunction of an interlocutory nature compelling the defendant to supply the plaintiff on a cash on delivery basis. This order was made by Carroll J. in circumstances where she was satisfied that there was a serious issue to be tried as to whether there had been an abuse of a dominant position resulting from a refusal to supply but she was also satisfied that there had been a serious question raised as to whether the refusal to supply the plaintiff was objectively justified. At face value this seems far from the 'strong and clear' case contem-plated in the earlier decisions and instead Carroll J. was content to apply the less restrictive test favoured in the context of interlocutory injunctions of a prohibitory nature. This approach is more in line with that followed by Murphy J. in *Bula Ltd v. Tara Mines Ltd (No. 2)* [1987] I.R. 95 where he stated that he would be reluctant to accept the proposition that the granting or withholding of a mandatory interlocutory injunction should be related to or dependent on the strength of the applicant's case although Murphy J. did go on to acknowl-edge that such relief will only issue in mandatory form in exceptional cases.

A further interesting comment made by Carroll J. is that 'since the advent of competition law commercial enterprises are being forced to do business with other persons against their will'. Certainly in the past the courts have been reluctant to grant relief which will force individuals to work together, or to a lesser extent to engage in business transactions, where a relationship of mutual trust and confidence is lacking. While Carroll J. did not directly address this issue, her conclusion would tend to suggest that a less restrictive attitude to this question is being pursued.

The question of the role which the adequacy or inadequacy of damages plays in the assessment made by a court as to whether an interlocutory injunction should be granted was further considered by Kelly J. in *Fitzpatrick v. Garda Commissioner* High Court, October 16, 1996. The applicant garda, who had been deployed with the UN civilian police in Cyprus for a temporary period, sought to challenge a decision by the respondent to repatriate him following an incident which allegedly had occurred there. In considering the applicant's entitlement to an interlocutory injunction restraining his repatriation, Kelly J. was satisfied that there was a serious question to be tried and he then proceeded to consider the adequacy of damages as a remedy from the applicant's point of view. Insofar as the applicant would suffer a loss of earnings or allowances should he be wrongfully repatriated, Kelly J. was satisfied that he could be completely compensated for the losses by an award of damages. He concluded furthermore that insofar as his constitutional entitlement to his good name and reputation was concerned, he could see no reason why these could not also be adequately compensated by an award of damages and as Kelly J. commented, damage to reputation as a result of libel or slander is regularly compensated by such an award. Kelly J. therefore concluded that the repatriation of the applicant even if it turned out to be unlawful would not give rise to any irreparable loss or damage being suffered by him. He was satisfied that the calculation of damages would not create any undue difficulty for the court and said that even if he was wrong in this view, he must bear in mind the statement of Finlay C.J. in *Curust Financial Services Ltd v. Loewe-Lack-Werk Otto Loewe GmbH & Co.* [1993] I.L.R.M. 723. However, in considering what he termed 'the other side of the equation', Kelly J. was satisfied that damages would be a wholly inadequate way of compensating the respondent for the damage which might be caused by the granting of an interlocutory injunction and concluded that on this basis he was justified in refusing the relief sought. Furthermore, he was satisfied that the general balance of convenience also favoured this result and he was satisfied that the injunction sought should be refused.

Mareva injunctions The fact that a Mareva injunction should only be granted if the plaintiff can establish that he has an arguable case that he will succeed in the action and that the anticipated disposal of the defendant's assets is for the purpose of preventing a plaintiff from recovering damages was clearly stated by the Supreme Court in *O'Mahony v. Horgan* [1996] 1 I.L.R.M. 161 (see 1995 Annual Review at 103, 272). This point that the court must be satisfied that a defendant must be acting with the motivation of seeking to avoid complying with an award or judgment was approved of again by the Supreme Court in *Tobin and Twomey Services Ltd v. Kerry Foods Ltd* [1996] 2 I.L.R.M. 1, although the court felt it unnecessary to give much attention to this aspect of the case. The plaintiff instituted proceedings seeking various orders under the Arbitration Act 1954 in relation to an arbitration award which had been made and a Mareva injunction. Blayney J. concluded that the trial judge, Carroll J., had been correct in holding that a Mareva injunction should be refused as she had found that there was nothing to sustain the plaintiff's suspicion that the first named defendant would seek to avoid any award or judgment obtained and in any event, there was no evidence to suggest that the defendant was dissipating its assets.

One comment made by Carroll J. in the paragraph in relation to which Blayney J. expressed his approval which may lead to some confusion was a statement that 'indeed there is no evidence that the first named defendant has assets within the jurisdiction'. While some residual doubt remains about the jurisdiction of the courts to grant a Mareva injunction on a worldwide basis in view of the comments of Murphy J. in *Countyglen plc v. Carway* [1995] I.L.R.M. 481, it is likely that the light of the decision of Costello J. in *Deutsche Bank Atkiengesellchaft v. Murtagh* [1995] 1 I.L.R.M. 381 that an order of this nature can be made. Therefore apart from the obvious practical difficulties in enforcing an order on such a basis, the fact that a defendant has no assets within the jurisdiction should not prevent the courts granting a Mareva injunction in relation to worldwide assets.

Undue influence   An issue which has provoked considerable controversy in recent years both in this jurisdiction and in England is the circumstances in which a wife who furnishes a guarantee as security for her husband's debts has an equity against him to set aside the transaction which may be enforceable against a third party, usually a bank or other lending institution. The position was clarified in England by the decision of *Barclay's Bank v. O'Brien* [1994] 1 A.C. 180 where it was stated by Lord Browne-Wilkinson that as a general principle where a wife was induced to stand as surety for her husband's debt as a result of his undue influence, misrepresentation or some other legal wrong, she had an equity against him to set aside the transaction and this right would be enforceable against a third party who had actual or constructive notice of the circumstances giving rise to the equity or for whom the husband was acting as agent. In the circumstances, The House of Lords found that the bank was fixed with constructive notice of the husband's wrongful misrepresentation and the wife was held to be entitled as against the bank to set aside the legal charge on the property securing the husband's liability to the bank. These general principles were approved subsequently by the House of Lords in *CIBC Mortgages plc v. Pitt* [1994] 1 A.C. 200 although on the facts it was held that the husband was not acting as an agent for the plaintiff, who had no actual notice of the undue influence, and in the circumstances, where there was no indication that the transaction was anything other than a normal advance to husband and wife for their joint benefit, it was held that the plaintiff was not fixed with constructive notice of the undue influence and it was therefore entitled to enforce the charge.

The circumstances in which a bank will be fixed with constructive notice of undue influence or misrepresentation were further considered by the English Court of Appeal in a number of recent decisions (see *Massey v. Midland Bank plc* [1995] 1 All E.R. 929, *Banco Exterior Intemacional v. Mann* [1995] 1 All E.R. 936, *TSB Bank plc v. Camfield* [1995] 1 All E.R. 951; for a recent comment on developments in that jurisdiction, see Lehane (1996) 59 MLR 675) but the application of the principles in *Barclay's Bank* remained in doubt in this jurisdiction until very recently. While the decision of the Supreme Court in *Bank of Ireland v. Smyth* [1996] 1 I.L.R.M. 241 clarified the position where a dispute arose between banks and the spouses of debtors who had given consent to the creation of a charge over the family home (see Sanfey (1996) CLP 31) as Sanfey pointed out its reasoning could not be extended to situations where a spouse had merely acted as a guarantor of the other spouse's liabilities. Mee had suggested (see (1996) 14 ILT 209) that the invocation of the principle of constructive notice by Blayney J might indicate a preference for the notice based approach of the House of Lords in *Barclay's Bank* to the issue, but until the recent decision of the Supreme Court in *Bank of Nova Scotia v. Hogan* [1997] 1 I.L.R.M. 407 the position remained unclear.

In *Bank of Nova Scotia*, the first named defendant borrowed money from the plaintiff on the security of equitable mortgages created over properties which he owned. Subsequently in return for releasing the security over two of these properties, the plaintiff took an equitable mortgage over a further property owned by the second named defendant, who was the first named defendant's wife. Prior to depositing the title deeds, a solicitor from a firm which had acted for the second named and her husband in the past, and also for the bank from time to time, explained to her that the plaintiff would be entitled to sell the property in the event of her husband's default. When the plaintiff subsequently brought proceedings to enforce the security, the second named defendant alleged that the security had been improperly obtained. In finding for the plaintiff, Keane J concluded that the legal advice received by the second named defendant had been adequate in all the circumstances.

In considering the appeal brought by the defendant against this order, Murphy J pointed out that while there was a similarity between the facts of the case before him and those in *Bank of Ireland v. Smyth* he said that the fundamental differences between them rendered the decision of little assistance, although he concluded that the decision of the House of Lords in *Barclay's Bank v. O'Brien* was 'both relevant and helpful'. He stated that notwithstanding the fact that the relationship between husband and wife has been held not to raise a presumption of undue influence some special status does appear to have been accorded to wives in a number of decisions. Murphy J concluded that whilst the matrimonial relationship as such did not give rise to a presumption of undue influence, it might be possible to identify circumstances which would more readily raise a presumption in favour of a wife than any outside party. However, as Murphy J pointed out the essential issue in this case was the dispute between the rights of the creditor and the wife and in relation to this, he was prepared to adopt and apply the principles of Lord Browne-Wilkinson in *Barclay's Bank v. O'Brien* referred to above. These were as follows:

> A wife who has been induced to stand as a surety for her husband's debts by his undue influence, misrepresentation or some other legal wrong has an equity against him to set aside that transaction. Under the ordinary principles of equity, her fight to set aside that transaction will be enforceable against third parties (e.g. against a creditor) if either the husband was acting as the third party's agent or the third party had actual or constructive notice of the facts giving rise to her equity.

Murphy J stated that even assuming – and he did not decide this issue – that married women in this jurisdiction might in certain circumstances enjoy as against their husbands a presumption that undue influence had been exercised, the fatal flaw in the case before him was that no undue influence was exercised by the husband; the wife had no equity against him to have the transaction set aside and that being so she had no equity on which she could rely to defeat the claim of the bank. Even if such equity had existed, Murphy J was still satisfied that the availability of appropriate legal advice to the wife would have afforded the bank a defence in relation to any claim by her in respect of an equity to set aside the transaction. Furthermore, he was satisfied that there was no evidence to support the claim that the bank itself had exercised undue influence over the wife; the relationship itself did not give rise to a presumption of undue influence and there was no suggestion of dealings which would raise an inference of wrongdoing.

In conclusion it would appear to have been accepted by the Supreme Court in *Bank of Nova Scotia v. Hogan* that where a wife furnishes a guarantee as security for her husband's debts as a result of his undue influence, misrepresentation or some other legal wrong, she has an equity against him to set aside the transaction which may be enforceable against a third party, who had actual or constructive notice of the circumstances giving rise to the equity or for whom the husband was acting as agent. While the facts of this case did not demand any detailed examination by the Supreme Court of the circumstances in which a bank may be deemed to have constructive notice of any wrong-doing, the *dicta* of Murphy J. would certainly suggest that the availability of appropriate legal advice to the wife would have been sufficient to enable the bank to reject any claim that they should have been fixed with notice of any impropriety. Clearly to avoid the application of the *Barclay's Bank* principles as adopted by the Supreme Court lending institutions should ensure that where they are put on inquiry by the circumstances of a transaction that they have taken adequate steps to ensure that the wife's agreement has been properly obtained and this requirement should be met by ensuring that an adequate explanation of the potential consequences of her actions have been explained to her by a legal adviser. As stated, it is clear from the judgment of Murphy J. that the fact that the wife had received 'appropriate independent legal advice' would have provided the bank with a defence against any equity to set aside the transaction. Whether these words could be used to describe advice received from a firm of solicitors which had previously acted, not only on the wife's behalf but also for her husband and even the bank, is open to some doubt. While the Supreme Court was not required to address this latter point in particular, the difficulties which such transactions may give rise to would suggest that such a practice it at least undesirable and that attention should be given to ensuring that the advice is not only 'appropriate' but also 'independent' if the spectre of constructive notice is to be avoided.

European Community Law

ARTICLE 177 RULING

Preliminary nature of reference In *McNamara v. An Bord Pleanála and Ors. (No. 2)*, High Court, July 31, 1996, Barr J. declined to refer a point of law to the European Court of Justice pursuant to Article 177 of the EC Treaty, since he had already delivered final judgment in the matter in dispute: see *McNamara v. An Bord Pleanála and Ors*, High Court, May 10, 1996, discussed in the Local Government chapter, 456, below. Barr J. noted that Article 177 referred to a 'preliminary' ruling in a case 'pending' before a national court, implying that the national court which received such a ruling from the European Court had not completed its function by delivering final judgment, but would do so, *inter alia,* in the light of the ruling received from the Court of Justice.

COMMON AGRICULTURAL POLICY

H.M.I.L. Ltd (formerly Hibernia Meats International Ltd) v. Minster for Agriculture and Food, High Court, February 8, 1996 was a lengthy judgment of Barr J. dealing with aspects of the Community regime for dealing with intervention storage of beef.

Background Regulation (EEC) No.2675/88 provides for the granting of aid for the private storage of beef. Article 4(4) provides that: 'The large tendons, cartilages, pieces of fat and other scraps left over from cutting for [*sic*] boning may not be stored.' It emerged during the case that the word 'for' should have read 'or' in Article 4(4), to which we will return. Regulation (EEC) No.1964/82 lays down conditions for granting export refunds on certain cuts of boned meat of bovine animals. Article 6 provides, *inter alia*, that the storage operator 'may . . . sell within the Community bones, large tendons, cartilages, pieces of fat and other scraps left over from boning.' Article 2(2) of Regulation (EEC) No.1208/81, provides that carcasses shall be presented without 'cod fat', that is, fat from the scrotal area of male animals. The defendant Minister, as the European Community's Intervention Agent in Ireland, operates the Aids for Private Storage Scheme (APS) and the Export Refund scheme.

In 1988, the plaintiff had entered into 138 contracts with the Minister in which the plaintiff agreed to store beef in accordance with Regulation (EEC) No. 2675/88. By means of circulars, the Minister had informed storage operators, including the plaintiff, that 'the large tendons, cartilages, pieces of fat, lean trimmings and other scraps left over from de-boning may not be put in store.' Between September and December 1988 the plaintiff and its sub-contractors packed 13,365 tonnes of beef which was then placed in storage pursuant to the 1988 APS scheme.

The appropriate advance payments under the scheme were made by the Minister; these totalled £5,344,605 in APS and £16,270,139 96 in export refunds. Much of the beef in store was later sold. Subsequently, the Minister's officials carried out a major sampling of the beef remaining in store in respect of which payments had been made for the 1988 season. The officials allowed all the product sampled to be exported except for 10 or 20 boxes of small trimmings. In May 1991, the Minister informed the plaintiff by letter that a number of infringements of the relevant regulations had been found, namely, that a number of cartons of 'plate and flank' and midrib were found to contain scraps and trimmings which were ineligible for APS aid or for the Export Refunds claimed, that a number of cartons of 'plate and flank' and midrib were found to contain non-individually wrapped pieces of meat which were ineligible for the export refunds claimed, that some cartons contained both trimmings and non-individually wrapped pieces of meat and, on the first day of sampling, cod fat (that is, fat adjacent to the sexual organs of the male animal) was found wrapped in 'plate and flank.'

The defendant claimed repayment of a total sum of £1,525,748 93 (made up of sums for APS aid, export refunds and forfeited contract securities). This sum had been calculated according to a "correction methodology" set out in the letter, which included the following criteria; the entire product contained in cartons found to contain trimmings, cod fat or non-individually wrapped pieces of meat were excluded from APS and export refunds, the sampling results were extrapolated across the total "plate and flank" and midrib production of the relevant sub-contractor and where the weight of trimmings in any carton was greater than or equal to 3kg, the weight of the entire carton was included in the extrapolation calculation. The plaintiff claimed that the Minister had misinterpreted the relevant Community Regulations and that the extrapolation methodology was *ultra vires*. In essence, Barr J. found for the plaintiff.

The issues   In carrying out the sampling, the Minister's officials had regarded trimmings of 100g or less as "scraps" within the meaning of Regulation (EEC) No.2675/88 and trimmings of greater weight than 100g as pieces of meat which were required to be individually wrapped under Regulation (EEC) No.1964/

82. Crucially, the Minister noted that, in the French and German language versions, of the Community Regulations the word "scraps" was rendered as "trimmings". The plaintiff submitted that "scraps" were small pieces of meat or fat which fell to the ground during the de-boning process and which were no longer fit for human consumption. The plaintiff did not consider that scraps included trimmings, whether large or small. The plaintiff stated that the '100g rule' had not been made known to it until after the sampling process. The plaintiff argued that the true interpretation of Regulation (EEC) No.1964/82 required that entire cuts or large pieces of meat must be individually wrapped, but that trimmings did not require individual wrapping and could be included in parcels of "plate and flank".

The evidence established that unlike other superior cuts, the cut "plate and flank" has no significance as a cut or piece of meat per se and is minced or chopped for sale as sausage, beefburger and other such products. The plaintiff's policy had been to wrap and store trimmings of all sizes from "plate and flank", midrib or other superior cuts such as fillet and striploin with pieces of "plate and flank". Four of the six contractors used by the plaintiff had instructed their deboners, with the plaintiff's approval, to store trimmings unless the Minister's officials objected. The Minister did not challenged evidence that the plaintiff's practice accorded with long standing practice in the Irish meat trade and internationally. As to cod fat, the evidence indicated that although it is readily identifiable at or about the time of slaughter, after a number of months in cold storage it is not easily distinguishable from the adjacent rose fat, permissible under the Community Regulations. Finally, the plaintiff also argued that there were no Community or national legislative basis authorising extrapolation of the sample results across the entire amount of beef in storage, as had been done by the Minister in the instant case. It appeared that such extrapolation had been insisted on by the European Commission, notwithstanding some misgivings by the Minister. As already indicated, Barr J. found in the plaintiff's favour on virtually all major issues.

The decision   Barr J. turned first to the correct interpretation of the Community Regulations. He held that the Court should confine itself to interpreting the English language version of the relevant Regulations, rejected the Minister's contention that the Court should examine the French or German language versions. He stated that any ambiguity between various Community language versions of particular Regulations was not a matter for the Irish courts. Despite this, he accepted as a primary rule of European law that he should adopt a teleological or schematic approach to the interpretation and construction of Community legislation, referring with approval to *Nestor v. Murphy* [1979] I.R. 326 (case involving domestic legislation), *Lawlor v. Minister for Agriculture* [1990] 1 I.R. 356; [1988] ILRM 400 (1987 Review, 92-4) and *Bosphorus Hava Yollari Turizm Ve Ticaret Anonim Sirketi v. Minister for Trans-*

port, Energy and Communications [1994] 2 I.L.R.M. 551 (1994 Review, 42 and in the Commercial Law chapter, 63, above). Adopting this approach, while not looking at the alternative translations opened to him, he was able to examine the legislation with a quite wide perspective. He held that there was no doubt that the purpose behind Regulations No.2675/88 and No. 1964/81 was that "scraps", being unfit for human consumption, should not be included in product for which APS or export refunds were claimed, and that it was not necessary under the export refund scheme and would be illogical to wrap separately individual trimmings of whatever size.

Applying the rule *noscitur a sociis*, Barr J. considered it evident that the common denominator between "scraps" and "large tendons, cartilages, pieces of fat" was that all are unfit for human consumption. Following from this, and applying the *ejusdem generis* rule, he concluded that the term "other scraps" was sufficiently wide to include all unspecified items which are not fit for human consumption. Thus, he concluded that the framers of Regulation No.2675/88 intended to set out a list of inedible items which ought not to be included in product for storage. In this context, the term "scraps" meant leavings from the de-boning process which are unfit for human consumption but which may have a minimal value as animal food and accordingly, may be sold within the Community pursuant to Regulation No. 1964/82. On this basis, he concluded that the Minister had failed to establish that the term "scraps" in the relevant Regulations includes trimmings, whether large or small, and there was thus no legislative or other lawful basis for the '100g rule'.

Turning to the interpretation of Art.1 of Regulation No.1964/82, Barr J. considered that the literal interpretation contended for by the Minister failed to achieve the apparent purpose of the Regulation and led to useless work and 'an exercise in bizarre bureaucracy of ultimate absurdity.' He considered that a requirement that trimmings included with "plate and flank" should be individually wrapped would create needless work for the exporter, would be bothersome for the purchaser and would achieve nothing. He held that once cuts or large pieces of meat are individually wrapped, Article 1 of the Regulation is satisfied and unwrapped trimmings may be included in rolls of "plate and flank" without infringing the Regulation.

While he accepted that some pieces of fat were discovered wrapped in "plate and flank" during the sampling, the defendant had not discharged the onus of proving on the balance of probabilities that the fat in question was cod fat rather than the permissible rose fat.

Moving to the extrapolation system used by the Minister, Barr J. accepted that although no Community or national legislative authority had been expressly put in place, the Minister as the national Intervention Agent, had implied power under the Community Regulations to devise and operate a system of financial corrections which was fair and reasonable, based on the actual weight of unlawful product found and including a system of extrapolation

across the appropriate unit of production. However, a system of financial corrections based only on the weight of unauthorised product actually found, as
here, fell far short of an equitable assessment of total actual infringements and
did not allow for the calculation of the benefit wrongfully obtained by the
contractor under the respective schemes. In addition, he held that the Minister's implied authority to devise and operate a system of financial corrections
did not include the authority to impose penalties, since they were of a quasi-
criminal nature and were in breach of the rule against retrospective criminal
offences in Article 15.5 of the Constitution (citing *King v. Attorney General*
[1981] I.R. 233 in this respect). Indeed, even if the penalties were not characterised as being quasi-criminal, he considered that the European Community
law requirement of legal certainty demanded that penalties be firmly based in
law at the time of the alleged offence (citing *Konecke v. Balm* [1984] E.C.R.
3291). Finally, he also held that the penal aspects of the extrapolation process,
the penal forfeiture of securities and the penal consequences of the '100g
rule' and the 3kg rule' offended the doctrine of proportionality in Community
law and he would have been struck down for that reason even if the scheme
for financial corrections had been specifically authorised by Community Regulations.

Since Barr J. held that the plaintiff was not in breach of the Community
Regulations, it was entitled to damages for any additional loss, over and above
the loss of the relevant contract securities, it may have suffered as a result.

FAILURE TO IMPLEMENT COMMUNITY OBLIGATIONS

In *Coppinger v. Waterford County Council (No. 1)*, High Court, March 22,
1996, Geoghegan J. considered the difficult question of alleged failure to implement a Community Directive correctly in the context of a road traffic personal injuries claim. For previous discussion, see *Tate v. Minister for Social
Welfare* [1995] 1 I.R. 419 (1995 Review, 363-5).

The plaintiff in *Coppinger* had sustained serious personal injuries when
he drove his car into the rear of a tipper truck, owned by the first defendant.
The plaintiff claimed that because the tipper truck was not fitted with rear
underrun protection his car went in some distance under the truck and that if
such protection had been fitted his injuries would have been minor. He claimed
that such rear underrun protection devices were required under the relevant
European Directives concerning the design and manufacture of motor vehicles, namely Directive 70/156/EEC and 70/221/EEC, as amended by Directive 79/490/EEC.

Directive 70/221/EEC laid down a general requirement that road vehicles
be equipped with rear underrun protective devices. As amended by the 1979

Directive, this general requirements does not apply to, *inter alia*, 'public works vehicles' or 'vehicles for which rear underrun protection is incompatible with their use.' The Road Traffic (Construction, Equipment and Use of Vehicles) (Amendment) Regulations 1985 purported to implement the 1970 Directives, as amended by the 1979 Directive. Article 4(1) of the 1985 Regulations provided that 'a vehicle, trailer or semi-trailer to which this article applies shall, on or after the 1st day of January, 1986 at all times while used in a public place, be equipped with a rear underrun protective device.' However, Article 4(3)(g) provides that 'a vehicle or trailer so constructed that it can be unloaded by part of the vehicle or trailer being tipped rearwards' is exempt from the requirements of Article 4(1).

The defendant Council argued that, having regard to the 1985 Regulations and to the general knowledge and understanding at the time of the accident, there was no legal duty to attach underrun protection to a tipper truck. Anticipating a claim based directly on the Directives, it also denied that it was an 'emanation of the State' so as to be liable to the plaintiff for non-compliance with the Directives, it denied that the Directives applied to the tipper truck in question, and also denied that the requirements of the Directives were sufficiently precise to have direct effect or that rear underrun protection would have saved the plaintiff from serious injury. Evidence was given on behalf of the defendant Council that the tipper truck would have been used for road surfacing between April and October and that, in the course of such work, a gritter would have been attached to it from time to time. Evidence for the defendant indicated that, in order to attach a gritter, an underrun protection device could be removed in a relatively simple operation taking no more than five minutes. Alternatively, a type of underrun protection device capable of being folded could have been used.

Geoghegan J. found for the plaintiff on the most significant issues raised. His judgment began promisingly for the defendant by finding that it was entitled to assume, in the absence of some clear evidence to the contrary, that the State had correctly interpreted the relevant Directives in the national implementing legislation (the 1985 Regulations). Thus, in this respect, it could not be held liable in negligence in not fitting rear underrun protection to the tipper truck.

Nonetheless, Geoghegan J. went on to hold the Council liable under principles of European law. He referred to much of the extensive case law on what constitutes an 'emanation of the State', in particular, *Foster and Ors v. British Gas plc* [1990] E.C.R. 3313, *Publico Ministero v. Ratri* [1990] E.C.R. 53, *Marshall v. Southampton and South West Hampshire Area Health Authority* [1986] E.C.R. 723, *Johnston v. Chief Constable of the R.U.C.* [1986] ECR 1651, *Marleasing SA v. La Commercial Internacional de Alimentacion SA* [1990] E.C.R. 4135 and *Fratelli Costanzo SpA v. Commune di Milano* [1989] E.C.R. 1839. Having reviewed these decisions, he found that the Council was an emanation of the State and that, accordingly, it had the same obligations towards a private individual under the Directives as the State.

As to whether the Directives in this instance were sufficiently precise to have direct effect, Geoghegan J. held that the mere fact that arguments might be made for differing interpretations of Directives did not mean that the obligations imposed by them were not sufficiently precise to be directly enforceable by a private individual against the State or an emanation of the State. Moving to the detailed arguments made, he rejected the Council's contention that the tipper truck was a 'public works vehicle' within the meaning of Directive 70/221/EEC. It seemed reasonably clear to him that 'public works vehicles' in this context was intended to apply to vehicles forming part of the machinery for the works themselves and not vehicles used for transporting materials to or from the works. Crucially, he also held that the onus of proving that a fitted rear underrun protection device was incompatible with the use of the tipper truck lay on the defendant Council and that it had failed to discharge that onus. He accepted the evidence that a rear underrun protection device could have been designed to be easily removable or folded when it was necessary to attach a gritter to the tipper truck. Thus, he also concluded that the fitting of rear underrun protection was not 'incompatible with the use of' the tipper truck, as defined in the 1970 Directive, as amended. Finally, he also accepted that the plaintiff's injuries would not have been as serious if the tipper truck had been fitted with a rear underrun protection device, thus concluding that the necessary causation had been established.

The other issues raised in the case, contributory negligence and quantum, are discussed in the Torts chapter, 601, below.

Evidence

Declan McGrath, Trinity College Dublin

BURDEN OF PROOF

Standard of Proof in Criminal Cases   In *The People (Director of Public Prosecutions) v. Shortt*, Court of Criminal Appeal, July 23, 1996, the summing up of the trial judge on the issue of the standard of proof was impugned on the ground that he should have contrasted the criminal standard with the civil standard of proof. Although, it is not cited in the judgment, this ground of appeal would seem to be based on the decision of the Court in *The People (Attorney General) v. Byrne* [1974] I.R. 1. In that case, Kenny J. in setting out the correct charge to be given to the jury in a criminal case as to the burden and standard of proof, said that it is helpful if the degree of proof required is contrasted with that in a civil case.

In *Shortt,* although it was accepted that such a contrast was frequently made by judges in their charges, it was held that there is no obligation to use this particular way of explaining the standard of proof. The Court was satisfied that the manner in which the trial judge had explained what was meant by a reasonable doubt could not be faulted and therefore, this ground of appeal failed.

This decision, quite sensibly, retains a degree of flexibility in the charge to be given to the jury on the issue of the standard of proof. It should therefore, serve to prevent any calcification of the charge laid down in *Byrne* into a ritualistic formula.

In *Convening Authority v. Doyle* [1996] 2 I.L.R.M. 213, the Courts Martial Appeal Court addressed the issue of the standard of proof to be met by an accused when a legal burden is placed upon him or her.

The appellant was appealing his conviction for desertion. Section 135(2)(a)(iii) of the Defence Act 1954 provides that a person deserts the defence forces if he absents himself without due authority from his unit with the intention of not returning. Section 135(2)(b) further provides that "a person who has been absent without authority for a continuous period of six months of more shall, unless the contrary is proved, be presumed to have had had the intention of not returning to his unit. . . ." The appellant had been absent from his unit for more than 12 years and the judge advocate, in summing up, dealt with the presumption in section 135(2)(b) by saying:

> Whereas the prosecution must establish the guilt of the accused beyond a reasonable doubt, the same degree of proof is not required of the accused in rebutting such a presumption as has been raised. It is enough if the accused satisfies you of the probability that he had not the intention of remaining away from the place where his duty required him to be. If he does so you must find him not guilty of desertion.

The appellant's contention that this direction was incorrect and breached the presumption of innocence was rejected by the Courts Martial Appeal Court. It stated that the direction was in accordance with the correct approach as laid down by the English Court of Criminal Appeal in *R. v. Carr-Briant* [1943] 1 K.B. 607, that:

> . . . in any case where, either by statute or at common law, some matter is presumed against an accused person 'unless the contrary is proved', the jury should be directed that it is for them to decide whether the contrary is proved, that the burden of proof required is less than that required at the hands of the prosecution in proving the case beyond a reasonable doubt, and that the burden may be discharged by evidence satisfying the jury of the probability of that which the accused is called upon to establish.

The Court was satisfied that this decision has been consistently followed in this jurisdiction and that the judge advocate's direction to the court was in accordance with it. Accordingly, the Court held that there had been no misdirection and upheld the conviction.

Standard of proof in civil cases   A number of cases decided in 1996 confirm that the effect of the decision of the Supreme Court in *Banco Ambrosiano S.P.A. v. Ansbacher & Co. Ltd.* [1987] I.L.R.M. 669, has been to give *quietus* to the contention that there are any categories of civil case where the standard of proof is any higher than that of proof on the balance of probabilities.

One type of case where it had been suggested that a higher standard of proof might apply was nullity suits but this submission was rejected by McCracken J. in *S.C. v. P.D.*, High Court, March 14, 1996. In reaching this conclusion, he relied on the *obiter* comments of McCarthy J. in *U.F. (Orse. C.) v. J.C.* [1991] 2 I.R. 330 (1990 Review 291-7), to the effect that the standard of proof on a petitioner in a nullity case was the same as in any other civil case, and on *Banco Ambrosiano* which he viewed as laying down the applicable principles.

In *Banco Ambrosiano*, Henchy J., speaking for the Court on this point, rejected the suggestion that there was any intermediate standard of proof between that applicable in criminal cases and that applicable in civil cases which was to be applied where allegations of fraud are made in civil proceedings. He did however, accept that the consequences of a finding of fraud should be taken into account in deciding whether it had been established. McCracken J. was satisfied that these comments applied equally to an issue of nullity and concluded that "the matter must be judged on a balance of probabilities rather than on any other basis, but that, as in cases of fraud, great care should be taken in drawing inferences".

A similar conclusion was reached in *P.C. v. C.M. (Orse. C.)*, High Court, 11 January 1996, although Laffoy J., in confirming that the correct standard of proof is that of proof on the balance of probabilities omitted any caveat as to the necessity of exercising caution in drawing inferences in nullity cases. However, this oversight should not be taken to indicate any dissent from the approach of McCracken J.

The issue of the standard of proof also arose in *Mehigan v. Duignan* [1997] 1 I.L.R.M. 171. This case concerned an application by a liquidator under section 204 of the Companies Act 1990 which makes provision for the imposition of personal liability on the officers of a company where proper books of account are not kept. Because no argument was addressed to Shanley J. to the effect that section 204 created a criminal offence, he approached the question of the standard of proof on the basis that the section created a civil wrong (on this point, reference should be made to the recent Supreme Court decision in *O'Keefe v. Ferris*, unreported, Supreme Court, February 19, 1997, which will be dealt with in the 1997 Review).

In considering the appropriate standard of proof, he rejected the approach which had been adopted in the New Zealand case of *Maloc Construction Ltd. v. Chadwick* [1986] 3 N.Z.C.L.C. 99. In *Maloc*, Tompkins J., considering the New Zealand equivalent of section 204, stated that although the civil standard of proof applied, a higher degree of probability than normal was required. This was because the subject matter of the enquiry involved facts, which if established, would constitute an offence. Thus, the learned judge endorsed the idea of degrees of probability which had been propounded by Denning L.J. in *Bater v. Bater* [1951] P. 35.

McCracken J. pointed out that this approach had not been followed in this jurisdiction, citing *Banco Ambrosiano*. He also referred to the decision of the Supreme Court in *Hanafin v. Minister for the Environment* [1996] 2 I.L.R.M. 161, where the Court had rejected the submission that the petitioner had to establish his claim to any higher standard than proof on a balance of probabilities. Therefore, he concluded that in considering whether to impose liability under section 204, no higher degree of probability is required than in any other civil matter.

Although the foregoing cases provide a trenchant reaffirmation that the standard of proof to be met in all civil cases is that of proof on the balance of probabilities, it is clear that this standard will not be met with the same ease in every case. This is because of the acceptance by Henchy J. in *Banco Ambrosiano* and by McCracken J. in *S.C. v. P.D.* of the proposition that the seriousness of the allegation is a factor which will be taken into account in deciding whether the civil standard is met. As it was put by Morris L.J. in *Hornal v. Neuberger Products Ltd.* [1957] 1 Q.B. 247, at 266:

> Though no court and no jury would give less careful attention to issues lacking gravity than to those marked by it, the very elements of gravity become a part of the whole range of circumstances which have to be weighed in the scale when deciding as to the balance of probabilities.

Implicit in this approach is the idea that the tribunal of fact should be more reluctant to find the burden of proof to be discharged where the allegation is a serious one and thus, it is arguable that it merely represents a veiled application of the idea of degrees of probability. This is because it is a distinction of form rather than of substance to say that while there is no higher standard for any specific categories of cases, it will be harder to reach the common standard in those categories. However, this 'soft' application of the notion of degrees of probability does offer the advantage of greater flexibility and spares the courts the task of expressly erecting and delineating the categories where the higher standard of proof is to apply.

By way of postscript, it is worth noting that section 8(2) of the Proceeds of Crime Act 1996, stipulates that the standard of proof required to determine any question arising under the Act is that applicable to civil proceedings.

Tribunals   It was held by Murphy J. in *Grant v. The Garda Síochána Complaints Board*, High Court, June 12, 1996 (below, 399) that the civil standard of proof is the appropriate standard of proof to be applied by a tribunal hearing complaints pursuant to the Garda Síochána (Complaints) Act 1986.

UNCONSTITUTIONALLY OBTAINED EVIDENCE

The decision of Carney J. in *Freeman v. Director of Public Prosecutions*, High Court, November 18, 1996 (above, 265) raises a number of issues relating to arrest and detention and the admission of unconstitutionally obtained evidence but only the latter will be dealt with here.

The background to the case was as follows. Two gardaí went to the appellant's house in Cabra where he had been seen, with two other men, unloading goods from a van and carrying them into the house. When the gardaí approached the house, they were spotted by the men who ran into the house and slammed the door behind them. After banging on the door and identifying themselves, the gardaí entered the house where they found cigarettes, spirits and other items. They gave chase to the men and arrested the appellant outside of the house pursuant to section 41 of the Larceny Act 1916 for the offence of handling stolen goods. The appellant was then taken to Cabra Garda station where he was detained pursuant to section 4 of the Criminal Justice Act 1984.

The appellant was subsequently convicted of handling stolen goods and of an offence under section 16 of the Criminal Justice Act 1984 and appealed by way of case stated. One of the questions raised on the case stated was the legality of the entry by gardaí into the appellant's dwelling and of his subsequent arrest. Although section 41 of the Larceny Act 1916 does not confer any express power to arrest on private property, Carney J. was of the view that the section was drafted in wide enough terms to permit a valid, legal arrest on private property by gardaí who were trespassers. However, he went on to hold that having regard to Article 40.5 which guarantees the inviolability of the dwelling "save in accordance with law", any interference with that right must be given express statutory effect. Therefore, the entry by gardaí was unconstitutional and he went on to consider the application of the exclusionary rule laid down in *People (Attorney General) v. O'Brien* [1965] I.R. 142, whereby evidence obtained in conscious and deliberate violation of the constitutional rights of an accused is excluded save where there are extraordinary excusing circumstances.

The entry by the gardaí was clearly deliberate and conscious and therefore the main question for consideration was whether there were any extraordinary excusing circumstances. In considering this point, Carney J. made the important observation that, contrary to the opinion of the District Judge, the presence of extraordinary excusing circumstances did not entitle the State or its agents to breach constitutional rights. This point had been made by Morris J. earlier in the year in *Director of Public Prosecutions v. Delaney* [1996] 1 I.L.R.M. 536 (above, 264). In that case, one of the questions on a case stated was whether the presence of persons outside a dwelling, who threatened to harm persons within it, was an extraordinary excusing circumstance *justifying* a forcible entry by the gardaí against the will of the occupier to a dwelling without warrant. Morris J. criticised the way in which this question had been formulated, opining that *O'Brien* was not (at 541):

> . . . authority for the general proposition that a member of An Garda Síochána may violate a constitutional right provided that there are extraordinary excusing circumstances. It is authority for no more than the proposition that where such a violation occurs and evidence is harvested as a result, it is for the court of trial to decide all the issues as to the admissibility of this evidence including a consideration of any extraor-

dinary excusing circumstances alleged. . . .

This point is one of more than mere semantics. The normal consequence of an intentional act which breaches the constitutional rights of an accused is the exclusion of any evidence obtained thereby. However, if there are extraordinary circumstances, these may *excuse* the breach in the sense that their presence may mitigate the normal consequences of the rule and thus, the judge may admit the evidence notwithstanding the unconstitutionality which has occurred. Thus, such circumstances do not absolve or deny the unconstitutionality, they merely temper the consequences which would otherwise follow. However, if these become extraordinary *justifying* circumstances, then the logical conclusion is that there was no violation at all (see Paul O'Connor, "The Admissibility of Unconstitutionally Obtained Evidence in Irish Law" (1982) 17 Ir. Jur. 257, at 268-73, commenting on the decision of the Supreme Court in *The People (Director of Public Prosecutions) v. Shaw* [1982] I.R. 1).

Carney J. went on to refer to the examples of extraordinary excusing circumstances enumerated by Walsh J. in *O'Brien* which included "the imminent destruction of vital evidence". He was conscious of the fact that to give too wide a scope to this exception might:

> . . . undermine the rationale of a rule which by its nature is invoked in circumstances where well meaning haste on the part of the gardaí may lead to unconstitutional acts. . . . [T]o excuse unconstitutional behaviour merely because it was designed to garner vital evidence is to adopt a lesser standard than that established in *Kenny*."

Thus, the exception is directed towards the 'imminent destruction' of vital evidence rather than the gathering of such evidence. However, he was of opinion that the facts of the case fell squarely within the exception. The gardaí had caught the appellant and his associates *in flagrante delicto* and there had not been enough time for the gardaí to obtain the necessary search warrant.

The gardaí had in fact subsequently obtained a search warrant and another issue was the validity of this search warrant in the light of preceding events. On this question, Carney J. took the view that the gardaí had had ample evidence available to ground the warrant independently from that which they perceived from their unconstitutional entry into the dwellinghouse and therefore the warrant was valid.

This decision is of interest for a number of reasons. Firstly, the decision of the Supreme Court in *Kenny* (1990 Review, 202-5) may well be viewed as the high watermark of that Court's endorsement of a due process model of criminal justice. Certainly, the language and the approach of the Court in that case seems to be somewhat removed from that of more recent cases such as *Heaney* (below, 329). In view of the changing public and political climate towards crime, some attempt to row back on the absoluteness of the exclusionary principle laid down in *Kenny* might be expected. This has already happened to some degree in a number of decisions such as *Walsh v. Ó Buachalla* [1991] 1 I.R. 56 (1990 Review 150-4) applying a strict requirement of causation and it would have been unsurprising to find the courts also willing to take a somewhat expansive approach to the idea of extraordinary excusing circumstances. Thus, the decision in *Freeman* is notable because of the acknowledgement by Carney J. that an expansive interpretation of the 'imminent destruction of evidence' exception would be likely to undermine the rationale of the exclusionary rule. Yet, there is somewhat of a divergence between his ostensible attachment to the exclusionary rule and the actual decision in the case. Although, the gardaí had come upon the appellant and his associates acting suspiciously and they fled into the house upon their arrival, it would seem as if the gardaí had no *specific* reason to believe that the appellant and his associates were about to destroy vital evidence other than a general belief to that effect. Indeed, the nature of the contraband involved was such that, unlike say drugs, it would be difficult to destroy or conceal the evidence. It would thus seem as if it was the element of haste and the lack of enough time to get a warrant which was determinative. If this is so, then 'the imminent destruction of evidence' exception may provide trial judges with a ready peg on which to hang decisions in favour of admissibility.

Another point of interest is the conclusion of Carney J. with regard to the validity of the search warrant. Although he does not employ the concept expressly, he implicitly applies the idea of idea of causation in order to atomise the sequence of events and uphold the validity of the warrant. It may well be that the gardaí had gathered sufficient evidence to ground the warrant prior to their unconstitutional entry into the dwelling. However, in view of the fact that the application for the warrant was made after the unconstitutional entry, it would be unrealistic to assume that the decision to apply for it was unaffected by what they perceived when they entered the dwelling. Thus, adopting a broad transactional approach, it could be argued that the issue of the warrant was coloured by the initial unconstitutionality. This is not to say that Carney J. was incorrect in the conclusion that he reached but it does demonstrate once again the potency of the causation requirement as a means of escaping the rigours of the exclusionary rule.

CONFESSIONS

Procedure where the admissibility of a confession is challenged The decision of the Courts Martial Appeal Court in *Finn and Mulraney v. Convening Authority*, Courts Martial Appeal Court, June 11, 1996, lays down the correct procedure to be employed by a court martial where the admissibility of a confession is challenged.

The appellants had been convicted at a general Court Martial of a number of offences including stealing a machine gun and treacherously or unjustifiably delivering up the gun to an unauthorised person or persons. They had been on UN service in Lebanon and a machine gun and tripod went missing while they were on sentry duty. An investigation by military investigators ensued and the appellants were interviewed on a number of occasions. Both of them initially made exculpatory statements but subsequently made inculpatory statements as to the misappropriation of the machine gun, though their accounts differed in certain important respects. Private Finn said that he had been complicit in the deed so as to discharge a debt which Private Mulraney owed a local inhabitant. However, Private Mulraney stated that he wanted to bring some form of retribution on the company commander of the post.

The admissibility of these statements was challenged by the appellants at their trial on the grounds that they were involuntary but after directions by the Judge Advocate, the Court Martial decided to admit the statements in evidence. Thereafter, counsel for the appellants sought to cross-examine the military investigators on matters going to the weight to be attached to these statements but was not permitted to do so because the Judge Advocate thought that such cross-examination would simply be a reiteration of matters which had already been canvassed. The appellants appealed their conviction on this ground and their appeal was upheld by the Courts Martial Appeal Court which quashed their convictions and ordered a re-trial.

The Court observed (citing *The People (Attorney General) v. Ainscough* [1960] I.R. 136, *The People (Director of Public Prosecutions) v. Conroy* [1986] I.R. 460 and *The People (Director of Public Prosecutions) v. Quilligan (No.3)* [1993] 2 I.R. 305) that the correct procedure to be employed where the admissibility of a confession is challenged on the ground of involuntariness was not now in doubt: it is for the trial judge to decide in a "trial within a trial" whether the statement should be admitted in evidence and for the jury to decide what weight to give to it, and in particular whether it is true. When a statement is admitted in evidence as being voluntary, the accused is entitled to traverse again all the ground that was covered before the trial judge.

Although this procedure had to be adapted in the case of a court martial because the officers that comprise the court martial must make findings both of law and fact, the same procedure should be adhered to with the exception that it should not be necessary to traverse again matters that have to do exclusively with the admissibility issue. It was acknowledged by the Court that sometimes, the distinction may be a difficult one to make but, when in doubt, it is better to give the defence a certain latitude than to rule out a line of cross-examination which may be useful in casting doubt on the truth or reliability of the contents of a confession.

This case affirms that considerations of due process and fair procedures require that accused persons should be afforded the maximum possible freedom to make their case, consistent with the due administration of justice. Thus, while a trial judge, or in the case of a court martial, a judge advocate, has a supervisory jurisdiction over the examination of witnesses, utilitarian considerations relating to speed or efficiency will in general have to give way to the fundamental right of an accused to make his or her case and challenge the evidence against him or her.

Custody regulations   The admissibility of a statement taken in breach of the Criminal Justice Act 1984 (Treatment of Persons in Custody in Garda Síochána Stations Regulations) 1987 was challenged in *The People (Director of Public Prosecutions) v. O'Shea*, Court of Criminal Appeal, [1996] 1 I.R. 556.

HEARSAY

The evidence of children   Two judgments of the President of the High Court in *Re K. (Infants)* (reported as *Re M., S., and W. Infants* [1996] 1 I.L.R.M. 370) and *Southern Health Board v. C.H.* [1996] 1 I.R. 219, and the decision of the Supreme Court in the latter case leave in a somewhat unsettled state, the law relating to the admission of hearsay evidence in wardship and analogous proceedings.

In *Re K. (Infants)*, the Eastern Health Board instituted proceedings seeking an order taking three children, M., S. and W. into wardship. At the hearing of the summons, Costello P. admitted certain contested hearsay evidence on a *de bene esse* basis. This evidence consisted of: (i) the evidence of Mrs. Halsham, a speech therapist, who stated that S. had confided to her that he had, with the knowledge of his mother, been subjected to sexual abuse by his father on a regular basis for a number of years; and (ii) the evidence of Mr. Kieran McGrath, a senior social worker with considerable experience of child abuse allegations, as to what S. said and did at an interview which he had with him in the Children's Hospital, Temple Street. A videotape of this interview had been made.

The President was satisfied that if the hearsay evidence was excluded, the rest of the evidence would not justify the making of an order of wardship and he therefore addressed the admissibility of this evidence as a preliminary issue. In the absence of any Irish authority, he engaged in a review of authorities from England, Northern Ireland and Canada including *Official Solicitor v. K.* [1965] A.C. 201, *Re P.B., a minor* [1986] N.I. 88, and *R. v. Khan* [1990] 2 S.C.R. 531.

Following this survey, he reached the conclusion that the hearsay rule has never been strictly applied in wardship proceedings. This is because a judge exercises a special jurisdiction in wardship proceedings which originated in the doctrine that infants are to be treated as specifically under the protection of the sovereign who, as *parens patriae*, had charge of persons not capable of looking after themselves. The judge exercising this jurisdiction has always acted in the interests of the welfare of the infant and this approach has been underpinned by section 3 of the Guardianship of Infants Act 1964, which provides that in any proceedings before any court where the custody, guardianship and upbringing of an infant is in question the court must regard the welfare of the infant as the first and paramount consideration.

He went on to say that although the court's wardship jurisdiction antedates the hearsay rule, the continued non-application of the rule is justified not by this historical fact but by reasons flowing from the nature of the jurisdiction which the court is exercising:

> In ordinary civil proceedings in litigation between parties the judge is acting as an arbitrator and is confined to reaching his or her decision on the evidence which the parties choose to produce before the court and is not free to call other witnesses or investigate the possibility of the existence of other evidence. The judge's function in wardship proceedings is entirely different. In these proceedings the judge is undertaking an inquiry and investigation for the purpose of deciding what orders should be made in the interests of the welfare of infants. The rules relating to the reception of evidence in litigation in which the judge is sitting as an arbitrator are inappropriate to this type of judicial process as they may not serve the object for which the jurisdiction has been granted, namely the welfare of infants. The court should therefore have a discretion to admit hearsay evidence in wardship proceedings.

The President proceeded to elaborate on when and how this discretion would be exercised. First, the court would have to be satisfied of the necessity of admitting the hearsay statement. He gave two examples of when such necessity would arise: (i) when the child is not old enough to give sworn testimony in court; and (ii) where the court concludes that to require the child to give evidence in court would be such a traumatic experience that in the interests of the welfare of the child he or she should not be required to undergo it.

Where this requirement of necessity is met and the statement admitted, the trial judge will have to decide what weight to give to the evidence. This assessment of the reliability of the statement is two-pronged. First, the judge might in some cases have to determine the reliability of the witness who is narrating what the child has said and in others whether the narrator has either consciously or unconsciously influenced the content of the out of court statement. Secondly, the court will be required to consider the reliability of the statement itself. For example, if the child has no motive to falsify a story, or if the child could not be expected to have prior knowledge of the acts which he or she has recounted these factors will be supportive of its reliability. Alternatively, where there is a bitter matrimonial dispute, the court might consider it unsafe to act on an accusation of wrongdoing made by a child against one parent when the risk of undue influence by the other was a very real one.

These twin criteria of necessity and reliability have been posited as the touchstones of any new exceptions to the hearsay rule (*R. v. Khan* [1990] 2 S.C.R. 531 and *R. v. Smith* (1992) 94 D.L.R. (4th) 590). However, it would appear from the judgment of Costello P. that as regards the admission of hearsay in wardship proceedings, only the requirement of necessity is a condition precedent, that of reliability merely goes to the weight to be attached to the statement. This is presumably because the hearsay rule does not apply in all its vigour to wardship proceedings.

The President concluded by saying that although in sexual abuse cases, the court may be required to adjudicate on an issue affecting the fundamental rights of one or even both of the child's parents, this was not a reason for refusing hearsay evidence, but was a reason for ensuring that the procedures adopted are scrupulously fair. No general rules could be laid down as to what fair procedures would require but generally a parent accused of abuse should be informed of the evidence to be given before the hearing (and, where available, furnished with copies of the statements of witnesses to be called) and if videotapes of interviews have been made, copies of the tape should be made available to the person affected by the evidence.

The President followed his decision in *Re K. (Infants)* in a decision handed down by him a few days later: *Southern Health Board v. C.H.* [1996] 1 I.R. 219. The case concerned a six year old girl who had been in the care of the Southern Health Board since the death of her mother in August 1990. Because of problems relating to access by the child's father, an information was sworn which led to a place of safety order being made on 27 July 1994. A fit persons order summons pursuant to section 58 of the Children Act 1908, was also issued on that date. The father subsequently issued an application under section 11 of the Guardianship of Infants Act 1964 against the Board and the two summonses were heard together. The Board proposed to call a social worker, Mr. O'Leary to give evidence as to allegations made by the girl of sexual abuse by her father and his opinion as to the validity of those allegations. Objection to the admission of this evidence was taken by the father's solicitor. The District Judge proposed to admit the evidence but stated a case for the opinion of the High Court pursuant to section 52 of the Courts (Supplemental Provisions) Act 1961, as to whether he was correct in so deciding.

The first question for determination by the High Court was whether the nature of the jurisdiction exercised by the court under section 58 was the same as that of the wardship jurisdiction. Costello P. agreed with the submissions of the Board that it was and held that the District Judge had a discretion as to whether to admit hearsay evidence in accordance with the principles laid down by him in *Re K. (Infants)*. He went on to elaborate further on what is required by the court's obligation to ensure fair procedures where hearsay evidence is contained in a videotape. In such circumstances, fair procedures require that the tape be given to a person against whom allegations of wrongdoing are made prior to the hearing and that an opportunity to submit evidence to rebut any suggested conclusions from the hearsay evidence be afforded.

On appeal, the Supreme Court agreed that the hearsay evidence could be considered by the District Judge but took a different approach to that of the President in reaching this conclusion. The Court, in a judgment delivered by O'Flaherty J. agreed that the nature of fit person proceedings was similar to that of wardship proceedings because they are both, in essence, an inquiry as to what is in the best interests of the child and not a *lis inter partes*. However, the Court stated, relying on its previous decision in *The State (D. and D.) v. Groarke* [1990] 1 I.R. 305 (1989 Review 265-7), that the correct approach to the evidence of Mr. O'Leary was to regard it as expert evidence rather than as hearsay evidence.

O'Flaherty J. emphasised that the videotapes were not independent evidence in the case but were instead part of the material on which the expert evidence of Mr. O'Leary would be based. The key evidence in the case would be that offered by Mr. O'Leary, not the tapes and the District Judge should approach the evidence of Mr. O'Leary as he would the evidence of any other expert witness.

Like the President, the Court laid emphasis on the procedural safeguards to be employed when evidence of this type was admitted. Thus, Mr. O'Leary would be subject to cross-examination and the respondent, having viewed the tapes in advance of the hearing, would have the right to adduce such expert or other evidence, in rebuttal or otherwise, as he thought best. O'Flaherty J. opined that this approach vindicated the rights of the child which were paramount, whilst protecting, as far as practicable, the rights of the father.

Although, the Supreme Court did not expressly endorse the portion of Costello P.'s judgment setting out when it would necessary to admit evidence of this type, the court set out the same criteria. Thus, it was only if the District Judge found that the girl was incompetent to give evidence (and he was directed to establish this fact anew) or, as a distinct condition, that the trauma that she would suffer would make it undesirable that she should give evidence, that the District Judge would be justified in admitting the videotapes. That the District Judge should not be reluctant to find the latter condition to be satisfied is perhaps indicated by the observation of O'Flaherty J. that a courtroom is, in general, an unsuitable environment for a child of such tender years.

We have in the judgments of Costello P. in these two cases and that of the Supreme Court in *Southern Health Board*, two different approaches to the admission of hearsay evidence in proceedings of this type, leaving the law in something of a state of confusion. Although both approaches gave rise to the same result in *Southern Health Board*, they would not seem to do so where the evidence of a non-expert, such as that of Mrs. Halsham in *Re K. (Infants)* is at issue. Of course, the approach of the Supreme Court in *Southern Health Board* does not foreclose the adoption of the approach of Costello P. where the evidence of a non-expert is at issue. However, it would seem to be preferable to have one clear rule governing the admission of hearsay evidence in cases of this type.

One criticism of the decision of the Supreme Court in *Southern Health Board* is that it does not accord with established jurisprudence governing the admission of expert testimony. While it is clear that experts are not subject to the hearsay rule in the same way as witnesses of fact and may therefore, draw on hearsay evidence as part of the process of arriving at their opinion, it is essential that the primary facts upon which their opinion is based are proved by admissible evidence (*R. v. Abadom* [1983] All E.R. 364). Therefore, it is only if the interview with the child was otherwise admissible by an exception to the hearsay rule that Mr. O'Leary could express an expert opinion based on it or refer to it in the course of his testimony. Thus, despite the assertion of the Court to the contrary, the case was really concerned with the admission of hearsay evidence. The real question raised by the testimony of Mr. O'Leary, as identified by Costello P., was whether and in what circumstances, such evidence should be admitted.

Both of these decisions highlight the urgent necessity for the reforms adopted in the Criminal Evidence Act 1992 governing the reception of the testimony of children, to be extended to civil proceedings. This is because, despite the various safeguards propounded by Costello P. in *Re K. (Infants)* and the Supreme Court in *Southern Health Board*, it is unsatisfactory that allegations as serious as those of sexual abuse should be proved by hearsay evidence, untested by cross-examination, where a better alternative exists.

Thus, to take the two situations of necessity identified by Costello P. The first is where the child is incompetent to give evidence. This proposition was criticised as illogical by the father in *Southern Health Board*, relying on *R. v. Burke* (1912) 47 I.L.T.R. 111, where in response to an application to admit the evidence of what a girl of unsound mind had said to her mother, Dodd J. asked: "How can the second-hand version of her evidence be good if her own testimony be deemed unfit for credence?" There is considerable force to this argument, yet to accede to it would render it impossible in many cases to prove allegations of sexual abuse. Sexual abuse is, of its nature, a crime which occurs generally in private. There may well be very little or no physical evidence of the crime. Thus, if a child is ruled to be incompetent, and his or her hearsay statement as to the fact of abuse and/or the identity of the abuser is not admitted, then it may well be impossible to prove that it has taken place. For example, the hearsay evidence in *Re K (Infants)* pointed to sexual abuse of a sustained and systematic nature, yet, Costello P. stated that in the absence of the hearsay evidence, the other evidence in the case would not justify the making of a wardship order. The real problem, is that in civil cases, there is no provision for the reception of unsworn testimony (*Mapp v. Gilhooley* [1991] 2 I.R. 253, 1991 Review 348-9). Thus, there is no analogue to section 27 of the Criminal Evidence Act 1992 which provides that the testimony of a person under 14 years of age may be received unsworn if the court is satisfied that he or she is capable of giving an intelligible account of events. If such a provision applied to civil cases, then the argument in favour of the reception of a hearsay statement of a child such as the girl in *Southern Health Board* would be considerably weaker.

The second situation where Costello P. indicated that the reception of a hearsay statement would be necessary is where the child would be traumatised by testifying. There is indeed considerable empirical research to support the proposition that testifying in the adversarial context of a courtroom may well harm, perhaps seriously, the welfare of a child. Yet, rather than eliminating this risk of harm by admitting hearsay, a much preferable course of action would be extend the provisions of Part III of the Criminal Evidence Act 1992, which make provision for the giving of evidence by television link, to civil proceedings in which allegations of sexual or violent offences against a child are made. This procedure, which affords a defendant or accused party, the opportunity of cross-examination offers a much better balance between the rights of children and accused persons (see *White v. Ireland* [1995] 2 I.R. 268 (above, 155) and *Donnelly v. Ireland*, High Court, 3 December 1996 (above, 154) where the constitutionality of section 13 of the 1992 Act which permits evidence to be given via live television link was upheld). Some of the problems relating to children's evidence are addressed by the Children Bill, 1997 which will be discussed in the 1997 Review.

Proof of character   The decision of the Supreme Court in *Murphy v. Times Newspapers Ltd.* [1996] 1 I.R. 169, raises some issues relating to the admission of hearsay evidence and the proof of character and reputation in a defamation action.

CONFLICT OF EVIDENCE BETWEEN EXPERT WITNESSES

O'Sullivan v. Sherry, Supreme Court, *ex tempore*, February 2, 1996, was an appeal on the question of damages (below, 617). One of the grounds of appeal was the contention that the trial judge had no reasonable grounds for, or had stated no grounds for, accepting the evidence of expert witnesses called on behalf of the plaintiff and by implication rejecting the evidence of the witnesses called on behalf of the defendants. However, the Supreme Court, in an *ex tempore* judgment delivered by Hamilton C.J., was of opinion that there is no obligation on a trial judge to give any reasons why he or she accepted the evidence of one witness rather than another, be they expert of otherwise. In many cases, it might be particularly invidious if the trial judge were to criticise the evidence of expert witnesses and give reasons why he or she rejected it.

The reason for such invidiousness is not apparent from the judgment but the reluctance to criticise expert witnesses may be attributable, at least in part, to a desire on the part of the judiciary not to damage the professional reputation of expert witnesses.

OPINION EVIDENCE

In *The People (Director of Public Prosecutions) v. Malocco*, Court of Criminal Appeal, May 23, 1996 (see also, 272 and 338), one of the grounds of appeal was that a garda detective had expressed his opinion as to the applicant's guilt and the trial judge had erred in failing to either discharge the jury or give them a strong warning to disregard the statement.

The Court, however, rejected this contention as unsustainable. The phrase which was impugned ("in my mind [I] tried to think was there anything in the file which would indicate his innocence in this matter. . . ."), had been used by the garda during the course of a relatively lengthy cross-examination. Even if it could be assumed that the witness was indicating his own view as to the guilt or innocence of the applicant, which was, at the least doubtful, the Court was satisfied that the risk that the jury would draw any inference from it unfairly adverse to the applicant was so extremely remote as not to have called for any specific warning in the charge, let alone the discharge of the jury.

Indeed, the view was taken that for the trial judge to have highlighted this reference in the course of his charge would, if anything, have been unfair to the applicant by reviving and giving fresh emphasis to a matter which, in the normal course, would probably have faded from their mind at the stage when they retired to consider their verdict.

Proceeds of Crime Act 1996   This statute which makes provision for the seizure and disposal of the proceeds of crime (below, 233) includes an evidential provision designed to make it easier to obtain interim and interlocutory orders freezing assets. Section 8 of the Act provides that where a member of the gardaí or an authorised officer states in proceedings for an interim order under section 2, on affidavit, (or if the Court so directs, in oral evidence), or in proceedings for an interlocutory order under section 3, in oral evidence, that he or she believes (i) that the respondent is in possession or control of specified property and that the property constitutes, directly or indirectly, proceeds of crime, and/or (ii) that the respondent is in possession of or control of specified property and that the property was acquired, in whole or in part, with or in connection with property that, directly or indirectly, constitutes proceeds of crime, and that the value of the property is not less than £10,000, then, if the Court is satisfied that there are reasonable grounds for the belief, the statement shall be evidence of the matter referred to and the value of the property.

This section renders admissible the opinion evidence of a garda or authorised officer which would otherwise be inadmissible on the twin grounds that it was opinion and hearsay. The admission of such evidence, especially on an application for an interim order will make it much easier for the authorities to move expeditiously to obtain an order. It is noteworthy that where this element of urgency is lacking, as in an application for a disposal order under section 4, evidence of belief is not admissible.

It should also be noted that the section does not raise any problems concerning the shifting of the burden of proof because it merely provides that if the Court is satisfied that there are reasonable grounds for the belief, the statement of opinion is *evidence* of the matters stated (see *O'Leary v. Attorney General* [1995] 2 I.L.R.M. 259, 1995 Review, 181, 243).

Domestic Violence Act 1996   Another section making provision for the admission of evidence of belief is section 3(4)(b) of the Domestic Violence Act 1996 (below, 358). Section 3(4)(a) of the Act provides that in respect of certain applicants, a court shall not make a barring order in respect of the place where the applicant resides where the respondent has a legal or beneficial interest in that place but (i) the applicant has no such interest, or (ii) the applicant's interest is, in the opinion of the court, less than that of the respondent. Section 3(4)(b) then goes on to provide that where in proceedings for a barring order, the applicant states the belief, in respect of the place to which paragraph (a) relates, that he or she has a legal or beneficial interest in that place which is not less than that of the respondent, then such belief shall be admissible in evidence.

This section is an example of a recent legislative trend to afford formal as opposed to substantive protection to certain constitutional rights. It attempts to head off any potential constitutional problems arising from the guarantee of property rights in Articles 40.3 and 43 by providing that a barring order cannot be made where the legal or beneficial interest of the respondent is greater than that of the applicant. But then, it uses an evidential device to undermine the protection conferred by providing that the opinion evidence of an applicant (who will usually be a person with minimal knowledge of the law) that he or she has a legal or beneficial interest which is equal or greater than that of the respondent is admissible. In view of the complexities of the question of beneficial ownership of the family home, it will be relatively easily for an applicant to state the *bona fide,* though perhaps ultimately mistaken, belief that his or her interest is not less than that of the respondent.

Of course, it is true to say that such belief is only evidence and a judge is not obliged to act on foot of it. However, it is likely that he or she will do so in many cases especially at the interim stage. Thus, any protection which the section affords to the property rights of a respondent will in many cases be more apparent than real.

Competition (Amendment) Act 1996   Section 4 of the Competition (Amendment) Act 1996 (above, 126) provides that in proceedings for an offence under section 2 of the Act, the opinion of any witness who appears to the court to possess the appropriate qualifications or experience as respects the matter to which his or her evidence relates shall be admissible in evidence as regards any matter calling for expertise or special knowledge that is relevant to the proceedings and, in particular and without prejudice to the generality of the foregoing, the following matters, namely (a) the effects that types of agreements, decisions or concerted practices may have, or that specific agreements, decisions or concerted practices have had, on competition in trade, (b) an explanation to the court of any relevant economic principles or the application of such principles in practice, where such an explanation would be of assistance to the judge or, as the case may be, the jury.

The purpose of this section is to ensure the admissibility of the expert evidence of economists in prosecutions under section 2 of the Act. Yet, the terms in which it is drafted, which mirror closely the common law requirements with regard to the admission of expert evidence, raise the question as to whether the section is in fact, superfluous. The evidence of economists is routinely admitted in civil cases regarding competition matters (see, for example, *Masterfoods Ltd. v. H.B. Ice Cream Ltd.* [1993] I.L.R.M. 145, 1992 Review 27-30) and it would seem as if such evidence would have been admissible in criminal prosecutions under section 2 even without section 4(1).

Section 4(2) goes on to provide that a court may, where in its opinion the interests of justice require it to so direct in the proceedings concerned, direct that evidence of a general or specific kind referred to subsection (1) shall not be admissible in proceedings for an offence under section 2 or shall be admissible in such proceedings for specified purposes only.

This subsection would seem to give the court a wider discretion to exclude expert evidence than exists at common law. At common law, a trial judge, as part of his duty to ensure that an accused receives a fair trial, has a discretion to exclude legally admissible evidence tendered by the prosecution where he is of opinion that its prejudicial effect on the jury would outweigh its probative value (*R. v. Sang* [1980] A.C. 402). Subsection (2) would seem to go further because the exclusionary discretion conferred thereby is not confined to expert evidence tendered by the prosecution. Also, the guiding criterion for the exercise of the discretion, namely, "the interests of justice" is broader than the idea of fairness to the accused. Thus, in appropriate circumstances, a trial judge could exclude expert evidence tendered by the defence under section 4 where he or she is of the opinion that the interests of justice require its exclusion. Undoubtedly, this jurisdiction will be sparingly exercised.

LEGAL PROFESSIONAL PRIVILEGE

In *Power City Ltd. v. Monahan*, High Court, October 14, 1996, the second and third named defendants sought to resist the discovery of a number of documents on the ground of legal professional privilege. The plaintiff's claim arose out of the theft of a consignment of hi-fi equipment while en route from the United Kingdom to Ireland. The plaintiff alleged that the theft occurred whilst the consignment was in the custody of the second or third named defendants and they were notified on October 6, 1992 that the plaintiff was holding them fully liable for all losses in connection with the theft. Privilege was therefore claimed by the second and third named defendants for a number of documents which came into existence after October 6 on the basis that from that point onwards, they believed that litigation would ensue.

Adjudicating on the claim of privilege, Kinlen J. approved and applied the decision in *Silver Hill Duckling Ltd. v. Minister for Agriculture* [1987] I.R. 289, which he said laid down the relevant principles. In that case, O'Hanlon J. held that a sustainable claim under the heading of legal professional privilege may be made in respect of a wider category of documents than the conventional communications passing between a client and his legal adviser in contemplation of litigation. Thus, privilege can be claimed for documents, the dominant purpose for the genesis of which, is preparation for litigation then apprehended or threatened.

One of the documents at issue in the case, No.59, was a letter written by the solicitors acting on behalf of the second and third named defendants to the Superintendent of Store Street Garda Station and Document No.65 was his reply. Although, these documents came into existence after the contemplation of litigation, this was not in itself, the only deciding factor. Kinlen J. cited the dictum of Costello J. (as he then was) in *Tromso Sparebank v. Beirne (No.2)* [1989] I.L.R.M. 257 (1988 Review 331-4), that "the Rules of Court are designed to further the rules of justice and they should be construed by the Court so that they assist in the achievement of this end". These documents could possibly be discovered by an order for third party discovery against the Superintendent or produced at the trial by a *subpoena duces tecum*. Thus, the matter was finely balanced, but, with some hesitation, he held the documents to be privileged on the grounds not merely that the correspondence was subsequent to the threat of proceedings but also on the basis that they would have had no reason for their existence save for the purpose of preparing a defence.

It should be noted that although the Superintendent could not have resisted discovery or production on the basis of the defendant's privilege (*Schneider v. Leigh* [1953] 2 Q.B. 195), the defendants themselves could have objected to disclosure by him on the grounds of privilege. Therefore, the relevance of the observation that an order for third party discovery could have been made against the Superintendent or a *subpoena duces tecum* issued is not entirely clear.

Another document which gave rise to difficulties was No.88. This was a fax message from a solicitor, on behalf of the second and third named defendants to their insurer's representatives, dated October 19, 1992, made with a view to the insurers dealing with any response to be made to the letters from the plaintiff. In dealing with the question of whether this document was privileged, counsel had referred to a note of a judgment of Dixon J. in (1949) 83 I.L.T.S.J. 103, in which he had held that a notice of accident form sent by an insured person to an insurance company was not privileged. Kinlen J., who received this note *de bene esse*, pointed out that it was not binding on the Court as it was not a law report. Thus, it could not be regarded as having been cited but only as having been adopted as part of the arguments. In any event, he was of opinion that Document No.88 differed from the document mentioned in the note as it was directly involved with the question as to what response should be made to letters from the claimants. He therefore, held that the document was privileged.

PUBLIC INTEREST IMMUNITY

Walker v. Ireland, High Court, [1997] 1 I.L.R.M. 363, raises the issue of public interest immunity in the context of inter-state communications. The case arose out of the delay in extraditing Father Brendan Smyth to Northern Ireland for alleged sexual offences involving minors. The plaintiff who was one of the alleged victims of these offences claimed that she had suffered personal injury, including psychiatric injury and mental distress, by reason of a negligent delay on the part of the Attorney General's office in processing the extradition request.

On a motion for full and better discovery by the plaintiff, public interest immunity was claimed by the defendants for a number of documents on the basis that they were supplied to the Irish Attorney General by the Attorney General for the United Kingdom and Northern Ireland on a confidential basis for the limited purpose of allowing the Irish Attorney General to decide whether to back the warrants for extradition. It was further claimed that public disclosure of such documents would be prejudicial to the proper and effective operation of the extradition arrangements between the two States and that if the claim of privilege (immunity) was not upheld, the free flow of information and consequently the effective operation of the extradition procedure would be seriously inhibited.

This was the first case in which the principles applicable to communications between sovereign states had arisen and in the absence of direct Irish authority on the point, Geoghegan J. had recourse to the English decision of *Buttes Gas and Oil Co. v. Hammer* [1981] 1 Q.B. 223. In that case, the Court of Appeal had refused to subscribe to the argument that an absolute public interest privilege attached to confidential communications between states. Having regard to the provisions of the Irish Constitution, Geoghegan J. said that there was an even stronger case in this jurisdiction for not countenancing any form of absolute privilege in relation to communications passing between sovereign states. He therefore proceeded to apply the principles laid down in *Murphy v. Dublin Corporation* [1972] I.R. 215 and *Ambiorix Ltd. v. Minister for the Environment (No.1)* [1992] 1 I.R. 277, [1992] I.L.R.M. 209.

The learned judge accepted, as a general proposition, that documents in connection with an extradition request would be assumed by both States to be confidential and that there was a public interest in the State maintaining that confidentiality as far as possible. However, that interest had to balanced against the public interest in having all relevant evidence before the Court for the purposes of the litigation.

Having read the documents, he came to the conclusion that the balance of public interest lay in favour of disclosure. In arriving at this view, he attached importance to four factors: (i) the criminal proceeding to which the action related had long been disposed of; (ii) the State had failed to discharge the onus on it of establishing that there was a greater public interest in non-disclosure; (iii) there was no evidence before the Court of any objection by the office of the Attorney General of Northern Ireland to the production of the documents; and (iv) while it would be understandable that both this State and the United Kingdom would want, as a matter of principle, to maintain the role of confidentiality in relation to such documentation, it was difficult to see any particular reason why the government of the United Kingdom would be concerned about the production of the particular documents sought to be produced in the case.

This case demonstrates once more how difficult it is to succeed in a claim of public interest immunity. It is not enough, as Geoghegan J. pointed out, to merely assert an expectation of confidentiality. To accept this as a basis for the claim would be to raise the spectre of a 'class claim' because that expectation of confidentiality would apply to all documents of this type (see the comments of Keane J. in *Breathnach v. Ireland (No.3)* [1993] 2 I.R. 458, 1991 Review 341-2). Therefore, it is necessary for the party raising the claim to point to some *particular* injury to the public interest which will be occasioned by disclosure and this the State failed to do.

IDENTIFICATION PARADES

In *The People (Director of Public Prosecutions) v. Maples*, Court of Criminal Appeal, February 26, 1996, the Court rejected the argument that there is a constitutional right to the holding of an identification parade.

The accused, who was suspected of involvement in a bank robbery, had been arrested pursuant to section 30 of the Offences Against the State Act 1939. Despite being handed a document which outlined the procedural safeguards, including his right to have a solicitor present, attendant upon the holding of an identification parade, the accused declined to take part in a parade. Thereafter, the gardaí made arrangements for informal identification. Three witnesses identified him outside the Circuit Court at Chancery Place on one date and another witness identified him at the same place on another occasion. A garda who was in the vicinity of the bank on the day of the robbery also identified the accused at in informal identification parade which was held in Store Street garda station when 9 or 10 people were led through a room.

The conviction of the applicant was challenged on the ground, *inter alia*, that the trial judge had erred in law in admitting evidence of the informal identification of the accused because it was not preceded by a clear and intelligent waiver by him, founded on a warning that his failure to stand on a formal parade might lead to an informal identification taking place. The argument was made that although there is no obligation on the gardaí to hold an identification parade in all circumstances, when they do hold a formal identification parade, it must be conducted in accordance with fair procedures. The corollary of this requirement of fair procedures was that it should have been explained to the accused that if he did not stand on the identification parade, then as happened in the instant case, recourse might be had to informal identification and so he might come to be identified in less favourable circumstances. Thus, it was submitted that there is a constitutional right to a formal identification parade and before that right can be waived, the consequences of such waiver must be explained to an accused so that he or she can give a full and free consent to the waiver.

The Court declined to hold that there was any constitutional right to the holding of an identification parade. Instead, it characterised the holding of a parade as a police procedure which, once embarked upon, must be carried out in accordance with fair procedures. O'Flaherty J. quoted his previous comments in *The People (Director of Public Prosecutions) v. O'Reilly* [1990] 2 I.R. 415 (1990 Review 207-9), that if a suspect refuses to take part in an identification parade or attempts to frustrate the parade, then he may have to live with the consequences. Thus, there is a limit, which had been reached in this case, as to what is to be expected of investigating officers in the way of explaining a suspect's options to him.

Due to the terms in which the Court construed the applicant's submission, the ultimate conclusion of the Court is unsurprising. However, there is considerably more merit to the applicant's submission than the judgment of the Court would seem to indicate. Decisions of the Supreme Court in cases such as *The People (Director of Public Prosecutions) v. Healy* [1990] 2 I.R. 73, [1990] I.L.R.M. 313 (1989 Review 137-9) and *The People (Director of Public Prosecutions) v. Hoey* [1988] I.L.R.M. 666 (1987 Review 124-5), indicate a commitment to a conception of the suspect in custody as an autonomous individual who is to be empowered to make free and fully informed decisions as to whether to co-operate with the gardaí or not. To hold that a suspect has a right to be informed of the consequences of refusal to participate in an identification parade is not to create a constitutional right to the holding of an identification parade but to recognise that, contrary to the comments of O'Flaherty J. in *O'Reilly*, fair procedures are to be accorded to both the co-operative and the non co-operative alike. If a suspect is to lose the benefit of a procedure conducted in accordance with the requirements of due process, then it is submitted that the consequences of that decision should be drawn to his or her attention.

During the course of its judgment, the Court made two observations in support of its conclusion that there was no obligation on the gardaí in the circumstances of the case to go any further in explaining the consequences of a failure to participate in a formal identification parade. Firstly, it was stated that any such intimation might have been construed as a threat or inducement by an accused. With respect, this is a specious point. Informing an accused of the consequences of non-compliance, while coercive to a certain degree, is surely fairer than not informing an accused and then making arrangements for informal identification in circumstances which are prejudicial to his or her interests.

Secondly, it was pointed out that the accused had the benefit of legal advice from his solicitor on at least one occasion prior to the invitation to stand on the identification parade and he knew how that parade would be conducted. This is true but there is nothing in the judgment to suggest that the accused actually discussed participation with his solicitor or that he consulted his solicitor *after* the request to take part in a parade. In such circumstances, it cannot be said that the accused made a free and fully informed decision not to take part in a parade. He may well have been labouring under the misapprehension, uncorrected by either the gardaí or his solicitor, that if he did not consent to the holding of a parade, no identification could be made.

THE RIGHT TO SILENCE

Constitutional status In *Heaney and McGuinness v. Ireland*, [1996] 1 I.R. 580, [1997] 1 I.L.R.M. 117, the plaintiffs challenged the constitutionality of section 52 of the Offences Against the State Act 1939. Section 52(1) provides that where a person is detained under Part IV of the Act, a member of the Garda Síochána may demand of such person, at any time while he is so detained, a full account of such person's movements and actions during any specified period and all information in his possession in relation to the commission or intended commission by another person of any offence under any section of the Act or any scheduled offence. Under section 52(2), it is an offence to fail or refuse to give such an account or information or to give an account or information which is false or misleading.

The background to the case was that the two plaintiffs were arrested under section 30 of the Offences Against the State Act 1939 on suspicion of being members of the I.R.A. and having been involved in the bombing of a British Army checkpoint in County Derry. While in detention, they were asked, pursuant to section 52 of the 1939 Act, to account for their movements. Both of the them refused to do so and they were convicted of an offence under section 52. They subsequently issued a plenary summons claiming that the section 52 was unconstitutional because, *inter alia*, it infringed their right to silence.

In a judgment, delivered by O'Flaherty J., the Supreme Court upheld the determination of Costello J. (as he then was) [1994] 3 I.R. 593, [1994] 2 I.L.R.M. 420 (1994 Review 128-33) that section 52 was not unconstitutional but the reasoning of the Court differs significantly from that of the High Court.

The first point of departure is that in the High Court, Costello J. had identified the guarantee of a fair trial contained in Article 38.1 as the *locus* of the right to silence. However, the Supreme Court expressly reserved the question of whether Article 38 was applicable in a case such as this. The Court accepted that what happens in the pre-trial period may have an adverse effect on the due course of a trial. However, it was of opinion that nothing touching on the due course of a trial arose as a result of the failure to answer questions because that failure constituted a separate and distinct offence.

Instead, drawing on the idea of correlative rights adopted in *Education Company of Ireland Ltd. v. Fitzpatrick (No.2)* [1961] I.R. 345, the Court preferred to rest its decision on "the proposition that the right to silence is but a corollary to the freedom of expression that is conferred by Article 40" (at 585, 123).

The Court then proceeded to consider whether section 52 impermissibly infringed this constitutionally protected right to silence. Attention was drawn to the qualifying language in Article 40 which states that the guarantee of freedom of expression is subject to public order and morality and it was stated that these restrictions also apply to the correlative right to silence. Therefore, the State is entitled to encroach on the right of the citizen to remain silent in pursuit of its entitlement to maintain peace and order. The question for the consideration of the Court was whether the power given to the Garda Síochána by the section is proportionate to the objects to be achieved by the legislation i.e. a test of proportionality had to be applied.

O'Flaherty J. identified the competing policy considerations. On the one hand, constitutional rights must be construed in such a way as to give life and reality to what is guaranteed. On the other hand, the interest of the State in maintaining public order must be respected and protected. He concluded that "there is a proper proportionality in the provision between any infringement of the citizen's rights with the entitlement of the State to protect itself" (at 590, 128).

Perhaps one of the most striking aspects of the decision is the *de facto* rejection by the Court of Article 38.1 in favour of Article 40.6.1.i as the *locus* of the right to silence. This is a surprising conclusion especially given that the arguments of the plaintiffs centred on Article 38.1 and it is submitted that the reasoning of the Court is unsatisfactory for a number of reasons.

In the first place, Article 38.1 would seem to be the more natural repository of the right to silence because most of the justifications for the right are based on the direct or indirect effect of the absence of such a right on the fairness of the trial process. It is noteworthy that in *Funke v. France*, Series A, No. 256-A, (1993) 16 E.H.R.R. 297, the European Court of Human Rights located the right to silence in the guarantee of a fair trial contained in Article 6(1) of the European Convention on Human Rights.

Secondly, it seems somewhat artificial to draw a distinction between the admission of statements obtained in breach of the right to silence and a prosecution to enforce a penalty for exercise of that right. Once it is acknowledged that a pre-trial right to silence exists, then it seems somewhat semantic not to invoke Article 38.1 merely because the plaintiffs were not in fact coerced to make potentially incriminating statements. The fact that section 52 was ineffective in this particular case to achieve its desired effect does not take the case outside the ambit of Article 38.1. Again, it is worth contrasting the decision in *Funke* in which it was held that the applicant's pre-trial right to silence had been infringed by his prosecution for failure to disclose documents.

Thirdly, the decision of the Supreme Court raises the prospect of a bifurcation in the protection of the right to silence. Will subsequent cases be taken pursuant to Article 38 or Article 40 or both? And will there be any difference in the principles applicable to each? It was probably in order to avoid such a bifurcation and its consequential problems that Costello J. in the High Court rejected the argument that the right to silence was also an unspecified personal right protected by Article 40.3.1.

Fourthly, by locating the right to silence in Article 40.6.1.i, the Supreme Court would appear to have overruled, *sub silentio*, a line of authority to the effect that the guarantee of free expression is restricted to the protection of convictions and opinions and does not extend to the dissemination of factual information (see *Attorney General v. Paperlink* [1984] I.L.R.M. 373, *Kearney v. Minister for Justice* [1986] I.R. 116 and *Oblique Financial Services Ltd. v. The Promise Production Co. Ltd.* [1994] 1 I.L.R.M. 74, 1993 Review 285-7). Instead, it was held by Costello J. (as he then was) in *Paperlink* that the right to communicate factual information is protected by Article 40.3.1.

One significant consequence of the decision to proceed under the aegis of the guarantee of freedom of expression is that it greatly increases the potential ambit of the privilege against self-incrimination. This is because Article 38.1 guarantees the conduct of *criminal* trials in due course of law and thus, has no application to civil trials. Article 40.6.1.i is not so limited and therefore, the right to silence may also apply in civil proceedings. This could potentially have implications for the various inquisitorial powers granted to, *inter alia*, liquidators and examiners but, as we shall see, it seems somewhat unlikely that any of these powers will fall foul of the right to silence.

This is because the most notable feature of *Heaney* is the lack of enthusiasm displayed by the Court for the right to silence. In his judgment, O'Flaherty J. cited the dictum of Lord Mustill in *R. v. Director of Serious Fraud Office, Ex p. Smith* [1993] A.C. 1, at 40, that "statutory interference with the right is almost as old as the right itself" and proceeded to catalogue, without any apparent doubt as to their constitutional validity, a number of statutory provisions which evinced "a legislative intent to abrogate, to various extents, the right to silence, in a myriad of contrasting circumstances" (at 588, 126). Thus, in an apparent reversal in the normal order of constitutional adjudication, it would appear that legislative encroachment sets the parameters of a right rather than the other way around.

The source of this disenchantment with the right is not difficult to identify. O'Flaherty J. noted a dichotomy between the absolute entitlement to silence as against the entitlement to remain silent when to answer would give rise to self-incrimination. He went on to say that (at 586, 124):

> Where a person is totally innocent of wrongdoing as regards his movements, it would require a strong attachment to one's apparent constitutional rights not to give such an account when asked pursuant to statutory requirement. So, the court holds, that the matter in debate here, can more properly be approached as an encroachment against the right not to have to say anything that might afford evidence that is self-incriminating.

Again, in justifying the conclusion of the Court that section 52 was proportional, he stated that (at 590, 125-6):

> ... the innocent person has nothing to fear from giving an account of his

or her movements, even though on grounds of principle, or in the assertion of constitutional rights, such a person may wish to take a stand. However, the Court holds that the *prima facie* entitlement of citizens to take such a stand must yield to the right of the State to protect itself. *A fortiori*, the entitlement of those with something relevant to disclose concerning the commission of a crime to remain mute must be regarded as of a lesser order.

In both of these passages, the Court appears to echo the Benthamite view that the right to silence is one which only benefits the guilty. Viewed in these terms, it is not surprising that section 52 was found not to infringe the right. Indeed, if this is really is the view of the Court, then the test of proportionality is likely to provide facile protection for the right.

In conclusion, it can be said that whilst the decision of the Court in *Heaney* elevates the right to silence to the constitutional plane, at the same time it gives at least an amber light to its curtailment on the grounds of the public interest in the detection of crime and prosecution of offenders.

Section 7 of the Criminal Justice (Drug Trafficking) Act 1996   The decision in *Heaney* sets the backdrop for the most recent legislative curtailment of the right to silence, section 7 of the Criminal Justice (Drug Trafficking) Act 1996. This section is important, not only in its own right, but also because it is very likely to provide the template for further restrictions on the right to silence.

Section 7(1) provides that where in any proceedings against a person for a drug trafficking offence, evidence is given that the accused on being questioned, charged, or informed that he or she might be prosecuted, failed to mention any fact relied on in his or her defence in those proceedings, being a fact which in the circumstances existing at the time he or she could reasonably have been expected to mention, the court (or, subject to the judge's directions, the jury) in determining whether the accused is guilty of the offence charged, may draw such inferences from the failure as appear proper. The subsection also provides that such failure may, on the basis of such inferences, be treated as corroboration of any evidence in relation to which the failure is material, but that a person shall not be convicted of an offence solely on an inference to be drawn from such failure. Section 7(2) further stipulates that inferences may not be drawn unless the accused was told in ordinary language when being questioned, charged or informed, what the effect of such failure might be.

The first question is whether this section would pass constitutional muster in the aftermath of *Heaney* and the answer must surely be an unequivocal yes. In view of the seriousness of the crimes involved, and the indirect nature of the interference with the right to silence, it seems unlikely that the section would not be held to be proportional.

This conclusion is reinforced by the decision in *Rock v. Ireland*, Unreported, High Court, November 10, 1995 (1995 Review, 182, 243), which was handed down in the interim between the High Court and Supreme Court judgments in *Heaney*. At issue in *Rock* was the constitutionality of sections 18 and 19 of the Criminal Justice Act 1984. These antecedents to section 7 are drafted in very similar terms and allow adverse inferences to be drawn from the failure of the accused to account for objects, substances or marks or the failure of the accused to account for his presence at a particular place respectively. Murphy J. was of the view that these sections were less draconian than section 52 and, following the decision of Costello J. in *Heaney*, dismissed the contention that they were unconstitutional.

A more difficult question is whether this section is compatible with the European Convention of Human Rights but again a tentative answer of yes is ventured. In *Murray v. United Kingdom* (1996) 22 E.H.R.R. 29, a challenge to the conviction of the applicant which was based in part on adverse inferences drawn from his pre-trial silence and his failure to testify at trial pursuant to provisions of the Criminal Evidence (N.I.) Order, 1988, was rejected. The European Court of Human Rights accepted that the drawing of inferences from silence involves "a certain level of indirect compulsion" but endorsed the opinion of the Commission that the provisions of the 1988 Order merely constituted "a formalised system which aims to allow common sense implications to play an open role in the assessment of evidence".

However, this decision should not be viewed as granting a blanket imprimatur to provisions of this type. In the circumstances of the case, the Court was of opinion that the inferences drawn were not unfair or unreasonable but stressed that:

> Whether the drawing of adverse inferences from an accused's silence infringes Article 6 is a matter to be determined in the light of all the circumstances of the case, having particular regard to the situations where inferences may be drawn, the weight attached to them by the national courts in their assessment of the evidence and the degree of compulsion inherent in the situation.

Therefore, it is possible that in an appropriate case, a challenge to a conviction based upon inferences drawn pursuant to section 7 might succeed. This is a factor which should be borne in mind by the courts in considering the construction and application of the section because of the presumption that Irish law is in conformity with the Convention (see *Desmond v. Glackin* [1992] I.L.R.M. 490).

In analysing the section, the first point to note is that it specifies that an inference may be drawn if the accused *at any time* while being questioned failed to mention any fact relied on in his or her defence. Similar wording was construed in the Northern Ireland case of *R. v. McLernon*, Belfast Crown Court, December 20, 1990, to mean that an inference may be drawn not only where an accused fails to disclose the fact relied on at any point during questioning but also where he or she initially fails to mention the fact but does so at a later stage of questioning.

The fact in question must be one *relied on* by the accused in his or her defence. The most obvious way in which a fact may be relied upon is where evidence as to the existence of that fact is given either by the accused or a witness called on his or her behalf. However, this is not the only way in which a fact may be relied upon. In *R. v. McLernon* [1992] N.I.J.B. 41, it was hypothesised by the Northern Ireland Court of Appeal that a fact would be relied upon where counsel for the defence suggested it to a prosecution witness in the course of cross-examination and it was accepted by that witness. Another decision of the Court of Appeal, *R. v. Devine*, Northern Ireland Court of Appeal, May 13, 1992, goes even further in indicating that it may be enough to suggest a fact even if it is not accepted by the witness. It seems clear, however, that an inference cannot be drawn where the defence does not rely on any particular fact but merely puts the prosecution on proof of its case.

The fact must be one which the accused could reasonably have been expected to mention at the time when he or she was questioned, charged or informed. This requirement of reasonableness seems to be directed at distinguishing 'tactical' from 'non-tactical' reasons for silence. Non-tactical reasons for failure to mention a fact would include confusion, intoxication, embarrassment, fear, desire to shield another, or perhaps a desire to conceal improper or immoral conduct. Also pertinent will be the importance of the fact to the accused's defence. An accused will be expected to mention matters which are central to his or her defence but will not be expected to have mentioned every fact relied on in that defence.

A contentious issue is whether an inference can be drawn if a suspect fails to mention facts because of the advice of his solicitor not to say anything. On the one hand, it might be argued that the section is clearly intended to curtail the right to silence and to allow a suspect to act on legal advice counselling silence would defeat the object of the section. On the other hand, the right of a suspect to receive legal advice is constitutionally protected. It would seem to follow that he or she should be able to act on that legal advice without being penalised for doing so.

In *R. v. Connolly and McCartney*, Belfast Crown Court, June 5, 1992, the view was expressed that legal advice to remain silent would not render reasonable, a failure to mention a fact which was objectively unreasonable. Thus, the view of the Northern Ireland courts would seem to be that it is the duty of a solicitor to inform his client of the consequences of remaining silent and that if the solicitor, in error, counsels silence this is no impediment to the drawing of adverse inferences.

A related issue is whether an inference may be drawn from the refusal of a suspect to speak before seeing a solicitor. In *R. v. Quinn*, Northern Ireland Court of Appeal, September 17, 1993, it was held that an inference could be drawn in such circumstances but whether the Irish courts would adopt this approach is open to question. In *The People (Director of Public Prosecutions) v. Healy* [1990] 2 I.R. 73, [1990] I.L.R.M. 313 (1989 Review 137-9), it was stressed by Finlay C.J. that the right to a solicitor was directed towards ensuring that a suspect in custody is aware of his rights and has the independent advice necessary in order for him to make a free and informed decision as to whether to make a statement, be it exculpatory or inculpatory. If this is the case, then surely a suspect cannot be penalised for waiting until he or she has obtained such legal advice before deciding to make a statement?

Where the foregoing conditions are satisfied, the tribunal of fact is permitted, though not obliged, to draw such inferences as appear proper. No guidance is provided as to what is a 'proper inference' but it appears from the decisions of the House of Lords in *R. v. Murray* [1994] 1 W.L.R. 1, and the Privy Council in *Haw Tua Tua v. Public Prosecutor* [1982] A.C. 136 that this question is to be answered by applying ordinary common sense in the circumstances of the particular case. and that in appropriate circumstances, a direct inference of guilt will be

One point of particular difficulty is whether an inference of guilt is a proper inference within the meaning of the section. Such an inference would appear to be open on the wording of the section. It provides that the court may draw such inferences from the failure of the accused to mention a fact relied on in his or her defence as appear proper in determining *inter alia* whether the accused is guilty of the offence charged and in *Murray* it was held by the House of Lords that a direct inference of guilt could be drawn where appropriate.

Cross-examination and comment on the exercise of the right to silence In *The People (Director of Public Prosecutions) v. Maples*, Court of Criminal Appeal, February 26, 1996, the accused was convicted at the Dublin Circuit Criminal Court of robbery and firearms offences arising out of a bank robbery. He had been arrested under section 30 of the Offences Against the State Act 1939 but having consulted his solicitor, refused to answer any questions. He sought leave to appeal on the grounds, *inter alia*, that the trial was rendered unsatisfactory by questions put to him in cross-examination as to why he had stayed silent during questioning and failed to give an account of his whereabouts on the date of the offence.

The Court, in a judgment delivered by O'Flaherty J., rejected this ground of appeal. While, it was of the opinion that the cross-examination was misconceived and did not serve any useful purpose, the Court was unable to detect that any injustice had resulted from it. Counsel had belatedly objected on the grounds that the accused had been cautioned as to his right to silence and couldn't be questioned as to his reasons for exercising that right and could have done so at an earlier stage.

The Court also rejected a challenge to the charge of the trial judge who, after a requisition was raised as to this matter, said to the jury:

> Likewise when he is being questioned, he is given a legal caution which stressed the fact that he is entitled to refuse to answer questions but you are entitled to *note* the fact that when questions were put to him that he did not make any answer. (emphasis added)

This direction was impugned on the ground that the jury might read more into the judge's invitation to note the accused's silence. However, the Court felt itself unable to put that construction on these words and was of opinion that "words should be taken to mean what they say".

In this case, the line of cross-examination pursued by the prosecution was designed to imply that an innocent man who had nothing to hide would not have declined to account for his whereabouts. Yet, such a suggestion completely undercuts the accused's exercise of his constitutional right to silence. If an accused has such a right, then it would seem to follow that he or she may not be penalised for the exercise of that right by having adverse inferences drawn therefrom, at least in the absence of a statutory provision to that effect. The prejudicial effect of the prosecution questioning was compounded by the invitation of the trial judge to the jury to 'note' the accused's exercise of his right to silence.

This decision should be contrasted with that of the Court in *The People (Attorney General) v. Saunders and Jasinski* (1963) 1 Frewen 283. In that case, the trial judge commented on the attitude of one of the accused, Saunders, when confronted with stolen goods as follows:

> She did not say 'we bought them' or 'I am surprised' or 'better ask Jasinski'. But remember this does not prove her guilty. But they are things you are entitled to take into consideration. Consider and examine them.

Relying on its previous decision in *Attorney General v. Durnan (No.2)* [1934] I.R. 540, the Court of Criminal Appeal was of the view that these remarks to the jury might have caused them to believe that Saunders was under an obligation to say something of an exculpatory nature. The Court pointed out that she was fully entitled to remain silent because of the caution given, and said that such silence should not have been adversely commented upon. Therefore, the observations made by the trial judge amounted to a misdirection in law, and her conviction was quashed on this ground. Other cases, including *The People (Attorney General) v. Trayers* [1956] I.R. 110, indicate that the discretion of a trial judge to comment on silence must be "discretely exercised".

A caveat to this criticism of *Maples* is that the holding of the Court of Criminal Appeal in this case may well be supported by the decision of the Supreme Court in *Heaney*. It has already been suggested that the Supreme Court in *Heaney* adopted an essentially negative attitude to the right to silence. It may be therefore, that the boundaries of permissible comment on the exercise of the right have been extended by that decision. If, as the Supreme Court seemed to do in *Heaney*, the view is taken that the right to silence is one which is only availed of by the guilty, then pointing out that an innocent person would not have exercised his or her right to silence in the circumstances of the case may well be permissible.

RIGHT TO A SOLICITOR

Barry v. Waldron, High Court, *ex tempore*, May 23, 1996, concerned an *habeas corpus* application by the applicant who was being detained at the time under section 4 of the Criminal Justice Act 1984. During the course of his *ex tempore* judgment, Carney J. made a number of comments pertaining to the right to a solicitor and the nature of detention.

Dealing with the issue of the applicant's right to a solicitor, Carney J. stated that the right is one of reasonable access and that a suspect does not have a right to have his solicitor present during questioning. His comments thus confirm that the decision in *The People (Director of Public Prosecutions) v. Healy* [1990] 2 I.R. 73, [1990] I.L.R.M. 313 (1989 Review 137-9), which held that the right to a solicitor is constitutional in origin, did not alter the nature of the right and that it is still confined to a right of reasonable access.

The learned judge observed that in this case, the applicant and his solicitor had a 'game plan' that the applicant would refuse to answer any questions and invoke his right to silence. To this end, the presence of the applicant's solicitor, Mr. O'Sullivan

> . . . was required during the statutory period which could and did go on for a period of up to 12 hours, so that Dr. Barry could continue with his formula of saying that he asserted his right to silence and refused to answer any questions and he would be supported and succored (*sic*) and maintained in that position by Mr. O'Sullivan for the statutory period of detention. If he did not have the support of an independent person, he would probably not be able to maintain such a stance which does require a considerable deal of strength against people who are trained in interrogation techniques, and let us not be frightened of the word "interrogation" because that is what it is all about and that is what the Statute

provides for.

Here, we have a frank admission of why the right to a solicitor is restricted to one of reasonable access; if it were otherwise then suspects who were advised by their solicitors to remain silent would actually be in a position to do so, instead of succumbing to what the U.S. Supreme Court in *Miranda v. Arizona* 384 U.S. 436 (1966) termed the inherently coercive nature of interrogation. The observations of Carney J. thus represent a rare judicial acknowledgement of the essentially illusory nature of the right to silence of the suspect in custody.

DOCUMENTARY EVIDENCE

A issue as to the proof of handwriting was taken in *The People (Director of Public Prosecutions) v. Malocco*, Court of Criminal Appeal, May 23, 1996. The applicant in the case who had practised as a solicitor in the firm of Malocco & Killeen, was convicted of six counts of forging documents and uttering forged documents. One of the grounds of appeal advanced by the applicant was that the evidence of a number of witnesses purporting to identify the signature of the applicant on some of the documents should not have been admitted by the trial judge and that the signature of the applicant could only properly have been proved by the evidence of a handwriting expert. It was submitted that, in the absence of any expert evidence as to the signatures, the jury should have been warned by the trial judge of the dangers of acting on the evidence of the witnesses.

The Court rejected this ground of appeal as unsustainable. Each of the witnesses who identified the applicant's signature on the various documents testified in evidence that they were well acquainted with the applicant's handwriting and signature, and in any case, the applicant himself had acknowledged that it was his signature on the documents in question.

Reliance was also placed by the applicant on section 8 of the Criminal Procedure Act 1865 (Lord Denman's Act) which provides that:

> Comparison of a disputed writing with any writing provided to the satisfaction of the judge to be genuine shall be permitted to be made by witnesses: and such writings and the evidence of witnesses respecting the same may be submitted to the court and jury as evidence of the genuineness of otherwise of the writing in dispute.

Dealing with this section, the Court said that it was intended to provide a machinery for the determination of the authenticity of a disputed writing, requiring as a precondition that the trial judge should satisfy himself that a genuine specimen of the disputed handwriting has been proved, before allowing witnesses to give evidence as to the genuineness or otherwise of the disputed writing. It had no application in the circumstances of the case where there was abundant evidence, in the form of the evidence of witnesses familiar with the applicant's writing and of the applicant's own admissions to satisfy the jury beyond a reasonable doubt that the documents in question had been executed by the applicant.

The essential point about section 8 is that it is concerned with, and establishes the procedure to be employed in the *comparison* of handwriting. In this case, no such comparison was being made.

DUTY OF THE PROSECUTION TO DISCLOSE EVIDENCE

The extraordinary facts of *The People (Director of Public Prosecutions) v. Flannery*, Central Criminal Court, June 25, 1996, cast into sharp relief the importance of the duty on the prosecution and gardaí to disclose all relevant and material evidence to the defence. The case reveals a catalogue of suppression of evidence which calls to mind previous miscarriage of justice cases on both sides of the Irish Sea.

The accused was charged with the murder of Patrick O'Driscoll and the first indication of impropriety came when, after he had been returned for trial, his solicitor wrote to the Chief State Solicitor seeking copies of all relevant documents in the possession of the gardaí in addition to those disclosed in the Book of Evidence. In response, they furnished 24 statements obtained from witnesses who alleged that they had seen the deceased after the date when the murder was alleged to have occurred. None of these statements had been furnished to the Director of Public Prosecutions, either originally or at that point, and it appeared that they would not have been given to him if he had not asked for them.

At the trial, the case for the prosecution depended substantially on the testimony of Michael Flannery, a nephew of the accused. He gave evidence that in December 1994, he was present in the deceased's flat with the accused and his brother John. He stated that the Flannerys had gone upstairs to the accused's flat with a saw and a knife and that sometime later that night he was asked by the accused to assist in the removal of a coal sack and two bags from the accused's flat to John Flannery's car which was parked outside. He also testified that the accused had shown him a hand and a foot in a cupboard in his kitchen and that he travelled in the car to his grandmother's house where the bags were stored. On a later date, he had been brought by his two uncles to a field where he was informed that they intended to dig up the body of the deceased, then buried nearby under a lane or path, and re-bury it in the field.

However, the plan was aborted because the ground was found to be too soft.

The witness conceded in cross-examination that at all material times he had a drink and drugs problem which necessitated in-patient treatment in a detoxification unit at Garryvogue, Co. Cork in early 1995. However, he denied the use of hallucinatory drugs or magic mushrooms and stated that his drug intake was limited to alcohol, marijuana and valium.

During cross-examination, it was revealed for the first time, that he had told some friends about what had happened and that the gardaí had obtained statements from them. As a result of this disclosure, Superintendent Brennan, the officer in charge of the investigation, furnished statements taken from two friends of the witness, two fellow patients at the unit in Garryvogue, and a statement from a Fás teacher to whom the witness had also confided. These various accounts differed significantly from his testimony in court and from statements made by him to the gardaí, copies of which were contained in the Book of Evidence.

The trial judge, Barr J., was of opinion that these statements were of major importance to the defence and copies ought to have been furnished at least in response to the letter of the defence solicitor and in fact long before then. He also thought it obvious that these statements ought to have been furnished to the Director of Public Prosecutions. Although the information therein contained would not have been admissible (because it was hearsay), the statements were important to an assessment by the Director of the credibility of the information supplied by the witness.

Consequent upon this disclosure, Barr J. asked specifically and was assured on behalf of the garda investigators that there were no other relevant documents in their possession which had not been made available to the Director of Public Prosecutions. However, when the trial resumed, more documents were furnished by the gardaí including a report in the form of a letter from a Garda Lynch to one of the senior investigating officers, concerning an interview which he had had with a fellow patient of Flannery in Garryvogue called Mason. Mason stated that Flannery had given him and the other inmates a substantially different account of what had happened. He also said that Flannery had told them, contrary to his evidence, that he had taken acid or some other such hallucinatory drug on the day that he alleged that the murder had been carried out. Following receipt of this report, no step had been taken by the investigating team to interview Mason nor had Garda Lynch's report been furnished either to the defence or the Director of Public Prosecutions.

Superintendent Brennan, who gave evidence in the absence of the jury, sought to explain the failure to disclose these statements on the basis of gross incompetence and negligence and denied that there had been a conscious and deliberate policy to suppress and conceal this information from the defence and the Director of Public Prosecutions. However, Barr J. rejected these explanations, concluding that:

... there was a conscious and deliberate policy probably orchestrated by him and involving at least one other member of his team of investigators to subvert the course of justice in this trial by suppressing documents in the possession of the police, the contents of which cast doubt upon the validity and value of the evidence of Mr. Michael Flannery junior on which the prosecution depends to establish the State case against the accused.

He reached this conclusion on the basis that any experienced garda investigator, *a fortiori* a team of investigators, could not have failed to appreciate the far-reaching significance of the documents in question, not only to the defence lawyers but also to the Director of Public Prosecutions. He was fortified in this conclusion by the failure to interview Mason which he attributed to a desire on the part of Superintendent Brennan not to add another statement to the collection he already had which cast doubt on Flannery's version of events. There was also the "alarming evidence" of Michael Flannery in the course of cross-examination that he had been coached by a garda on how to deal with questions which might be put to him in cross-examination.

The next question was what course of action to take in the light of these revelations. Three alternatives were canvassed: (i) to continue with the trial, having allowed the defence an appropriate adjournment to provide time for further investigations in the light of the information which had been revealed; (ii) to declare a mistrial and adjourn the trial to take place at a later date before a new jury; or (iii) to direct the jury to acquit the accused or to permanently stay the indictment against the accused.

Barr J. rejected the first alternative as clearly untenable because the trial had been so tainted by the garda misconduct that it could not be satisfactorily retrieved. As between the second and third alternatives, he concluded that in the light of what had happened, the accused could not be assured of his constitutional right to a fair trial if a new trial were directed to taken place.

Two factors were of importance in reaching this conclusion. The first was that the "drip feed" emergence of documents during the trial and the explanations put forward by Superintendent Brennan to explain their non-disclosure, which he regarded as "bordering on the absurd", raised a significant doubt as to whether full disclosure had been or ever would be made by the investigating team. Secondly, the likelihood that Michael Flannery had been coached was not something which could be undone.

Therefore, he ordered that the case be withdrawn from the jury and the indictment against the accused stayed permanently, saying:

> The right of the citizen to a fair trial is a fundamental principle in a democratic society. Our courts have a duty under the Constitution to defend that right with the utmost vigor [*sic*]. The mendacious conduct of

> Superintendent Brennan and other police officers have grievously un-
> dermined the integrity and legality of the criminal process in this case. I
> am satisfied that irreparable harm has been done which militates against
> the accused's right to a fair trial now or at a future date.

This decision illustrates once more the desirability of legislation which would
place a statutory obligation on the prosecution to disclose any information
which it did not intend to use but which either undermined its case or helped
that of the defendant. It would also be necessary, in order to prevent a recurrence of a case such as *Flannery* where the policy of suppression was aimed at
the prosecution as well as the defence, to place a statutory obligation on the
gardaí to record and maintain information and material gathered in the course
of a criminal investigation and disclose all such information to the prosecution.

The English legislature has acted to pass legislation along these lines in
the Criminal Procedure and Investigations Act 1996 though some of the provisions contained therein, especially those relating to reciprocal discovery on
the part of the defence have proved controversial (for an analysis of the discovery provisions in the Act, see John Sprack, "The Criminal Procedure and
Investigations Act 1996: (1) The Duty of Disclosure" [1997] Crim.L.R. 308).

It is regrettable that in the absence of any comparable legislation in this
jurisdiction, the Court of Criminal Appeal in *The People (Director of Public
Prosecutions) v. Kavanagh*, Court of Criminal Appeal, February 26, 1996,
passed up the opportunity to issue guidelines on the duty of disclosure.

The applicant had been convicted of rape and other sexual offences in
respect of a minor. After the accused was convicted, the court of trial and the
defence were supplied with a copy of a report, prepared by a senior social
worker, which had apparently been furnished to one of the investigating garda
shortly after it had been compiled. The report contained an account of an
interview which the social worker had had with the complainant and there
were material differences between the story of the complainant as set out in
the report and the evidence which she had given at trial. The prosecution conceded that the report was relevant but gave no explanation as to why it had not
been disclosed in advance of the hearing.

The Court of Criminal Appeal, speaking *per* O'Flaherty J., stated that it
was "highly unfortunate" that the report had not been disclosed and was unable to conclude that the course of the trial might not have been altered significantly if the report had been available and questions asked arising from it.
Accordingly, the convictions of the applicant were quashed and a retrial ordered.

The Court was at pains to stress that it was not laying down any guidelines
as to what should be disclosed to the defence in advance of a hearing: "To say
that every statement in every possible circumstances should be made avail-

able to the defence in every case might place an impossible burden on the prosecution. Not everyone has the expertise in taking statements that members of the garda [*sic*] have".

Such judicial reluctance to enunciate guidelines is as disappointing as it is unwarranted. It is not contended that there is, or should be, an obligation on the gardaí to disclose every statement to the defence but they should be obliged to disclose all material evidence (defined in *R. v. Ward* [1993] 1 W.L.R. 619 as evidence which tends either to weaken the prosecution case or strengthen the defence case).

Such judicial reticence is not evident in two other cases decided in 1996, namely, *The People (Director of Public Prosecutions) v. Kelly*, Court of Criminal Appeal, 4 March 1996, and *Maher v. O'Donnell* [1996] 2 I.L.R.M. 321, both of which endorsed the decision of *R. v. Ward* [1993] 1 W.L.R. 619, in which the English Court of Appeal summarised the principles governing the disclosure of evidence by the prosecution before trial.

In *Kelly*, one of the grounds of appeal of the applicant who had been convicted on two counts of possession of drugs, was that he had been deprived of fair procedures by the manner in which the prosecution's fingerprint expert had carried out his duties.

It was submitted that the value of fingerprint evidence can be twofold. It can be used towards establishing the guilt of the accused, or alternatively, establishing the innocence of the accused. While it was accepted that the fingerprints found on the bag containing the drugs failed to disclose a sufficient number of characteristics to enable the fingerprints to be used for positive identification of the applicant, it was argued that there was an onus upon the prosecution to make such evidence as it did have available to the applicant for his use and the mere fact that it did not support the prosecution case was no reason for disregarding the evidence.

The Court of Criminal Appeal accepted counsel's summary of the obligations which are cast on the prosecution and the decision in *Ward* as laying down principles which would be accepted in this jurisdiction. However, it was pointed out that the submission of the applicant suffered from a fundamental fallacy in that all the expert found were 'smudges' which had no value as fingerprints. Accordingly, they could not be of assistance either in helping the prosecution to establish the guilt of the applicant or in helping the defence in establishing his innocence. That being so, the applicant had not been deprived of any material evidence in the case.

Counsel for the applicant also submitted that there is an obligation on the prosecution to retain and make available to the defence all permanent records and material created during the course of the fingerprint examination and that a failure on the part of the prosecution to make available this material constitutes a denial of fair procedures. The Court accepted as a general principle that there is an obligation upon the prosecution to make such material available if it exists. But there must be evidence that it does exist and in this case, there was no evidence that any such material existed.

Furthermore, the bag had at all stages been available to the defence and the defence's fingerprint expert had an opportunity of examining the bag for the purpose of observing the smudges. Therefore, the Court could not identify any area in which there had been any material irregularity in the course of the prosecution.

The decision in *Ward* was also endorsed in *Maher v. O'Donnell*, a case in which Laffoy J. made the important point that the duty on the prosecution is one of disclosure and is therefore, directed towards evidence of which the accused is not already aware.

The applicant in the case sought an order of certiorari quashing his conviction on the ground that he had been tried otherwise than in due course of law because of (i) the failure of the Director of Public Prosecutions to furnish to the defence on request the statements of all material witnesses and, (ii) the failure of the Director of Public Prosecutions to adduce in court all material witnesses or to make available to the applicant such material witnesses that were not being called by him.

In dealing with these contentions, Laffoy J. referred to the decision of the Supreme Court in *Director of Public Prosecutions v. Doyle* [1994] 2 I.R. 286, [1994] 1 I.L.R.M. 529 (1994 Review, 210-11) and pointed out that the underlying rationale of the proposition that the interests of justice may necessitate that the accused be furnished before his trial with statements and other documents is that the accused is entitled, in advance of his trial, to adequate information of the accusations against him and the case he has to meet and any matters which might affect his defence.

In this case, the applicant was aware of all the facts recorded in the documents sought. Therefore, no injustice was perpetrated by the failure to produce those documents to the applicant before the trial. Further, in relation to the failure of the prosecution to call a particular garda witness or to have him available in court to give evidence, that witness would only have given evidence of matters of which the applicant was aware. Even assuming that the witness's testimony would have strengthened the applicant's defence, in order to sustain the claim that, by reason of the non-attendance of that witness, the applicant was deprived of a trial in due course of law, the applicant would have to establish that there was a duty on the prosecution to procure the garda's attendance in court and the applicant had failed to establish that the prosecution was under such a duty. The non-attendance of the garda witness, whom the accused expected to attend was a mere 'mishap', which if not remedied by the adjournment of the trial, should be sought to be remedied by way of appeal, not by way of certiorari.

In the course of her judgment, Laffoy J. endorsed the principles laid down in *Ward* that where the prosecution have taken a statement from a person whom they know can give material evidence but decide not to call him as a witness, they are under a duty to make that person available as a witness for the defence. This duty is performed, unless there are good reasons for not doing so, by supplying copies of the witness statements to the defence or allowing them to inspect the statements and make copies, or, where there are good reasons for not supplying copies, by supplying the name and address of the witness to the defence.

Therefore, it is clear that the duty placed upon the prosecution is confined to one of disclosure. The criminal justice system retains its adversarial character to the extent that it is not the duty or function of the prosecution to make the defence's case for it. Thus, provided that the defence have been apprised that a witness may have material evidence to give, the obligation of calling that witness to give evidence falls upon the defence and not upon the prosecution.

The duty is a continuing one It is clear from the decision in *The People (Director of Public Prosecutions) v. Scannell*, Court of Criminal Appeal, June 18, 1996, that the duty of disclosure on the prosecution is a continuing one and therefore the prosecution must provide the defence with any material evidence in its possession as soon as it comes into its possession.

The applicant had been convicted on two counts of raping and falsely imprisoning a woman. One of the grounds of appeal was that the complainant gave evidence during the trial of oral intercourse although her statement included in the Book of Evidence made no mention of this. The prosecution had been in possession of an additional statement made by the applicant in which an account was given of oral intercourse having taken place, for over a month before the trial. However, this statement had never been furnished to the defence, although the solicitor for the applicant had written to the Chief State Solicitor and specifically requested the prosecution to furnish the defence with any additional statements prior to the trial.

After the complainant gave evidence of oral intercourse, an application was made by counsel for the applicant for the discharge of the jury on the ground that he had no notice of this evidence. However, the trial judge held that the essential issue in the case was whether sexual intercourse had taken place without the consent of the complainant, the evidence as to the oral intercourse was part of one incident and it was not necessary, in the circumstances to discharge the jury. He thus adjourned the trial for an hour and a half to enable the prosecution to serve the defence with a formal notice of additional evidence and to give the defence time to consider that evidence.

The Court of Criminal Appeal took the view that the course adopted by the trial judge amounted to a breach of fair procedures. It was held that having regard to the gravity of the charges against the applicant, it was of the utmost importance that he and those advising him were fully aware before the trial began of the account of the events on that night given by the complainant to the Gardaí and which, it should have been anticipated, would be the account given by her in the witness box. The failure of the prosecution to furnish them with an additional statement by the complainant which contained significant new material of which the defence was unaware was a breach of the fair procedures to which the applicant was entitled.

While there are cases in which the presentation of evidence at the trial additional to that contained in the book of evidence may be permitted without unfairly prejudicing the defence, this was not such a case. Thus, the appropriate course would have been for the trial judge to discharge the jury and the conviction of the applicant was quashed and a retrial ordered.

Discovery in criminal proceedings   In *The People (Director of Public Prosecutions) v. Flynn and Keely* [1996] 1 I.L.R.M. 317, the accused were charged with conspiracy to defraud a company ALH which was a subsidiary of the notice party, Aer Lingus. The defence of the accused was that the acts alleged to constitute the fraud were done with the consent of, and pursuant to a policy approved by, ALH. Keely alleged that investigations by his solicitor had turned up a record of a garda interview with the managing director of ALH, which was a vital document and had not been disclosed to him, that one vital witness was not going to testify, and that others had suffered failures of recollection. He therefore argued that discovery of certain specified classes of documents was necessary. The Director of Public Prosecutions contended that he had taken all reasonable steps to secure disclosure of information to the accused.

Judge Moriarty in the Dublin Circuit Criminal Court refused the application for discovery on the basis that the duty upon the prosecution to ensure full disclosure of relevant documents and information to the accused was sufficient in the circumstances of the case. He advanced three grounds for his decision.

Firstly, although Order 31, rule 29 of the Rules of the Superior Courts, 1986, did admit of the possibility of third party discovery in criminal cases, no authority for the making of such an order was cited to him and he was of the view that the case was not appropriate for a watershed decision allowing it.

Secondly, the reasoning of the English Court of Appeal in *Compagnie Financière du Pacificque v. Peruvian Guano Co.* (1882) 11 Q.B.D. 55, that a party applying for discovery was entitled to discovery of any document that might enhance his own case or destroy that of his adversary was less applicable in criminal proceedings where the entire burden of proof rests on the prosecution and the accused does not have to prove anything.

Thirdly, discovery is intended to be a mutual procedure. However, in a criminal case it was far-fetched to suppose that an order for discovery would be made against an accused in the light of factors such as the right to silence, the presumption of innocence and the privilege against self-incrimination. It would, therefore, be inequitable to require a third party to comply, on the application of an accused, with an obligation that could not be required of the accused himself. Furthermore, there was the delay in seeking discovery.

The first point to be made in relation to this decision is that it does not foreclose the possibility of an order for discovery being made in a criminal case. Although, Judge Moriarty declined the opportunity to hand down a seminal decision, such an order might be made in an appropriate case if the view was taken that the duty of disclosure on the prosecution was not adequate to secure fair procedures. Such a situation may well arise where information or documentation material to the case is in the possession of a third party. Such a third party is not under a duty of disclosure to the defence and in such circumstances, an order of discovery might be the only means of securing the information.

As regards the point that the burden of proof rests solely on the prosecution and the accused does not have to prove anything, it is worth noting that this is not always the case. It is true that the prosecution has to prove its case beyond a reasonable doubt but the legal burden of proving insanity rests upon the accused and a number of statutes also place a legal burden in relation to a specific issue upon the accused. In addition, the accused bears an evidential burden in raising any defence which is more than a mere denial of the prosecution case (see *Director of Public Prosecutions v. Collins* [1981] I.L.R.M. 447). Therefore, the accused may well have to 'prove' a defence or at least adduce sufficient evidence to raise the defence.

Regarding the mutuality point, discovery is not always mutual. Order 31, rule 29, which was at issue in this case, allows for the making of orders of discovery against third parties. By definition, such a procedure cannot be mutual. In addition, in the criminal context, fair procedures may well demand procedures characterised by a lack of mutuality. Thus, there is a general obligation on the prosecution to disclose material evidence to the defence but there is no corresponding obligation on the defence save in respect of alibi evidence (see section 20 of the Criminal Justice Act 1984).

It should be remembered that one of the rights of an accused identified by O'Higgins C.J. in *The State (Healy) v. Donoghue* [1976] I.R. 325, is the right to have an opportunity for the preparation of his or her defence. If it can be shown by an accused that discovery is necessary for the preparation of his or her defence, then it would seem as if fair procedures would require such an order to be made.

BREACH OF NATURAL JUSTICE

The case of *Ryan v. Walsh and Galway County Council*, Supreme Court, *ex tempore*, July 18, 1996, arose out of an accident in which the husband of the plaintiff was killed and the plaintiff suffered personal injuries. The trial judge found both the first named defendant, Walsh (who was the personal representative of the husband of the plaintiff) and the second named defendant, Galway County Council, to be negligent and apportioned liability, two thirds to Walsh and one third to the County Council. The latter appealed the decision of the trial judge on the ground, *inter alia*, that part of the judgment was based on conclusions reached by the trial judge which had no foundation in the evidence given by any party at the hearing of the action.

The accident had occurred on the Loughrea to Oranmore road at a point where the County Council were in the process of constructing a roundabout. Expert evidence was given on both sides as to the adequacy of the signs and other precautions taken by the County Council at the site but the trial judge based his judgment in part upon matters and theories which had not been advanced by any of the experts who gave evidence.

The Supreme Court acknowledged that trial judges frequently find themselves confronted by a conflict between expert witnesses. In such a situation, the trial judge has to use his or her common sense in deciding which of the two bodies of expert opinion to accept. A trial judge does not have to accept a view which may affront his or her own concept of common sense simply because it comes from an expert witness. However, this case was not concerned with a conflict of expert witnesses. What the trial judge had done was effectively to decide the case in favour of one party and against the other party on a basis which the latter party had not been given an opportunity of refuting.

The criticisms of the precautions taken by the County Council on which the trial judge had laid emphasis in delivering his judgment, had not been advanced by the experts giving evidence on behalf of either the plaintiff or the first named defendant. Thus, the experts called on behalf of the County Council had no opportunity of dealing with them and this was fundamentally unfair. The case was therefore remitted to the High Court for a retrial.

One of the fundamental principles of our adversarial system of justice is that, subject to the limited exceptions provided for pursuant to the doctrine of judicial notice, a judge must decide the issue before him or her solely on the basis of the evidence adduced by the parties to the action. Thus, as a general rule, the judge may not draw directly or indirectly on facts within his or her knowledge in contradiction of the evidence adduced (*The Queen v. Justices of Antrim* [1895] 2 I.R. 603). Similarly, if a judge wishes to draw any inferences or rely on any theories from the evidence in the case which have not been advanced by the parties to the action, he must inform the parties. Failure to do so is a breach of natural justice and will render the trial unfair.

Family Law

ADOPTION

In *In re L., and Infant; E.F. & F.F. v. An Bord Uchtála*, Supreme Court, July 17, 1996, the Supreme Court unanimously upheld Costello J.'s judgment to the effect that a mother had made a fully informed and free decision to place her child for adoption and that the subsequent refusal by the mother to give her consent to the child's adoption should be overridden in the best interests of the child.

The facts of the case, as so often in adoptive litigation, were sad. The mother, who already had a child, gave birth to another child in November 1989. Within a day of the birth the mother had signed a consent to fostering her daughter, 'at a stage when she must have undoubtedly been in a vulnerable condition'. Two months later the mother signed the appropriate form (Form 10), consenting to place her child for adoption. The social worker sought to ensure that she understood it fully. The father also signed a document stating that he had no objection to his daughter's being placed for adoption.

Five months later, the social worker wrote to the mother requesting to see her. Having received no response she wrote again a few weeks later. This time the mother replied, apologising for not having replied, and the meeting took place. In a phonecall to the administrator of the adoption society, the mother indicated at least a tentative desire to have her daughter returned to her. This desire was not apparently expressed quite so strongly at the meeting, though the evidence on this issue was conflicting.

Two months after this, the mother made it plain to the social worker and the administrator that she wished to withdraw her consent. They sought to persuade her to continue with the adoption. The following month, An Bord Uchtála, which had been informed of the situation by the adoption society, wrote to the mother, referring to the withdrawal of her consent and stating that, if the prospective adopters refused to give up custody of the child, the mother could institute legal proceedings and that it was in her interest that these proceedings should be brought as quickly as possible.

Matters drifted for a further five months. At a further meeting with the administrator of the adoption society, the mother and father reaffirmed their wish to have their daughter returned. Following this meeting, the administrator wrote to the mother a letter which ended as follows:

> In the meantime, I will urge you yet again out of the love you have for
> [your daughter] to prove that love by doing what is best for her, painful
> though that may be for you and [the father].

It took a further eleven months before the prospective adopters issued a special summons claiming an order dispensing with the mother's consent. Nine
months after this, the mother and father issued a special summons claiming
custody of their daughter. This was three years after the child had been fostered.

Not surprisingly the expert psychiatric evidence was coercively in favour
of leaving the child with the prospective adopters, with whom she had long
since bonded.

Costello J. held, first, that the mother had freely consented to placing her
child for adoption. He preferred the evidence of the social worker and the
administrator of the adoption society, 'whose recollections were clear and who
had, for a lot of their evidence, contemporary records to support the accuracy
of their recollection.' He did not find the mother to be a reliable witness, being
of the view that 'her very natural desire for the return of her little girl' had led
her to give testimony which he could not accept as true or accurate. Costello J.
rejected the argument that emotional pressure of any sort had been exercised
on the mother.

On the question of dispensing with the mother's consent, Costello J. considered that 'the overwhelming evidence in the case' was to the effect that it
was in the child's best interests that she remain with the prospective adopters.
To return her to her mother 'would represent a major trauma to her and . . .
cause both immediate and long term psychological damage.'

A notice of appeal was served in March 1993 but books of appeal were not
lodged until around May 1996, at which stage it was given an expedited hearing. The Supreme Court was informed that the delay was attributable to the
inability of the appellants to obtain a transcript of the High Court proceedings
because of the absence of legal aid.

The Supreme Court dismissed the appeal. Keane J. (Hamilton C.J., Blayney,
Denham and Barrington JJ. concurring) emphasised the reluctance of an appellate court to reverse findings of fact which depend on assessment by the
trial judge of the credibility of witnesses. He nonetheless acknowledged that
there was 'at least some justification' in the criticism of the conduct of the
adoption society which counsel for the child's parents had made.

Expanding of this criticism, Keane J. observed that it was:

> not unfair to say that, so far as the evidence goes, no serious considera-
> tion seems to have been given by the Adoption Society to the possibility
> of the child being restored to its parents at any time between the handing
> over to foster care and the signing of the Form 10 by the mother on
> January 11th [1990].

The letters written by the social worker and the administrator to the mother from July 1990 onwards, when the mother had evinced, at the very least, a tentative desire to have her baby back, reflected 'a somewhat disquieting approach' on the part of the adoption society:

> Far from taking steps to see whether that obviously desirable reunion could be effected, at the cost of some natural disappointment and frustration to the prospective adopters, they seem to have seen their function as persuading the mother to continue with the adoption.

As to the criticism by the parents of the failure of the social worker, when explaining the meaning of Form 10 to the mother, to state that, if a successful application were brought, under section 3 of the Adoption Act 1974, the mother might never see her child again, Keane J. commented:

> It is also to be said that the wording of the passage relating to section 3 in the Form 10 in use at the time might well have been confusing for someone unaccustomed to dealing with legal phraseology. (The form now in use . . . , while significantly better in other respects, is couched in much the same language so far as section 3 is concerned.) It would also be clearly preferable for a person explaining the effect of the placement to the mother to use blunt and uncompromising language: she should be told that, while she may withdraw her consent, the prospective adopters may always apply under Section 3 and that if an order is made under that Section followed by an adoption order, she will lose custody of her child forever. However, while language of that precise nature was not used, on her own admission by [the social worker] in the present case, the trial judge, who had the opportunity of seeing and hearing the witnesses, was clearly satisfied that the consequences of a section 3 order were fully explained to the mother and, most importantly, understood by her. That is a finding of fact with which this court cannot interfere.

Once the mother's consent to placing her daughter for adoption was held to be valid, the issue of dispensing with her consent to the adoption simply had to be decided in favour of upholding the dispensation. By now, nearly seven years had gone by since the child had gone to the prospective adopters. Keane J. made an express finding that the prospective adopters had not been responsible for the delay.

DIVORCE

Legislation   In the 1995 Review, 138, 285, we analysed the constitutional change which re-introduced a divorce jurisdiction into the Irish legal system. The Family Law (Divorce) Act 1996 prescribes the legislative detail, the existence of which, it should be noted, is not a constitutional precondition to the entitlement to obtain a divorce: *R.C. v. C.C.* [1997] 1 I.L.R.M. 401. The Act came into force on February 27, 1997.

Part II of the Act sets out the conditions for obtaining a decree. Section 5(1), echoing the language of the constitutional amendment, provides as follows:

> Subject to the provisions of this Act, where, on the application to it in that behalf by either of the spouses concerned, the court is satisfied that:
>
> (a) at the date of the institution of the proceedings, the spouses have lived apart from one another for a period of, or periods amounting to, at least four years during the previous five years, and
> (b) there is no reasonable prospect of a reconciliation between the spouses, and
> (c) such provisions as the court considers proper having regard to the circumstances exists or will be made for the spouses and any dependent members of the family,
>
> the court, may, in exercise of the jurisdiction conferred by Article 41.3.2° of the Constitution, grant a decree of divorce in respect of the marriage concerned.

Sections 6 and 7 include provisions, described as 'safeguards', requiring the solicitors for the parties to discuss with their client the possibility of reconciliation, mediation or drawing up a separation agreement and to inform the client of the option of judicial separation. Section 8 requires the court to 'give consideration' to the possibility of reconciliation and to adjourn the proceedings to enable attempts at reconciliation to be made by the spouses 'if they both so wish'.

The 'living apart' ground is a *tabula rasa*. Two particular issues need to be resolved. The first relates to the mental element involved. It is possible to envisage cases where, over a period of five years, the spouses are in each other's physical presence for less than a year; yet, if they clearly got on well with each other, and made these arrangements for health or even employment reasons, we might hesitate in describing them as 'living apart'. The judicial tendency in other common law jurisdictions, therefore, has been to incorporate a mental element into the concept.

Once this is done, further, and more disturbing, questions arise. If one spouse is incarcerated in prison or is a patient in a hospital, does the clock start ticking when the key is first turned in the cell or when the spouse is placed in a ward? The answer given by most courts in other common law jurisdictions has been that when either of the spouses, on whom this compulsory physical separation has been imposed, chooses to embrace that fact freely, the period of 'living apart' commences, even where this secret repudiation of the other spouse is not conveyed to the other spouse: *Santos v. Santos* [1972] 2 All E.R. 246; *Sullivan v. Sullivan* [1958] N.Z.L.R. 912; *Joe v. Joe* [1985] 3 N.Z.L.R. 675.

This means, in practice, that prisoners and long-term hospital patients are at risk of being divorced after a period of four years, regardless of the apparent quality of their relationship with their spouse over that period. For who can contradict a spouse who asserts that he or she made an internal mental withdrawal from the incarcerated or hospitalised spouse?

Some may regard the outcome as satisfactory rather than inhumane. After all, in many cases the prisoner has brought the problem on himself or herself; but the hospital patient has not. If judicial concern for the liberty of the other spouse to pursue his or her own happiness enables the court to hold that the partners were 'living apart' on the basis of a private uncommunicated repudiation of one by the other, what implications does this have for the other substantial issue, relating to whether it is possible for spouses, living under the same roof, to be regarded nonetheless as 'living apart'?

Section 2(3)(a) of the Judicial Separation and Family Law Reform Act 1989 provides some element of clarity on this matter so far as proceedings for *judicial separation* are concerned. Spouses are to be treated as living apart from each other 'unless they are living with each other in the same household'. Significantly, neither the constitutional amendment nor the legislation on *divorce* contains any similar restriction.

So what is the position where spouses are admittedly living together under one roof but one of them asserts that in truth he or she was 'living apart' from the other spouse in the sense that he or she had withdrawn from the relationship, being constrained through poverty or a sense of obligation to their children to continue living under the same roof as the privately rejected spouse? There are several decisions from other common law jurisdictions which accept the possibility that the spouses may be held to have been living apart in such circumstances, at all events where there is a demonstrable distance in their living patterns. Courts, a couple of decades ago, used to test this by asking such practical questions as whether the wife continued to wash her husband's dirty clothes and put a meal on the table for him in the evenings. One suspects the Irish judges will not frame an identical test. With changing, and more equal, work patterns, which impact on family relationships, it seems likely that courts would be open to the argument that a significant emotional distance between the spouses should be capable of being interpreted as according to 'living apart' in some cases.

The statutory requirement that the court, before granting a divorce, be satisfied that proper provision exists or will be made for 'the spouses and any dependent members of the family' is in an important respect narrower than what is required by the constitutional amendment on divorce, which speaks of provision 'for the spouses, any children of either or both of them and any other person prescribed by law'. The expression 'dependent member of the family', defined by section 2 (1) of the Act, excludes most children over the age of eighteen.

Part III of the Act deals with preliminary and ancillary orders in (or after) divorce proceedings. They bear many similarities to the equivalent provisions in the Family Law Act 1995. Thus, for example, the court may make maintenance pending suit orders, periodical payments orders, secured periodical payments orders, lump sum orders, financial compensation orders, property adjustment orders and orders for occupation or sale of the family house, pension adjustment orders, orders for provision for a spouse out of the estate of his or her former spouse and orders for the sale of property. For consideration of some of these provisions, see Muriel Walls, 'No Place Like Home', 91 *Law Soc. of Ireland Gazette,* p. 24 (April 1997), Rosemary Horgan, 'Till Debt Do We Part, id., p. 22 (May 1997).

In determining whether to make more of these orders and, if so, in determining the provision of these orders, the court is to have regard, in particular, to several specified factors: section 20(2). The conduct of each of the spouses is to be taken into consideration only if it is 'such that in the opinion of the court it would in all the circumstances of the case be unjust to disregard it': section 20(2)(i). A spouse's desertion no longer has any decisive effect and is not mentioned on the list. While capable of falling under the 'conduct' rubric, its removal from the code of family legislation dealing (*inter alia*) with maintenance can be seen as a legislative statement that desertion is no longer regarded by the law as stigmatic conduct. Why should it be when four years' desertion generates a constitutionally prescribed right to divorce?

Part IV of the Act deals with taxation matters. For a comprehensive, highly accessible, analysis of these provisions, see Anne Corrigan's paper, 'Taxation Aspects of the Family Law (Divorce) Act 1996', delivered at the Conference entitled *The Family Law (Divorce) Act 1996: Implications for Practice*, held by the Law School of Trinity College Dublin on February 15, 1997.

Part V of the Act contains a series of miscellaneous provisions, many of which involve technical amendments to the family law code and other statutes, such as the Criminal Damage Act 1991, the Criminal Evidence Act 1992 and the Domestic Violence Act 1996, to take account of the introduction of divorce. Section 37 is a substantive provision giving the court wide-ranging powers to deal with transactions intended to prevent or reduce a claim for financial relief in divorce proceedings. A similar provision has existed in relation to proceedings for judicial separation since 1989.

The Circuit Court, concurrently with the High Court, has jurisdiction to hear and determine proceedings under the Act: section 38(1). This jurisdiction may be exercised by the judge of the circuit in which any of the parties to the proceedings ordinarily resides or carries on business: section 38(3).

It may be useful to note the wider international dimension. Section 39(1) of the Act confers jurisdiction on the Irish court to grant a decree of divorce *if*:

(a) either of the spouses was domiciled in the State on the date of the institution of the proceedings, or

(b) either of the spouses was ordinarily resident in the State throughout the period of one year ending on that date.

Thus the *domicile* or *one year's ordinary residence* of *either* spouse will suffice.

The large majority of applicants for divorce under the 1996 Act are likely to fulfill the ordinary residence requirement under section 39(1)(b). So what kind of cases will have to rely on the domicile requirement?

The first will arise where a person asserts that, although he or she (or his or her spouse) has been ordinarily resident here for less than a year before the divorce application, his or her intent (or the spouse's intent) to reside here permanently can be established. Domicile of choice requires proof of the requisite residence plus intention. There is no need to prove that the residence was for any specified duration – certainly nothing like as long as a year. It would be quite possible to establish a domicile of choice on the basis of a very short period of residence, provided, of course, the requisite intent to stay here permanently can be established.

The second case will arise where a person who has admittedly not been ordinarily resident here for the requisite one-year period and who cannot prove sufficient residence and intent to establish the acquisition of a domicile of choice here within the year before the divorce application, nonetheless asserts a domiciliary connection within the State. This could occur in a wide variety of ways. A person who was born and brought up here will normally have an Irish domicile of origin. If, when he or she is twenty, that person goes to England and lives there for a couple of years, it may be that his or her sense of attachment to England is so tenuous as not to generate an acquisition of an English domicile of choice in spite of the loss of the Irish residence. Not having acquired an English domicile, the Irish domicile of origin applies. That person would therefore fulfil the requirement of section 39(1)(a).

As a practical matter, many Irish people who are living abroad may have an opportunity to petition for divorce *either* in the foreign country where they

live (on the basis of residence) *or* in Ireland under the provisions of the 1996
Act. The entitlement to apply under the 1996 Act will depend on the crucial
issue of whether that person has lost his or her Irish domicile.

Why would an Irish person living abroad wish to avail of himself or herself of the Irish divorce jurisdiction rather than the divorce jurisdiction where
he or she is now living? The answer will depend on how that person weighs
the advantages and disadvantages of this course. This will involve a comparison of the ancillary orders in Part III of the 1996 Act and the orders that are
likely to be made under the foreign divorce code, as well as the question of
ease or difficulty in enforcing the orders. There are, admittedly, ways of enforcing ancillary orders internationally but, even so, some people will take the
view that an order obtained in a court in the jurisdiction where they reside
tends to be easier to enforce than one obtained abroad.

A further factor to be taken into consideration relates to the question of
recognition of foreign divorces under private international law. Irish jurisdictional rules relating to divorce are wider than our rules relating to recognition
of foreign divorces, since ordinary residence is not a ground for recognition.
Unless an English domicile of choice could be established (under Irish private
international law), the English divorce would not be recognised here, even
though obtained on the same jurisdictional ground as would support divorce
proceedings in Ireland. Under the rules of English private international law, a
divorce obtained in Ireland on the basis of one year's ordinary residence would
be likely to be recognised since habitual residence is a ground for recognition
(as well as nationality): see Dicey & Morris, *The Conflict of Laws*, Rule 81
(12th ed., 1993).

There is little point in seeking to parse the words 'ordinarily resident'. In
State (Goertz) v. Minister for Justice [1945] I.R. 45, at 55, Maguire C.J. commented that earlier cases which had considered the meaning of these words
were:

> of very little help. They are of assistance, however, in showing that the
> word 'resident', not being a term of art, must be construed by reference
> to the statute in which it is found.

(See also, in this context, *Deutche Bank Aktiengesellschaff v. Murtagh* [1995]
1 I.L.R.M. 381, which we note in the 1995 Review, 271-2).

In the context of divorce jurisdiction, the words seem unproblematic. Note
again that there must have been a year's ordinary residence immediately preceding the institution of proceedings.

Neither the domicile ground nor the ordinary residence ground requires
that the *applicant* be domiciled or resident here. It is sufficient that *either*
spouse is domiciled here or has been ordinarily resident here for the past year.
This means that spouses who have absolutely no connection with Ireland apart
from the fact that the person they married has an Irish domicile or ordinary

residence may initiate proceedings for divorce here. The kind of strategic calculations which have already been mentioned in relation to a person living abroad without having lost his or her Irish domicile thus apply equally to *that person's spouse*. So the English wife of a young Irishman who went to England when he was twenty but never put sufficient roots down to acquire an English domicile will be entitled to apply for an Irish or an English divorce.

Section 39(2) to (4) of the 1996 Act sets out the broad principle that, if one fulfills the jurisdictional requirement for obtaining a decree of divorce, nullity or judicial separation, as the case may be, and these proceedings are pending (either in the court of first instance or on appeal), the court has jurisdiction to grant either of the two other decrees notwithstanding that one does not fulfil the jurisdictional requirement for this other decree. Since section 31(4) of the Judicial Separation and Family Law Reform Act 1989 and section 39(1) of the Family Law Act 1995 set out jurisdictional criteria for judicial separation and nullity proceedings which are identical to those of section 39(1) of the Family Law (Divorce) Act 1996, it is hard to see what is added by subsection (2) to (4) of section 39 of the 1996 Act.

It may be worth reflecting for a moment on the impact of Barron J.'s decision in *R.C. v. C.C.* [1997] 1 I.L.R.M. 401, holding that there is an entitlement to divorce by virtue of the Constitution, as amended on November 24, 1995, without basing that entitlement on any legislation. If the applicant in that case had not been so obviously of strong Irish connections, what would have been the position? If, for example, he had been an Irish citizen, resident and domiciled abroad, would the court have had jurisdiction to grant a divorce? Conversely, if he had been a foreign national resident here for only eleven months, would he have been entitled to a decree?

Had there been no divorce legislation or had the legislation not contained a jurisdictional provision such as section 39, then these questions would have had to be confronted as a matter of urgency. Now that we do have legislation in place, the matter must have lost most (though not all) of its practical importance. There is a real prospect that a court, faced with an application for divorce which falls outside the jurisdictional grounds prescribed by section 39 of the Act, would hold that, since the jurisdictional issue has now been dealt with by legislation, the constitutional entitlement has properly been delimited and that no jurisdictional grounds outside the scope of section 39 should thus be recognised. The idea that there is an ancillary divorce jurisdiction, based on the Constitution, supplementing the legislation, is one that is unlikely to appeal to a court since it would introduce huge uncertainty to no great advantage. It is interesting to note in this context that section 39(1) makes it plain that, for the purposes of the legislation, the grounds based on domicile and one year's ordinary residence constitute a closed list: 'The court may grant a decree of divorce *if, but only if*, one of the following requirements is satisfied. . . .' (emphasis added).

DOMESTIC VIOLENCE

Legislation   The Act came into effect on March 27, 1996, is a most important piece of legislation. For analysis of its provisions, see Raghnal O'Riordan
B.L., 'New Domestic Violence Law Enacted', 1 *The Bar Review* 28 (1996)
and Joan O'Mahony, 'Domestic Violence Act 1996', 90 *L. Soc. of Ireland
Gazette* 136 (1996). The provisions of the legislation reflect the recommendations of the Law Reform Commission in its *Report on Child Sexual Abuse*, the
Second Commission on the Status of Woman and the Kilkenny Incest Investigation Team.

The Act introduces important changes in the *types of order* that the courts
may make, the *persons eligible to apply for these orders* and in other *miscellaneous respects*.

As to the *types of order* that the courts may make, the Act provides for
three principal orders: the *safety order* (section 2), the *barring order* (section
3) and the protection order (section 5(3)). An *interim* barring order is permitted under section 4 in emergency situations, on an *ex parte* basis if, in exceptional cases, the court considers this necessary or expedient in the interests of
justice.

The *safety order* is, in effect, 'a long-term protection order available to or
against all members of a household' (*Explanatory Memorandum to the Bill as
Initiated*, para. 4(d)). In contrast to the protection order under the 1981 legislation, a safety order is not an interim order between the making of an application for a barring order and its determination. It requires the respondent not to
use or threaten violence against the applicant or any dependent person, not to
molest them and not to put them in fear. If the respondent is not living with
them, he or she must not watch or beset their place (or places) of residence.
The court has power to attach exceptions or conditions to the safety order.

The *barring order* is largely modelled on the barring order of the 1981
legislation, though the scope of applicants has been significantly extended.
The test for granting an order is whether there are reasonable grounds for
believing that the safety or welfare of the applicant or any dependent person
so requires: section 3(2)(a). This is the same criterion as that formulated in the
Family Law (Protection of Spouses and Children) Act 1981, but with one
important difference. In the Bill as initiated in the Dáil, section 1(1) had defined 'welfare' as including the physical, emotional and mental welfare of the
person in question. This was designed to reflect the Supreme Court judgment
in *O'B. v. O'B.* [1984] I.R. 182, which made it clear that domestic violence is
not confined to physical abuse and can include emotional and mental cruelty.
Experience at District Court level suggested that in practice a more stringent
test was applied.

At Committee Stage, Dr Michael Woods moved an amendment substituting a definition of 'welfare' which included the physical and psychological welfare of the person in question. He argued that reference to an applicant's emotional welfare might encourage the court to take into account matters for which the respondent was responsible but which might not involve any legal or moral blame on his (or her) part. As the original definition was not exhaustive 'it would not in extreme circumstances prevent the court from considering the applicant's emotional response to the respondent's behaviour': *Select Committee on Legislation and Security,* column 408 (November 1, 1995). Dr Woods was of the view that, since a barring order was a severe remedy for the person who was barred, it should not extend to cases of emotional trauma following the breakdown of a marriage where there was no intention to cause harm to the other partner.

The Minister for Equality and Law Reform, Mr Taylor, accepted the merits of the argument and on Report Stage introduced an amendment in identical terms, even though the language of the original draft was closer to the wording used in the Supreme Court judgment.

The *protection order*, prescribed by section 5 of the Act, is a re-creation of the order prescribed by section 3 of the 1981 Act. Section 5 provides for the granting of a protection order pending the determination of an application for a barring order or safety order.

The *interim barring order* is a statutory novelty. Section 4(1) empowers the court to grant an order of this kind, before the determination of an application for a barring order, when of opinion that there are reasonable grounds for believing that there is an immediate risk of significant harm to the applicant or a dependent person if the order is not made immediately *and* the granting of a protection order would not be sufficient protection. Section 4(3) enables the court to grant an interim barring order *ex parte* (or without service of notice of the originating documents) 'in exceptional cases' where the court considers it 'necessary or expedient in the interests of justice'.

Probably the most important changes brought about by the legislation, from a cultural standpoint, are in relation to the *person eligible to apply* for safety orders, barring orders and protection orders. Broadly speaking, the legislation permits spouses, cohabitees, parents and health boards to apply for any of these orders and it permits a novel category of persons, residing with the respondent 'in a relationship the basis of which is not primarily contractual' to apply for safety orders.

Conferring an entitlement on a cohabitee to evict a violent partner was seen by Deputies as a crucial new change. Deputy Willie O'Dea described it as '[t]he most fundamental reform introduced by the legislation' and Deputy Helen Keogh regarded it as 'the crux' of the legislation.

A cohabitee may apply for a safety order if he or she has lived with the respondent as husband or wife for at least six of the previous twelve months: section 2(1)a)(ii). The requirements in relation to a barring order are considerably stricter: the applicant must have lived with the respondent as husband or wife for at least six of the previous *nine* months (section 3(1)(b)) and the court may not make a barring order where the respondent has a legal or beneficial interest in the place where the applicant or dependent person resides, while the applicant either has no such interest or it is, in the court's opinion, less than that of the respondent.

Section 3 (4)(b) provides that an assertion by the applicant of the *belief* that he or she has a legal or beneficial interest in the place which is not less than that of the respondent should be *admissible in evidence*. It is hard to find a sound basis for its admissibility. Not expert opinion, surely. Most people are untroubled by an expert knowledge of the refinements of real property law. It is to be noted section 3(4)(b) merely provides for the admissibility of this belief as evidence. The weight of the evidence in any particular case is for the court to decide. The provision does not quantify the weight of the evidence or prescribe that it generates any presumption, not even one of the fact. Nevertheless, one suspects that in practice this provision is designed to achieve an accommodation with the constitutional concerns which will in many cases have the effect of enabling the court to comply formally with the need to address these concerns without doing so in any meaningful substantive way. It may be argued that constitutional principles are worthy of greater attention. Is it worrying that the tradition rules of evidence, which do not admit non-expert belief, should be modified in this context. A constitutional issue may arise as to the justification for admitting the opinion of evidence of the applicant but not the respondent.

Section 17(1) provides that contravention of a safety order, barring order or protection order is a statutory offence with a maximum penalty of £1,500 or twelve months' imprisonment or both. Section 17(2) provides that subsection (1) is without prejudice to the law as to contempt of court or any other liability, civil or criminal that may be incurred by the respondent. This cumulative approach has a long legislative pedigree but it is hard to see how it does not raise a question of double jeopardy so far as criminal contempt is concerned. Criminal contempt is an offence, albeit one with distinct rules as to prosecution, the role of the jury and sanction. If contravention of an order is both a statutory offence and criminal contempt, surely the defendant should be exposed to only one prosecution? Possibly the courts will interpret the provision as enabling a criminal contempt charge to be made, but subject to a double jeopardy restriction that only one charge may be brought.

It was clear at all stages of the Oireachtas Debates that Mr. Taylor would have preferred a more extensive change in the law. He emphasised that he was restricted by the advice of the Attorney General that to go further would create a constitutional doubt as to the validity of the legislation in that it could be considered to infringe a person's property rights protected under Article 40.3. During the Committee Stage he expanded on these concerns:

> The advice available to me . . . is that a provision . . . which would allow a respondent other than a spouse with an ownership interest to be barred on the application of a person with no such interest or with a lesser interest than the respondent might not survive constitutional scrutiny. This is so by virtue of the fact that a barring order would constitute an infringment o[f] that person's property rights which the State and its laws must respect under Article 40.3 of the Constitution. The position is different – where parties are named. An infringement of a spouse's property rights is presumed to be justified on the basis that the rights of a family founded on marriage are protected by the Constitution and take precedence over property rights. (*Select Committee on Legislation and Security*, column 454 (November 7, 1995).)

Mr Taylor went on to say that the format of the Bill was the product of exhaustive discussion and intensive examination by the Attorney General:

> The reason for it is understandable. For example, where a man owns or is tenant of a house which is in his sole name and a woman comes to cohabit with him in his house, he may become violent towards her and she brings an application against him for a barring order to bar him from his house. He may say that although they have been cohabiting until now, as of now they are no longer cohabitants. He may say: 'this is my house, please leave. We are no longer cohabitants.' A man cannot say that to his wife; a woman cannot say that to her husband, but cohabitants do not have the connection that spouses have. He can say that the house is in his name and protected under the Constitution. That is the difficulty. (*Id.*, column 458.)

The opposition deputies stressed the need to examine further the conflict between the rights of property and of bodily integrity, especially where children were concerned.

The Minister, making his discomfiture plain, emphasised that he had referred the matter to the Constitutional Review Group 'to establish its thinking in this area': *id.*, col. 455. The Review Group's recommendations in relation to Article 41 involve the proposal that non-marital families should come within the scope of the Article. This would mean that the property-based concern as to the exclusion of a violent cohabitee from his (or her) home would lose much, if not all, of its force.

Opposition deputies suggested that the restrictions contained in the legislation would mean that up to 90% (or more) of cohabitees would be excluded from the entitlement to apply for a barring order. Deputy Willie O'Dea commented:

If one takes the typical example of a couple living in a local authority home under a tenancy from the local authority – they may be a tenant or on tenant purchase – and if their marriage breaks up and somebody else moves in with them, then the original tenant is still the person in whose name the tenancy is made, or perhaps it is made in the name of him and his wife. In the case of tenant purchase, the same situation applies: *id.*, column 452.

The Minister pointed out that there was no reason to suppose that the cohabitee who took in the other party was necessarily the party who would be bringing the application. Furthermore, it was very usual among cohabitees to buy or rent a property jointly.

Undoubtedly cohabitation by married persons is likely to present the kind of difficulty identified by Deputy O'Dea, though by no means in every case. It is of relevance to note that international experience is that the facility of divorce has not resulted in a decrease of cohabitation by married persons but rather an increase.

It is worth considering why the Oireachtas extended the power to apply for safety orders (but not barring orders) to persons in a relationship with the respondent 'the basis of which is not primarily contractual'. The Minister gave a short, and relatively unenlightening, explanation during the Second Reading in the Dáil:

Violence in the home is not confined to violence by one spouse against another or children. It transcends all relationships. For this reason I have provided that the safety order remedy will be widely available. An exception is where the relationship is primarily contractual in order to ensure that the remedy is confined to what are genuine domestic disputes and does not, for example, become a feature of disputes between landlords and tenants for which there are adequate alternative legal remedies. Of course, the nature of a relationship may change over time from being primarily contractual to primarily non-contractual. Each case will have to be decided by the court on its merits and subsection (1)(b) sets out some factors to which the court must have regard in reaching a conclusion. 455 *Dáil Debates*, column 1103 (July 4, 1995).

It was clear to Deputies from the outset, however, that the provision was designed in substantial part to bring homosexual relationships within the scope of the legislation. No doubt this was regarded as an important ideological statement. Clearly it is indeed that. Yet, in the manner by which it was executed in the legislation, it was more a statement out of the corner of the mouth. The Minister could not bring himself to announce directly what was the true intent of the Bill. Moreover, the legislation itself makes no reference to the sexual component of the relationship. Its list of factors to which the court is to have regard in deciding whether the applicant is in a relationship the basis of which is not primarily contractual studiously avoids reference to any emotional, psychological, physical or sexual elements. These are sanitised by the catch-all factor (iv), which requires the court to have regard to 'such matters as [it] considers appropriates in the circumstances'. These factors are to guide the court in determining *whether or not the relationship has been established, not whether or not the court should grant a safety order*. Thus, considerations of public policy or of sexual morality are not intended to play any part in the court's decision.

At Committee Stage, Deputy O'Dea pointed to an anomaly between homosexual partners and heterosexual cohabitees : the former may obtain a safety order without establishing a particular period of residence with the respondent whereas the latter must establish that for six of the previous twelve months they have 'lived with the respondent as husband or wife.' The Minister sought to justify the distinction on the basis that an applicant in the former case had to establish that he (or she) is actually living with the respondent at the time of the proceedings whereas a cohabitee has merely to show that he or she '*has* lived', not 'is residing with', the respondent. 'In other words', said the Minister, 'it would be open to a cohabitant who is actually living with the other cohabitant at the time of the application to avail also of the provisions of subsection (iv) without the time limitation, always provided, of course, the qualifiers in (b) were taken into account by the court, the length of time and so on' : 455 *Dáil Debates*, column 472.

This seems an unconvincing interpretation of section 2. It appears to offend the *noscitur a sociis* principle.

The new power of Health Boards to intervene in relation to domestic violence by seeking a safety order or a barring order is worth noting. This was recommended by the Law Reform Commission in it *Report on Child Sexual Abuse* and the Kilkenny Incest Investigation Team. The court must be satisfied that there remains a parent in the home who is willing and able to provide reasonable care for the child : section 6(5). Section 25(2) provides that section 6 and so much of the other provisions of the Act relate to that section come into operation on January 1, 1997. This is to ensure that the necessary staffing and administrative arrangements have been put in place.

The Act contains several other important provisions. They include the integration of the legislation with the Child Care Act 1991 (section 7), section 9(2) of the Family Home Protection Act 1976 (section 8) and, more broadly, other remedies relating to maintenance and guardianship (section 9). Family law practitioners will have to pay close attention to the detailed procedural requirements as to notice of the effect of the orders (section 10) and the giving of copies of the orders to several parties, including the Garda' (section 11). The court's power to discharge an order, under section 13, is more restricted than under the 1981 Act. It may do so only when of opinion that the safety and welfare of the applicant or dependent person for whose protection the order was made does not require that the order should continue in force: section 13(1).

Section 17 increases the penalties for contravention of orders and section 18(1) extends the Garda"s power of arrest without warrant to breaches of the new safety order and interim barring order procedures. Section 18(2) confers a similar power in respect of the offences of assault occasioning actual bodily harm or grievous bodily harm against a person who appears to be one who could apply for, or gain protection from, a safety order or barring order. It permits members of the Garda Síochána, for the purpose of making the arrest, to enter, if necessary by force, and search any place where they suspect, with reasonable cause, the person they intend to arrest to be present. This place need not necessarily be the family home. The Minister, during the Second Stage Debate, explained that these broad powers are essential to deal with situations where, for example, the perpetrator has forced or convinced the victim not to let the Garda' into the home after a scene of domestic violence.

Jurisdiction is based (*inter alia*) on where the applicant resides : section 14(1). Section 14(2) permits the court to treat a person as residing at a place where that person would, but for the conduct of the respondent, be residing. This provision is designed to cover situations where the respondent's violence (or other misconduct) has driven the applicant from the home. The question whether the respondent's conduct was of this nature will in some cases be contested. It seems that a court may have to assume jurisdiction on the basis of an allegation which may prove unfounded. In theory, if a court came to the conclusion that it lacked jurisdiction on this account it would be required to dismiss the proceedings (assuming, of course, that jurisdiction was not estab-lished by virtue of the situation of 'the place in relation to which th[e] applica-tion was made' (section 14(1)), even where it was satisfied that grounds for making of a barring order had been established. One may wonder whether courts will in fact adopt such a fastidious approach.

FAMILY COURTS

There has been an international debate for over forty years on the subject of family courts. Much of the discussion has been symptomatic of wider philo-sophical concerns: the desire to place less, or no, emphasis on the matrimonial 'fault', the perception of marital disharmony as a symptom of a pathology in the relationship and the notion of the judge as a benevolent inquisitor, hand-ing out authoritative prescriptions for the best interests of the spouses and the children. The early models of family courts therefore emphasised a strongly intrusive role for the judges, with a focus on the totality of the spouses' relationship as a proper subject for scientific analysis.

This view of the family court was consistent with the philosophy of the English Law Commission in 1966, which recommended a 'no-fault' divorce jurisdiction based on a judicial investigation on whether the marriage had irretrievably broken down. Once 'irretrievable breakdown' became a ground for divorce in 1969, the perceptions changed because it became obvious very quickly that a system of divorce which is based on irretrievable breakdown of marriage actually is one that provides for divorce by consent and by unilateral repudiation.

In truth, with a divorce jurisdiction that allows for unilateral repudiation there is nothing really left for the judge to decide in determining whether the marriage has 'irretrievably broken down'. If one spouse says that, so far as he or she is concerned, the marriage is over, the denial by the other spouse will carry no weight. The judge may have to make sure that any minimum period of 'living apart' has been established, but there is no judicial role in examining the nature of the parties' matrimonial relationship and in coming up with authoritative scientific prescriptions. A modern 'no fault' divorce regime is entirely hostile with such intrusion and lays strong emphasis on *non*-judicial strategies, epitomised by mediation.

The apotheosis of the contemporary divorce philosophy is that courts should have no role in the curtailing the autonomy of the individual in the pursuit of his or her life plans. One may find the odd statutory provisions requiring a court to have regard to the welfare of collateral victims – most obviously children – but no legal system takes them seriously. Once divorce based on unilateral repudiation is accepted, there is no credible judicial attempt in any country to modify that jurisdiction on the basis of the damage caused to others.

It is against this background that the Law Reform Commission published its *Report on Family Courts* (LRC 52 – 1996) in March 1996, when the referendum introducing divorce was still under a judicial cloud of uncertainty.

The Commission proposes the establishment of a system of Regional Family Courts, operating as a division of the Circuit Court, in about fifteen regional centres. These courts would be presided over by judges nominated to serve for a period of at least one year and assigned on the basis of their suitability to deal with family law matters.

The jurisdiction of the Regional Family Court would be comprehensive and include all emergency remedies under the Child Care Act 1991 and the Domestic Violence Act 1996 (cf. above, 358-64), for example. The District Court's jurisdiction in family law matters would be limited to the making of emergency orders and interim orders 'especially in situations of emergency': para. 4.43.

The Commission proposes that each Regional Family Court should have attached to it a Family Court Information Centre, with responsibility for providing to the parties information relating to available alternatives to litigation.

Parties involved in proceedings for judicial separation would be required to attend the Centre to receive this information; parties involved in other family litigation would be given the opportunity to do so.

The Commission places a strong emphasis on mediation and recommends the development of a mediation service in conjunction with the Regional Family Courts. It proposes that mediated agreements should normally be reviewed by the parties' respective legal advisers. The courts should have a power of review, supplemented by a power of variation, in relation to agreements concerning maintenance and property, on the basis of newly discovered facts or a change in the economic circumstances of the parties.

The Commission proposes that the court should have power to appoint an independent legal representative for a child in family proceedings where this appears necessary in the child's interests. Such a need might arise where the extent of hostility between the parents is severe, involving frequent resort to litigation, or where mental illness or child abuse is in issue.

The Commission takes the position in relation to proceedings which involve an active dispute between the parties that, save in two very specific and limited respects, the adversarial tradition should continue to hold sway. This is because of the need to respect the requirements of a fair hearing, adhering to the principles of constitutional and natural justice. The two new exceptions it proposes are, first, extension of the judicial power to procure a report on any question affecting the welfare of the infant in guardianship proceedings so that it applies to *any* proceeding in which the welfare of a dependent child is relevant and, secondly, the establishment of a discretionary judicial power to procure a financial report from an accountant or other qualified independent person in proceedings involving maintenance or other financial orders or property orders.

Whilst opposed to compulsory training for family court judges, the Commission favours the taking of measures, as a matter of urgency, to enable the judiciary to organise judicial studies on a systematic basis, with a management board, chaired by the Chief Justice (or nominee), comprising a majority of judges, backed by adequate financial and administrative support. It recommends also that specialist courses on family law should be made availing to practising lawyers, with, downstream, the possibility of certification attaching to their successful completion.

THE FAMILY HOME

In the Land Law Chapter, below, 416-18, Paul Coughlan analyses the Supreme Court decision of *Allied Irish Banks Ltd. v. Finnegan* [1996] 1 I.L.R.M. 401. In the present context, we may merely note that the scope of the holding, whilst professedly narrow, has potentially wider effects in practice. It is not news that the burden of proof of establishing compliance with section 3(3)(a) of the Family Home Protection Act 1976 rests on the purchaser: section 3(4) expressly so provides. What is noteworthy about the decision, formalistic though Blayney J.'s judgment may be, is its apparent willingness to countenance the argument that the consent of the non-owning spouse (usually the wife), to be valid, must be fully informed and legally sophisticated. No doubt, if the Court wishes in the future to resile from such an implication, it will be easy for it to do so without any defiance of the (loose enough) limitations of precedent, but practitioners advising banks should heed the amber light that *Finnegan* has placed in their path.

GUARDIANSHIP OF INFANTS

In the 1989 Review, 248-57, we analysed in some detail the Supreme Court's determination in *K v. W (No. 1)* [1990] I.L.R.M. 121 of questions posed in a case stated by Barron J. regarding the correct approach to determining an application by a natural father under section 6A of the Guardianship of Infants Act 1964 (inserted by section 12 of the Status of Children Act 1987) to be appointed guardian of his child. In a crucial passage, Finlay C.J. said that he was satisfied that the submission on behalf of the father that he had a constitutional or natural right identified by the Constitution to the guardianship of his child which was acknowledged in section 6A was:

> not correct and that although there may be rights of interest or concern arising from the blood link between the father and the child, no constitutional right to guardianship in the father of the child exists. This conclusion does not, of course, in any way infringe on such considerations appropriate to the welfare of the child in different circumstances as may make it desirable for the child to enjoy the society, protection and guardianship of its father, even though its father and mother are not married.
>
> The extent and character of the rights which accrue arising from the relationship of a father to a child whose mother he is not married to must vary very greatly indeed, depending on the circumstances of each individual case.
>
> The range of variation would, I am satisfied, extend from the situation of the father of a child conceived as a result of a casual intercourse, where the rights might well be so minimal as practically to be nonexistent, to the situation of a child born as a result of a stable and established relationship and nurtured at the commencement of his life by his father and mother in a situation bearing nearly all the characteristics of a constitutionally protected family, when the rights would be very extensive indeed.

This analysis presented commentators with some difficulties. It appeared to represent a shift from _State (Nicolaou) v. An Bord Uchtála_ [1966] I.R. 567, which treated *all* unmarried fathers, regardless of differences among them as to the level of commitment they showed towards their child, in an identical constitutional way, namely, that they had no constitutionally protected rights by virtue of their paternity. Finlay C.J. seemed to envisage varying 'rights of interest or concern', depending on the intensity of the particular relationship between the father and child.

But what was the juridicial nature of these rights? The Chief Justice appeared to deny them constitutional status. If lacking that status, where should they be located? As natural rights? Or, perhaps, rights inhering in the *children*, rather than their fathers?

In *W. O'R. v. E.H.*, Supreme Court, July 23, 1996, the Supreme Court returned to the issue. The Court was called on to answer a series of questions on a consultative case stated submitted by Judge Moran of the Circuit Court, on appeal from the District Court which had refused to make the appellant guardian of his children, pursuant to section 6A of the 1964 Act (as amended).

The applicant and respondent had been involved in a relationship from 1981 to 1992. Two children had been born to them: a daughter in 1982 and a son in 1991. The parties had resided together as a family from 1986 to 1992. The birth of their son had been planned as they had intended to stay together at that time. During the course of the relationship, the parties had considered marriage. They separated permanently eleven months after the birth of their son.

The respondent married another man in July 1993. A month later she and her husband appealed to An Bord Uchtála for the adoption of both children. Four months after this, the applicant unsuccessfully applied to the District Court to be appointed guardian of both children, under section 6A of the Guardianship of Infants Act 1964 (as amended). He was, however, granted liberal access to the children under section 11 of the 1964 Act (as amended). He exercised this entitlement, with the approval of the respondent and her husband. An Bord Uchtála indicated that it would not make an adoption order in favour of the respondent and her husband until the access order was vacated.

The natural father intended to oppose the making of an adoption order should he be appointed guardian but did not intend to oppose the children's existing custodial status.

The Circuit Court Judge submitted for the determination of the Supreme Court the following questions:

1. On hearing of an application by a natural father to be appointed under section 6A of the Guardianship of Infants Act, 1964, is it proper for the court to take into account a specific pending application for adoption of the children of the natural parents by the natural

mother's husband when deciding whether or not to appoint the natural father as a guardian to his children, in particular in circumstances where the natural father is not seeking to change the custodial status of the children?

2. If the answer to No. 1 is in the affirmative, is it proper for the Court to take into account the natural father's intention to oppose the adoption application?

3. If the answer to No. 1 is in the affirmative, is it proper for the Court to have regard to this specific adoption application pending?

4. What are the character and extent of the rights of interest or concern of the natural father (referred to by the Supreme Court in the decision of *K. v. W.*) and when do same arise in the context of a guardianship application and are such matters within the sole of discretion of the trial judge?

5. Is the concept of *de facto* family ties as referred to in the European Court of Human Rights decision of *K. v. Ireland* (1994) 18 E.H.R.R. 142 afforded recognition under the Constitution and what rights, if any, accrue to the applicant arising from same?

6. Is a natural father's right to apply for guardianship and/or access or an order for access already made extinguished on the making of an adoption order?

7. If the answer to No. 6 is in the negative, does the Adoption Board have the right to direct that an access order already made be vacated before making an adoption order?

In addressing these questions, the Supreme Court had to revisit its earlier decision in *K. v. W.* as well as assessing the potential impact of the decision of the European Court of Human Rights in *K. v. Ireland*. The majority of the Court favoured a conservative strategy, battening down the hatches and resorting to a formalistic resolution of the issues presented.

Thus, Hamilton C.J. stated that:

[a] *de facto* family, or any rights arising therefrom, is not recognised by the Constitution or by any of the enactments of the Oireachtas dealing with the custody of children.

The Chief Justice did not consider it necessary 'to refer to or purport to deal in any way' with *Nicolaou*, other than to state that the view of the Supreme Court in that decision that it 'had not been established that the father of an illegitimate child has any natural right, as distinct from legal rights, to . . . the custody of that child would appear to be reinforced by the statement made by Finlay C.J. in the course of his judgment in *K. v. W.*, where he stated that "no constitutional right to guardianship in the father exists."'

Hamilton C.J. rejected the submission by counsel for the father that the 'rights and concerns' referred by Finlay C.J. were 'constitutional rights in the natural father.' They were 'matters to be taken into account in determining the welfare of the children when the natural father avails of his statutory right to apply to the Court for guardianship or custody of the children or access thereto.' Thus, according to the Chief Justice, the Court's consideration of 'the father's position should focus, not on his rights, but rather on the welfare of the children which might (or might not) be advanced by maintaining their relationship with their father.

The Chief Justice proceeded to dispose of the seven questions submitted to the Court. The first three questions should be answered in the affirmative. The fourth question, arising from *K. v. W.*, generated the following response:

> The rights of interest or concern in the context of the guardianship application arise on the making of the application. However, the basic issue for the trial judge is the welfare of the children. In so determining, consideration must be given to all relevant factors. The blood link between the natural father and the children will be one of the many factors for the judge to consider, and the weight it will be given will depend on the circumstances as a whole. Thus, the link, if it is only a blood link in the absence of other factors beneficial to the children, and in the presence of factors negative to the children's welfare, is of small weight and would not be a determining factor. But where the children are born as a result of a stable and established relationship and nurtured at the commencement of life by father and mother in a *de facto* family as opposed to a constitutional family, then the natural father on application to the Court under Section 6(A) of the Guardianship of Infants Act, 1964 has extensive rights of interest and concern. However, they are subordinate to the paramount concern of the Court which is the welfare of the children.

The fifth question raised the issue of whether the concept of *de facto* ties, endorsed in *Keegan v. Ireland*, was afforded recognition under the Constitution. The Chief Justice answered in the negative.

The decision of the European Court was not part of the domestic law of Ireland. The family referred to in Articles 41 and 42 of the Constitution was the family based on marriage. The concept of a *de facto* family was unknown to the Irish Constitution. The Irish Supreme Court, however, in its decision in *K. v. W.*, had recognised the existence of '*de facto* families' and also the fact that a natural father who lived in such a family might have extensive rights of interest and concern of the kind referred to in the reply to Question No. 4.

The Chief Justice answered Question No. 6 in the affirmative. It was clear from section 24 of the Adoption Act 1952, and from the Status of Children Act, 1987, that an adopted person was from the date of the adoption to be regarded as the child of the adopters and not the child of anyone else. 'A natural consequence of such a law' was that the right to apply for guardianship or access was extinguished on the making of the adoption Order. Since the answer to Question No. 6 was in the affirmative, Question No. 7 did not arise.

In her concurring judgment, Denham J. identified the father's 'rights of interest or concern' as impacting on the welfare of the children. These rights, she said,

> are directly in proportion to the circumstance that exist in the case between the father and the children. The greater the beneficial contact there has been, the more important it is to the welfare of the children and so the higher the rights of interest and concern of the father. Thus, variable degrees of interest and concern of the father arise on the making of the guardianship application.

Later in her judgment, again emphasising the centrality of the issue of the children's welfare, Denham J. observed that:

> where the children are born as a result of a stable and established relationship and nurture at the commencement of life by father and mother in a *de facto* family as opposed to a constitutional family, then the natural father on an application to the Court under section 6A [of the] Guardianship of Infants Act 1964 has extensive rights of interest or concern. However, they are subordinate to the paramount concern of the court, which is the welfare of the child.

It has to be said that this passage presents the rights of the father and the welfare of the child as potentially *conflictual* rather than as involving simply an enquiry as to the child's welfare in the light of the child's relationship with his or her father. The problem is the inevitable consequence of Finlay C.J.'s language in *K. v. W.* which, in truth, did purport to ascribe rights to the father.

The attempts by the Court in the instant case to force this language into a procrustean welfare test is understandable, but unconvincing.

Murphy J.'s strategy of denying any juridical status to paternal rights is of some interest. Placing heavy emphasis on English decisions (as well the decision of the Irish Court of Appeal ninety seven years ago in *In re O'Hara* [1900] 2 I.R. 232), he took the view that fatherhood, in conjunction with a long-standing and active commitment to the welfare of the child, was a factor to which the court would be bound to give serious consideration and which might well be of decisive importance in some cases. Murphy J. summarised his conclusions as follows:

1. What are described as 'natural rights' whether arising from the circumstance of mankind in a primitive but idyllic society postulated by some philosophers but unidentified by any archeologist, or inferred by moral philosophers as the rules by which human beings may achieve the destiny for which they were created, are not recognised or enforced as such by the courts set up under the Constitution.

2. The natural rights aforesaid may be invoked only insofar as they are expressly or implicitly recognised by the Constitution; comprised in the common law; superimposed on to common law principles by the moral intervention of the successive Lord Chancellors creating the equity jurisdiction of the courts or expressly conferred by an Act of the Oireachtas or other positive human law made under or taken over by, and not inconsistent with, the Constitution.

3. The Constitution does not confer on or recognise in a natural father any right to the guardianship of his child (see the *Nicolaou* case and *K. v. W.*).

4. The common law right of parents – and *a fortiori* the father to guardianship and custody of their or his child was moderated by equitable principles (see the *O'Hara* case).

5. Such rights as the family or father had in equity to guardianship of their or his child were supplanted by the provisions of the Guardianship of Infants Act. . . .

6. The undoubted statutory right of the natural father to apply for guardianship of his child carries with it the right to have the application properly considered by the court to which the application is made. That analysis will involve the consideration of a multiplicity of material facts varying with the particular circumstances of the case and in particular the actual personal, financial and emotional relationship that has existed between the father and his child and above all the value to the child of that relationship being continued but only in the context of how such benefits would interact with all or any other relevant considerations.

Discernible here is the positivist ideology which has gained recent dominance in the Supreme Court. In genuflecting to the formal sovereignty of the Constitution, the judicial enthusiasts of positivism have failed to recognise, and consequently, to protect, the coherence and integrity of the philosophic understanding of human capacities, entitlements and obligations which is integral to the Constitution. Even a strictly positivist approach should not yield such an outcome. The task of the positivist judge is to identify and give effect to the norms that constitute the particular legal order, regardless of whether the judge is sympathetic or hostile to those norms. One suspects that a certain lack of judicial sympathy for some of the norms which manifestly are integral to the Constitution underlies the rush to positivism, without the appreciation that positivism does not enable the court to discard a philosophy that forms part of the legal system which it is called on to implement.

Murphy J.'s judgment is of interest for another reason: it represents the first consideration by an Irish judge of the constitutional implications of recent developments in reproductive technology. Whilst the *Nicolaou* decision has been criticised for many years on the basis of its alleged harshness to unmarried fathers, Murphy J. found merit in its approach in the context of these recent developments. He stated:

> The question of the rights of a natural father has heretofore involved the acceptance of the fact that natural (or illegitimate) fathers may comprise a range of males extending from loving and caring fathers participating in an enduring relationship with the mother and children, to the psychopathic rapist whose only purpose was to do violence and bring humiliation to the mother. In more recent times one has to recognise a category of biological parenthood within which the male contributes sperm which is provided by means of artificial insemination in a female recipient unknown to the donor. This must be the case by which can be tested the basic proposition whether the mere donation of sperm confers on the donor any natural or constitutional right over any child that may subsequently be identified as having been conceived as a result of such a procedure. In my view that cold and clinical scenario would do much to strengthen the view expressed in the *Nicolaou* case that the mere fact of fatherhood does not give rise to natural or constitutional rights.
>
> Scientific advances may pose even greater problems in relation to the rights of mothers. If it is possible – as I understand it to be – to transplant a fertilised ovum in a woman who in due course gives birth to a child, 'Who is the mother for the purposes of Article 40 of the Constitution? The woman who provided the ovum or the woman who gave birth to the child?'
>
> These very questions illustrate the fundamental distinction between the line which may have to be drawn between the provision of the genetic material on which life depends and the nurturing of the being not merely from the time of birth but from the moment of conception.

This analysis, which asks rather than answers questions, is of particular interest because it represents the invocation of what might be called traditional constitutional principles to support conclusions which are far from traditional and which have been proposed or implemented in some other countries. Thus, for example, there is much support internationally for the view that, in cases of artificial insemination by donor (A.I.D.), the husband of the woman who gives birth by this method should be treated as though he were the child's father and the donor should be treated as having no legal status as father. The idea that *Nicolaou* should be called on to support this approach is as ironic as the invocation of Article 41, in *Attorney General v. X.* [1992] 1 I.R. 1; [1992] I.L.R.M. 401 in support of a family decisions that a member of the family should have an abortion.

Barrington J., in contrast to his judicial colleagues, departed from the approach adopted by the Supreme Court in *Nicolaou*. Acknowledging frankly that he had been counsel for Mr. Nicolaou, he observed that he found the reasoning in *Nicolaou* inadequate. He stated:

> [O]nce the court had accepted that the prosecutor was a concerned and caring parent it was not logical to justify his exclusion by a reference to natural fathers who had no interest in the welfare of their children. This was to fall into the logical trap . . . [of] treating equally persons who were in different situations and amounted therefore to unfair discrimination.

> The logical flaw in the argument can more easily be seen if one reduces it to a syllogism:

> (1) Many natural fathers show no interest in their offspring and the State may properly exclude them from all say in their children's welfare.
> (2) The prosecutor is a natural father.
> (3) Therefore the State may properly exclude him from all say in his child's welfare.

Barrington J. invoked Walsh J.'s famous statement on the natural law and its interpretation, in *McGee v. Attorney General* [1974] I.R. 284, at 318, and Walsh J.'s statement in *East Donegal Co-op Ltd. v. Attorney General* [1970] I.R. 317, as to the presumption that all statutorily-prescribed proceedings and procedures should be conducted in accordance with the principles of constitutional justice, in support of his view that a modern court would depart from *Nicolaou*.

Barrington J. regarded Article 40.3 of the Constitution as the best avenue for developing a theory of how a complex of rights and duties for parents of children born outside marriage might be given constitutional status. He reasoned as follows:

The Irish Constitution . . . stresses the relationship between parent and child and derives from that relationship a system of moral rights and duties which the law is enjoined to respect.

These reciprocal rights and duties may derive from the blood tie between parents and child but they are not the same thing as that blood tie. Rather do they amount to a moral code based upon it. It appears to me that they can be referred to as natural rights or duties or constitutional rights and duties and that in the context of Articles 41 and 42, the two terms are indistinguishable. . . .

The relationship between natural parents and their child can be compared with that existing between married parents and their children under Article 42 of the Constitution but the group does not form a unit group or institution within the meaning of Article 41. The relationship will give rise to reciprocal duties and rights but the manner in which these will, or can, be expressed will vary greatly with the circumstances. On the one hand the parents may be living together in what could be described as a de facto family. On the other hand the circumstances attending the child's conception or birth may be so horrific as to make it undesirable, or unthinkable, that the parents should live together.

. . . [I]llegitimate children are not mentioned in the Constitution. Yet the case law acknowledges that they have the same rights as other children. These rights must include, where practicable the right to the society and support of their parents. These rights are determined by analogy to Article 42 and are captured by the general provisions of Article 40.3 which places justice above the law. Likewise a natural mother who has honoured her obligation to her child will normally have a right to its custody and to its care. No-one doubts that a natural father has the duty to support his child and, I suggest, that a natural father who has observed his duties towards his child has, so far as practicable, some rights in relation to it if only the right to carry out these duties. To say that the child has rights protected by Article 40 Section 3 and that the mother, who has stood by the child, has rights under Article 40.3 but that the father, who has stood by the child has no rights under Article 40.3 is illogical, denies the relationship of parent and child and may, upon occasion, work a cruel injustice.

Barrington J. derived support for his analysis from Finlay C.J.'s judgment in *K. v. W.* It has to be said that Barrington J. has provided an impressive conceptual model for locating the unmarried father's 'rights of interest or concern' in the constitutional framework. The only problem is that Finlay C.J. denied any constitutional status to these rights.

NULLITY OF MARRIAGE

Lack of Consent: Relational Incapacity   In *P.C. v. C.M. (otherwise C.)*,
High Court, January 11, 1996, Laffoy J. had to analyse the crucial concepts
underlying the ground of relational incapacity first articulated in 1981. In *R.S.J.
v. J.S.J.* [1982] I.L.R.M. 263, Barrington J. held that a marriage might be
invalidated where one of the parties, on account of illness, lacked the capacity
to enter into a 'caring or considerate relationship with the other' at the time of
the celebration of the marriage. In *U.F. (otherwise U.C.) v. J.C.* [1991] 2 I.R.
330, the Supreme Court made it clear that the basis of the incapacity was
wider than simply illness. It could also be attributable to 'some inherent quality or characteristic of an individual's nature or personality which could not be
said to be voluntary or self-induced'.

   In *P.C.*, the respondent had had a child by another man before she married
the petitioner. After the marriage she resumed her relationship with the father
of her child; she also had an affair with a counsellor. There were, however,
periods where the marriage relationship was happy.

   The psychiatrist who gave evidence on behalf of the petitioner considered
that the respondent suffered from an immature personality disorder, involving
egocentricity and a lack of 'the empathy which is the fundamental quality of a
mature relationship.' The two highly inappropriate sexual relationships in which
she had engaged during the marriage indicated that she lacked the capacity for
a mature and empathetic relationship. This witness stated that an immature
personality disorder was classified in the tenth edition of the *International
Classification of Diseases*, published by the World Health Organisation, in
the category of 'Other Specific Personality Disorders'. He acknowledged that
personality disorder is common – as high as 13% of the population – although
he could not indicate the percentage of the population who suffer from immature personality disorder.

   In contrast, the psychiatrist who gave evidence on behalf of the respondent did not consider that she had a personality disorder. To justify such a characterisation, the insensitivity, vulnerability, and poor self-esteem would have
to be gross and serious. This witness stated than an immature personality disorder did not appear in the classification of personality disorders in the fourth
edition of the *Diagnostic and Statistical Manual* published by the American
Psychiatric Association.

   Laffoy J. approached the issue as follows. Since it was common case that
mental *illness* was not involved, the matter to be resolved, on the basis of the
U.F. decision, was whether the respondent was incapable of entering into and
sustaining 'a proper marital relationship, that is say, a life long union embodying an emotional and psychological relationship between [her] and the petitioner', because of some inherent quality or characteristic of her nature or

personality which was not voluntary or self induced. It was not, therefore, necessary to evaluate the conflicting psychiatric opinions of the two witnesses with a view to determining which opinion was correct, nor was it necessary to determine whether the best psychiatric practice recognised immature personality disorder or whether the respondent satisfied the criteria which justified classification as a person with an immature personality disorder. Laffoy J. noted that this was:

> not to say that [the psychiatrists'] evidence . . . is of no import. It rules out the existence of any psychiatric or mental illness and provides an insightful analysis of the personalities and mental attitudes of the parties on the basis of what the psychiatrists were told by the parties. However, in the final analysis it is for the court to decide, on the basis of the evidence adduced in court, whether the petitioner has established that the respondent was incapable of entering into and sustaining a proper marital relationship by reason of incapacity attributable to some inherent quality or characteristic, or whether a valid marriage has disintegrated by reason of wilful conduct on the part of the respondent.

In Laffoy J.'s view, several aspects of the respondent's life suggested that she was a resourceful and capable person but above all a strong willed person. When she had become pregnant she had received 'very little, if any, familial support' from her family, yet she had resisted her mother's suggestion that she have an abortion. She had got through the pregnancy 'largely on the basis of her own physical and emotional resources. . . .' After the birth of her child, while she was living at home with her family in difficult circumstances, she had resisted the suggestion that she have him fostered or adopted. When the father of the child, having initially agreed to marry her, changed his mind, the respondent had accepted the position and set herself up in her own establishment with her son, regulating her relationship with the father by a legal agreement dealing with custody and access.

In Laffoy J.'s view, the respondent's actions after the marriage represented 'wilful and voluntary conduct on her part' rather than revealing an incapacity to enter into and sustain a proper marital relationship. The renewal of her relationship with the father of her child had not been 'involuntary or . . . something she could not curb'; it was because she was attracted to him and wanted to act in this way. Similarly her affair with the counsellor occurred 'because the intimacy was comforting at a time when she was in low spirits, not because of a personality trait which impelled her.'

In an important passage, Laffoy J. stated:

> The respondent by her conduct has ruined her marriage and created adverse consequences not only for herself but also for her husband and her

children. From an objective viewpoint one might conclude that the respondent was immature in failing to foresee the consequences of her
conduct and in failing to regulate her conduct so as to avoid those consequences. The issue, however, is not whether the respondent was immature by objective norms. The issue is whether her nature, or personality,
as originally formed or as it developed, inherently predisposed her to act
in such a way as to preclude the existence of a normal marital relationship with her husband. In my view, it did not. . . .

I believe that the respondent did enter into the marriage with good
intent and that [for a number of years], by and large she tried to make her
marriage work. However, consistent with her conduct before her marriage, she did what she wanted to do, even in circumstances where she
was resiling on agreements with her husband and breaking her marriage
vows. The position here is that a valid marriage broke down . . . , not that
the marriage was void *ab initio*.

Laffoy J.'s approach provokes a number of observations. First, it represents a
strong reassertion by the court of control over the ultimate issue, which other
judges had let slip to the psychiatrists to determine. As far as Laffoy J. is
concerned, psychiatric evidence is crucial on whether incapacity *on account
of mental illness* has been established but, where mental illness is not in issue,
the views of psychiatrists on the existence or non-existence of 'some other
inherent quality or characteristic of an individual's nature or personality which
could not be said to be voluntary or self-induced' are far from central to the
court's determination of the question.

It should be noted that the issue of the scope of voluntary human conduct
is one that has tantalised philosophers for millennia. The present age is one in
which a determinist philosophy rules most of the sciences; it is no surprise to
find many psychiatrists saturated with determinist premises underlying their
assessment of human behaviour and relationships. Laffoy J. has made it plain
that the court should not impotently surrender the difficult task of assessing
the limits of human freedom to witnesses, however expert in their own disci-
plines, whose philosophic preferences have no necessary entitlement to be
elevated into principles of law.

Nonetheless, Laffoy J.'s perception of the boundaries of freedom seems
considerably broader than some of her judicial colleagues. Once the respondent's conduct could be characterised as 'wilful' or voluntary, it fell outside the
test for invalidity prescribed by the Supreme Court in *U.F.* There are echoes
here of the narrow interpretation traditionally afforded to the *M'Naghten* rules.
One may wonder whether this is quite what the Supreme Court envisaged. It
has to be said that Finlay C.J.'s formula is less than helpful on the delimitation
between voluntary conduct and personality. The Court in *U.F.* was dealing
with the matter of a homosexual orientation. It was naturally disinclined to

characterise this as a mental illness; the formula of 'some other inherent quality or characteristic of an individual's nature or personality which could not be
said to be voluntary or self-induced' seems to apply comfortably to those of
homosexual orientations. But what is the position where the orientation inclines a person to act in a way that offends the moral code but the conduct is
scarcely capable of being characterised as completely involuntary? Few juries
will easily acquit a paedophile, compulsive shoplifter or arsonist. There appears to be a zone of orientations which inspire conduct where that conduct
has an element of voluntariness. If one looks closely at Finlay C.J.'s formula,
it requires that the *inherent quality or character* of the individual's nature or
personality not be voluntary or self-induced; it says nothing about the voluntariness of the *conduct* attributable to such quality or character.

Of course the ground first stated in *R.S.J.* and amplified in *U.F.* is based on
an incapacity rather than on any particular conduct (or the lack of conduct).
Nevertheless, in order to determine whether the alleged incapacity exists, it
will be necessary for the court to scrutinise all relevant conduct.

B.J.M. v. C.M., High Court, July 31, 1996 is a troubling decision. Flood J.
granted a decree of nullity of marriage where the marriage had been celebrated
in 1974, the parties had lived together until 1991 (when the petitioner's sexual
relationship with another woman 'came to light'), the respondent having given
birth to at least two children during the currency of the marriage. (The judgment merely refers to 'children'.) The ground for the decree was a generic
one: that the petitioner's consent to the marriage had been 'apparent rather
than real in that it was not a full, free and informed consent'. The essence of
the petition was that the respondent had failed to disclose the petitioner the
fact that, when she was three years old, she had been extensively burned,
resulting in very significant disfigurement to parts of her body which the petitioner had not seen before the marriage. The discovery of the true position
'created in him a revulsion'. The marriage was not consummated for about
eight weeks.

Flood J. considered that the petitioner's revulsion was:

> a very human reaction. He has spent a courtship with a very attractive
> person both outwardly physical and in personality. She behaves with
> great modesty consistent with her manifest religious and moral beliefs
> and on his honeymoon where all inhibitions no longer exist, he is con-
> fronted not with 'a snowy breasted pearl' but with a partner for life who
> is seriously disfigured and in the sensual province gives rise . . . in his
> mind not to desire but to revulsion. To any partner or intended partner,
> the concept of relationship – a lifelong relationship – prior to marriage
> is based on a mixture of respect and desire and if the reality or near
> reality of his basic concept proves wholly illusory and has in fact no
> foundation in fact but on the contrary creates a revulsion, he has in fact

not entered into a contract of marriage with a full, free and informed consent and accordingly . . . his consent was apparent rather than real.

Flood J. was willing to go further. The petitioner's psychological revulsion rendered it improbable that he could maintain an emotional and psychological relationship such as was required to support a marriage and for this reason too the marriage was 'flawed'. (Presumably this amounts to an invalidation of the marriage on the *R.S.J.* ground. Immediately before this passage in his judgment, Flood J. quoted from Costello J.'s judgment in *D. v. C.* [1984] I.L.R.M. 173, at 188.)

One must have severe misgivings about this decision. It appears to place an undue emphasis on surface attractions and not enough on the deeper aspects of personality, psychology and relationship. Of course physical attraction is an important part of the sexual dimension of an interpersonal relationship and the sexual dimension is itself an important part of the whole relationship. That is why impotence has always been a ground for annulment. It is possible to envisage cases where bodily disfigurements could be so serious as to provoke a state of revulsion which would, in effect, foreclose the possibility of a sexual dimension to the relationship, but that was not the situation here. Consummation was admittedly delayed but, so far as the parties' sexual relationship was concerned, the petitioner was the more enthusiastic party. Flood J. noted that the respondent 'has unquestionably had physical sexual relations with her husband, not in my opinion on an ad lib basis but as her husband says after much persuasion.'

Flood J. went to some length to acquit the respondent of any bad faith in her failure to tell the petitioner about the disfigurements before the marriage:

> To her they were something to which she did not have regard and, while on an objective test she was lacking in frankness and indeed objectively in honesty to her intended partner for life in not detailing their extent, subjectively she was not conscious of any deceit.

If one has to categorise precisely the first ground on which the decree is based, therefore, it would seem wrong, for future cases, to require proof of deception. Nevertheless it could perhaps be argued that Flood J, while undoubtedly sympathetic to the respondent, regarded her as having culpably failed to give the necessary degree of disclosure of relevant information, such culpability being judged by an objective test.

The grant of a decree for nullity on the *R.S.J.* ground surely cannot be unsupported. The psychiatrist who gave evidence on behalf of the petitioner expressed the opinion that:

this is not a breakdown of an established marriage but evidence of a preexisting lack of information and an inability to sustain a normal marriage relationship because of the circumstances of which [the petitioner] had no real prior knowledge.

Flood J, while noting that his judicial task was 'to form a view' which could not be delegated even to a most distinguished psychiatrist, observed that he could 'take comfort in the correspondence of the psychiatrist's view and mine'. Yet the psychiatrist's opinion placed the non-disclosure in a central position in explaining the long-term outcome. The *R.S.J.* ground has no connection with non-disclosure. The petitioner in the instant case was clearly not suffering from a mental illness. Nor could it be said that he had 'some other inherent quality or characteristic of [his] nature or personality which could not be said to be voluntary or self-induced', as Finlay C.J. prescribed in *U.F. (otherwise U.C.) v. J.C.* [1991] 2 I.R. 330 at 356. Nothing useful is to be gained by trying to squeeze a case of non-disclosure into the language of a ground which is based on an inherent characteristic of one of the parties. The idea that the victim of non-disclosure has, as a result, a psychiatric condition is frankly preposterous.

Flood J. made no reference to the possible bar of approbation. This is curious, since the marriage had lasted nearly twenty-two years, there were children and the respondent had 'attempted to provide the material side of marriage in a very formal, fine and proper manner, [now] feel[ing] that all her efforts have been in vain as she has been rewarded by infidelity.' There is one passage in Flood J.'s judgment that is possibly capable of referring obliquely to the approbation issue. He was:

> very conscious that the marriage has continued to exist from 1974 to 1991 or thereabouts. I think this is entirely due to the petitioner's commitment and belief that he had no way out, that once he had been married there was really no going back and he adjusted to the best he could. But in the years that pas[sed], notwithstanding the undoubted efforts of the respondent, he could not sustain the relationship when it came under stress from an alternative source.

The more convincing interpretation of this passage is that it is addressing the question of the petitioner's relational capacity rather than the issue whether he should not be considered to have approbated the marriage on the basis that he was not for many years aware of the existence of an entitlement to a decree for nullity of marriage.

In *S.C. v. P.D. (falsely called C.)*, High Court, March 14, 1996, McCracken J. was called on to address difficult conceptual questions relating to the ground for annulment based on a party's incapacity to form and sustain a normal marital relationship with the other party. The parties had gone through a ceremony of marriage in 1974. Three children were born subsequently, the first in 1976 the last in 1980. The marriage relationship broke down in 1984 though the parties continued to reside under the same roof, living totally separate lives. During her teenage years, the respondent had consulted a child psychiatrist who treated her for anxiety symptoms.

On the day of the marriage, the respondent had behaved somewhat bizarrely, laughing and crying at inappropriate moments.

During her first pregnancy the respondent went into a hypermanic state with 'a marked paranoid trend'. She was successfully treated with Largactyl and Valium. A similar pattern emerged with her two subsequent pregnancies. In each case she was hospitalised for a period.

After the birth of the third child, the marital relations began to deteriorate and the respondent's illness recurred on several occasions, being hospitalised four times between 1982 and 1989. In 1987 she was diagnosed as suffering from manic depression. She was treated with Lithium and was 'fairly stable' thereafter.

McCracken J. refused to grant a decree of nullity of marriage on the basis of the respondent's inability to enter into and sustain a normal marriage relationship. In his view, the manic depressive illness which the respondent suffered was a latent one which did 'not manifest itself or affect the ability of the respondent to have normal relations, marital or otherwise, unless triggered by some event.' The incidents before and at the time of the marriage were not a manifestation of the manic-depressive order and did not affect the respondent's ability 'to contract or sustain a marriage in latter years.' The first 'trigger' of the respondent's condition had been her first pregnancy and each of the subsequent pregnancies had similarly acted as 'triggers'.

McCracken J. stated that, on the balance of probability, he was

> satisfied that at the time of the marriage, while the respondent suffered from a latent illness, that illness did not render her incapable of forming and sustaining a normal life long marital relationship. She was clearly capable of forming that relationship, and while, perhaps with hindsight, she ought not to have had children, and in fact a normal marital relationship was not sustained, I am satisfied that her illness was not such as to render her incapable of sustaining the relationship. Obviously, she was incapable of doing so during her periods under treatment, but with the aid of modern drugs these were comparatively short lived. It is most unfortunate that her illness was not properly diagnosed before the marriage had disintegrated beyond the point of no return, as it has shown itself to be an illness which can be kept under control for most of the time. I am particularly impressed by the fact that neither the death of her third child in 1992 nor the death of her father triggered off an incident, and I believe, had she been treated with Lithium at a much earlier stage, she would have been perfectly capable of sustaining this marriage, and indeed it might well have survived because I think in the early years the

petitioner did try to make a success of the marriage.

The holding in the case can clearly be defended on the basis of the express finding that the respondents' illness was not in fact such as to prevent her from forming or sustaining a normal life-long marital relationship. Nonetheless, McCracken J. ventured into deeper philosophical waters when he addressed the question of how the courts should regard an insidious condition, marital or physical, which exists, but has not yet manifested itself, at the time of the marriage. What he had to say is of great interest:

> What I must look at is the situation at the time of the marriage, and I do not think that the law has been extended so far as to say that a decree of nullity may be granted where a person suffered from a latent illness which did not affect her ability to enter into a marriage, but which might subsequently affect the ability to sustain that marriage. If it were otherwise, there are a host of illnesses which could give rise to a nullity where the illness was latent in the person at the time of the marriage, but did not manifest itself until subsequently. An obvious example which come to mind also have a logical extension of the principle, if it is to be correct, to physical defects, such as a brain tumour, which may have existed at the time of the marriage, and might subsequently manifest itself and grossly incapacitate the party.

One may hesitate before committing oneself to the proposition that a latent illness or other condition, existing *at the time of the marriage* ceremony, should not render a marriage voidable if it renders the party incapable of sustaining a normal marriage relationship merely because it does not render the party incapable of entering into the relationship. Once the vitiating element was there from the start, even if it did not initially manifest itself, it can be argued that the marriage suffers from an invalidating factor from day one.

As against this, it is possible to conceive of cases, as McCracken J. makes clear, where a *potential* to suffer an illness, existing at the time of the marriage ceremony, may be *actualised* at some later date. This should not, on principle, be a ground for annulment, since the vitiating element did not exist at the time of the marriage.

Undoubtedly there will be many illnesses or conditions, especially *mental* illnesses or conditions, where it will be genuinely hard to differentiate between a pre-existing latent condition, on the one hand, and a potential to develop a particular condition, on the other. We are treading here on dangerous philosophical waters: the very concept of actualisation of potential, supported by Aristotle and denigrated by many other philosophers, is hard to apply in particular contexts involving the human mind. Nonetheless, if the comparison is not an unfortunate one, it is worth noting that courts have to make these kind of judgment calls in other contexts. Take, for example, the notion of a defect in a product that did not exist at the time it was placed on the market. And what about the notion that, for the purposes of limitation of actions, the clock might start ticking before damage is actually sustained if a building is 'doomed from the start'? cf. *Pirelli General Cable Works Ltd. v. Oscar Faber & Partners* [1983] 2 A.C. 1.

Psychiatric examination   In *J. Section v. C. Section (otherwise C.T.)*, High Court, October 14, 1996, Budd J. held that the Master of the High Court had competence to appoint a psychiatrist as medical inspector for both parties in a nullity petition, under Order 36, rule 4 and Order 70, rule 32 of the Rules of the Superior Courts 1986. The Master's jurisdiction traditionally has been exercised in nullity petitioners where the ground was impotence; two medical inspectors, a gynecologist and a urologist, would be appointed to carry out the necessary examinations. Budd J. considered it 'preferable that there should be one consultant psychiatrist so as to minimise the intrusion into the private lives of the parties and the stress of attending a psychiatric examination.'

Budd J. was satisfied that, in the light of the development of the grounds for nullity of marriage, especially those involving an assessment of the psychiatric condition of a party to an alleged marriage, it was proper to extend the Master's capacity as to the appointment of medical inspectors beyond the impotence cases to other cases of nullity. The ecclesiastical matrimonial courts had always proceeded on a more inquisitorial basis than other courts and this approach had been maintained by the civil courts which succeeded them after the passing of the Matrimonial Causes and Marriage Law (Ireland) Amendment Act 1870.

Budd J. derived support for his approach from Henchy J.'s judgment in *C.D. v. E.D.*, High Court, June 21, 1971, holding that the Master had been mistaken, in proceedings for impotence *quoad hanc*, to appoint a psychiatrist as an inspector. As to the word 'inspection', Budd J. observed that, 'while it may mean literally to look at, it seems to me that a gynecological or urological examination would probably be tactile as well as visual and, accordingly, "inspection" has a wide connotation and includes interview, although not including any invasive test procedures or treatment.'

Budd J. rejected arguments that the appointment of a psychiatric medical inspector infringed the respondent's rights to bodily integrity, privacy and marital privacy. It was not obligatory for her to attend the interview. Budd J. observed:

> Obviously, adverse comment may be made if a party refuses to attend, but this may well be subject to a reasonable explanation, for example, the recommendation of a person's treating psychiatrist in this respect.

Standard of Proof   In *S.C. v. P.D. (falsely called C.)*, High Court, March 14, 1996, McCracken J. took a firm position on the question of the proper standard of proof in nullity proceedings. Having quoted from Henchy J.'s judgment in *Banco Ambrosiano v. Ansbacher & Co. Ltd.* [1981] I.L.R.M. 669, at 701-2, McCracken J. expressed himself

> quite satisfied that these remarks apply equally to an issue of nullity, and that the matter must be judged on a balance of probabilities rather than on any other basis, but that, as in cases of fraud, great care should be taken in drawing inferences.

Fisheries and Harbours

AQUACULTURE LICENCES

In *Madden and Ors. v. Minister for the Marine* [1993] 1 I.R. 567 (H.C.); [1993] I.L.R.M. 436 (H.C.); [1997] 1 I.L.R.M. 136 (Section C.), the Supreme Court upheld a decision of Johnson J. in the High Court (1992 Review, 377-9) that the Minister had acted *ultra vires* in attempting to use the Foreshore Act 1933 and the Fisheries (Consolidation) Act 1959 to grant what amounted to aquaculture licences and thus circumvent the more stringent terms of the Fisheries Act 1980. Section 54 of the Fisheries Act 1980 authorises the Minister for the Marine to designate by Order an area for which licences to engage in aquaculture can be granted. Section 54 of the 1980 Act is hedged around with a number of procedural requirements before such an Order can be made: see *Courtney v Minister for the Marine* [1989] I.L.R.M. 605 (1988 Review, 256).

In the *Madden* case, the applicants had read a notice in their local newspaper indicating that a company, Vestobrook Ltd (the notice party in the case), intended to apply to the Minister for the Marine under section 19 of the Foreshore Act 1933 for permission under section 3 of the 1933 Act to moor cages on an area of the foreshore at Ballyvaughan Bay, Clare, for the cultivation of trout. As required by section 19 of the 1933 Act, the notice also stated that objections to the grant of permission should be made to the Department of the Marine. The applicants lodged objections with the Department, and these were acknowledged by letter of February 1, 1989. The first applicant then requested, by letter of May 7, 1989, a copy of the environmental impact assessment carried out in respect of the area concerned. This was furnished by the Department by letter dated May 18, 1989. In response to a further request from the applicants' solicitor, the Department by letter of June 20, 1989 sent him a copy of a licence issued on June 1, 1989 by the Minister to Vestobrook Ltd. pursuant to section 3 of the 1933 Act and section 15 of the Fisheries (Consolidation) Act 1959 (the latter relating to fish culture licences) which in turn had replaced a licence issued to the company under section 3 the 1933 Act by the Minister on April 28, 1989. As indicated, Johnson J. held that the Minister had acted *ultra vires* in attempting to use the 1933 and 1959 Acts to grant what amounted to aquaculture licences and thus circumvent the more stringent terms of the 1980 Act, particularly those concerning objections. The Supreme Court (Hamilton C.J., Blayney and Barrington JJ.) affirmed and dismissed the Minister's appeal.

Delivering the Court's decision, Blayney J. stated that section 15 of the 1959 Act had to be construed in the context of both the 1959 Act and the 1980 Act, since the 1980 Act provided that both were to be construed as one. It was clear in his view that section 15 of the 1959 Act would empower the Minister to grant a fish culture licence in respect of an inland several fishery. It was also clear from section 8 of the 1959 Act that the only matter in respect of which the Minister could cause an inquiry to be held was "the fisheries.. or any of them" in any fishing district. This power It did not extend, in his view, to causing an inquiry to be held into the grant of a fish culture licence in respect of part of the open sea.

Blayney J. went on to say that the Minister could have directed an inquiry under section 3(9) of the Foreshore Act 1933 but he thought it was extremely doubtful whether such an inquiry would have been able to deal with anything other than the consequences of the physical presence of the cages moored in the sea as the 1933 Act was not concerned with fishing. He noted that if s 15 of the 1959 Act were to be construed as allowing the grant of a culture licence in respect of part of the sea, it would mean that it could be granted without any worthwhile inquiry being held and without the prospect of an appeal to the High Court. He stated that the Court would be reluctant to give the section such a construction 'since there would clearly be a risk that it would be unconstitutional.' When the section was looked at in the context of the 1980 Act it was open to be construed as applying only to a licence granted in respect of inland several fisheries. On that basis, the Court rejected the Minister's appeal.

FISHERIES

Detention of boat: application to court   In *Attorney General v Walley (Andrew, Notice Party)*, High Court, June 18, 1996, Geoghegan J. held that, while generally an application for the detention of a boat and the persons on board pursuant to section 234 of the Fisheries (Consolidation) Act 1959 (which provides the application is to be made 'as soon as may be') should be made to a judge of the District Court within 24 hours, where there was no court available within that time a lapse of 32 hours did not fall outside the 1959 Act.

Section 234 of the 1959 Act, as amended provides, *inter alia*, that where a sea fisheries protection officer in exercise of his powers under the Act has detained a boat and the persons on board at a port, an officer shall, 'as soon as may be', bring the Master of the boat and any other relevant persons on board before a judge of the District Court. The judge, if satisfied that proceedings for an offence under the Act have been or are about to be instituted, shall by order require the officer to detain the boat and relevant persons on board until the proceedings have been adjudicated upon by a judge of the District Court.

An application was made under this section to the respondent judge of the District Court but he refused to entertain it on the grounds that the application had not come before the court 'as soon as may be'. The State Solicitor for the county had been informed at 7 a.m. on September 17 that the vessel in question was arriving. He undertook to obtain a 48 hour detention order under section 234 of the 1959 Act. At 9 a.m., he contacted the District Court Clerk and requested him to arrange a special court to obtain the 48 hour order. The Court Clerk indicated that to his knowledge no judge was available as they were attending a statutory meeting out of the county. Later that morning the clerk stated that the respondent would deal with the matter the next day at 3 p.m. As indicated, the respondent concluded that he believed that an order should have been made under section 234 the previous day and that a lapse of about 32 hours from the time of the handing over of the vessel did not come within the phrase 'as soon as may be'. On judicial review, Geoghegan J. granted an order of *certiorari* quashing the respondent's order.

He accepted, in accordance with the decision in *Rederij Kennemerland BV v Attorney General* [1989] I.L.R.M. 821 (1990 Review, 326), that ordinarily the application under section 234 of the 1959 Act should be made within 24 hours. However, he considered that the position was different where there was no court available within that time, as here. In such as case, the matter should be decided on the basis of the ordinary interpretation of section 234. In his view, there was no difference between the words 'as soon as may be' and the words 'as soon as practicable.' The State had taken all reasonable steps to have the matter heard as soon as practicable and its obligation did not go beyond that. While Geoghegan J. not surprisingly took judicial notice of the system of District Courts established by the Oireachtas under the Constitution which were reasonably available for both ordinary and special sittings throughout the country and throughout the year, he also accepted that peculiar circumstances could arise resulting in more delay in setting up a court than would normally be the case and that this had happened in the instant case. Accordingly, he concluded that the officer had made the application 'as soon as may be' and that the respondent was not entitled to refuse to entertain it.

Emergency bye-law: drift net restrictions   In *Needham v Western Regional Fisheries Board and Minister for the Marine*, High Court, November 6, 1996, Murphy J. dismissed a challenge to a bye-law made by the Minister for the Marine in 1994 under section 9 of the Fisheries (Consolidation) Act 1959. The bye-law allowed for the creation of 'salmon sanctuaries' off the coast of County Mayo where salmon could not be caught. The bye-law also prohibited the use of drift nets for the purposes of catching salmon in the sanctuaries. The bye-law did not to apply to vessels of less than 26 feet in length. The plaintiff challenged the validity of the bye-law, pursuant to section 11 of the 1959 Act. He argued that his constitutional rights to a livelihood and his property rights under Article 40.3 and 43 of the Constitution were infringed by the bye-law, particularly having regard to the fact that he was the only licensed drift fisherman in the area in question.

Murphy J. held that since the bye-law in question was introduced every year as an emergency measure and had not been intended to last more than one year, it could be justified as an emergency measure under section 9(1)(gg) of the 1959 Act. Since there was no policy by the Fisheries Board to either phase out or abolish drift net fishing, and since the Minister was not seeking to do such under the guise of emergency legislation, the plaintiff's constitutional arguments did not stand up to scrutiny.

Murphy J. held that the purpose of section 9 of the 1959 Act was not the preservation of an endangered species, but the protection and improvement of a food supply, an industry and a leisure pursuit. In that sense, he considered that section 9 required a political decision which reconciled existing and to some extent conflicting decisions, and that the High Court must review the decision by reference to those criteria rather than those of some academic standard of commercial excellence divorced from the needs and interests of the public. In this context, since there was a serious reduction in the national and regional salmon catch, this justified the Minister in adopting the emergency measures.

He was not prepared to test the validity of the bye-law solely by reference to its impact on the plaintiff, even though he was the only licensed drift-net fisherman operating in the affected area. He accepted that the bye-law was intended to protect the fishing in the area; he considered that the further protection of the river mouths from excessive fishing was desirable and the prohibition contained in the bye-law was reasonable whether it impacted on one or many fishermen. While he accepted that the extent to which drift-net fishermen impinged on sea trout fishing was minimal, he held that it was appropriate that protective measures be taken so as to avoid even that minimal exploitation. He thus upheld the bye-law as an emergency measure under section 9 of the 1959 Act.

Inland several fishery In *Gannon and Ors v Walsh and Ors*, High Court, June 20, 1996, the plaintiffs successfully sued the defendants for interference with a several fishery along the River Moy between Foxford and Ballina in County Mayo. In the course of his judgment in the case, Keane J. reviewed in detail the history of the fishery in question. He held, *inter alia*, that the defendants were not entitled to set up a *jus tertii* against the plaintiffs' possessory title, that section 13 of the Land Act 1913 entitled the plaintiffs to a right of access to the fishery, that the defendants had interfered with the plaintiffs' enjoyment of the fishery by erecting fencing around the area of access (and awarded £5,000 in damages) and held that the plaintiffs had acted in breach of their fishery rights to the extent of bringing an excessive number of cars along the access route to the fishery. In order to avoid any future difficulties between the parties, Keane J. made a form of speaking order, reciting that the plaintiffs were entitled to a several fishery in the River Moy between the points to be delineated on a map annexed to the order, and to the soil and bed of the river *usque ad medium filium.* The order would also recite that the plaintiffs were entitled to a right of access without vehicles along the access road to the river bank and along the bank between the relevant points for the purpose of exercising the right of fishery. Finally, the order also included an injunction restraining the defendants from interfering with the plaintiffs' in the exercise of their rights and directing them to remove the lock on the gate on the access road and any fences obstructing the use of the pathway along the river bank.

Irish exclusive waters: offences   The Sea Fisheries (Control Of Catches) Order 1985 (Amendment) Order 1996 (SI No.6 of 1996), made under section 223A of the Fisheries (Consolidation) Act 1959, made any infringement of Council Regulations 2847/95 and 2870/95 (which provide new control measures for designated fishing areas including the Irish exclusive waters and the Irish box) an offence. The 1996 Order came into force on January 1, 1996.

HARBOURS

Harbours Act 1996   The Harbours Act 1996 is a lengthy piece of legislation, which updates in significant respects the Harbours Act 1946. The principal provisions of the 1996 Act deal with the following:

(a) laying down a framework for the establishment of State commercial companies to manage and operate the ports of Arklow, Cork, Drogheda, Dublin, Dundalk, Foynes, Galway, New Ross, Shannon, Waterford and Wicklow, and to provide for their functions and powers. Prior to the 1996 Act, these ports were managed by harbour authorities under the Harbours Act 1946.

(b) to provide for the setting up of a State commercial company to manage and operate Dun Laoghaire Harbour; prior to the 1996 Act, this harbour was managed by the Department of the Marine (see the Dun Laoghaire Harbour Act 1994, discussed in the 1994 Review, 279-80);

(c) to revise the law relating to pilotage.

Establishment and administration of companies   Sections 7 and 8 of the 1996 Act provide for the setting up of 12 commercial State companies and their capital formation. The new State companies are as follows: Arklow Harbour Company, Port of Cork Company, Drogheda Port Company, Dublin Port

Company, Dundalk Port Company, Dun Laoghaire Harbour Company, Foynes Port Company, Galway Harbour Company, New Ross Port Company, Shannon Port Company, Port of Waterford Company and Wicklow Port Company. The limits of each company's harbour are set out in Part I of the Third Schedule. These may be varied by Ministerial Order.

Section 11 sets out the principal objects of each company. Each company shall: (a) take all proper measures for the management, control, operation and development of its harbour and the approach channels thereto and provide reasonable facilities, services and accommodation in the harbour for vessels, goods and passengers; (b) promote investment in its harbour; (c) engage in any business activity, either alone or in conjunction with other persons, that it considers to be advantageous to the development of its harbour; (d) utilise and manage the resources available to it in a manner consistent with these objects; (e) take such steps either alone or in conjunction with other persons as are necessary for the efficient operation and management of its harbour; (f) appropriate any part of its harbour to the exclusive use of any person; and (g) engage in activities outside the State (related to functions in respect of its harbour) which will promote the interests of trade and tourism in the State. Section 12 imposes a duty on each company to operate in a cost-effective manner and to ensure that it generates enough revenue to cover its costs and remunerate its capital. Section 13 empowers each company to impose charges, as determined by it, on goods, vessels, passengers and the provision of any facility or service. It sets out who shall be liable to pay such charges and it provides that different rates of charges may be imposed in different circumstances. Section 14 provides that where default is made in payment each company may, under certain circumstances, detain and sell goods or ships for the purpose of recovering unpaid harbour charges. Section 16 provides that a company may compulsorily acquire land required for port development purposes, where the land is essential for the development to proceed. The provisions relating to compulsory acquisition are set out in the Fourth Schedule to the 1996 Act. The number of directors of each company shall be not more than 12. The directors (with the exception of the chief executive, the worker director and local authority directors) will be appointed and may be removed from office by the Minister for the Marine with the consent of the Minister for Finance. Each director, except the chief executive, shall be appointed for five years. Remuneration for directors shall be determined by the Minister for the Marine with the consent of the Minister for Finance. Section 19 provides for shares in each company to be issued to the Minister for the Marine. Both the Minister for the Marine and the Minister for Finance are prevented from selling their shares in the company to ensure that each company remains in public ownership. Section 35 provides for the appointment of a chief executive of each company. The first chief executive of each company (other than Dun Laoghaire) will be the person who on the day before vesting day was the

General Manager or Secretary (as the case may be) of the relevant harbour authority. The first chief executive of Dun Laoghaire Harbour Company will be appointed by the Board following consultation with the Minister. Each subsequent chief executive will be appointed to and be liable to be removed from office by the directors of the companies. The functions of the chief executive will be to carry on, manage and control generally the administration of the company, subject to the lawful directions of the directors of the company.

Harbour master   Section 37 requires that a harbour company shall employ a harbour master and such other employees as are required to perform its functions effectively. The harbour master may delegate some of his powers to one or more members of the staff of the company.

Harbour bye-laws   Section 42 empowers a company to make harbour bye-laws for the use of and safety of navigation in its harbour. Any bye-laws in force immediately before the vesting day shall remain in place until amended or revoked by a company. A person who contravenes a bye-law shall be guilty of an offence under the Act.

Ministerial powers   Section 44 confers general powers on the Minister for the Marine in connection with general policy decisions made by the Minister concerning development of harbours, safety of operations and levels of harbour charges. The Minister may, in consultation with a company and with the consent of the Minister for Finance, stipulate financial targets to be met and dividends to be paid by any company.

Safety of navigation and security in harbours   Section 45 of the 1996 Act requires each company to place buoys and lights in its harbour as necessary. Section 46 confers on the harbour master of a company the power to give directions to the master of a ship relating to the times of entry and egress of vessels to and from the harbour, the dismantling of a ship, the loading and discharging of cargo and related matters. Any shipmaster refusing to carry out such instructions shall be guilty of an offence under the 1996 Act. Section 47 empowers the harbour master, in certain circumstances, to direct the master of a ship to remove such ship from a place in the harbour to such other place or anchorage as he may consider necessary. Any master refusing to carry out such instructions shall be guilty of an offence. Sections 48 and 49 relate to information required by a harbour master. A harbour master may require the master of a ship to supply statements on the draught of the ship, the cargo on board, insurance documents, certificates of competency and any other relevant documentation. The harbour master may enter a ship to obtain such information. Any master of a ship refusing to comply with the terms of these sections shall be guilty of an offence under the 1996 Act. Section 50 provides that any person who obstructs or impedes the harbour master in the exercise of his or her powers shall be guilty of an offence. Section 51 provides that any direction or requirement of a harbour master under the 1996 Act shall not diminish the responsibility of the master of a ship in relation to the ship or the cargo thereof under, in particular, the Merchant Shipping Acts 1894 to 1992. Section 52 provides that a company may refuse entry to its harbour of a ship or other vehicle carrying nuclear/radioactive material, or any other material which would be likely to endanger persons or property. Any person who contravenes this section shall be guilty of an offence. This provision does not prejudice the provisions of the Sea Pollution Act 1991 (see the 1991 Review, 366) as they relate to harbours. Section 53 provides that a person who interferes with anything provided by a company for the purpose of safety in its harbour shall be guilty of an offence. Section 54 deals with the appointment of harbour police at the ports of Dublin and Dun Laoghaire. Staff who on vesting day are employed as harbour constables at Dublin and Dun Laoghaire shall be designated as harbour police at the new companies. The section deals with the powers of arrest afforded to the harbour police, the training required before such powers can be exercised and the furnishing by each company of warrants of appointment to such employees. Any person obstructing the harbour police in the performance of their duties shall be guilty of an offence under the 1996 Act.

Pilotage   Section 56 provides that port companies shall organise and ensure the provision of pilotage services either by employing pilots as members of their staff, or by licensing persons to perform acts of pilotage. It also provides that the harbour master shall be the superintendent of pilots and pilotage. Section 58 provides for the grant and renewal by port companies of pilots' licences and/or warrants of employment. The port company may, in granting a licence/warrant attach such conditions thereto as it thinks fit including conditions as to the area(s) within the pilotage district that the licensee/employee may act as a pilot and the type of ship he or she may pilot. Different classes of licences may be issued. The grant or renewal of a pilots licence will not render the port company liable for any act or default of the holder of the licence. It also provides for the continuation in force of a pilot's licence granted by the former pilotage authority and which is in force immediately before the coming into force of the 1996 Act. Section 59 provides for a pilotage agreement between a port company and its licensed pilots. The pilots will nominate a person or persons for the purpose of concluding such an agreement. A pilotage agreement will provide for the number of licensed pilots who shall provide pilotage services and an increase or reduction in the number of such pilots in the event of an increase or reduction in traffic in the pilotage district; the carrying out of the following duties by the port company or the licensed pilots: (a) collection and recovery of pilotage charges and the disbursement of these after all lawful deductions have been made as well as their payment to the harbour companies and (b) the making of a scheme for the grant of pensions, gratuities and other allowances on death or retirement of pilots. A pilotage agreement may be varied or cancelled by the harbour company provided the majority of licensed pilots vote (by secret ballot) in favour. Section 60 provides that a ship which is being navigated in a pilotage district in circumstances in which pilotage is compulsory shall be under the pilotage of a licensed or employed pilot *or* be under the pilotage of a master or first mate who is the holder of a pilotage exemption certificate. If, for some reason, the services of an appropriately qualified pilot are not available the master may navigate the ship in the pilotage district provided the harbour master authorises such navigation. The master of a ship who fails to comply with these provisions will be guilty of an offence. Section 63 provides that the fact that a ship is being navigated in a pilotage district in circumstances in which pilotage is compulsory for it shall not affect any liability of the owner or master of the ship for any loss or damage caused by the ship or by the manner in which it is navigated.

Pilotage charges   Section 64 provides that a harbour company may fix pilotage charges for its pilotage district; and that such charges shall be recoverable by the company or the pilots (as the case may be) as a simple contract debt in any court of competent jurisdiction. Section 65 provides that pilotage charges may be imposed on either the owner or master of the ship or a consignee or agent. A port company may require a person to give a bond of a specified amount in favour of the company to recover pilotage charges. Section 67 provides that a dispute or disagreement as to whether a thing done or to be done in relation to the navigation of a ship is a pilotage service shall be referred to the harbour master for determination. While it also provides that his or her decision in the matter shall be final, this is clearly subject to the overriding principle that a patently incorrect decision would be subject to some form of judicial review.

Retiring age for pilots   Section 69 provides that the retiring age for pilots shall be 60 years of age, but this provision does not apply to a person who, before the coming into operation of the 1996 Act, was the holder of a pilot's licence.

Pilotage bye-laws   Section 71 provides for the making of pilotage bye-laws by port companies. The Minister for the Marine shall direct that the bye-law be introduced, modified or not introduced. The purposes for which pilotage bye-laws may be made are set out in Part II of the Sixth Schedule. A person who contravenes a pilotage bye-law shall be guilty of an offence under the 1996 Act.

Pilotage exemption certificates Section 72 provides for the granting by port companies of pilotage exemption certificates to the master or first mate of a ship provided that he or she is (a) an Irish citizen, (b) a national of another Member State of the European Union or (c) a national of a State with which the State has reciprocal arrangements for the grant of such certificates. Before granting a pilotage exemption certificate the company will have to be satisfied that the applicant has sufficient skill, experience and local knowledge, and that he or she is the holder of a certificate referred to in Regulation I/2 of the International Convention on Standards of Training, Certification and Watchkeeping for Seafarers (1978), made under the aegis of the International Maritime Organisation (IMO). Section 73 provides for the suspension or revocation of a pilot's licence or a pilotage exemption certificate if the holder has conducted himself or herself in a manner that amounts to a contravention of the provisions of the 1996 Act or otherwise to misconduct, incompetence or neglect of duty. A company may not suspend or revoke a licence or certificate otherwise than in accordance with a direction given to it by a Board of Inquiry. The members of any such Board of Inquiry shall consist of the chief executive of the company (or a person nominated by him or her), a person nominated by the Minister for the Marine and a person nominated by the holder of the licence or certificate. Subject to any bye-laws that may be in force, the Board of Inquiry shall determine the procedure to be followed at an oral hearing. The Board of Inquiry may obtain the assistance of assessors in determining any matter of a technical nature that arises during the course of an oral hearing. The company shall comply with a direction given to it by a Board of Inquiry. Where a licence or certificate is suspended or revoked the holder or former holder thereof may appeal the decision to the Circuit Court. A company may suspend a licence or certificate without a direction from a Board of Inquiry being given to it if the gravity of the particular conduct is such as to warrant the immediate suspension of the licence. Such a suspension shall not prejudice the operation of the Board of Inquiry. Section 74 provides that a person may appeal to the Minister against the conduct of a port company with respect to a pilot's licence or a pilotage exemption certificate. The Minister shall consider the complaint and is empowered to make an order redressing the matter complained of and the company shall give effect to any such order made by the Minister. Section 75 states that a master of a ship shall be obliged to furnish to a pilot in respect of a ship which he or she is piloting the ship's draught of water, air draught, length and beam and to provide him/her with such other information relating to the ship (including any defects in, and matters peculiar to, the ship and its machinery and equipment which might materially affect the navigation of the ship) as the pilot considers necessary to enable him or her to carry out his or her duties. A master who fails to comply with this requirement or makes a false statement shall be guilty of an offence under the 1996 Act.

Duty of pilots   Section 77 provides that if a pilot in the course of piloting a ship does any act or omits to do something which endangers or is likely to endanger the ship, another ship, persons or structures he or she shall be guilty of an offence. In proceedings for an offence under this provision, it shall be a defence to prove that in all the circumstances the loss, damage, death or injury in question or, as the case may be, the likelihood of its being caused either could not reasonably have been foreseen by the accused person or could not reasonably have been avoided, or, if the act or omission alleged against the accused person constituted a breach or neglect of duty, the accused person took all reasonable steps to discharge that duty.

Dissolution of harbour authorities   Section 81 provides for the dissolution of harbour authorities in respect of which companies have been set up and also for the contemporaneous dissolution of pilotage authorities to be, where appropriate.

Dublin quay walls and bridges   Section 88 of the 1996 Act, *inter alia*, provides for the transfers of responsibility for the quay walls and bridges of the River Liffey in Dublin from and including Rory O'More Bridge at Heuston Railway Station up to and including the Matt Talbot Memorial Bridge to Dublin Corporation.

Powers of harbour authorities   Sections 91 and 93 amended section 47 of the Harbours Act 1946 by conferring additional powers on harbour authorities to become engaged, either alone or in conjunction with other persons, in any business activity that would be advantageous to the development of their harbour or to do anything that would facilitate, either directly or indirectly, the performance by them of their functions under the 1946 Act. Section 93 also added a new section 47A to the 1946 Act authorising the harbour master to refuse entry to any vessel he considers is dangerous. A general prohibition is placed on nuclear vessels, subject to specific permission authorised by the Radiological Protection Institute of Ireland (RPII).

Lighthouse authority   Section 94 provides that nothing in the 1996 Act affects the powers of any general or local lighthouse authority.

Penalties   Section 6 of the 1996 Act provides that persons guilty of an offence under the Act shall be liable (a) on summary conviction to a fine not exceeding £1,500 and/or imprisonment for a term not exceeding 12 months or both or (b) on conviction on indictment to a fine not exceeding £100,000 and/or imprisonment for a term not exceeding two years.

Garda Síochána

ASSOCIATIONS

In *Minister for Justice v. Garda Representative Association*, High Court, September 13, 1996, Geoghegan J. dealt with an aspect of a highly publicised dispute concerning the running of one of the Garda staff representative associations. A series of disputes within the defendant Garda Representative Association (GRA), which represents rank and file Gardaí, had led to the establishment of a breakaway organisation which became known as the Garda Federation. In response to this, and with a view to re-establishing a single representative association, the Minister for Justice had proposed introducing legislation under which elections would have taken place to the GRA in March 1997. The legislation had not been passed in time to facilitate this and, in July 1996, the Minister made the Garda Síochána (Associations) (Amendment) Regulations 1996 (SI No.222 of 1996), which removed the requirement to hold elections in September 1996 and substituted March 1997 in its place. The Minister then applied for an injunction restraining the defendant from holding September elections. Geoghegan J. granted the relief sought. Resisting the application, the defendant argued that the 1996 Regulations were in conflict with the right of association under Article 40.6 of the Constitution. Geoghegan J. held that it was not appropriate to consider constitutional issues at an interlocutory stage unless the Minister's Regulations were 'manifestly unconstitutional' and that was not the case here, in his view. He considered that, since the Minister had made what were *prima facie* a lawful set of Regulations, the defendant had nothing more than an arguable case that they were *ultra vires*. Thus, he concluded that there was at least a serious issue to be tried. He concluded that the balance of convenience lay in favour of granting the injunction, in particular because the Garda Síochána were a special category of public servants having responsibility for public security and the Minister's fears of the effect of a double election were well founded and also because very little inconvenience would be caused to the defendants by the type of injunction sought by the Minister. At the time of writing (July 1997) it would appear that, although the dispute has not been finally resolved, substantial steps have been taken to re-establish a unified GRA under which it would appear that the breakaway Garda Federation would be re-integrated into a reformed GRA.

COMPENSATION

Fatality award   In *Reid v. Minister for Finance*, High Court, July 29, 1996, Budd J. awarded the applicants, the widow and three children of a member of An Garda Síochána who was killed on duty with the United Nations in Bosnia Herzegovina in May 1995, over £380,000 under the Garda Síochána (Compensation) Acts 1941 and 1945. In awarding this sum, Budd J. took into consideration the deduction factors referred to in *Reddy v. Bates* [1983] I.R. 141. He also awarded a sum for bereavement under section 2(1)(a)(iv) of the Civil Liability Act 1961. Budd J. also took the rather unusual, but certainly welcome, step of directing that, in view of the dearth of reported judgments on the making of compensation awards under the 1941 and 1945 Acts, since the State was a party in each of these cases, a stenographers note should be made in respect of any *ex tempore* judgment relating to the 1941 and 1945 Acts in the future. It is greatly to be hoped that this expression of opinion will be acted on.

Trivial injuries: effect of Minister's certificate   In *McGee v. Minister For Finance*, High Court, April 19, 1996, Carney J. awarded the applicant damages under the Garda Síochána (Compensation) Acts 1941 and 1945, even though of the view that the injuries suffered were trivial, where the Minister for Justice had certified that the application should be brought.

The incident giving rise to the claim occurred in a Garda station in September 1993, when the applicant Garda was injured when a prisoner head butted him. The applicant's injuries consisted of a nose bleed and associated bruising which cleared up within a couple of weeks. He brought an application under the Garda Síochána (Compensation) Acts 1941 and 1945. Carney J. noted that the 1941 Act was in the first instance designed to compensate the dependants of members of the Gardaí who had died from injuries inflicted in the course of or in relation to the performance of their duties. Secondly it provided for like compensation for members of the Gardaí on whom personal injuries not causing death had been inflicted. He opined that the frequent use of the expression 'personal injuries not causing death' in the 1941 Act suggested that the minimum level of injury required to attract the benefit of the compensation regime was considerably above that of a nosebleed and some associated bruising and discomfort.

Nonetheless, since the applicant had come before the High Court on foot of a certificate from the Minister for Justice authorising him to apply to the court, section 6 of the 1941 Act indicated that such ministerial authorisation necessarily implied that the Minister considered that the applicant's injuries were non-minor. In Carney J.'s view, the Minister's certification did violence to the English language and represented a failure on her part to filter out the advancement of trivial and minor claims. He went on to state that in the course of these proceedings the Minister for Finance had come to share the Court's view and had asked him either to set aside or disregard the Minister for Justice's certification as being perverse. However, Carney J. was of the view that he was precluded from doing this by virtue of section 6(3) of the 1941 Act, which provided that the decision of the Minister for Justice in this matter was 'final and conclusive' and also by reason of the fact that the Minister for Justice was not a party to these proceedings. He thus felt obliged to proceed to assess compensation., which he found to be £300. As required by section 7(h) of the 1941 Act, Carney J. also awarded the applicant his costs. He noted that an examination of previous cases showed that the costs would amount, at a minimum, to a sum five times greater than that assessed for compensation.

It is clear that Carney J. took little pleasure in dealing with the case, but the level of distaste expressed is unusually forthright. As to whether he was obliged to accept the Minister's certification as 'final and conclusive', we should comment that, in *Maher v. Attorney General* [1973] I.R. 140 the Supreme Court found such a designation inconsistent with the independence of the judiciary guaranteed by Article 34.1 of the Constitution. Nonetheless, the trenchant tone of Carney J.'s judgment is likely to have a salutary effect on future such cases.

COMPLAINTS

Procedural principles   In *Grant v. Garda Síochána Complaints Board*, High Court, June 12, 1996, Murphy J. held that the appropriate standard of proof to be applied at hearings by the adjudicative bodies established under the Garda Síochána (Complaints) Act 1986 was the civil standard and also rejected the contention that the principle of *autrefois acquit* should be applied to their deliberations.

The Garda Síochána (Complaints) Act 1986 established procedures for the investigation and determination of complaints by members of the public concerning the conduct of members of the Garda Síochána. Section 7(5) of the 1986 Act provides for the referral of complaints to a tribunal. Section 9(2) of the 1986 Act provides that the function of such a tribunal is to decide: '(a) that the member concerned has not been in breach of discipline, or (b) that such member has been in breach of discipline as alleged, or (c) that the facts established constituted another breach of discipline.' Section 11 of the 1986 Act provides that a member of the Garda Síochána may appeal to the Garda Síochána Complaints Appeal Board from a decision of a tribunal finding him to be in breach of discipline and that the Appeal Board may 'affirm or set aside a decision of a Tribunal finding a member to be in breach of discipline or set aside such a decision and find that the member concerned was in breach of discipline other than as found by the Tribunal.'

It had been reported to the applicant, a member of the Garda Síochána, that a car had been interfered with by a named person. The applicant had arrested the named person and had interviewed him. A crucial issue in the case was that the person being interviewed averred that he had informed the applicant during this interview that he had been in St. Patrick's Institution, the place of detention for young offenders, on the day the interference with the car had been committed. The applicant denied that he had been told this. The applicant charged the person he had detained with interfering with a motor car. The applicant later withdrew the charges in the District Court. He maintained that he withdrew the charges when his informant stated that he could not positively identify the person interviewed as the person who had interfered with the car in question. A tribunal established under the Garda Síochána (Complaints) Act 1986 heard a complaint of three breaches of discipline, namely, (a) that the applicant had failed to carry out a proper investigation into the allegations made against the person he had detained; (b) that he had failed to take a statement from the relevant informant until almost two months after the case had been withdrawn; and (c) that he had charged the person who had been interviewed with an offence when, given the quality of evidence immediately available to him and the availability of the suspect, he should have carried out further inquiries before so charging him. Crucially, the tribunal accepted that the person who had been detained had advised the applicant during the interview that he had been in St. Patrick's Institution on the date the offence had been committed. The tribunal then found the applicant guilty of the third charge (c), above and imposed a reduction of two weeks pay. The tribunal also took the view that charges (a) and (b), above amounted to duplications of the third charge. The applicant appealed to the Garda Síochána Complaints Appeal Board which found him guilty of charge (a), above and affirmed the fine imposed by the tribunal.

The applicant sought an order of *certiorari* quashing the decision of the Appeal Board on the grounds that, in breach of his constitutional rights, he had been convicted on appeal of a charge dismissed against him by what he described as a court of first instance. In particular, he argued that the principle of *autrefois acquit* should apply and that the tribunal and Appeal Board should have applied the criminal standard of proof in determining the complaint. Murphy J. refused the relief sought and allowed the cause shown by the respondents.

Murphy J. noted that the Appeal Board had an express statutory power under section 11(2)(c) of the Garda Síochána (Complaints) Act 1986 to find a member in breach of discipline otherwise than as found by the tribunal. He rejected the applicant's argument that the investigating bodies established under the 1986 Act constitute courts set up under the Constitution to administer justice. While he accepted that the principles of constitutional and natural justice must be applied by the tribunal and Appeal Board, there was no justification for importing the practice and procedure of the High Court, or the common law principles governing the conduct of the courts, into proceedings under the 1986 Act.

Specifically, Murphy J. concluded that there was no basis for importing the principle of *autrefois acquit* into the regime set down in the 1986 Act. Analysing the different approaches of the tribunal and the Appeal Board, he noted that both had found that the applicant had been informed of the alibi which the person being interviewed had, and that the tribunal and Appeal Board had differed only on the issue of when the alibi should have been investigated. The tribunal had concluded that this should have been investigated before charges had been brought, while the Appeal board did not express a view on this point but did conclude that the applicant had not investigated the allegations properly. Murphy J. concluded that the finding of the Appeal Board did not involve any possible injustice to the applicant and declined to apply the *autrefois acquit* principle.

As to the standard of proof to be applied, Murphy J. held that the tribunal should apply the civil standard of proof, that is, proof on the balance of probabilities, in determining complaints pursuant to the 1986 Act. In this respect, he expressly followed his own decision in *Georgopoulos v. Beaumont Hospital Board* [1994] 1 I.L.R.M. 58 (1993 Review, 21-3).

DISCIPLINE

Delay In *McNeill v. Garda Commissioner* [1995] 1 I.L.R.M. 321 (H.C.); Supreme Court, July 30, 1996 the applicant appealed successfully against the refusal of Morris J. in the High Court (1994 Review, 281-3) to quash a disciplinary decision made under the Garda Síochána (Discipline) Regulations 1989, the main ground for objection being the delay in having a disciplinary hearing under the 1989 Regulations.

In December 1989, the applicant, a member of An Garda Síochána was interviewed in connection with alleged false claims made for overtime. The applicant explained that the claims were in relation to work he had taken home. The matter was referred to the Director of Public Prosecutions who decided that the applicant should be prosecuted. In June 1991 he was suspended from duty with pay and in July 1991 was served with 87 District Court summonses. He elected for trial on indictment, but the trial did not go ahead as the applicant's explanatory statements had been made without caution and were felt to be presumptively inadmissible. All summonses against the applicant were withdrawn.

In February 1992 the applicant was served with a notice under Regulation 40 of the Garda Síochána (Discipline) Regulations 1989, the 'fast track' procedure which empowers the Garda Commissioner in specified circumstances to dismiss certain members from the Garda Síochána. The Regulation 40 power may only be exercised where the Commissioner has decided that dismissal is merited and that the holding of an inquiry could not affect his decision. The consent of the Minister for Justice must be obtained in order to proceed under Regulation 40. In May 1992 the Regulation 40 notice was withdrawn, the Minister advising that the Regulation 40 procedure was inappropriate and that the holding of an inquiry could affect the Commissioner's decision. In July 1992 the applicant's suspension was lifted and he resumed full duties.

Later in July 1992, procedures under Regulation 8 of the Garda Síochána (Discipline) Regulations 1989 , which provides that an alleged breach of discipline shall be inspected 'as soon as practicable' by a Garda not below the rank of inspector, were commenced. The investigation commenced in September 1992 and in October 1992 the applicant was served with a notice indicating that an Inspector had been appointed to investigate the alleged breaches, which mirrored the summonses originally served on the applicant. The applicant's solicitor wrote three letters requesting time to prepare the defence and subsequently notified the Inspector of his intention to apply for judicial review. In January 1993, notice of witnesses to be called was served on the applicant, but it proved necessary to alter some of the charges and a new notice was served on the applicant in October 1993.

As already indicated, in the High Court Morris J. refused the applicant judicial review, holding that the delays involved in the case did not preclude the holding of the disciplinary inquiry but the Supreme Court reversed and granted the applicant an injunction restraining the holding of an inquiry under the 1989 Regulations. The Court held that, by December 1989 or January 1990 it would have been practicable to carry out an investigation into the alleged breaches of discipline in accordance with the 1989 Regulations; the respondents were thus in breach of the obligation imposed on them by Regulation 8(1) of the 1989 Regulations to investigate the alleged breaches of discipline as soon as practicable after they became aware of them. The Court rejected the submission that the reference of the matter to the Director of Public Prosecutions and the serving of the notice under Regulation 40 relieved them of the obligation imposed on them by Regulation 8.

Futility of hearing In *Hughes v. Garda Commissioner,* High Court, July 23, 1996, McCracken J. quashed a disciplinary hearing decision made against the applicant Garda. In the context of a complex inquiry made under the Garda Síochána (Discipline) Regulations 1989, it had been decided not to investigate a particular complaint on the basis that such investigation would have been futile. McCracken J. accepted that it might be the case that it would have been pointless to hold a further investigation in the instant case, but he concluded that that was not the issue. The Regulations had been put in place to ensure that fair and proper procedures were carried out in every investigation into an alleged breach of discipline by a member of the Garda Síochána. He held that the procedures set out in the Regulations had to be followed in every case and it was not for the investigating officer or the complainant in relation to any particular breach of discipline to decide whether it would be futile to follow the procedures as set out in the Regulations.

Trainee: medical reports   In *O'Brien v. Garda Commissioner*, High Court, August 19, 1996 Kelly J. quashed a decision that the applicant, a trainee Garda, should not be permitted to graduate from the Garda Training College pursuant to the Garda Síochána (Admissions and Appointments) Regulations 1988 where the decision had been made on the basis of medical reports of which the applicant had no notice. The matter was remitted to the Garda authorities pursuant to O.84, r.26 of the Rules of the Superior Courts 1986.

Trainee: oral hearing   In the 1995 Review, 337, we noted that in *McAuley v. Garda Commissioner*, High Court, July 4, 1995; Supreme Court, February 15, 1996, Barr J. held in the High Court that an oral hearing should have been conducted in the inquiry into whether the applicant, a trainee Garda, should be dismissed from the Garda Training College pursuant to the Garda Síochána (Admissions and Appointments) Regulations 1988. We also noted that Barr J. held that the procedures were quasi-judicial, though in this respect he did not appear to consider the effects of the Supreme Court decision in *Beirne v. Garda Commissioner* [1993] I.L.R.M. 1 (1992 Review, 382). Nonetheless, the Supreme Court upheld the High Court decision.

The background was that the applicant was a trainee in the Garda Síochána. Disciplinary proceedings had been initiated against him arising from an incident in a licensed premises, during which it was alleged that he exposed himself while drunk and assaulted a fellow female Garda trainee. The applicant had conceded that he placed his T-shirt over a female trainee's head but had denied that he was drunk, exposed himself or assaulted her. During the disciplinary investigation, the applicant was interviewed and informed that he could be reprimanded, cautioned or fined if the charges were proven. All trainees at the premises were interviewed and statements taken; there were significant discrepancies between the accounts given but the applicant was denied access to them. A recommendation was made to terminate the applicant's appointment as a trainee and the Commissioner proceeded to carry this into effect. As already indicated, Barr J. held that the dismissal was *ultra vires* and this was upheld by the Supreme Court.

The Court agreed (citing *Kiely v. Minister for Social Welfare* [1977] I.R. 267) that Barr J. had been correct in holding that the applicant had been deprived of his rights under the disciplinary code contained in the 1988 Regulations, of his basic right to constitutional justice and fair procedures and that the purported termination of his traineeship was thus unlawful. While the Court accepted that the Commissioner is entitled to terminate the contract of the applicant in accordance with the conditions of service accepted and signed by him if in the opinion of the Commissioner the applicant is unsuitable for continued employment as a trainee by reason of misconduct, the Commissioner was obliged to have regard to the provisions of the disciplinary code and the requirements of natural and constitutional justice. The Court also noted that the Commissioner was entitled to take further disciplinary against the applicant provided that they were conducted in accordance with the requirements of the disciplinary code and the requirements of natural and constitutional justice. The Court concluded that in view of the breach of the applicant's constitutional rights and breach of contract by the Commissioner he was entitled to damages. While the decision appears to conform with a sound procedures-based approach, the Court failed to address the remaining issue as to whether the Commissioner's decision may be characterised as being primarily related to contract or a quasi-judicial decision. It seems that the difficulties raised by the failure to categorise the decision as either private (contract) or public (quasi-judicial), which were adverted to in *Beirne v. Garda Commissioner* [1993] I.L.R.M. 1 (see the 1992 Review, 382), will remain for the foreseeable future.

Health Services

CORONERS

Fees   The Coroners Act 1962 (Fees And Expenses) Regulations 1996 (SI No. 151 of 1996), made under the Coroners Act 1962, prescribed revised fees and expenses for the purposes of the holding of inquests and consequential matters under the 1962 Act. They applied retrospectively from January 1, 1995.

HEALTH BOARDS

Financial accountability and removal of controls   The Health (Amendment) (No.3) Act 1996 was enacted to strengthen the arrangements governing the financial accountability of health boards and to clarify the respective roles of the members of health boards and their chief executive officers. The Explanatory Memorandum to the legislation when it was introduced in the Oirteachtas indicated that it was also part of the process of removing the Department of Health from detailed involvement in operational matters. Section 2 provides that health boards must have regard to certain matters in carrying out any of their functions. These relate to securing the most beneficial, effective and efficient use of resources; co-operating and co-ordinating their activities with other health boards, local authorities and public bodies; and giving due consideration to the policies and objectives of Ministers and of the Government. The Act came into effect on November 6, 1996 on its signature by the President.

Reserved and executive functions   Section 3 provides that certain functions, to be known as 'reserved functions' (a terminology familiar from local authority legislation) will be carried out directly by the members of health boards. These include the adoption, supervision and amendment of service plans, the appointment and removal of the chief executive officer, the purchase and disposal of assets, the borrowing of money and decisions to discontinue the provision and maintenance of any premises. Section 4 provides that, generally, any function that is not a 'reserved function' will be performed by the chief executive officer and the staff of the board and shall be known as an 'executive function.'

Annual budget Section 5 requires the Minister to determine in respect of each health board for each financial year the maximum amount of net expenditure that may be incurred for that year. The term 'net expenditure' is defined as the gross expenditure of a health board for a year less the income of the board, other than grants made to the health board by the Minister under the Health Act 1970. The Minister is required to notify health boards in writing of the amount so determined within 21 days of the publication of the Estimates by the Government. Section 6 requires a health board, within 42 days of the receipt of a determination, or a shorter period not less than 21 days as the Minister may direct, to adopt and submit to the Minister a service plan in respect of the period to which that determination relates. A service plan shall include a statement of the services to be provided by the board consistent with the financial limits determined by the Minister under section 5. The Act also allows for a determination by the Minister that a health board may run a deficit for a financial year.

Health promotion programmes Section 17 contains a number of amendments to the Health Act 1970. These include a new statutory obligation on health boards to develop and implement health promotion programmes.

HEALTH INSURANCE

Health Insurance Regulations A number of Regulations were introduced in 1996 in order to implement the general provisions of the Health Insurance Act 1994 (1994 Review, 284-7). The Health Insurance Act 1994 (Registration) Regulations 1996 (SI No. 80 of 1996) provide for a Register of Health Benefit Undertakings as envisaged by section 13 of the 1994 Act and set out conditions for registration of restricted membership undertakings. The Health Insurance Act 1994 (Open Enrolment) Regulations 1996 (SI No. 81 of 1996) provide that registered health undertakings cannot refuse health insurance to a person under 65 except in certain limited circumstances, as envisaged by section 8 of the 1994 Act. They also deal with waiting periods for payment under a policy. The Health Insurance Act 1994 (Lifetime Cover) Regulations 1996 (SI No. 82 of 1996) provide, as envisaged by section 9 of the 1994 Act, that once a person is insured an undertaking cannot terminate or refuse to renew cover except in specified limited circumstances. The Health Insurance Act 1994 (Minimum Benefits) Regulations 1996 (SI No. 83 of 1996) prescribe in great detail the minimum level of cover for various health services, as envisaged by section 10 of the 1994 Act. The Health Insurance Act 1994 (Risk Equalisation Scheme) Regulations 1996 (SI No. 84 of 1996) provide for the implementation of a risk equalisation scheme with an equalisation fund, as envisaged by section 12 of the 1994 Act. Much of the four sets of regulations came into effect on March 28, 1996. As indicated in the 1994 Review, the 1994 Act and the 1996 Regulations were intended to introduce competition to the health insurance market in the State, dominated until 1997 by the Voluntary Health Insurance Board (see below). This became a reality with the arrival of the British insurance provider BUPA in 1997. Its arrival was not without some controversy, as one of its proposed products was asserted by the then Minister for Health to be in breach of the 'community rating' requirements in section 7 of the 1994 Act (1994 Review, 285-6). The Minister indicated that he was unwilling to licence BUPA under the 1994 Act and there were some indications that litigation would follow. However, after some well-publicised negotiations between the Department of Health and BUPA, a modified proposal was placed on the market and the British company was granted a licence to trade. Its products became available on the market in early 1997.

Voluntary Health Insurance Board   The Voluntary Health Insurance (Amendment) Act 1996 amended the Voluntary Health Insurance Act 1957 to enable the Voluntary Health Insurance (VHI) Board, with the consent of the Minister for Health, to develop new health insurance products and activities beyond its indemnity based insurance business to areas such as cash schemes in respect of serious illness. The Act came into effect on March 6, 1996 on its signature by the President.

Section 2 of the 1996 Act repealed section 4 of the 1957 Act but retains the provision which defines the VHI as a not-for-profit organisation. The Act also conferred explicit powers on the Board as to the basis on which it may make agreements and enter into arrangements with health service providers for the treatment and care of its member and subscribers.

The 1996 Act increased the number of persons on the VHI Board from not more than five to not more than 12. It was stated during the Act's passage in the Oireachtas that this was to enable the Minister to ensure that the balance and range of skills and expertise available at Board level was sufficient to meet the demands of a modern health insurance business operating in the Single Market. This referred to the introduction of competition in the health insurance market: see the discussion of the Health Insurance Act 1994 in the 1994 Review, 284-7 and the discussion above of the various Regulations made under the 1994 Act in 1996.

The Act requires the VHI Board to give the Minister for Health specified prior notice of an intention to increase premiums. Such proposed increases will have effect unless the Minister issues a direction to the contrary within a specified period and provides his/her reason(s) for doing so. Section 5 of the 1996 Act provides a statutory basis to the creation of the post of Chief Executive of the VHI; it repealed section 13(4) in the 1957 Act which dealt with the appointment of a general manager.

HEALTH SERVICE EMPLOYERS AGENCY

The Health Service Employers Agency (Establishment) Order 1996 (SI No.213 of 1996), made under the Health (Corporate Bodies) Act 1961, established the Agency to provide certain services to health service employers, including health boards, public voluntary hospitals or other corporate bodies which the Agency may admit to membership. It is intended, for example, to promote value for money in pay cost management and to assist health service employers in the management of industrial relations and conditions of employment. The Agency was established on 15 July 15, 1996.

HEPATITIS C CONTROVERSY

The Health (Amendment) Act 1996 was enacted to deal with certain aspects of the mass infection of thousands of women with Hepatitis C arising from the use of contaminated Anti-D blood products between the late 1970s and early 1990s. The 1996 Act conferred on health boards the power to make available medical and counselling services without charge to persons who had contracted hepatitis C directly or indirectly from the use of Human Immuno-globulin-Anti-D or the receipt within the State of another blood product or a blood transfusion. The Act came into effect on September 23, 1996: Health (Amendment) Act 1996 (Commencement) Order 1996 (SI No.255 of 1996). The 1996 Act must be seen in the context of a huge controversy surrounding the cause of this mass infection and the subsequent establishment in 1996 of a Tribunal of Inquiry into the matter. The Report of the Tribunal, published in 1997, will be discussed in the 1997 Review. A non-statutory Tribunal of Compensation had been established to compensate those who had contracted Hepatitis C; some aspects of the Tribunal's activities were discussed in *Ryan v. Compensation Tribunal* [1997] 1 I.L.R.M. 194, discussed in the Administrative Law chapter, 5, above. We note here that the Compensation Tribunal was established on a statutory basis in 1997 pursuant to the Hepatitis C Compensation Tribunal Act 1997, which we will discuss in the 1997 Review. The Consultative Council on Hepatitis C (Establishment) Order 1996 (SI No.339 of 1996), made under section 98 of the Health Act 1947, established a Consultative Council to advise the Minister for Health on all aspects of hepatitis C, with effect from November 26, 1996. Other aspects of the Hepatitis C controversy were discussed in *Roe v. Blood Transfusion Service Board and Ors.* [1996] 1 I.L.R.M. 555 (H.C.) (see the Constitutional Law chapter, 139, above).

HOSPITAL CHARTERS

The Health (Amendment) (No. 2) Act 1996 amended section 76 of the Health Act 1970 (which deals with the amendment, by Ministerial Order, of a hospital Charter) in order to enhance the powers of the Minister for Health in circumstances of any re-organisation or extension of the provision of hospital services. The immediate objective of the Act was explained by reference to the need to facilitate the provision of the necessary statutory basis for the establishment of the governing body of a new hospital being built in Tallaght, Dublin, comprising and amalgamation of three existing Dublin city hospitals. The title of the new hospital, namely. *the Adelaide and Meath Hospital, Dublin, Incorporating the National Children's Hospital*, reflects these origins. While section 76 of the 1970 Act empowered the Minister for Health to amend by Order the Charter of a hospital, it did not provide for the establishment of a new body corporate to govern a new hospital such as that being provided at Tallaght. Section 2 of the 1996 Act, by amending section 76 appropriately, fills this legislative gap. The Act came into effect on July 15, 1996 on its signature by the President. The detailed amendments to the existing charters were effected by the Health Act 1970 (Section 76) (Adelaide and Meath Hospital Dublin, Incorporating the National Children's Hospital) Order 1996 (SI No.228 of 1996), which came into effect on August 1, 1996.

INFECTIOUS DISEASES

The Infectious Diseases (Amendment) Regulations 1996 (SI No.384 of 1996), made under the Health Act 1947, amended the Infectious Diseases Regulations 1981 in order to add Creutzfeld Jakob Disease (CJD) and new variant Creutzfeld Jakob Disease (nv CJD) as notifiable diseases. They came into effect on December 16, 1996. The addition should be seen against the background of the BSE controversy, with which nv CJD is associated: see the Agriculture chapter, 18, above.

LICENSING OF HUMAN MEDICINES, BLOOD PRODUCTS AND CLINICAL TRIALS

Advertising The Medical Preparations (Advertising) (Amendment) Regulations 1996 (SI No.308 of 1996) amended the Medical Preparations (Advertising) Regulations 1993 (1993 Review, 344) to permit the advertising of medical preparations authorised for the treatment of alopecia (including male pattern baldness), with effect from October 15, 1996.

Irish Medicines Board: fees   The Irish Medicines Board (Fees) Regulations 1996 (SI No.44 of 1996) provide for the payment of relevant fees to the Irish Medicines Board, established under the Irish Medicines Board Act 1995 (1995 Review, 339).

Irish Medicines Board: transfer of functions   Four sets of Regulations provided for the transfer of various licensing functions from the Minister for Health to the Irish Medicines Board, established under the Irish Medicines Board Act 1995 (1995 Review, 339). The Medical Preparations (Wholesale Licences) (Amendment) Regulations 1996 (SI No. 41 of 1996) amended the Medical Preparations (Wholesale Licences) Regulations 1993 (1993 Review, 345) and provided for the transfer of the authority to grant wholesale licences for medical preparations from the Minister to the Board. The Medical Preparations (Licensing Of Manufacture) (Amendment) Regulations, 1996 (SI No. 42 of 1996) amended the Medical Preparations (Licensing Of Manufacture) Regulations 1993 (1993 Review, 344-5) and provided for the transfer of the authority to grant manufacturing licences for medical preparations from the Minister to the Board. Similarly, the Medical Preparations (Licensing And Sale) Regulations 1996 (SI No. 43 of 1996) transferred the authority to grant licences for human medicines from the Minister to the Board: see also below. These three sets of 1996 Regulations came into effect on 19 February 1996. Finally, the Medical Preparations (Advertising) (Amendment) Regulations 1996 (SI No.308 of 1996) amended the Medical Preparations (Advertising) Regulations 1993 (1993 Review, 344) and provided for the transfer of the authority to regulate the advertising of medical preparations from the Minister to the Board.

Licensing and sale   The Medical Preparations (Licensing and Sale) Regulations 1996 (SI No. 43 of 1996) consolidated previous legislative requirements concerning the licensing of human medicines as required by Directive 65/65/EEC. The 1996 Regulations also regulated for the first time homeopathic medicines, as required by Directive 92/72/EEC. In keeping with other Regulations already discussed, they transferred the authority to grant licences for human medicines from the Minister for Health to the Irish Medicines Board: see above. They came into effect on February 19, 1996.

Prescription and supply   The Medicinal Products (Prescription and Control of Supply) Regulations 1996 (SI No. 256 of 1996), made under the Medicines Board Act 1995 (1995 Review, 339), revoked the Medical Preparations (Prescription and Control of Supply) Regulations 1993 (1993 Review, 345) and specify updated arrangements for the control of the sale of medicinal products to the public. In accordance with Directive 92/26/EEC, they contain an updated list of those products which may only be supplied on prescription, 'delisting' certain products which were previously subject to sale only by prescription and which thus may be sold 'over-the-counter' in a pharmacy. The 1996 Regulations also specify the form of an individual prescription, which differs from that contained in the 1993 Regulations. They also specify the circumstances excluding medicinal products from prescription control, most such products now forming a new category of pharmacy-only products. The Regulations provide special arrangements for emergency supply of medicinal products. They also lay down requirements on the labelling of dispensed medicinal products and the keeping of pharmacy records. As with the 1993 Regulations, the 1996 Regulations provide that while a manual prescription book record may be used for this purpose, they also provide that, where prescription labels are prepared with the aid of a computerised data base, as is the case in many pharmacies, a daily computer printout or a prescription book containing adhesive labels from the computer which generated the prescription labels will suffice. The Regulations also prohibit the sale of medicinal products after the expiry date specified by the manufacturer and also prohibit the supply of medicinal products by mail order. The Regulations also provide for a number of significant exemptions from their general terms; these appear to allow for greater dispensing of medicinal products by a registered nurse in a hospital, thus restricting the powers of a pharmacist in this context. Finally, the Regulations provide for their enforcement by relevant officers, together with powers of entry and inspection. Penalties for non-compliance are provided for in the 1995 Act. The 1996 Regulations came into effect on September 1, 1996. They were amended by the Medicinal Products (Prescription and Control of Supply) (Amendment) Regulations 1996 (SI No. 309 of 1996) with a view to clarifying certain provisions relating to the classification of insulins, the recognition of dental prescriptions; operative on October 15, 1996 as health prescriptions and the nature of certificates to be given for the purpose of evidence.

NURSING

An Bord Altranais Section 21 of the Health (Amendment) (No. 3) Act 1996 (whose principal provisions are discussed above, 405) empowered the Minister for Health to extend by Order the term of office of An Bord Altranais, the Nursing Board which was due to expire on October 3, 1996, pending the enactment of a Bill to revise the Nurses Act 1985. See the Health (Amendment) (No.3) Act 1996 (Extension of Bord Altranais) Order 1996 (SI No.331 of 1996).

NURSING HOMES

Offences   Section 20 of the Health (Amendment) (No. 3) Act 1996 (whose principal provisions are discussed above, 405) makes it an offence to carry on a nursing home that is not registered under the Health (Nursing Homes) Act 1990 (the 1990 Act is discussed in the 1990 Review, 340).

Subvention   The Nursing Homes (Subvention) (Amendment) Regulations 1996 (SI No.225 of 1996), made under the Health (Nursing Homes) Act 1990 (1990 Review, 340), amended the Nursing Homes (Subvention) Regulations 1993 (1993 Review, 348). They provide that a Health Board may offer alternative care to a person who has qualified for a subvention, may contract out beds in registered nursing homes and provide for increased personal allowances when assessing the circumstances of adult children of applicants for subventions. They came into effect on July 19, 1996.

PHARMACY

Community pharmacy agreements   The Health (Community Pharmacy Contractor Agreements) Regulations 1996 (SI No. 152 of 1996), made under the Health Act 1970, set out the criteria and procedure for the issue of community pharmacy contractor agreements. In effect, the Regulations prescribe limits to the number of pharmacy outlets with which health boards may enter into such agreements (including the provision of general medical services under the Health Act 1970, the 'medical card scheme'), particularly where existing pharmacies are already providing such services within specified distances from other existing pharmacy premises. The 1996 Regulations came into effect on May 31, 1996.

REGISTRATION OF BIRTHS AND DEATHS

Amalgamation of Registrars' Districts   In 1995, three further statutory instruments were made to amalgamate certain Superintendent Registrars' Districts and, where applicable, Registrars' Districts so as to reduce the number of such districts, continuing a process begun in 1993: see the 1993 Review, 348, 1994 Review, 290-1 and 1995 Review, 341. The relevant Orders were the Registration of Births and Deaths (Ireland) Act 1863 (Section 18) (Waterford) Order 1996 (SI No. 140 of 1996), the Registration of Births and Deaths (Ireland) Act 1863 (Section 18) (Limerick) (No. 2) Order 1996 (SI No. 200 of 1996) and the Registration of Births and Deaths (Ireland) Act 1863 (Section 18) (Kerry) (No. 2) Order 1996 (SI No. 224 of 1996).

Revised form of birth certificate   The Registration of Births Act 1996 amended the form of the birth certificate in order to remove gender inequalities in the particulars registered. In presenting the legislation, the then Minister for Equality and Law Reform explained that the prior format of the birth certificate dated from the Registration of Births and Deaths (Ireland) Act 1863 and reflected the social attitudes of the time. It recorded the address and occupation of the father, but not of the mother of the child; it asked for the mother's maiden name; it did not record the child's surname, giving rise to the assumption that the child automatically took the surname of the father. In providing for a new format of birth certificate, it was noted that the 1996 Act thus gave effect to one of the recommendations of the Second Commission on the Status of Women. The 1996 Act came into effect on October 1, 1997: Registration of Births Act 1996 (Commencement) Order 1997 (SI No. 45 of 1997).

Section 1 of the 1996 Act provides that the new format, as described in the Schedule, is to apply to births registered or re-registered after the Act came into effect (that is, after October 1, 1997). The child's surname registered can be that of either the mother or the father or both. Another surname can, however, be registered if either parent requests this and the Registrar General considers that the circumstances so warrant. In the case of a re-registration of a birth which has already been registered in the new format, the surname of the child on re-registration remains unchanged. Other elements of the new form also differ in some significant respects from the existing format. The birth certificate will record the occupation and address of the mother, as well as those of the father. The former name or names of both mother and father will be shown, instead of the mother's maiden name.

Land Law

Paul Coughlan, School of Law, Trinity College Dublin

AIRSPACE

Right to control of airspace over land   In *Keating & Co. Ltd. v. Jervis Shopping Centre Ltd.*, unreported, March 1, 1996, the plaintiff was the owner of licensed premises on the corner of Jervis Street and Mary Street in Dublin. The defendants were engaged in an extensive development of neighbouring premises. The plaintiff complained that the building work being carried out by the defendants interfered with the use of its premises and deterred potential customers from entering those premises. It brought proceedings claiming damages for nuisance, negligence, trespass and wrongful interference with its contractual relations with its customers. It sought an interlocutory injunction restraining the use of a tower crane on a site adjoining its premises to the extent that the jib of the crane moved into the airspace above the licensed premises. It also sought an interlocutory injunction restraining the defendants from parking lorries and other vehicles close to its premises. The defendants argued that there was a fair question to be tried as to whether the movement of the jib of the crane into the airspace above the plaintiff's premises was impliedly licensed and thus did not amount to a trespass. This was based on an agreement dated September 30, 1994 whereby the plaintiff and the first named defendant agreed to co-operate in the construction and re-development of their respective premises.

Keane J. observed that a landowner, whose title is not in issue, is prima facie entitled to an injunction to restrain a trespass and that this was also the case where the claim is for an interlocutory injunction. However, this principle was subject to the qualification that the defendant may seek to establish that he has a right to do what would otherwise be a trespass and in those circumstances the ordinary principles governing the grant or refusal of an interlocutory injunction apply. Here the defendants were asserting such a right and there was a serious question to be tried between the parties as to whether the defendants were entitled to move the jib of the crane across the plaintiff's airspace. Accordingly, the plaintiff would not be entitled to an interlocutory injunction unless it could satisfy the court that damages would not be an adequate remedy, which it had failed to do. Any loss of trade was capable of being quantified in damages and the defendants were in a financial position to meet an award. In any event, Keane J. felt that an interlocutory injunction would not have been appropriate having regard to the behaviour of the parties. He referred to the observation of Stamp J. in *Woollerton and Wilson Ltd. v. Richard Costain Ltd.* [1970] 1 All E.R. 483 that the airspace in question had assumed value only by reason of the defendant's necessities.

As to the parking of vehicles in the vicinity of the plaintiff's premises, there was a fair question to be tried as to whether this was lawful. A trader who owns premises bordering a highway was prima facie entitled to use the highway in a reasonable way for the purpose of loading and unloading goods from and into vehicles for the purpose of his business and such loading and unloading was not necessarily an unreasonable use of the highway because it caused inconvenience to others. However, the owner of premises adjoining a highway, such as the plaintiff in this case, enjoys a private right of access to the highway which must also be available to its customers. Here the plaintiff had failed to establish that if it was shown that the defendants had acted unlawfully damages would not be an adequate remedy. Accordingly, no interlocutory injunction would be granted.

FAMILY HOME PROTECTION ACT 1976

Dispensing with the need for prior consent in writing In *Kavanagh v. Delicato*, unreported, December 20, 1996, the plaintiffs sought specific performance of a contract for the sale of a room and a yard at the rear of the defendant's premises which had previously been used as a café but had been closed down for three years. The defendant and his wife had living accommodation above the café. After hearing a great deal of conflicting evidence Carroll J. held the defendant and his wife had agreed to the sale of the yard and the room to the plaintiffs for £30,000. A deposit of £3,000 was paid and an auctioneer who had been retained by the defendant's wife in connection with the sale wrote identical letters to both the plaintiffs' and the defendant's solicitor confirming that the yard had been sold to the plaintiffs or a company to be nominated by them for the sum of £30,000. Subsequently, a third party offered a higher price for the entire premises owned by the defendant and a contract was concluded.

The defendant argued that there was not a sufficient note or memorandum in writing of the contract with the plaintiffs to satisfy the Statute of Frauds (Ireland) 1695 and that the contract did not comply with the provisions of the Family Home Protection Act 1976 in that his wife did not give her prior consent in writing to the sale. As regards the latter argument, the first issue was whether the subject matter of the sale fell within the definition of a family home contained in section 2 of the 1976 Act. While the room had been described as a 'living room' in the map drawn up for the purposes of the sale,

Carroll J. found that it had never been used as such since the café had closed in 1986. However, the defendants and their family had used the yard in the summer and for hanging out washing. Carroll J. felt that this made it part of the curtilage of the family home and thus within the scope of the Act. Nevertheless, Carroll J. refused to regard the absence of the wife's consent as vitiating the sale. She observed at pp. 12-13:

> The Family Home Protection Act 1976 is an Act to avoid alienation against the wishes of the non-owning spouse, i.e. in this case Mrs. Delicato. However, she was the prime mover who initiated the sale and concluded it with the agreement of her husband. A statute should not be made an instrument of fraud. . . . In my opinion her husband, who is the defendant, is estopped from raising the statute as a defence. He cannot be allowed to plead that there was no written consent when it was his wife, with his approval, who arranged the sale. It is an appropriate case for an application to dispense with consent under section 4.

There is authority to the effect that a spouse may be estopped from invoking the sanction of voidness provided for in section 3(1) of the 1976 Act (e.g. *A.D. v. D.D.*, unreported, June 8, 1983, McWilliam J.) and the principle that a statute may not be used as an instrument of fraud would seem to be a logical ground upon which to find that such an estoppel has arisen. But the basis upon which Carroll J. apparently went on the dispense with the need for the consent of the defendant's spouse under section 4 of the 1976 Act may be open to question. An application to the court for an order under section 4 must be brought before the intended conveyance is effected. In *Somers v. W.* [1979] I.R. 94 it was held by the Supreme Court that there is no jurisdiction to grant a retrospective dispensation where it is subsequently discovered that the consent of a spouse was required. It may have been the case in *Kavanagh v. Delicato* that the dispensation was directed not towards the contract which had already been concluded, but the conveyance by the defendant which would be required to complete the sale on foot of the decree of specific performance made by the court.

Necessity for plenary hearing when adequacy of consent put in issue in mortgage proceedings   In *Allied Irish Banks plc v. Finnegan* [1996] I.L.R.M. 401 the first and second named defendants were husband and wife. In 1989 they decided to purchase a new family home and £100,000 was borrowed from the plaintiff in order to finance the transaction. On December 1, 1989 the second named defendant signed a consent form for the purposes of the Family Home Protection Act 1976. This related to the creation of a mortgage over the new home by the first named defendant in favour of the plaintiff. On December 5, 1989 the house was conveyed to the first named defendant. On December 15, 1992 the first named defendant executed a mortgage in favour of the plaintiff as security for the loan. In 1992 the first named defendant ceased making repayments of the loan and on March 24, 1994 the plaintiff instituted proceedings by special summons seeking possession of the family home. By this time £121,888.49 was due to the plaintiff and only the second named defendant was in possession of the house, the spouses having separated in February 1992. The special summons claiming possession was issued against the first named defendant, but the second named defendant was subsequently joined as a defendant. While the first named defendant did not defend the proceedings, the second named defendant resisted the plaintiff's claim for possession on the grounds that she did not give a valid consent to the mortgage for the purposes of the 1976 Act. The second named defendant swore an affidavit to the effect that prior to the purchase of the house it had been agreed between the spouses that the purchase would be in their joint names and that she would not have agreed to the purchase if she had been told that the house was going to be purchased in her husband's sole name. She further averred that she went with the first named defendant to the offices of his solicitors where she signed a document which she thought related to the purchase in joint names. She did not receive any advice and the effect of the document was not explained to her. This version of events was disputed in an affidavit sworn by the solicitor of the first named defendant who averred that he told the second named defendant that her consent was necessary for the mortgage as the house was being purchased in her husband's sole name.

The second named defendant argued that as there was an issue of fact as to whether her consent was valid there would have to be a hearing on oral evidence. The plaintiff argued that the validity of the consent was irrelevant as it was a *bona fide* purchaser for value and thus entitled to rely upon section 3(3) of the 1976 Act. In the High Court Carroll J. made an order for possession in favour of the plaintiff. She held that the plaintiff was entitled to rely on the documentation signed by the second named defendant which had been sent to it by the first named defendant's solicitor. As the plaintiff was a bona fide purchaser for value the mortgage was valid. The second named defendant appealed. In separate family law proceedings which the second named defendant instituted against the first named defendant the Circuit Court made an order on March 6, 1995 declaring that she was entitled to a half share in the family home.

The Supreme Court allowed the appeal and remitted the matter to the High Court for determination at a plenary hearing on oral evidence. Blayney J. with whom Hamilton C.J. and O'Flaherty J. concurred, observed that there was a clear dispute of fact as to the circumstances in which the second named defendant signed the consent form and the issue as to the validity of the consent turned upon how this dispute was resolved. The question as to whether the plaintiff was a bona fide purchaser for value was disputed by the second named defendant and involved issues of fact which would have to be established by the plaintiff as section 3(4) of the 1976 Act placed the onus of proof on it. The plaintiff had to establish that it did not have any actual or constructive notice of the possible invalidity of the consent and this was not an issue which could be decided by the court on affidavit. Blayney J. added that the declaration made by the Circuit Court that the second named defendant was beneficially entitled to a half share in the family home would not affect the plaintiff's claim if it had a valid mortgage. In that event the second named defendant would have a half share in the equity of redemption.

Postponement of sale of family home in the event of bankruptcy   By virtue of section 61(4) of the Bankruptcy Act 1988, where the property of a bankrupt, arranging debtor or person dying insolvent comprises a family home, no sale can be effected without the prior sanction of the court and any disposition made without such sanction is void. Section 61(5) goes on to provide:

> On an application by the Official Assignee under this section for an order for the sale of a family home, the Court, notwithstanding anything contained in this or any other enactment, shall have power to order postponement of the sale of the family home having regard to the interests of the creditors and of the spouse and dependants of the bankrupt as well as to all the circumstances of the case.

In *Rubotham v. Duddy*, unreported, May 1, 1996, the defendant, who was the wife of the bankrupt, was entitled to a 60% share in the family home which she occupied along with the bankrupt and one of their seven children, with the remaining 40% vested in the official assignee. While the house was valued at £65,000, the creditors of the bankrupt were owed approximately £20,000. The official assignee sought an order for sale in lieu of partition under the Partition Acts 1868-76 and an order under section 61 of the Bankruptcy Act 1988 sanctioning the sale. The defendant suffered from hypertension, arthritis and agoraphobia and had been in receipt of psychiatric care. Of the children that did not reside with her and the bankrupt, one suffered from epilepsy, one was an alcoholic and two were unemployed.

Shanley J. adopted the observation of McCracken J. in *Official Assignee v. Young*, unreported, May 23, 1995, to the effect that if discretion is to be exercised in favour of the family of a bankrupt this must only be done under exceptional circumstances. Shanley J. went on to follow the approach applied in the English case of *Re Mott* [1987] C.L.Y. 212 where the sale was postponed until after a widow's death. In the present case Shanley J. felt that there were exceptional circumstances which would justify postponing the sale of the family home. However, unlike *Re Mott*, the sale would be postponed for only ten years.

FISHERY

Use of words of limitation in reservation of fishing rights In *Gannon v. Walsh*, unreported, June 20, 1996, the plaintiffs claimed that the defendants had wrongfully interfered with their right to fish a stretch of the River Moy between Foxford and Ballina in County Mayo. A lease of a fishery comprising that part of the river had been granted to the mother of the first named plaintiff in 1989 by Sir James Langham. The lease had been taken in order to provide fishing facilities for guests staying in a bed and breakfast run by some of the plaintiffs, who also owned a field near the river which was used as a car park by the anglers. The defendants objected to the large number of people who were gaining access to the river on the grounds that they were crossing their fields, damaging crops and leaving litter behind them. On a number of occasions they ordered anglers who were fishing on the river bank to leave and ultimately they locked a gate across the road which gave access to the river bank. They also placed fences and trenches along the river bank which prevented the plaintiffs and their licensees from moving along the stretch of river over which they claimed fishing rights.

The lands in question, which formed part of what was known as the Rashleigh Estate, had been the subject matter of a number of marriage settlements in the nineteenth century. In 1906 the Congested Districts Board bought the land subject to the vendor, Arthur Rashleigh, reserving to himself 'or his assigns' the exclusive right of fishing over the River Moy together with such rights of way and rights of entry as would be necessary to enjoy it. Arthur Rashleigh died in 1952 and his will left the residue to his two daughters. In 1982 one of the daughters executed an indenture purporting to transfer the fishery to Sir James Langham. By her will dated May 10, 1989, the other daughter left the residue of her estate to Sir James Langham, who was her son. During the course of the Circuit Court proceedings Sir James Langham transferred his entire interest in the fishery to the first named plaintiff.

In the Circuit Court the plaintiffs' claims were dismissed by Judge Cassidy. On appeal to the High Court Keane J. granted an injunction and awarded the plaintiffs £5,000 damages. Among the many arguments advanced by the defendants, it was claimed that the bed of the River Moy had never vested in the Rashleigh Estate and furthermore that as the documents pertaining to the 1906 sale referred to the 'vendor or his assigns' reserving the fishing rights, the appropriate words of limitation for a fee simple had not been used and so only a life estate had been reserved in favour of Arthur Rashleigh. The defendants

also argued that the failure of Sir James Langham's mother to convey or release her interest as a tenant in common of the fishery to her sister prior to the
execution of the 1982 indenture was not remedied by the vesting in Sir James
Langham of his mother's property on her death. However, Keane J. felt that
any defect in title had been cured by the grant of probate in favour of Sir
James Langham in respect of his mother's estate and the fact that an assent
was not executed until sometime in 1996 did not assist the defendants.

Keane J. applied the principle that a person entitled to a several fishery in
non-tidal waters is, in the absence of an indication to the contrary, presumed
to be the owner of the bed of the river over which the right is exercised. Keane
J. held that the plaintiffs had established a title to the soil and the bed of the
river and to an exclusive right of fishing therein. He expressly rejected the
defendants' argument that because a map produced in 1831 delineated only
the west bank of the river there must have been an intention to exclude the bed
of the river from the marriage settlement which constituted the root of title. It
was also clear that the bed of the river had been excluded from the rest of the
Rashleigh Estate which had been vested in the Congested Districts Board.

Having found that the plaintiffs had rights of ownership in respect of the
bed of the river, Keane J. went on to point out that even if the plaintiffs had
been entitled to only a profit a prendre, they could still seek an injunction and/
or in respect of any wrongful interference by the defendants. Moreover, while
the proceedings were in the form of an action for nuisance, they were akin to
an action for trespass and it was well established that where a plaintiff is in
possession of a several fishery it was not open to a defendant to put the plaintiff's title in issue if in doing so he was merely asserting a *jus tertii* (i.e. pointing to a weakness in the plaintiff's title suggesting or showing that some person
other than the defendant might be entitled to the property in issue).

Turning to the question of gaining access to the river bank for the purpose
of exercising the right to fish, at common law it was clear that a grant of
fishing rights necessarily implied a right of access to the banks save where the
beneficial use of the fishing could be enjoyed by the person entitled by the use
of boats, which was not the case here. However, the right of access to the bank
had to be exercised in a manner which was as least detrimental to the riparian
owners as would be consistent with the full beneficial use of the right of fishing. Here the plaintiffs had a right of access to the bank for the purpose of
exercising the right to fish both at common law and under section 13 of the
Irish Land Act 1903. The road which the defendants had obstructed was the
appropriate means of access to the river bank. However, in deciding whether
this access should be on foot or by car, Keane J. adopted the approach taken in
the Scottish case of *Middletweed Ltd v. Murray* 1989 SLT which determines
the parameters of the right of access in the light of an angler of average strength
and mobility. Here there was no need for the anglers using the fishery to have
a right to drive along the road leading to the river bank.

Having referred to the doubts which exist as to whether appropriate words of limitation are required in the grant or reservation of a *profit à prendre*, Keane J. rejected the defendants' argument that appropriate words of limitation had not been used in respect of the reservation of the fishery. Here the critical documents were orders by the Irish Land Commission vesting parts of the Rashleigh Estate in various tenants which went on to reserve the fishing rights to 'Arthur Rashleigh, his heirs and assigns.' Keane J. commented at pp. 63-64:

> Those are accepted to be appropriate words of limitation for the conveyance of an estate in fee simple so that, even if appropriate words of limitation were required for the reservation of a right of fishing in gross, on which it is not necessary to express any concluded view, these words would still be apt to effect a reservation of the freehold. Even if that were not so, the reversion would remain vested in the Land Commission only and that body, even if it were minded to do so, would not be allowed to assert such a title in opposition to the plaintiffs in a court of equity.

LANDLORD AND TENANT

Breach of covenant In *Crofter Properties Ltd. v. Genport Ltd.*, unreported, March 15, 1996, the plaintiff was the lessor and the defendant was the lessee of premises known as Sachs Hotel' located on Morehampton Road in Dublin. It had brought proceedings claiming that the leasehold interest of the defendant had been forfeited. In an unreported judgment delivered on December 6, 1995 McCracken J. dismissed the plaintiff's claim for possession on foot of the purported forfeiture because the plaintiff had failed to give the defendant a reasonable time to remedy the alleged breaches of covenant, as required under section 14 of the Conveyancing Act 1881. In addition to seeking relief against forfeiture, the defendant counterclaimed for breach of contract and breach of the plaintiff's covenant for quiet enjoyment. It also alleged malicious prosecution, conspiracy and negligence, but these claims were rejected by McCracken J. The covenant for quiet enjoyment contained in the lease provided as follows:

> That the lessee paying the rents and other charges herein before reserved and performing and observing the covenants' stipulations, conditions and agreements on the part of the lessee herein before contained, shall peacefully and quietly hold and enjoy the premises for the term hereby demised without any interruption from or by the lessor or any person lawfully claiming through under or in trust for the lessor.

Section 41 of the Landlord and Tenant Law Amendment Act Ireland 1860 ('Deasy's Act') implies a covenant for quiet enjoyment in favour of the tenant 'so long as the tenant shall pay the rent and perform the agreements contained in the lease to be observed on the part of the tenant.' In *Whelan v. Madigan* [1978] I.L.R.M. 136 it was held that the covenant could not be implied if the tenant was in arrears of rent. McCracken J. held that this was also the case in respect of the express covenant set out above. He rejected the defendant's argument that the clause contained two separate covenants, one by the lessee to pay the rent and perform its covenants, and the other by the lessor for quiet enjoyment.

McCracken J. held that it had been reasonable for the plaintiff to institute forfeiture proceedings because it appeared that it might have a cause of action against the defendant for breach of certain covenants in the lease. First, monies were outstanding in relation to the insurance of the premises. Secondly, the defendant had entered into concession or franchise agreements with third parties for the running of parts of the hotel such as the public bar, the bar in the nightclub and the taking of reservations. These agreements contained many of the terms which would ordinarily be found in a tenancy agreement and therefore suggested that there might have been a breach of the covenant in the defendant's lease which prohibited underletting, parting with or sharing possession of the premises. Thirdly, while McCracken J. was highly critical of the manner in which a schedule of dilapidations had been drawn up for the plaintiff because the person who drew it up was not familiar with what had been the condition of the premises at the start of the lease, there appeared to be a lack of repair on the part of the defendant such that the plaintiff had reasonable grounds for relying upon a breach of the repairing covenant in claiming forfeiture. Fourthly, there were serious breaches by the defendant of the covenant that the premises would not be altered without the prior consent of the lessor and that any alterations or changes could only be made in accordance with plans and specifications previously approved by the lessor in writing. McCracken J. held that agreement in principle to some of the alterations was not sufficient as there had been no approval of plans and specifications. However, inaccuracies in an inventory of chattels in the hotel which were included in the lease were such that it could not provide the basis for a claim that there had been a breach of a covenant in the lease providing that missing chattels were to be replaced with chattels of similar value and quality.

McCracken J. rejected the defendant's argument that the plaintiff had waived the breaches of covenant or was estopped from making a claim on foot of them. Section 43 of Deasy's Act provides that nothing done or suffered by a landlord shall be deemed to be a waiver of the benefit of covenants in respect of any breach thereof unless it is signified by the landlord or his lawfully authorised agent in writing. During the course of argument in *Foott v. Benn* (1884) 18 I.L.T.R. 90 Palles C.B. expressed the view that section 43 was confined to a general waiver, that is to say the waiver of the entire benefit of a covenant, as opposed to a waiver of a single breach of that covenant. McCracken J. declined to follow Palles C.B. and pointed to the wording of section 43 which refers to 'any breach thereof.' According to McCracken J., the only reasonable interpretation which could be given to this is that there cannot be a waiver of any specific breach unless that waiver is in writing. McCracken J. rejected the defendant's argument of estoppel because the plaintiff never represented that any of the covenants were being waived, that any specific breaches were being waived or that any set of facts or circumstances existed which would permit the defendant to commit breaches of covenant.

Construction of insurance covenant　In *Sepes Establishment v. KSK Enterprises Ltd.*, unreported, May 21, 1996, the plaintiff was the lessor and the defendant was the lessee under a 38-year lease which was to run from July 1, 1978. The premises comprised two buildings in Westmoreland Street in Dublin save for two ground floor shops and the basements thereunder. A dispute arose between the parties concerning the amount which the lessee was obliged to pay to the lessor by way of a contribution to the insurance premiums payable by the lessor in respect of the premises. Clause 1(v)(e) of the lease required the lessee to pay:

> by way of further rent a yearly sum equal to 80 per cent of the sum or sums which the lessor shall from time to time pay by way of premiums (including any increased premium payable by reason of any act or omission of the lessee) for keeping the Building insured against loss or damage by fire and such other risks under the lessor's covenant in that behalf hereinafter contained. . . .

Clause 2(10) provided that the lessee covenanted not to carry on in the demised premises any trade or occupation or do anything which render void or voidable any policy of insurance for the building or by virtue of which the premium would be increased, and that the lessee would 'repay the lessor all sums paid by the lessor by way of increased premium on the building and all expenses incurred by the lessor in or about any renewal of such policy or policies rendered necessary by a breach of this covenant. . . .'

Subsequent to the grant of the lease, the lessee began to use the premises as an amusement arcade. At the time when the lease was granted the lessor was aware that the lessee intended this use for the premises. The insurance premium payable in the event of the premises being used as an amusement arcade was significantly higher than that which would have been payable if the building was used as offices. It appeared that the clauses had been inserted into the lease with the intention that the lessee should meet the cost of any consequent increase in premium. The lessor claimed that the lessee owed

£11,521.42 in respect of the insurance premium and on July 20, 1992 O'Hanlon J. held in its favour and gave judgment for the amount claimed.

In the Supreme Court Blayney J., with whom Hamilton C.J. and Barrington J. concurred, observed that prima facie it appeared that effect could not be given to both clause 1(v)(e) and clause 2(10). It seemed that under the former the lessee in effect had to pay 80 per cent of any increase in the premium (including 80 per cent of the basic premium), while under the latter the lessee had to pay the entire amount of the increase, so that if the lessor could enforce both clauses it would receive 180 per cent of any increase in premium. Blayney J. felt that the parties could not have intended this and that the two clauses could be reconciled. Quite simply, having paid 80 per cent of the entire premium under clause 1(v)(e), the lessee should be given credit for this when the lessor sought to recover the increase in premium under clause 2(10). This construction had been adopted by O'Hanlon J. and seemed to have been followed by the parties between 1978 and 1990.

Finally, Blayney J. upheld the lessee's contention that the lessor was not entitled to recover parts of the premiums in respect of the risks of loss of rent and public liability. The risks referred to in clause 1(v)(e) had to be risks to the building. The risk of losing rent (principally the risk of the lessee being unable to pay the rent in the event of a fire) and the risk of incurring civil liability to a member of the public did not come within the category of risks causing loss and damage to the building. Blayney J. rejected the lessee's argument that the same could be said of insuring against the cost of demolition, professional fees in connection with reinstatement and the engineering policy on the lift.

MORTGAGES

Delay in execution on foot of order for possession In *Bank of Ireland Finance Ltd. v. Browne*, unreported, June 24, 1996, the defendants charged certain registered land in County Louth in favour of the plaintiff in 1982. The charge was registered as a burden and the plaintiff was registered as owner of the charge. In 1985 the plaintiff instituted proceedings seeking an order for possession of the land and on July 15, 1985 Costello J. ordered the defendants to deliver up possession to the plaintiff. By means of a transfer dated March 3, 1994, the plaintiff transferred the charge to Bio Enterprises Limited ('the applicant') in consideration of £300,000. The applicant was subsequently registered as owner of the charge. The applicant applied to the High Court for an order under Order 17, rule 4 of the Rules of the Superior Courts 1986 substituting it as the plaintiff in the proceedings in place of Bank of Ireland Finance Ltd., and an order under Order 42, rule 24 giving it liberty to execute the order for possession made by Costello J. The latter order was necessary because Order 42, rule 23 provides that as between the original parties to a judgment or order, execution may issue at any time within six years from the recovery of the judgment or the date of the order. Where more than six years has expired the leave of the court is required under Order 42, rule 24.

After making an order substituting the applicant as plaintiff, Laffoy J. went on to consider whether execution should be permitted. The defendants argued that the transfer of the charge had occurred in the context of an agreement whereby funds were to be advanced for the development of a regional airport and as those funds had not been forthcoming execution should not take place. The defendants had commenced separate proceedings in respect of what they claimed was a breach of contract by, inter alia, the applicant and they submitted that the matter should be remitted to plenary hearing or adjourned pending the outcome of the proceedings which they had instituted.

Laffoy J. pointed out that the liability of the defendants qua mortgagors under the charge and the entitlement of the applicant qua mortgagee had already been determined and the only matter left outstanding was whether leave to execute should be granted. The charge entitled the plaintiff to transfer the security to a third party without the consent of the defendants after its power of sale became exercisable. This had occurred prior to the making of the order on July 15, 1985. Laffoy J. rejected the argument of the defendants that it had been agreed between the defendants and the applicant that the transfer of the charge, which did not require the consent of the defendants, would not carry with it a right to proceed to execution on foot of the order. None of the correspondence generated in relation to the transfer of the charge supported the defendants' contention. In those circumstances Laffoy J. gave the applicant leave to execute on foot of the order for possession.

POWERS OF ATTORNEY

Statutory provision for enduring powers of attorney At common law a power of attorney was automatically revoked on the death, insanity, bankruptcy or marriage of the donor. The fact that a power would be extinguished in the event of mental incapacity meant that a person could not make provision as to how his or her property and affairs should be dealt with in the event of their faculties becoming impaired. The only means of supervising the estate of someone who became mentally incapable was an application to the President of the High Court under the Lunacy Regulation (Ireland) Act 1871 to have that person made a ward of court. In a working paper on the subject the Law Reform Commission noted that with increases in life expectancy the number of people suffering from senility would grow and so there was a need for the introduction by statute of enduring powers of attorney which, as the name suggests, continue in force notwithstanding the fact that the donor has become mentally incapable. Section 6 of the Powers of Attorney Act 1996 permits the creation of enduring powers of attorney and the Enduring Power of Attorney Regulations (S.I. No. 196 of 1996) set out the format which an enduring power should adopt and the steps required to execute it. Under section 7 of the Act an enduring power of attorney cannot come into force until it has been registered with the Registrar of Wards of Court. For a detailed discussion of the legislation see Costello, 'The Powers of Attorney Act 1996' (1996) 90 *Law Society of Ireland Gazette* 197.

SALE OF LAND

Authority of auctioneer to produce sufficient note or memorandum in writing for the purposes of the Statute of Frauds (Ireland) 1695 In *Kavanagh v. Delicato*, unreported, December 20, 1996, the facts of which are outlined above, Carroll J. rejected an argument advanced by the defendant that the letters sent by the auctioneer were insufficient to satisfy the Statute of Frauds. Following the decision of Kenny J. in *Law v. Robert Roberts & Co. (Ireland) Ltd.* [1964] I.R. 292, she held that this was a case of an offer being made to an agent who in turn communicated it to the owner of the land who authorised the agent to accept it. The letter was signed by the agent with the authority of the defendant. The defendant also argued that the letter was insufficient because it failed to mention a right of way attaching to the yard and the reservation by the defendant of the right to use the sewers, watercourses and drains. Carroll J. held that there had been a sufficient indication of the right of way in the map which had been drawn up for the sale. In any event, the right of way was appurtenant to the premises and even if not mentioned would have passed on the conveyance of the yard. Recourse to the doctrine of stipulations submitted to answered the argument concerning the defendant's right to use the sewers, watercourses and drains because the plaintiffs had not disputed the existence of this right.

Exchange of contracts   In *Embourg Ltd. v. Tyler Group Ltd.*, unreported March 5, 1996, which is fully discussed in the chapter on Contract (above, 211), the plaintiffs sought specific performance of an alleged contract for the sale of premises in Mary Street in Dublin. This claim was dismissed by Costello P. in an ex tempore judgment on the grounds that no contract was ever executed and his decision was affirmed on appeal by Blayney J., with whom Hamilton C.J. and Barrington J. concurred. One interesting aspect of this case was the recourse to the English practice whereby no binding contract of sale exists until signed copies of the contracts are exchanged by the parties. The plaintiffs sought to argue that this was not a feature of Irish conveyancing practice and thus irrelevant to the present case. However, Blayney J. was satisfied in the light of the correspondence between the parties and their conduct that it was their intention that no contract should come into existence until contracts had been exchanged. Blayney J. was careful to add that this conclusion was reached having regard to the special facts of this case. It did not follow that whenever there is a sale which is expressed to be 'subject to contract' no binding contract comes into existence until contracts have been exchanged. Each case had to be decided on its own facts.

SUCCESSION

Capacity to make a will In *Blackall v. Blackall*, unreported, June 28, 1996, the principal issue concerned the validity of a will purportedly made by the deceased on 23 September 1976. The deceased died on March 10, 1977 aged 100. Having heard the evidence of the persons who witnessed the execution of the will, McCracken J. held that there had been compliance with the formal requirements relating to the making of a will as laid down in section 78 of the Succession Act 1965. Turning to the question as to whether the deceased knew and approved of the contents of the will, and whether she was of sound mind, memory and understanding at the time of its execution, McCracken J. pointed out that while the onus of proving the formal validity of a will is on the person who propounds the will, where there is a challenge to a will based on the state of knowledge or state of health of the testator the onus is upon the person who challenges the will. As confirmed by the Supreme Court in *Re Glynn* [1990] 2 I.R. 326, there is a presumption of due execution and testamentary capacity where a will is formally valid. Here the evidence established that the will had been read over to the deceased by her solicitor and that the deceased had commented that it was fair. McCracken J. felt that this was the comment of a person who had understood what had been read to her. While the deceased was slightly hard of hearing and bed ridden, she had sufficient mental capacity when she made the will and the presumption to this effect had not been rebutted.

Extrinsic evidence In *Lindsay v. Tomlinson*, unreported, February 13, 1996, the testatrix devised and bequeathed the residue of her estate, which was valued at in excess of £50,000, 'to the British Legion Republic of Ireland Area Office, 3 Crosthwaite Terrace, Dun Laoghaire in the County of Dublin and the National Society for the Prevention of Cruelty to Animals (Dogs and Cats Home), 1 Grand Canal Quay in the City of Dublin to be divided equally between them.' The difficulty encountered in construing the will was that there was no entity known as 'the National Society for the Prevention of Cruelty to Animals (Dogs and Cats Home).' However, there was the Dublin Society for the Prevention of Cruelty to Animals and the Irish Society for the Prevention of Cruelty to Animals. The latter was a federation of independent societies and the Dublin society was a member of it and operated the Dogs and Cats Home at Grand Canal Quay.

Carroll J. held that there was an ambiguity in the will and accordingly extrinsic evidence was admissible under section 90 of the Succession Act 1965. Having considered evidence as to the testatrix's love of dogs, the fact that she had been a volunteer in a clinic devoted to the care of animals, her membership of the Dublin Society and the fact that the Irish Society for the Prevention of Cruelty to Animals was an administrative body not involved in active field work, Carroll J. concluded that on the balance of probabilities the testatrix intended the Dublin Society to be the beneficiary.

In *O'Connell v. Bank of Ireland*, unreported, March 27, 1996, the testatrix and her husband had made mutual wills leaving their respective estates to each other with provision for alternative dispositions in the event of the other having already died. The testatrix's husband died in 1991 and in 1993 the testatrix made a new will. Prior to doing so she informed a close friend that she intended to leave her house to the plaintiffs. Her friend told her to be sure to leave them the contents as well because otherwise they would have no right to them. On the evening of December 15, 1993, the day on which she made her new will, the testatrix told her friend that she had left the house and its contents to the plaintiffs. Subsequently she informed the plaintiffs that she had done so. However, the will as drafted provided that the plaintiffs were entitled to only the contents of the testatrix's house. The plaintiffs sought a declaration that they were entitled to the house.

Given the decision of the Supreme Court in *Rowe v. Law* [1978] I.R. 55, which makes the presence of an ambiguity or contradiction in the will a pre-condition to the admission of extrinsic evidence, the plaintiffs disclaimed any attempt to have such evidence admitted under section 90. However, they argued on the basis of the Supreme Court's decision in *Re Curtin* [1991] 2 I.R. 562 that the intention of the testatrix should not be frustrated. However, Barron J. held that *Re Curtin* was wholly distinguishable because unlike the circumstances of that case, here there was no question of the testatrix's intention being frustrated by the manner in which the will was drawn and the will itself gave no suggestion that what was provided therein might not be the intention of the testatrix. Consequently, the will had to be construed in accordance with its terms, regardless of the fact that the testatrix had intended to leave the house and its contents to the plaintiffs.

Nature of interest enjoyed by next of kin of intestate pending administration of the estate The decision of the Supreme Court in *Gleeson v. Feehan* [1997] 1 I.L.R.M. 522 reaffirms the principle that pending the administration of a deceased person's estate property comprised within that estate cannot be regarded as belonging to the persons entitled to share in the estate. James

Dwyer had been the registered owner of lands described in Folios 11057 and 3371 of the Register of Freeholders for County Tipperary. He died intestate on November 27, 1937, leaving a wife and six children. Edmond Dwyer, the son of James Dwyer, took possession of the land following the death of James Dwyer. James Dwyer's other children left the land either before their father's death or shortly thereafter. On June 16, 1953 Edmond Dwyer was registered as the owner of lands described in Folio 28973 of the Register of Freeholders for County Tipperary pursuant to a fiat of the Irish Land Commission dated June 16, 1953. Edmond Dwyer died on October 22, 1971 leaving neither a spouse nor issue. Following the death of Edmond Dwyer, Jimmy Dwyer, the illegitimate son of Edmond Dwyer's sister, remained in possession of the lands comprised in Folios 11057, 3371 and 28973. In 1978 Jimmy Dwyer entered into an agreement to sell the lands comprised in folios 11057 and 3371 to Patrick Purcell, the father of Francis Purcell. This agreement was completed by means of a deed dated March 3, 1978. In 1978 Jimmy Dwyer entered into an agreement to sell the land comprised in Folio 28973 to Donal Feehan and the purchase monies were paid on or before January 11, 1978. The sale was completed by a deed dated March 3, 1981.

Under a power of attorney dated December 15, 1980 and granted by the next of kin of Edmond Dwyer, on January 14, 1983 the plaintiff obtained letters of administration intestate in respect of the estate of Edmond Dwyer and, on February 8, 1983, letters of administration intestate in respect of the estate of James Dwyer. The plaintiff in his capacity as administrator of these estates instituted Circuit Court proceedings against Donal Feehan and Francis Purcell on March 1, 1983 by means of an ejectment civil bill on the title. The defendants pleaded that the plaintiff's claim was statute barred and this claim was tried as a preliminary issue. In a judgment delivered on June 20, 1991 (reported at [1993] 2 I.R. 113; [1991] I.L.R.M. 783) it was held by the Supreme Court that the plaintiff's claim was not statute barred. The case was remitted back to the Circuit Court where the plaintiff was granted a decree for possession. The defendants appealed to the High Court.

At the hearing of the appeal before Morris J. it was conceded by the plaintiff that the registration of Edmond Dwyer as full owner of the lands comprised in Folio 28973 was effected by fiat of the Irish Land Commission as a graft on his interest in the lands comprised in Folios 11057 and 3371 and, being subject to the equities affecting the lands comprised in Folios 11057 and 3371, conferred on Edmond Dwyer no better or greater title than that which was enjoyed by him in respect of the lands comprised in Folios 11057 and 3371. The defendants did not seek to rely upon the doctrine of notice as provided for in section 3 of the Conveyancing Act 1882 and accepted that the title conferred on them by Jimmy Dwyer was no better or greater than that enjoyed by him in 1978. All of the parties accepted that as Jimmy Dwyer had been illegitimate he could not have inherited a distributive share in the estates of James Dwyer and Edmond Dwyer. It followed that the only issue to be determined was whether Jimmy Dwyer was entitled to be registered as owner of the lands comprised in Folios 11057, 3371 and 28973 to the exclusion of Edmond Dwyer's next of kin. By way of case stated Morris J. posed the following questions for the Supreme Court:

1.(a) Where, prior to the Succession Act 1965, several next of kin in actual occupation of lands of a deceased person acquired title to those lands by adverse possession against the personal representative, was the title so acquired the title to which they would have been beneficially entitled on due administration?

(b) Where such next of kin acquired title by adverse possession against other next of kin not in occupation, was such title acquired as joint tenants?

2. Where such next of kin in actual occupation shared such occupation with persons other than next of kin, was the possession of such other persons adverse possession against (a) the personal representative or (b) next of kin not in occupation?

3.   If the answer to 1(a) or 1(b) is yes, was such title acquired jointly with the next of kin in occupation as (a) joint tenants or (b) tenants in common?

In the Supreme Court Keane J., with whom Blayney and Barrington JJ. concurred, pointed out that using the term 'interest' in a loose and imprecise sense, the next of kin of an intestate owner of property have an interest in ensuring the administration of his property is carried out in accordance with law by the administrator. The next of kin have a right, in the nature of a chose in action, to payment to them of the balance of the estate after the debts have been discharged. This right can be enforced against the personal representative. Regardless of the legal nature of the estate vested in an executor or administrator, he does not hold the property for his own benefit. To that extent, he is properly regarded as a trustee who must perform the duties of his office in the interests of those who are ultimately entitled to the deceased's property, whether as beneficiaries or creditors, and not in his own interest.

Keane J. felt that until such time as the extent of the residuary estate of a deceased person has been ascertained and the executor is in a position either to vest the proceeds of sale of the property comprised in the residue in the residuary legatees or, where appropriate, to vest individual items of property *in specie* in an individual residuary legatee, it would be contrary to elementary legal principles to treat the persons entitled to the residuary estate of a deceased person as being the owners in equity of specific items forming part of that residue. The same considerations applied to the rights of the next of kin in relation to the estate of a person who dies intestate. In both situations it is unnecessary and inappropriate to analyse the ownership of the deceased's estate in terms of who is entitled to the legal estate and who is entitled to the equitable estate as the court will control the personal representative's exercise of his rights in respect of the assets comprised in the estate.

Even if the next of kin of an intestate owner of land had an equitable interest in the land from the time of the owner's death, Keane J. observed that it would not follow that they would also have a right to possession which they could enforce against the personal representative. Furthermore, such a right to possession, even if it existed, could not depend on the purely fortuitous circumstance that a person who was one of the next of kin happened to be in possession of the land at the time of the intestate's death. If the administrator were to institute ejectment proceedings against any other person in possession, it would be no defence for that person to say that he was entitled to remain in possession of the land until such time as the administrator put up the property for sale with a view to paying the debts of the deceased. There was no reason in principle why different considerations should apply to one of the next of kin who happened to be in possession of the land at the time of the intestate's death.

Turning to the facts of the instant case, Keane J. held that as from the deaths of James and Mary Dwyer, the possession of the lands by Edmond Dwyer and Jimmy Dwyer was at all times adverse to the title of the true owner, the President of the High Court, in whom the entire estate in the lands was vested by statute pending the raising of representation. Section 15 of the Probate and Letters of Administration (Ireland) Act 1859 had provided that after the death of a person dying intestate and until letters of administration were granted in respect of his estate, the personal estate and effects of that person would vest in the President of the High Court. This provision was replaced by section 13 of the Administration of Estates Act 1959 which in turn was replaced by section 13 of the Succession Act 1965. By virtue of their adverse possession during the relevant period Edmond Dwyer and Jimmy Dwyer acquired a title to the lands as joint tenants. Accordingly, on the death of Edmond Dwyer, Jimmy Dwyer became the sole owner of the lands by virtue of survivorship. As section 24 of the Statute of Limitations 1957 extinguished the title of the President of the High Court to the lands and his right to bring an action to recover the land, no estate or interest could thereafter be vested by anyone in the next of kin, regardless of whether the next of kin were in or out of possession. The grant of letters of administration to the estate of James Dwyer could not revive the title to the land which had been extinguished by section 24.

Provision made during lifetime of testatrix precluding failure of moral duty under section 117 of the Succession Act 1965   In *Browne v. Sweeney*, unreported, July 5, 1996, the applicant brought a claim under section 117 in respect of his mother's estate. The testatrix was a widow who died in 1992 leaving four children including the applicant. With the exception of gifts of personal items, the testatrix made no provision in her will for any of her children. Instead, her estate, which was worth approximately £300,000, was left to five named charities. However, in 1987 the testatrix had made inter vivos gifts of shares in favour of each of her children. The applicant sold his shares which realised a sum of £270,000 after tax. By the time of the testatrix's death in 1992 this money had been completely dissipated by the applicant. The applicant was 40 years of age and unemployed. He was married with three children and had a history of alcohol and drug abuse for which he had been treated.

Lavan J. found that the applicant had been well provided for by both of his parents. After leaving school he had attended University College Dublin to study Commerce, but he left after one year. He then went to work in his father's business and later went to work in England and then Holland. He returned to Ireland where his father set him up in a haulage business on his own account. However, that business was not a success and at the age of 29 he decided to study History and German at Trinity College Dublin. The applicant's father financed this course of study and supported the applicant and his family while he was a student between 1983 and 1986. The applicant and his family lived rent free in a house which the applicant's father had put into the joint names of the applicant and one of his sisters.

Lavan J. concluded that proper provision had been made for the applicant throughout his life. He had received the same inter vivos gifts as his sisters and in some respects had been better provided for than them. However, despite having a university degree which improved his job prospects, since receiving the gift in 1987 he had not taken up any form of employment. Lavan J. rejected the argument that notwithstanding the making of provision for a child, a parent remains under a moral duty to make such continued provision for the child as is necessitated by changes in the child's circumstances, even if such changes are brought about by the child's own actions or inaction. Lavan J. observed that save where a child is mentally or physically handicapped, when a parent has made provision for a child during their lifetime there must come a time when that child can be regarded as having been established in life and the parent is thereby relieved of his or her moral duty. Lavan J. felt that if the courts were to hold otherwise, parents might be reluctant to make gifts during their lifetimes for the purpose of giving the child a start in life because they could still be required to make further provision by will.

Time at which legal right share of spouse arises   Section 111(1) of the Succession Act 1965 provides that 'if the testator leaves a spouse and no children, the spouse shall have a right to one half of the estate.' In *Re Urquhart* [1974] I.R. 197 the Supreme Court held that as the deceased had not elected under section 115 to take the legal right share provided for in section 111(1) instead of the gift provided for in his wife's will, the deceased's estate could not be regarded as comprising one half of the estate of his wife who had pre-deceased him. The issue to be decided in *O'Dwyer v. Keegan* [1997] 1 I.L.R.M. 102 differed in that there was no question of there being an election between the legal right share and an entitlement under the deceased's will. Thomas Cummins ('the husband') died on February 2, 1995. At the time of his death his wife, Kathleen Cummins ('the wife'), was comatose. She died twelve hours after her husband. Both husband and wife died testate and without children. The husband made no provision for his wife in his will. The wife had not renounced her legal right under section 111(1) in an antenuptial contract or in writing after marriage and during the life of her husband as she was entitled to do under section 113.

The defendant, who was a residuary legatee under the wife's will, argued that on the death of the husband, the wife automatically became entitled to one half of his estate by virtue of section 111(1) and so when she died twelve hours later her estate had been enhanced by having added to it one half of her husband's estate. The plaintiffs, who were the executors of the wife's will, argued that section 111(1) did not effect an automatic transfer, but merely created a right to one half of her husband's estate exercisable by the wife if she so wished and as she had not exercised that right her estate did not include one half of her husband's. This argument was supported by the notice parties who were the husband's next of kin.

Kelly J. that the wife's estate did not include one half of the husband's estate. The word 'right' in section 111(1) had to be given its ordinary and natural meaning. The conferring of a right gives the recipient an interest which will be recognised and protected by law. However, the recipient is free to decide whether to exercise such a right. Not every right need be exercised and there are circumstances where, if it is not exercised, it may be lost. There was nothing in section 111(1) which suggested that the right which is given to the surviving spouse operated automatically in favour of that spouse regardless of his or her wishes. As with any other right, the surviving spouse might choose to exercise it or not. If he or she does not or cannot exercise the right, the benefits of that right do not accrue. Therefore section 111(1) did not give rise to an automatic transfer of half of the husband's estate to the wife. Rather it created a right exercisable on the part of the wife, if she so wished, to one half of her husband's estate. Kelly J. adopted the description of the legal right proffered by Walsh J. in *Re Urquhart* [1974] I.R. 197, at 215 to the effect that it was in the nature of a statutory offer which was not binding on the spouse unless and until she accepted it.

The defendant's appeal from the decision of Kelly J. was allowed by the

Supreme Court in an unreported judgment delivered on May 8, 1997. Barron J., with whom Murphy and Lynch JJ. concurred, observed that it was clear from sections 3, 111 and 112 of the Succession Act 1965 that the surviving spouse has a right to share in the estate and this right has the same quality as an interest arising under a will or a share arising on intestacy. Section 112 provides that 'the right of a spouse under section 111 is to be known as a "legal right".' The term 'legal right' is defined in section 3 of the 1965 Act as meaning 'the right of a spouse under section 111 to share in the estate of a deceased person.' Section 3 defines 'share' as including 'any share or interest, whether arising under a will, on intestacy or as a legal right, and includes also the right to the whole estate.' According to Barron J., just as an interest arising under a will or a share arising on intestacy vests on death, so also does the legal right share of the surviving spouse. The absence of any procedure whereby the surviving spouse could be notified of the right and given the opportunity to exercise it was fatal to the plaintiffs' argument that section 111(1) merely created a right to one half of her husband's estate exercisable by the wife if she so wished. This may be contrasted with the obligation of the personal representatives under section 115(4) to notify the surviving spouse in writing where he or she has an election between the legal right and a gift under the will, together with any share on intestacy if the deceased died partially testate.

Barron J. concluded by pointing out that here it must be presumed that in the absence of a renunciation of the legal right under section 113, both spouses realised that the survivor of them would be entitled to the legal right and, even accepting that this was an interest conditional on acceptance, so could distribute the relevant assets as he or she wished. He added that it was important that the law should be certain so that those who rely upon it when they make their wills should be in no doubt as to how their assets will be distributed not only in expected circumstances but in unexpected circumstances also.

Limitation of Actions

AIR TRANSPORT

In the 1993 Review, 565, we analysed Barr J.'s decision in *Galvin v. Aer Rianta*, High Court, 13 October 13, 1993, which was concerned with liability under Article 17 of the Warsaw Convention 1929. The same article raised an issue relating to limitation of actions in *Burke v. Aer Lingus plc* [1997] 1 I.L.R.M. 148.

The point was a simple one of characterisation. Article 29(1) of the Convention prescribes a two-year limitation period for liability arising, *inter alia*, under Article 17. This contrasts with the normal three-year period for personal injury tort litigation. Article 17 imposes strict liability for damage suffered by a passenger 'if the accident which caused the damage so sustained took place on board the aircraft or in the course of any operations of embarking or disembarking.' In *Burke*, the plaintiff claimed that she had been injured when a shuttle bus conveying passengers from a plane to the terminal braked suddenly. She initiated proceedings within the three-year period but later than two years after the accident. If Article 17 applied, therefore, her claim would fall outside the limitation period prescribed by Article 29(1).

In an elaborate judgment, reviewing the international jurisprudence on Article 17, Barr J. held that Article 17 did indeed apply. He considered that its use of the phrase 'any of the operations . . .' suggested that it was not confined solely to the act of entering or leaving the airplane *per se* but that it had a wider meaning which included 'some activity by the passenger prior to entering or after leaving the aircraft.'

The crucial questions related to whether the plaintiff was at the time under the continuous control of the airline or its agent and whether the close temporal and spatial relationship with the flight itself' (*per* Selya J. in *McCarthy v. Northwest Airlines* 25 Aviation Cas. 17, 101 (1st Circ., 1995) still have vitality.

The shuttle-bus journey was an 'air related risk having regard to the nature and purpose of that part of the airport where it takes place'; during it the passengers remained in the exclusive control of the airline.

Barr J.'s decision is surely correct. This does not mean, of course, that every time a passenger uses vehicular transport within the confines of an airport, Article 17 applies.

MARITIME PROCEEDINGS

In *Carleton v. O'Regan* [1997] 1 I.L.R.M. 370, Barr J. in a maritime action declined to exercise his discretion in favour of extending the two-year limitation period, as section 46(2) of the Civil Liability Act 1981 permits. The litigation resulted from a collision at Castletownbere. The defendant's insurers did not dispute liability but seriously contested the quantum of damages. The plaintiff's insurers sent a fax to the defendants' insurers three days before the period ran out requesting their consent to extend the time limit by a further year. The defendant's insurers replied that they had passed the request on to the defendant. The time ran out without any further response from, or on behalf of, the defendant.

Barr J. gave a thorough review of the English decisions. He distinguished Sheen J.'s judgment in *The 'Seaspeed America'* [1990] 1 Lloyd's Rep. 150, which granted an extension, on the basis that there had been a formal undertaking on behalf of the defendants to pay such sums as might be due to the plaintiffs in respect of their claim; all that the plaintiffs had to establish was the reasonableness of the cost of repairing their vessel. In the instant case, in contrast, the parties were a long way from agreement on quantum and no basis for negotiating a settlement on that issue had been established.

THE CONSTITUTIONAL DIMENSION

The relationship between the rights-based language of the Constitution and the wrongs-based vocabulary of the law of torts has puzzled our courts. The easy solution is to characterise claims based on constitutional rights as being a species of tort claim, thus capable of being tamed by the Statute of Limitations 1957. Carroll J. so held in *Tate v. Minister for Social Welfare* [1995] 1 I.L.R.M. 507: see the 1995 Review, 363, 541, 543.

Carroll J. reiterated this view, twice, in 1996. In *McDonnell v. Ireland* [1996] 2 I.L.R.M. 222, the plaintiff, a civil servant who had been convicted in 1974 of IRA membership, had lost his employment by virtue of section 34 of the Offences Against the State Act 1939, which provided for forfeiture of civil service positions in such circumstances. After the institution of An Post in 1984 the plaintiff had unsuccessfully sought reinstatement from the newly established body. The Supreme Court, in *Cox v. Ireland* [1992] 2 I.R. 503, had held section 34 to be unconstitutional: see the 1991 Review, 105-7. The plaintiff shortly afterwards took proceedings claiming that the purported dismissal had been unconstitutional and of no legal effect and claiming damages for breach of his constitutional rights resulting from the operation of the impugned statutory provision. The damages consisted of loss of income, pension and gratuity entitlements.

Carroll J. cited her judgment in *Tate*, stating that she saw no reason to change the views she had there expressed. It 'flow[ed] logically' that section 11(2) of the 1957 Act applied to breach of a constitutional right in the nature of a tort as it did to breaches of obligations of the Sate under community law, as in *Tate*. The plaintiff's cause of action had arisen when he had been notified that his position as a civil servant was forfeited. His application to An Post in 1984 had not affected the matter and, had not served to revive any claim then barred.

Carroll J. admitted to seeing merit in the argument by the plaintiffs counsel that the forfeiture had been inoperative but she considered that:

> the argument applies only for as long as the cause of action is not barred. Once the cause of action was barred, the *de facto* forfeiture which was an act done on foot of an unconstitutional law, became immune from suit. It follows that the plaintiff is not entitled to the declarations sought. It would be futile to make any declaration since no consequence could flow from it. Since the Statute of Limitations applies, laches does not arise.

One may perhaps question the adequacy of this analysis. A person who has wrongly been treated as having forfeited an entitlement may surely make two claims: first that that entitlement has not in fact been validly forfeited and secondly that those who wrongly acted to his or her detriment by treating him or her as though it had been validly forfeited. It is worth noting that the statutory code on limitation of actions is perfectly capable of distinguishing between the denial of a right of action on the one hand and the retention of an entitlement in respect of which that action can no longer be maintained. Thus, for example, prior to the enactment of section 12 of the 1957 Act, although an owner's right to sue for conversion became statute-barred in relation to the converter, he or she could pursue a subsequent converter whose act of conversion was less than six years old and his or her title to the goods was not extinguished: see James Brady & Anthony Kerr, *The Limitation of Acts* (2nd ed., 1994), 88-9.

Carroll J. revisited the issue in *Murphy v. Ireland* [1996] 2 I.L.R.M. 461. The plaintiff was another victim of section 34 who had lost his employment as assistant county engineer in 1973.

Carroll J. derived support from the crucial part of Henchy J.'s judgment in *Hanrahan v. Merck Sharp & Dohme* [1988] I.L.R.M. 629, at 636:

> So far as I am aware, the constitutional provisions relied on have never been used in the courts to shape the form of any existing tort or to change the normal onus of proof. The implementation of those constitutional rights is primarily a matter for the State and the courts are entitled to

intervene only when there has been a failure to implement or, where the implementation relied on is plainly inadequate, to effectuate the constitutional guarantee in question. In many torts - for example, negligence, defamation, trespass to the person or property - a plaintiff may give evidence of what he claims to be a breach of a constitutional right, but he may fail in the action because of what is usually a matter of onus of proof or because of some other legal or technical defence. A person may of course, in the absence of a common law or statutory cause of action, sue directly for a breach of a constitutional right (see *Meskell v. Coras Iompair Éireann* [1973] I.R. 121); but when he founds his action on an existing tort he is normally confined to the limitations of that tort. It might be different if it could be shown that the tort in question is basically ineffective to protect his constitutional right.

It should be noted that Henchy J. was addressing the question of whether the constitutional provisions should be used to shape, or vary the shape, of existing torts. His reply, in essence, was that generally the courts should not engage in the process of refashioning existing torts, whether of common law or statutory derivation, unless the particular tort is 'basically ineffective to protect' the particular constitutional right that has been injured or placed in jeopardy. Henchy J. was not addressing the quite different question as to whether, with respect to a claim for infringement of a constitutional right which, as it were, is not sailing under the flag of any particular tort, section 11(2) of the 1957 Act, which is restricted to actions 'founded on tort', should [scupper] the constitutional claim.

It is not at all unreasonable that, in a case where a claim for infringement of a constitutional right is proceeding under the characterisation of a tort, it should be capable of being defeated by section 11(2). It is far less clear, however, that this generic statutory provision should be considered lethal to claims for infringement of constitutional rights which have not been reduced to a tortious characteristic.

Carroll J.'s disposition of the issue raises some further questions in this context. Having quoted Henchy J.'s observations in *Hanrahan*, she stated:

> To my mind, that passage confirms the view that, where the existing law of tort provides adequate protection for the enforcement of constitutional rights the State has implemented its duty under article 40.3.1° of the Constitution 'as far as practicable by its laws to defend and vindicate the personal rights of the citizen.' If the plaintiff's constitutional rights are protected by being able to sue under the law of tort, then the statutory limitation periods applicable to torts must also apply. It is only in the absence of a common law or statutory cause of action that here is a necessity to sue directly for a breach of constitutional right (as happened

in *Kearney v. Minister for Justice* [1986] I.R. 116; [1987] I.L.R.M. 52
where it was held that non-delivery of letters in prison was not a tort but
was an unjustified infringement of a constitutional right).

This passage appears to support the view that the statutory limitation periods
applicable to torts apply only to cases where the plaintiff's constitutional rights
are protected by an action in tort. On that approach, Mr. Kearney's action
would not be defeated by the 1957 Act (though, as we shall see, it would be
subject to the principle of laches).

If this was Carroll J.'s view, why should the plaintiff's claim in the case
before her have been held to be tortious in character? At no point in her
judgment did Carroll J. expertly hold that the claim should be characterised as
an action for a specific tort. Instead, echoing her language in *McDonnell*, she
identified it as a breach of a constitutional right 'in the nature of a tort'. At
one point in her judgment, she stated that '[i]n this case the action of the State
has all the hallmarks of the tort of procuring a breach of contract.' It seems,
however, that in doing so, she was merely summarising the argument of counsel for the State rather than necessarily endorsing it.

Carroll J. went on to reject the plaintiff's argument that his cause of action
had not arisen until he knew that section 34 had been held to be unconstitutional. The plaintiff had had the right to bring proceedings once he had been
notified that his job was forfeited. The forfeiture complained of 'was a single
act and not a continuing wrong.'

Carroll J. considered that, if she was wrong about the Statute of Limitations applying to breaches of constitutional rights in the nature of a tort, the
plaintiff's claim should still be rejected on the ground of laches. In *Murphy v.
Attorney General* [1982] I.R. 241, Henchy J. had recognised the application
of their equitable ground to constitutional claims. In the instant case, Carroll
J. did not think that proof of public policy was necessary:

> The matter speaks for itself. If the plaintiff did nothing for twenty years
> resulting in an extremely large claim for damages based on actuarial
> evidence, that, in my view, is sufficient proof that, the state has been
> prejudicial.

DISMISSAL FOR WANT OF PROSECUTION

In *Carroll Shipping Ltd. v. Mathews Mulcahy & Sutherland Ltd.*, High Court,
December 18, 1996, McGuinness J. applied the principles laid down by the
Supreme Court in *Primor plc v. Stokes Kennedy Crowley* and *Primor plc v.
Oliver Freaney & Co.*, Supreme Court, December 19, 1995, in dismissing the

plaintiffs case for want of prosecution. The plaintiffs, marine contractors and shipping charterers, had sued the defendants, insurance brokers, for breach of contract and negligence arising out of a shipping accident in 1975. The plaintiffs' insurance had allegedly left them exposed to the loss and damage resulting from that accident. Judgment was given in the accident claims against the plaintiffs in 1980. The plaintiffs issued and served their plenary summons against the defendants in 1981. The statement of claim was delivered four years later. The plaintiffs filed a motion for judgment in 1987. T The defendant sought particulars and the plaintiffs replied July 1987. The plaintiffs delivered notice of trial in 1989. A discovery procedure then began. It lasted for three years.

In November 1993, the plaintiffs unsuccessfully sought the consent of the defendants' solicitor to the serving of an amended statement of claim. The plaintiffs' solicitors served a notice of intention to proceed in January 1996.

McGuinness J. held that the delay of fifteen years since the issue of the plenary summons was 'undoubtedly inordinate, especially when one bears in mind that the actual events given rise the claim date back to 1973 to 1975.' The situation was aggravated by the fact that the plaintiff was seeking substantial amendments to the statement to claim which would 'inevitably lead to a whole new round of particulars, discovery and so on before the case could come on for trial?

McGuinness J. went on to hold that the delay was also inexcusable. The framing of the original statement of claim had not involved complex calculations. The delays in the discovery procedure could be attributed to both sides but the delay in dealing with the amended statement of claim was purely that of the plaintiffs. A 'crucial factor was that from 1990 until 1995 the plaintiff company had had no existence, having been struck off the Companies Register, apparently for failure to file returns.

The final question to be decided was whether a fair and just trial might now be had between the parties. McGuinness J. noted that:

> [w]here in any trial the issues between the parties which fall to be decided by the Court can clearly be established by documentary evidence only, it may well be that delay, however inordinate or inexcusable, will not in fact prevent the holding of a fair and just trial. However, where matters are at issue which are not, or are not fully, covered by documentary evidence, there is a greater likelihood of prejudice resulting from delay.

McGuinness J. considered that, inspite of the difficulties and delays involved in keeping documents since 1981, it would have been 'wise and prudent' for the defendants to have done so until they were absolutely certain that the proceedings had been withdrawn or completely struck out by the court. If the case had been wholly dependent on documentary evidence, it would not warrant dismissal on account of these difficulties, which included the restructuring of the defendants interval administrative activities following computerisation and the dispersal of files following a move of premises in 1975. It appeared, however, that 'important issues' as to the *verbal* advices given by the defendants and as to the state of information and state of mind of the plaintiffs were certain to arise at trial. In this context, the defendants had particular difficulties. Their principal negotiator who had advised the plaintiffs during the relevant period had died in 1986. Moreover, persons who might have either supervised or assisted him in dealing with the plaintiffs' businesses were no longer employed by the defendants. Even were they available for the purposes of giving evidence, there was no doubt that their memory of the events of over twenty years previously would be 'dangerously defective.'

McGuinness J. was therefore satisfied that the prejudice caused to the defendants by the inordinate and inexcusable delay on the part of the plaintiffs was such as to place an unfair burden on the defendants in defending these proceedings and was such as to make it impossible that a fair trial between the parties could now be had. She was also satisfied that the interests of justice required that the proceedings brought by the plaintiffs should be dismissed.

NEGLIGENT MISREPRESENTATION

In *Murphy v. Minister for the Marine* [1996] 2 I.L.R.M. 297, Morris J., following the Supreme Court decision of *Hegarty v. O'Loughran* [1990] I.L.R.M. 403; [1990] 1 I.R. 148 (analysed in the 1990 Review 389-98), held that the cause of action for negligent misrepresentation accrued, not when the "representation was allegedly *made*, but when it was allegedly *breached*. In the instant case, the plaintiff, a fisherman, claimed that he had made certain investment decisions on the basis of a ministerial assurance that he would be given a licence, and that the Minister had later gone back on that assurance resulting in the plaintiff's sustaining economic loss. The alleged assurance had been made more than six years prior to the making of the claim but the alleged breach had occurred within that period. Accordingly Morris J. held that the claim had been made within time.

Local Government

COMPULSORY PURCHASE

Entry on lands: judicial discretion to refuse In *McKeen v. Meath County Council*, High Court, April 13, 1996 Barron J. held that the respondent Council had been wrongly refused permission by a District Court judge for permission to enter lands with a view to ascertaining whether they were suitable for compulsory acquisition. The lands were required for use as a cemetery. The applicant, whose lands were the subject of the Council's interest, had applied to the District Court for an order restraining entry under section 13 of the Local Government (No. 2) Act 1960. She objected to the proposed entry on the grounds that there were alternative lands available, that other lands had already been donated by her family and that the lands in question had been planted under a scheme funded by the European Community which might be jeopardised. The District Court judge was of the view that, in exercising his discretion under section 13 of the 1960 Act, he was required to balance the constitutional right to private property with the statutory right to enter the land. He felt that unless the Council could show that there were no alternative lands available, the constitutional rights of the applicant should prevail; on this basis he granted the applicant the order she sought.

On a case stated was made to the High Court, Barron J. held that the District Court judge had erred. Barron J. accepted that section 13 of the 1960 Act contemplated that there may be reasons why a District Court judge may conclude that entry on lands should be prohibited or subject to certain conditions. However, the discretion ought to be exercised in accordance with the objectives of the 1960 Act in relation to compulsory purchase and to seek to give effect to that intention. He considered that the question of alternative sites was not one which came within the proper exercise of discretion. As to the constitutional dimension to the case, Barron J. stated that it was implicit from the presumption of constitutionality which the 1960 Act enjoyed that the power of entry would be exercised in accordance with fair procedures. On this basis, he concluded that there were no grounds in the instant case on which the District Court judge could have refused to permit the entry.

Unconditional offer In *Manning v. Shackleton* [1994] 1 I.R. 397 (H.C.); [1994] 1 I.L.R.M. 346 (H.C.); [1997] 2 I.L.R.M. 26 (SC), the Supreme Court held that an unconditional offer within the meaning of section 5 of the Acquisition of Land (Assessment of Compensation) Act 1919 had not been made in the instant case: see the discussion in the Administrative Law chapter, 10, above.

CONTROL OF ANIMALS

Dogs The Control of Dogs (Restriction of Certain Dogs) (Amendment) Regulations 1996 (SI No. 295 of 1996), made under the Control of Dogs Acts 1986 and 1992 (1992 Review, 439-10), provide that the muzzling restrictions imposed by the Control of Dogs (Restriction of Certain Dogs) Regulations 1991 (1991 Review, 308-9) do not apply to harbour police rescue dogs or airport police dogs.

Horses The Control of Horses Act 1996 was enacted to introduce legislative controls over wandering horses, particularly in urban areas. As indicated by the Explanatory Memorandum which accompanied its presentation to the Oireachtas, its main provisions are: (a) the declaration, by means of local authority bye-laws, of control areas where horses may not be kept without licences, (b) the granting of licences to horse owners in control areas subject to compliance with conditions to be set out in bye-laws, (c) disqualification from keeping a horse or from obtaining a licence, (d) a ban on the sale of horses to minors under the age of 16 years, (e) the seizure, detention and disposal of stray, unlicensed or unidentifiable horses or horses causing a nuisance or posing a danger, in particular a power to dipose of horses detained for non-compliance with bye-laws on three or more occasions (an Irish version of the 'three strikes and out' policy); (f) criminal liability for injury or damage caused by horses, (g) powers of enforcement for authorised persons and members of the Garda Síochána and (h) powers of arrest and the issue of search warrants. The Act also provides penalties on conviction for offences under the legislation. Finally, the Act provides for amendments to the Protection of Animals Act 1911, the Pounds (Provision and Maintenance) Act 1935, the Protection of Animals (Amendment) Act 1965, and the Animals Act 1985. The Act (other than Part IV, which came into effect on March 4, 1997) came into effect on March 18, 1997: Control of Horses Act 1996 (Commencement) Order 1997 (SI No. 99 of 1997).

Control areas and disposal of horses Section 2 of the Act defines horse in the same manner as that contained in the Protection of Animals (Amendment) Act 1965. Section 2 defines control areas as areas (likely to be mainly urban) in which horses may not be kept without licences and will be designated in bye-laws made by local authorities under section 17 of the Act. Section 2 also defines disposal of a horse as including selling, giving away or destruction. A

stray horse is defined as a horse apparently wandering at large, lost or unac-
companied by any person apparently in charge of it in a public place or on any
premises without the owner's or occupier's consent.

Arrest Section 4 empowers a member of the Garda Síochána to arrest without
warrant persons suspected of having committed certain offences under the
Act, including: failure to remove an unlicensed horse from a public place or a
control area; failure to give name and address to an authorised person of the
local authority or the Garda where the commission of an offence under the
Act is suspected; failure to desist from dangerous use of a horse, from infringing bye-laws relating to horse control and welfare, or from having a horse in
an area from which it is excluded; obstruction of an authorised person of a
local authority or a member of the Garda Síochána in the exercise of their
duties; failure to adhere to bye-laws relating to the control and welfare of
horses; keeping, having or riding a horse in an exclusion area.

Penalties Section 6 provides that the maximum penalties for offences under
the Act (other than section 42) will be a fine of £1,500 and/or 6 months imprisonment. For an offence under section 42 (which deals with wilfully allowing a horse to cause injury to person or property) similar penalties apply in
summary proceedings, but a change may also be on indictment, where the
maximum penalties are a fine of £10,000 and/or 2 years imprisonment. Section 7 provides that, on conviction of an offence, a person may, in addition to
the penalty imposed, be disqualified from keeping a horse for such period as
the court sees fit, while section 8 empowers the court to order the forfeiture of
a horse to a local authority on conviction of the owner of an offence where the
welfare of the animal so demands. The local authority may seize and detain
the horse and dispose of it as it thinks fit.

On-the-spot fines Section 10 allows the imposition of an on-the-spot fine of
£50 (variable by Ministerial Regulation) for offences such as: failure to licence a horse kept in a control area (section 18); to inform the local authority
in relation to the disposal or change of ownership of a horse (section 25); to
produce a horse licence for inspection by the local authority or the Garda
(section 26); to remove an unlicensed horse from a public place or control
area (section 27); to comply with bye-laws (section 44); or to keep a horse out
of an exclusion area or to comply with a requirement of an authorised officer
or a member of the Garda Síochána that a horse be removed from an exclusion
area (section 45).

Increased penalties Section 47 of the 1996 Act increases the maximum penalties under section 1(1) of the Protection of Animals Act 1911 as follows: on
summary conviction a fine of £1,500 and/or 6 months imprisonment; on con-

viction on indictment a fine of £10,000 and/or 2 years imprisonment. Maximum fines for offences under ssection 8(2) and 9 of the Pounds (Provision and Maintenance) Act 1935 were also increased. Finally, section 47 provides for an increase in the maximum fine to £1,500 under section 5(5) and (6) of the Animals Act 1985.

ELECTIONS

Electoral divisions and boundaries   The Local Government Act 1994 (Commencement) Order 1996 (SI No. 191 of 1996) brought section 63 of the Local Government Act 1994 into force on June 24, 1996. Section 63 of the 1994 Act (1994 Review, 347) replaced the long-established terms 'wards' and 'district electoral divisions', provided for in sections 88 and 89 of the Electoral Act 1963 (now repealed by the coming into force of section 63 of the 1994 Act) with the single term 'electoral divisions'. The Local Government Act 1991 (Commencement) Order 1996 (SI No. 215 of 1996) brought Part V of the Local Government Act 1991 (1991 Review, 312), which concerns local authority boundary changes, into force on 16 September 1996. The Local Government (Boundary Alteration) Regulations 1996 (SI No. 217 of 1996) set out the relevant procedural matters in relation to local authority boundary alterations under Part V of the 1991 Act, also with effect from 16 September 1996. The Local Government Act 1994 (Commencement) (No. 2) Order 1996 (SI No. 216 of 1996) brought section 24 of the Local Government Act 1994, which concerns local electoral areas, into force, also on 16 September 1996

HOUSING

Housing grants   The Housing (New House Grants Etc.) Regulations 1990 (Amendment) Regulations 1996 (SI No. 88 of 1996), made under the Housing Act 1966, increased the minimum floor area for houses and apartments qualifying for grants. They came into effect on April 4, 1996.

House purchase   The Housing Regulations 1980 (Amendment) Regulations 1996 (SI No. 148 of 1996), made under the Housing Act 1966 and the Housing (Miscellaneous Provisions) Act 1992 (1992 Review, 441-4), amended the Housing Regulations 1980 in relation to house purchase and improvement loans made by local authorities. They increase the amounts of local authority house purchase and improvement loans; provide a formula for taking into account second incomes in the assessment of income; the extension of repayment periods in cases of hardship and the consolidation of loans; and provide that loans may be made to persons who previously owned a house (for example, following marital breakdown). They came into effect retrospectively from May 1, 1995.

Registration   The Housing (Registration of Rented Houses) Regulations 1996 (SI No.30 of 1996), made under the Housing (Miscellaneous Provisions) Act 1992, provided for the registration with housing authorities of most premises rented to private persons. They came into effect on May 1, 1996.

Temporary halting sites   *Ward and Ors. v. South Dublin County Council,* High Court, July 31, 1996 was another case concerning the difficulties experienced on the one hand by members of the travelling community in seeking to maintain their nomadic lifestyle and on the other hand by local authorities charged with the duty of providing suitable accommodation and restraining unlawful encampments. The applicants were representatives of a number of travelling community families who had halted their vehicles and caravans on land which was not a designated halting site. Section 10 of the Housing Act 1992 provides that where a person without lawful authority retains a temporary dwelling in a public place within five miles of a site provided, managed or controlled by a housing authority under section 13 of the Housing Act 1988 and the temporary dwelling could in the authority's opinion appropriately be accommodated on that site, the authority may serve a notice on the person requiring him within a specified period to remove the said dwelling to the said site.

The applicants were issued with notices served on them by the respondent Council in purported exercise of the provisions of section 10 of the 1992 Act, but challenged their validity, primarily on the basis that the site to which they were being directed was a designated temporary halting site under section 13 of the 1988 Act which already housed a number of travelling families and was unsuitable in terms of facilities to accommodate the additional burden which would be placed on it by the applicants. In what was an important test case on the duties of the defendant authority, Laffoy J. in effect accepted the applicants' arguments. She held that it was a precondition to the serving of a valid notice under section 10 of the 1992 Act that there was within five miles from the location of the offending temporary dwelling a halting site provided by the housing authority under section 13 of the 1988 Act on which the offending temporary dwelling could 'appropriately be accommodated.' She considered that the halting site provided by the Council in the instant case did not meet this statutory duty.

Laffoy J. reasoned that a traveller family which was entitled to be provided with a dwelling had to be offered a dwelling. If this was refused because the family pursued a nomadic, traveller way of life, this did not mean that the Council had a discretion as to whether to provide that family with a caravan site. The correct approach, she held, was that section 13 of the 1988 Act obliged the local authority to provide serviced halting sites to those who required them instead of conventional dwellings and a housing authority could not meet its statutory obligations by offering a conventional dwelling only to travellers. She referred to the decision of Barron J. in *University of Limerick v. Ryan and Ors.,* High Court, February 21, 1991 (1991 Review, 309-10) and of Flood J. in *Meath Vocational Education Committee v. Joyce* [1994] 2 I.L.R.M. 210 (1994 Review, 347-10) in this respect.

Laffoy J. accepted that the respondent Council was committed to providing accommodation for the travelling community and it was not the Court's function to direct a local authority as to how it should deploy its resources or as to the manner in which it should prioritise the performance of its various statutory functions; these were policy matters which were outside the ambit of judicial review. Nonetheless, she added that section 13 of the 1988 Act had to be implemented in a rational and reasonable manner, and had to involve the adoption of a coherent and fair system of allocating halting site units. She considered that the respondent Council, as housing authority, was required to have regard to the fact that housing needs and traveller accommodation needs in its area were continuing to grow, if that were the case, or to change, and it could not ignore the fact that there were people without accommodation, even though at a particular point in time they did not qualify under an existing scheme or system. Thus, it was for the housing authority to determine priorities in relation to allocation of halting site units, the court having no function in ordering the provision of a halting site unit for any particular applicants or in any particular order.

Laffoy J. noted that it was the clear purpose of section 10 of the 1992 Act to control unauthorised encampment and parking of caravans and mobile homes generally. But, as already indicated, she stated that in this case there was no halting site within five miles provided by the housing authority on which the offending temporary dwelling could "appropriately be accommodated". On the evidence, she was satisfied that by reason of the physical condition of and the inadequacy of the services at the bays at the relevant halting site the applicants' temporary dwellings could not have been appropriately accommodated there. Thus, the Council had not been entitled to invoke section 10 of the 1992 Act. However, she did not base this conclusion merely that the halting site in question had been designated as a temporary halting site and was not intended to be maintained as a permanent halting site. The key factor was whether the halting site to which a person was directed under a section 10 notice was in proper physical condition and adequately serviced. Rather than making a final order in the matter, Laffoy J. directed the Council to ascertain the accommodation requirements of the applicants and to assess their eligibility for accommodation under the Housing Acts as soon as reasonably practicable. Pending this, she restrained the Council from taking any action on foot of the section 10 notices. See also Laffoy J's judgment in *O'Reilly and Ors. v. O'Sullivan and Dun Laoghaire-Rathdown County Council*, High Court, July 25, 1996, below, another traveller-related case.

LOCAL AUTHORITY MANAGEMENT

Emergency works In *O'Reilly and Ors v. O'Sullivan and Dun Laoghaire-Rathdown County Council*, High Court, July 25, 1996, Laffoy J. dealt with the interaction between the legislative regime for local authority management and the housing and planning code, against the background of the ongoing difficulties associated with providing accommodation for the travelling community. Section 2(7) of the City and County Management (Amendment) Act 1955 provides that the county manager shall inform the members of a local authority before any works (other than maintenance and repair) of the local authority are carried out. Section 2(9) of the 1955 Act provides that nothing in section 2(7) shall prevent a county manager from dealing forthwith with any situation which he considers is an emergency situation calling for immediate action without regard to those provisions. Section 2(10) of the 1955 Act (as inserted by section 27 of the Housing Act 1988) provides that an emergency situation within section 2(9) 'shall be deemed to exist where, in the opinion of the manager, the works concerned are urgent and necessary (having regard to personal health, public health and safety considerations) in order to provide a reasonable standard of accommodation for any person.'

The second respondent Council had agreed, in settlement of High Court proceedings, to cease using a particular site in County Dublin as a halting site not later than June 1995. Within its administrative area, over 30 families of the travelling community were living at unauthorised locations in County Dublin without any basic amenities. The first respondent, the Council's County Manager, was of the opinion that an emergency situation existed within the meaning of section 2(10) of the 1955 Act. By order dated June 23, 1995, he directed that a halting site for 40 caravans be established at a particular location in County Dublin. The proposed site was located in an area zoned F in the 1993 Dublin County Development Plan, which had as its objective "to preserve and provide for open space and recreational amenities". The Development Plan "permitted in principle" halting sites in an area zoned F "subject to compliance with relevant policies, standards and requirements" set out in the Development Plan. The applicants, local residents, objected to the Order made on the grounds, *inter alia*, that the decision constituted a material contravention of the 1993 Dublin Development, that it was unreasonable and irrational and that the first respondent had failed to prepare an environmental impact study (EIS) pursuant to the European Communities (Environmental Impact Assessment) regulations 1989 and the Local Government (Planning & Development) Regulations 1994. Laffoy J. refused the relief sought.

As to the 1989 and 1994 Regulations, she held that, since the proposed development was for a maximum of 40 caravans, it did not come within their terms, since an EIS was required only where such a development would involve more than 100 caravans. As to whether the decision was irrational, she applied the principles set out by the Supreme Court in *O'Keeffe v. An Bórd Pleanála* [1993] 1 I.R. 39 (1991 Review, 16-18). She held that the onus was on the applicants to show that the emergency procedure had not been properly invoked and they had failed to do so, in her view. She was not prepared to conclude that their judgment on these matters, or the managerial order based on these judgments, was irrational. In particular, while the decision involved a departure from previous practice, this did not in itself render the decision irrational. She also noted that the relevant Council officials were aware of the material provisions of the 1993 Development Plan and had adverted to them in considering whether to proceed with the proposed development. On this basis, she concluded that all relevant factors had been adverted to by the officials and their decision could not be held to be *ultra vires*.

Request for information by elected official In *Cullen v. Wicklow County Manager and Wicklow County Council*, High Court, June 13, 1996, McCracken J. held that information requested by an elected local authority member from a local authority official could include information requested verbally. The applicant was chairman of the defendant County Council. In 1994, the Council had approved a draft development plan for the Blessington area which included the zoning of certain lands as "forestry and amenity". Later, a revised draft plan was drawn up in which those lands were zoned so as to allow the extraction of sand and gravel from them and the revised draft plan was approved by the Council and placed on public display. In the meantime, the owner of the lands had started works on those lands in contravention of the then zoning and the Council instituted proceedings under the Local Government (Planning and Development) Act 1963. In the course of these proceedings, the Council's law agent amassed a file in relation to the proceedings. Subsequently, the applicant wrote to the Council County Secretary (and copied the letter to the Council's law agent) expressing concern at the status of the lands in question, formally requesting that all papers concerning those lands be made available and requesting that if any papers were missing that such fact be communicated to him before the meeting. The applicant was offered a number of documents for inspection but was refused access to the law agent's files. Section 27 of the County Management Act 1940 provides that every county manager "shall, whenever requested by the council of his county . . . or by the chairman of such council . . . afford . . . all such information as may be in the possession or procurement of such county manager in regard to any act, matter or thing appertaining to or concerning any business or transaction of such council or body . . . which is mentioned in such request".

The applicant sought judicial review of the refusal to provide him with information. The Council argued that the applicant had not made any request to the county manager in accordance with section 27 of the 1940 Act as the request was made to the County Secretary and to the law agent. It was also submitted that as the request made was verbal in character, this did not come within the 1940 Act. Finally, the Council contended that the applicant was entitled to "information", not documents, and that he had been given general information regarding the progress of the proceedings against the land owner. McCracken J. granted the applicant the relief sought.

He held that it was the function of the County Secretary to pass a request such as that made by the applicant to the County Manager. It had not suggested in evidence that the County Manager was unaware of the request and thus section 27 of the 1940 Act applied and the request had been made to the County Manager through the proper channels. McCracken J. was satisfied that a verbal request for information came within section 27 of the 1940 Act. He noted that there were many examples of statutory provisions where communications were directed to be "in writing". This was not so in the case of section 27 of the 1940 Act and there was no reason why, in the absence of such express provision, the section should not cover a verbal request. The applicant had requested that all papers be made available, but this request was made in the context of his stated concern to be up-to-date on the status of the lands in question. There was no doubt that the law agent's files contained information, in the words of the section, "appertaining to or concerning" a transaction of the Council, namely, the progress of proceedings taken by the Council in connection with the lands. He was therefore satisfied that such information was within the possession or procurement of the County Manager.

Commenting on the general purpose of section 27 of the 1940 Act, which was only applicable to the County Manager or the Council as a whole, McCracken J. noted that it seemed to have been intended to allow the administration of a local authority to proceed as efficiently as possible without interference from individual members of the Council, while also ensuring that there was some procedure whereby the executive of the local authority could be overseen, though not necessarily controlled, by the elected members. As to the argument concerning the word 'information' in the 1940 Act, McCracken J. referred with approval to the views expressed in *Commissioners of Police v. Ombudsman* [1985] 1 N.Z.L.R. 578, where it had been held that the use of the word "information" without any express limitation gave to it a very wide and general meaning, which seemed to be in accordance with what had been intended by the Oireachtas. The word was not defined in the 1940 Act and there was nothing in the legislative context to limit the scope of what was, *prima facie*, a word with a very wide meaning. On this basis, he held that the applicant was entitled, on request, to see all information which might be in written form as well as to be verbally informed in regard to any act, matter or thing appertaining to or concerning any business or transaction of the Council and that his request for such information could be written or verbal. Since the applicant had made a valid request for all information in writing and this included a request to see the law agent's files, he was entitled to the information.

MALICIOUS INJURIES

In *Ó Faoláin v. Dublin Corporation*, High Court, December 10, 1996, Lavan J. held that there had been sufficient evidence of intent to commit violence within section 6 of the Malicious Injuries Act 1981 in the following circumstances. The applicant sought to recover under the 1981 Act for damage caused to his premises by four men removing goods. Their actions were witnessed by a person who observed them from the door of her flat situated at the rear of the applicant's premises and who was caused to go back into her flat when one of the men fumed and stared at her. Lavan J. held that this stare was sufficient to indicate the intent required by section 6 of the 1981 Act which provides that an award is to be made where damage is caused to property "unlawfully by one or more of a number of persons riotously assembled together". It was accepted that the applicant had complied with the following requirements of the test to obtain compensation, namely, that there were at least three people involved, that they were assembled for the common purpose of damaging the applicant's property and that this common purpose had been executed. The case thus revolved around whether there was an intent by the persons present to use force if necessary against any person who might oppose them and that the force be displayed in such a manner as to alarm at least one person of reasonable firmness and courage. Lavan J. held (applying the decision in *John Section Sellers Ltd. v. Donegal County Council* (1937) 71 I.L.T.R. 43) that, in the absence of statements to the contrary, it had to be inferred that the person who was stared at was a person of reasonable firmness and courage and thus as there was no mention of that person witnessing any actual violence, the effect of the stare had to be enough to infer a measure of violence displayed in same. He concluded that, while the evidence was only in relation to one of the four men, since it established that they had been acting in concert, the witnessed behaviour could be considered as reflecting the common determination of the group. Thus, considering the overall circumstances of the case, there was enough evidence to indicate that the applicant's claim came within the definition of a 'riot' under the 1981 Act. This decision would appear to have taken a wide approach to the definition of 'riot' than that of the Supreme Court in *Duggan v. Dublin Corporation* [1991] I.L.R.M. 330 (1990 Review, 412-3), though we should note that Lavan J. expressly referred to the test laid down in the *Duggan* case.

PLANNING

Advertisement In *Blessington & District Community Council v. Wicklow County Council*, High Court, July 19, 1996, Kelly J. held that the applicant was not entitled to judicial review of a planning permission, where the applicant had raised a number of grounds concerning the published advertisement seeking permission. The premises in question had been used, without permission, for a number of years as an outdoor youth centre, and the advertisement referred to the premises as a youth centre. Kelly J. held that , although the use of the premises as an outdoor youth centre was unauthorised, the use had continued for so long that the premises was known by the public as a youth centre and the public might have been misled had this description not been used. Referring to the Supreme Court's decision in *Monaghan UDC v. Alf-a-Bet Promotions Ltd.* [1980] I.L.R.M. 64, he stated that since the primary purpose of a newspaper notice published in pursuance of Art.14 of the Local Government (Planning and Development) Regulations 1977 (since replaced by the Local Government (Planning and Development) Regulations 1994) is to ensure that adequate notice is given to members of the public so that they may make such representations or objections as they consider proper, the description of the premises in the instant case as a youth centre did not invalidate the notice. The notice had also failed to use the word 'Limited' after the name of the company applying for permission. Kelly J. held that this omission was so insubstantial that it did not invalidate the notice either. On this basis, he held that the applicant had not made out any 'substantial grounds' within the meaning of section 82(3B) of the Local Government (Planning & Development) Act 1963, as inserted by section 19(3) of the Local Government (Planning and Development Act 1992.

Afforestation The Local Government (Planning And Development) Regulations 1996 (SI No. 100 of 1996) amended the principal 1994 Regulations (1994 Review, 350) reduced the area of afforestation which requires planning permission from 200 hectares to 70 hectares, with effect from October 1, 1996. Similarly, the European Communities (Environmental Impact Assessment) (Amendment) Regulations 1996 (SI No.101 of 1996) reduced the threshold at which afforestation requires an environmental impact assessment from 200 hectares to 70 hectares, also with effect from October 1, 1996.

Conditions: details delegated to planning authorities In *Boland v. An Bord Pleanála and Ors.*, High Court, December 20, 1994; Supreme Court, March 21, 1996, the Supreme Court examined the extent to which the respondent Planning Board is empowered to grant planning permission subject to conditions, the details of which are to be agreed between the developer and local authority. Section 14(4) of the Local Government (Planning and Development) Act 1976 provides that where there is attached to a planning permission a condition which provides that a contribution or other matter is to be agreed between the planning authority and the person to whom the permission is granted, the condition shall be construed as providing that in default of agreement the contribution or other matter is to be determined by the Board. The applicant sought to have set aside a permission connected with an extensive extension and refurbishment of a ferry terminal at Dun Laoghaire Harbour, Co Dublin on the grounds that the Board had no power to impose three of the conditions subject to which the permission had been granted. Two of the conditions concerned regulating traffic and the third with provision for pedestrians. All three conditions, while setting out detailed instructions and accompanied by reasons for their imposition, required that the details of the work to be done should be agreed between the Minister for the Marine and the relevant local authority. In the High Court, it was held that the matters left to be agreed between the Minister and the local authority were of such a technical nature as to render the imposition of detailed conditions impractical. The Supreme Court upheld this view.

The Court held that, while the regulation of traffic was of crucial importance to the applicant it would be incorrect to describe it as the central issue in the appeal before the respondent Board; indeed the Court described it as peripheral. The Court noted that the development in question was a major one and the nature of the conditions imposed had to be considered against this background. Citing with approval Murphy J's decision in *Houlihan v. An Bord Pleanála*, High Court, October 4, 1993 (1993 Review, 425), the Supreme Court concluded that whether the imposition of a condition by the Board was an abdication of its statutory powers depended on the nature of the matter to be agreed between the planning authority and developer and this had to be resolved having regard to the nature and the circumstances of each particular development.

In imposing a condition and providing that certain details were to be agreed, the Court held that the Board was entitled to have regard to, *inter alia*, three matters: (a) the desirability of leaving to a developer a limited degree of flexibility having regard to the complexity of the enterprise (b) the desirability of leaving technical matters or matters of detail to be agreed and the impracticability of imposing detailed conditions; and (c) whether any member of the public could have reasonable grounds for objecting to the work to be carried out having regard to the precise nature of the instructions laid down by the Board. In imposing such conditions, the Court considered that the Board was obliged to set out the purpose of such conditions and to state clearly the reasons for them.

In the instant case, the conditions were essentially technical matters and contained sufficient detail to enable the Minister and the local authority to comply with the Board's requirements. Nor did the Court consider that the applicant's rights could be prejudiced by it nor could any member of the pub-

lic have had any grounds of objection to it. In those circumstances, as indicated, the Court dismissed the application for judicial review.

County manager's powers   In *East Wicklow Conservation Community Ltd.
v. Wicklow County Council* [1995] 2 I.L.R.M. 16 (H.C.); [1997] 2 I.L.R.M. 72
(S.C.), the Supreme Court affirmed the High Court decision of Costello J. (as
he then was) in which he had upheld the refusal by a county manager to comply with a resolution passed by the elected local authority representatives to
authorise approval for a municipal dump (1994 Review, 354). The case arose
against the following background.

Wicklow County Council had engaged consultants to investigate possible
waste disposal sites and prepare an environmental impact statement in respect
of the chosen site. The consultants recommended that certain land be developed as a dump. The elected members of the Council passed a resolution
which rejected the proposed site and directed that further investigations should
be carried out in order to find other land where the dump could be located.
The county manager refused to regard this resolution as having any legal effect and directed that work should continue in the preparation of an environmental impact statement pertaining to the proposed site. The applicants were
local residents who sought an order of *certiorari* quashing the decision of the
county manager to ignore the resolution and to proceed with the consultants'
proposals.

The statutory provisions involved in the case were as follows. Section 52
of the Public Health (Ireland) Act 1878 provides that every sanitary authority
may themselves undertake or contract for the removal of house refuse from
premises. Section 55 of the 1878 Act provides that a sanitary authority shall
provide fit buildings or places for the deposit of any matters collected by them
pursuant to the 1878 Act. Section 2(7) of the City and County Management
(Amendment) Act 1955 provides that the city or county manager shall inform
the members of the local authority before any works (other than works of
maintenance or repair) of the local authority are undertaken, or before committing the local authority to any expenditure in connection with proposed
works (other than works of maintenance or repair). Section 3 of the 1955 Act
provides that where the members of a local authority are informed pursuant to
section 2 of the 1955 Act of any works (not being works which the local
authority are required by or under statute or by order of a court to undertake),
the local authority may by resolution direct that the works shall not be proceeded with, and the manager shall comply with the resolution.

Costello J. held that the proposed development of the site constituted
'works' within the meaning of section 2(7) of the 1955 Act. As the development of a waste disposal site was work which the Council was required to
undertake under section 55 of the 1878 Act, he concluded that the elected
members had no power under section 3 of the 1955 Act to direct that it should

be pursued. As indicated, on appeal the Supreme Court (Hamilton C.J., Blayney and Murphy JJ.) upheld Costello J.'s decision.

Delivering the only judgment, Blayney J. noted that the general scheme of local government legislation distinguished between functions exercised by local authorities in pursuance of an express statutory duty and others carried out in pursuance of a discretion conferred upon them;. The word "required" as used in the phrase "works required by or under statute" clearly referred, he held, to works carried out in pursuance of a mandatory requirement imposed on a local authority;. In the instant case, the works had to be carried out if the council was to fulfil its duty under section 55 of the 1878 Act, which it has embarked on by choosing a site. Accordingly, the works came within the exception in section 3 of the 1955 Act and the members of the council could not direct that the works should not proceed.

Intensification of use In *Westmeath County Council v. Michael F. Quirke & Sons Ltd*, High Court, May 23, 1996, the applicant Council sought an injunction pursuant to section 27(1) of the Local Government (Planning and Development) Act 1976 preventing the respondent company from operating a quarry until planning permission for its operation had been obtained under the Local Government (Planning and Development) Act 1963. The quarry was a limestone quarry, and had been operated intermittently for over one hundred years. Prior to 1965, the applicant Council had used the quarry for the extraction of stone on a small scale, but in 1965 that use was discontinued. In 1967, a company had obtained planning permission to produce ground limestone (lime), which was produced until 1971, when production ceased. The Council contended that the quarry was then abandoned, and was used for feeding cattle. There was no blasting or quarrying on the site between 1971 and 1985. There was minor activity in 1988, but none such that elicited any complaints from the local residents. In 1990, the respondent company had taken over the operation of the quarry. The Council contended that there was a huge change in the nature and scale of the operations at the quarry and that the intensification of use constituted development within the meaning on the 1963 Act for which the respondent was required to obtain planning permission. Budd J. granted the relief sought by the Council.

He held that there were considerable differences between the production of lime carried on prior to 1971, and the production of quarry run rock as a road making material as carried on by the respondent company. It is notable that he opined that there was a significant difference in the two operations in planning terms and there was a real and material effect in their impact on the environment. He also pointed out that an entrance to the quarry created by the respondent was of such a nature as to endanger public safety by reason of being a traffic hazard and that the entrance constituted an unauthorised development under the 1963 Act. Applying the decisions in *Patterson v. Murphy*

[1978] I.L.R.M. 85 and *Stafford v. Roadstone Ltd.* [1980] I.L.R.M. 1, Budd J. held that intensification of an existing use of land, if marked and considerable, could amount to a material change of use. The evidence in the instant case that about 80,000 tonnes of rock was removed from the quarry in 1993 was objective evidence of massive intensification at the quarry, and was a scale of operations greatly different from that prior to October 1, 1964, the relevant date for exempt development under the 1963 Act.

Judicial review: specificity of grounds   In *McNamara v. An Bord Pleanála and Ors.*, High Court, May 10, 1996 Barr J. held that, in seeking judicial review of a planning decision an applicant must specify with some particularity the grounds on which relief is sought. The background was that Dublin County Council had applied in 1992 to Kildare County Council (both Councils were notice parties in the case) for planning permission for a municipal dump to be created at Kill in County Kildare. The dump would be the largest of its kind in Ireland, serving the needs of Dublin city and county. An Environmental Impact Statement (EIS), required under the relevant Regulations (see now the Planning Regulations 1994: 1994 Review, 350), was carried out prior to the application being made. In 1993, Kildare County Council refused the permission sought. The refusal was appealed to the respondent Planning Board. After an oral hearing lasting over 20 days, it was recommended to the Board that the appeal be refused. The Board decided not to accept the report, and in July 1994 it granted permission subject to 26 conditions.

In September 1994, the applicant sought leave to apply for judicial review of the Board's decision. The relevant motion and grounding affidavit was served within the two months time limit specified in the Local Government (Planning and Development) Act 1992 (1992 Review, 448-50). A further affidavit was filed in support of the application in December 1994. In January 1995, the applicant was granted leave to seek judicial review. Another affidavit was filed by the applicant in June 1995. The Board submitted that the December 1995 and June 1995 affidavits introduced new grounds of opposition which were not referred to in the original documentation, and which could not be reasonably be inferred or implied from the original documentation filed in support of the motion. Citing the decision of the Supreme Court in *KSK Enterprises Ltd. v. An Bord Pleanála* [1994] 2 I.L.R.M. 1 (1994 Review, 359), the Board contended that it could only be aware of any challenge to a planning permission within the two month time limit if the challenge or challenges in question were notified to the relevant parties within that period. It was also submitted that the applicant could not expand the grounds of challenge beyond the statutory time limit.

Barr J. accepted the Board's principal procedural objections and also went on to dismiss the application for judicial review. He pointed out that O.84, r.20(2) of the Rules of the Superior Courts 1986 required that an applicant had to specify the relief sought and the grounds on which it was sought. In the context of a planning judicial review, he concluded that a developer was entitled to know within the required period that its planning permission was being challenged, and also the specific grounds on which the challenge was based. In the instant case, he considered that the grounds of objection in the original documentation upon which the applicant had sought to rely in support of the new grounds of objection disclosed in the supplemental affidavits, were too wide, broad and general, and told the developer little or nothing as to the actual nature and basis for the challenge. The applicant was thus not entitled to rely upon a general complaint as an umbrella to justify subsequent specific allegations not notified as grounds within time. Where there was an allegation of irrationality against the Board, the nature of the irrationality alleged ought to have been specified in the grounds of objection submitted by the applicant within the two month limitation period.

Although this approach limits the basis on which judicial reviews may be brought, nonetheless Barr J. accepted that an applicant was not precluded from introducing evidence after the expiration of the two month time limit in further support of or amplification of the grounds of objection relied on; provided that such grounds were specified in the original documentation which was served on all the relevant parties within the time limit.

Examining the grounds on which he was prepared to review the grant of permission, Barr J. accepted the approach taken by Murphy J. in *Houlihan v. An Bord Pleanála*, High Court, October 4, 1993 (1993 Review, 425) that there could be little doubt that in relation to a major development it would be impractical for the Board to concern itself directly in every aspect of the proposed development, and it was reasonable to provide that certain details, which were not fundamental to the project *per se* should be delegated to the planning authority for ultimate decision as they arose. As to whether the Board had acted reasonably in the instant case, Barr J. referred to the criteria laid down by Hamilton CJ. and Blayney J. in *Boland v. An Bord Pleanála*, Supreme Court, March 21, 1996 (see above, 452) and held that the Board had acted within these criteria. As already indicated, Barr J. dismissed the applicant's challenge to the decision to grant planning permission. Subsequently, in *McNamara v. An Bord Pleanála and Ors (No. 2)*, High Court, July 31, 1996, Barr J. declined to refer the matter to the European Court of Justice pursuant to Article 177 of the EC Treaty, since he had already delivered final judgment in the matter. He noted that Article 177 referred to a 'preliminary' ruling in a case 'pending' before a national court, implying that the national court which received such a ruling from the European Court had not completed its function by delivering final judgment, but would do so, *inter alia,* in the light of the ruling received from the Court of Justice.

Judicial review: substantial grounds   In *RGDATA Ltd. v. An Bord Pleanála*

and Ors, High Court, April 30, 1996 Barron J. applied the principles laid
down in *Scott v. An Bord Pleanála* [1995] 1 I.L.R.M. 424 (1994 Review, 352-
3) and *McNamara v. An Bord Pleanála* [1995] 2 I.L.R.M. 125 (1995 Review,
374), namely that in deciding whether to grant leave to apply for judicial review, the court must determine whether there is a submission of substance
which it is reasonable to permit to go to a full hearing. Planning permission
had been granted by granted by Monaghan County Council for a development
in the centre of Monaghan town. An appeal against this decision was refused
by the respondent Planning Board and the applicant then applied for leave to
apply for judicial review. The applicant argued that, since the area of the site
of the proposed development exceeded two hectares, an environmental impact statement should have been furnished by the developer, and that, failing
this one should have been requested by the Board. The applicant referred to
Regulation 56(1) of the Local Government (Planning and Development) Regulations 1994, which provides that where there is an appeal against the decision
of a planning authority which relates to a development which, in the opinion
of the Board, is a development in respect of which an environmental impact
statement would be required and no such statement has been submitted to the
planning authority, the Board shall require the applicant to submit to the Board
such a statement. The Board contended that the area did not exceed two hectares, and the applicant argued that the Board ought to have permitted it to
demonstrate how its measurements had been calculated showing the area to
be in excess of two hectares rather than relying on the evidence adduced by
the developer. The Board submitted that the applicant had not established
'substantial grounds', within the meaning of section 19(3) of the Local Government (Planning and Development) Act 1992, as interpreted in the *Scott*
and *McNamara* cases. In the instant case, Barron J. noted that no submission
had been made in the notice of appeal to the Board that the site area exceeded
two hectares, it merely indicated that the area of the site had not been set out in
any of the documents. In his view there was no evidence of a substantial reme-
diable error by the Board and he concluded that neither of the applicant's
submissions constituted a substantial ground.

Judicial review: Supreme Court appeals   In *Irish Asphalt Ltd. v. An Bord
Pleanála*, Supreme Court, May 22, 1996, the Supreme Court held that the
Local Government (Planning and Development) Act 1992 had restricted the
right of appeal from the High Court to the Supreme Court, as envisaged by
Article 34.4.3 of the Constitution: see the discussion in the Practice and Pro-
cedure chapter, 468, below.

Navigational aid system   In *Keane v. An Bord Pleanála (No. 2)*, High Court,
October 4, 1995; Supreme Court, July 18, 1996, the Supreme Court affirmed
the decision of Murphy J. in the High Court (1995 Review, 378) that the Com-

missioners of Irish Lights were not empowered to seek planning permission for the erection of a particular type of navigational aid system. The Commissioners had applied to Clare County Council for planning permission to erect a navigational aid, including a 750ft high radio mast, at Feeard Cross in County Clare. The navigational aid, known as the Loran-C system, uses electromagnetic impulses to allow positions to be fixed. The application was refused by the Council but, on appeal, the respondent Planning Board granted the permission sought. The case turned on whether the Loran-C system came within the powers granted to the Commissioners under the Merchant Shipping Act 1894. Section 638 of the 1894 Act empowers the Commissioners to erect or place any 'lighthouse, buoy or beacon.' Section 742 of the 1894 Act provides that '"lighthouse" shall in addition to the ordinary meaning of the word include any floating and other light exhibited for the guidance of ships, and also any sirens and any other descriptions of fog signals, and also any addition to a lighthouse of any improved light, or any siren, or any description of fog signal' and that '"buoys and beacons" includes all other marks and signs of the sea'. Thus, the question was whether the Loran-C was a 'lighthouse, buoy or beacon' within the 1894 Act. As indicated, the Supreme Court held, by a 3-2 majority (Hamilton C.J., Blayney and Barrington JJ.; O'Flaherty and Denham JJ. dissenting) that it did not.

The Supreme Court unanimously accepted that the general approach it should take (as Murphy J. had in the High Court) was that laid down in *Howard v. Commissioners of Public Works in Ireland* [1994] 1 I.R. 101 (1993 Review, 430-2), namely, that the powers of a corporation created by a statute are limited and circumscribed by the statutes which regulate it, and extend no further than is expressly stated therein or is necessarily and properly required for carrying into effect the purposes of incorporation or may be fairly regarded as incidental to or consequential upon those things which the legislature has authorised.

The Court then turned to the central issue in the case, namely was whether the Loran-C system came within the express or implied ambit of the 1894 Act. Since the system had not been invented when the 1894 Act had been enacted, this raised a particular problem of statutory interpretation, namely whether the 1894 Act could be given an updated meaning. In this respect, the Court divided, the majority contenting itself with expressly following the approach of Murphy J. in the High Court, quoting with express approval the following passage:

'I have no difficulty in accepting the desirability and, in general, the necessity for giving to legislation and 'updating construction'. Where terminology used in legislation is wide enough to capture a subsequent invention, there is no reason to exclude it from the ambit of the legislation. But a distinction must be made between giving an updated construction to the general scheme of the legislation and altering the meaning of particular words used therein.'

The majority in the Supreme Court held that the 1894 Act enabled the Commissioners to provide only the navigational aids specified in section 638 and did not give them any general power to provide navigational aids. Although the Court accepted that the proposed radio mast fell within the current definition of 'beacon' this does not determine its meaning for the purposes of the 1894 Act, which envisaged navigational aids that would provide aural and visual guidance or warning for ships within the area of responsibility of the Commissioners as specified in section 634 of the 1894 Act. Since the Loran-C system was designed to enable ships and aircraft to pin-point their position at sea or in the air and extended far beyond the area of responsibility of the Commissioners, it was thus outside the scope of the 1894 Act. In dissent, Denham J. did not accept that the word "beacon" was expressly limited by the 1894 Act to navigational aids which may be seen or heard. Both she and O'Flaherty J. were of the view that, while section 634 of the 1984 Act limited the area in which the Commissioners might erect a beacon, it did not limit the range of signal which the beacon may emit. However, as indicated, this view did not prevail. Connected litigation concerning the Loran-C application, *Keane v. An Bord Pleanála (No. 3)* [1997] 1 I.L.R.M. 508 (H.C.), is discussed immediately below.

Proper planning and development   In *Keane v. An Bord Pleanála (No. 3)* [1997] 1 I.L.R.M. 508 (H.C.), another aspect of the planning application for the Loran-C navigation system discussed above was at issue. In the instant case, the question was whether, in deciding what amounted to proper planning and development within the 'area' of a planning authority's jurisdiction, as provided for in section 26 of the Local Government (Planning and Development) Act 1963, the Planning Board was entitled to have regard to have regard to an international resolution made in Oslo in August 1992 in which the Government had committed itself to the Loran-C system, together with a Dail Resolution approving that agreement and also to the fact that the Loran-C system would operate up to 500 miles offshore. In essence, the argument as to the Oslo Resolution was that this was irrelevant to the 1963 Act and that the fact that the Loran-C system would operate up to 500 miles offshore with extra-territorial brought it outside section 26 of the 1963 Act which referred to planning consideration within the 'area' of the planning authority. Carroll J. rejected these arguments. She considered that the Board was entitled to have regard to both these matters under section 26 of the 1963 Act. In particular, she noted:

> If the argument about extra-territorial effect were taken to its logical conclusion, planning permission could not be granted for a Telecom Éireann development which would provide telecommunications with the whole world because it would have extraterritorial effect.

In the instant case, Carroll J. held that there was an element of common good within the territorial waters and in providing a link in an international network in compliance with international obligations. Therefore, she did not accept that because there would be an added benefit outside territorial waters the Board was precluded from taking that into consideration. As this was only one factor among many, it could not be equated with extending the operation of a statute beyond the State's jurisdiction. Since the development was a development within the State which gave a benefit within the State and it was only in addition that it provided a benefit outside the jurisdiction. On this basis, she held that the Board had not acted *ultra vires* in granting the permission. Nonetheless, she certified that the point raised was of sufficient public importance to warrant having the matter heard by the Supreme Court, and its decision is still pending at the time of writing (July 1997). In addition, there remains the (as yet) unsurmounted difficulty of the previous decision of the Supreme Court in *Keane v. An Bord Pleanála (No. 2)*, High Court, October 4, 1995; Supreme Court, July 18, 1996, above, that the Commissioners of Irish Lights lacked the power to apply for permission pursuant to the Merchant Shipping Act 1894.

Residential use excludes use as holiday homes In *McMahon and Ors v. Dublin Corporation* [1997] 1 I.L.R.M. 227 (H.C.), Barron J. held that use of residential homes as holiday homes constituted a material change of user within the meaning of section 28(6) of the Local Government (Planning and Development) Act 1963. Thus, such change required planning permission. Where the original permission for the houses was for residential use only, use for holiday homes was thus not within the permission granted.

Rezoning: consideration of sporting facilities irrelevant In *Malahide Community Council Ltd. v. Fingal County Council*, High Court, December 19, 1994, Kinlen J. held that the decision of a local authority to rezone land for residential use was *ultra vires* and unreasonable where, as in the instant case it was based, almost exclusively, on the benefits to be received by sporting clubs in the relevant area on the rezoning of the land as a result of an agreement entered into by them with the owners and proposed developers of the land. The case concerned the decision made at a meeting of the respondent Council in April 1993 to amend the 1991 Draft Development Plan for County Dublin by rezoning lands at Malahide, County Dublin from 'Green Belt' to 'Residential' for a maximum number of 250 dwellings. Prior to this meeting, three sporting clubs from Malahide and Portmarnock had entered into an agreement with the owners and proposed developers of the relevant lands by which considerable financial and other benefits would accrue to the clubs if the lands were rezoned to provide a minimum number of 250 residential units. Widespread publicity had been given to the agreement and its terms were brought to the attention of members of the respondent Council. One of the Council members, Bernadette Malone (since elected an MEP) deposed that, at the relevant meeting of the Council, no debate had taken place on the housing or planning requirements of the area affected by the rezoning and that the only subject of debate was the availability of moneys and facilities for sports clubs in the area Kinlen J. accepted that at its meeting the Council had introduced illegitimate considerations and rejected legitimate ones. It had not considered the housing or planning requirements of the area in detail and had regard, almost exclusively, to an agreement to which it was not a party and which it could not enforce. On this basis, he declared null and void the decision to grant the permission. He referred in support to much of the recent case law ion this area, including *O'Keeffe v. An Bord Pleanála* [1993] 1 I.R. 39; [1992] I.L.R.M. 237 (1991 Review, 16-8) and *P. & F. Sharpe Ltd. v. Dublin City and County Manager* [1989] I.R. 701 (1988 Review, 296-301).

Substantial works   *Littondale Ltd. v. Wicklow County Council* [1996] 2 I.L.R.M. 519 (H.C.), involved whether the applicant company had carried out 'substantial works' on foot of a permission which would entitle it to an extension of time pursuant to section 4 of the Local Government (Planning and Development) Act 1982. Laffoy J. held that the works effected could not be regarded as 'substantial works' for the purposes of section 4 of the 1982 Act. Section 2 of the Local Government (Planning and Development) Act 1982 imposes a limitation on the duration of a planning permission. Section 4(1) of the Local Government (Planning and Development) Act 1982 provides that a planning authority 'shall' extend the period of a planning permission if there has been compliance with certain requirements, including that the planning authority is satisfied that the development to which such permission relates commenced before the expiration of the appropriate period sought to be extended, that 'substantial works' were carried out pursuant to such permission during such period and that the development will be completed within a reasonable time. In the *Littondale* case, the applicant was the owner of property comprising a hotel in respect of which a permission had been granted in 1981 to its predecessor in title to build 51 holiday chalets beside the hotel. Arising from various difficulties and legal proceedings, there were substantial delays in completing the building works. By 1987, when the 1981 permission ran out, the following had been completed: seven of the proposed chalets together with a sewage system, foul sewer pipes, an electrical ring main and water main. In December 1987 the respondent Council refused to extend the 1981 permission on the basis that the works carried out were not considered to be substantial and it was considered that the work would not be completed within a reasonable time. When the applicant purchased the property in 1994, it renewed the application for an extension of the 1981 permission, adding that other works should be taken into account, namely the refurbishing of the hotel and resurfacing of the car park around it. The Council again declined to extend the 1981 permission, and the applicant then applied for judicial review. Laffoy J. refused the relief sought.

Laffoy J. referred to the judicial consideration given to the phrase 'substantial works' in recent years, including *dicta* of Lynch J. in *Frenchurch Properties Ltd. v. Wexford County Council* [1992] 2 I.R. 268; [1991] I.L.R.M. 769 (1991 Review, 315-6) and of Geoghegan J. in *Garden Village Construction Co Ltd. v. Wicklow County Council* [1994] 3 I.R. 413; [1994] 1 I.L.R.M. 354 (1994 Review, 358). She did not accept that 'substantial works' should be equated with 'other than trivial or insignificant', as was contended for by the applicant. Rather, she felt it should be given its natural or ordinary meaning and turned to the definition of 'substantial' in the *Shorter Oxford Dictionary*, 3rd ed, namely 'of ample or considerable amount, quantity, or dimensions.' As indicated by the judicial *dicta* she had cited, this was to be considered having regard to the nature and extent of the works in question. In the instant case, it could not be said that the Council's conclusion that the works carried out were not substantial flew in the face of reason and common sense, within the meaning of the Supreme Court decision in *O'Keeffe v. An Bórd Pleanála* [1993] 1 I.R. 39 (1991 Review, 16-18), and thus she dismissed the application.

Time limits: judicial review In *O'Connor v. Nenagh UDC and Dunnes Stores Ltd*, High Court, July 16, 1996, Geoghegan J. declined to grant the applicant leave to apply for judicial review of a planning permission granted by the UDC in 1974 for the erection of a supermarket to the predecessor in title of Dunnes Stores Ltd. The applicant had claimed that the siting and orientation of the buildings differed to the permission and sought to quash the certificate of correctness granted by the Council to Dunnes. Geoghegan J. accepted that, since the applicant was a member of the Council and in that capacity would be entitled to be concerned that the public functions of the Council were being carried out properly, he had sufficient *locus standi* to seek relief and that the certificate which he sought to be quashed was of a sufficiently public nature to be amenable to judicial review. Nonetheless, as indicated, he held that the application was long out of time. He relied on the public policy reasons behind the decision of the Oireachtas in section 27 of the Local Government (Planning and Development) Act 1963 for imposing time limits on both the section 27 review and the enforcement notice procedures and unless there was some proven element of fraud or public corruption, it would be wrong for the courts to circumvent those time limits by the route of judicial review. While he accepted that an order of *certiorari* or a declaration would not have the effect of compelling Dunnes to demolish and rebuild, it would throw into doubt whether there had been compliance with the planning legislation and could have adverse effects on Dunnes.

Time limits: meaning of 'month' In *McCann v. An Bórd Pleanála* [1997] 1 I.L.R.M. 314 (HC), the applicant had received a planning permission from Sligo County Council on June 7, 1995, subject to certain conditions. The applicant's appeal against these conditions was received by the respondent Planning Board on July 7, 1995 and it declined to consider the appeal on the grounds that it had not been received within the period prescribed by section 26(5) of the Local Government (Planning and Development) Act 1963, as amended by the Local Government (Planning and Development) Act 1992. Section 26(5) of the 1963 Act, as amended, provides that an appeal from a decision of a planning authority shall be brought within the period of one month beginning on the day on which the decision was made is mandatory. Section 11(h) of the Interpretation Act 1937 provides that 'where a period of time is expressed to begin on or be reckoned from a particular day, that day shall, unless the contrary intention appears, be deemed to be included in such period, and, where a period of time is expressed to end on or be reckoned to a particular day, that day shall, unless the contrary intention appears, be deemed to be included in such period.' Para. 19 of the Schedule to the 1937 Act provides that the word 'month' means a calendar month. The applicant sought unsuccessfully for an order of *certiorari* quashing the Board's decision. The applicant submitted that the corresponding date rule applied in reckoning the prescribed period and that, accordingly, the prescribed period ended on July 7, 1995, the day of the relevant month bearing the same number as the day on which the decision was made. Lavan J. rejected this argument.

He held that, since in the 1963 Act the word "month" means calendar month and since a calendar month cannot include two days bearing the same date and since, by virtue of section 11(h) of the 1937 Act, the prescribed period must include 7 June 1995, the prescribed period did not include July 7, 1995. In this respect, he followed the decision of McMahon J. in *McGuinness v. Armstrong Patents Ltd.* [1980] I.R. 289 in preference to the *obiter* comments of Flood J. in *Max Developments Ltd. v. An Bord Pleanála* [19941 2 I.R. 121. He also held that, because section 17(1)(a) of the Local Government (Planning and Development) Act 1992 provides that an appeal to the Board after the expiration of the prescribed period 'shall be invalid' as not having been made in time, the requirement that an appeal be brought within the prescribed period is mandatory. Although he accepted, in accordance with the decision in *The State (Elm Developments Ltd) v. An Bórd Pleanála* [1981] I.L.R.M. 108, that strict compliance with a mandatory requirement may be waived, the breach in the instant case could not be regarded as trivial or subject to the *de minimis* rule in *Monaghan UDC v. Alf-a-Bet Promotions Ltd.* [1980] I.L.R.M. 64. Accordingly, he dismissed the application for judicial review.

RATING (VALUATION)

Hypothetical tenant basis for valuation In *Waterford Crystal Ltd. v. Commissioner of Valuation*, High Court, December 10, 1996, Costello P. held that the Valuation Tribunal had erred in its valuation of the principal manufacturing premises owned by the appellant, the well known crystal manufacturing company, in Waterford. The property in question comprised of the main Waterford Crystal plant and incorporated head offices and showrooms in a large industrial complex. Commissioner had fixed a rateable valuation of £7,145 on the buildings and the company had appealed this to the Valuation Tribunal. The company argued that there should be a reduction in the valuation to take account of under-utilisation of the premises, which arose from changes in technology. The Tribunal held that, although the entire complex was not a specialised plant, in determining the net annual value it should allow a 40% reduction for obsolescence to the net value of the furnace house and it should apply a 25% reduction for overcapacity to the net value of the remainder of the premises, thus reducing the rateable value to £5,660. On a case stated to the High Court, Costello P. held that the Tribunal had erred. He accepted that, if the plant had been a specialised one and not capable of any use other than that of manufacturing crystal, the Tribunal would have been correct in its approach in making an allowance for under-utilisation, but it had made a specific finding that the complex was not specialised. In addition, he noted that the Tribunal had only taken into account as a hypothetical tenant a crystal manufacturer and failed to have regard to the existence of other hypothetical tenants who would use the entire premises (other than the furnace house) for manufacturing purposes. But he also held that whether doing so would produce a rateable valuation higher than that already fixed was a matter entirely for the Tribunal. He therefore remitted the case to the Tribunal for reconsideration on the basis of this different test.

ROAD MAINTENANCE

In a well-publicised decision, *Brady v. Cavan County Council* [1997] 1 I.L.R.M. 390 (H.C.), Carroll J. granted the applicants an order of *mandamus* to compel the respondent local authority comply with its statutory duty under section 13 of the Roads Act 1993 (1993 Review, 588-9). The applicants, residents of County Cavan, claimed that the Council had failed in its statutory duty to maintain a particular stretch of road and that it was dangerous. The Council did not deny that the road was dangerous, but it indicated that £140,000 would be required to repair it and that £40 million would be required to repair all the roads in the county in a similar condition. The Council submitted it did not have an absolute duty to repair the road and, alternatively, that an order of *mandamus* should not be made as it would give the applicants priority over the users of the other roads requiring repair, that it would lead to similar applications in respect of these roads and that the Council could not raise the necessary funds from local taxes and could not compel the central government to provide the funds.

Carroll J. reviewed the statutory background. She referred to section 82(1) of the Local Government (Ireland) Act 1898, which provides that it is the duty of every local authority to keep all public works maintainable at the authority's cost 'in good condition and repair, and to take all steps necessary for that purpose.' Section 109 of the 1898 Act defines 'public works' as including a road. More specifically, section 13(2) of the Roads Act 1993 provides:

> It shall be a function of the council of a county, the corporation of a county or other borough or the council of an urban district to maintain and construct all local roads—
>
> (a) in the case of the council of the county – in its administrative county, excluding any borough or urban district,
> (b) in the case of any other local authority – in its administrative area.'

As already indicated, Carroll J. granted the order of *mandamus* sought. She held that since section 82 of the 1898 Act and section 13 of the 1993 Act impose a clear duty on local authorities to repair and maintain roads and since this duty had not been qualified by reference to the money made available by the central government, *mandamus* would lie, citing *R. (Westropp) v. Clare County Council* [1904] 2 I.R. 569 in support. She rejected the argument that the applicants could be denied the relief sought on the grounds that they would achieve priority over others in the same situation or that similar applications would be made as a result. On the argument that the Oireachtas had not made available funds to enable the local authority to carry out its statutory duties, Carroll J. responded with the answer that such funds simply had to be made available once the legislation had been enacted. She also drew a comparison with the decision concerning the maintenance of courthouses in *Hoey v. Minister for Justice* [1994] 3 I.R. 329 (H.C.); [1994] 1 I.L.R.M 334 (1993 Review, 443-5). She also relied on the decision concerning strict liability offences, *Shannon Regional Fisheries Board v. Cavan County Council*, High Court, December 21, 1994; Supreme Court, July 30, 1996 (Carroll J. referred to the Murphy J., and did not appear to have been made aware that his decision had been upheld by the Supreme Court. We note here that the decision in *Brady* has, not surprisingly perhaps, been appealed to the Supreme Court.

Practice and Procedure

Hilary Delany and Raymond Byrne

An invaluable addition to all practitioners was the publication of Ó Floinn and Gannon, *Practice and Procedure in the Superior Courts* (Butterworths, 1996). Practitioners would have been greatly served merely by the fact that the volume includes the amended text of the Rules of the Superior Courts 1986 up to SI No. 5 of 1996. However, its particular strength lies in the comprehensive annotation on the Rules, as amended, referring to the great accumulation of indigenous case law in this area. The year also saw the welcome emergence of a journal, *Practice and Procedure*, which provides specialist comment in this area.

APPELLATE JURISDICTION

Fresh evidence   In *Foran v. Cobbe and Kelly*, Supreme Court, June 13, 1996, the Supreme Court permitted the plaintiff to introduce additional evidence in an application under Order 8, rule 8 of the Rules of the Superior Courts 1986. The plaintiff's action for damages for personal injuries arising out of a road traffic accident was dismissed by the High Court. On appeal to the Supreme Court, she was given liberty to introduce further evidence at the appeal. The evidence was that of a Garda, who was one of two called to the scene of the accident. The other Garda had given evidence at the trial of the action. The role of the Garda who had not been called as a witness had been to assist the Garda who had been called in taking measurements. The Garda who had not been called notified the plaintiff's solicitor that he had been present at the scene when he became aware that the action had been tried. He gave evidence on commission that the defendant's car had been moved onto the grass margin of the road after the accident; this had not been stated at the trial of the action. The Garda also gave evidence which placed the point of impact on the plaintiff's side of the road and this also differed from the evidence given in that regard by the Garda who gave evidence at the trial of the action. The Supreme Court concluded that the new evidence was relevant, would have been of such weight that it would of necessity have been taken into account by the trial judge and might have influenced his decision. On this basis, the Court set aside the decision of the High Court and directed a new trial.

Supreme Court: limitation on In *Irish Asphalt Ltd. v. An Bord Pleanála*, Supreme Court, May 22, 1996, the Supreme Court held that the Local Government (Planning and Development) Act 1992 had restricted the right of appeal from the High Court to the Supreme Court, as envisaged by Article 34.4.3 of the Constitution. Section 82(3)(a) and (b) of the Local Government (Planning and Development) Act 1963, as inserted by the 1992 Act, provides that a decision of the planning board or authority may only be challenged by judicial review. Section 82 (3)(b)(i) provides that the decision of the High Court shall be final and conclusive and no appeal would lie to the Supreme Court unless the High Court certified that the case involved a point of excepional public importance. In the instant proceedings, the High Court had refused to allow the applicant's application to seek judicial review of the respondent's decision and then refused to certify that an appeal to the Supreme Court should be granted. The Supreme Court held that, in those circumstances, it had no jurisdiction to entertain an appeal.

The Court accepted, in accordance with its jurisprudence in *The People v. Conmey* [1975] I.R. 341 and *Hanafin v. Minister for the Environment* [1996] 2 I.L.R.M. 141, that any law excluding the appellate jurisdiction of the Supreme Court must be clear and unambiguous. It concluded that the 1992 Act clearly excepted cases from the appellate jurisdiction of the Supreme Court, and having so excepted those decisions, the provision went on to create an exception to the exception, allowing the High Court to certify an appeal to the Supreme Court for those excepted cases involving a point of exceptional importance. Referring to the decision in *Attorney General v. Murray (No. 2)* [1926] I.R. 300 (which concerned the certification by the Court of Criminal Appeal under section 29 of the Courts of Justice Act 1924), the Court held that the High Court alone may issue the certificate that a case involved a point of law of exceptional public importance. The Court concluded that this interpretation of the 1992 Act accorded best with what appears to have been the policy of the Act, namely the speeding up of the planning process by shortening litigation and by eliminating applications for judicial review which were devoid of substance.

CASE STATED

Constitutional issue may not be raised In *Director of Public Prosecutions v. Dougan* [1997] 1 I.L.R.M. 550 (H.C.), *sub nom. The People v. Dougan* [1996] 1 I.R. 544 (H.C.), Geoghegan J. confirmed that a District Court judge is precluded by Article 34.3.2 of the Constitution from using the case stated procedure to challenge the constitutional validity of a statutory provision. In the instant case, the defendant had been charged, *inter alia*, with refusing to comply with the request of a medical practitioner to provide a sample of blood or urine, contrary to section 13(3) of the Road Traffic Act 1994 (1994 Review, 219). The District Court judge sought to raise the question whether the penalties provided for in the 1994 Act rendered the offence one which was not minor and therefore incapable of being tried summarily under Article 38.5 of the Constitution. In effect, Geoghegan J. held that such an issue could not be raised in such a bald manner by means of a case stated. In this respect, he followed the decision of the Supreme Court in *Foyle Fisheries Commission v. Gallen* [1960] Ir. Jur. Rep. 35, which had in turn been applied by O'Hanlon J. in *Minister for Labour v. Costello* [1988] I.R. 235 (discussed generally in the 1988 Review, 269). Thus, the mere fact that the High Court was given jurisdiction under the Constitution to determine a question of the constitutionality of a statutory provision did not mean that this could be done by way of case stated. In some respects, however, Geoghegan J. entered into the issues raised in the case by holding that the District Court judge was entitled to state a consultative case under section 52 of the Courts (Supplemental Provisions) Act 1961 where, on its face, the judge took the view that he was not challenging the constitutionality of any provisions of the 1994 Act as such, but was concerned in relation to the case before him that he should not breach the express provisions of Article 38.5 of the Constitution. However, Geoghegan J. stated that if the High Court took the view that the District Court was bound to assume that any offence made a summary offence only by the legislature was a "minor offence" within the meaning of the Constitution, the High Court would have to decline to give specific answers to the questions posed. The judge of the District Court would therefore be required to proceed on the assumption that the powers conferred by an Act of the Oireachtas may be lawfully exercised by him unless and until the statute has been successfully impugned in proceedings appropriate for that purpose.

Despite these comments which seemed to indicate that he was not prepared to enter into the substantive issue, Geoghegan J. gave some hints to the effect that he did not consider section 13 of the 1994 Act was in breach of Article 38.5 of the Constitution. He was wary of the defendant's argument that there existed a form of statutory provision which, although not unconstitutional, was 'inoperative'. He doubted whether such a concept could ever be countenanced, but that in any event it could not be appropriate in a case such as the present where there was a range of discretion in determining whether an offence was minor or non-minor and that discretion was prima facie vested in the Oireachtas. In a case where summary trial only was provided for, any challenge by a judge of the District Court to the mode of trial must necessarily be an attack on the constitutionality of the enactment. Such a challenge was tantamount to suggesting that the Oireachtas might have gone badly wrong and acted unconstitutionally. Nonetheless, Geoghegan J. formally declined to answer the question posed in the instant case.

Remittal: power of trial judge In *O'Toole v. Revenue Commissioners*, Supreme Court, May 15, 1996, the Supreme Court held that where a case stated is returned to a Circuit Court judge under section 38 of the Courts of Justice Act 1936, he has the jurisdiction to hear further evidence or to make further findings of fact, or to amend the pleadings, and is not confined to the findings already made. In this respect, the Court expressly followed the decision of the Court in *Dolan v. Corn Exchange* [1975] I.R. 315. While this reflects the unanimous view of the Supreme Court in the instant case, it is regrettable that the Court did not take the opportunity to address the confused state of authority on this particular point, since the *Dolan*. case merely reflects one previous judicial attempt to determine this important point. See further the discussion in Delany, *The Courts Acts 1924-1991* (Round Hall Press, 1994).

COSTS

Advisers and witnesses: restrictions on costs outside Rules In *Minister For Finance v. Flynn*, High Court, February 9, 1996, Carroll J. considered the extent to which an order for costs may fetter the general discretion of a Taxing Master

The application for review of taxation arose out of the Tribunal of Inquiry into the Beef Processing Industry (see 1993 Review, 11-12). Pursuant to section 6 of the Tribunals of Inquiry (Evidence) (Amendment) Act 1979, the Chairman of the Tribunal made orders as to costs and certain issues arising under these were referred to the respondent Taxing Master. The respondent ruled, *inter alia*, that he would allow the costs of those witnesses who had given oral evidence before the Tribunal. He also ruled that, taking into account the 1979 Act and the discretion conferred on him by Order 99, rule 37(18) of the Rules of the Superior Courts 1986, he was empowered to allow such costs, charges, and expenses as would appear to him to have been necessary or proper for the attainment of justice or for enforcing or defending the rights of any parties to the Tribunal. This was to include the costs of expert witnesses. The applicant Minister challenged this ruling on two grounds: that there was an inconsistency between the ruling that, on the one hand, only those witnesses who gave oral evidence would tax and, on the other hand, that the respondent was retaining a general discretion to tax costs in the interests of justice. The Minister was particularly concerned to ensure that the expenses incurred by the parties to the Tribunal in the retention of advisers who had not given oral evidence would not tax.

Carroll J. granted the Minister some relief, to the extent of indicating that the Taxing Master did not have the breadth of discretion conferred by the 1986 Rules in the instant case. She held that the order for costs made by the

Tribunal of Inquiry affected the ordinary application of the 1986 Rules, and it was not practicable to apply those Rules where they were in conflict with certain aspects of the Tribunal's order. In particular, the Order would appear to have precluded taxation of advisers expenses where they did not come into the category of witnesses, even where they had been directed by counsel to be retained. While the Taxing Master's discretion was thus limited, Carroll J. went on to say that it remained a matter for the respondent to determine whether a person was to be considered as an adviser or as a potential witness. It was also for the respondent to determine if and when someone who was originally retained to give advice moved into the category of a witness, even though they did not give oral evidence. She therefore declined to grant the wider declaration sought by the Minister seeking to prevent the recovery of the costs of persons who did not give evidence. She held that some elements of the costs, charges and expenses of advisers might be recoverable under the (circumscribed) discretion conferred on the Taxing Master by the Tribunal's order for costs. The case was remitted to the Taxing Master on that basis.

Counsel's fees: complexity of case In *Commissioners of Irish Lights v. Maxwell Weldon & Darley*, High Court, May 15, 1996, Barron J. dealt with the taxation of counsel's brief and refresher fees. The defendant firm of solicitors had acted as the plaintiffs' solicitors in a planning appeal, for which the plaintiffs were, in effect, acting on behalf of the Department of the Marine: see *Keane v. An Bord Pleanála (No. 2)*, High Court, October 4, 1995; Supreme Court, 18 July 1996 (1995 Review, 378 and, above, 458). The plaintiffs disputed the defendant's costs of briefing senior counsel. The defendants had been instructed to brief one particular senior counsel and it had been indicated that his brief fee would be a minimum of 30,000 guineas and his refresher fees would be 3,000 guineas a day. The plaintiff had believed this to be excessive and consulted the Attorney General's office as to what it would recommend. The office recommended that a brief fee of £7,500 and refresher fees of £1,500 per day should suffice. Counsel indicated that he would mark whatever fee he considered appropriate having regard to the amount of work done but that he would take into account the Attorney General's recommendation. A marked brief fee of £31,500 and a refresher fee of £2,100 were allowed in full on taxation. The solicitor dealing with the matter from the defendant firm gave evidence that this was a case on which their clients had been working for five to six years and it was considered vital that the planning permission be obtained; and that the case had been the most important one in which he had been involved in his 25 years as a solicitor. Evidence was given that counsel had been in constant touch with the clients during the four months in which he was involved in the case. In addition the case had run for two and a half weeks longer than expected and counsel had therefore had to obtain releases from a number of other cases at the last moment, exposing himself to dissatisfaction from solicitors and clients. Counsel acted without the assistance of junior counsel in the case and the hearing each day had been very long with consultations before and after the days' work for which no additional fees had been charged. It was also claimed that the case involved technical and scientific issues of great complexity. Both parties adduced expert evidence from legal cost accountants who presented cases which they claimed were of comparable length and complexity, where the fees were either of a similar magnitude to those being claimed or substantially lower.

Barron J. allowed the fees claimed. He stated that, while only one counsel had been required in this particular case, the fee claimed could not be measured by reference to the totality of the fees that more than one counsel would have received. Nonetheless, he accepted that the fact that counsel had to commit himself to a date and to give exclusive attention would be a factor to be taken into account since this might be expected to require him to refuse or return work. However the work actually lost had to be disregarded. As a general proposition, he accepted that the level of fees marked by counsel depended on the nature of the case, the attendant complexities and its importance to the parties. In addition the care and prudence of the solicitor briefing counsel and experience of fees marked in other cases also had to be taken into account. In this respect, he noted that counsel's fees had been taxed on the basis that the particular counsel was experienced and practised in the field to which the case related. He also accepted the averment that the issues in the case had been particularly complex as they had covered many scientific specialities and the matter had been of extreme importance to the clients. He accepted that, while on the basis of the cases relied on by the defendant the fees claimed would not appear to be unreasonable, they were out of line with the cases relied on by the plaintiffs. However, having regard to the fact that counsel had taken into account the views of the Attorney General's office when marking his final fee, he concluded that although the fees, looked at as a total figure appeared very large, they were not so large in comparison with other fees agreed or determined on taxation as to be excessive on that ground alone. On this basis, he concluded that it would not have been unreasonable for a reasonably careful and prudent solicitor to have agreed the fees in question. Barron J. therefore allowed the fees under Order 94 of the Rules of the Superior Courts 1986.

Counsel's fees: test case   In *Gaspari v. Iarnród Éireann/Irish Rail and Ors.* [1997] 1 I.L.R.M. 207 (H.C.), Kinlen J. dealt with an aspect of the costs arising from rather complex litigation. The plaintiff was one of a number of people injured while travelling on a train owned by the first defendant which was in collision with cattle owned by the third defendant. The land on both sides of the track was owned by the second defendant. At one time it appeared that proceedings instituted by another person injured in the train crash would be the first to come before the High Court, but ultimately the plaintiff's case was heard first and it became a test case for the other proceedings. The first and third defendants were held liable in negligence, the first defendant being held 30% liable. The first defendant subsequently instituted an action (in which the plaintiff was joined) claiming that sections 12 and 14 of the Civil Liability Act 1961, by which as concurrent wrongdoer it was liable to indemnify the plaintiff to the extent of 100% of the damages awarded, were in breach of the Constitution: see *Iarnród Éireann/Irish Rail v. Ireland and Ors.* [1996] 2 I.L.R.M. 500. However, the judgment of Kinlen J. as to costs concerned the test case claim by the plaintiff for damages, not the constitutional action. The central issue was whether counsel for the plaintiff should be entitled, in view of the test case nature of the proceedings, to a proportionately larger fee than that marked and claimed by counsel for the second defendant, who had been held not liable and whose costs had been awarded against the plaintiff.

Kinlen J. referred with approval to the decisions in *Dunne v. O'Neill* [1974] I.R. 180 (described by Kinlen J. as the seminal decision), *Kelly v. Breen* [1978] I.L.R.M. 68 and *The State (Gallagher Shatter & Co) v. deValera (No. 2)* [1991] 2 I.R. 198 (1990 Review, 430-1) to the effect that the sole matter for the taxing master was whether the amounts claimed should be assessed on the basis of what a practising solicitor who is reasonably careful and prudent would consider a proper and reasonable fee. Kinlen J. accepted that the plaintiff's case had become a 'test case' when it was apparent that it was going to be the first to be heard and the taxing master had applied the correct principles when assessing costs on that basis. Bu he considered that the taxing master had been wrong in allowing only a £20,000 differential in the instructions fees of counsel for the plaintiff and counsel for the second defendant, namely £90,000 and £70,000 respectively. The difference in the scale of work done by the plaintiff compared the second defendant showed, he considered, a lack of proportionality in what had been allowed and, in the circumstances, Kinlen J. allowed an instructions fee of £120,000 to the plaintiff.

Interest: repayment of portion of interim award In *Best v. Wellcome Foundation Ltd. (No. 4)*, High Court, March 8, 1996, a further issue arose in this difficult litigation (1992 Review, 610-11). The defendant had raised a number of objections to the bill of costs. After a review in the High Court of taxation, in *Best v. Wellcome Foundation Ltd. and Ors. (No.3)* [1996] 1 I.L.R.M. 34 (1995 Review, 384), it transpired that there had been a considerable overpayment on foot of the interim certificate originally granted by the Taxing Master. The defendant sought repayment of this sum together with interest, pursuant to Order 99, rule 38(1) of the Rules of the Superior Courts 1986. Barron J. agreed. He held that, as the original order for costs carried interest, it would be unjust not to direct repayment with interest of the overpaid sum. He also awarded costs against the plaintiff's next friend and wardship committee (his mother).

Public importance of issue raised *In re La Lavia (No. 2)*, High Court, October 14, 1996 involved the application for costs by the plaintiffs in the case which involved the salvage and/or right to reward concerning the Spanish Armada shipwrecks: see *In re La Lavia* [1996] 1 I.L.R.M. 194 (S.C.). Barr J. awarded the plaintiffs their costs on the basis that their claim had been essentially successful. The plaintiffs had presented their claim in the action on the alternate grounds that they were entitled to a reward either as salvors in possession of the wrecks in admiralty law or as finders of valuable historical wrecks. Although Barr J. acknowledged that they had failed on the first ground, the issue had given rise to the first judgment on the status of archaeology in admiralty law. In view of the obvious importance of the issue, he concluded that there should be no deduction in their costs as a result of the adverse finding of the High Court. In this respect, he referred to a similar decision on costs in *Hanafin v. Minister for the Environment* [1996] 2 I.L.R.M. 141 (S.C.). Finally, he stated that the lodgements made by the defendants could be relevant to the issue of costs only if the court had been informed of their amount and if they had been such that they could reasonably exceed the reward, including expenses, which would ultimately be paid. But since the court had not been informed of the amount of the lodgements, they could not be taken into account in awarding costs.

Security for costs Traditionally an order for security for costs was sought where the plaintiff resided outside the jurisdiction. This point is reflected in the principle laid down by Finlay P. in *Collins v. Doyle* [1982] I.L.R.M. 495, that: '[p]*rima facie* a defendant establishing a *prima facie* defence to a claim made by a plaintiff residing outside the jurisdiction has a right to an order for security for costs', although he acknowledged that this is not an absolute right and that the court must exercise a discretion based on the facts of each case. The question of whether an individual who is resident outside the jurisdiction but within the European Union can be ordered to give security for costs on the basis of these principles was considered in 1995 in two High Court decisions, *Maher v. Phelan* [1996] 1 I.L.R.M. 359 and *Proetta v. Neil* [1996] 1 I.L.R.M. 457 (both discussed in the 1995 Review, 390-1). In the light of the findings and conclusions of the European Court of Justice in *Mund & Fester v. Hatrex International Transport*, Case C-398/92 [1994] ECR I-467, in which the Court had re-appraised the question of whether such forms of indirect discrimination based on grounds of nationality could be justified in the light of current practice in relation to enforcement of judgments, it was held that as an individual litigant who is resident in Ireland cannot be ordered to provide security for costs, a plaintiff resident outside Ireland but within the EU should not be so ordered. In addition, as Carroll J. pointed out in *Maher*, the rationale for granting an order for security for costs no longer exists as far as EU countries are concerned in which judgments are enforceable with comparative ease under the Brussels Convention and the Jurisdiction of Courts and Enforcement of Judgments (European Communities) Act 1988.

An attempt was made to distinguish these decisions in a recent case on the basis that the plaintiff while a national of an EU country was not ordinarily resident there. In *Pitt v. Bolger* [1996] 2 I.L.R.M. 68 (H.C.) the plaintiff, who was a farmer and bloodstock breeder, was prior to the events giving rise to the proceedings, the full owner of a valuable thoroughbred filly. She alleged that she was encouraged by the first named defendant, a race horse trainer who received a commission on the sale, to enter into a partnership agreement in relation to ownership of the filly with the second named defendant, a stud farm owner, and under the terms of this agreement the second named defendant paid her £100,000 for a half share in the filly and took possession of it with a view to selling it at its maximum value. The plaintiff averred that, acting on the advice of the first named defendant, she subsequently accepted the sum of £200,000 in total for her share of the filly in the belief that an offer had been made to buy out the entire interest for the sum of £400,000. The second named defendant alleged that this sale fell through and after he had bought out the plaintiff's share, he agreed to sell to another buyer for £800,000. The plaintiff claimed that the defendants had acted fraudulently and in breach of their duty to her or in the alternative had been negligent in failing to advise her of the true value of the filly. The second named defendant sought an order for security for costs on the basis that the plaintiff resided out of the jurisdiction, namely in the Isle of Man, and claimed that affidavits had been sworn which should satisfy the court that he had a defence on the merits within the meaning of Order 29, rule 3 of the Rules of the Superior Courts 1986. The plaintiff averred that while she had resided in the Isle of Man, she had recently acquired a property in England, that she was currently living in both places and intended to reside in England permanently as soon as she had sold her home in the Isle of Man. Counsel for the second named defendant sought to distinguish the decisions in *Maher v. Phelan* and *Proetta v. Neil* on the basis that at the time the proceedings were initiated, the plaintiff was ordinarily resident in the Isle of Man which is neither a member state of the European Union or one of the contracting parties to the Brussels Convention. Counsel for the plaintiff submitted that as a citizen of the United Kingdom she was entitled to the benefit of the principle laid down in *Mund & Fester*.

Keane J. embarked upon a comprehensive review of the relevant authorities in the area and said that the nature of the jurisdiction of the court had been explained in *Collins*, namely that *prima facie* a defendant establishing a *prima facie* defence to a claim made by a plaintiff residing outside the jurisdiction is entitled to an order for security for costs but this was not an absolute right and, amongst the matters to which a court might have regard in exercising its discretion against ordering security, was a *prima facie* case that the plaintiff's inability to give security flowed from the wrong committed by the defendant. Keane J. said that the Brussels Convention had effected a 'radical change' in the enforcement of judgments throughout the member states of the EU and the rules of private international law in this context had been entirely altered.

On this basis Keane J. concluded that: 'the undoubted discretion under the rule should never be exercised by an Irish court to order security to be given by an individual plaintiff who is a national of and resident in another member state which is a party to the convention' subject to the possible qualification referred to by Bingham MR in the recent decision of the English Court of Appeal in *Fitzgerald v. Williams* [1996] 2 W.L.R. 447 namely, where there is 'very cogent evidence of substantial difficulty in enforcing a judgment in another member state'. Finally, Keane J. had to consider whether the fact that the plaintiff was ordinarily resident in the Isle of Man at the time proceedings were instituted should alter the position. He concluded that where, as in the case before him, the plaintiff was a national of a member state of the EU and the evidence was that while resident in the past in a non-member state she had significant assets in the member state and intended to reside there permanently in the future, it seemed to him that the principles in *Mund* were clearly applicable. Accordingly he refused to grant the order for security for costs.

It would appear therefore that the courts should not exercise their discretion under Order 29 of the 1986 Rules to order security for costs to be given by an individual plaintiff who is a national of and resident in another member state of the EU which is a party to the Brussels Convention. Equally, on the authority of *Pitt v. Bolger* this would seem to be the case even in the context of a EU national whose place of residence is not altogether unproblematic, provided the court is satisfied that any judgment will be enforced within the framework of the Brussels Convention.

Solicitor and client costs: time limit   In *Meagher v. O'Boyle and Ors. (Peter O'Boyle & Co)*, High Court, February 20, 1996, McCracken J. made an order for taxation of solicitor and client costs under section 10 of the Attorneys and Solicitors (Ireland) Act 1870. The defendant firm had been retained by the plaintiff in judicial review proceedings arising from the plaintiff's prosecution for breach of various statutory Regulations concerning animal growth promoters (see *Meagher v. Minister for Agriculture and Food* [1994] 1 I.R. 329; [1994] 1 I.L.R.M. 1 (S.C.), discussed in the 1993 Review, 299-304). The plaintiff had made various payments to the defendants on foot of bills of costs presented between September 1991 and October 1993. Although these had not been in the form provided for under Order 99, rule 29 of the Rules of the

Superior Courts 1986, McCracken J. accepted that the plaintiff had requested the bills be in the form presented and that the format prescribed by the 1986 Rules was solely for the purpose of taxation of costs. Thus, the fact that they were not in the prescribed form did not render them invalid. This was central to the claim by the plaintiff in the instant proceedings, who challenged the entire amount of costs paid by him between 1991 and 1993. He had instituted the proceedings in September 1993. In accordance with the 12 month time limit specified in the 1870 Act, McCracken J. held that he was confined to challenging the sums paid within the previous 12 months and was thus precluded from challenging any payments made between October 1991 and September 1993, notwithstanding that, as indicated, the bills of costs from the defendants were not in the form prescribed by the 1986 Rules. McCracken J. also declined to order that the payments received by the defendants between October 1991 and October 1993 (totalling over £50,000) be paid into court pending taxation. He held that, since the defendants had fully accounted to the plaintiff for all sums received by them, such an order would be inappropriate.

Standby fees: civil servant as consultant In *Staunton v. Durkan and Ors.* [1996] 2 I.L.R.M. 509 (S.C.), the Supreme Court upheld a claim for the standby fees of an employment consultant. The consultant was a full-time civil servant seconded to FÁS, the State Training and Employment Agency. Outside his office hours, he also carried on a practice as an employment consultant. The plaintiff had recovered damages in his personal injuries action against the defendants arising from an injury sustained to his right hand. The plaintiff's solicitor had been directed by counsel to retain the consultant to advise and give evidence on the plaintiff's prospects of obtaining employment, as his hand had been permanently affected by the injury he had sustained. On taxation of the costs, the Taxing Master had disallowed the consultant's fees for attending the High Court hearing for eight days and a further two days on standby for court, principally on the basis that he refused to sanction payment to civil servants when they were at the same time being paid out of public funds. The High Court upheld this decision, but on further appeal, the Supreme Court reversed.

The Court referred to Order 94, rule 37 of the Rules of the Superior Courts 1986, which provide, *inter alia*, that on taxation of costs those expenses which appear to have been properly incurred in procuring evidence are to be allowed; and that no costs should be allowed which appear to have been incurred through caution, negligence or mistake or by payment of special charges or expenses to witnesses. The Supreme Court reiterated and approved the principles laid down in *Kelly v. Breen* [1978] I.L.R.M. 63, *The State (Gallagher, Shatter & Co) v. DeValera (No. 2)* [1991] 2 I.R. 198 (1990 Review, 430-1) and *Aspell v. O'Brien* [1993] 3 I.R. 516; [1993] I.L.R.M. 590 (1993 Review, 442-3). From these it was clear that the Taxing Master, in the exercise of his discretion under the 1986 Rules, was only entitled to disallow any part of a solicitor's disbursement if satisfied that no solicitor acting reasonably carefully and prudently, based on experience in the course of practice, would have agreed to such fees. The Court rejected the suggestion accepted in the High Court that the charges which it was proper to pay a witness were those which might be necessary to recoup any financial losses which that witness had suffered because of attendance at court. Instead, the Supreme Court accepted the plaintiff's submission that the test to be applied was not whether the witness had been at a loss but whether the solicitor had acted reasonably in discharging the fees claimed by the witness. Because the consultant had been retained in compliance with a direction from counsel, the Court concluded that the plaintiff's solicitor had been obliged to pay him. If the Taxing Master had applied that principle in the instant case, he could not have been satisfied that no careful and prudent solicitor would have paid the consultant for attending court and giving evidence. On this basis, the Court remitted the case to the Taxing Master to determine whether a reasonably careful and prudent solicitor would have required the consultant to attend court for eight days and to be on stand by for two days.

Submissions in court must be responsible   In *Bloomer and Ors. v. Incorporated Law Society of Ireland* [1995] 3 I.R. 14 (H.C.); Supreme Court, February 6, 1996 (the circumstances of which are discussed in the Solicitors chapter, 567, below), the Supreme Court held that the awarding of costs to a successful party may not always 'follow the event' where that party's submissions failed to deal in an objective manner with the facts of the case and the issues of law involved and any authorities which would be of assistance to the court in the determination of the issue before it. In particular, the Court considered that submissions should not be made, as in this case, consisting of contemptuous language and unfounded allegations. In that case, the successful plaintiffs were awarded a portion only of their costs.

COURTS AND COURT SERVICES

Against a background of dissatisfaction with court facilities and delays in the court system, the then Government established a Working Group on a Courts Commission in December 1995, chaired by Denham J. The Denham Working Group had published three reports by the end of 1996. If and when implemented, the recommendations in these reports would radically transform the face of the Irish court system. We discuss here briefly these three reports.

Managing and Financing the Courts: the Proposed Courts Service   The *First Report of the Working Group on a Courts Commission: Management* *and Financing of the Courts* (Pn 2690, April 1996) recommended the establishment of a State agency to be called the Courts Service, headed by a chief executive officer, subject to overall control by the Department of Justice. The establishment of an independent Court Service would bring the State into line with similar systems established in the United Kingdom, Australia and New Zealand. See also the discussion of the Report in Byrne and McCutcheon, *The Irish Legal System* (3rd ed., Butterworths, 1996), pp.140-6.

Deficiencies and delays The Report discussed in detail the deficiencies within the existing structures. On the administrative side, it found there was no clear management structure for the 800 persons who staffed the different courts and no strategic plan on the work of the courts. The Report identified with some particularity different delays at the various court levels. In the Supreme Court list in February 1996, it found that the length of time between the High Court hearing and a Supreme Court date for hearing varied from two to eight years. In the High Court, there was an average delay in personal injuries cases of almost three years from the date of setting down and hearing. As for criminal trials in the High Court (Central Criminal Court) delays in returns for trial varied from between two months to almost six years. Delays in High Court family law cases between readiness and hearing varied from a week to six months, but in the Circuit Court, delays in family law cases varied from three months to two years in the different Circuits. In other civil matters, delays in the Circuit Court ranged from one to three years. In the District Court, there were delays of up to eight months from the issuing of a summons in criminal prosecutions under the Road Traffic Acts.

The cost of the court service The Report also found that there was a lack of financial or statistical information on the courts in any understandable format. Indeed, the Report itself constitutes the first attempt to cost the different elements of the court system. It estimated that the cost of the court system, including salaries, building work, pensions, administration, legal aid, law reporting and witness expenses was about £46.77m in 1995, up from £24.73m in 1990. The court system earned an estimated income of £10.3m in 1995, largely from stamp duty imposed on pleadings, and this was similar to the amount raised in 1990. Because of the rise in overall costs between 1990 and 1995, the net cost of the court system to the State had thus risen from £13.8m in 1990 to £36.4m in 1995. This sum represented about 0.28% of total Government expenditure (estimated at just over £14bn) for 1996. This compared with estimated Government spending of about £2bn each in the Departments of Education and Health. It is not surprising, therefore, that the Report concluded that the State was receiving good value for money from the courts service.

Complete self-financing inappropriate The Report rejected the concept of complete self-financing of the courts system, as this would be inappropriate having regard to the constitutional right of access to the courts. Nonetheless, it was accepted that certain reforms could increase State income from the courts. By way of example, the Report suggested that a Commercial Court managed by High Court judges with specially trained Registrars could facilitate speedier litigation, with consequent benefits to business and commerce as well as the State through the generation of more court fees.

The Proposed Courts Service The Working Group rejected a number of proposed models for the court system, including ironically a Courts Commission (thus rendering the Working Group's title somewhat anomalous) in which responsibility for the management of the courts would have resided in the judiciary. Instead, the Working Group recommend the establishment of an independent statutory State agency, to be called the Courts Service, to manage a unified court system. The functions of the Court Service would include: management of the courts system; management of the budget; publication of annual performance reports; the provision, management and maintenance of suitable court buildings; the provision of secretarial, research and other administrative services to the judiciary; the establishment of a communications system between staff and judges; provision of a public information system on the court service, including the introduction of a Charter for Court Users and improved communication with the various media. The Courts Service would be accountable to the Oireachtas through the Minister for Justice for issues concerning finance and administration, and its funding would be audited by the Comptroller and Auditor General. It would not be accountable to the Oireachtas for judicial decisions, as the Report considered this would be in breach of the doctrine of the separation of powers in the Constitution.

Detailed arrangements The Working Group's proposal was accepted in principle by the then Government. The *Third Report of the Working Group on a Courts Commission: Towards the Courts Service* (Pn 3273, November 1996) laid down some of the detailed administrative arrangements required to bring the Courts Service into being, including the draft heads of a Courts Service Bill. In the wake of the 1997 General Election and change of government, the promised Courts Service has yet to be established, but the incoming administration was committed to establishing the proposed independent Service.

Case management and court management The *Second Report of the Working Group on a Courts Commission: Case Management and Court Management* (Pn 3070, July 1996) proposed significant reforms to the manner in which individual litigation is managed, through the mechanism of judicial case management. This element of the Report reflects to a large extent the recommendations of Lord Woolf in respect of the courts of England and Wales. Indeed, the Report makes express reference to Lord Woolf's Report, *Access to Justice, Interim Report to the Lord Chancellor on the Civil Justice System*. The Working Group quoted with approval Lord Woolf's definition of judicial case management as:

> ... the court taking the ultimate responsibility for progressing litigation along a chosen track for a pre-determined period during which it is subjected to selected procedures which culminate in an appropriate form of resolution before a suitably qualified judge. Its overall purpose is to encourage settlement of disputes at the earliest appropriate stage; and, where trial is unavoidable, to ensure that cases proceed as quickly as possible to a final hearing which is itself of strictly limited duration.

In effect, case management is intended to avoid unnecessary delay or 'drift' in civil litigation. The Working Group noted that, in June 1996, the President of the High Court, Costello P., had published a Practice Direction entitled 'Personal Injury Actions in Which Liability is Admitted' which introduced on a voluntary and trial basis a system of case conferences for personal injury cases. The Working Group's Report contains the full text of the Practice Direction (see also *Practice and Procedure*, June 1996, p.16) and a pre-trial check list which must be prepared prior to any case conference. This check list deals with whether any amendments to pleadings are proposed, whether pre-trial applications (such as for particulars or interrogatories) are to be made, an estimation of the length of the trial, whether attempts to settle have been made, whether medical reports have been exchanged, whether special damages have been calculated and whether it is wished that the judge presiding at the case conference will be asked to assist in settlement of the action. Clearly, the advent of case management, even on a trial basis, represents a fundamental shift in the manner in which the judiciary participate in civil proceedings.

Presidents of Courts and other aspects of court management The *Second Report of the Working Group on a Courts Commission: Case Management and Court Management* (Pn 3070, July 1996) (discussed in the context of case management, above) also proposed significant reforms to the manner in which Presidents of the various courts are appointed. The Report recommended that, in future, each President (whether the Chief Justice or the Presidents of the High Court, Circuit Court and District Court) should be appointed for a fixed term, and the Report suggested that this be of seven years duration. The Working Group considered that the current arrangements, where a person was appointed as Chief Justice or President of a court until retirement age, was not adequate where there is a greater need to respond to changes in the courts regime (proposed by the Working Group itself). The Report accepted that a person who had held a Presidency for many years might be unable to respond rapidly to change; indeed, the Report noted that its proposal would bring the courts into line with normal practice in other areas of public and professional life.

The Report also recommended that the Presidents of each bench be empowered to request a judge to work in a specialised area of as required in order to develop a level of expertise, for example, in the listing of cases or the co-ordination of specialist areas such as family courts. This would appear to envisage a return to a more formal structured division of courts which disappeared with the passing of the Courts of Justice Act 1924. It is also consistent with the references in the Working Group's *First Report*, discussed above, to the establishment of a specialist Commercial Court in the High Court.

Rules of Courts Committees   The Second Report of the Working Group also recommended that the various Rules of Courts Committees be enabled to be more active vehicles for introducing improvements in the court system. In effect, the Report recommended that they be better resourced so that they could meet more regularly and respond to perceived problems in practice and to introduce rule changes where required.

Judicial numbers   The Courts Act 1996, which amended section 10 of the Courts and Court Officers Act 1995 (1995 Review, 393-401) in order to provide for an increase from 24 to 27 in the maximum number of ordinary judges of the Circuit Court, may be seen against the background of a package of anti-crime legislation enacted in the middle of 1996 (see the Criminal Law chapter, above, 228). The additional judges thus provided were intended to ensure that any extra judicial business created in the Circuit Criminal Court would not result in any backlogs. It is notable that the Explanatory and Financial Memorandum published when the legislation was presented to the Oireachtas indicated that it would give rise to an estimated total annual salary cost of approximately £311,000, including provision for judicial salaries and additional support staff. Thus, the annual cost in 1996 terms of a judge of the Circuit Court, including ancillary support staff, was approximately £104,000. These figures may be seen against the general background of the cost of the court system, discussed in the *First Report of the Working Group on a Courts Commission: Management and Financing of the Courts* (Pn 2690, April 1996): see above.

DISCOVERY

Privilege   The decisions in *Walker v. Ireland*, High Court, October 7, 1996 and *Power City v. Monaghan*, High Court, October 14, 1996, which concern public interest immunity and legal professional privilege, respectively, are discussed in the Evidence chapter, 324-7, above.

Relevance   As O'Flaherty J. has recently stressed in *Stafford v. Revenue Commissioners*, Supreme Court, March 27, 1996, 'the most singular thing about discovery is that the documents sought to be discovered have to be relevant to the matter in issue'. So the fact that documents must be relevant to the matter which the court is being called upon to resolve is 'an essential prerequisite' if discovery is to be ordered. A dispute arose about the importation of a bronze statute and the Revenue Commissioners sought and obtained an order for discovery in wide terms relating to previous importations carried out by the appellant. O'Flaherty J. concluded that the documents dealing with previous importations were not relevant to the matter that would have to be resolved in the litigation and amended the order made by the Master on this basis.

In relation to the plaintiff's argument that if the application had been brought to attack his credit it was not a proper ground for discovery, O'Flaherty J. approved a passage from Matthews and Malek on *Discovery* to the effect that it will not be ordered of material which would be used solely for cross-examination of a witness as to credit since it would be oppressive if a party was obliged to disclose any document which might provide material for cross-examination as to his credibility as a witness. One further point about this judgment which is interesting to note is that O'Flaherty J. stated that 'these interlocutory matters are used to hold up the business of the courts', a comment which he said he was making 'not for the first time.'

In *Radiac Abrasives Inc v. Prendergast*, High Court, March 13, 1996, the plaintiff brought a motion to strike out the defence for failure to make discovery and in the alternative sought an order for further and better discovery. The plaintiff complained that discovery which had been made was inadequate; that it had been made by files and not by documents and that the files which had been furnished were not complete. Barron J. accepted that some of the documents furnished had not been discovered at all and that others had not been furnished without condition. He stated that it was not appropriate that this information should have been kept from the plaintiff; in his view discovery had not been made in accordance with the rules and reference had not been made to many documents which had existed but were said to exist no longer. Barron J. concluded that while there were elements in the defendants' conduct which suggested that they had acted deliberately, he said that they should be given a further opportunity to place a full affidavit of discovery before the court. (See also the discussion below, 485).

In *Irish Permanent Building Society v. Utrecht Consultants Ltd. and Ors.*, Supreme Court, October 31, 1996, the Court, in a brief judgment, dismissed an appeal against a High Court refusal to grant discovery against the plaintiff.

The defendants, who included a former chief executive of the plaintiff (but who was not involved in the instant application) had sought additional discovery against the plaintiff in relation to a general consultancy fee. The plaintiff did not dispute that there were documents which would record or affirm the provision of such services but submitted that they could not advance the case of the defendants or damage that of the plaintiff or put the defendants on a train of enquiry which would have either consequence. They relied on the test of relevance set out in *Compagnie Financiere du Pacifique v. Peruvian Guano Co.* (1882) 11 Q.B.D. 55. As indicated, the Supreme Court held for the plaintiff, concluding that none of the documents sought were material or relevant to any of the issues to be determined in the proceedings.

Striking out defence for failure to comply with order for discovery   Order 31, rule 21 of the Rules of the Superior Courts 1986 provides that if any party fails to comply with an order for discovery or for interrogatories, he shall be liable to attachment, and also if a plaintiff, to have his action dismissed for want of prosecution, or if a defendant, to have his defence struck out. This latter aspect of the rule was considered by the Supreme Court in *Mercantile Credit Co. of Ireland Ltd. v. Heelan*, Supreme Court, February 14, 1995 (1995 Review, 407) and the principles outlined by Hamilton C.J. in *Heelan* were reiterated by Barrington J. in similar language when the Supreme Court was called upon to consider the matter in *Murphy v. J. Donohoe Ltd. and Ors.* [1996] 1 I.R. 123; [1995] 2 I.L.R.M. 509 (HC); [1996] 1 I.L.R.M. 481 (SC). The plaintiffs had brought proceedings in respect of personal injuries sustained by them when a car belonging to their father caught fire. The fourth named defendant (the father) brought a motion against the second and fifth named defendants (Fiat) pursuant to Order 31, rule 21 of the 1986 Rules seeking to have their defences struck out on the grounds that they had failed to comply with an order for discovery. It was argued on behalf of these defendants that the failure to make discovery - of documents in relation to earlier problems with and complaints about the car – was attributable to inefficiency, stupidity, confusion and incompetence. Johnson J. did not accept this and held that they could not be relied on to comply with the orders of the court and made an order striking out the defences of these defendants (1995 Review, 407). The Supreme Court allowed their appeal. Barrington J. stated that 'Order 31 rule 21 exists to ensure that parties to litigation comply with orders for discovery. It does not exist to punish a defaulter but to facilitate the administration of justice by ensuring compliance with the orders of the court.' He said that, undoubtedly, cases exist in which one party may not be able to get a fair trial because of the other party's wilful refusal to comply with an order for discovery and in such cases it may be necessary to dismiss the plaintiff's claim or to strike out the defendant's defence – but such cases will be extreme ones. While he accepted that Johnson J. had taken the view that the case before him was an extreme one, there were matters to which the learned trial judge did not appear to have attached sufficient weight. Barrington J. concluded that having regard to a number of factors, such as the fact that the defendants' legal advisers had placed a restrictive interpretation on the order and that they had declared they would make further and better discovery, he would allow the appeal.

A similar conclusion was reached by Barron J. in *Radiac Abrasives Inc v. Prendergast*, High Court, March 13, 1996 in which the plaintiff brought a motion to strike out the defence for failure to make discovery and in the alternative sought an order for further and better discovery. Barron J. pointed out that the motion had been argued on the basis that the defendants had deliberately concealed information which would establish or at any rate materially support the plaintiff's case. He stated that the defendants denied this but accepted that if it had been the case, then the proper remedy would have been to strike out the defence. As he commented: 'A party to proceedings who has deliberately concealed documents in its discovery cannot when it has been found out, be allowed merely to amend its discovery'. However, on the facts before him, Barron J. concluded that while there were elements which suggested deliberate conduct on the defendants' part, they should be given a further opportunity to place a full affidavit before the court.

DISMISSAL FOR WANT OF PROSECUTION

As McGuinness J. pointed out in *Carroll Shipping Ltd. v. Mathews Mulcahy and Sutherland Ltd.*, High Court, December 18, 1996 there is a considerable amount of authority on the circumstances in which an action may be struck out for want of prosecution where there has been inordinate and inexcusable delay. The essence of the plaintiffs' claim in this case was that the defendant, as their insurance broker, had purported to insure them fully against all risks but in fact had failed to do so and had left them exposed to loss and damage arising from an accident. McGuinness J. quoted in detail from the judgment of the Supreme Court in *Primor plc v. Stokes Kennedy Crowley*, Supreme Court, December 19, 1995 (1995 Review, 401) which in her view showed that it must be asked whether the delay was inordinate and inexcusable and if so whether it was such that a fair trial between the parties could not proceed in the circumstances. Similarly O'Flaherty J. in *Primor* had identified the essential question to be whether after inordinate and inexcusable delay a just and fair trial might still take place.

Approaching the facts of the *Carroll Shipping* case in the light of these principles, McGuinness J. stated that a delay of over 15 years since the plenary summons had been issued was 'undoubtedly inordinate', especially bearing in mind that the events which gave rise to the claim dated back to the period

1973 to 1975. She found that the plaintiffs' delay was inexcusable given the history of the matter as a whole and said that while the defendant was not blameless in the matter of delay, she was satisfied that the defendant's conduct did not amount to acquiescence in the plaintiffs' delay. McGuinness J. then proceeded to consider whether a fair and just trial might now be had between the parties. She pointed out that where matters at issue are not, or are not fully covered by documentary evidence, there is a greater likelihood of prejudice resulting from delay. McGuinness J. was of the view that documentary evidence alone was not the only issue in the case before her and said that important questions about the verbal advice given by the defendant and the degree of the plaintiffs' knowledge were certain to arise at the trial. She referred to the fact that the employee of the defendant who had primarily dealt with the plaintiffs had died and to the fact that others who had either supervised or assisted were no longer employed by the defendant, and even if available to give evidence, they might have dangerously defective memories of the events which had transpired over 20 years previously. McGuinness J. was therefore satisfied that the prejudice caused to the defendant by the inordinate and inexcusable delay on the plaintiffs' part was such as to place an unfair burden on the defendant in defending the proceedings and was such as to make it impossible that a fair trial between the parties could now proceed. She concluded that the interests of justice required that the proceedings brought by the plaintiffs should be dismissed.

DISMISSAL OF FRIVOLOUS OR VEXATIOUS CAUSE OF ACTION

Order 19, rule 28 of the Rules of the Superior Courts 1986 provides that a court may order a pleading to be struck out on the grounds that it discloses no reasonable cause of action or in any case where the action is shown by the pleadings to be frivolous or vexatious.

It has been accepted that the court can only make an order under r.28 where the statement of claim discloses *on its face* no reasonable cause of action (see *McCabe v. Harding Investments Ltd.* [1984] I.L.R.M. 105) and in addition, the court has an inherent jurisdiction to strike out a plaintiff's claim where the proceedings are frivolous or vexatious or clearly unsustainable. However, it has been stressed that this jurisdiction 'should be exercised sparingly and only in clear cases' (*per* Costello J. in *Barry v. Buckley* [1981] I.R. 306, 308) and that the courts 'should be slow to entertain an application of this kind' (*per* McCarthy J. in *Sun Fat Chan v. Osseous Ltd.* [1992] 1 I.R. 425, 428: 1991 Review, 325-6).

Further consideration has been given to the circumstances in which this inherent jurisdiction may be exercised in a number of decisions this year. In

McSorley v. O'Mahony, High Court, November 6, 1996, Costello P. confirmed that this jurisdiction is only to be exercised 'in clear and exceptional cases'. However, he was satisfied that the case before him fell into this category and ordered that the action should be stayed on the grounds that it was vexatious and an abuse of the court's process. In his view the first cause of action between the parties no longer existed and in the second, the plaintiff could obtain no benefit from maintaining the proceedings. As he stated:

> It is an abuse of the process of the courts to permit the court's time to be taken up with litigation which can confer no benefit on a plaintiff. It is also an abuse to permit litigation to proceed which will undoubtedly cause detriment to a defendant and which can confer no gain on a plaintiff.

In *Mehta v. Marshs*, High Court, March 5, 1996 motions were brought to strike out the proceedings against the defendants on the grounds that they were vexatious, groundless and an abuse of the process of the courts. However, Carroll J. pointed out that the inherent jurisdiction of the court to dismiss an action on these grounds must be on the basis that on agreed facts the plaintiff could not succeed. In the case before her, she stated that there were no agreed facts and so the inherent jurisdiction of the court to dismiss the action could not be invoked.

Finally in *Ennis v. Butterly* [1997] 1 I.L.R.M. 28 (H.C.) the plaintiff instituted proceedings claiming that she had suffered loss and damage as a result of representations allegedly made to her by the defendant that she would be financially secure and that he would marry her - although he was already married to someone else - and seeking damages for breach of contract and misrepresentation. The defendant argued that any agreements were unenforceable as a matter of public policy and that the plaintiff's action was unsustainable and should be struck out. Kelly J. referred to the court's inherent jurisdiction to stay proceedings and quoted with approval from *Barry v. Buckley* [1981] I.R. 306 and *Sun Fat Chan v. Osseous Ltd.* [1992] 1 I.R. 425 (1991 Review, 325-6). He also referred to the decision in *D.K. v. A.K.* [1994] 1 I.R. 166; [1993] I.L.R.M. 710 (1992 Review, 365-7) in which Costello J. had stressed that in exercising this jurisdiction the court is required to consider whether a claim is so clearly unsustainable that it should be struck out. Kelly J. found that even if an implied contract were contended for, it would still be unenforceable on grounds of public policy and he held that the claim for damages for breach of contract must, as a matter of law, fail. However, he concluded that he could not say that the plaintiff's claim for damages for misrepresentation *must* fail and so he declined to strike out this part of the action on this basis.

INTERROGATORIES

In *McCole v. Blood Transfusion Service Board*, High Court, June 11, 1996 the plaintiff sought leave to deliver interrogatories to the first named defendant (for other aspects of this highly-publicised litigation, see *Roe v. Blood Transfusion Service Board and Ors.* [1996] 1 I.L.R.M. 555 (H.C.), discussed in the Constitutional Law chapter, 141, above). Laffoy J. took the opportunity to reiterate in full the principles by which the court should be guided in determining whether such leave should be granted, set out previously by Costello J. (as he then was) in *Mercantile Credit Co of Ireland Ltd. v. Heelan* [1994] 2 I.R. 105; [1994] 1 I.L.R.M. 406 (1994 Review, 381-3) (The Supreme Court decision in *Mercantile Credit*, considered in the 1995 Review, 407, dealt with striking out a defence for failure to comply with an order for discovery: see above). In *McCole* Laffoy J. stated that interrogatories must relate to 'matters in question' in the action as provided for in Order 31, rule 1 of the Rules of the Superior Courts 1986 and that leave will only be given when they are considered necessary for 'disposing fairly' of the matter or for saving costs. In this regard the court must bear in mind that actions are generally to be heard on the basis of oral evidence and that the use of affidavit evidence given in reply to interrogatories is an exception which must be justified by some special exigency. Laffoy J. reiterated that interrogatories may be delivered either to obtain information from the interrogated party about the issues which arise in the action or to obtain admissions and that where information is sought it must relate to the issues raised in the pleadings and not to the evidence which a party wishes to adduce in order to establish his case. Laffoy J. further stated that interrogatories which seek admissions as to the existence of documents and signatures to documents identified in discovery will normally be allowed unless there are special reasons why in the interests of justice an order should not be made. In addition, interrogatories which seek admissions about facts surrounding documents identified in discovery affidavits must relate to the issues raised in the pleading and cannot be used as a means of proving the interrogating party's case. While interrogatories may be served for the purpose of saving costs, the paramount consideration is to do justice between the parties and an order will be refused if a fair hearing might be prejudiced by it, even if the costs would thereby be reduced.

Counsel for the defendant submitted that particular regard should be had to the difference between an interlocutory procedure and the trial of the action and to the distinction between eliciting information at an interlocutory stage and through cross-examination at trial. Laffoy J. agreed that the principle that requests for information ascertainable by cross-examination at trial are generally inappropriate unless it can be established that it is essential for the proper preparation of the case was consistent with the fundamental rubric identified by Costello J. in *Mercantile*. Applying these principles to the facts of the case before her, Laffoy J. granted leave to deliver some of the interrogatories at issue.

JOINDER OF PARTIES

Order 15, rule 13 of the Rules of the Superior Courts 1986 provides that the court may at any stage of the proceedings and on such terms as it thinks just, add the name of any party who should have been joined as a defendant. However the point has recently been made that this jurisdiction will not be exercised where the claim against the proposed additional party must fail as it would serve no useful purpose. In *Allied Irish Coal Supplies Ltd. v. Powell Duffryn International Fuels Ltd.* [1997] 1 I.L.R.M. 306 (H.C.) the plaintiff had instituted proceeding against the defendant claiming damages for breach of contract and misrepresentation. Subsequently the plaintiff sought an order joining another company as a co-defendant, averring that the defendant was a wholly owned subsidiary of this other company and alleging that the defendant was not a separate entity in any respect. The defendant objected to the joinder of the parent company as a co-defendant on the basis that any claim which the plaintiff had against that company was statute-barred. While Laffoy J. accepted that the plaintiff was correct in asserting that the onus on the plaintiff was no greater than to show that it had a stateable case against the parent company she decided that the relief sought should be refused. She held that even if the plaintiff had a stateable case the court would not order the joinder of the parent company as co-defendant because as the claim against it was statute-barred, it would serve no useful purpose to do so.

LEGAL AID

Civil Legal Aid Act 1995 and Regulations As discussed in the 1995 Review, 407, the Civil Legal Aid Act 1995 (Commencement) Order 1996 (SI No. 272 of 1996) brought the Civil Legal Aid Act 1995 into effect on October 11, 1996. The Civil Legal Aid Regulations 1996 (SI No. 273 of 1996), which lay down eligibility criteria are also discussed in the 1995 Review, 409.

Appointment of solicitors not function of court In *D.I. v. F.T and the Legal Aid Board*, High Court, February 16, 1996, Murphy J. held that the courts had no power or authority in any circumstances to appoint a solicitor on behalf of any of the parties appearing before them in civil matters on the basis that the costs of such solicitor would be defrayed by the Legal Aid Board. In this respect, he noted that this applied both to the (then existing) non-statutory Scheme of Civil Legal Aid and to the statutory arrangements put in place under the Civil Legal Aid Act 1995 (1995 Review, 407-13). As to whether a court might adjourn proceedings (as had occurred in the instant case) in order to have the Legal Aid Board determine whether a party to proceedings might be granted legal aid, he considered that judges must exercise their discretion in granting or withholding an adjournment based on the facts as they appear before them, and he was strongly of the view that a discretion so exercised should not be reviewed by any other court. In this respect, his comments allow some margin of appreciation where the justice of case so requires. While strictly speaking Murphy J's comments on the 1995 Act were *obiter*, they are of some significance nonetheless.

Unaided person seeking costs from Board'   In *G.D. v. St. Louis Adoption Society and Ors.*, High Court, February 1, 1996, Budd J. held that where a party retains a private solicitor and, by the cogency and value of the submissions made on his behalf, makes a worthwhile contribution to the hearing of a case, he may be described as a "successful person" and "unaided person" within the meaning of paragraph 8.3.2 of the non-statutory Scheme of Civil Legal Aid and Advice, which preceded the Civil Legal Aid Act 1995 (1995 Review, 407). The case arose against the following background. The applicant wished to challenge the adoption of her child in the High Court. She had approached the Legal Aid Board on a number of occasions prior to the High Court proceedings but was told that there was a very considerable waiting list. She contacted her solicitors, who decided to represent her. Following a 13 day hearing, the High Court had made an order pursuant to section 3(2) of the Adoption Act 1974 dispensing with the consent of the applicant to the adoption of her child. The court made no order as to the costs of the adoptive parents, who had been granted legal aid by the Legal Aid Board. The High Court recommended strongly that the applicant's costs be paid by the Board. The Board considered that it was precluded by paragraph 8.3.2 of the non-statutory Scheme from paying the applicant's costs. Paragraph 8.3.2 provided, *inter alia*, "It will be open to an unaided person (in the remainder of this paragraph referred to as the successful person) who has been awarded costs against a legally aided person (in the remainder of this paragraph referred to as the unsuccessful person) to submit a bill of costs to the Board and the Board may make an *ex gratia* payment towards those costs of such amount as it considers appropriate . . .' Budd J. awarded the applicant her costs against the adoptive parents, thus paving the way for the application of paragraph 8.3.2. He noted that the High Court had, in making the order as to costs, retained liberty to apply so that there had been no final determination of the issue. He noted that the cogent submissions made on behalf of the applicant had greatly assisted the High Court and therefore the applicant had made a worthwhile contribution to the case. He adopted the reasoning of the Supreme

Court in *M.F. v. Legal Aid Board* [1993] I.L.R.M. 797 (1993 Review, 334-5) in holding that the applicant could be said to have been successful in the proceedings and to come within the meaning of "unaided person" and "successful person" in paragraph 8.3.2. of the non-statutory Scheme. He concluded that, if the applicant was awarded costs against the adoptive parents, the Board would be enabled, pursuant to paragraph 8.3.2., to make an *ex gratia* payment towards her costs. He considered that the applicant should have little difficulty in satisfying the Board that she had taken all reasonable steps necessary to recover her costs from the adoptive parents since they were not in a position to pay her costs. Budd J. put a stay on the order to allay the fears of the adoptive parents that it would adversely affect their credit rating and also recommended that the Board deal with the matter with expedition.

PRECEDENT

Stenographer's note directed in cases involving State   In *Reid v. Minister for Finance*, High Court, July 29, 1996, discussed in the Garda Síochána chapter, 398, above, Budd J. took the rather unusual, but certainly welcome, step of directing that, in view of the dearth of reported judgments on the making of compensation awards under the Garda Síochána (Compensation) Acts 1941 and 1945, since the State was a party in each of these cases, a stenographers note should be made in respect of any *ex tempore* judgment relating to the 1941 and 1945 Acts in the future. It is greatly to be hoped that this expression of opinion will be acted on. Whether the comments should be extended to all litigation involving the State is a matter for another day.

RULES OF COURT

Air pollution   The Rules of the Superior Courts (No. 2) 1996 (SI No. 377 of 1996) made provisions for applications to the High Court under the Air Pollution Act 1987. They added a new Order 103A to the 1986 Rules and came into effect on January 1, 1997.

District Court: water supply disconnection   The District Court (Local Government (Delimitation Of Water Supply Disconnection Powers) Act 1995) Rules 1996 (SI No. 93 of 1996) prescribe the procedures to be followed and forms to be used by a local authority acting as sanitary authority in making applications for an order to discontinue a supply of water for domestic purposes under the Local Government (Delimitation Of Water Supply Disconnection Powers) Act 1995. The 1996 Rules came into effect on April 19, 1996.

Planning and development: unknown persons The Rules of the Superior Courts (No. 1) 1996 (SI No. 5 of 1996) provide for the making of orders against unknown persons carrying on unauthorised development and are in addition to Order 103 of the 1986 Rules. The 1996 Rules came into effect on January 15, 1996.

District Court areas The District Court Areas (Variation Of Days And Hours) (No. 1) Order 1996 (SI No.8 of 1996) provided for the days and hours for the holding of the District Court in Kilelly, Co. Mayo; with effect from March 1, 1996.

SERVICE OF SUMMONS

Order 11, rule 1(h) of the Rules of the Superior Courts 1986 provides that service out of the jurisdiction of an originating summons may be allowed by the court whenever any person out of the jurisdiction is a necessary or proper party to an action properly brought against another person duly served within the jurisdiction. The correct interpretation of this provision was considered by the Supreme Court in *Short and Ors. v. Ireland* [1997] 1 I.L.R.M. 161 which dealt with the plaintiffs' claim that they had been adversely affected through radioactive contamination by the activities of the third named defendants, British Nuclear Fuels, at the Sellafield nuclear reprocessing plant in Cumbria. The plaintiffs were granted leave to serve notice of the plenary summons on the third named defendant out of the jurisdiction and the latter brought a motion to have this order set aside. O'Hanlon J. refused this application and on appeal, the Supreme Court upheld this decision. The Supreme Court held that the learned High Court judge had been correct in finding that the plaintiffs had established a good arguable case for the purposes of their application for service out of the jurisdiction. In considering the interpretation of Order 11 rule 1 (h), Barrington J. stated that that the test to be applied when deciding whether to allow service out of the jurisdiction in accordance with this rule was whether the person out of the jurisdiction would, if he were within the jurisdiction, be a proper person to be joined as a defendant in the action against the other defendants. He was satisfied that the third named defendant would have met this requirement had it been resident within the State and held accordingly that O'Hanlon J. had been correct in allowing service out of the jurisdiction under Order 11, rule 1(h).

Order 11, rule 8 of the Rules of the Superior Courts 1986 provides that where a defendant is not, or is not known or believed to be a citizen of Ireland, notice of a summons and not the summons itself shall be served on him. This rule was considered by Morris J. in *O'Connor v. Commercial General and Marine Ltd.* [1996] 2 I.L.R.M. 290 (HC) which concerned the plaintiff's claim to recover monies which he alleged were due to him on foot of an insurance policy in respect of a vessel which had been lost at sea. The plaintiff believed the second named defendant to be the underwriter of the policy and an original plenary summons was served on the second named defendant at an address in Belgium. The second named defendant disputed the fact that it was the underwriter and brought a motion to have service of the summons set aside on a number of grounds, including non-compliance with the requirements of Order 11, rule 8. Morris J. agreed to set aside service of the plenary summons on the basis that notice of the summons rather than the summons itself should have been served. He therefore concluded that the service which had been effected was bad and should be set aside pursuant to Order 12, rule 26 of the 1986 Rules.

Finally, in *Petronelli v. Collins*, High Court, July 19, 1996 the court had to consider whether Order 9, rule 3 of the 1986 Rules, which provides that personal service shall be effected by delivering a copy of a summons to a defendant in person and showing him the original or duplicate original of the summons, had been complied with. Costello P. accepted the evidence of the summons server that she had handed a copy of the summons to the defendant and shown him the original despite the conflicting evidence of the defendant and other witnesses, and concluded that the defendant had therefore been properly served with the summons in accordance with the provisions of the rule.

SUMMARY JUDGMENT

Leave to defend: refusal   In *First National Commercial Bank Plc v. Anglin* [1996] 1 I.R. 75 (S.C.), the Supreme Court refused the defendant leave to defend a summary summons under Order 37, rule 3 of the Rules of the Superior Courts 1986. The plaintiff had issued proceedings against the defendant in the High Court claiming £950,000 on foot of a guarantee dated February 1989 whereby the defendant guaranteed the payment by a named company of all or any moneys due by that company to the plaintiff up to but not exceeding the sum of £950,000. The High Court entered summary judgment in the plaintiff's favour and declined to allow the defendant enter a substantive defence. On the defendant's appeal, the Supreme Court upheld the decision of the High Court.

The defendant had argued that the guarantee had in fact been executed in September 1989 and was therefore void as having been given for past consideration. The detailed factual background may be summarised as follows. The defendant was chairman of the company in respect of whom the guarantee had been given and managing director of its parent company. The guarantee was required by the plaintiff as part of the security of a loan for £4,050,000 to the company. A facility letter from the plaintiff to the company dated October 12, 1988 referred to the defendant's personal guarantee. This facility was accepted by the company by resolution and a certificate of that resolution was signed by the defendant and furnished to the plaintiff. By letter dated 16 December 1988, the defendant's solicitors explained that the defendant had previously given guarantees and was conversant with the obligation he was taking on himself. In December 1988, facility letters were reissued by the plaintiff, in each case referring to the defendant's guarantee. By a letter dated February 13, 1989, the defendant's solicitors returned to the plaintiff all the required documentation including a guarantee by the defendant expressed to be 'executed in escrow.' The plaintiff alleged that this letter had in fact been received on January 13, 1989, that the draw down had been planned for February 1, 1989 and that it took place on that date. The plaintiff also argued that, subsequent to 1 February, correspondence took place between the parties seeking and providing copies of the documentation that had been executed on that date.

The Supreme Court referred to relevant case law in this area, including *Irish Dunlop Co. Ltd. v. Rolph* (1958) 95 I.L.T.R. 70, *Banque Nationale de Paris v. de Naray* [1984] 1 Lloyd's Rep. 21 and *National Westminister Bank plc v. Daniel* [1993] 1 W.L.R. 1453. Thus, the Supreme Court confirmed that, in considering whether to grant leave to defend a summary summons under Order 37, rule 3 of the Rules of the Superior Courts 1986, it must look at the whole situation to satisfy itself as to whether there is a reasonable probability of the defendant having a *bona fide* defence. Crucially, the Court accepted the plaintiff's evidence that the letter dated February 13, 1989 had in fact been received by it on January 13, 1989. The court also accepted that the defendant had not signed the guarantee in question on February 1, 1989 nor had he been present when the transaction had been completed. Indeed, the Court acknowledged that it was common practice, to avoid inconveniencing business people, that such documents were made available in advance and then dated when the transaction was perfected. The Court concluded that the guarantee had been executed by the defendant before February 1, 1989 and probably before January 13, 1989. On this basis, there was no credible evidence for the defence the defendant wished to assert. In any event, the Court commented that, even if the guarantee had been executed subsequent to the drawdown of funds, it was questionable whether it would have been invalidated, for two reasons: first, the loan had been made expressly on terms that the guarantee would be given and, second, the guarantee extended to the present as well as future indebtedness of the company.

Oral hearing: refusal In *Goodman and Ors. v. Kenny*, High Court, July 30, 1996, Kinlen J. declined to refer proceedings commenced by way of summary summons to an oral hearing because he was not satisfied that there was a genuine issue of fact between the parties. Thus, in accordance with the principles in *Tennant v. Associated Newspapers Group Ltd.* [1979] F.S.R. 298 and

Mellowhide Products Ltd. v. Barry Agencies Ltd. [1983] I.L.R.M. 152, he held that he was obliged to give judgment since he was satisfied that the matters advanced by the defendant were advanced for the purpose of delaying and avoiding judgment. The case involved a sum of almost ST£23m advanced to the defendant by the plaintiffs.

THIRD PARTY PROCEDURE

Section 27(1)(b) of the Civil Liability Act 1961 provides that any party who wishes to make a claim for contribution under the Act shall if the person from whom he wishes to claim contribution is not already a party to the action serve a third party notice as soon as is reasonably possible. In *Kelly v. Governors of St Laurences Hospital* [1990] 2 I.R. 31; [1989] I.L.R.M. 877 (1989 Review, 354-5) Finlay C.J. made it clear that a claim for contribution must be made 'as soon as is reasonably possible' and held that as the defendants' had known of the particulars of negligence alleged against them more than three years before they had sought to join the third party, the claim had not been made in accordance with this requirement. Further consideration has recently been given to this phrase in *Dowling v. Armour Pharmaceutical Co Inc* [1996] 2 I.L.R.M. 417.

The plaintiffs claimed damages for negligence against the defendants in relation to the manufacture and preparation of contaminated blood products. It emerged from replies to particulars that the plaintiffs had been treated with another company's products prior to being diagnosed HIV positive. The second named defendant sought leave to add this company as a third party and the plaintiffs sought leave to join it as a co-defendant. The company opposed the applications on the grounds that its joinder as a third party would delay the hearing of the actions and that the application had not been made as soon as reasonably possible within the meaning of section 27(1)(b) of the 1961 Act. Morris J. held that in the circumstances it had been wholly reasonable for the second named defendant to postpone its decision on whether to apply to join the company as a third party until after the final replies to particulars had been delivered, by which time it had become clear that the product had not just been administered in isolated cases. In the circumstances he was therefore satisfied that there had been no undue or unreasonable delay on the part of the second named defendant in seeking to join the company as a third party. While Morris J. concluded that this would have been an appropriate case in which to give liberty to issue and serve a third party notice, in the circumstances, he felt that the best course of action was to grant the plaintiff's application to join the proposed third party as a co-defendant.

Another point relating to third party procedure which has emerged recently is that a motion to set aside a third party order should only be brought before the third party has taken an active role in the proceedings and it would appear that such a motion will not be successful where the third party has entered a defence in the third party proceedings. This became clear from the decisions of Morris J. in *Carroll v. Fulflex International Co.*, High Court, October 18, 1995 and *Tierney v. Sweeney*, High Court, October 18, 1995 (both discussed in the 1995 Review, 415) and this point was reasserted in *Grogan v. Ferrum Trading Co. Ltd.* [1996] 2 I.L.R.M. 216 (H.C.). The plaintiff sustained injury when a lorry driven by the second named defendant struck steel girders belonging to the first named defendant which fell as they were being loaded. Two third parties applied to set aside the order made granting the second named defendant liberty to issue and serve third party notices against them. One of them, the owner and occupier of the premises in which the accident had taken place, had originally been named as a defendant until a notice of discontinuance was served against him and Morris J. found that the delay of nine months in bringing the application against this party was reasonable and within the time scale envisaged by section 27 of the 1961 Act. However, in the case of the other third party, he was satisfied that the delay – of two and a half years since the statement of claim had been delivered – was quite unreasonable in the circumstances. However, Morris J. concluded that in both cases, in view of the fact that a defence to the third party claim had been delivered, by adopting this procedure the third parties had forfeited their rights to apply to the court to have the procedure set aside. In his opinion at the stage when a third party enters a defence to a third party claim, he must be assumed to have received all appropriate advice in relation to the matter and such advice would, presumably, have included a consideration of the desirability of setting aside the third party notice. As Morris J. stated: 'the delivery of the defence is, in my view, an election by the third party which precludes him thereafter from moving the court to set aside the notice.' Therefore it must be remembered that in cases where a third party might have good grounds for seeking to have a third party notice set aside, he should proceed to take steps to achieve this rather than seeking to become further involved by delivering a defence to the third party claim.

Prisons

ACCESS TO LEGAL ADVICE

In *Walsh v. Governor of Limerick Prison (No. 2)*, High Court, July 31, 1996, Laffoy J. rejected a number of claims by the applicant, a convicted prisoner, that his continued detained in Limerick Prison was not in accordance with law within the meaning of Article 40.4.2 of the Constitution. He claimed, *inter alia*, that he had been denied access to his legal adviser, contrary to the Rules for the Government of Prisons 1947, inhibiting him in processing his appeal to the Court of Criminal Appeal and that the only manner in which the court could vindicate his rights was by ordering his release. The applicant's solicitor had visited him on a particular occasion and the supervising prison officer had furnished the solicitor with a docket of the type used for ordinary prison visits and not professional visits. The prison officer positioned himself in the visiting room about 16 to 18 feet away from applicant and his solicitor. Neither party complained to the prison officer about his presence in the room within earshot of the parties, nor did either disabuse the prison officer of the misconception he was under as to the nature of the visit. The applicant's complaints concerning visits by his solicitor had already been the subject of separate legal proceedings, *Walsh v. Governor of Limerick Prison* [1995] 2 I.L.R.M. 158 (1995 Review, 417) and the respondent had given an undertaking to the Supreme Court that a consultation room would be made available to enable the applicant consult his solicitor and counsel without the presence of a prison officer.

As indicated, Laffoy J. rejected the applicant's for release. She was satisfied that there had been no intentional breach of the undertaking given to the Supreme Court or a deliberate denial of the applicant's rights. She was satisfied that the respondent intended to fulfil the undertaking in the future and to ensure that the applicant received his entitlement under the 1947 Rules to visits from his legal advisers in the sight but not the hearing of a prison officer. She concluded that the breach of the applicant's rights during visits by his solicitor fell short of the type of "default of fundamental requirements that the detention may be said to be wanting in due process of law" which the Supreme Court had indicated in *The State (McDonagh) v. Frawley* [1978] I.R. 131 would be required to render invalid the applicant's detention as a convicted person.

DISCIPLINE

Disciplinary code for officers   The Prison (Disciplinary Code for Officers) Rules 1996, made under section 12 of the General Prisons (Ireland) Act 1877, lay down a detailed disciplinary code for the investigation of allegations of breaches of discipline against prison officers. The Schedule to the Rules contain a detailed list of breaches of discipline. The Rules were made after extensive consultation over a number of years between the Department of Justice and representatives of prison officers. The 1996 Rules are stated to be expressly override anything contained in the rather less specific provisions of Rules for the Government of Prisons 1947, in particular, Rule 102 of the 1947 Rules. The 1996 Rules came into effect on October 1, 1996.

REMISSION

In *O'Brien v. Governor of Limerick Prison*, High Court, July 31, 1996; Supreme Court, February 13, 1997, the Supreme Court, reversing Geoghegan J, held that where a sentence of imprisonment has been suspended in part, remission may be earned by a prisoner on the part which has not been suspended rather than the whole of his sentence.

The case was, in effect, a 'test' case concerning the effect of suspended sentences on the granting of remission. The applicant had been convicted on counts of burglary and aggravated sexual assault and was sentenced to two terms of ten years to run concurrently. The High Court judge ordered that the last six years of the sentence be suspended on condition that the applicant enter into a peace bond to keep the peace for the suspended portion of the sentence. The judge appeared to indicate in his remarks that he intended the applicant to serve four years, though he did not expressly advert to the position as to the executive's power to grant remission of sentences. The applicant did not appeal the order but, having served three years imprisonment, claimed that he was eligible for remission under Rule 38(1) of the Rules for the Government of Prisons 1947, which provides that a convicted prisoner sentenced to imprisonment, for a period exceeding one month, shall be eligible, by industry and good conduct to earn a remission of a portion of his imprisonment, not exceeding one fourth of the whole sentence. The Department of Justice initially agreed with him. This appeared to be based on the views expressed by Carroll J. in *The State (Beirnes) v. Governor of the Curragh Military Detention Barracks* [1982] I.L.R.M. 491, in which she dealt with the identical wording in Reg. 35(1) of the Prisons Act 1972 (Military Custody) Regulations 1972. However the respondent Governor was concerned that if the applicant was released on the basis of this interpretation of the 1947 Rules, he might be in breach of the High Court order and therefore in contempt of court.

He was also concerned that if the applicant was released on this basis, he would be at large for approximately a year before he would be obliged to enter into the bond with the conditions attached which the Court had imposed. An application was made to the trial judge to have the position clarified, but he refused to entertain it as he felt the sentence was quite clear. The applicant then sought an order for his release under Article 40.4.2 of the Constitution. Geoghegan J. refused the relief sought, but as already indicated the Supreme Court reversed.

Geoghegan J. accepted that the validity of a High Court order could be challenged in the context of an inquiry under Article 40. However, he was satisfied that the order sentencing the applicant did not have the meaning contended for by the applicant. He held that any remarks by the trial judge about remission could not be construed as affecting the power of the executive concerning remission. Geoghegan J. concluded that remission could only be earned on the whole of a prisoner's sentence, that is, the aggregate of the custodial and the proposed suspended part. In this respect, he declined to follow the contrary views expressed by Carroll J. in *The State (Beirnes) v. Governor of Curragh Military Detention Barracks* [1982] I.L.R.M. 491. Finally, he also found it difficult to interpret the expression "the whole sentence" in Rule 38 of the 1947 Rules as meaning in the case of a part suspended sentence only the custodial part of the sentence.

The conflicting views expressed by Carroll J. in *Beirnes* and by Geoghegan J. in *O'Brien* left an unsatisfactory state of affairs. It is not surprising therefore that an appeal was taken to the Supreme Court. While the Court's decision was given in February 1997, we refer to it briefly here because of its importance. In effect, the Court upheld the views expressed by Carroll J. in *Beirnes*, though without expressly drawing attention to the differences in the judicial views expressed. The Court unanimously held that the sentence imposed in the instant case could only properly be understood as a sentence of four years imprisonment and that, accordingly, the applicant was, *prima facie*, entitled to remission once he had served three years. The Court thus ordered the applicant's release, which led to a substantial number of consequential releases.

The Supreme Court accepted that the 1947 Rules, and the Prisons (Ireland) Act 1907 on which they were based, were difficult to reconcile with the type of sentence imposed in the instant case where the trial judge had not retained seisen of the matter, as had been indicated in the case law on suspended sentences, such as *The People v. Cahill* [1980] I.R. 8 and *The People v Aylmer*, Supreme Court, December 18, 1986 (1987 Review, 160). Despite these difficulties, the Court expressly declined to make any general judgment on the desirability of the partly suspended sentence, though it noted that the Court of Criminal Appeal retained an appellate jurisdiction in these matters. Nonetheless, by declining to rule out such sentences, it gave them a *nihil obstat*, if not an *imprimatur*. For the present, therefore, the sentences imposed in such cases will be dealt with in accordance with the interpretation given to the 1947 Rules in the *O'Brien* case, though the Court accepted that this interpretation is difficult to reconcile with the wording of the 1947 Rules. It is to be hoped that the position will be clarified in any new Prison Rules to be made under the general power now conferred by the Criminal Justice (Miscellaneous Provisions) Act 1997, which we will discuss in general in the 1997 Review.

RULES OF PRISONS AND PLACES OF DETENTION

Castlerea   The Detention Of Offenders (Unit A Castlerea) Regulations 1996 (SI No.3 61 of 1996), made under the Prisons Act 1970, specify the classes of prisoners who may be detained at the newly-built prison at Castlerea, County Roscommon, and also provide for their management. They came into effect on December 2, 1996. In so far as relevant, the Saint Patrick's Institution Regulations 1960 and the Rules for the Government of Prison 1947 are also to apply to the new prison.

Curragh   The Detention Of Offenders (The Curragh) Regulations 1996 (SI No. 390 of 1996), also made under the Prisons Act 1970, specify the classes of prisoners who may be detained at the refurbished former military detention barracks at the Curragh, County Kildare, and also provide for their management. They came into effect on 16 December 1996. In so far as relevant, the Saint Patrick's Institution Regulations 1960 and the Rules for the Government of Prison 1947 are also to apply to the refurbished prison.

TEMPORARY RELEASE

Discretion to grant   In *McHugh v. Minister for Justice*, Supreme Court, June 7, 1996, the Supreme Court rejected a challenge to the refusal of the respondent Minister to grant the applicant temporary release. The applicant had been convicted of murder of a member of the Garda Síochána, which until 1990 was a capital offence carrying the death penalty (see now the Criminal Justice Act 1990: 1990 Review, 195). His sentence had been commuted by the President to 40 years imprisonment without remission. The applicant sought relief in the form of *mandamus* on the ground that he had not been given temporary release by the Minister when he wished to visit his mother who was not in good health. He submitted that he would have been happy to have had a release under escort and that a similar concession had been extended to other prisoners, some also serving long sentences. The High Court refused leave to seek judicial review at the *ex parte* stage on the basis that this was a matter exclusively within the discretion of the Minister and that the court had no jurisdiction to intervene.

On appeal, the Supreme Court invited counsel for the applicant and respondent to appear before it. Section 2 of the Criminal Justice Act 1960 provides that the Minister may make rules providing for the temporary release of prisoners, subject to such conditions, if any, as may be imposed in each particular case. The relevant rules made under section 2 are the Criminal Justice (Temporary Release) Rules 1960. Section 5 of the 1960 Act provides that the currency of the sentence, if any, of a person temporarily released under the Act may at the time of the release or at any time during or after the period of release be suspended by the Minister if he thinks fit in respect of the whole or part of the period.

Rejecting the application, the Supreme Court held that no distinction fell to be made between temporary release in the generally understood meaning of that term or any form of release under escort, and that both were exclusively a matter within the Minister's discretion. The Court considered that there was nothing to be inquired into and that no useful purpose would be served by sending this matter back to the High Court with an indication that an order granting such inquiry should be made. It is unfortunate that the matter was dealt with in this summary manner, since the Court made no comment on the extent to which the Minister's discretion was to be exercised. It cannot have intended to convey the impression that the discretion was not subject to judicial review, since this would be inconsistent with existing authority on the matter: see *The State (Murphy) v. Kielt* [1984] I.R. 458 (H.C. & S.C.); [1982] I.L.R.M. 475 (H.C.); [1985] I.L.R.M. 141 (S.C.), discussed by Byrne, (1983) *D.U.L.J. (n.s.)* 69.

Rules for prisons and places of detention   The Temporary Release of Offenders (Unit A Castlerea) Rules 1996 (SI No. 360 of 1996), made under the Criminal Justice Act 1960, provide for the temporary release of offenders held at the prison in Castlerea. They came into effect on December 2, 1996. The Temporary Release of Offenders (The Curragh) Rules 1996 (SI No. 391 of 1996), also made under the Criminal Justice Act 1960, provide for the temporary release of offenders held at the prison at the Curragh. They came into effect on December 16, 1996.

Restitution

Eoin O'Dell, Trinity College, Dublin

The genius of the Common Law is its capacity for organic growth and evolution. Though this process may be quite slow at certain times and in certain legal areas, recent years have borne witness to a spectacular and exciting construction of a modern law of Restitution in common law jurisdictions throughout the world. This year saw Irish law participate in that development.

In the case concerning *The Bricklayers' Hall*, Keane J. in the Supreme Court described Restitution as "separate from both contract and tort" (*Dublin Corporation v. Building and Allied Trade Union* [1996] 2 I.R. 468, 483; [1996] 2 I.L.R.M. 547, 558). By means of the law of contract, the common law recognises and enforces obligations which are assumed voluntarily by the parties to an agreement; by means of the law of tort, the common law recognises and enforces obligations which are imposed by operation of law to compensate for wrong. It is now clear that by means of the law of Restitution, "in a variety of distinct categories of cases", the law recognises and enforces "an obligation on the part of the defendant to make fair and just restitution for a benefit derived at the expense of the plaintiff" (*Pavey & Matthews v. Paul* (1987) 162 C.L.R. 221, 256 *per* Deane J.; approved [1996] 2 I.R. 468, 483; [1996] 2 I.L.R.M. 547, 558 *per* Keane J.).

As to the manner in which such an obligation arises, Keane J. observed that "while there is seldom any problem in ascertaining whether two essential preconditions for the application of the doctrine have been met – *i.e.* an enrichment of the defendant the expense of the plaintiff – considerably more difficulty has been experienced in determining when the enrichment should be regarded as 'unjust' and whether there are any reasons why, even where it can be regarded as 'unjust', restitution should nevertheless be denied to the plaintiff." ([1996] 2 I.R. 468, 483; [1996] 2 I.L.R.M. 547, 558). This passage seems to predicate the obligation to make restitution upon four "essential preconditions": whether there was (i) an enrichment to the defendant (ii) at the expense of the plaintiff, (iii) in circumstances in which the law will require restitution (*i.e.* the 'unjust' phase of the enquiry), (iv) where there is no reason why restitution will be withheld. Of course, since they are all described as essential, all four enquiries will have to be answered in the plaintiff's favour before an order for restitution can be made. Consequently, the light sketch of the law of Restitution in this chapter will be organised around these four enquiries, (and the treatment will be more concerned with what the law now is rather than with where it has come from; on which see generally O'Dell, "The Principle Against Unjust Enrichment" (1992) 14 *DULJ* (*ns*) 27).

ENRICHMENT

As Keane J. observed, there is often little difficulty in determining whether a defendant has received a benefit. This is particularly true where the defendant has received money: it "has the peculiar character of a universal medium of exchange. By its receipt, the recipient is inevitably benefited." (*BP v. Hunt* [1979] W.L.R. 783, 799 *per* Goff J.). Thus, the recipient of money is incontrovertibly benefited.

Where, however, the benefit is not in money but in kind, such as the receipt of property or of a service, some difficulties may arise. "By their nature, services cannot be restored; nor, in many cases can goods be restored ..." (*ibid*). Furthermore, since the focus of this enquiry is upon the position of the defendant, it may be that the defendant could credibly claim in the circumstances that the good or benefit received did not in fact result in an enrichment: "benefits in kind have value to a particular individual only so far as he chooses to give them value" (Birks *An Introduction to the Law of Restitution* (Oxford, rev. ed., 1989) p. 109). This argument from "subjective devaluation" (*ibid*) reduced the value of the benefit received by the defendant in *Ministry for Defence v. Ashman* (1993) 66 P&CR 195 (CA). To counter a defendant's argument from subjective devaluation, a plaintiff may seek to show that the receipt of the benefit in kind has as incontrovertibly benefited the recipient as the receipt of money would have done. Judicially approved as "a neat phrase" (*Proctor & Gamble v. Peter Cremer, The Manila* [1988] 3 All E.R. 843, 855 *per* Hirst J.), such an "incontrovertible benefit" will be made out where "the defendant gained a financial benefit readily realisable without detriment to himself or has been saved expense which he must inevitably have incurred" (*ibid*, citing Goff and Jones *The Law of Restitution* (3rd ed, Butterworths, 1986), p. 148; see now (4th ed., 1993), p. 172; *cp* pp. 22 *et seq*; see also *Peel v. Canada* (1993) 98 D.L.R. (4th) 140). Thus, where a defendant has received either a readily realisable benefit or has been saved an inevitable expense, "no reasonable man" in the position of the defendant "could seriously deny that he has been benefited" (Burrows *The Law of Restitution* (Butterworths, 1993), pp. 9-10), and no recourse to the argument from subjective devaluation will be possible.

Apart from demonstrating an incontrovertible benefit, Prof Birks (pp. 114-115) argues that the argument from subjective devaluation may also be rebutted if the plaintiff shows that the defendant, as a reasonable man, "freely accepted" the benefit in question "with an opportunity of rejection and with actual or presumed knowledge that they were to be paid for" (Goff and Jones, (1st ed., 1966), pp. 30-31; compare now (4th ed., 1993), p. 19). In so accepting, the defendant has demonstrated that the goods or services in question represented a benefit or an enrichment to him, thus denying to him the argument from subjective devaluation. However, as a test of enrichment, free acceptance has had its critics (e.g. Beatson "Benefit, Reliance and the Structure of Unjust Enrichment" in *The Use and Abuse of Unjust Enrichment* (Oxford, 1991), p. 21), and Prof Burrows has suggested as a narrower alternative that a defendant is enriched "where the plaintiff has performed what the defendant bargained for" because, in general, a defendant who has bargained for a performance will consider himself to be benefited by it, and thus cannot have recourse to the argument from subjective devaluation. (Burrows, *The Law of Restitution* (Butterworths, 1993), p. 14). Notwithstanding the critics, Prof Birks has continued to defend the utility of free acceptance (Birks "In Defence of Free Acceptance" in Burrows (ed.), *Essays on the Law of Restitution* (Oxford, 1991), p. 105) and, in the context of enrichment, it has been adopted in Australia in *Brenner v. First Artists Management Pty Ltd* (1993) 2 V.L.R. 221, 258-259 *per* Byrne J.

All of these tests are concerned to establish the fact of a defendant's enrichment. It must be borne in mind that once the fact of enrichment has been determined, the extent or value of that enrichment must thereafter also be determined. Very often, of course, especially where the defendant has received money, to answer the first question will also be to answer the second. But where he has received a benefit in kind, the above tests will merely demonstrate that he has been enriched; it will then be necessary to calculate the value of that benefit in kind, the amount by which he has been enriched.

AT THE PLAINTIFF'S EXPENSE

If it has been determined – on whatever test of enrichment – that the defendant has been enriched, it is necessary that such a benefit, have been derived at the plaintiff's expense. It is the equivalent of a causation requirement, linking in any given case this particular defendant with this particular plaintiff. The phrase "serves to identify the person by or on whose behalf the payment was made and to whom repayment is due" (*Kleinwort Benson v. Birmingham City Co.* [1996] 3 All E.R. 733, 742 *per* Evans L.J.); the words "do no more than to point that the immediate source of the unjust enrichment [in the defendant's hands] must be the plaintiff. ([1996] 3 All E.R. 733, 749 *per* Morritt L.J.).

First, the most obvious sense in which a defendant's enrichment can be at a plaintiff's expense is when the plaintiff's benefit has directly "passed to the defendant from the plaintiff. This sense can be rendered by the words 'by subtraction from' . . .", in that the defendant has been enriched "by subtraction from" the plaintiff (Birks, p. 23).

Second, Prof Birks has argued that where the defendant intercepts money certainly intended for the plaintiff, he is as surely enriched at the plaintiff's expense: "[i]f the wealth in question would certainly have arrived in the plaintiff if had not been intercepted by the defendant *en route* from the third party, it is true to say that the plaintiff has lost by the defendant's gain" (Birks, pp. 133-134). Though this notion of "interceptive subtraction" has proved controversial (e.g. Smith (1991) 11 *OJLS* 481), it seems to form part of Irish law. For example, in *HKN Invest OY v. Incotrade PVT Ltd* [1993] 3 I.R. 152, Costello J. held that where a promoter purports to contract in the name of a company to be incorporated, and without fraud receives a commission for services which the company is to render, "he has received the commission for the benefit of the company which is to be incorporated and not for his own benefit". ([1993] 3 I.R. 152, 162). The commission was certainly meant for the company, and in intercepting it, the promoter has been enriched at the company's expense. Again, where a donor had instructed a life assurance company to name the plaintiff as beneficiary, but the company had failed to do so and paid out to the defendant who was the beneficiary originally named in the policy, the defendant's enrichment was at the expense of the plaintiff. (See O'Dell [1997] *LMCLQ* 197, 201-202, discussing *Shanahan v. Redmond* (High Court, June 21, 1994, Carroll J.)).

Third, (and whether enrichment is direct or interceptive) it is possible to adopt a narrow approach to the question of whether a plaintiff's benefit has reached a defendant, by insisting for example upon rules akin to tracing to identify the route by which the enrichment left the one and reached the other (*semble* as done by Stoljar *The Law of Quasi-Contract* (2nd ed, Sydney, 1989) chapter 5). However, cases such as *Kleinwort Benson* (above, and following it *Brennan v. Brighton BC* (*The Times*, 15 May 1997) demonstrate a much more robust approach, rejecting the defence of passing on (below), and eschewing a strict interpretation of this requirement (see in particular [1996] 3 All E.R. 733, 749e *per* Morritt L.J.) in favour of seeking merely to discover whether there was a sufficient nexus between the plaintiff and the defendant.

Restitution for Wrongs A defendant who been enriched by subtraction from a plaintiff is therefore enriched at the plaintiff's expense. It has also been held that a defendant who has done a wrong to the plaintiff is likewise enriched at the plaintiff's expense: thus, the "requirement that the defendant be unjustly enriched 'at the expense of' of the plaintiff can mean that the enrichment is 'by doing wrong to' or 'by subtraction from' the plaintiff. Hence a plaintiff can succeed by showing that he or she was the victim of a wrong which enriched the defendant ... or that the defendant was enriched by receiving the plaintiff's money or property." (*Commissioner v. Royal Insurance* (1994) 182 C.L.R. 51, 73 *per* Mason C.J.; see also *Macmillan v. Bishopsgate Investment*

Trust (No. 3) [1995] 3 All E.R. 747, 757-758 *per* Millett L.J. (*rvsd* on other grounds [1996] 1 All E.R. 585); *Halifax BS v. Thomas* [1995] 4 All E.R. 673, 677 *per* Peter Gibson L.J.; see generally Birks, 39-44; 132; 313 *et seq*). In principle, it seems therefore that a defendant who has profited by his wrong is liable to make restitution of those profits to the plaintiff. As to what constitutes a wrong, at least as a matter of Irish law, it encompasses torts, breaches of contract, infringements of intellectual property rights, and breaches of equitable duties. In all such cases, the principle against unjust enrichment supplies a justification for the availability of damages in the restitution measure to strip the wrongdoer of the profits of his wrong.

Thus, as to damages in the restitution measure for torts, in *Maher v. Collins*, the Supreme Court affirmed that the primary measure of damages in tort is the compensation measure, but continued that this "is not to say that there may not be exceptional and particular cases where the defendant's conduct has been calculated by him to make a profit for himself which may well exceed any compensation likely to be payable to the plaintiff. In such rare and exceptional circumstances other considerations may apply" ([1975] I.R. 232, 238 *per* O'Higgins C.J.). The stripping of such profits, the reversal of such unjust enrichment, from the defendant, and consequent restitution to the plaintiff, is plainly envisaged here. Again, in *Hickey v. Roches Stores* [1993] *Restitution Law Review* 196 (July 14, 1976), Finlay J. envisaged a similar restitutionary remedy both for breach of contract and for tort: thus, his statement of principle that an intentional *mala fide* wrongdoer can be stripped of his profits "whether the form of his wrongdoing constitutes a tort or a breach of contract" ([1993] *RLR* 196, 208) is plainly consistent with the approach of the Chief Justice in *Maher v. Collins* and confirms that damages in the restitution measure are available as a matter of Irish law for torts and for breach of contract. Further, as to infringement of intellectual property rights, it has been held that a plaintiff whose copyright has been infringed can have restitution of the profits which the defendant gained from his infringement (*Allied Discount Card v. Bord Fáilte Eireann* [1991] 2 I.R. 185). Furthermore, as to breaches of equitable duties, where a plaintiff has been held liable to account to the defendant for profits from breaches of confidence, the "basis on which such an account of profits should be ordered is that there should not be unjust enrichment on the part of the wrongdoer" (*House of Spring Gardens v. Point Blank* [1984] I.R. 611, 707 *per* Griffin J.).

THE UNJUST FACTOR

"Unjust" is an open-textured concept, which, in the particular context of the principle against unjust enrichment, has often engendered judicial unease. In the *Bricklayers' Hall* case, Keane J. deftly deflected such fears by pointing out that "the law, as it has been developed, has avoided the dangers of 'palm-tree justice' by identifying whether the case belongs in *a specific category* which justifies so describing the enrichment: possible instances are money paid under duress, or as a result of a mistake of fact or law or accompanied by a total failure of consideration" ([1996] 2 I.R. 468, 484; [1996] 2 I.L.R.M. 547, 558; emphasis added; cp *Moses v. Macferlan* (1760) 2 Burr. 1005, 1012). Thus, an enrichment to the defendant at the plaintiff's expense will be unjust because the enrichment was transferred by mistake, or under duress, or for a consideration which had failed.

Mistake   In *Barclays Bank v. Simms* [1980] Q.B. 677, Goff J. deduced from the authorities the principles which govern liability to make restitution of money paid under a mistake:

> (1) If a person pays money to another under a mistake of fact which *causes* him to make the payment, he is *prima facie* entitled to recover it as money paid under a mistake of fact. (2) His claim may however fail if (a) the payer intends that the payee shall have the money *at all events*, whether the fact be true or false, or is deemed in law so to intend; or (b) the payment is made for *good consideration*, in particular if the money is paid to discharge, and does discharge, a debt owed to the payee (or a principal on whose behalf he is authorised to receive the payment) by the payer or by a third party by whom he is authorised to discharge the debt; or (c) the payee has *changed his position* in good faith, or is deemed in law to have done so.

> . . . The following propositions are inconsistent with the simple princi-ple of recovery established in the authorities: (i) That to ground recov-ery, the mistake must have induced the payer to believe that he was liable to pay the money to his payee or his principal. (ii) That to ground recovery, the mistake must have been 'as between' the payer and the payee. Rejection of this test has led to its reformulation . . . in terms which in my judgment mean no more than that the mistake must have caused the payment. . . . ([1980] Q.B. 677, 695)

On the facts, a bank which had mistakenly paid on foot of a cheque, for-getting a stop order; was held entitled to recover their mistaken payment. As to the Goff J.'s first proposition that if "a person pays money to another under a mistake of fact which *causes* him to make the payment, he is *prima facie* entitled to recover it as money paid under a mistake of fact" a mistake will be said to have caused a payment if it appears that "without the mistake on the part of the payer, the payment would not have been made" (*ANZ. v. Westpac* (1987-1988) 164 C.L.R. 662, 672 *per curiam*). In the later *David Securities v.*

Commonwealth Bank of Australia (1992) 175 C.L.R. 353 the High Court of Australia approved and adopted the *Simms* formulation, preferring it to formulations which predicated liability upon whether the mistake was fundamental or as to a liability to pay: both were rejected on the grounds that if "the payer has made the payment because of a mistake, his or her intention to transfer the money is vitiated and the recipient has been enriched." ((1992) 175 C.L.R. 353, 378 *per* Mason C.J. and Deane, Toohey, Gaudron and McHugh JJ.; emphasis added. Dawson J. concurred; Brennan J. delivered a judgment to like effect on this point.)

Irish law is probably to the same effect. The starting point is the decision of Budd J. in the High Court in *National Bank v. O'Connor & Bowmaker* (1969) 103 I.L.T.R. 73. Thornton was an employee of the National Bank. He ran a large, criminally fraudulent, investment scheme. O'Connor, an investor in the scheme was owed £17,000. Thornton fraudulently obtained two National Bank drafts in that amount and gave them to O'Connor, who placed £12,000 on deposit in Bowmakers Bank. The plaintiffs claimed to be entitled to recover that £12,000 "on the basis that it was recoverable in law as money paid under a mistake of fact." ((1969) 103 I.L.T.R. 73, 88). The National Bank mistakenly believed that the drafts presented by O'Connor were valid, whereas in fact they were invalid as a consequence of Thornton's fraud. Budd J. had to face largely the same questions as would face Goff J. eleven years later in *Simms*, and Budd J.'s conclusions were largely similar to those reached later by Goff J. First, after a review of the authorities, Budd J. concluded that actionable mistake is not "confined to such a mistake, as would, if the mistaken fact were true, have placed on the payer, as between him and the payee, a liability to pay the money". Second, Budd J.'s decision seems ambiguous as between fundamental and causative mistakes, since he held that "it is has been proved that it has been paid under a mistake of fact. *It must be a fundamental mistake* but no question really arises here as to that since such mistakes as arose were obviously of that nature in this case. It is of course necessary, in order to establish a mistake of fact to show that the fact supposed to be true was untrue and that *the money would not have been paid if was known that the fact was untrue.*" ((1969) 103 I.L.T.R. 73, 94; emphasis added). The first italic suggests that Budd J. leaned towards fundamentality, the second, that he leaned towards causative mistakes. For the reasons given in *David Securities*, this ambiguity must be resolved in favour of the view that if a mistake causes a payment, that is *prima facie* sufficient for an action in restitution. Furthermore, in the later case of *Webb v. Ireland* [1988] I.R. 353 Blayney J. in the High Court seems to have assumed such a test.

In a dispute over the ownership of the hoard including the Derrynaflan chalice, Blayney J. in the High Court held that the plaintiffs had title. The plaintiffs had delivered the hoard into the custody of the National Museum, which restored the chalice: the "staff of the National Museum honestly believed that the State was the owner of the hoard, and what work was done was done in that belief" ([1988] I.R. 353, 370). The Museum was held entitled to recover the value of the service so mistakenly rendered from the plaintiffs who had thereby received the benefit of the restoration of the chalice. It is quite clear that the museum staff's mistake *caused* the enrichment, and for Blayney J. that was sufficient. The plaintiffs' duty to make such restitution would be set-off against the defendants' *prima facie* liability in detinue for having detained the hoard to which the plaintiffs had title. On appeal, the Supreme Court held that the defendants had title, so the restitution issue did not arise. However, it is submitted that the decision of Blayney J. on that issue ought to be followed, since it resolves the ambiguity in Budd J.'s judgment in *O'Connor* consistently with the decisions in *Simms* and *David Securities*.

Blayney J.'s judgment in *Webb* also illustrates another very important point: on the facts (and following *Greenwood v. Bennett* [1973] 1 Q.B. 195) the plaintiff who had mistakenly improved a chattel was entitled to restitution; more generally, a plaintiff who mistakenly renders a service which thereby enriches a defendant is entitled to restitution of the value of the service so rendered (e.g. *Rover International v. Canon Film Sales (No. 3)* [1989] 1 W.L.R. 912; [1989] 3 All E.R. 423; Birks (1990) 2 *JCL* 227). The action for restitution for mistake, though often described as an action to recover *money* paid under mistake, is not confined to money, but applies to *all* enrichments, such as goods and services: thus, a plaintiff who mistakenly transfers an enrichment is entitled to recover back the amount of money so transferred or the value of the goods or services so transferred. More generally, since "enrichment" and "unjust" are independent enquiries, a plaintiff who successfully fulfils each element will make out a case for restitution.

Finally, it was at one time thought that a plaintiff who paid under a mistake of law could not recover (e.g. *Casey v. The Irish Sailors and Soldiers Land Trust* [1937] I.R. 209 (SCt)); but that rule had been substantially undermined by exceptions (e.g. *Dolan v. Neligan* [1967] I.R. 247; *Rogers v. Louth County Council* [1981] I.R. 265; [1981] I.L.R.M. 143; *cp East Cork Foods v. O'Dwyer Steel* [1978] I.R. 103, 108-109 *per* Henchy J.); so that in *Pine Valley v. Minister for Environment* Henchy J. held that "so much of the purchase price as was attributable to the planning permission was paid under a mistake of law, but in my opinion it would be recoverable no less than if it had been paid under a mistake of fact" ([1987] I.R. 23, 42); and in the *Bricklayers' Hall* case, Keane J. referred to the cause of action as being based upon "a mistake of fact *or law*". [1996] 2 I.R. 468, 484; [1996] 2 I.L.R.M. 547, 558 (emphasis added)). Similar conclusions have been reached in other common law jurisdictions. In Canada, it has been argued that "[o]nce a doctrine of restitution or unjust enrichment is recognized, the distinction as to mistake of law and mistake of fact simply becomes meaningless". (*Hydro Electric Commission of Nepean v. Ontario Hydro* (1982) 132 D.L.R. (3d) 193, 210 *per* Dickson J, dissenting).

Thus, both "species of mistake, if one can be distinguished from the other, should, in an appropriate case, be considered as factors which can make an enrichment at the plaintiff's expense 'unjust' . . .". (*Air Canada v. British Colombia* (1989) 59 D.L.R. (4th) 161, 192 *per* La Forest J. for the majority, approving Dickson J. in *Nepean*, and overruling the mistake of law bar as a matter of Canadian law). This is because, if the proper focus of the enquiry is to be the effect of the mistake upon the mind of the plaintiff, then to focus on the type of mistake is illogical, whether that is a liability mistake or a mistake of law, as the High Court of Australia explained in *David Securities*, (above)).

Duress   Where a plaintiff has been compelled to transfer an enrichment, as where he has made a payment under duress, he can restitution of that enrichment. For example, in *Astley v. Reynolds* (1731) 2 Str. 915 and *Somes v. British Empire Shipping Co.* (1860) 8 H.L.C. 338, where the defendants threatened to retain the plaintiffs' property unless the plaintiffs paid higher sums than were due, the plaintiffs had restitution of the excess as money paid under duress. So far as the law of restitution is concerned, such duress is made out by duress of the person (e.g. *Barton v. Armstrong* [1976] A.C. 104), duress of goods (*Astley, Somes*), and economic duress (e.g. *Universe Tankships of Monrovia v. ITWF, The Universe Sentinel* [1983] 1 A.C. 366; *Dimskal Shipping Co. v. ITWF, The Evia Luck (No. 2)* [1992] 2 A.C. 152). Though once explained as turning on the overbearing of the plaintiff's will, the cases now stress that underlying these categories of duress is the common theme that the defendant's illegitimate pressure caused the enrichment.

As to when pressures are to be regarded as "illegitimate", though there are in the judgments in the cases so far mentioned traces of an argument that if a pressure is otherwise unlawful it must be illegitimate and if it is otherwise lawful it must be legitimate, the law has not in fact adopted this position. For example if a breach of contract is unlawful, then it would follow that a threat to breach a contract would constitute illegitimate pressure, and a payment exacted by such a threat would for that reason be recoverable; however, although there are many cases in which such a threat has been held to be illegitimate thus allowing for restitution (e.g. *The Universe Sentinel* (above); *The Evia Luck* (above)), there are others in which the threat has not been held to be illegitimate (e.g. *B & S v. Victor Green* [1984] I.C.R. 419). It follows that some unlawful pressures are not illegitimate. On the other hand, the Court of Appeal has also accepted that a threat to do a lawful act may nonetheless be illegitimate (*CTN Cash and Carry v. Gallagher* [1994] 4 All E.R. 714; on the facts, the Court held that a threat by a monopoly to refuse to supply was not illegitimate (though in Ireland this may be contrary to section 5 of the Competition Act 1991)). It follows that some lawful pressures are not legitimate. As to the alternative test for illegitimacy, although some commentators seem to favour a test based on the *mala fides* of the threatener (Birks, p. 183; Burrows,

p. 181), the Court of Appeal in the *CTN* case seemed prepared to answer, on a case by case basis, the question of whether a particular pressure is illegitimate; and it is submitted that this approach is, on balance, preferable to the *mala fides* test. Further, the Court in that case, and Lord Goff in the House of Lords in the earlier *Woolwich v. IRC (No. 2)* [1993] A.C. 70, emphasised that the heads of illegitimacy are not closed.

As to when such illegitimate pressure may be said to have "caused" the enrichment, it seems that it is enough that the pressure is *a* reason (not *the* reason, nor the *predominant* reason nor the *clinching* reason) for the plaintiff's actions (*Barton v. Armstrong* (above); *The Evia Luck* (above)).

Three further points must be made. First, as with mistake, the action for restitution for duress, though often described as an action to recover *money* paid under duress, is not confined to money, in principle it applies to all enrichments, such as goods and services. Thus, where a local authority is statutorily liable to abate a nuisance, and compels a plaintiff to abate the nuisance, the authority has received an enrichment by duress for which it must make restitution: the plaintiff "can recover the expenses from the sanitary authority as money paid . . . as the result of the duress or *prima facie* compulsion of the notice served by themselves." (*Hackett v. Smith* [1917] 2 I.R. 508, 528 *per* Campbell C.J.; cp *id* at p. 520). Second, the action for the recovery of benefits transferred on foot of actual undue influence is the equitable counterpart of the common law doctrine of duress: in both cases, the plaintiff has been subject to actual pressure, and recovers any benefits transferred as a consequence. "In the days in which common law duress was thought to be confined to two or three restricted types, it made sense to see equitable actual undue influence as a supplement" (Birks p. 184; cp the speech of Lord Cross in *Barton v. Armstrong* (above)); but, at least from the perspective of the law of restitution, there is probably nowadays no practical distinction between illegitimate pressure and actual undue influence. Third, equity also contains policy motivated supplements to its actual undue influence jurisdiction: it can presume undue influence or find improvidence or unconscionability; and if the presumption is not rebutted or if a transfer has been found improvident or unconscionable, restitution of any benefits transferred can be ordered, (though the precise theoretical basis for such restitution is a matter of debate in the texts, compare Birks, p. 204; Burrows, p. 189; Bamforth [1995] *LMCLQ* 538; O'Dell [1997] *CLJ* 71).

Such coercion as is comprised by duress, undue influence and so on, does not exhaust the range of compelled enrichments for which the law will order restitution: a plaintiff who has been compelled to discharge the debt of another, can have restitution from that other in the amount of that enrichment (*Moule v. Garrett* (1872) L.R. 7 Exch. 101; *Brooks Wharf v. Goodman* [1937] 1 K.B. 543). Take, for example, a tort action, in which D1 has been compelled to pay the full amount of damages to the plaintiff in circumstances in which it is subsequently found on appeal that D2 is 100% liable to the plaintiff: D1 has been compelled to discharge D2's debt, and can have restitution from D2. There were the facts of the leading Irish case of *East Cork Foods v. O'Dwyer Steel* [1978] I.R. 103, and in the Supreme Court, Henchy J, following *Moule v. Garrett*, held that D1 "could recover the £20,000 in an action for money had and received, ...because it would be unjust and inequitable to allow D2 to keep the money. To refuse the claim would mean that D2 would be unjustly enriched." ([1978] I.R. 103, 110-111). However, since the basis of the action is that the plaintiff must have been *compelled* to discharge the defendant's debt, if the plaintiff is held voluntarily so to have discharged, he has not made out the unjust factor and his claim must fail (*Owen v. Tate* [1976] Q.B. 402 states the rule, though controversially – see e.g. Beatson, pp. 177-205).

Although the plaintiffs in *Moule* and *East Cork Foods* were compelled to discharge their defendants' debts by operation of law, it has been held that if the circumstances are such that the practical compulsion felt by the plaintiff is equivalent to that in *Moule* and *East Cork Foods*, such a plaintiff may again recover. The leading case is *Exall v. Partridge* (1799) 8 T.R. 308. The plaintiff had left his carriage on the defendant's premises for repair. The defendant had failed to pay his rent, so the defendant's landlord distrained, and took the carriage. To recover the carriage, the plaintiff paid off the defendant's rent to the landlord, and successfully sought restitution from the defendant. *Exall* did not fare well in the later *England v. Marsden* (1866) L.R. 1 C.P. 529, but was rehabilitated in England in *Edmunds v. Wallingford* (1885) 14 Q.B.D. 811. In Ireland, its status is unclear in the light of *Beresford v. Kennedy* (1887) 21 I.L.T.R. 17 and *Gormley v. Johnston* (1895) 29 I.L.T.R. 69 (in both cases, the plaintiffs' cattle on the defendants' lands were seized to pay the defendants' debts; the plaintiffs discharged those debts, but failed in their actions against the defendants substantially on the grounds that the plaintiffs' cattle were trespassing, so that the plaintiffs' claims arose *ex turpi causa*), but it is submitted that the logic of Henchy J. in *East Cork Foods* applies here *mutatis* so that a plaintiff who is compelled by circumstances to discharge the debt of another can have restitution from that other.

In modern terms, the traditional action arising out the compulsory discharge of the debt of another seems to be composed of an unjust factor (compulsion) and an enrichment (the discharge of the other's debt saves that other an inevitable expense and thus constitutes an incontrovertible benefit). If that separation is made, at least two consequences follow: first that any unjust factor may be combined with that enrichment to generate an action in restitution; and second, conversely, the unjust factor of compulsion may be combined with another enrichment to generate an action in restitution. There is a third point related to the second: if the action arising out the practically compelled discharge of the debt of another (in *Exall*) is seen to be composed of an unjust factor (the practical compulsion) and an enrichment (the discharge), then that unjust factor of practical compulsion may be combined with another enrichment to generate an action in restitution. Let us take each such point in turn (in each case assuming that the other relevant enquiries have been resolved in the plaintiff's favour).

First, as to whether any unjust factor may be combined with an enrichment arising from the discharge of another's debt to generate an action in restitution, there would seem to be no possible objection in principle. For example, if a plaintiff mistakenly discharges the debt of another, the mistake would supply the unjust factor, the discharge would again constitute the enrichment, and the plaintiff can have restitution (cp Birks, pp. 189-190). Indeed, it "is clearly established in Canadian law that one who, acting under a mistake, discharges the obligation of another may succeed in a restitutionary claim . . ." (Maddaugh and McCamus, *The Law of Restitution* (Ontario, 1990), p. 282 citing *County of Carleton v. City of Ottawa* (1965) 52 D.L.R. (2d.) 220). An excellent Irish example is supplied by the old case of *Rochfort v. Earl of Belvidere* (1770) Wall L. 45. The real and personal estate of the deceased had devolved independently. The successor to the real estate, mistakenly believing that he had a liability to do so, had paid off a portion of a debt which it was held in this case had attached to the personal estate, and in this case recovered from the personal estate the amount so paid. As Budd J. put it in the High Court in the *Bricklayers' Hall* case, it "would seem from the report that *Moses v. Macferlan* [(1760) 2 Burr 1005] was employed to justify restitution in circumstances where the plaintiff had paid off the debt of the personal estate of the [deceased]. This would appear to be an example of a case in which the plaintiff had himself conferred the benefit on the defendant through mistake and where to allow the defendant to retain such a benefit would result in his being unjustly enriched at the plaintiff's expense." (High Court, March 6, 1996, at pp. 20-21 of the transcript). As it is with compulsion and mistake, so can it be in principle with other unjust factors.

Second, as to whether the unjust factor of compulsion (in *East Cork Foods* (above)) may be combined with another enrichment to generate an action in restitution, there would seem to be no possible objection in principle. For example, if a plaintiff is compelled by the defendant to render a service which the defendant is under a duty to render, the compulsion is again the unjust factor, and the discharge of the service would save the defendant the inevitable expense of providing it, thus incontrovertibly benefiting and thereby enriching him, and the plaintiff can again have restitution. An excellent example is supplied by *Gebhart v. Saunders* [1892] 2 Q.B. 452. The defendant was statutorily required to keep drains in repair, but the local authority compelled the plaintiff to repair them, (by serving a notice to abate the nuisance). The plaintiff successfully sued the defendant for the value of the service so rendered. Although there was a statutory ground for the plaintiff's claim, Charles J. affirmed that "the ordinary principle of law is applicable to this case apart from statute, the principle applicable to all cases where one man has been legally compelled to expend money on what another man ought to have done". ([1892] 2 Q.B. 452, 458). Again, since the basis of the action is that the plaintiff must have been *compelled* to discharge the defendant's liability, if the plaintiff is held voluntarily so to have discharged, he has not made out the unjust factor and his claim must fail: here the leading case is *Hackett v. Smith* [1917] 2 I.R. 508. The plaintiff was the owner of property which the defendant had leased, and the tenant had the duty under the lease to pay for all "impositions". The local authority served upon the plaintiff a notice to abate a nuisance. However, the plaintiff was a minor and ward of court, the notice of abatement was served upon the receiver of his estate, who merely handed it over to the solicitor "having carriage in the minor matter, who thereupon brought it to the notice of the Lord Chancellor, and an order was made directing that the required works be carried out" ([1917] 2 I.R. 508, 515). The plaintiff sued the defendant, claiming to have discharged an "imposition" which it was the defendant's duty to pay. Dealing with *Gebhart v. Saunders*, Campbell C.J. found the *dictum* of Charles J. in *Gebhart* "incomprehensible" since he was "at a loss to understand where, apart from the statute, the legal compulsion upon the plaintiff came from" (p. 521). He found "the greatest difficulty in attributing any element of duress or compulsion to the service of the notice on the occupier so long as he has a complete defence to any legal proceedings founded upon the notice" (p. 528). Thus, it seems that Campbell C.J. accepted that the plaintiff could in principle sue for duress or compulsion, but held that on facts like those of *Gebhart*, since the plaintiff had a defence, he could not be said to have been compelled. Likewise, here, Campbell C.J. held that "where the claim, based upon the service of a notice, is made by the person served to recover the expense of his compliance . . . from a third party, . . . the claimant can only succeed upon proof that the provisions of the Act have been strictly complied with, as otherwise his act will be that of a mere volunteer" (p. 520). Given that failure to comply with the particular notice on the facts did not "subject the person served to any liability for a penalty, *prima facie* or otherwise" (p. 529) there was no compulsion, and thus the payment was voluntary. Two points therefore emerge from *Hackett v. Smith*: first, support for the proposition that an action will lie for the compulsory discharge of the obligation of another to supply a service, and, second a holding on the facts that the plaintiff was not so compelled.

Third, as to whether the unjust factor of practical compulsion (in *Exall* (above)) may be combined with another enrichment to generate an action in restitution, there would seem to be no possible objection in principle. For example, if a plaintiff is practically compelled – by a necessity arising from a "political, social or moral responsibility" (*Peel v. Canada* (1993) 98 D.L.R. (4th) 140, 157; *cp* Birks, p. 193) – to render a valuable service to the defendant, the plaintiff can again have restitution. Thus, a plaintiff who buried a deceased, or hired an undertaker to bury the deceased, was compelled by the circumstances to render a valuable service to estate of the deceased, and recovered in restitution from the estate (respectively: *Rogers v. Price* (1829) Y.&J. 28 (the plaintiff-undertaker recovered *quantum meruit* for burial); *Jenkins v. Tucker* (1788) 1 H. Bl. 90 (the father of the deceased, in her husband's absence, arranged her burial, and, by analogy with *Exall* (above) succeeded against her estate)). Likewise, a party who rendered a necessary service to an *incapax*, or who paid for that service to be rendered, can have restitution (respectively: *Matheson v. Smiley* (1932) 2 D.L.R. 787 (a surgeon who sought to save the life of a suicide recovered the value of his services from the next of kin of the suicide); *Re Rhodes* (1890) 44 Ch.D. 94 (relatives paid for the treatment of the *incapax* in an asylum for over a quarter of a century; the Court of Appeal accepted that their action would lie in principle). And the railway company which stabled a horse, which it had carried but which had not been collected, was entitled to restitution from the owner of the horse (*Great Northern Rly v. Swaffield* (1874) L.R. 8 Ex. 132; though such a plaintiff probably would have no proprietary interest in the horse, whether by lien (*id, Nicholson v. Chapman* (1793) 2 H. Bl. 254) or by bailment (*Flannery v. Dean* [1995] 2 I.L.R.M. 393)).

In all such cases, the plaintiff must genuinely have been acting under the practical compulsion arising from the necessity of the circumstances; so the plaintiffs are subjected to particular scrutiny by the courts. It was important, in *Rogers v. Price* that the undertaker had been set in motion by a relative of the deceased, in *Jenkins v. Tucker* that the plaintiff had been the deceased's father, in *Matheson v. Smiley* that the plaintiff was a doctor. On the other hand, in *Re Rhodes*, the Court characterised the plaintiffs' actions as voluntary – since they did not confer the benefit with an intention to be repaid – and the claim therefore failed. Furthermore, though the action is sound in principle, the authorities do not speak with one voice, and natural caution has often become outright hostility (e.g. *Falcke v. Scottish Imperial Insurance Company* (1886) 34 Ch.D. 234) as a consequence of which courts in England – unlike in Canada after *Peel* – have failed to take the step to rationalise the law in favour of this cause of action (e.g. *The Goring* [1988] A.C. 831 (the House of Lords refused to extend maritime salvage to fresh water rescues); see Rose (1989) 9 *OJLS* 167).

Failure of Consideration   The third example of an unjust factor given by Keane J. in the *Bricklayers' Hall* case is failure of consideration. In this, the plaintiff claims that the basis upon which a benefit had been conferred upon the defendant had failed, so that the defendant consequently should not retain it and ought to make restitution. Thus, for example, in the context of a payment in advance on foot of a contract which was frustrated "the payment was originally conditional. The condition of retaining it was eventual performance. Accordingly, when that condition fails, the right to retain the money must simultaneously fail." (*Fibrosa Spolka Ackyjna v. Fairbarin Lawson Combe Barbour* [1943] A.C. 32, 65 *per* Lord Wright). Again, "... where a plaintiff has paid money in pursuance of his obligations under a contract and the consideration for which he entered into the contract totally fails, he may bring an action for the return of the money so paid (as money had and received to his use). . . ." (*United Dominions Trust v. Shannon Caravans* [1976] I.R. 225, 231 *per* Griffin J.).

The word "consideration" is used by the common law in at least two senses, first in the context of the formation of a contract where it is a doctrine of the law of contract, and second in the context of a cause of action in restitution – usually consequent upon the failure of a contract – where it is a doctrine of the law of restitution. Though in the law of contract, "consideration" means the promise or its price, in the law of restitution "when one is considering the law of failure of consideration and of the quasi-contractual right to recover money on that ground, it is generally speaking, not the promise which is referred to as the consideration, *but the performance of that promise*. The money was paid to secure performance, and, if performance fails, the inducement which brought about the payment is not fulfilled." (*Fibrosa v. Fairbairn* [1943] A.C. 32, 47 *per* Lord Simon, emphasis supplied). Thus, if a plaintiff has paid for a *performance* which he did not receive, he may recover back his payment as money paid for a consideration which had failed. In the 1995 Review (p. 202), it was suggested that to transcend any ambiguity caused by using the word "consideration" in two distinct senses, the cause of action in restitution could be described as "failure of basis" since that is what it is (cp Swadling [1993] *All E.R. Rev* 349, 351). But "[o]ld habits die hard. The phrase 'total failure of consideration' is one on which common lawyers cut their teeth" (Birks "Failure of Consideration" in Rose (ed.), *Consensus ad idem* (London, Sweet & Maxwell, 1996), p. 179) and such a change may be difficult to make.

Another has proven even more difficult. In *Fibrosa*, Lord Wright stated that the rationale for the cause of action was that the condition of performance under which the defendant had received was not fulfilled; Birks argues in that essay that as a matter of logic, that condition is as much unfulfilled by a part performance as by none, and that a plaintiff who has paid but received only a partial performance is as much entitled to restitution of the payment as the plaintiff who has paid and received no performance; though in the context of the plaintiff who has received a partial performance, that plaintiff as a condition of restitution, must also make counter-restitution of the value of any benefit so received by that partial performance (see also McKendrick, "Total Failure of Consideration and Counter-Restitution" in Birks (ed.), *Laundering and Tracing* (Oxford, 1995), p. 217). Instead of undertaking this apportionment exercise, however, the law seems to deny any remedy to the plaintiff who has received a partial performance by insisting that the failure of consideration upon which the plaintiff claims is a *total* failure (by which is meant that the plaintiff received *no* part of that performance for which he had bargained) rather than a partial failure. Despite this absolute position, there are many cases in which the courts have discounted receipts by the plaintiff so as to char- acterise the relevant failure as total and not partial (Burrows p. 260; Barker [1993] *LMCLQ* 291; Birks and Swadling [1996] *All E.R. Rev* 366, 385), and others in which the courts seem prepared to undertake the apportionment exercise (*David Securities v. Commonwealth Bank of Australia* (1992) 175 C.L.R. 353, 383; *Goss v. Chilcott* [1996] A.C. 788, 798). Consequently, signs "are appearing in judgments throughout the common law, as appropriate cases arise for decision" that failure of consideration is being reformulated "upon a more principled basis" (*Westdeutsche Landesbank v. Islington* [1996] 2 W.L.R. 802, 807 *per* Lord Goff) such as that outlined above by which a partial failure of basis will generate a cause of action in restitution subject to the plaintiff making counter-restitution for any benefits received.

The circumstances in which the action for failure of basis will lie are various; in particular, it will lie for the recovery of benefits transferred under an ineffective contract: as where the contract is unenforceable for non-compliance with statutory formalities (*Delgman v. Guaranty Trust* [1953] 3 D.L.R. 785) or because it is 'subject to contract' (*Lowis v. Wilson* [1949] I.R. 347); or where it is void *ab initio* for the non-incorporation or incapacity of one of the parties (*Rover v. Canon* (above); *Westdeutsche* (above); *In re PMPA Garage (Longmile) Ltd (No. 2)* [1992] 1 I.R. 332); or where the contract becomes void for frustration (*Fibrosa* (above)); or where the contract is discharged by breach (for example, where a defendant has failed to make good title, as in *Woodchester Investments v. O'Driscoll* (High Court, July 27, 1995, Barron J.), discussed in the 1995 Review, 203-4), though in the context of breach, it is a matter of dispute whether the right to restitution is to be denied to the party in breach (e.g. Birks, p. 234, Burrows, p. 272). Further, is an important theme of the work of Prof Birks that failure of basis as an unjust factor is not confined to contracts, but extends to non-contractual, but still clearly conditional, transfers where the condition is unfulfilled (*e.g.* Birks, pp. 225, 461; Birks, *Restitution – The Future* (Sydney, 1992), p. 9: discussing, *inter alia*, *P. v. P.* [1916] 2 I.R. 400; *Barclays Bank v. Quistclose Investments* [1970] A.C. 567 and *Muschinski v. Dodds* (1985) 160 C.L.R. 583; the reasoning of Henchy J. in *RF v. MF* (October 24, 1985) [1995] 2 I.L.R.M. 572, 577-578 is similar).

If failure of basis constitutes an unjust factor, then, in principle, it may be combined with any enrichment to generate a cause of action. Thus, whilst the cases traditionally speak of the recovery of *money* paid for a consideration which has failed, there is no reason in principle why they could not also speak of the recovery of the value of services rendered upon a basis which has failed. Thus, in *Delgman* (above), Rand J. held that in the "principle of restitution against what would otherwise be an unjust enrichment of the defendant at the expense of the plaintiff" applied equally as between enrichments based upon money and upon services rendered ([1953] 3 D.L.R. 785, 788; cp Birks (1990) 2 *JCL* 227). Though sound in principle, this has not been consistently observed in the cases. Thus, the difficulties in the way of restitution for the party in breach become greater where that party is seeking restitution for benefits in kind (e.g. *Sumpter v. Hedges* [1898] 1 Q.B. 673; *Coughlan v. Moloney* (1905) 39 I.L.T.R. 153).

The nature of the unjust factors   In the *Bricklayers' Hall* case, Keane J. iterated mistake, duress and failure of consideration as "possible instances" of unjust enrichments. There is a single idea underlying these three instances. In *Jones v. Warring & Gillow*, Lord Sumner explained that the mistaken payor had "no real intention . . . to enrich" the defendant ([1926] A.C. 670, 696; cp *David Securities* ((1992) 175 C.L.R. 353, 378; (above)). Similarly, in *Rogers v. Louth County Council*, Griffin J. held that "a plaintiff may . . . recover monies so paid in an action for money had and received upon proof that the monies were paid by him involuntarily, that is, as the result of some extortion, coercion or compulsion in the legal sense" ([1981] I.R. 265, 271; [1981] I.L.R.M. 143, 147). And in *Fibrosa v. Fairbairn*, Lord Wright explained of failure of basis that where an intention to enrich is conditional upon a performance which never materialises, there is again "in such circumstances no intention to enrich the payee" ([1943] A.C. 32, 61).

In other words, unifying all three such unjust factors is the idea that the plaintiff *did not intend* the defendant to have the enrichment: in the case of mistake and duress, the plaintiff's intent was *vitiated*; whereas in the case of failure of consideration, it was conditional or *qualified* (Birks, pp. 99-104; 140 *et seq*). Thus, in *David Securities v. Commonwealth Bank of Australia*, the majority of the High Court of Australia accepted that recovery in such circumstances "depends upon the existence of a *qualifying* or *vitiating* factor such as mistake [or] duress ..." ((1992) 175 C.L.R. 353, 379, emphasis added) and in the same case, Brennan J. explained that "[e]nrichment is unjust because the defendant has no right to receive, or as the case may be, to retain the money or property which the plaintiff has transferred to him" ((1992) 175 C.L.R. 353, 393).

Therefore it can be said that an enrichment is unjust because the plaintiff did not intend the defendant to have the enrichment. Thus, if a plaintiff proves that his intent was vitiated by mistake or duress, or qualified by an unfulfilled condition, the plaintiff has shown that the defendant has no right to receive or retain any enrichment. As a consequence, such an enrichment may be described as "unjust", where that adjective simply states a conclusion. There is nothing here of palm-tree justice. Instead, as Prof Birks points out, the adjective "unjust" simply identifies "a general way those factors which, *according to the cases themselves*, called for an enrichment to be undone". (Birks, p. 19, emphasis added).

At least three further points must be made about the nature of the unjust factors. First, Deane J. in *Pavey & Matthews v. Paul*, in a passage which was approved by Keane J. in the *Bricklayers' Hall* case, saw the principle against unjust enrichment as explaining why "the law recognises, in a variety of distinct categories of cases, an obligation on the part of the defendant to make fair and just restitution for a benefit derived at the expense of the plaintiff" and as assisting "in the determination, by the ordinary process of legal reasoning, of the question of whether the law should, in justice, recognise the obligation in a new and developing category of case" ((1987) 162 C.L.R. 221, 256; approved [1996] 2 I.R. 468, 483; [1996] 2 I.L.R.M. 547, 558). Again, "new situations can arise which do not fit into an established category of recovery but nevertheless merit recognition" on the basis of the general principle (*Peel v. Canada* (1993) 98 D.L.R. (4th) 140, 154). An important consequence of concluding that unifying the unjust factors of mistake, duress and failure of basis is the idea that the plaintiff did not intend the defendant to have the enrichment, is that if there is another category in which it can also be said that the plaintiff likewise did not so intend, it becomes difficult to resist the conclusion that this unintentional transfer should also be characterised as unjust and trigger restitution. Thus, where a plaintiff does not intend to enrich because he is unaware of (ignorant of) the defendant's enrichment, that enrichment should likewise be characterised as unjust. Birks therefore argues that "ignorance" should be explicitly accepted as an unjust factor in the modern law of restitution (Birks, pp. 140-142). An excellent example is provided by the case of theft: the victim does not intend to enrich the thief, but his intent is neither vitiated by mistake or coercion nor qualified by condition; at the time of the theft, he simply was unaware the enrichment. The oft-stated duty of the thief to make restitution seems intuitively obvious (*Bristow v. Eastman* (1794) 1 Peake 291; *Neate v. Harding* (1851) 6 Exch. 349; *O'Hehir v. Cahill* (1912) 97 I.L.T.R. 274; *Moffat v. Kazana* [1968] 3 All E.R. 271; *Lipkin Gorman v. Karpnale* [1991] 2 A.C. 548), and is best explained on the basis that since the plaintiff did not intend to enrich the defendant, the enrichment is unjust. Furthermore, if the personal equitable duty to account as constructive trustee for receipt of trust funds is to be explained on restitutionary grounds (*Royal Brunei Airlines v. Tan* [1995] 2 A.C. 378, 386f *per* Lord Nicholls; cp the *Bricklayers' Hall* case, High Court, March 6, 1996, Budd J. at pp. 50-51 of the transcript), the fact that the plaintiff whose funds were misdirected was unaware of the misdirection to the defendant means that the appropriate unjust factor is ignorance (e.g. Birks (1989) 105 *LQR* 352; (1989) 105 *LQR* 528; [1989] *LMCLQ* 296; [1991] *LMCLQ* 473; [1993] *LMCLQ* 218. Such cases often also provide examples of enrichment to the defendant by interceptive subtraction from the plaintiff; for an example in an Irish context of the concepts ignorance and interceptive subtraction being deployed to explain a restitutionary result, see O'Dell [1997] *LMCLQ* 197, 200-202, discussing *Shanahan v. Redmond* (High Court, June 21, 1994, Carroll J.)).

Second, ignorance, mistake, duress, compulsion, and failure of basis, all focus on the consent of the plaintiff. To that extent they are plaintiff-sided unjust factors. Logic poses the question whether there may be cases where the focus is not on the quality of the plaintiff's giving but on the quality of the defendant's receipt. In other words, is there a defendant-sided unjust factor (independent of and irrespective of the consent of the plaintiff) ? There is a strong argument that the law recognises an obligation upon a defendant to make restitution to a plaintiff who has, non-gratuitously to the knowledge of the defendant, conferred a benefit upon the defendant, who, with an opportunity to reject it, chooses nevertheless to accept it. Since the defendant has "freely accepted" the benefit, the plaintiff can have restitution (see *BAGS v. Gilbert* [1994] F.S.R. 723, 743; *Angelopoulos v. Sabatino* (South Australia, unreported, September 8, 1995); the controversy surrounding this unjust factor of "free acceptance" is referred to in the 1994 Review, 139-140, and the 1995 Review, 227). Thus, the liability of the defendants in the leading Canadian case of *Pettkus v. Becker* (1980) 177 D.L.R. (3d) 257 and in the leading Australian case of *Pavey & Matthews v. Paul* (above) was expressed by those courts as turning on the respective defendants' free acceptance of the enrichment (and see Mason and Carter, *Restitution Law in Australia* (Butterworths, Sydney, 1995), pp. 341-344, para 1025, for a defence of free acceptance in that context). This unjust factor is peculiarly well adapted to plaintiffs who seek restitution of benefits conferred pursuant to contracts which never materialise (Birks, pp. 271-276; *Angelopoulos* (above)), though the critics of free acceptance are driven to explaining such cases as turning on an expanded notion of failure of basis (e.g. Burrows, 11-14; 293-299). Finally, here, (assuming the category of free acceptance to be established) it will be noticed that the defendant's free acceptance not only supplies the unjust factor here, but also helped (above) to establish that the defendant was enriched.

Third, as a matter of observation, there are some cases in which a strong policy elsewhere in the law has mandated a restitutionary response. Public law policies as to the scrupulousness and legality by which public bodies and the like gather their funds through taxes and rates have generated an unjust factor, a cause of action in restitution, by which the tax-payer can recover any such taxes exacted *ultra vires* the public bodies. And similar policies underlie the right of the government to recover money expended *ultra vires*. Thus, where a rate-payer or taxpayer pays such rates or taxes pays pursuant to a statute which is unconstitutional, or to a statutory instrument which is *ultra vires*, or pursuant to an invalid or overstated demand, both mistake and duress will often supply such a plaintiff with a cause of action (see e.g. *Air Canada v. British Colombia* (1989) 59 D.L.R (4th) 161 (mistake); *Murphy v. Attorney General* [1982] I.R. 241 (duress *colore officii*); see Burrows "Public Authorities, *Ultra Vires* and Restitution" in Burrows (ed.), *Essays in the Law of Restitution* (Oxford, 1991), p. 39 for the view that such unjust factors should be sufficient). Nevertheless, in *Woolwich v. IRC (No. 2)* [1993] A.C. 70, the plaintiff building society had paid tax on foot of an *ultra vires* statutory instrument, and Lord Goff, for the majority, held that money paid by a citizen to a public authority in the form of taxes or other levies paid pursuant to an *ultra vires* demand by the authority is *prima facie* recoverable by the citizen as of right. Although the law had not before then clearly recognised such a claim of right (*pace* Birks, "Restitution From the Executive: A Tercentenary Footnote to the Bill of Rights" in Finn (ed.), *Essays on Restitution* (Sydney, 1990), p. 164) the recognition of a new unjust factor in *Woolwich* was accepted as part of Irish law in *O'Rourke v. The Revenue Commissioners* [1996] 2 I.R. 1. There, Keane J. ultimately held that the *Woolwich* principle applied where the tax was overpaid simply by virtue of a misapplication of the tax code. And, conversely, in *Auckland Harbour Board v. R* , Viscount Haldane held that "[a]ny payment out of the consolidated fund made without Parliamentary authority is simply illegal and *ultra vires* and may be recovered by the Government . . ." ([1924] A.C. 318, 327). A strong public law principle therefore underlies the restitutionary causes of action recognised in *Woolwich* and in *Auckland*, and supplies an excellent example of that rare phenomenon, a strong policy outside the law of restitution which mandates a restitutionary response.

In summary then, at the level of one remove from the cases, it might be said that an enrichment can be unjust for one of three reasons: (i) because the plaintiff did not *intend* the defendant to have it (ignorance, mistake, duress, compulsion, failure of basis); (ii) because the defendant freely accepted it; or (iii) because a strong policy elsewhere in the law so requires.

DEFENCES

Of the four "essential preconditions" for liability in restitution recognised by Keane J. in the *Bricklayers' Hall* case, the fourth – "whether there are any reasons why, even where [an enrichment] can be regarded as 'unjust', restitution should nevertheless be denied to the plaintiff" – essentially focuses upon the availability of defences. These can be grouped into three broad categories: (i) those which deny an essential element of the principle against unjust enrichment, ie, those which answer one of the first three enquires in the defendant's favour; (ii) those which would deny restitution even if the terms of the first three enquiries were answered in the plaintiff's favour; and (iii) those which reflect defences more generally in the law.

As to the first category of defences, those which deny an essential element of the principle against unjust enrichment: first, the defence of change of position denies that a defendant has been relevantly enriched on the basis that the enrichment is no longer in the defendant's hands; second, a defendant who received as agent for a principal can rely on the defence of ministerial receipt to show that it is the principal and not the agent who is relevantly enriched; and, third, a defendant who gave value in return for the enrichment can rely on the defence of *bona fide* purchase for value without notice.

Change of position   As a matter of Irish law, in *Murphy v. AG* Henchy J. held that it "is one of the first principles of the law of restitution on the ground of unjust enrichment" that there be a defence of change of position by which "the defendant should not be compelled to make restitution, or at least full restitution when, after receiving the money in good faith, his circumstances have so changed that it would be inequitable to compel him to make full resti- tution", and (citing a New Zealand statute) he clarified that the defendant's relevant change of position have been "in reliance on the validity of the pay- ment" ([1982] I.R. 241, 319). The State had received income tax pursuant to an unconstitutional statutory provision, and were thus *prima facie* liable to make restitution to the tax payers. In holding that the State could rely upon the defence of change of position, Henchy J. found that it had received the rel- evant taxes in good faith, and had spent the revenue in reliance upon its belief – engendered by a protracted absence of a claim to the contrary – that it was legally and constitutionally proper to spend the money so collected. This ap- plied in respect of receipts "in every tax year from the enactment of the [un- constitutional section] . . . until the institution of these proceedings" ([1982] I.R. 241, 320). However, the present plaintiffs would be entitled to restitution for the subsequent tax years; but if no other taxpayers had formulated a claim impugning the relevant section, no other taxpayers would be entitled to resti- tution ([1982] I.R. 241, 324). Presumably, for so long as there was no objec- tion, the government's receipt was *bona fide*; and the terms of the defence of change of position were fulfilled; thereafter, once the statute had been im- pugned, the receipt was still *bona fide* from those who did not object; whilst in respect of those who had objected, and from the date of the objection, that receipt was no longer *bona fide*, and the terms of the defence were no longer fulfilled.

The defence seems to have been accepted in principle as a matter of Aus- tralian law, (*David Securities v. Commonwealth Bank of Australia* (1992) 175 C.L.R. 353, 385-386) where its contours have yet to be mapped out. When the defence was finally recognised as a matter of English law in *Lipkin Gorman v. Karpnale* Lord Goff was "most anxious that, in recognising this defence to actions of restitution, nothing should be said at this stage to inhibit the devel- opment of the defence on a case by case basis, in the usual way . . ." ([1991] 2 A.C. 548, 579) and Lord Bridge likewise felt that "it would be unwise to attempt to define its scope in abstract terms, but better to allow the law on the subject to develop on a case by case basis" ([1991] 2 A.C. 548, 558). Nevertheless, certain matters have been regarded as clear: "the defence is not open to one who has changed his position in bad faith, as where the defendant has paid away money with knowledge of the facts entitling the plaintiff to restitution; and it is commonly accepted that the defence should be available to a wrongdoer" ([1991] 2 A.C. 548, 579 *per* Lord Goff). The first example is illustrated by *Murphy v. AG* (above). Lord Goff went on to hold that "the mere fact that the defendant has spent the money, in whole or in part, does not of itself render it inequitable that he should be called upon to repay, because the expenditure might in any event have been incurred by him in the ordinary course of things". (*id.* p. 580). A good illustration of payment over being insufficient is provided by *Goss v. Chilcott* [1996] A.C. 788 where the payees allowed the money to be paid to a third party, and the Privy Council held that the mere fact of this payment over was not sufficient to make out the defence of change of position. Though some defendants have successfully invoked the defence (*Murphy*; *RBC Dominions Securities v. Dawson* (1994) 111 D.L.R. (4th) 230), other courts have treated its invocation with caution (e.g.: the leading case in Canada *Storthoaks v. Mobil Oil Canada* (1975) 55 D.L.R. (3d.) 1; at first instance in *Westdeutsche Landesbank v. Islington LBC* [1994] 4 All E.R. 890 (this point was not taken on appeal (above)); *South Tyneside MBC v. Svenska* [1995] 1 All E.R. 545; for a view of a likely shape of the defence, see Birks "Change of Position" in McInnes (ed.), *Restitution: Developments in Unjust Enrichment* (LBC, Sydney 1996) 49)).

Ministerial receipt In *Holland v. Russell* (1861) 1 B.&S. 424; *affd* (1863) 4 B.&S. 14 it was held that when money is paid to an agent in circumstances in which the payor has a cause of action in restitution to recover the money, and the agent, without notice of that claim *bona fide* pays on to his principal, the liability of the agent ceases and the claim can only be brought against the principal. A similar decision was reached in by Barron J. in *Woodchester Investments v. O'Driscoll* (High Court, July 27, 1995; see the 1995 Review, 203-4).

***Bona fide* purchase for value without notice** A defendant, who has given value to a third party in exchange for the enrichment which the plaintiff now seeks to recover, may be able to rely on the defence of *bona fide* purchase. "The general rule is that where a person purports to pay money directly to another ... and that other has notice that they payment has been induced by fraud, the payee ... does not get any title to the money" (*Carey v. Ryan* [1982] I.R. 179, 185 *per* Henchy J.) and can therefore be made liable in an action in restitution; from which it follows that if the payee has no such notice, he gets title and can resist such a claim.

Despite a controversy over whether such a defence should be confined to proprietary claims (see O'Dell [1997] *CLJ* 71, 79 n 34), courts seem to have accepted the defence, though it seems difficult for defendants to fulfil its terms.

For example, in *Nelson v. Larholt* [1948] 1 K.B. 339, a defendant paid a third party on foot of a cheque drawn on the plaintiff; and Denning J. held that the defendant, despite having given value (and thereby purchased), had not made reasonable enquires and thus had notice of the plaintiff's claim. Again, in *Lipkin Gorman v. Karpnale* [1991] 2 A.C. 548, a partner in a firm of solicitors had gambled the firm's money at the defendant club, and in the firm's action to recover the money, the club sought to argue that since it had given value to the solicitor, it could rely on the defence of *bona fide* purchase; but the House of Lords held that the nullity of the gaming contract between the club and the partner meant that the club were not purchasers for value.

As to the first category of defences, those which deny an essential element of the principle against unjust enrichment, the above three deny that the defendant has been relevantly enriched; the defence of passing on (if it exists) denies that an enrichment in the hands of the defendant is at the expense of the plaintiff.

Passing on   As a matter of logic, in every successful claim, it is necessary to draw a causal link between the matter of which the plaintiff complains and the defendant. In the law of restitution, this is supplied by showing that the defendant's enrichment *was at the expense of the plaintiff*. If the defendant can show that his enrichment was at the expense of some other party, T, he is not enriched at the expense of the present plaintiff, whose claim must fail. For example, let P. charge T a given amount for the provision of a service; if the government D were to impose upon P. a tax in respect of that receipt, P. will simply increase his charge to T to take account of the tax. P. will have passed on his loss. If, thereafter, the tax were to be found unconstitutional, and P. were to sue D for restitution of the taxes paid, it would be open to D to argue that, since P. passed on his loss in the increase to T, any enrichment in its [D's] hands is not at P's expense but at T's. Thus, in *Air Canada v. British Colombia* (1989) 59 D.L.R. (4th) 161, La Forest J. for the majority, (Wilson J. dissenting on this point) held that payments of airport tax were *prima facie* recoverable as mistake payments (overruling the mistake of law rule), but, since the plaintiffs had passed on the increased taxes charges to their customers, any enrichment in the hands of the plaintiffs was not at the plaintiffs' expense (see in particular at (1989) 59 D.L.R. (4th) 161, 193-194).

Though it seems sound in principle, this argument has not met with much support, and Wilson J.'s dissent *Air Canada* has commended itself to subsequent courts: (e.g. Lord Goff in *Woolwich* (above); Hobhouse J. in *Westdeutsche* (above)). Thus, Mason C.J. in the High Court of Australia in *Commissioner v. Royal Insurance*, denied the defence on the ground that "[b]ecause the object of restitutionary relief is to divest the defendant of what the defendant is not entitled to retain, the court does not asses the amount of its award by reference to the actual loss which the plaintiff has sustained" ((1994) 182 C.L.R. 51, 74; cp p. 90 *per* Brennan J, McHugh and Toohey JJ. concurring); and, in the Court of Appeal in England in *Kleinwort Benson v. Birmingham City Council*, Evans L.J. simply focused on the P. and D relationship, and considered whether as between P and D, D's enrichment was at P's expense ([1996] 4 All E.R. 733, 742). For Saville L.J., D was "unjustly enriched by receiving and retaining money he has received from [P] and to which he has no right. He does not cease to he unjustly enriched because [P] for one reason or another is not out of pocket" ([1996] 4 All E.R. 733, 744). There are, in the cases denying the defence of passing on, traces of the view that P. having recovered from D may hold on trust for T (see *Commissioner v. Royal Insurance* (1994) 182 C.L.R. 51, 75-78 *per* Mason C.J. and *Kleinwort Benson v. Birmingham City Council* [1996] 4 All E.R. 733, 739 *per* Evans L.J., both citing the dissenting judgment of Hand J. in *123 East 54th St v. US* (1946) 157 F 2d 68), to ensure that P. is not in turn enriched at T's expense.

Underlying the judgment of La Forest J. in *Air Canada v. British Colombia* (1989) 59 D.L.R. (4th) 16, there is a strong public policy in favour of security of the public purse, which is given expression both in the proposition that there ought as a consequence to be a special defence for the state which had received taxes on foot of an unconstitutional taxing statute, and as a justification for the application of the further defence of passing on. Similar considerations underlie the judgment of Henchy J. in *Murphy v. AG* giving the state the benefit of the defence of change of position: "the position had become so altered, the logistics of reparation so weighted and distorted by factors such as inflation and interest," that it would be inequitable to expect the State to make full restitution ([1982] I.R. 241, 320). It may be, therefore, that Irish law might be less hostile to the defence of passing on in an appropriate case.

The defences so far examined assert either that the defendant was not relevantly enriched (change of position, ministerial receipt, *bona fide* purchase), or that any enrichment was not at the plaintiff's expense (passing on); to complete the defences in the category of those which deny an essential element of the principle against unjust enrichment, it is necessary to examine those which deny the existence of an unjust factor. It was explained above that an enrichment can be said to be unjust for one of three reasons: (i) because the plaintiff did not intend the defendant to have it; (ii) because the defendant freely accepted it; or (iii) because a strong policy elsewhere in the law so requires. If the defendant demonstrates that the enrichment was, or should be taken to be, voluntary, the effect is to preclude reliance upon the argument that the plaintiff did not intend to enrich the defendant, and thus provides an defence to a claim arising from an intention-based unjust factor. It follows from that, of course, that the fact that an enrichment was voluntary would not, for that reason, defeat a claim based upon an unjust factor in either of the other two categories. More generally, in principle, that which denies unjust in relation to one category of unjust, by its nature, is silent as regards the other two.

Voluntary enrichment   There are many examples, in respect of each of the intention-based unjust factors, of cases in which the plaintiff's claim has failed because the court characterised the plaintiff's transfer of the enrichment as voluntary. For example, in the context of mistaken payments, in *Barclays Bank v. Simms* (above) Goff J. held that a plaintiff's claim would fail if he "intends that the payee shall have the money *at all events*, whether the fact be true or false, or is deemed in law so to intend" (similar is Budd J. in *National Bank v. O'Connor* (above)). Again, in the context of mistakenly rendered services, in *Webb v. Ireland* where Blayney J. in the High Court had held that the Museum was entitled to restitution for restoring the chalice in the mistaken belief that the state was the owner of the hoard, he went on to hold that, once they were aware of the plaintiff's claim, the defendants were no longer mistaken, and though they continued to work on the chalice, they "accepted the risk" that the plaintiff's claim was valid ([1988] I.R. 353, 370). In effect, the enrichment in the circumstances was voluntary. Furthermore, it is said to be a defence to an action for restitution on the grounds of mistake that the plaintiff voluntarily submitted to the plaintiff's honest claim to the enrichment (*Brisbane v. Dacres* (1813) 5 Taunt 143; Andrews [1989] *LMCLQ* 43; Arrowsmith "Mistake and Role of Submission to an Honest Claim" in Burrows (ed.), *Essays on the Law of Restitution* p. 17; *David Securities v. Commonwealth Bank of Australia* (1992) 175 C.L.R. 353; *Commissioner v. Royal Insurance* (1994) 182 C.L.R. 51).

Similar considerations are to be found defeating claims for duress or compulsion. Once again, it is said to be a defence to an action for restitution on the grounds of duress that the plaintiff voluntarily submitted to the plaintiff's honest claim to the enrichment (*Maskell v. Horner* [1915] 3 K.B. 106; McMeel *Casebook on Restitution* (Blackstone, London, 1996) queries whether *CTN Cash and Carry v. Gallagher* [1994] 4 All E.R. 714 is "an example of a 'submission to an honest claim' ?" (p. 142). And in the context of duress *colore officii*, if the payment is held to be voluntary, again recovery is precluded (*Rogers v. Louth County Council* (above)). Furthermore, the payor of the debt of another will not have been compelled, nor will the renderer of a service be found to have acted out of necessity, if they have acted voluntarily (*Owen v. Tate* [1976] Q.B. 402; *Hackett v. Smith* [1917] 2 I.R. 508).

As to the second category of defences, those which would deny restitution even if the terms of the first three enquiries were answered in the plaintiff's favour, if a plaintiff had transferred the enrichment pursuant to a valid obligation, or if he cannot make counter restitution, then his claim to restitution will fail.

Enrichment pursuant to obligation   If "the plaintiff conferred the benefit as a valid gift or in pursuance of a valid common law, equitable or statutory obligation which he owed to the defendant", the plaintiff's claim to restitution may nonetheless fail. "The most important illustration of this is where he had contracted . . . to confer the benefit . . .". (Goff and Jones, pp. 44, 45) a proposition which has many illustrations in the cases in Ireland (*Pigs and Bacon Commission v. McCarren* (1978) *JISEL* 7, 107-108 *per* Costello J.; *Galvin Estates v. Hedigan* [1985] I.L.R.M. 295, 301-302 *per* Costello J.) and in England (*Dimskal Shipping Co. v. ITWF, The Evia Luck (No. 2)* [1992] 2 A.C. 152, 165 *per* Lord Goff; *Pan Ocean Shipping v. Creditcorp, The Trident Beauty* [1994] 1 W.L.R. 161, 164f, 165d-e, 166e-f *per* Lord Goff). Thus, a plaintiff, seeking restitution in circumstances where there is or has been a contract, must first demonstrate that the contract is ineffective (e.g. void, unenforceable, and so on) and then successfully answer the four enquiries described in this chapter.

Counter-restitution   The essence of this matter was well captured by Palles C.B. in *In re Irish Provident Assurance Co.* In an action for restitution of benefits transferred under void contracts, Palles C.B. held that "if the applicant had received anything under that void agreement, the Court will compel him to do equity, and as far as possible, to bring back all that he has received under that agreement, either *in specie* or by making compensation to the extent of its value. ... It is a condition for granting relief" ([1913] 1 I.R. 353, 370 – 371; cp at 377 *per* Cherry L.J., Holmes L.J. concurring). Thus, a company seeking, first, restitution of payments on foot of *ultra vires* insurance policies had to make counter-restitution of the amounts of the *premia* received (which amounts the Court of Appeal unanimously equated); and, second, restitution of money paid *ultra vires* by the company for shares in itself and certain other benefits had to make counter-restitution of the shares and those benefits. Since the majority (Cherry and Holmes LL.J.; Palles C.B. dissenting) held that those benefits were not quantifiable, the company could not comply with the precondition of counter-restitution, and the claim for restitution failed.

As to the third category of defences, those which reflect defences more generally in the law (see e.g. Mason and Carter, p. 801, para 2208), a plaintiff may be estopped from relying upon his right to restitution if he had expressly or impliedly represented to the enriched defendant that it was entitled to it (e.g. *Avon CC v. Howlett* [1983] 1 W.L.R. 605). A plaintiff may also be met by a limitation period: claims at common law for restitution were at one time described as claims for quasi-contract, and section 11(1)(b) of the Statute of Limitations, 1957 provides six year limitation period for "actions founded on quasi-contract". Further, claims in restitution fail because the plaintiff's arose *ex turpi causa* in exactly the same way as a claim in contract would fail for illegality (recall that in *Beresford v. Kennedy* (1887) 21 I.L.T.R. 17 and *Gormley v. Johnston* (1895) 29 I.L.T.R. 69 (above) the plaintiffs' claims failed as arising *ex turpi causa*). Again, claims in restitution are subject to the defence of *res judicata*: in the *Bricklayers' Hall* case, where the defendants had received payment pursuant to an arbitrator's award, Keane J. in the Supreme Court held that the award attracted the protection of the principle of *res judicata*, and the plaintiff's claim for restitution of the award was dismissed (*Dublin Corporation v. Building and Allied Trade Union* [1996] 2 I.R. 468; [1996] 2 I.L.R.M. 547; see O'Dell (1997) 113 *L.Q.R.* 245).

In earlier sections, there are many examples of the law of restitution recasting the terms of causes of action to reflect more accurately the principle against unjust enrichment. Thus, the ambit of mistake was widened by the abolition of the mistake of law bar; again, it is argued that failure of basis should not be confined to total failure of consideration. Fears of too much restitution as a consequence have been met by the introduction of the defences sketched above sensitive to the principle against unjust enrichment. Thus, in *Air Canada v. British Columbia*, where the Supreme Court of Canada abolished the mistake of law rule, they affirmed the defence of change of position and proposed the defence of passing on. Again, in *David Securities v. Commonwealth Bank of Australia*, the High Court of Australia saw in many of the previous mistake of law cases the defence of voluntary submission to an honest claim (which may also explain the early and leading Irish case on the (former) mistake of law bar: *O'Loghlen v. O'Callaghan* (1874) I.R. 8 C.L. 116). Thus, as Millett L.J. has written, in the context of the development of the defence of change of position "the introduction of this defence not only provides the court with a means of doing justice in future, but also allows a re-examination of many decisions of the past in which the absence of the defence may have led judges to distort basic principles in order to avoid injustice to the plaintiff" (*Boscawen v. Bajwa* [1995] 4 All E.R. 769, 776-777; cp *Lipkin Gorman v. Karpnale* [1991] 2 A.C. 548, 581 *per* Lord Goff). The presence of that and similar defences therefore allows judges to restate the basic principles in a more coherent manner. For example, in the context of failure of basis, the argument in favour of allowing a partial failure to ground restitution is based partly upon the premiss that the pre-condition of counter-restitution achieves the same policy objectives as the requirement that failure be total but in a more coherent manner.

In *Moses v. Macferlan*, having explained that what we now call the principle against unjust enrichment was at the heart of the action for money had and received, Lord Mansfield held that the defendant "may defend himself by every thing which shews that the plaintiff, *ex æquo et bono*, is not entitled to the whole of his demand, or to any part of it" ((1760) 2 Burr. 1005, 1010). This important *dictum* must be treated with care; Lord Goff in *Lipkin Gorman v. Karpnale* treated the *dictum* as referring to the defence of change of position. Any tendency to import palm tree justice on the fourth enquiry (defences) having forcibly ejected it on the third (unjust) must be resisted. Thus, it is because a plaintiff is mistaken, for example, that a defendant's enrichment can be characterised as unjust, not for reasons of judicial discretion. Likewise, it ought to be understood that it is because of the existence of a recognised defence that a plaintiff's claim fails, not for reasons of judicial discretion. Thus, in *Lipkin Gorman v. Karpnale* Lord Goff observed that a "claim to recover money at common law is made as a matter of right; and, even though the underlying principle of recovery is the principle of unjust enrichment, *nevertheless, where recovery is denied, it is denied on the basis of legal principle.* . . ." ([1991] 2 A.C. 548, 578 emphasis added). The organisation of the defences here is intended to illustrate just that point.

Safety and Health

CHEMICAL SAFETY

Cosmetics   The European Communities (Cosmetic Products) (Amendment) Regulations 1996 (SI No. 164 of 1996) amended the European Communities (Cosmetic Products) Regulations 1990 and gave effect to Directives 94/32/EC 95/32/EC and 95/34/EC. They permit the use of certain additional substances in cosmetic products and prohibit or restrict the use of certain other substances, with effect from June 1, 1996.

Explosives: land mines   The Explosives (Land Mines) Order 1996 (SI No. 175 of 1996), which was made under the Explosive Act 1875, prohibits the manufacture, keeping, importation, conveyance or sale of land mines in the State. The Order came into effect on June 31, 1996. It may be seen against the background of the State's support for a world-wide ban on the manufacture and use of land mines, on which the United Nations has been engaged in recent years.

ENVIRONMENTAL SAFETY

Access to information   The Access to Information on the Environment Regulations 1996 (SI No. 185 of 1996), made under section 110 of the Environmental Protection Agency Act 1992 (1992 Review, 533), give effect in amended form to Directive 90/313/EEC, which had previously been implemented by the Access to Information on the Environment Regulations 1993. The 1993 Regulations, revoked by the 1996 Regulations, had been criticised as being an incomplete implementation of the 1990 Directive: see the 1993 Review, 475. The 1996 Regulations set out the procedures for public access to information relating to the environment held by public authorities and provide certain grounds for refusal. They came into effect on July 22, 1996.

Air pollution: emission limits for combustion plant   The Air Pollution Act 1987 (Emission Limit Values for Combustion Plant) Regulations 1996 (SI No. 264 of 1996), in implementing Directive 88/609/EEC as amended by Directive 94/66/EC, lay down emission limit values for sulphur dioxide, nitrogen oxide and dust emissions from industrial combustion plant using solid fuels. They came into effect on October 1, 1996 and also revoked the Air

Pollution Act 1987 (Combustion Plant) Regulations 1992 (1992 Review, 534). Whereas the 1992 Regulations also provided directions on the best practicable means for limiting and monitoring emissions, the 1996 Regulations do not as this is now provided for in a general manner by the Environmental Protection Agency Act 1992 (1992 Review, 531-2).

Air and water pollution: extension of EPA powers The Environmental Protection Agency Act 1992 (Commencement) Order 1996 (SI No. 13 of 1996) brought sections 100 and 101 of the Environmental Protection Agency Act 1992 into operation on January 22, 1996. These sections envisaged the transfer to the Environmental Protection Agency of responsibility for enforcement of elements of, respectively, the Local Government (Water Pollution) Acts 1977 and 1990 and the Air Pollution Act 1987. Such transfer would then be effected by means of a further Ministerial Order under sections 100 and 101 of the 1992 Act. This was effected by the Environmental Protection Agency (Extension Of Powers) Order 1996 (SI No. 126 of 1996). The Order extended a number of powers to the EPA, including: applications to the High Court to prohibit, terminate or reduce discharges and emissions; service of notices specifying measures to prevent air or water pollution; prosecutions of offences under general statutory prohibitions on air and water pollution not already covered by the Integrated Pollution Control (IPC) regime; powers of entry, inspection, monitoring, gathering of information and prosecutions for the purposes of the extended powers; and the recovery of the EPA's costs in bringing prosecutions as well as payment of fines to the EPA in certain circumstances. The Order also provided for consequential changes to the relevant Acts. The 1996 Order came into effect on May 27, 1996.

Bathing water The Quality of Bathing Waters (Amendment) Regulations 1996 (SI No.230 of 1996), made under the Local Government (Water Pollution) Act 1977, amended the Quality of Bathing Waters Regulations 1992 (1992 Review, 534) and applied the water quality standards of the 1992 Regulations to an additional eight bathing areas, bringing the total number covered to 124 areas. The 1996 Regulations also provide that results of bathing water samples be provided to the EPA rather than the Minister, as had been provided for under the 1992 Regulations. The 1996 Regulations came into effect on July 31, 1996.

Emission levels from vehicles The relevant statutory regime regulating emission levels from vehicles is outlined in the Transport chapter, 629, below.

Energy labelling of household appliances Council Directive 92/75/EEC envisages a series of specific Commission Directives providing consumers with information on the energy efficiency of certain household electrical goods, a limited kind of eco-labelling regime. Two of these specific Directives were implemented in 1996. The European Communities (Energy Labelling of House-hold Electric Washing Machines) Regulations 1996 (SI No. 109 of 1996) gave effect to Directive 95/12/EC. The Regulations prohibit the placing on the market for sale, hire or reward electric mains operated household washing machines unless accompanied by information relating to the consumption of electric energy conveyed by a specified label and fiche for which the supplier is responsible and also provide for inspection and penalties for offences. They came into effect on 30 September 1996, with transitional provisions for certain machines. Similarly, the European Communities (Energy Labelling of Household Electric Tumble Driers) Regulations 1996 (SI No. 110 of 1996) gave effect to Directive 95/13/EC. They also prohibit the placing on the market for sale, hire or reward electric mains operated household tumble driers unless accompanied by information relating to the consumption of electric energy conveyed by a specified label and fiche for which the supplier is responsible and also provide for inspection and penalties for offences. They also came into effect on 30 September 1996, again with transitional provisions for certain machines.

EPA: Advisory Committee The Environmental Protection Agency (Advisory Committee) Regulations 1996 (SI No. 229 of 1996) prescribe various organisations for selecting candidates for consideration for appointment by the Minister for the Environment to the EPA Advisory Committee envisaged by section 27 of the Environmental Protection Agency Act 1992 (see the 1992 Review, 530).

Genetically Modified Organisms (GMOs) The Genetically Modified Organisms (Amendment) Regulations 1996 (SI No. 348 of 1996), made under section 111 of the Environmental Protection Agency Act 1992 (1992 Review, 533-4), amended the Genetically Modified Organisms Regulations 1994 (1994 Review, 397-8) and gave effect to Commission Decisions concerning the information to be notified pursuant to Directives 90/219/EEC and 90/220/EEC, which had been implemented by the 1994 Regulations. The 1996 Regulations came into effect on December 2, 1996.

IPC regime Environmental Protection Agency Act 1992 (Commencement) (No. 2) Order 1996 (SI No. 77 of 1996), the Environmental Protection Agency (Established Activities) Order 1996 (SI No. 78 of 1996), the Environmental Protection Agency (Licensing) (Amendment) Regulations 1996 (SI No. 79 of 1996), the Environmental Protection Agency (Licensing Fees) (Amendment) Regulations 1996 (SI No. 239 of 1996) and the Environmental Protection Agency (Licensing) (Amendment) (No.2) Regulations 1996 (SI No. 240 of

1996) provided for the further introduction to specified classes of industrial activities of the integrated pollution control (IPC) regime in the Environmental Protection Agency Act 1992 (1992 Review, 531) and revised the related fees for applying for such licences.

Maritime pollution: Dumping at sea   The Dumping at Sea Act 1996 is discussed separately, below, 536.

Strict liability offences   In *Shannon Regional Fisheries Board v. Cavan County Council*, High Court, December 21, 1994; Supreme Court, July 30, 1996 (discussed in the Criminal Law chapter, 278, above), the Supreme Court confirmed that certain offences under section 171 of the Fisheries (Consolidation) Act 1959, concerning discharges of effluent into watercourses, were strict liability offences.

Waste management   The Waste Management Act 1996 is discussed separately, below, 546.

Water pollution: repeal and replacement   The Local Government (Water Pollution) Act 1977 (Commencement) Order 1996 (SI No. 18 of 1996) made under section 33 of the Local Government (Water Pollution) Act 1977 brought section 34 of the 1977 Act into force, providing for the repeal of the Rivers Pollution Prevention Acts 1876 and 1893, with effect from 22 January 1996. Note also the effect of the Environmental Protection Agency (Extension Of Powers) Order 1996 (SI No. 126 of 1996), discussed above.

Water pollution: discharge into sewers   The Local Government (Water Pollution) (Amendment) Regulations 1996 (SI No. 184 of 1996) amended the provisions of the Local Government (Water Pollution) Regulations 1978 concerning the application of the two month period allowed for the determination of licence applications for effluent discharges to combined drains declared to be sewers for the purposes of the Local Government (Water Pollution) Acts 1977 and 1990. They also amended the Local Government (Water Pollution) Regulations 1992 (1992 Review, 535) on the control of discharges to aquifers in small quantities which pose no risk to the quality of groundwaters. The 1996 Regulations came into effect on June 24, 1996.

FOOD SAFETY

Animal origin: pesticide residues   The European Communities (Pesticide Residues) (Foodstuffs Of Animal Origin) (Amendment) Regulations 1996 (SI No. 35 of 1996) and the European Communities (Pesticide Residues) (Foodstuffs Of Animal Origin) (Amendment) (No. 2) Regulations 1996 (SI No. 412 of 1996) amended the European Communities (Pesticide Residues) (Foodstuffs of Animal Origin) Regulations 1988 and gave effect to Directives 95/39/EC and 96/33/EC, respectively. They extended the list of pesticides for which maximum residue levels have been set, with effect from 13 February 1996 and December 20, 1996, respectively. The European Communities (Pesticide Residues) (Cereals) (Amendment) Regulations 1996 (SI No. 47 of 1996) implemented Directive 95/39/EC and amended the European Communities (Pesticide Residues) (Cereals) Regulations 1988 by extending the list of pesticides for which maximum residue levels have been set. They came into effect on February 13, 1996.

Feedingstuffs: additives The European Communities (Additives in Feedingstuffs) (Amendment) Regulations 1996 (SI. No. 15 of 1996) gave effect to Directives 95/11/EC, 95/37/EC and 95/55/EC with effect from January 24, 1996. The European Communities (Additives in Feedingstuffs) (Amendment) (No.2) Regulations 1996 (SI. No. 252 of 1996) gave effect to Directive 96/7/EC, with effect from August 22, 1996. They both amended the European Communities (Additives in Feedingstuffs) Regulations 1989 specified updated list of additives authorised in feedingstuffs and the conditions for their use.

Fish products The European Communities (Fishery Products) (Health Conditions and Hygiene Rules for Production and Placing On The Market) Regulations 1996 (SI No.170 of 1996) gave effect to Directives 91/493/EEC and 92/48/EEC and prescribe the detailed conditions for the production and placing on the market of fishery products in general. They apply primarily at the ship and wholesale end of the process, not the retail end. They came into effect on 10 June 1996 and revoked and replaced the Demersal Fish (Handling, Storage and Transport) Regulations 1967 to 1983 and the Pelagic Fish (Handling, Storage and Transport) Regulations 1979. The European Communities (Live Bivalve Molluscs) (Health Conditions for Production and Placing On The Market) Regulations 1996 (SI No. 147 of 1996) gave effect to Directive 91/492/EEC. They lay down the detailed conditions for the production and placing on the market of live bivalve molluscs. They came into effect on May 27, 1996.

Inspection generally The Health (Official Control of Food) Regulations 1996 (SI No. 241 of 1996) lay down the general arrangements imposed on health boards to ensure the effective supervision and inspection of premises, raw materials, semi-finished products, cleaners and materials coming into contact with food. They implemented Directive 89/397/EEC, as amended by Directive 93/99/EEC and revoked the Health (Official Control of Food) Regulations 1991 (1991 Review, 367). The 1996 Regulations came into effect on September 1, 1996, with the exception of Reg. 17, which deals with the approval of official laboratories, which is operative with effect from November 1, 1998. The Health (Official Control of Food) Approved Laboratories Order 1996 (SI No. 242 of 1996) specified an approved list of laboratories for the analysis of food samples taken by authorised officers under SI No. 241, above, and revoked the Health (Official Control of Food) Approved Laboratories Order 1991 (1991 Review, 367).

Materials coming into contact with foodstuffs: plastics The European Communities (Materials and Articles intended to come into Contact with Foodstuffs) (Amendment) Regulations 1996 (SI No. 226 of 1996) amended the European Communities (Materials and Articles intended to come into Contact with Foodstuffs) Regulations (1991 Review, 366) (see also the amending Regulations of 1993 and 1994, 1993 Review, 480, and 1994 Review, 401) in order to give effect to Directive 95/3/EC. They further deal with the use of plastic materials coming into contact with food and came into effect on September 16, 1996.

Milk production: hygiene The European Communities (Hygienic Production and Placing on the Market of Raw Milk, Heat-Treated Milk and Milk-Based Products) Regulations 1996 (SI No. 9 of 1996) gave effect to Directives 92/46/EEC, 92/47/EEC and 94/71/EEC and Commission Directive 89/362/EEC. They provide for the hygienic production and placing on the market for sale of milk and milk based products and came into effect on January 15, 1996.

Minced meat European Communities (Minced Meat and Meat Preparations) Regulations 1996 (SI No. 243 of 1996) implemented Directive 94/65/EC. They lay down detailed requirements for the production and marketing of minced meat and meat preparations for human consumption and set out hygiene standards for premises producing such products. They came into effect on August 14, 1996 and revoked the European Communities (Minced Meat) Regulations 1994 (1994 Review, 401-2).

Potatoes: quality and grading The Food Standards (Potatoes) (Amendment) Regulations 1996 (SI No. 4 of 1996), made under the Food Standards Act 1974 amended the grading and quality standards for potatoes sold for human consumption within the State and amended the information to be provided on packages or at the point of sale. The Regulations came into effect on February 1, 1996.

Poultry: production The European Communities (Fresh Poultrymeat) Regulations 1996 (SI No. 3 of 1996) gave effect to Directive 71/118/EEC as amended by Directives 92/116/EEC and 94/65/EC. They lay down the health rules for the production and placing on the market of fresh poultrymeat intended for human consumption and set out the structural and hygienic standards for premises, veterinary supervision of premises and health marking of poultrymeat. They came into effect on January 8, 1996.

MANUFACTURING STANDARDS

The important National Standards Authority of Ireland Act 1996 is considered separately below, 538. As in previous Reviews, we also note Regulations which gave effect to further 'New Approach' EC Directives linked to the CE technical conformity marking and European Norms (ENs), that is technical manufacturing standards.

Construction plant: noise levels   The European Communities (Construction Plant and Equipment) (Permissible Noise Levels) (Amendment) Regulations 1996 (SI No. 359 of 1996) amended the European Communities (Construction Plant and Equipment) (Permissible Noise Levels) Regulations 1988 and gave effect to Directive 95/27/EC. They set down revised permissible noise levels for the equipment covered by their terms, such as excavators, dozers and loaders. They came into effect on December 3, 1996.

National Standards Authority of Ireland   The National Standards Authority of Ireland Act 1996 is discussed separately, below, 538.

Pressure vessels   The European Communities (Simple Pressure Vessels) Regulations 1996 (SI No. 33 of 1996) implemented Directive 87/404/EEC, as amended by 90/488/EEC and 93/68/EEC. They require the manufacturer of simple pressure vessels (as defined in the Directive and Regulations) to affix the CE conformity marking on simple pressure vessels, with transitional provisions for pressure vessels that complied with the previous statutory requirements, contained in the European Communities (Simple Pressure Vessels) Regulations 1991 (1991 Review, 369). The 1991 Regulations were revoked with effect from February 13, 1996 when the 1996 Regulations came into effect.

MARITIME POLLUTION

Dumping at sea   The Dumping At Sea Act 1996 gave effect in Irish law to the 1992 Paris Convention for the Protection of the Marine Environment of the North-East Atlantic, which had updated previous Oslo and London Conventions in this area. The Act, apart from section 5, came into effect on June 19, 1996 on its signature by the President. The 1996 Act repealed and re-enacted with amendments the Dumping at Sea Act 1981, which had given effect to the Oslo and London Conventions. The State's annual contribution towards the operational budget of the Commission established under the Paris Convention to police its operation was expected to be in the order of just over £20,000, based on 1994 prices.

Section 2 of the 1996 Act provides for restrictions on dumping in the State's maritime area, that is, an area extending out to 200 miles from certain designated baselines and in some cases out to 350 miles. It provides that it an offence to dump in the maritime area or to load for the purpose of dumping in the maritime area a substance, material, vessel and aircraft unless it is in accordance with a permit granted by the Minister for the Marine or it can be proven that it was as a result of an accident or it was necessary for the purpose of saving life. Similarly, section 3 makes it an offence to cause the incineration of substances or materials in the maritime area.

Section 4 makes it an offence to deliberately dump or permit the dumping of: (a) an offshore installation or any substance or material from an offshore installation; (b) radioactive substances or materials in the maritime area except for those substances or materials containing background levels of radio-activity; and (c) toxic, harmful or noxious substances. This general prohibition is subject to the exemptions provided for in section 5 of the 1996 Act.

Section 5 enables the Minister for the Marine, in consultation with the Ministers for the Environment, for Enterprise and Employment and for Transport, Energy and Communications, to grant or refuse to grant a permit for the disposal of a specified substance, material, vessel and aircraft in the maritime area subject to certain considerations. The considerations which the Minister must take into account when deciding whether to grant or refuse to grant a permit are outlined in the Schedules to the Act. The First Schedule to the Act sets out the criteria governing the grant of a permit, while the Second Schedule lists the exemptions to the prohibition on dumping. Section 5 also makes provision for the Minister by Order to modify or amend any provision of the First or Second Schedule in conformity with any alteration which from time to time may be made to the relevant Conventions. Finally, provision is also made for the Minister, with the consent of the Minister for Finance to charge fees in respect of an application for a permit and in respect of the cost of any monitoring, surveys and examinations carried out for the purpose of enabling the Minister to determine whether dumping may take place.

Section 6 of the Act enables the Minister for the Marine, the Minister for Transport, Energy and Communications and harbour authorities (or harbour companies under the Harbours Act 1996: see the Fisheries and Harbours chapter, 390, above) to appoint authorised officers. It makes provision for members of the Defence Force to be authorised officers. It also provides for powers of authorised officers in respect of the enforcement of the 1996 Act and makes it an offence to obstruct or interfere with an authorised officer in the course of the officer's performance of functions.

Section 10 provides that the maximum penalties for an offence under the Act shall be: on summary conviction, a fine not exceeding £1,500 and/or 12 months imprisonment; on conviction on indictment, a fine without limit and/ or 5 years imprisonment. Section 11 of the 1996 Act, by stating that the provisions of the Prosecution of Offences Act 1974 do not apply to the 1996 Act, provides, in effect, that prosecutions on indictment under the Act shall be by the Attorney General rather than the Director of Public Prosecutions. Similarly, section 12 of the 1996 Act provides that prosecutions on indictment under the Sea Pollution Act 1991 (1991 Review, 366) shall be by the Attorney General rather than the Director of Public Prosecutions. This is consistent with the arrangements under the Fisheries Acts 1959 to 1992.

NATIONAL STANDARDS AUTHORITY OF IRELAND

The National Standards Authority of Ireland Act 1996 provided for the establishment of the National Standards Authority of Ireland (NSAI) as an independent statutory body. Prior to the 1996 Act, the NSAI operated as a semi-autonomous committee of Forfás, the State industrial development agency, set up under the Industrial Development Act 1993 (1993 Review, 8-10). The functions of the NSAI, formerly known as Eolas and prior to that the Institute for Industrial Research and Standards (IIRS) are set out in Part V of the Industrial Research and Standards Act 1961; in general, they involve the promulgation and formulation on behalf of the Minister for Enterprise and Employment of manufacturing standards, recognised by the prefix IS, and the certification of products and processes that comply with these standards. They are the Irish equivalent of the British BS standards promulgated by the British Standards Institution (BSI). Indeed, such national standards should be seen in the context of the European Standards or Norms (ENs) or those of the International Standards Organisation (ISO). The NSAI provide two broad categories of services, namely standards development and product and process certification. It was explained during the passage of the 1996 Act that within the context of the European Union's Internal Market, the key requirements for a national certification body, such as the NSAI, are that it should be independent, impartial and have a separate legal identity. The 1996 Act was thus required to meet these requirements. The 1996 Act became fully effective on April 14, 1997 on the establishment of the NSAI as a separate legal entity: National Standards Authority of Ireland Act 1996 (Commencement and Establishment) Order 1997 (SI No. 176 of 1997).

National Standards Authority of Ireland   Section 6 provides for the establishment of the National Standards Authority of Ireland to carry out the functions assigned to it by the Act. In particular, section 7 specifies the functions of the Authority as being the promotion, fostering and encouragement of the use of standard specifications as a means of improving the technical processes and methods used in the industries of the State. The functions include the formulation, on the request of the Minister, of specifications for commodities, processes and practices, the declaration of specifications so formulated to be Irish Standards Specifications and the making of recommendations to the Minister on matters concerning standards and certification. The functions also include responsibilities in regard to the certification of commodities, processes and practices as conforming with an Irish Standard Specification, the supervision of the use of standard marks and the testing and analysis of commodities, particularly in relation to certification and approval schemes. The functions also envisage the Authority entering into agreements with bodies in other countries and, in particular, agreements relating to mutual recognition of certificates of conformity.

Section 10 provides for the consultation by the NSAI with such authorities, persons or bodies as it considers necessary to perform its functions. In particular, it allows the NSAI to appoint such and so many consultative committees as it considers proper to advise and assist it on the technical content of such standards. Section 12 provides that the NSAI may make such charges as it considers appropriate in consideration of the provision by it of services and the carrying on by it of the activities set out in the Act.

Standard specification and standard marks   Section 16 provides for the declaration by the NSAI of Irish Standard Specifications for such commodities, processes and practices as the Minister may from time to time request. Section 20 provides that the Authority may, by notice in *Iris Oifigiúil,* specify a standard mark or other marks for use in accordance with the Act and in connection with commodities, processes and practices generally or with any class or kind of commodity, process or practice to indicate conformity with an Irish Standard Specification. A standard mark shall include the words 'Caighdeán Éireannach' or the initials 'C.É.' and may include the words 'Irish Standard' or the initials 'I.Section ' or any other mark. Section 21 provides that the NSAI may grant to a person a licence to use, subject to such conditions as may be expressed in the licence, a standard mark in connection with any commodity, process or practice for which there is a standard specification. The most commonly visible example of such licence under the pre-1996 arrangements were the NSAI-approved 'IS/EN/ISO 9000' marks. Section 22 provides that, except under a licence granted under the Act, no person shall use in connection with any commodity, process or practice, a standard mark approved by the NSAI or an imitation thereof. Any person who contravenes this section shall, unless that person proves that there was no intention to defraud, be guilty of an offence. Section 23 provides that the NSAI may procure the registration, in any register maintained in any place outside the State, of a standard mark and may procure that the Authority be entered in the register as the proprietor of the mark.

Register of standards   Section 24 requires the NSAI to keep a register of standard specifications, a register of standard marks and a register of licensees under the Act. Section 25 provides that, after the commencement of the Act, a person shall not be registered under the Registration of Business Names Act 1963 by a name containing or consisting of the word 'Caighdeán', or the word 'Standard', or the initials 'C.É.' or 'I.Section ' or by a name which so nearly resembles any such word or initials as to be likely to deceive. Similarly, section 26 provides that, after the commencement of the Act, a company shall not be registered under the Companies Acts 1963 to 1990 by a name containing or consisting of the word 'Caighdeán', or the word 'Standard', or the initials 'C.É.' or 'I.Section ' or by a name which so nearly resembles any such word or initials as to be likely to deceive. Finally, section 27 provides that, after commencement of the Act, no trade mark or design shall be registered under the Industrial and Commercial Property (Protection) Acts 1927 to 1958, or the Trade Marks Act 1996 if it contains or consists of the word the word 'Caighdeán', or the word 'Standard', or the initials 'C.É.' or 'I.Section ' or if it so nearly resembles any such word or initials or any standard mark as to be likely to deceive.

Regulations requiring compliance with standards   Section 28 provides that, for the purpose of promoting the safe use by the public of a commodity intended for sale to the public and for promoting safe practices the Minister may by Regulations prohibit the manufacture, assembly, storage, supply, offer to supply or the exhibiting of commodities or the exercise of certain practices, unless such commodities or practices comply with the Irish Standard Specification for that commodity or practice published under the seal of the Authority, in accordance with the Act, or with the standard of another Member State of the European Union which is equivalent to the Irish Standard Specification declared under the Act, or with a specification or condition set down by the Minister. While this reflects comparable provisions in the 1961 Act, the reality is that many standards are now, and will continue in the future, to be determined at European and international level. Indeed, where European Community Standards Directives are adopted, national standards are in effect prohibited on the ground that these would inhibit freedom of trade under the EC Treaty. Thus, it has become common for the NSAI to adopt and approve national standards in the context of European obligations; where this is done, the standard is published as an IS/EN standards and, in the context of increasing linkages with the International Standards Organisation, as an IS/EN/ISO standard. We have already referred to the sight of the quality standard IS/EN/ISO 9002 in this respect.

Offences and penalties Section 30 provides that any person who contravenes any provision of the Act, or any Regulation made thereunder, shall be guilty of an offence. Section 31 provides that a person guilty of an offence under the Act shall be liable, on summary conviction, to a fine not exceeding £1,500 and/or to imprisonment for up to 12 months. Section 32 provides that an offence under the Act may be prosecuted summarily by the Minister.

OCCUPATIONAL SAFETY AND HEALTH

Prosecutions: time limits The correct interpretation of the time limits prescribed by section 51 of the Safety, Health and Welfare at Work Act 1989 (1989 Review, 379-93) for the institution of criminal prosecutions under the Act arose in two High Court cases decided within a week of each other in 1996, *National Authority for Occupational Safety and Health v. Fingal County Council* [1997] 1 I.L.R.M. 128 (H.C.) and *National Authority for Occupational Safety and Health v. O'K Tools Hire and Sales Ltd*, High Court, July 11, 1996.

In the first of these decisions, *National Authority for Occupational Safety and Health v. Fingal County Council* [1997] 1 I.L.R.M. 128 (H.C.), Murphy J. dealt with the time limit applicable where an inquest has been held into a workplace fatality. Section 51(3) of the 1989 Act provides that a summary prosecution 'may be instituted at any time within one year after the date of the offence.' Section 51(4) of the 1989 Act provided that where a statutory report on foot of an investigation under the 1989 Act is made or a coroner's inquest is held concerning the death of any person which may have been caused by an accident which happened while he was at work and it appears that any of the relevant statutory provisions was contravened, summary proceedings 'may be commenced at any time within six months of the making of the report or . . . within six months of the conclusion of the inquest.' An employee of the Council had been killed while at work on April 29, 1993. An inquest was held on the death and a verdict recorded on October 7, 1993. On April 22, 1994 the Authority applied for the issue of summonses in relation to offences allegedly arising out of the fatality. The Council argued that the time limit for instituting the proceedings was governed by section 51(4) and accordingly the time limit was six months from the conclusion of the inquest, so that a summons should have been issued by April 7, 1994. The Authority contended that the relevant time limit was determined by section 51(3) so that they could be instituted at any time within 12 months after the date of the offence, that is, not later than

April 29, 1994. Murphy J. held in the Council's favour. He applied the maxim *generalia specialibus non derogant*, namely that general words should not be taken to undermine or abrogate a special word where used to deal with a particular situation, citing the decision of the Supreme Court in *Hutch v. Governor of Wheatfield Prison*, Supreme Court, November 17, 1992 (1992 Review, 305-6) as being a particularly good example of its application. While Murphy J. stated that he 'suspect[ed] that it had been intended . . . that the effect of section 51(4) . . . would be to extend the time for instituting proceedings by the Authority . . . the intention of the legislature must be obtained from the words used and the application of the appropriate principles of construction.' On this approach, since section 51 of the 1989 act was penal in nature it should be construed in a manner favourable to the accused and in the circumstances it seemed that section 51(4) restricted the period within which particular prosecutions might be brought. On this basis, he held against the Authority. Finally, it is notable that Murphy J. stated that, if it had been intended that the 'report' or 'inquest' offences could have been prosecuted within a year from the contravention, as the Authority had submitted, this could have been achieved by inserting the words 'or within one year after the date of the offence, whichever shall be the later.' in section 51(4) of the 1989 Act. This judicial hint was accepted by the legislature, who made precisely this amendment to section 51 in section 38 of the Organisation of Working Time Act 1997, which we will discuss in the 1997 Review.

The second case in which time limits under the 1989 Act arose was *National Authority for Occupational Safety and Health v. O'K Tools Hire and Sales Ltd*, High Court, July 11, 1996, decided just one week after the *Fingal County Council* case, above. In this case, a somewhat different issue arose though against the background of the 12 month time limit in section 51(3) of the 1989 Act. In the instant case, the question posed was whether the time limit prescribed in section 51 applied to the 'third party' procedure provided for in section 48(18) of the 1989 Act. Section 48(18) provides that where a person is charged with a summary offence under the 1989 Act, that person is entitled, 'upon information duly laid by him and on giving to the prosecution not less than three days notice in writing of his intention, to have any other person whom he charges as the actual offender brought before the Court' and if the Court is satisfied of the other person' guilt, 'that other person shall be summarily convicted of the offence' in the place of the person initially summoned. It also provides that the person ultimately convicted may, in the Court's discretion, be liable to pay any costs of the proceedings.

In the *O'K Tools and Hire* case, the defendant was prosecuted for the alleged breach of various provisions of the 1989 Act and of the Factories Act 1955, alleged to have taken place on October 23, 1992. The summonses had been issued on October 13, 1993, ten days before the 12 month time limit in the 1989 Act had expired. They were served on the defendant on December

13, 1993 and made returnable for January 26, 1994. The defendant submitted that it could not avail of the third-party procedure in section 48(18) of the 1989 Act as the 12 month time limit in section 51 of the 1989 Act had expired before it was made aware of the charges and it was therefore deprived of a statutory defence. It should be noted that, at this stage of the case, the defendant had not sought to issue a notice under section 48(18).

In any event, Laffoy J. did not accept the defendant's argument. She held that the third party procedure under section 48(18) was not subject to the time limit prescribed in section 51(3). Where section 48(18) was invoked, proceedings were not being instituted for that offence, since the proceedings had already been instituted by the making of the complaint against the person originally charged. However, she accepted that, in a particular case, a person charged as the actual offender under section 48(18) might be able to establish that an unfair prejudice in making a defence might arise because of undue delay in bringing the case before the Court and might be able to have the charges dismissed arising from some form of prejudicial delay. However the person originally charged would only be unfairly prejudiced arising from any delay if able to establish a separate element of prejudicial delay unconnected with the delay associated with the third party. Thus, in the instant case the District Court should apply the principles laid down by the Supreme Court in *Director of Public Prosecutions v. Byrne* [1994] 2 I.L.R.M. 91 (1993 Review, 223-6) and examine whether there was any prejudice suffered by the defendant because the summonses were not applied for and issued until October 13, 1993 and were not served until December 13, 1993. While the Authority was in some respects more successful in the *O'K Tools Hire and Sales* case than in the *Fingal County Council* case, it remains the case that the question of delay remains a continuing matter of concern in future prosecutions.

Young persons   The Protection of Young Persons (Employment) Act 1996 implemented Directive 94/33/EC, a health and safety at work Directive, and repealed and replaced the Protection of Young Persons (Employment) Act 1977. The 1996 Act came into effect on January 2, 1997: Protection of Young Persons (Employment) Act 1996 (Commencement) Order 1996 (SI No. 371 of 1996).Some of the key provisions of the 1996 Act include the following.

Section 3(1) of the 1996 Act provides that, in general, an employer shall not employ a child to do work, but section 3(2) provides that the Minister may, by licence, authorise in individual cases the employment of a child in 'cultural, artistic, sports or advertising activities which are not likely to be harmful to the safety, health or development of the child and which are not likely to interfere with the child's attendance at school, vocational guidance or training programmes'. Section 3(4) of the 1996 Act provides that an employer may employ a child who is over the age of 14 years to do light work during any period outside the school term, subject to certain limitations on the hours, including a general limit that the hours of work do not exceed 7 hours in any day or 35 hours in any week. Section 3(5) of the 1996 Act provides that an employer may employ a child who is over the age of 15 years to do light work during school term time, provided that the hours of work do not exceed 8 hours in any week.

Section 4 of the 1996 Act deals with night work and rest periods for a child, as defined in the Act. Section 4(1) provides that an employer shall not employ any child on any work between 8 p.m. on any one day and 8 a.m. on the following day. Section 4(2) provides that an employer shall ensure that an employee who is a child receives a minimum rest period of 14 consecutive hours in each period of 24 hours, while section 4(4) provides that an employer shall ensure that an employee who is a child receives, in any period of seven days, a minimum rest period of two days which shall as far as is practicable be consecutive.

Section 5 of the 1996 Act deals with the obligations on an employer to require the production of a copy of the birth certificate of, or other satisfactory evidence of the age of, a young person or child before employing them and, before employing a child, to obtain the written permission of the parent or guardian of the child. The employer must also maintain a register, or other satisfactory record, containing, in relation to every young person or child employed by him or her, specified particulars.

Section 6 of the 1996 Act deals with the limitations on employing a young person. Section 6(1) provides that an employer shall not employ a young person on any work unless the employer:

(a) does not require or permit the young person to work for more than 8 hours in any day or 40 hours in any week,

(b) does not require or permit the young person to work—

(i) between 10 p.m. on any one day and 6 a.m. on the following day, or

(ii) between 11 p.m. on any one day (provided the day is not before a school day during a school term where such young person is attending school) and 7 a.m. on the following day, where the Minister is satisfied, following consultation with such representatives of employers and representatives of employees as the Minister considers appropriate, that there are exceptional circumstances affecting a particular branch of activity or a particular area of work as may be prescribed,

(c) ensures that the young person receives a minimum rest period of 12 consecutive hours in each period of 24 hours,

(d) ensures that the young person receives in any period of 7 days a minimum rest period of 2 days which shall, as far as is practicable, be consecutive, and

    (e)   does not require or permit the young person to do for him or her any work for any period exceeding 42 hours without a break of at least 30 consecutive minutes.'

These conditions, while not as strict as those for a child, nonetheless impose somewhat more stringent limitations than those in the 1977 Act which they replace. It had been argued during the passage of the 1996 Act that even more stringent restrictions contained in the legislation as published would have prevented young persons attending school or college from working at night, particularly in bars and other licensed premises. The 1996 Act, as passed, provides a degree of flexibility in this respect while at the same time respecting the focus on safety and health which the 1994 Directive it implements was intended to achieve.

Section 7 of the 1996 Act empowers the Minister, by licence, to permit an individual employer to employ young persons on terms specified in the licence in lieu of any of those referred to in section 6(1) of the Act, and may attach to the licence such conditions as the Minister sees fit. This is subject to the proviso that the Minister must be satisfied that: (a) the terms of the licence are in compliance with the terms of the 1994 Directive, (b) the health, welfare and safety of the employees affected will not be endangered, and (c) compliance with one or more of the terms of section 6(1) would be impractical due to the seasonal nature of the work or the technical or organisational requirements of the work or for other substantial reason. Section 8 of the 1996 Act allows a similar Regulation-making power to the Minister. Section 9(1) of the 1996 Act empowers the Minister to provide by Regulations that sections 3, 5, and 6 of the Act shall not apply to the employment of close relatives, but in the absence of such Regulations the Act applies. The Act also establishes an appeals procedure which may be invoked by a young person or a parent or guardian before a Rights Commissioner and also provides for offences, penalties and the prosecution of offences by the Minister.

We also note here that some detailed safety and health at work Regulations were also envisaged by the 1994 Directive. Such Regulations, to be made under the Safety, Health and Welfare at Work Act 1989, would deal with restrictions on the employment of young persons in particularly hazardous activities, such as where they might be exposed to heavy concentrations of certain dangerous chemicals, such as lead or lead derivatives. At the time of writing, no such Regulations had been made.

RADIOLOGICAL PROTECTION

Section 93 of the Harbours Act 1946, which authorises a harbour master to refuse entry to any vessel he considers is dangerous, and in particular nuclear vessels, subject to specific permission authorised by the Radiological Protection Institute of Ireland (RPII), is referred to in the Fisheries and Harbours chapter, 393, above.

TOBACCO

Advertising and promotion The Tobacco Products (Control of Advertising, Sponsorship and Sales Promotion) (Amendment) Regulations 1996 (SI No. 408 of 1996), which came into effect on January 1, 1997, amended the Tobacco Products (Control of Advertising, Sponsorship and Sales Promotion) Regulations 1991 (1991 Review, 376). They placed further restrictions on advertising by tobacco manufacturers and promotion of tobacco products by corporate sponsors.

WASTE MANAGEMENT

Introduction The Waste Management Act 1996, which began its legislative life as the Waste Bill 1995, aimed to provide a legislative framework for the prevention, minimisation, management, control ands recovery of waste, whether industrial packaging and/or chemical waste or domestic waste. In implementing a number of European Community Directives in this area, the Act provides for new or redefined roles for the Minister for the Environment, the Environmental Protection Agency and local authorities. The implementation of the Waste Management Act 1996 will have economic and financial implications for both the private and public sectors. Measures to facilitate waste prevention and recovery will impact mainly upon industry, the services sector and consumers. The disposal of municipal, industrial and agricultural wastes will be subject to greater regulatory control and more stringent environmental standards, in accordance with ongoing European Community environmental policy requirements. Regulatory costs will be recouped from local authorities and the commercial waste sector. Increased costs will therefore arise, either directly or indirectly, for all waste producers. National waste management infrastructure will be subject both to rationalisation and qualitative development, and Exchequer and EC grant assistance will be available in respect of selected infrastructure matters. The Act (apart from sections 6(2), 32(2), 57 and 58) came into effect on July 1, 1996: Waste Management Act 1996 (Commencement) Order 1996 (SI No. 192 of 1996).

Scope of Act Section 2 of the 1996 Act lists various Directives of the European Community which the Act implements. These include Directives 75/442/EEC and 91/689/EEC, the 'framework' Waste Directives. Section 3 specifies those matters to which the Act will not apply, namely:

- an emission into the atmosphere, other than an emission from a waste related activity;

- sewage and sewage effluent;

- the treatment or discharge of effluent to waters or sewers, other than such treatment at or discharge from a waste facility;

- dumping of waste at sea (see the Dumping at Sea Act 1996, discussed above);

- a radioactive substance or product.

Section 5 defines 'environmental pollution' in connection with waste as being the holding, recovery, or disposal of waste in a manner which would, to a significant extent, endanger human health or harm the environment, and in particular:

    (a) create a risk to waters, the atmosphere, land, soil, plants or animals,
    (b) create a nuisance through noise, odours or litter, or
    (c) adversely affect the countryside or places of special interest.

As in the case of the Environmental Protection Agency Act 1992 (1992 Review, 531-2), section 5(2) uses the term 'best available technology not entailing excessive costs' (BATNEEC). The use of BATNEEC is a precondition for the grant of a waste recovery or disposal licence under section 40 of the 1996 Act, and may also be required in respect of waste activities which are exempted from such licensing.

    Section 6 and the Fifth Schedule provide for the eventual repeal or revocation of the following when the 1996 Act is fully operational: various provisions of the Public Health (Ireland) Act 1878 dealing with matters such as street cleansing, refuse removal, sewage works and street paving; section 26 of the Public Health Acts Amendment Act 1890 which enables a local authority to make byelaws in relation to removal or carriage of offensive substances and to household refuse removal; section 63 of the Dublin Corporation Act 1890 which enables the Corporation to make byelaws on household refuse removal; provisions of the Public Health Acts Amendment Act 1907 dealing with removal of trade refuse, deposit of building materials and repairs to private streets; section 10A of the Water Supplies Act 1942 dealing with the relationship between enquiries under that Act and environmental impact assessment; section 96(4) of the Environmental Protection Agency Act 1992, on the measurement of prescribed emissions; the European Communities (Waste) Regulations 1979 (which had implemented the 1975 Waste Directive; the European Communities (Toxic and Dangerous Waste) Regulations 1982; the European Communities (Waste) Regulations 1984; the European Communities (Asbestos Waste) Regulations 1990 and 1994; the European Communities (Use of Sewage Sludge in Agriculture) Regulations 1991; the European Communities (Waste Oils) Regulations 1992; the European Communities (Transfrontier Shipment of Waste) Regulations 1994; and the European Communities (Batteries and Accumulators) Regulations 1994.

Prosecutions and penalties Section 10 specifies the maximum penalties which may be imposed on a person convicted of an offence under the Act. A person will be liable on summary conviction to a fine of £1,500 and/or imprisonment for 12 months, and on conviction on indictment to a fine of £10,000,000 and/or imprisonment for 10 years. Certain minor offences specified in section 10(2) may only be prosecuted summarily. Under section 10(4), courts are required in imposing penalties to have particular regard to the risk or extent of environmental pollution arising from an offence. Section 11 specifies that the Agency, the appropriate local authority or prescribed persons may prosecute summarily for offences under the Act and provides that summary prosecutions can be taken up to five years after the offence in certain circumstances. Section 12 provides that the costs of prosecution and the expenses incurred in investigating and prosecuting offences shall, where a conviction is obtained, be paid to the Agency, local authority or person which brought the proceedings, unless there are special reasons for not so doing.

Powers of inspectors Section 14 provides for the powers of authorised persons, that is, a person appointed by the Minister, a local authority, the Agency or such other person as may be prescribed pursuant to regulations made by the Minister. Authorised persons are empowered by the Act to enter premises and stop or detain vehicles, and generally to carry out inspections, make tests and take samples as necessary for the purposes of the Act. Under section 14(2), 24 hours notice of intended entry to a private dwelling will be required, except where a District Court warrant is obtained. Section 14(5) permits an authorised person to issue directions to a holder of waste in order to remove a risk of environmental pollution, and where there is a failure to comply with such directions, the authorised person may take any necessary steps and recover any costs from the holder concerned.

Monitoring of emissions Section 15 deals with monitoring of emissions from, and inspection of, waste recovery and disposal facilities and other waste activities. It requires each local authority and the Agency to carry out or arrange for such monitoring and inspections as they consider necessary for the purpose of their functions under the Act. The cost of monitoring and inspection undertaken by local authorities and the Agency may be defrayed by charges upon the relevant persons concerned, in accordance with Regulations which may be made under the Act.

Waste register   Section 19 provides that a register shall be kept by each local authority and the Agency in which information such as details of waste licences and waste collection permits issued, particulars of notices served must be entered. Members of the public will be entitled to inspect the register at the principal office of the relevant local authority or the Agency during office hours and to obtain extracts, for which a reasonable charge may be made.

Waste management planning   Part II of the 1996 Act provides for the making of waste management plans by local authorities and the Agency, having regard to their respective functions. Each local authority will be required to make a waste management plan addressing all aspects of the prevention, minimisation, collection, recovery and disposal of non-hazardous waste within its functional area (such plans are already required for air and water pollution). These plans will be subject to review at least once every five years. Two or more local authorities may if they wish make a joint waste management plan for their combined functional areas. The Agency is required to develop a national hazardous waste management plan, to which other public authorities must have regard in carrying out their functions.

Reducing the production, and promote recovery, of waste   Part III of the 1996 Act provides for wide ranging measures in support of waste prevention and minimisation, and waste recovery, including the making of relevant regulations by the Minister. It requires the Minister to promulgate a programme for the prevention, minimisation and recovery of waste arising from the performance of their functions by public authorities, and empowers local authorities to engage in waste recovery activities.

Section 28 deals with measures which may be taken to promote support or facilitate waste prevention and minimisation. It enables any Minister or a local authority to support or assist research and development projects in respect of waste prevention or minimisation, in accordance with appropriate programmes or otherwise and empowers the Minister to make regulations for the purpose of preventing, minimising or limiting the production of specified classes of waste. Such Regulations may include requirements upon business concerns to implement waste audits and waste reduction programmes, and the prohibition, limitation and control of the production or use of specified substances or products.

Section 29 deals with measures which may be taken to promote, support or facilitate the recovery of waste. Section 29(2) enables any Minister or a local authority to support or assist the development of waste recovery activities. Again, it also enables the Minister to make Regulations governing the recovery of waste and such Regulations may include requirements in relation to the design, composition and use of products and packaging, the operation of deposit and refund schemes, and the taking back of specified wastes by relevant commercial interests. It also provides that a person or body may be exempted from all or any of the requirements of Regulations under the section if they are satisfactorily participating in a voluntary waste recovery programme which has been approved by the Minister; the Minister's powers of approval in this regard are also specified. In certain cases, Regulations may provide for targets to be achieved by relevant persons.

Section 30 specifies measures to be undertaken with regard to the prevention, minimisation and recovery of waste arising from the performance of their functions by public authorities. The Minister is required to promulgate a programme in this regard. It also requires the Minister to publish relevant guidelines and criteria, to which public authorities must have regard in the performance of their functions.

Holding, collection and movement of waste Part IV of the 1996 Act specifies the basic responsibilities of a person holding waste, and provides for controls in relation to the presentation, collection and movement of waste. The functions of local authorities in relation to the collection of waste are specified, and authorities are empowered to make bye-laws in respect of the presentation of household and commercial waste for collection. Provision is made for a permit system, to be operated by local authorities, in respect of commercial waste collection services. The Minister is empowered by Regulations to provide for the supervision and control of waste movements within, into or out of the State.

Section 32 imposes certain general duties on a holder of waste. A person shall not hold, recover or dispose of waste in a manner which causes or is likely to cause environmental pollution. The section provides that it is a good defence to a charge of causing environmental pollution to prove that the activity concerned was in accordance with a waste collection permit under Part IV of the Act, a waste licence under Part V of the 1996 Act or a licence granted by the Agency under the Environmental Protection Agency Act 1992. Section 32(2) provides that, save under circumstances specified by Regulations under the section, control of waste shall not be transferred to anyone other than an appropriate person, that is, any local authority or person duly authorised to collect, recover or dispose of waste.

Section 33 deals with the collection of waste by local authorities. It places a duty on local authorities to collect or arrange for the collection of household waste within their functional area, and enables, but does not require, non-county borough corporations and urban district councils to collect such waste. It provides that local authority collection is not mandatory where an adequate collection service is available, or collection would be unreasonably costly, or adequate means of waste disposal are available to a householder. It also provides that notwithstanding any other provisions, a local authority shall be under no obligation to collect household waste where a provision of relevant bye-laws regarding the presentation of waste for collection are not being complied with or where the waste contains anything contrary to Regulations under section 29 of the 1996 Act. Finally, it also specifies various offences relating to interference with or obstruction of authorised waste collection activities.

Section 34 provides for a local authority permit system in respect of commercial waste collection operations. It provides that after a date to be prescribed in Regulations, a person other than a local authority cannot engage in commercial waste collection unless such activity is carried on under and in accordance with a permit issued by the relevant local authority, or a valid application for a permit has been made, or the activity is, in accordance with Regulations which may be made by the Minister, exempt from the permit requirement and subject to alternative regulatory controls. The Agency may issue guidance and directions to local authorities in relation to their management of hazardous waste collection activities, and requires local authorities to have regard to same. Section 34(3) provides for the grant or refusal of a waste collection permit. A permit may not be granted unless the relevant authority is satisfied that the collection activity will not cause environmental pollution and is in accordance with the relevant waste management plan and the national hazardous waste management plan.

Section 35 empowers a local authority to make bye-laws controlling the presentation of household and commercial waste for collection, which are to be construed as being made in accordance with the Local Government Act 1994. To facilitate uniform waste collection arrangements, section 35(4) enables a local authority to provide, or require a relevant permit holder to provide, at a reasonable charge, receptacles into which household or commercial waste shall be deposited prior to collection. Finally, section 35(5) enables the Minister to direct a local authority to take specified steps (including the making of bye-laws) for the purpose of segregated collection, recovery or disposal of specified wastes.

Section 36 authorises the Minister to make Regulations providing for the supervision and control by the Agency and local authorities of the movement of waste within, into or out of the State.

Recovery and disposal of waste Part V of the 1996 Act provides for the control and supervision of waste recovery and disposal activities, and requires local authorities to ensure adequate infrastructure for household waste recovery and disposal in their areas. With certain exceptions, which include waste activities licensed under the Environmental Protection Agency Act 1992, and the recovery of sewage and water treatment sludges and specified agriculture wastes, waste disposal or recovery activities will be required to obtain an integrated licence from the Agency. Such activities will not be required to obtain licences under other environmental legislation. Waste recovery and disposal activities which are not subject to licensing will be subject to alternative controls, to be exercised by the relevant local authority.

Section 38 deals with the provision of waste management facilities. It requires each local authority to ensure that adequate facilities are available for the recovery or disposal of household waste arising in its functional area. A local authority has power to provide, or arrange for the provision of, any other waste management facilities which it may consider appropriate. A local authority may enter into an agreement with any person, including another local authority, for the provision and operation of waste recovery or disposal facilities. The section empowers a local authority or the Agency to issue directions as to the disposal of specified classes of waste, and in particular allows them to require the disposal of specified waste at a specified facility. Under section 38(7), the Agency may classify waste disposal facilities in accordance with prescribed criteria; this provision was inserted to anticipate EC Directives on landfill of waste.

Section 39 prohibits, as and from dates to be prescribed in Regulations, the recovery or disposal of waste at a facility (subject to specified or prescribed exceptions), unless the recovery or disposal is in accordance with a waste licence authorising the carrying on of the activity at the facility. Established activities will be entitled to continue in operation after any relevant prescribed date, provided an application for a waste licence is properly made and, where appropriate, the activities are currently subject to a waste permit under existing Regulations, pending a decision on the licence application. Certain waste activities are excluded from the requirement of licensing under this section, in addition to the recovery of sewage and water treatment sludges and specified agriculture wastes excluded under section 51; these include activities licensed under the Environmental Protection Agency Act 1992, the deposit of waste at civic waste facilities and public landfills, and the disposal of specified animal by-products.

Section 40 provides for the grant of a waste licence, with or without conditions, or the refusal of a licence, by the Agency. Under section 40(4), licences will not be granted by the Agency unless the Agency is satisfied that emissions from the activity comply with any relevant standard, that the activity will not cause environmental pollution and will use the best available technology not entailing excessive costs (BATNEEC) to minimise emissions, and that the applicant, if he or she is not a local authority, is a fit and proper person to hold a waste licence, and has complied with any financial requirements under section 53. Activities licensed under this section will not require licences under other specified legislation, and any such licence that is in force in relation to a waste activity shall cease to have effect.

Section 42 sets out the procedures to be followed in processing applications for waste licences or in reviews of licences, and includes a public consultation process. More detailed procedures may be specified in Regulations to be made by the Minister under section 45. Before giving a final decision on an application or review, the Agency must give specified notice of the decision it proposes to take.

Section 50 provides for the making of regulations by the Minister governing the payment of fees to the Agency or a local authority, as appropriate, in relation to specified matters.

Section 51 provides for special controls in relation to the recovery of sludges from local authority water and sewage treatment plants and certain non-hazardous agricultural wastes. These wastes are or may be recovered by means of application to land, for the purpose of benefiting agriculture, silviculture, or ecological systems. A waste licence will not be required in respect of the recovery of such wastes. However, the Minister may make regulations prohibiting, limiting or controlling such recovery activities, which may require that the prior written consent of the relevant local authority be obtained, except where relevant agricultural waste is being applied to land on the farm on which it originates.

Section 52 provides that section 97 of the Environmental Protection Agency Act 1992 will also apply in relation to the grant of a waste licence. This provision will have the effect that the Agency, where it proposes to grant a waste licence for an activity which involves the discharge of trade effluent to a sewer, must obtain the consent of the relevant sanitary authority. A consent by a sanitary authority may be granted subject to such conditions as it sees fit and these conditions, or conditions of a more stringent nature, must be included in the waste licence. A sanitary authority may request the Agency to review a licence to which this section relates in specified circumstances.

Section 53 enables the Agency before it grants, transfers or reviews a waste licence to require details in relation to the ability of the applicant, transferee or licence holder to meet financial commitments arising from compliance with requirements of or under the licence concerned, and to require appropriate financial provision (which may include a bonding arrangement or another form of financial security) in this regard.

Section 54 deals with the overlap between Part V of the 1996 Act and the Local Government (Planning and Development) Acts 1963 to 1992, insofar as they apply to waste recovery or disposal activities. It provides that where a licence is granted under the 1996 Act in relation to a waste activity, any conditions attached to a planning permission relating to that activity which are for the purpose of the prevention and limitation of environmental pollution shall cease to have effect. The Agency is required in specified circumstances to consult a planning authority in relation to any development necessary to comply with a waste licence condition and may attach to the licence such additional conditions in this regard as the planning authority may specify. Such development, and the provision of waste collection receptacles under section 29, are deemed 'exempted development' under the Local Government (Planning and Development) Acts. Conditions under planning legislation relating to environmental impact assessment for the purpose of activity licensed under the Environmental Protection Agency Act 1992 will also apply in respect of activity licensed under the 1996 Act. In accordance with the relevant EC Directives, the Minister may exempt certain local authority development within its functional area from any requirement to carry out an environmental impact assessment. The question of such local authority development carried on outside of its functional area is dealt with under planning legislation).

General provisions regarding environmental protection   Part VI of the 1996 Act contains provisions, paralleling similar provisions under air and water legislation, dealing with the powers of courts, local authorities and the Agency to take action for the purposes of the prevention or remediation of environmental pollution. It also specifies the general functions of local authorities in relation to the holding, recovery and disposal of waste under the Act.

Section 56 allows a local authority to take such measures as they consider necessary to prevent or to limit environmental pollution and to recover the cost of such measures as a simple contract debt. Nothing in the Act or any other enactment shall preclude the taking of necessary action by a local authority under this section.

Section 57 enables the High Court, on the application of a local authority or any other person, to make an order requiring measures to be taken to prevent or limit, or prevent a recurrence of, environmental pollution, where waste is being held, recovered or disposed of other than in compliance with a waste licence. An application for an order may be made whether or not there has been a prosecution for an offence under the Act, and shall not prejudice such subsequent prosecution.

Section 64 inserted a new section 96A into the Environmental Protection Agency Act 1992 for the purpose of making available information on releases to the environment of specified substances. Section 96A of the 1992 Act enables the Minister to make Regulations requiring a person carrying out a specified process or operation to determine, and provide to the Agency and specified public authorities, or otherwise publish, details of releases of substances to environmental media and of the relationship ('mass balance') between such releases and the consumption of specified substances in the process or operation concerned.

Section 67 deals with indemnification of the Agency, local authorities and their employees. It provides that the Agency or a local authority shall not be liable for damages as a result of failure to perform or comply with any function provided for in the 1996 Act. On the validity of such exclusion of liability, see the 1989 Review, 384. Section 67(2) provides for the indemnification of any authorised person, officer or employee of a local authority or the Agency against any actions in relation to their duties, provided such duties have been carried out in a *bona fide* manner.

Section 70 provides that section 107 of the Public Health (Ireland) Act 1878 and section 27 of the Public Health Acts Amendment Act 1890 does not apply to waste within the meaning of the 1996 Act.

Abandonment of vehicles Finally, section 71 of the Act prohibits (subject to criminal penalty) the abandonment of any vehicle on any land. It also empowers a local authority to impound such a vehicle.

Social Welfare

Gerry Whyte, Law School Trinity College Dublin

SOCIAL WELFARE ACT

A number of interesting changes to the welfare code were effected by the Social Welfare Act which contains, in all, eleven Parts.

Parts II and III make provision for the annual changes in welfare rates and in the calculation of social insurance contributions respectively. Part II also provides, in section 7, for the continued payment of child dependant allowances for up to 13 weeks to people unemployed for a minimum of 12 months who take up employment expected to last for at least 4 weeks – see further S.I. No. 188 of 1996, referred to below, 561 – while Part III also provides for the extension of full social insurance to Community Employment workers or workers participating in the Part Time Job Opportunities Programme who commence such employment after April 6, 1996. People already participating in such schemes are given the option of becoming fully insured – see also S.I. No. 97 of 1996, referred to below, 560.

Part IV provides for the introduction of a new social assistance scheme, Disability Allowance, to replace the former Disabled Person's Maintenance Allowance administered by the Health Boards. Entitlement to the new allowance will be subject to the same conditions as those applicable to DPMA, subject to certain improvements. In particular, a claimant dissatisfied with a decision in relation to his claim for the new allowance will now be able to appeal against that decision to an appeals officer, an option not available in relation to DPMA. See also S.I. Nos. 296 and 297 of 1996, referred to below, 563.

Part V provides for the amalgamation of the existing means-tested Lone Parent's Allowance and the insurance-based Deserted Wife's Benefit into the new means-tested One-Parent Family Payment. Deserted Wife's Benefit, Deserted Wife's Allowance and Prisoner's Wife's Allowance will no longer be payable to new claimants, though they will continue to be paid to existing recipients. This move amost completes the process of purging the family payments of any gender-based discrimination, a process which was commenced by the Department in 1989 with the introduction of allowances for widower's and deserted husbands with children – see also S.I. Nos. 425 and 426 of 1996, referred to below, 564. However, childless widows continue to qualify for Widow's (Non-Contributory) Pension while there is no comparable payment for childless widowers.

Part VI provides for certain improvements in relation to Unemployment Assistance. First, claimants who go straight on to unemployment assistance, as opposed to unemployment benefit, on becoming unemployed will be able to claim assistance for those days of that first week of unemployment on which they worked. (A week of unemployment consists of any three days of unemployment, whether consecutive or not, within a period of six consecutive days.) As against that, claimants continue to be disentitled to unemployment assistance in respect of the first three days of unemployment in any continuous period of unemployment. Thus, it would appear that, on entering into a continuous period of unemployment, a claimant may be entitled to unemployment assistance in respect of days on which he worked but not entitled to such assistance in respect of the first three days on which he is unemployed! (Where the claimant subsequently obtains work but then becomes unemployed again, the three day waiting rule does not apply if the subsequent period of unemployment occurs within one year of the first week of unemployment.) Second, claimants who were in receipt of Carer's Allowance or Lone Parent's Allowance (now One-Parent Family Payment) immediately before claiming unemployment assistance are entitled to the higher rate of assistance. Third, the means test for unemployment assistance is amended to provide for the disregard of allowances paid by a Health Board in respect of accommodation provided by a child under the Supported Lodgings Scheme and for the disregard of moneys, up to a prescribed amount, received under the Rural Environment Protection Scheme. See further S.I. Nos.96, 372 and 375 of 1996, referred to below, 560, 563, 564.

Part VII contains a number of provisions dealing with different pensions. Section 24 incorporates into primary legislation, and amends, existing regulatory provisions which relax contribution requirements for the Old Age (Contributory) Pension in the case of homemakers. Section 25 extends the Pre-Retirement Allowance scheme to separated people aged 55 or over who have not had an attachment to the labour force within a preceding period to be specified in regulations – see further S.I. Nos. 425 and 426 of 1996, below, 564. Section 26 amends existing provisions to allow a person with a mixed insurance record, *i.e.* periods of full and modified insurance) to qualify for either a pro-rata Old Age (Contributory) or Retirement Pension on the one hand, or an EU Pension or pension payable under a Reciprocal Agreement on the other, whichever is the higher. The section also provides for consequential technical amendments to the welfare code consequent on the extension of full social insurance to new entrants to the public service from April, 1995. See also S.I. Nos. 142 and 143 of 1996, referred to below, 561. Section 27 provides for Survivor's Pension to be renamed as Widow's or Widower's (Contributory) Pension, as the case may be. It also provides that a claimant who remarries and who does not qualify for pension on the death of their second spouse or who qualifies for pension at a rate lower than that payable prior to their remarriage, may requalify for pension at the rate which would have been payable had they not remarried. See further S.I. Nos. 142 and 143 of 1996, referred to below, 561. Section 28 provides for the extension of entitlement to Widow's and Widower's (Contributory) Pension to a person, whose marriage has been dissolved, on the death of the former spouse. This provision has been brought into effect by the Social Welfare Act, 1996 (Sections 20 and 28) (Commencement) Order 1997 [S.I. No. 195 of 1997].

Part VIII makes a number of amendments to the decision-making processes of the welfare system. Perhaps the most significant of these is the extension of the jurisdiction of the Social Welfare Appeals Office to deal with claims under the Supplementary Welfare Allowance scheme – sections 30 and 31 – though at the time of writing this change has not yet been brought into effect. Section 32 is intended to confirm the discretion of deciding officers, appeals officers and, in the case of Supplementary Welfare Allowance, officers of the Health Boards, to determine the effective date of a decision revised in the light of new evidence or new facts and which results in a reduction in a person's entitlement. Section 33 enables a person disqualified from receiving unemployment payments due to participation in a trade dispute to apply directly to the Social Welfare Tribunal for an adjudication without first having to appeal to the appeals officer. Finally, section 34, essentially reversing the decision of Barron J. in *O'Sullivan v. Minister for Social Welfare*, High Court, May 9, 1995, (see 1995 Review, 462), implicitly denies appeals officers any power to award the costs (as opposed to expenses) incurred by a party to a social welfare appeal.

Part IX contains a number of miscellaneous amendments to the social welfare code. Section 35 empowers the Minister to make regulations permitting claimants who have reached pensionable age to continue to receive welfare payments such as unemployment benefit or assistance up to the date on which payment of pension commences. Section 36 similarly empowers the Minister to provide for the payment of Supplementary Welfare Allowance by the Department of Social Welfare, as opposed to the Health Boards. To date, no regulations have been made pursuant to either of these sections. Section 37 provides for a number of changes to the means tests for various social assistance payments. In particular, it provides for the disregard of: (a) a prescribed amount of earnings from employment of a rehabilitative nature and the maintenance portion of Higher Education Grants in the case of Blind Pension – see further S.I. No. 143 of 1996, below, 561; (b) Health Board payments in respect of the provision of accommodation for a child under the Supported Lodgings Scheme; (c) in the case of Old Age (Non-Contributory) Pension, a prescribed amount of moneys received under the Rural Environment Protection Scheme and all moneys received under the EU Early Retirement Scheme from Farming – see further S.I. No. 96 of 1996, below, 560; and d) in the case of Supplementary Welfare Allowance, income received by way of Blind Welfare Allowance, earnings from employment of a rehabilitative nature and the maintenance portion of Higher Education Grants. Sub-section 3 also purports to give the Minister power to modify, by means of regulations, the provisions of the Third Schedule to the Social Welfare (Consolidation) Act 1993 dealing with the assessment of capital for the purpose of means-testing. On the face of it, however, this would appear to violate Article 15.2 of the Constitution which reserves the power to legislate exclusively to the Oireachtas. Section 38 provides that increases for dependent children up to age 22 in full-time education, payable to claimants of long-term social welfare payments, will continue to be payable up to the end of the academic year in which the student reaches 22. Section 39 allows the Minister to make regulations granting a reduced rate of Constant Attendance Allowance to claimants of Disablement Pension whose degree of disablement is assessed at less than 100%. Section 40 provides that fees paid to the Comptroller and Auditor General in respect of an audit of the accounts of the Social Insurance Fund will be met by the Fund. Section 41 increases, from 2 to 6 years, the period within which legal proceedings may be brought against the estate of a deceased person for the recovery of overpayments of social assistance. It remains to be seen whether this provision results in delay in the administration of estates. Section 42 extends the scope of the Household Budgeting scheme under which claimants of certain welfare payments can opt to have deductions made from their weekly payments in respect of regular household expenses and paid over to specified bodies. Section 43 provides for a technical amendment to the 1993 Consolidation Act to replace a reference to the Minimum Notice and Terms of Employment Act 1973 with a reference to the Terms of Employment (Information) Act 1994.

Penultimately, Part X provides for an amendment to the Combat Poverty Agency Act 1986 to enable the Minister to extend, by not more than six months, the period within which the Agency is required to draw up and submit a strategic plan.

Finally, sections 45 and 46, in Part XI, increase the weekly earnings below which employees are exempt from liability for the Health Contributions and the Employment and Training Levy. They also increase the annual income limit below which self-employed people are exempt from these levies.

REGULATIONS

Thirty three regulations pertaining to income maintenance schemes were passed during 1996. They were as follows:

Social Welfare (No. 2) Act, 1995 (Section 10(3)) (Commencement) Order 1996 [S.I. No. 94 of 1996] – This order brings into effect section 10(3) of the 1995 (No. 2) Act which provides for regulatory powers for determining the circumstances in which a person is to be regarded as wholly or mainly maintaining another person for the purposes of determining entitlement to adult dependant allowances.

Social Welfare (Consolidated Payments Provisions) (Amendment) Regulations 1996 [S.I. No. 95 of 1996] – These are companion regulations to the aforementioned S.I. No. 94 of 1996 and provide that a person will be regarded as wholly or mainly maintaining another person where the person either (a) is one of a married couple living together or one of a cohabiting couple and the person's spouse or partner does not have weekly income in excess of £60; (b) is separated from his/her spouse and is contributing at least £37.50 per week to that spouse's maintenance where the spouse is not cohabiting with someone else and his/her income does not exceed £60 per week; or (c) being an unmarried, widowed or separated person, is residing with a person aged 16 or over who does not have weekly income in excess of £60 and who is caring for a child dependant of the person. In this last category, a separated person must not be wholly or mainly maintained by his/her spouse. Finally, the regulations specify the manner in which weekly income is to be calculated for the purposes of determining whether a person is being wholly or mainly maintained by another person.

Social Welfare (Consolidated Payments Provisions) (Amendment) (No. 2) Regulations 1996 [S.I. No. 96 of 1996] – These regulations provide for the exemption of the first £2,000 of income per year from the Rural Environment Protection Scheme in excess of any expenses necessarily incurred in that year for the purpose of assessing means for Unemployment Assistance, Pre-Retirement Allowance and Old Age (Non-Contributory) Pension.

Social Welfare (Contributions) (Amendment) Regulations 1996 [S.I. No. 97 of 1996] – These regulations provide that people participating in Community Employment or in the Part Time Job Opportunities Programme prior to April 6, 1996 may elect to become fully insured with effect from April 6, 1996 by notifying the employer to this effect prior to April 30, 1996.

Social Welfare (Modifications of Insurance) (Amendment) Regulations 1996 [S.I. No. 107 of 1996] – These regulations effect relatively minor changes in the conditions of insurability of certain categories of employee. (Both this regulation and S.I. No. 97 of 1996 were subsequently consolidated in S.I. No. 312 of 1996.)

Social Welfare (Treatment Benefit) (Amendment) Regulations 1996 [S.I. No. 125 of 1996] – These regulations extend to recipients of Carer's Allowance the exemption from the requirement of having to have 13 paid contributions in the governing contribution year in order to quality for Treatment Benefit. In addition, the regulations also provide that where an insured person dies and his/her dependent spouse was entitled to Treatment Benefit at the date of death, the spouse will retain entitlement for so long as s/he remains a widow or widower.

Social Welfare Act, 1996 (Sections 26 and 27) (Commencement) Order 1996 [S.I. No. 142 of 1996] – These regulations bring sections 26 and 27 of the 1996 Act (see above, 557) into effect from 17 May 1996.

Social Welfare (Consolidated Payments Provisions) (Amendment) (No. 3) Regulations 1996 [S.I. No. 143 of 1996] – These regulations are made pursuant to the aforementioned sections 26 and 27. They also provide that in assessing means for Blind Pension, the first £34.10 per week of earnings from employment of a rehabilitative nature will be disregarded.

Social Welfare (Rent Allowance) (Amendment) Regulations 1996 [S.I. No. 144 of 1996] – These regulations provide for increases in the amount of means disregarded for people affected by the decontrol of rents and the minimum rent for the purposes of the Rent Allowance scheme.

Social Welfare (Employers' Pay-Related Social Insurance Exemption Scheme) Regulations 1996 [S.I. No. 145 of 1996] – These regulations provide for an ongoing Employers' PRSI Exemption Scheme whereby employers who take on certain categories of person as additional employees are exempted from having to pay the employer's portion of PRSI in respect of such employees for a period of two years.

Disabled Person's Maintenance Allowances Regulations 1996 [S.I. No. 165 of 1996] – These regulations consolidate the provisions governing the payment of Disabled Person's Maintenance Allowance and also provide for the budgetary increases in such allowance. (However they are now overtaken by the activation of Part IV of the 1996 Act by S.I. No. 296 of 1996, see below, 563.)

Infectious Diseases (Maintenance Allowances) Regulations 1996 [S.I. No. 166 of 1996] – These regulations provide for the annual budgetary increases in the rates of this allowance.

Social Welfare (Occupational Injuries) (Amendment) Regulations 1996 [S.I. No. 171 of 1996] – These regulations provide for increases in the reduced rates of certain occupational injuries benefits, following on the changes announced in the 1996 Budget.

Social Welfare (Consolidated Payments Provisions) (Amendment) (No. 4) Regulations 1996 [S.I. No. 172 of 1996] – These regulations provide for increases in the reduced rates of certain welfare payments, following on changes arising from the 1996 Budget.

Social Welfare Act, 1996 (Section 7) (Commencement) Order 1996 [S.I. No. 188 of 1996] – This order brings section 7 of the 1996 Act (see above, 556) into effect on June 10, 1996.

Social Welfare (Consolidated Payments Provisions) (Amendment) (No. 5) Regulations 1996 [S.I. No. 189 of 1996] – These regulations relax the conditions of eligibility for Family Income Supplement in a number of ways. First, they reduce the minimum period for which employment is expected to last in order to qualify for supplement from six to three months. Second, they reduce the number of hours which must be worked from 20 hours per week to 38 hours per fortnight. Third, they extend the scheme to cover job-sharers. Penultimately, they provide for an increase in the rate of supplement payable on the birth of a new child rather than at the time of the annual review of entitlement. Finally, they extend some of the existing claims and payments provisions to the payment of child dependent allowances for up to 13 weeks to people who have been unemployed for 12 months or more who take up employment expected to last for at least 4 weeks.

Social Welfare (Consolidated Supplementary Welfare Allowance) (Amendment) Regulations 1996 [S.I. No. 190 of 1996] – This regulation effects a number of changes to the operation of the Supplementary Welfare Allowance scheme. Principally, it provides for the disregard of a portion of any Carer's Allowance received by a claimant in the assessment of means for the purpose of determining entitlement to rent and mortgage interest supplements. It also provides for the disregard of the first £34.10 of weekly earnings from employment of a rehabilitative nature in determining entitlement to Supplementary Welfare Allowance and for minor amendments to existing provisions relating to diet supplements.

Social Welfare (Consolidated Supplementary Welfare Allowance) (Amendment) (No. 2) Regulations 1996 [S.I. No. 202 of 1996] – The purpose of these regulations is to enable payment of Supplementary Welfare Allowance to be made under a computerised system known as the Integrated Short-Term Schemes system.

Social Welfare (Code of Practice on the Recovery of Overpayments) Regulations 1996 [S.I. No. 227 of 1996] – This important regulation implements a code of practice governing the repayment of all overpayments of social welfare which a person is liable to repay under the Social Welfare Acts. First promised in 1993, (see 1993 Annual Review, 505), this is the first occasion on which a code of practice has been used in the social welfare code. Unfortunately the relevant statutory provision, section 282 of the Social Welfare (Consolidation) Act 1993, does not explicitly prescribe the legal status of the code, simply stating that an officer of the Minister or, in the case of Supplementary Welfare Allowance, of the health board "may, in accordance with such code of practice as shall be prescribed, defer, suspend, reduce or cancel repayment of any [amount of welfare which a person is liable to repay]." However certain provisions of the code appear to impose clear obligations on the officials involved, (such as article 3 which requires the official to provide certain information to the claimant), and as such are arguably binding in law on the administrators. At the very least, the code would appear to provide the basis for bringing claims based on legitimate expectations. However, as the code is not administered by deciding officers of the Department, but rather by officers of the Minister, there would appear to be no statutory right of appeal against a decision made pursuant to the code to an appeals officer.

Social Welfare (Treatment Benefit) (Amendment) (No. 2) Regulations 1996 [S.I. No. 261 of 1996] – These regulations exempt people aged 55 or over who are signing for credited contributions in respect of proved unemployment from the requirement of having to have 13 paid contributions in the relevant contribution year in order to qualify for Treatment Benefit.

Social Welfare (Social Welfare Tribunal) Regulations 1996 [S.I. No. 262 of 1996] – These regulations provide for a technical amendment to the time limit for making an application to the Social Welfare Tribunal arising from the amendment made in section 33 of the Social Welfare Act 1996 whereby the applicant who is disqualified for receipt of welfare because of involvement in a trade dispute no longer has to appeal to an appeals officer before taking a case before the Tribunal.

Social Welfare Act, 1996 (Part IV) (Commencement) Order 1996 [S.I. No. 296 of 1996] – This order brings into effect Part IV of the 1996 Act, which part provides for the introduction of a new Disability Allowance administered by the Department to replace the former Disabled Person's Maintenance Allowance scheme, administered by the Health Boards.

Social Welfare (Consolidated Payments Provisions) (Amendment) (No. 6) Regulations 1996 [S.I. No. 297 of 1996] – These regulations provide for the introduction of the new Disability Allowance, by defining the circumstances in which a person may be regarded as substantially handicapped in undertaking suitable employment, by prescribing rules of behaviour which must be observed by claimants of the allowance, by providing for certain disregards in the assessment of means and by extending existing claims and payments provisions and overlapping benefits provisions to the new allowance.

Social Welfare (Consolidated Contributions and Insurability) Regulations 1996 [S.I. No. 312 of 1996] – Over the past few years, the Department of Social Welfare has made commendable progress in consolidating the hundreds of statutory instruments on social welfare. This regulation marks further significant progress with this task, consolidating as it does the regulations dealing with the payment and collection of social insurance contributions, the crediting of contibutions, the refund of contributions, modifications of insurance and a number of miscellaneous provisions relating to insurability.

Maintenance Allowance (Increased Payment) Regulations 1996 [S.I. No. 346 of 1996] – These regulations provide for the Christmas bonus payment to claimants of infectious diseases (maintenance) allowance.

Social Welfare Act, 1996 (Section 22) (Commencement) Order 1996 [S.I. No. 372 of 1996] – This order brings into effect section 22 of the 1996 Act which provides for certain improvements in the Unemployment Assistance scheme.

Social Welfare (Temporary Provisions) Regulations 1996 [S.I. No. 373 of 1996] – These regulations provide for the payment of a Christmas bonus to long-term social welfare claimants and to certain claimants of unemployment benefit.

Social Welfare (Consolidated Payments Provisions) (Amendment) (No. 8) Regulations 1996 [S.I. No. 374 of 1996] – These regulations provide that any money received by way of compensation awarded to persons who have contracted Hepatitis C and to persons who have disabilities caused by Thalidomide will be disregarded in the assessment of means for social assistance purposes.

Social Welfare (Consolidated Payments Provisions) (Amendment) (No. 7) (Unemployment Assistance) Regulations 1996 [S.I. No. 375 of 1996] – These regulations prescribe the manner in which earnings from insurable employment are to be assessed for the purposes of qualifying for Unemployment Assistance, specify the method of determining average weekly earnings for this purpose and provide, pursuant to the new section 121A of the 1993 Consolidation Act, (see above, 557) for the payment of Unemployment Assistance in respect of days of unemployment.

Social Welfare (Consolidated Payments Provisions) (Amendment) (No. 9) (Treatment Benefit) Regulations 1996 [S.I. No. 383 of 1996] – These regulations mark yet another step forward in the process of consolidating the social welfare statutory instruments by consolidating the regulations in respect of Treatment Benefit.

Social Welfare (Consolidated Contributions and Insurability) (Amendment) (Regulations 1996 [S.I. No. 416 of 1996] – These regulations deal with the modified social insurance status of employees of Bord Telecom Éireann.

Social Welfare Act, 1996 (Sections 17, 18, 19 and 25) (Commencement) Order [S.I. No. 425 of 1996] – This order brings into effect sections17 to 19 and section 25 of the 1996 Act which deal, respectively, with the new One-Parent Family Payment and Pre-Retirement Allowance.

Social Welfare (Consolidated Payments Provisions) (Amendment) (No. 10) Regulations 1996 [S.I. No. 426 of 1996] – These regulations provide for the introduction of the new One-Parent Family Payment contained in Part V of the 1996 Act (see above, 556). They also deal with the entitlement of separated spouses to Pre-Retirement Allowance and introduce a new obligation on an unmarried parent applying for One-Parent Family Payment to make such reasonable efforts as may be required to obtain maintenance from a liable relative. On this last point, it is understood that the Department's intention was to require the claimant to pursue the other parent of the child for maintenance for that child. However the relevant article – article 10 – arguably does not properly reflect this intention as it refers to the claimant making "such reasonable efforts, as may be required from time to time by an officer of the Minister, to obtain maintenance from a liable relative." Because it fails to make clear that such maintenance is in respect of the child of the claimant, article10 is open to the interpretation that the maintenance is in respect of the claimant and that the relevant liable relatives are the claimant's own parents where s/he is under the age of 18.

EQUAL TREATMENT

Somewhat unusually, there do not appear to have been any cases involving social welfare matters before the Irish courts this year. However, the Court of Justice has handed down three decisions on the interpretation of Directive 79/7/EEC on the progressive implementation of the principle of equal treatment of men and women in matters of social security. (Readers are referred to the 1993 Review, pp.512-523, for an overview of the impact of this Directive.)

Scope of the Directive: Ratione materiae In *Atkins v. Wrekin District Council*, Case C–228/94, July 11, 1996; [1996] 3 C.M.L.R. 863, the Court of Justice held that a scheme of concessionary fares on public transport services which benefitted, *inter alia*, elderly persons did not fall within the scope of the Directive. According to the Court, such a scheme did not afford "direct and effective protection against one of the risks listed in Article 3(1) of the Directive." However, one commentator has suggested that the Court has refined its jurisprudence on the scope of the Directive in this case.

The Court relies less on the function of the benefit, defined in terms of the risks against which the benefit provides protection, and more on the character of the benefit, whether it is 'social security' or 'social protection'. In *Atkins*, the primary focus is not the risk against which the benefit protects, but the nature or character of the benefit concerned. Although the character of the benefit itself remains functionally defined, after *Atkins* there may be greater scope for States to provide measures of social protection which protect *inter alia* against the risks specified in Directive 79/7, without falling within its scope.[1]

In passing, one should note that in *Meyers v. Chief Adjudication Officer*, Case C–116/94, July 13, 1995, [1995] E.C.R. I–213; [1996] 1 C.M.L.R. 461, the Court held that social welfare payments designed to supplement the income of low paid workers with children had to comply with the principle of equal treatment contained in Directive 76/207.

Scope of the Directive: Ratione Personae In *Zuchner v. Handelskrankenkasse (Ersatzkasse) Bremen*, Case C–77/95, November 7, 1996, the Court held that the term 'activity', referred to in relation to the expression 'working population' in Article 2, had to be construed as referring, at the very least, to an

---

[1] Hervey, "The European Court of Justice and equal treatment in Social Security: *equality versus subsidiarity?*" in *Beyond Equal Treatment: Social Security in a Changing Europe* (Department of Social Welfare, 1996), at p.53.

economic activity, *i.e.*, an activity undertaken in return for remuneration in the broad sense. The applicant in the instant case had to provide specialised therapeutic and home nursing care for her husband who became paraplegic as a result of an accident. However as she was not engaged in an occupational activity when her husband suffered the accident and as she received no remuneration for caring for him, she did not constitute a member of the working population for the purposes of Article 2.

Indirect discrimination In *Laperre v. Bestuurscommissie beroepszaken in de provincie Zuid-Holland*, Case C–8/94, February 8, 1996, [1996] E.C.R. I–288, the Court of Justice upheld the validity of dependency additions to a non-means-tested scheme specifically for older or partially incapacitated long-term unemployed. Similarly, in *Posthuma-van Damme v. Bestur ven de Bedrijfsvereniging voor Detailhandel, Ambachten en Huisvrouwen*, Case C–280/94, February 1, 1996; [1996] E.C.R. I–194, the Court upheld the validity of a condition requiring claimants of a benefit for incapacity for work to have received a certain income from or in connection with work in the year preceding the commencement of incapacity. These cases emphasise the Member States' discretion in relation to social policy and social security matters – the Member States can decide how to secure minimum levels of income (whether contributory or non-contributory) for households, even if this discriminates indirectly against women.

PUBLICATIONS

Finally, as part of Ireland's Presidency of the European Union, the Department of Social Welfare hosted a conference in October 1996 on the theme of equal treatment in social security. The papers of that conference are now published in *Beyond Equal Treatment: Social Security in a Changing Europe* (Department of Social Welfare, 1996).

Solicitors

EXEMPTIONS FROM PROFESSIONAL EXAMINATIONS

As we noted in the 1995 Review, 464, prior to 1995, pursuant to Regulation 15 of the Solicitors Acts 1954 and 1960 (Apprenticeship and Education) Regulations 1991, the Law Society of Ireland had granted exemptions from FE-1, the 'entrance examination' to their professional course, to law graduates from the universities of the State provided they had successfully completed the relevant 'core' subjects in their law degrees. In *Bloomer and Ors. v. Incorporated Law Society of Ireland* [1995] 3 I.R. 14 (HC); Supreme Court, 6 February 6, 1996, Laffoy J held in the High Court that the exemption in Regulation 15 of the 1991 Regulations for law graduates from the universities in the State was invalid because it was in conflict with the prohibition of discrimination on grounds of nationality in Article 6 of the EC Treaty. The plaintiffs, law graduates of Northern Ireland universities, had sought parity with their counterparts from the State. In light of the High Court decision, the Law Society stated that it would henceforth require all persons to sit the FE-1 Examination rather than extend the prior exemption. However, pursuant to Regulation 30 of the 1991 Regulations, which empowers it to modify any requirement of the Regulations 'in exceptional circumstances,' it decided that the plaintiffs in *Bloomer* be granted an exemption from FE-1. The effect of this was that the plaintiffs in *Bloomer* had achieved the objective of their proceedings, namely, exemption from FE-1. The plaintiffs had already appealed the High Court decision to the Supreme Court, but the Law Society's decision rendered this moot. Consequently the Supreme Court *ex tempore* judgment in *Bloomer* was concerned primarily with the question of costs, though the Court's formal order confirmed the High Court decision that Regulation 15 of the 1991 Regulations was invalid. The plaintiffs had also alleged in their proceedings that the Law Society and its officers, and in particular the members of its education committee, were motivated by *mala fides* and improper considerations in the determination of the issues which came before them with regard to the application by Queen's University for recognition on the same basis as the universities which were mentioned in Regulation 15 of the 1991 Regulations. In the High Court, Laffoy J. had rejected the claim that there had been any conspiracy between the members of the Society, the relevant officers and committees to cause injury of any kind to the plaintiffs; she also held that the members of the education committee had not in any way been motivated by any *mala fides* towards the plaintiffs. Laffoy J. had awarded costs against the plaintiffs and, as already indicated, the Supreme Court judgment dwelt primarily on this point. The Court ultimately set aside Laffoy J.'s order on costs, awarded the plaintiffs the costs of eight days in the High Court and half the costs of the appeal to the Supreme Court.

Delivering the Court's *ex tempore* judgment in *Bloomer*, Hamilton C.J. commented that a major portion of responsibility for the award of costs against the plaintiffs rested, in his view, on confrontational attitude adopted by the plaintiffs, in particular their persistence in the allegations of conspiracy and *mala fides* against the Law Society. The Court completely accepted that the Law Society had, at all times, acted on a *bona fide* (though ultimately incorrect) interpretation of Regulation 15 of the 1991 Regulations. The Chief Justice also pointed out that it was clear that Laffoy J had been willing to make a declaration that Regulation 15 of the 1991 Regulations was invalid having regard to Article 6 of the EC Treaty, but that counsel for the plaintiffs had refused to accept a declaration as sufficient remedy for them. He stated that if Laffoy J. had simply been asked by the plaintiffs to make a declaration of invalidity, she would in all probability have awarded the plaintiffs their costs. Nonetheless, despite the attitude of the plaintiffs in the High Court, it allowed the appeal against Laffoy J's order and concluded that the plaintiffs were entitled to an order for the costs of the proceedings in the High Court limited to the costs attributable to the issue of determining the validity of Regulation 15, which the court estimated as constituting eight days of the hearing in the High Court. As to the costs of the appeal, the Court disallowed any fees incurred in connection with submissions which did not bear the hallmark of propriety having regard to the Court's jurisprudence. The Chief Justice commented that submissions should deal in an objective manner with the facts of the case and the issues of law involved and any authorities which would be of assistance to the court in the determination of the issue before it, and should not be made, as in this case, consisting of contemptuous language and unfounded allegations.

The *Bloomer* case had a sequel later in 1996, *Abrahamson and Ors. v. Law Society of Ireland* [1996] 1 I.R. 403; [1996] 2 I.L.R.M. 481. In *Abrahamson*, over 800 undergraduate law students in the State's universities successfully argued that they should also be granted exemptions from FE-1 under Regulation 30 of the 1991 Regulations. In the High Court, McCracken J. held that, since Regulation 15 had been declared invalid in *Bloomer*, it was a judgment *in rem*, and the 800 applicants in *Abrahamson* were bound by its terms. He cited the well known decision in *O'Brien v. Keogh* [1972] I.R. 144 as an example of a decision (in that case a declaration of unconstitutionality) whose effect could not be avoided. In effect, McCracken J. held that the matter was now *res judicata*. He went on to consider whether the applicants were entitled to rely on a suggested legitimate expectation that they would be exempt from FE-1. In this respect, he engaged in a comprehensive analysis of the existing case law on legitimate expectation. Because he also provided a summary of the case law to date, we have discussed this aspect of the decision in the Administrative Law chapter, 9, above. He concluded that the applicants would, in any other situation, have succeeded on this ground, but because Regulation 15 of the 1991 Regulations had been declared invalid in the *Bloomer* case, he felt he could not grant any substantive relief. However, while not prepared to grant mandatory relief, he ultimately held that the position of the 800 applicants constituted 'exceptional circumstances' under Regulation 30 of the 1991 Regulations and made a declaration to that effect, which required the Law Society to consider exercising its discretion to grant the applicants the exemptions they would have had if Regulation 15 had been a valid subsisting statutory provision. The Law Society subsequently decided that all law students attending the previously exempted law degrees at the time of the decision in *Abrahamson* were exempt from FE-1, thus restoring the position prior to *Bloomer*, but only for those already studying for law degrees. But for students who began their law studies in universities in the Republic from the academic year 1996-97, there is no longer any exemption from FE-1.

NEGLIGENCE

Cases involving solicitors' liability in negligence are discussed in the Torts chapter, 580, below.

REGULATIONS

The following Regulations were promulgated in 1996.

Advertising   The Solicitors (Advertising) Regulations 1996 (SI No. 351 of 1996) place certain restrictions on advertising 'free' or 'no foal, no fee' services, particularly in personal injuries actions. In particular, solicitors are required to indicate that clients may be exposed to potential costs if unsuccessful, or at least refrain from indicating that liability for costs can never arise (as had been claimed in certain advertisements). The Regulations, which came into effect on January 1, 1997, may be seen against the background of claims that unregulated advertising had fuelled unjustified personal injuries claims. While the legal profession had denied such claims, the 1996 Regulations may be seen to accept, at least in part, that certain excesses had taken place.

Notepaper   The Solicitors (Practice, Conduct and Discipline) Regulations

1996 (SI No. 178 of 1996) prescribe details concerning the matters to be included in the names, nameplates and notepaper of solicitors practices. They came into effect on October 1, 1996.

Practising certificates   The Solicitors (Practising Certificate 1997) Regulations 1995 (SI No. 401 of 1996) prescribed the form of practising certificate for 1997. The Solicitors (Practising Certificate 1997 Fees) Regulations 1996 (SI No. 400 of 1996) set out the relevant fees for a practising certificate for 1997 and the appropriate contribution to the Compensation Fund.

Statutory Interpretation

European Community legislation: different languages   In *H.M.I.L. Ltd. (formerly Hibernia Meats International Ltd.) v. Minster for Agriculture and Food*, High Court, February 8, 1996 (discussed in the European Community chapter, 300, above) Barr J. held that, in interpreting EC legislation (in that case, a number of Community Regulations, he would confine himself to the English language version of the relevant Regulations. He rejected the contention that the Court should examine French or German language versions and held that any ambiguity between various Community language versions of particular Regulations was not a matter for the Irish courts. He went on to apply the teleological or schematic approach to the interpretation and construction of the relevant Community legislation.

Generalia specialibus non derogant   In *National Authority for Occupational Safety and Health v. Fingal County Council* [1997] 1 I.L.R.M. 128 (H.C.), discussed in the Safety and Health chapter, 541, above, Murphy J. applied the maxim *generalia specialibus non derogant* in interpreting section 51 of the Safety, Health and Welfare at Work Act 1989.

Implied Regulation-making power   In *Blascaod Mór Teo v. Minister for the Arts, Culture and the Gaeltacht*, High Court, December 19, 1996, Kelly J. held that the defendant Minister had an implied power pursuant to An Blascaod Mór National Historic Park Act 1989 (1989 Review, 4) to make statutory Regulations under the Act: see the Arts and Culture chapter, 38, above.

Parliamentary history   In *The People v. McDonagh (M.)* [1996] 1 I.R. 565; [1996] 2 I.L.R.M. 468, discussed in the Criminal Law chapter, 274, above, the Supreme Court discussed the comparative parliamentary origins of section 2 of the Criminal Law (Rape) Act 1981, with a view to determining its true interpretation. The decision establishes authoritatively the use of such external sources in the interpretive context.

Preservation of rights under repealed or revoked legislation   In *Allen & Hanbury Ltd and Anor v. Controller of Patents, Designs and Trade Marks and Clonmel Healthcare Ltd. (No. 2)* [1997] 1 I.L.R.M. 416 (H.C.), discussed in the Commercial Law chapter, 57, above, Carroll J. considered the effect of section 22 of the Interpretation Act 1937, which deals with the preservation of rights under repealed or revoked legislation.

Time limits: meaning of 'month'   In *McCann v. An Bórd Pleanála* [1997] 1 I.L.R.M. 314 (H.C.), discussed in the Local Government chapter, 464, above, Lavan J. considered the meaning of section 11(h) of the Interpretation Act 1937, which concerns reckoning of periods of time, and Para. 19 of the Schedule to the 1937 Act, which provides that the word 'month' means a calendar month.

Torts

DUTY OF CARE

Economic loss   In the wake of the House of Lords decision in *Murphy v. Brentwood DC* [1991] A.C. 398, commentators have been waiting with hushed breath to see whether the Irish courts would join the undignified retreat from the expansive approach to the duty of care which was articulated in *Anns v. London Borough of Merton* [1978] A.C. 728 and endorsed by the Supreme Court in *Ward v. McMaster* [1989] I.L.R.M. 400; [1988] I.R. 337. See McMahon & Binchy, *Irish Law of Torts* (2nd ed., 1991), ch. 6.

McShane Wholesale Fruit and Vegetables Ltd. v. Johnston Haulage Co Ltd., [1997] 1 I.L.R.M. 86 appeared on its facts to be the watershed case. The plaintiffs' factory had been brought to a halt by the loss of electrical power caused by a fire in the defendants' adjoining premises. The plaintiffs sued for damages for the economic loss that they sustained, claiming breach of statutory duty (under the Dangerous Substances Act 1972), public nuisance and liability under the Accidental Fires Act 1943; their central plank was, however, a claim in negligence.

Flood J. was called on to try a preliminary issue as to 'whether economic loss consequent on a negligent act is recoverable as damages, within this jurisdiction.' He disposed of the issue in twelve sentences:

> In Ireland since the Supreme Court decision in *Ward v. McMaster* [1989] I.L.R.M. 400, the test for actionable negligence is:
>
> (a) A sufficient relationship of proximity between the alleged wrong-doer and the person who has suffered damage.
> (b) Such relationship that in the reasonable contemplation of the former carelessness on his part may be likely to cause damage to the latter – in which case a prima facie duty of care arises.
> (c) Subject always to any compelling exemption based on public policy.
>
> Mr. Justice McCarthy at page 409 stated the position as follows:-
>
> "I prefer to express the duty as arising from the proximity of the parties, the foreseeability of the damage and the absence of any

> compelling exemption based on public policy. I do not in any fash-
> ion seek to exclude the latter consideration although I confess that
> such a consideration must be a very powerful one if it is to be used
> to deny any injured party his right to redress at the expense of the
> person or body that injured him."

The quality of the damage does not arise. It can be damage to property, to the person, financial or economic – see *Sweeney v. Duggan* [1991] I.R. 274. The question as to whether the damage (of whatever type) is recoverable is dependent on proximity and foreseeability subject to the caveat of compelling exemption on public policy.

In short, the proximity of the parties giving rise to the duty of care must be such, as a matter of probability to be causal of the damage. If it is not, the damage is too remote and the action will fail. It will fail not because the damage is of a particular type but because the relationship between the wrongdoer and the person who suffers the damage does not have the essential, of sufficient relationship of proximity or neighbourhood.

It therefore follows that the fact that the damage is economic is not in itself a bar to recovery where the other elements above stated are present.

Whether the damage in this instance is or is not too remote is a question of fact to be determined on evidence.

This analysis provokes a number of observations. The first, and most obvious, is that Flood J. appears to regard claims based on pure economic loss as essentially non-controversial and non-distinctive: the fact that the damage is economic 'is not in itself a bar to recovery where the other elements above stated are present'. This perception of such claims may be contrasted starkly with the approach presently adopted by the courts in Britain. The House of Lords in *Murphy* held that no liability attaches to one who negligently produces or sells a product that endangers life or limb where the victim of that negligence discovers the danger before it eventuates and suffers economic loss as a result of taking steps to avoid the catastrophe.

Secondly, Flood J. appears content to endorse the 'two step' test articulated by Lord Wilberforce in *Anns*, in spite of its subsequent repudiation in Britain. Indeed, McCarthy J.'s rendition of that test in *Ward v. McMaster* shrinks the remit of the second step almost to vanishing-point: it would only be in the rarest of circumstances that a 'compelling exemption based on public policy' should prevent the application of the *prima facie* duty of care.

Housing authority   In *Howard v. Dublin Corporation*, High Court, July 31, 1996, Lavan J. was called on to deal with a fact situation similar to that which arose in *Burke v. Dublin Corporation* [1991] 1 I.R. 341, which we analyse in the 1989 Review 117-25, but different from *Burke* in a number of crucial respects. It will be recalled that, in *Burke*, the Supreme Court held that the defendant housing authority owed a continuing duty of care to its tenants in regard to its premises being fit for human habitation, so that it was liable in negligence for failing to remove a heating system which it ought to have known was injuring its tenants' health.

In *Howard*, in distinction to *Burke*, the plaintiffs were tenant-purchasers, rather than simply tenants, who had bought their heater from a third party, rather than having it installed by the Corporation, though they did so with the benefit of a loan from the Corporation as housing authority.

Lavan J., following the Supreme Court decision in *Ward v. McMaster*, held that housing authorities had a duty of care under section 40 of the Housing Act 1966 to persons obtaining loans for the repair and improvement of houses, just as they had a duty of care to purchasers qualifying for loans under section 39 of that Act:

> The defendants would be in breach of their statutory duty under subsection 40(1) (a) were they to make loans which rendered houses unfit for human habitation by the installation of a seriously defective heating system. Breach of this public law duty could give rise to a private law action in negligence in circumstances where a relationship of proximity exists. Just such a relationship of proximity exists here given the specific objectives of the Housing Acts and the straitened circumstances of the legislation's beneficiaries.

In *Ward v. McMaster* the defendant local authority had been careless in failing to have a proper valuation carried out by a person competent to do so. The plaintiffs in the instant case had failed to establish any such breach of the defendants' duty of care. In *Burke* it had been held by Blayney J. in the High Court and accepted by the Supreme Court that Dublin Corporation were not negligent in their initial installation of the conserva warm air heaters. Blayney J. had stated ([1990] 1 I.R. 18 at 32):

> Could the defendant reasonably have foreseen that its choice of the conserva would be likely to injure any of the occupants of its houses in Tallaght? In my opinion there is no evidence that it could reasonably have foreseen this. It was not suggested that there was anything in the report in the demonstration of the conserva in Cork, or in the pilot period during which two conservas were installed in houses in Tallaght which would have led it to foresee the possibility of injury.

In the instant case, the test was whether the defendants had been negligent in making the section 40 loan and not whether they had been negligent in the direct choice of, and actual installation of, the heating system. The plaintiffs had not established a breach of the duty of care in the making of the loan.

It was clear from the judgment of Finlay C.J. in *Burke* that, in circumstances where the original installation was not negligent, a housing authority might nevertheless be in breach of a *continuing* duty of care as regards its premises being fit for human habitation if subsequently the fact of unfitness was established or ought to have been discovered. This finding appeared to be based on the status of a plaintiff as tenant under a letting agreement. In the instant case, the plaintiffs were tenant-purchasers. The Supreme Court further held in *Burke* that the implied warranty as to fitness arising under the Housing Acts 1966 applied as equally to transfers under that Act as to lettings, and accordingly displaced the rule of *caveat emptor*. Lavan J. stated:

> The position may be summarised as follows:
> (a) A *tenant* under a letting agreement enjoys the benefit of an implied warranty of fitness for human habitation;
> (b) A *tenant-purchaser* is entitled to the same implied warranty with respect to a transfer under Section 90;
> (c) A *resident* not party to the letting agreement may nevertheless have a claim in negligence for breach of a duty which continues for the currency of the letting agreement.

The duty in the instant case was tenuous: a duty to take care with respect to such representation as to approval of the heating system as might be implicit in the making of a section 40 loan. It had not been established that the defendants were negligent in this regard. The implied warranty identified in *Burke* was inapplicable to the facts of the instant case, since the plaintiffs themselves had installed the heating system *after* the transfer. The making of a loan was 'at a clear remove' from the transfer of a house with the defective system already installed.

A plaintiff's status as tenant-purchaser must shift the balance of the relationship between him and the housing authority and the duties of the latter are relaxed accordingly. Such warranty as to fitness for human habitation as existed at the time of the transfer must be regarded as spent by the time of the installation. In the absence of negligence on the housing authority's part, no breach of duty is established. Nor is there a continuing duty (as in the case of a letting agreement), breach of which can give rise to liability in negligence, because of the status of the plaintiffs as tenant-purchasers.

Lavan J. accordingly dismissed the plaintiffs' claim. His thorough and incisive analysis of the issues is a helpful contribution to the development of the law of negligence in this murky no-man's-land between public and private law duties.

Later in this Chapter, in the Section on Remoteness of Damage, below, 592, we discuss Flood J.'s decision in *Turner v. Iarnród Éireann/Irish Rail*, High Court, February 14, 1996, which involves and important examination of the scope of the duty of care of housing authorities arising from the construction of a housing estate close to a railway track.

Voting entitlement In *Graham v. Ireland*, High Court, May 1, 1996, Morris J. held that a returning officer at a general election was not guilty of the negligent deprivation of the plaintiff's right to vote when she permitted the plaintiff's father, whose name was the same as the plaintiff's, to vote and denied the plaintiff his entitlement to do so. The plaintiff, though by then living elsewhere, had taken 'comprehensive measures' to ensure that his name remained on the register. It continued to do so, being entered, correctly, as 'Graham, Patrick (Jnr.)'. His father was no longer registered. When the plaintiff's father came to vote, in the company of his wife and daughter, both of whom appeared on the list of electors, the returning officer decided to issue him with a ballot paper, believing incorrectly that, since the plaintiff had left the area and his father's name did not appear elsewhere on the register, the appellation on the register must apply to his father.

Morris J. held that this did not amount to negligence. The returning officer had been 'required to and did in fact exercise a judgment upon the problem with which she was faced and . . . she had valid grounds for reaching the decision which she reached.' There is an aura of judicial review about this language, with its concentration on minimum criteria for procedural due process rather than on the inherent reasonableness or unreasonableness of the conduct, judged by the standard of the reasonable returning officer.

Morris J. did not address the question whether there might be a remedy for the *non-negligent* interference of a person's constitutional right to vote or the question of whether interference with this right is actionable *per se*: cf. *Ashby v. White* (1703) 2 Lord Raym. 938, *Cosgrove v. Ireland* [1981] I.L.R.M. 548.

Contractual immunity from duty to protect others from violent assault Morris J in *McCann v. Brinks Allied Ltd. and Ulster Bank Ltd.*, High Court, May 12, 1992, imposed liability in negligence on a security firm which exposed its employees to danger in making deliveries to a bank by requiring them to park their vehicle on the roadside, some distance from the bank. The plaintiffs had been violently attacked when attempting to make a delivery to the bank. The bank had refused to let the vehicle drive closer to the premises over a slabbed forecourt, saying that the slabs were not intended to support the weight of vehicles such as the van the employees were using. In the previous three years, two attempted robberies had taken place outside this bank. The security firm had requested the bank to provide a better access to its premises and a Garda Síochána inspector had given the bank similar advice. This could have been done by strengthening the forecourt or by providing a chute at the side of the bank.

Morris J., while holding the security firm liable, held that the bank was not guilty of negligence in unreasonably exposing the plaintiffs to the danger of criminal assault. The security firm appealed to the Supreme Court, arguing that the bank should be held a concurrent wrongdoer. The Supreme Court, controversially, dismissed the appeal.

The only judgment delivered in the Court was by O'Flaherty J., which whom Blayney and Murphy JJ. concurred. O'Flaherty J. reasoned as follows. If it could be held that the bank owed a duty of care to the plaintiffs, then it was 'clear that there was enough to have alerted the bank to take steps to minimise, at least, the risk of injury to [them]'. But, in his view, no such duty was owed:

> The legal solution to the problem posed is to say that the parties reached an agreement that the risk would lie with Brinks to make sure that the cash was delivered safely; that was the extent of the bank's interest; possibly the bank could have done more. in the way of co-operating with Brinks as regards the proposal made about easier access to the bank premises and so forth but the fact that it did not do more does not give rise to any liability in law. In this case the contract was a circumstance which prevented any duty of care arising on the part of the bank *vis-à-vis* Brinks' employees. It is, therefore, a preventative factor, rather than an intervening one, which negatives the existence of a duty of care here.

The contractual provision which had the effect of thus immunising the bank from liability in negligence to the plaintiffs was to the following effect:

> The company [Brinks] reserves to itself absolute discretion as to the means, route and procedure to be followed in the storage, guarding and transportation of any goods to which this contract relates. Further, if in the opinion of the company it is at any stage necessary or desirable in the customer's interests to depart from any instructions given by the customer as to such matters the company shall be at liberty to do so.

This clause, as O'Flaherty J. conceded, did not amount to an agreement by Brinks to assume the risk of any damage or injury to its employees. Quite clearly, on the facts of the case, the parties had acted on the basis that the bank's demands had secured the acquiescence of Brinks. Far from running the operation as it wanted, in pursuance of its contractual entitlement, Brinks had deferred to a policy adopted by the bank which, to the bank's own knowledge, exposed the plaintiffs to a danger which both Brinks and the Garda inspector understood to be unacceptable. It seems frankly astounding that the bank should be considered not to have owed, and breached, a duty of care to the plaintiffs, whose lives and physical safety were placed at risk.

The judgment contains no analysis of the reason why the contractual provision should have had the effect of extinguishing a duty of care that would otherwise have arisen. It seems as if O'Flaherty J. regarded the very existence of a contract as being, of itself, the explanation by the putative duty expired. He took a somewhat similar view in *Madden v. Irish Turf Club* [1997] 2 I.L.R.M. 148, at 155 where, on an appeal from Morris J.'s judgment of April 2, 1993 (noted in the 1993 Review, 531), O'Flaherty J. stated that the fact that the plaintiff's contractual relationship was with the tote management 'erected a barrier so as to prevent such close and direct relations to occur as is necessary to give rise to a duty of care between the plaintiff and the defendants'. In the nineteenth century, courts in England (*Winterbottom v. Wright* ((1842) 10 M. & W. 109) and Ireland (*Corry v. Lucas* I.R. 3 C.L. 208 (1868)) used to favour such an approach but what became known as the 'privity of contract fallacy' was repudiated over six decades ago in *Donoghue v. Stevenson* [1932] A.C. 562. Even within the law of contract itself, the privity doctrine is under increasing attack: see Friel, 'The Failed Experiment with Privity,' 14 I.L.T. (n.s.) 86 (1996).

One further aspect of *McCann* should be noted. O'Flaherty J. rejected the argument by the bank that the contract represented a *novus actus interveniens*. It seems that he did not regard the negligence of Brinks as superceding that of the bank. On his approach, the injury sustained by the plaintiffs was a foreseeable consequence of what the bank had done, unbroken by the conduct of Brinks; the bank was not liable simply because, in acting as it had done, it had not breached a duty of care to the plaintiffs.

NEGLIGENT INFLICTION OF 'NERVOUS SHOCK

In *McDaid v. Letterkenny Seafoods* [1996] I.L.L.W. 397 (Circuit Court (Northern-Letterkenny), Judge Smyth awarded £10,000 to the mother of an infant child who had suffered mild gastro-enteritis when she consumed muesli which contained maggots. The muesli had been bought by the child's father and the mother had fed it to her. The child and her mother sued the defendant (whose role was not clarified in the report but may be presumed to have been that of producer of the muesli). The child was awarded £2,500. The mother's claim was for nervous shock suffered by her as a result of seeing her child become ill and knowing that she had fed the contaminated food to her three children on the successive mornings.

Judge Smyth reviewed the earlier caselaw on the subject. *Kelly v. Hennessy* [1995] 3 I.R. 253 had established that, where nervous shock contributed post-traumatic stress disorder, damages should be awarded. In the instant case, however, the shock was not enough to constitute post-traumatic stress disorder. Under Irish law it was settled that shock could attract an award of damages. *Mullally v. Bus Éireann* [1992] I.L.R.M. 722 (analysed in the 1991 Review, 401-4, 446-7) was cited in support of this proposition.

The report states that:

> [i]n this case the mother is in such a proximate relationship to the child that it comes within the reasonable foreseeability necessary to attract liability. The mother was shaken and distressed and suffered guilt that she had fed contaminated food to her children, breaching the trust that they placed in her. Her anxiety was accentuated by the fact that her husband was ill at the time and that she had been acutely aware and vigilant at the time that all food was clean and fresh. Nervous shock could be equated with a mild psychiatric condition, a condition this lady was suffering from, albeit minor.

For a thorough analysis of the Supreme Court decision in *Kelly v. Hennessy*, see Dr. Eamonn G. Hall, 'PTSD – Post – Traumatic Stress Disorder', 90 *Law Society of Ireland Gazette* 227 (1996).

PROFESSIONAL NEGLIGENCE

Legal malpractice   In the 1995 Review, 474, we analysed Costello P.'s decision in *Hussey v. Dillon*, High Court, June 23, 1995, holding that the defendant, who had been the plaintiff's solicitor, was not guilty of professional negligence. We there gave details of the main facts of the case. Here we need merely note that the Supreme Court, on June 26, 1996, dismissed the appeal. O'Flaherty J. (Barrington and Keane JJ. concurring) commented:

> It goes without saying that if solicitors were required to conduct company office searches to try and detect changes of names of companies and the like in every bankruptcy proceedings in which the petitioner is a company, it would add greatly, and in the opinion of the court unnecessarily, to the cost of such proceedings.

Even if the defendant had carried out the search and found out about the change of the company's name, and if an application had been brought to the Court, the trial judge would 'indubitably' have availed himself or herself of section 128 of the Bankruptcy Act 1857.

Medical malpractice In *Collins v. The Mid-Western Health Board*, High Court, May 14, 1996, Johnson J. dismissed a wrongful death action taken by the dependants of a man who died in hospital after suffering from a brain hemorrhage. Johnson J. held that the general practitioner whom the deceased had originally consulted, some weeks beforehand, had not been negligent in misdiagnosing his condition as an upper tract respiratory infection as the deceased had failed to communicate his true symptoms to him. Another general practitioner, whom the deceased had subsequently consulted (again failing to communicate his true symptoms) made what he believed was an admission arrangement for the deceased at a hospital. In addition he wrote a letter which he gave to the deceased to bring with him to the out-patients' department of the hospital. It was in the following terms:

> Thank you for admitting the above as arranged. He has been unwell for the past five weeks. Severe headaches not relieved by analgesics, anorexia and weight loss. Past history nil relevant. Then details of his smoking habits. Examination. Looks unwell. c. and s. examination grossly normal. R.S. alright. E.N.T. alright. Abdomen alright. He had never been unwell previously and usually is reluctant to seek medical advice. Accordingly I feel he needs admission to rule out anything sinister underlying his symptoms.

A senior house officer at the hospital examined the deceased and took his history. The system operating in this hospital (as also, apparently in other hospitals in Ireland and in England) was that, unless the general practitioner had contacted a consultant in the hospital 'to arrange on a physician-to-physician basis for the admission', no emergency admission would take place unless the senior house officer formed the opinion that an emergency admission was necessary. After a very thorough examination, the senior house officer decided that an emergency admission was not warranted but that the deceased should be referred to the medical out-patients for further examination.

The deceased returned home. His failure to be admitted caused the general practitioner who had sought his admission 'some distress and surprise'. The following day the general practitioner rang the hospital. He was told by the senior house officer that, if he brought the patient back, he would refer to him the medical team, but that he could not guarantee over the phone that he would be admitted. The general practitioner at this point decided with the deceased that they would not do anything for the time being.

At approximately 2.30 a.m. the following day the deceased suffered a very sudden deterioration. He became agitated, appeared to lose consciousness and developed lateral symptoms and paralysis. The general practitioner was called and he was admitted to hospital as an emergency. Another doctor at this point examined the deceased. Having regard to the fact that by now the deceased was unable to communicate, he took a collateral history from the deceased's wife which was fuller and more accurate than any which the deceased had given all the other doctors.

The doctor produced a differential diagnosis of meningitis, tumour, migraine, infarct or subarachnoid hemorrhage. He carried out a lumbar puncture on the deceased, being satisfied that there was no raised intracranial pressure, because there was no papilloedema in the deceased's eyes. Nor were there any of the other signs which would suggest such a condition.

The deceased's condition continued to deteriorate. He died some time later in another hospital.

Johnson J. held that the senior house officer had not been negligent in failing to admit the deceased as an emergency patient. The deceased had failed to communicate his symptoms fully (as he had also failed to do so to the two general practitioners). Johnson J. rejected the plaintiff's attempt to stigmatise as negligent a system which gave a senior house officer the right to countermand a request by a general practitioner for a patient's admission. He commented:

> I must say when I first saw it I was somewhat taken by surprise that his G.P. could not by a letter alone have achieved admission. However, I was then told in the evidence, and I accept as a fact, that this is the situation which pertains not only in Ireland but in England and also that in the event of a G.P. really wishing to admit that the usual route is by making a person to person contact with the consultant in the hospital under whom it would be hoped that the patient would be admitted. This appears to be a perfectly regular and normal course that is taken by G.P.s when they wish to have an admission of an emergency nature. Under those circumstances, I find that there is no negligence on the defendants in having this system in place, it being the system which apparently applies throughout the country and indeed in our neighbouring jurisdiction.

Johnson J. was, of course, bound by the principles set down by the Supreme Court in *Dunne v. National Maternity Hospital* [1989] I.R. 91, which we analyse in the 1989 Review, 421. One may, however, question whether health service providers should be permitted to benefit from the deference given to professionals where what is in issue is essentially a policy of *management* rather than a question of diagnosis or treatment. The fact that some, most or indeed all hospitals in Ireland may adhere to a particular management practice should not, it is respectfully submitted, be given the same weight as should be afforded decisions and practices that savour of genuine professional judgment. It has to be said that some doubt must arise about a practice of admission to hospital which leaves a general practitioner thinking that a patient will be admitted when in fact the patient may be denied admission to the hospital. Even on the *Dunne* test such a practice might be stigmatised.

EMPLOYERS' LIABILITY

The duty to provide training for employees Part of any safe system is a well-trained workforce. If a plaintiff employee can show that he or she was injured as a result of an inadequate training, there is a prospect of impugning the system of work. Not every action based on this ground succeeds. Each depends on the strength of the evidence that is adduced.

In *Delaney v. United Frames Ltd.*, [1996] I.L.L.W. 169, (Circuit Court (Dublin) Judge Smith, March 11, 1996), the defendant's training regime passed critical scrutiny. The plaintiff injured her back when lifting glass panels on to a table in the course of her work assembling picture frames in the defendant's factory. She accepted that the defendant had brought in physiotherapists to train employees in lifting techniques but she contended that here had been no specific instruction regarding the manual handling of glass. An engineer who gave evidence on behalf of the plaintiff acknowledged that the size of the glass she had handled was within a safe limit but he argued that she should have been shown correct techniques for handling glass and been warned about the dangers. He conceded that the system operated by the defendant was standard in the industry.

Judge Smith, after hearing the plaintiff's witness, held that the defendant had no case to answer. The plaintiff had been doing the work for nearly three years previous to the accident, without incident. (She had assembled around 150,000 frames!) The training she had received in the safe lifting, handling and carrying of objects at work covered the description of the accident that had occurred. The system was accordingly a safe one and the training was adequate.

Safe premises In the 1995 Review, 483, 485, we analysed *Mulligan v. Holland Dredging (Ireland) Ltd.*, High Court, January 23, 1995, where O'Hanlon J. dismissed an action for negligence by a deck-hand who had fallen from a vertical ladder, linking the deck of the vessel to a stony area beneath. The plaintiff claimed that he fell while beginning a descent; other evidence, accepted by O'Hanlon J., was to the effect that he fell while ascending the ladder. The ladder complied with the safety requirements of the law of the Netherlands; it had been regularly inspected and was of a type to be found on other vessels.

The plaintiff appealed unsuccessfully to the Supreme Court. O'Flaherty J. (Hamilton C.J. and Murphy JJ. concurring) was 'inclined to agree' with counsel for the plaintiff that O'Hanlon J. had stated the test too narrowly in terms of whether the ladder presented any real or significant danger to crew members. (We expressed a similar concern in the 1995 Review, 486.) O'Flaherty J. thought that:

> [i]n general, . . . in deciding whether he has any liability, it is sufficient to ask whether an employer has taken reasonable care for the safety of his employees to prevent injury or damage to them from a foreseeable risk, having regard to all the circumstances of the particular case.

The Supreme Court was nonetheless in as good a position as the trial judge to determine the issue of negligence in the case (cf. *Moore v. Fullerton* [1991] I.L.R.M. 29) and it also came to the conclusion that the plaintiff had not established negligence on the part of the defendant. In the circumstances, O'Flaherty J. decided to reserve his position on 'the interesting issues' that might arise in a future case concerning the duty of care owed by an employer to an employee where the employee had to work on premises and the employer had no control of the situation. It should be noted that the issue at trial was not so much that of the duty of an employer whose employee works off the premises but rather whether the duty of a person (or company) who is not, in substance, the employer of the plaintiff by reason of the absence of capacity to control the discharge of the plaintiff's duties as employee: cf the 1995 Review, 486.

Safe system of work   In *Coughlan v. Birr Urban District Council,* Supreme Court, July 22, 1996, the plaintiff, working on a FÁS scheme as a stone mason, was injured when building a wall. A narrow channel, about ten inches wide and three inches deep, had been dug between the wall and the kerb of an adjoining footpath. It was intended that this gap would be filled in by blockwork 'which would improve the appearance of the wall and the footpath generally'. The plaintiff was obliged to stand with the rear portions of his feet on the kerb and the front portions of his feet in the channel. He tripped when placing a stone on the wall.

Lavan J. dismissed the plaintiff's action for negligence against the employer. The Supreme Court by a majority (Hamilton C.J. and Blayney J., O'Flaherty J. dissenting) reversed. Hamilton J. considered that stone masons should be entitled to work on a level surface, at least to the extent that they should not be required to expose themselves to danger from an artificially created uneven surface, as was the situation in the instant case. Both Hamilton C.J. and Blayney J. considered that the fact that the plaintiff had not complained about the difficulties caused by the channel was irrelevant. No witness had asserted that the area or the system of work was safe.

O'Flaherty J., dissenting, stated:

In my judgment what happened here was an accident pure and simple –
such that cannot be divorced from the ordinary misfortunes and vicissi-
tudes of life whether they occur at home, at play, or at work. To hold the
employer liable as a *wrongdoer* on the facts of this case would be to
impose a duty on employers to take extravagant precautions -as far as
the circumstances of this case are concerned, for example – to place
planks etc. to ensure a level ground surface. When we impose such a
duty of care v/e do no service either to workers or employers. The worker
with a true cause of action for negligence against an employer will naturally be affronted when he discovers that, in a case where no blame in
any meaningful sense of that term should be attached to the employer,
recovery of damages is equally possible. Employers will legitimately
argue that to allow these standards to be set is to put in place a disincen-
tive to the giving of employment.

It is interesting to contrast O'Flaherty J.'s observations with those of Hederman
J. in *Coyle v. An Post* [1993] I.L.R.M. 508, where O'Flaherty J. was dissenting. See our comments in the 1992 Review.

In *McDonagh v. Brian O'Connell Ltd.*, High Court, October 24, 1996, the
plaintiff, who was engaged in archeological excavations at King John's Castle in Limerick, was injured when he fell into a trench. He was at the time
leaning across it to pick up an artifact from the top of the opposite bank. Barr
J. held that his '*de facto* employer', Limerick Corporation, was guilty of negligence. The risk that unprotected vertical banks might collapse was substantial and could have been obviated either by securing appropriate horizontal
shuttering along the walls of the trench or by digging the trench in such a way
that its sides were not vertical but sloped outwards in an approximate V-
shape. The latter method was the one normally adopted by local authorities
and public utilities which had occasion to dig such trenches for pipe-laying
and other similar purposes. It seemed to Barr J. to be the more convenient
strategy.

An interesting question of what level of care the law demands of an employer arose in *McCann v. ESB* [1996] I.L.L.W. 178 (Circuit Court (Dublin),
Judge Carroll, March 21, 1996). The issue was a simple one. The plaintiff's
task was to remove an electricity pole which had earlier been removed from
the ground by other employees of the defendant. There was a hole in the
ground where the pole had been. The plaintiff fell into it. He argued that the
work team who had taken out the pole could have rendered the hole safe by
the simple device of placing a board over it.

Judge Carroll dismissed the action. He is reported as having said that:

the law was not that he who is injured must be compensated. Rather it is
that he who is injured through the negligence of another must be com-

pensated. The work the plaintiff was engaged in was one of those practical tasks that involves some slight risk. The negligence must be clear.
In this particular case, everything happened quickly. The plaintiff knew
the hole had been made and that there was a danger in moving the pole
before the pole was tied down. This was just one of those areas where
the law must leave the plaintiff to take care of himself.

It has to be said that Judge Carroll has consistently displayed a concern that
the law of negligence should be true to its requirement of proof of fault on the
part of the defendant and that some other judges, not merely in the Circuit
Court, are disposed to set an easier test, from the standpoint of the plaintiff. It
is more than possible that another judge, on the facts of *McCann* case, would
have held in favour of the plaintiff, with some reduction for the plaintiff's
contributory negligence.

**The duty to protect physically infirm employee from exposure to an un-
safe working environment**   In *Bolger v. Queally Pig Slaughtering Ltd.*,
High Court, March 8, 1996, the plaintiff, a boner employed by the defendant,
developed a swelling around his left elbow as a result of the pressure he
applied when doing his work. He complained to his foreman and the floor
manager but they told him he just had to get on with his work. His condition
worsened and he sued his employer for negligence.

   Barron J. imposed liability. He considered that the employer could not be
blamed for having failed to anticipate the injury, but that the failure to respond to the plaintiff's complaint was culpable:

> It could not just ignore the complaint as it did. It had a duty to consider
> the cause of the complaint and, if necessary, to do what was required to
> ensure the safety of the plaintiff. By doing nothing, it was in breach of
> its duty to him.

The employer argued that no damage had flowed from its default since "there
was no obligation to move the plaintiff to any other job in the factory and the
only remedy for the plaintiff would have been to cease work". Barron J. rejected this contention. He thought that:

> it would be unfair to the plaintiff to accept such an argument. The de-
> fendant owed the plaintiff an obligation to consider his complaint and
> to see what could be done about it. I am quite sure that if the complaint
> was taken seriously . . . some arrangement would have been made to
> enable the plaintiff to work but at the same time would have enabled
> him to work without injuring himself.

It has to be said that this disposition of the causal issue was somewhat kind to the plaintiff. Barron J.'s emphasis on the employer's obligation to consider the plaintiff's complaint has the aura of a judicial review proceeding, with its concentration on procedural due process. It is somewhat similar to the approach that Barron J. favoured in *Mullen v. Vernal Investments Ltd.*, High Court, December 15, 1995, where he held that an employer has a duty to *give consideration* to the health and safety of employees who, in the course of their employment, have to leave their main place of work to carry out their duties elsewhere. See the 1995 Review, 481, 485. (See also, in this context, *Graham v. Ireland*, High Court, May 1, 1996, which we analyse earlier in this Chapter in the section on the Duty of Care, above, 577.)

The *Bolger* case may be contrasted with *Sammon v. Flemming GmbH*, High Court, November 23, 1993, which we analysed in the 1993 Review, 539.

OCCUPIERS' LIABILITY

The Occupiers' Liability Act 1995 (See 1995 Review, 493-519) did not feature in judicial decisions in 1996, as many actions were already in progress before its enactment. What the courts had to say is nonetheless of some general interest.

Safety on the dance floor   In *Duffy v. Carnabane Holdings Ltd. t/a The Glencarn Hotel*, Supreme Court, March 25, 1996, (*ex tempore*) the Supreme Court upheld a finding of liability against the defendant hotel (reduced by 20% for the plaintiff's contributory negligence) where the plaintiff slipped on the dance floor when attending a disco. The plaintiff gave evidence that alcoholic beverages were sold at bar areas adjacent to the dancing area and that there were spillages and broken glass on the dance floor.

In the course of his judgment, O'Hanlon J. observed:

> I think it is one of those situations where the law recognises that the demand on people carrying on this is very difficult and at the same time it is a fact that the law compels the factory owner to insure that his machinery is guarded in such a manner that it is virtually impossible for an accident to happen. That involves a certain expense in running a factory and these rules have to be implemented by the factory owner. Similarly with the disco scene when there is a level or pattern of drink being brought onto the dance floor and glasses being broken, it creates something very close to an absolute liability on the part of the proprietor for accidents which may occur.

On appeal, counsel for the defendant argued that the analogy with the duty of factory owners to their employees had set an inappropriately high standard of care for proprietors of dance halls. O'Flaherty J. (Blayney and Barrington JJ. concurring) agreed that this would be too high. The proper test had been stated by Griffin J. in the earlier Supreme Court decision of *Mullen v. Quinnsworth* [1990] 1 I.R. 59, at 62 as follows:

The plaintiff was an invitee of the defendant on the occasion of the accident. As such, the defendant was not an insurer of her safety, but it owed her a duty to take reasonable care, in all circumstances, to see that the premises were reasonably safe for her. Whilst this is the general principle which applies in cases of invitees, each case must necessarily depend on its own particular facts.

O'Flaherty J. did not, however, interpret the trial judge's remarks as actually applying the analogy. It was

> inconceivable that a judge with the experience of O'Hanlon J., having spent most of his career at the bar doing these type[s] of cases, and after a long time on the bench, that coming towards the close of his judicial career that he would not be *au fait* with what the standard of care was in a situation such as this. So I take what he was saying as being largely discursive and it is important to note that he did stop short of saying that there was an absolute duty of care. He said it was something approaching that but stopping short of it.

I think the important point in this case is that the evidence was there to make the finding that he did and while I would reject his formulation as regards the standard of care as having been pitched too high, in fact when he came to deal with the matter he dealt with it in an impeccable way.

It has to be said that certain operations, even though they achieve desirable social goals, are designed in such a way that there is an attrition rate which simply cannot be removed by any system of accident prevention, however well managed. Perhaps large supermarkets involve such a risk: no 'sweeper' system can entirely remove the possibility that customers will slip on items that have been very recently knocked from the aisles. Similarly in the context of discos, once alcohol – or indeed any other drink – is permitted to be consumed in the vicinity of the dancing area, a risk of spillage and slippage inevitably arises and no system of monitoring the floor can afford full protection.

Three options thus present themselves. The first is to hold that the high social utility of the particular operation means that it is not negligent to carry it on. On such an approach the cost of preventing the injury would be regarded as socially or economically prohibitive. The second option is to stigmatise the operation as being negligently structured. In the context of discos, this would mean that even an excellent system of monitoring for spillages would not exempt a defendant proprietor from liability in negligence because the negligence would be considered to consist in permitting beverages to be consumed in the dancing area, not in failing to clear up the spillages properly.

The third option would have the same outcome as the second but would be based on a different conceptual model. It would decline to stigmatise the operation as negligent but would nonetheless impose *strict* liability, without fault. There is nothing new about such an approach. The tort of trespass was originally one of strict liability, the rule of *Rylands v. Fletcher* was for long so regarded and, of course, the statutory regime of product liability prescribed by Europe, implemented (belatedly) by the Liability for Defective Products Act 1991, imposes liability for damage caused by a defective product without the need to show negligence on the part of the producer: see the 1991 Review, 420.

It should be kept in mind that the Occupiers Liability Act 1995 has overtaken the common law: see the 1995 Review, 493-519. Thus, the category of invitee has become a thing of the past. It is, however, worth noting that O'Flaherty J. was not willing to categorise a dance floor 'bestrewn with spillages and with broken glass' as an 'unusual danger' under the test laid down by Willes J. in *Indermaur v. Dames* (1866) L.R. 1 C.P. 274, because a floor in that state would constitutes no obvious danger as to take it outside the category of an unusual one. (On the facts of the case, the floor was held to have been less obviously dangerous than the plaintiff had described.)

Access areas   In *Flynn v. McGoldrick*, High Court, October 25, 1996, Flood J. imposed liability on the lessees of licensed premises where the plaintiff, a patron, tripped on a kerbing that was used to confine the pavement of the forecourt. Flood J. held that the accident had occurred 'on an area which was the legitimate access to the defendants' premises and on an area over which they certainly had a right-of way and that she was a lawful invitee on the said right-of way and had been in their premises on business.' The point where she fell 'was a danger to users of the said right-of-way and ought to have been within the defendants' knowledge.'

It is noteworthy that Flood J. did not speak of the danger as an 'unusual' one, which was required by Willes J. in the classic formulation of the occupier's duty to invitees in *Indermaur v. Dames*.

Railway and housing authorities   Later in this Chapter, in the section on Remoteness of Damage, below, 592, we discuss Flood J.'s decision in *Turner v. Iarnród Éireann/Irish Rail*, High Court, February 14, 1996.

ROAD TRAFFIC ACCIDENTS

Transporting school-children by bus In *Connolly v. Bus Éireann/Irish Bus*, High Court, January 29, 1996 the question of the duties surrounding the transport of school-children fell for consideration. The plaintiff, a fourteen-year-old girl, was seriously injured when crossing the road at 5 pm on a summer's evening, having just alighted from a bus. The bus was on a scheduled run from Ballyshannon to Sligo. Whereas primary school children in the area were transported by school buses dedicated to that function, with distinct identification as such, secondary school children were transported in the ordinary scheduled bus service. The bus which carried the plaintiff served two secondary schools in Bundoran; that afternoon it had collected about thirty pupils and twelve adult passengers.

The driver of the vehicle which struck her was found to have been guilty of negligence; but a question arose as to whether the bus should have had attached to it some suitable sign or writing to indicate that it was in part school transport and therefore was likely to contain a substantial number of children returning from school. Barr J. rejected such a basis of liability, stating:

> That might be a counsel of perfection but in my view it was not a duty in negligence which Bus Éireann owed to other road users. The distinction between the standard type of school bus and a bus operating on a scheduled service is that the former is concerned with conveying primary school children to and from schools. Such children, who may be as young as four years of age, have a potential for causing traffic hazards on leaving the bus. There is no doubt that such vehicles should be clearly identified. A scheduled service bus which incidentally carries secondary school children at certain times of day is in a quite different situation. First, the children are substantially older, being from twelve to eighteen years of age, and their presence on the bus is for a comparatively short part of the total bus journey, i.e. in the ordinary course, in circumstances such as those under review, all of the children will have dismounted long before the bus reaches its destination. In short, for the greater part of hits route the bus leads a normal existence and cannot be regarded as a partial school bus. I am not satisfied that Bus Éireann had any obligation to warn other road users that for part of its scheduled journey it carried a large number of secondary school children.

Barr J.'s differentiation between primary school children and secondary school children is surely sensible. More troublesome is the problem of a bus which has schoolchildren on board for only part of its journey. It can hardly be right that liability should not be imposed on a bus authority if, on a systematic basis, it conveyed *primary* school children on a scheduled service for part only of the route and sought to justify the failure to alert other road users of the fact that young children were on board for part of the route by invoking the fact that it carried other passengers further. It is true that the way in which this message could most effectively be conveyed presents room for argument but the need for some such communication would seem imperative.

In determining how safety for transporting schoolchildren can be fostered, Irish courts could with benefit examine the practice in the United States of America where, in some states, not only is the schoolbus painted a distinctive colour but an artificial barrier, stretching across the opposite lane of the highway, protrudes from the bus when children are alighting. Drivers are under the obligation, in both criminal and civil law, to stop before the barrier.

Road authority's duty to provide adequate signposting   In *Ryan v. Walsh and Galway County Council*, Supreme Court, July 18, 1996, the Supreme Court ordered a retrial where Lynch J., in an action for negligence against (*inter alia*) Galway County Council, had held in favour of the plaintiff on the basis of a particular theory of the case without giving the expert witnesses called on behalf of the County Council a full opportunity to refute it. The essence of the plaintiff's claim was that the signposting leading to an incompleted roundabout was confusing and misleading.

Cyclists   In *Buckley v. Maloney*, Supreme Court, July 2, 1996, (*ex tempore*), the Supreme Court affirmed Johnson J.'s finding of negligence against the defendant driver where he had collided with the plaintiff cyclist who had come onto the road from the hard shoulder to avoid some potholes. O'Flaherty J. stated:

> The law on this matter I would lay down as follows: that when vehicles are travelling in the same direction and when one is a lorry travelling at some speed, at about 30 miles an hour .... and there is a cyclist on the hard shoulder, and then it is clear that the cyclist must move out from the hard shoulder to the main carriageway – it was his entitlement to be on the main highway in the first instance – then a duty devolves on the lorry driver to give him a goodly clearance. [The defendant driver] felt that he had done this but I am clear in my mind that he did not do so. Further, he could have checked further in advance that there was no traffic behind; in addition, he could have slowed down sufficiently to give the cyclist a chance to come outside the potholes and could, indeed, have stayed behind him for some distance. It is clear that he had many options open to him in the circumstances because there was no traffic behind, nor was there any traffic approaching. None of these options were effectively exercised, I am satisfied.

The Supreme Court altered the trial judge's 50%-50% of liability to 80% for the defendant's negligence and 20% for the plaintiff's contributory negligence. The plaintiff had to bear some responsibility for the accident as he ought to have checked behind him when he knew that he had to go onto the road to avoid the potholes.

Motorcyclists   In *Healy v. Jeudermann*, Supreme Court, July 9, 1996 (*ex tempore*), the Supreme Court affirmed Carroll J.'s dismissal of the plaintiff motorcyclist's action for negligence against the defendant car driver arising from a collision between the vehicles. The defendant was turning right at the time; the plaintiff was driving his vehicle along the road in the same direction. The defendant gave evidence that she was driving at only 15 mph and that she had indicated her intention to turn about sixty yards before she did so. She had also checked in her mirror.

In upholding the dismissal, O'Flaherty J. asked rhetorically, 'What more could she have done?'

Road junctions   Later in this Chapter, in the Section on Remoteness of Damage, below, 595, we discuss the decision of *Grace v. Fitzsimon and O'Halloran*, Supreme Court, June 14, 1996 (*ex tempore*), which analyses the duty of a driver who enters the yellow hatched area at a road junction.

Technical evidence versus witness's recollection   In *Dunne v. Clarke Oil Products Ltd.*, Supreme Court, June 7, 1996 (*ex tempore*), the Supreme Court affirmed Johnson J.'s dismissal of an action for negligence where the plaintiff, the defendant's employee was injured when driving an oil tanker which struck another vehicle at the wrong side of the road, from the tanker's standpoint. The plaintiff claimed that bald tyres caused the accident. The technical evidence in relation to the extensive skid-marks was to the opposite effect. Johnson J., while being impressed with the plaintiff's honesty, held against him on the basis of the technical evidence. O'Flaherty J. (Blayney and Keane JJ. concurring) was affected by the plaintiff's certainty that he had lost control of the tanker. The evidence of a person who was believed by the trial judge should always be given special weight; but in this case the gap between what the plaintiff perceived and the physical evidence observed at the scene of the accident had not been crossed.

REMOTENESS OF DAMAGE

Rescuer   In *Turner v. Iarnród Éireann/Irish Rail*, High Court, February 14, 1996, a six year old girl, permitted by her mother to play in front of her house in a local authority housing estate in Tralee on a summer's afternoon, wan-dered away down the road, went through an opening in a post-and-wire fence and proceeded onto the Tralee-Mallow railway line. Her mother went looking for her, naturally became agitated, ran along the track and tripped on some signal wires, injuring her knee. The child emerged unscathed.

The mother sued the railway company and the local authority which had responsibility for the housing estate, claiming negligence. She argued that the railway track was an allurement and danger to young children and that the railway company had failed to take reasonable care to ensure that they did not get onto the track. She characterised herself as a rescuer.

Flood J. had little difficulty in dispatching the railway's contention that section 73 of the Railway Clauses Consolidation Act 1845 specified its maximum obligation in relation to fencing. That section provides as follows:

> The company shall not be compelled to make any further or additional accommodation works for the use of owners and occupiers of lands adjoining the railway after the expiration of the prescribed period, or if no period be prescribed, after five years from the completion of the works and the opening of the railway for public use.

In Flood J.'s view, the purpose of the obligation to fence, prescribed by section 68 of the Act, was to preclude trespass by animals either adjacent lands. It was never intended to constitute a discharge of a common law duty of care to anyone to whom the railway company could be said to owe such duty.

Equally Flood J. had no time for the argument that, because the danger had not existed before the housing estate was built, the railway had no responsibility for the present danger. He stated:

> In my opinion the existence or non-existence of a duty of care is always circumstance-related. If you are the owner of lands upon which an operation has a potential for being dangerous but in the circumstances in the past in which it was conducted was unlikely to give rise to injury, and if the circumstances change and it is foreseeable that injury could result to a person or class of person then a duty of care is imposed upon the person operating the said potential source of danger.

The circumstances under which a duty of care arose had been crystallized by McCarthy J. in *Ward v. McMaster* [1988] I.R. at 349 when he said:

> I prefer to express the duty as arising from the proximity of the parties, the foreseeability of the damage and the absence of any compelling exemption based upon public policy. I do not in any fashion seek to exclude the latter consideration although I confess that such a consideration must be a very powerful one if it is to be used to deny an injured

party his right to redress at the expense of the person or body that injured him.

In the instant case, the railway must have been aware that many children could get down to the track through the railway boundary fence 'even if it were in good condition, which it clearly was not'. Likewise, it would have been aware that children on a railway track were in serious danger of injury. 'Thus', said Flood J., 'the ingredients of proximity to the source of danger and foreseeability of damage are clearly present and in my opinion there is a total absence of any compelling exemption based on public policy'. The railway had owed, and breached, a duty of care to the plaintiff's daughter. The plaintiff's agitation was natural and her failure to see the wires was due to that agitation and concern which in turn was created by the absence of a proper fence to prevent children going onto the railway line. The plaintiff's injuries were 'a direct consequence' of the railway company's breach of the duty of care in failing to provide adequate fencing. Accordingly the railway was liable to the plaintiff. The local authority was similarly liable. It was not sufficient for it to say that because the railway track was there before the housing estate was built, the railway had the sole obligation to have its track appropriately fenced:

> If a local authority constructed a housing estate adjacent to a disused mill and mill-race, it would be no answer to a claim against the local authority for injury to a child that it was the duty of the mill-owner to fence off the mill-race. . . .

Flood J. divided the liability equally as between the defendants.

Turner may usefully be compared with the Supreme Court decision in *Phillips v. Dargan* [1991] I.L.R.M. 321, which we analysed in the 1990 Review, 493-500. In that case a husband was injured when dragging his wife away from a fire. The main features of a negligence claim by a rescuer have now been established. The courts are clear that the claim is based on the defendant's breach of duty of care *to the rescuer* and is not, in essence, a derivative action, parasitic upon the actionability of the claim of the person in danger. It is not essential for the plaintiff to establish that, in fact, anyone was in danger: it is sufficient if the defendant negligently induced the rescue attempt by creating a situation of *apparent* danger.

Flood J.'s reference to the plaintiff's injuries as 'the direct consequence' of the railway's breach of its duty of care should not, it seems, be interpreted as an attempt to revive the directness test for the remoteness of damage, which the English Court of Appeal favoured in *In re Polemis* [1921] 3 K.B. 560. It is clear from the facts, and Flood J.'s view of them, that the plaintiff's agitation, and consequent stumble, were entirely foreseeable: cf. McMahon &

Binchy, *op. cit.*, 372.

An interesting conceptual question might have arisen if the defendants had sought to argue that the plaintiff had been negligent in the supervision of her daughter. (No such claim was made and Flood J. said nothing indicating any support for such a notion.) From the standpoint of legal theory, in a case where a rescuer's negligence in placing a person at risk is part of the story of the accident, that negligence would be capable of also being characterised as *contributory* negligence if it foreseeably induced him or her to engage in the rescue attempt. There is nothing strange about conduct in the context of rescue attempts being capable of being characterised as both negligence and contributory negligence: if a person carelessly places himself or herself in a situation of danger (by climbing a mountain, for example, without the proper equipment), that contributory negligence will also amount to negligence to those who engage in a foreseeable rescue attempt: see our comments in the 1990 Review, 498.

Intervening conduct In *Grace v. Fitzsimon and O'Halloran*, Supreme Court, June 14, 1996 (*ex tempore*), the Supreme Court affirmed a finding by Barr J. that the first defendant was 40% to blame and the second defendant 60% to blame for an accident causing injury to the plaintiff. The first defendant, wishing to turn left into a street in the direction that the plaintiff was approaching, nudged out into a yellow "box" on the street and stopped there for perhaps a minute, waiting for a clearance. The second defendant came 'at some speed' in the opposite direction. He collided with the plaintiff. He argued later that he had been forced onto the wrong side of the road because of the obstruction created by the first defendant.

The first defendant unsuccessfully sought to convince the Supreme Court that, although he should not have needlessly been in the yellow hatched area, nevertheless, since he had been there for so long, the second defendant ought to have seen him, so that the first defendant's wrong should not be regarded as having contributed to the accident at all. In essence this was an invocation of the doctrine of *novus actus interveniens* or at least an attempt to apply the doctrine of the 'last clear opportunity', abolished by section 56 of the Civil Liability Act 1961. O'Flaherty J. observed that the first defendant

> was in a place where he should not legally have been. There is no doubt that if [the first defendant] was going somewhat slower he would have been able to stop and not have had to swerve onto the wrong side of the road. But that is where [the first defendant] was at fault.

In *Roche v. K.M.B. Investments Ltd.*, Supreme Court, June 21, 1996, the plaintiff, a married woman, received a groin injury caused by the defendants' negligence. Her husband's insensitivity had contributed to exacerbating her psycho-sexual difficulties resulting from the accident. The trial judge, in assessing damages for pain and suffering, was of the view that the husband's insensitivity should not be treated as a factor that reduced the *quantum* of damages:

> [W]hat has happened [the plaintiff,] certainly up to date . . . was reasonably foreseeable and even though the role of the husband played a major part, that role does not come into the category of, if you like, a completely new intervening third party coming in that would remove any further liability from the defendants.

The Supreme Court held that this was not the correct approach. Keane J. (Hamilton C.J. and Murphy J. concurring), noted that, if the plaintiff had had a more understanding and sympathetic husband, the detrimental consequences for her sexual life following the accident would have been more limited in time:

> As it was, however, her husband's unreasonable behaviour made the resumption of a normal sexual life significantly more difficult.

This was not the direct consequence of the defendants' negligence or of the injuries the plaintiff had received; it was 'the direct consequence of her husband's insensitivity'. That distinction should have been reflected in the award of general damages, which the Supreme Court accordingly reduced from £55,000 to £35,000.

The invocation by the Supreme Court of a directness test seems hard to support in the light of the repudiation of *In re Polemis* [1921] 3 K.B. 560 by *Overseas Tankship Ltd. v. Morts Dock and Engineering Co. Ltd. (Wagon Mound (No. 1))* [1961] A.C. 388. The Irish courts have not cast doubt on the foreseeability test proposed by the Privy Council in *Wagon Mound (No. 1)*. Unsympathetic spouses, it may be sad to acknowledge, are quite foreseeable.

RES IPSA LOQUITUR

The Supreme Court has had continuing difficulty over the past decade in coming to terms with the doctrine of *res ipsa loquitur*. See our observations in the 1988 Review, 447-52.

Merriman v. Greenhills Foods Ltd. [1997] 1 I.L.R.M. 46 prolongs the agony. The facts were relatively straightforward. The plaintiff, a truck driver employed by the defendant, was injured when a truck that he was driving suddenly veered off the road. The trial judge, Hamilton P, concluded that one of the leaves of the offside front spring had fractured before the impact, that the truck had been driven 'for some time' after the fracture and that there was no evidence of a pre-existing defect in the leaf. He held that the maintenance of the truck had been of a reasonable standard and that the principle of *res ipsa loquitur* did not apply. He dismissed the plaintiff's claim for negligence against his employer, the essence of the plaintiff's case being that the defendant had not taken due care in the maintenance of the truck.

On appeal, the Supreme Court was divided, the majority ordering a new trial. Blayney J. (O'Flaherty J. concurring) considered that the case fell within Erle C.J.'s much-cited principle in *Scott v. London and St. Katherine Docks Co.* (1865) 3 H. & C. 596 that:

> [t]here must be reasonable evidence of negligence, but, when the thing is shown to be under the management of the defendant, or his servants, and the accident is such as, in the ordinary course of things, does not happen if those who have the management of the machinery used proper care, it affords reasonable evidence, in the absence of explanation by the defendant, that the accident arose from want of care.

The reason why, in Blayney J.'s view, this principle applied was that:

> [i]n the instant case the facts bearing on causation and on the care exercised by the [defendant] are unknown to the [plaintiff] and are or ought to be known to the [defendant]. All that the [plaintiff] knows is that the leaf of the spring broke. He does not know why it broke and he does not know what care the [defendant] exercised in the maintenance and servicing of the truck. I am satisfied that to enable justice to be done the doctrine should be applied so as to throw the onus on the [defendant] to prove that it was not negligent.

The tenor of this analysis is that the inability of the plaintiff to explain the accident should be a substantial factor in determining whether to shift the onus onto the defendant to show that it was not negligent. Yet this is not what Erle C.J. prescribes. Unless the 'thing' causing the plaintiff's injury 'is shown to be under the management of the defendant', no onus shift occurs.

Was the vehicle under the defendant's management? Certainly not at the time of the accident. If one in obliged to speak in such terms, the *plaintiff* was surely managing the truck when it crashed. Perhaps it could be argued that the defendant's ongoing right to control should enable the court to draw the defendant within the remit of the doctrine (cf. McMahon & Binchy, *op. cit.*, 135-6), but on the facts of the case this would seem harsh on the defendant.

Now it is, of course, reasonable for a court to investigate the possibility that an employer, whose obligation it is to keep its vehicles well maintained, may not have properly discharged that obligation, but this does not shift the onus onto the employer. On the facts of the case, as Murphy J.'s dissenting judgment makes plain, although the shackle pin, which held the spring in place, was worn to the extent of a sixteenth of an inch, the permitted tolerance was one eighth of an inch, so Hamilton P.'s express finding that there was 'no evidence of a defect in the truck' should not have been disturbed.

Blayney J. was, however, surely correct in distinguishing *Barkaway v. South Wales Transport Co.* [1950] 1 All E.R. 392, which held that, if the cause of the accident is established, the *res ipsa loquitur* doctrine no longer applies. In the instant case, it is true that in one sense it could be said that the cause of the accident had been identified: the leaf of the spring broke. But this was only a partial explanation: the reason *why* it broke remained a mystery. The *Barkaway* principle should apply only where the explanation proffered is directed to facts which are relevant to the issue of the defendant's possible negligence.

CONTRIBUTORY NEGLIGENCE

Occupiers' Liability   In *Roche v. K.M.B. Investments Ltd.*, Supreme Court, June 21, 1996, the plaintiff, a young woman, was a patron in the defendant's public house. She was invited to take part in a singing competition. Having made her contribution she was handing [*sic*] back the microphone and turning round when she fell over a box which provided amplification for the music. The defendant admitted that it had been negligent but armed that the plaintiff was guilty of contributory negligence. The trial judge did not agree. He stated:

> I do not think a person called up in a public house to sing a song on a microphone in a crowded pub, that he or she can reasonably be expected to anticipate that there would be some danger, some object on the floor that could cause an accident and that she would have to be at all stages keeping her eyes glued to the floor to prevent any injury due to some obstacle. I think it is unreasonable to suggest in this case where the defendant has admitted liability, has admitted it was negligent to have the box in the way it was, to suggest the liability should be reduced by finding contributory negligence.

The Supreme Court dismissed the defendant's appeal. Keane J. (Hamilton C.J. and Murphy J. concurring) considered that the trial judge had been perfectly entitled to draw the inference he had drawn on the facts as he had found them.

The sparse recitation of the facts in the case makes one cautious about commenting on the legal aspects of the holding but one may perhaps wonder why the issue of the defendant's negligence was considered so coercively in the plaintiff's favour as to warrant the concession by the defendant without argument that it had been negligent. Sound amplifiers are notoriously bulky and positioned in close proximity to singing areas. The idea that a singing area in a public house should be free of these obstructions seems to involve a very high standard of care. Equally, the notion that a person should be entitled to assume the absence of these obstructions to the extent of not looking out for them seems remarkably indulgent. In retrospect, the defendant may have regretted the strategy of conceding the negligence issue since this appears to have made it harder to convince the trial judge and the Supreme Court that the allegation of contributory negligence had a sound basis.

Employers' liability   In the section on Employer's Liability, earlier in this Chapter, above, 585, we discuss *McDonagh v. Brian O'Connell Ltd.*, High Court, October 24, 1996, where Barr J. imposed liability on Limerick Corporation, the plaintiff's '*de facto* employer', for having negligently constructed a trench where he was engaged in archeological excavations. Barr J. reduced the award by 25%, however, on the basis that the plaintiff had on two earlier occasions fallen into trenches in the course of his work in similar circumstances and therefore ought to have appreciated the danger. In that knowledge he had stood at the edge of such a trench and added to the risk of collapse by leaning across it to pick up an artifact from the top of the opposite bank.

This holding seems somewhat harsh on the plaintiff. He had reported the earlier incidents to his employers and what he did on the fateful day could be regarded as no more than part of his duties. The idea that he should be obliged to take extra care because his employers had taken less than they should is difficult to reconcile with some of the earlier authorities.

Traffic accidents   In *Ward v. Dawson*, High Court, July 26, 1996, Flood J. held that the plaintiff had behaved 'as any ordinary motorist would behave in the circumstances unfolding before him' in braking sharply when 'a confusion of cars ahead of him' was involved in a collision.

In *Wilson v. McGrath*, High Court, January 17, 1996, Flood J. reiterated the principle stated by the Supreme Court in *Hamill v. Oliver* [1977] I.R. 73, that the onus rests on the defendant to establish that the plaintiff, injured in a traffic accident, was not wearing a seat-belt. Since no positive evidence of any kind had been advanced by the defendants in the instant case, the defence of contributory negligence for failure to wear a seat-belt foundered.

Euro-tort   Later in this Chapter, below, 601, in the section entitled *Euro-tort*, we analyse Geoghegan J.'s decision in *Coppinger v. Waterford County Council*, High Court, March 22, 1996, imposing liability on the defendant, as an 'emanation of the State', for breach of certain safety directives relating to road transport. He reduced the plaintiffs' damages by 75%, however, on ac-

count of the plaintiffs' contributory negligence. In our analysis of the decision, we discuss Geoghegan J.'s approach to the important conceptual issues
relating to the operation of the defence of contributory negligence in this
context.

FATAL ACCIDENT

Legislation   The Civil Liability (Amendment) Act 1996 raises the statutory
cap on damages for mental distress in fatal accident litigation to £20,000 and
extends the definition of 'dependant' to include a spouse whose marriage
with the deceased has been dissolved by a decree of divorce and a person, not
married to the deceased but who, 'until the date of the deceased's death, had
been living with the deceased as husband or wife for a continuous period of
not less than three years', provided the divorced spouse or cohabitee has suffered injury or mental distress as a result of the death of the deceased. For a
comprehensive analysis of the new legislation, see Tony Kerr's *Annotation*,
I.C.L.S.A.

The statutory cap, when the entitlement was first introduced in 1961, was
£1,000. This was raised to £7,500 by section 28 (1) of the Courts Act 1981:
see McMahon & Binchy, *op. cit.* 740. As the inflation of the early Eighties
began to bite, the revised limit began to look parsimonious: cf. *Coppinger v.
Waterford County Council* [1996] 2 I.L.R.M. 427, which we discuss below,
601. S. 2 of the 1996 Act facilitates further increases (or, in these anti-infla-
tionary times, decreases) by Ministerial order, to take account of future changes
in the value of money.

S. 3 prohibits an award for marital distress being made in favour of a
former spouse. One may question the justice of this irrebutable presumption
that a divorced spouse (whether the applicant or respondent in the divorce
proceedings) will suffer no mental distress on the death of his or her partner.
It can scarcely be the case that every former spouse will have no close feel-
ings of this type. If, for example, a wife is devastatingly injured in an accident
and is consigned to permanent hospital care, her husband, for good or ill,
may decide to divorce her (without, it seems, having to communicate to her
his unilateral decision to withdraw from the relationship); is there any reason
for proceeding coercively on the basis that he cannot suffer mental distress
when she dies or that, if he does, it should not be cognisable by the law?

The extension of the statutory entitlement to cohabitees is to be noted. It
will be recalled that in *Hollywood v. Cork Harbour Commissioners* [1992] 1
I.R. 457, O'Hanlon J. proceeded on the basis that a long-term cohabitee was
capable of coming within the scope of section 47 of the 1961 Act as being a
person in respect of whom her deceased partner had been *in loco parentis*.
The moral obligation discerned by O'Hanlon J. as arising in such a case was

not professedly contingent on the existence of a sexual relationship between the parties. The 1996 legislation requires such a relationship and further that it should have existed for a continuous period of at least three years, up to the date of the death of the deceased. Does this mean that a cohabitee of (say) two years' duration could have any serious prospect of successfully invoking *Hollywood*? We think not. We did not find O'Hanlon J.'s analysis fully convincing: see the 1992 Review, 611-2. A future court, even if more sympathetic to that analysis, would be likely to take the view that the policy underlying the express statutory change modifies the former law as tentatively interpreted by O'Hanlon J.

If cohabitees as well as spouses are entitled to claim, how is the court to deal with a situation where a man has deserted his wife and lived for three years with a new partner? If he has, in essence, transferred the bulk of his economic support to his new partner and gives his wife relatively modest support, then, on his death caused by the wrongful act of another, the new partner will receive very substantial compensation and the wife less compensation. It might be thought that this should not happen because of the provisions of the Family Law (Divorce) Act 1996. But the computation of economic loss in wrongful death actions is ruthlessly frank. It cuts through the rhetoric and faces the actuality of the character and propensities of the deceased as well as the real probable future developments.

Finally, in relation to the Civil Liability (Amendment) Act 1996, we should note that it changes section 18 of the Air Navigation and Transport Act 1936 (as amended) in the same way as it changes section 47 of the 1961 Act.

EURO-TORT

In *Coppinger v. Waterford County Council* [1996] 2 I.L.R.M. 427, the plaintiff collided into the rear of a stationary tipper truck, owned by the defendant. His injuries were greatly exacerbated by the absence of an under-run protection barrier on the rear of the truck. E.C. directives (notably 79/490/EC) required the installation of such barriers, save in certain circumstances, two of which were relevant. The first was in respect of public service vehicles;, the second exempted vehicles for which rear under-run protection was 'incompatible with their use'. In Ireland, the Road Traffic (Construction, Equipment and Use of Vehicles) (Amendment) Regulations 1985 (SI No. 158 of 1985), which professedly give effect to these directives, exempted tipper-trucks from their remit.

Geoghegan J. held that in these circumstances the defendant council had not been guilty of common law negligence in failing to have a rear under-run safety device on its tipper truck:

The County Engineer and other officers of Waterford County Council advising the County Manager on technical matters and the County Manager himself would in the context of these surrounding circumstances have been entitled to regard it as reasonable that the Council's tipper trucks should not be fitted with under-run devices. In my view, the County Engineer was entitled to assume in the absence of some clear indication to the contrary, that the State had correctly interpreted the E.C. Directive.

The Council was, however, liable, as an 'emanation of the State' for breach of the directives. As to the exemption for 'public works vehicles' which was made by Article 1 of the Council Directive of March 20, 1970 (70/221/EEC) Geoghegan J. considered that this exemption:

> must be interpreted in its context, particularly the context of the other exceptions in the same Article which are 'vehicles which run on rails, agricultural tractors and machinery'. I think it is reasonably clear that what is meant by 'public service vehicles' in this context is vehicles forming part of the machinery for the works themselves and not vehicles used for transporting materials to or from the works. If it meant the latter it would be an extraordinarily wide exemption from what were clearly intended to be important safety obligations.

As to the second exemption, Geoghegan J. held on the technical evidence that it was 'perfectly possible' to have in place a safety under-run barrier in a tipper truck in compliance with the directives.

Geoghegan J. went on to hold on the evidence that the breach of the directives had caused 'the serious aspect' of the plaintiff's injuries. Agreeing with the views that Carroll J. had expressed in *Tate v. Minister for Social Welfare* [1995] I.L.R.M. 503 (which we noted in the 1995 Review, 363, 541, 543), he held that this breach was a tort which should be characterised as a 'wrong' with the meaning of the Civil Liability Act 1961.

That being so, the question of the plaintiff's contributory negligence fell for consideration. Even it had not, because the breach was capable of characterisation as a wrong under the 1961 Act, Geoghegan J. took the view that, 'in assessing fair compensation for breach of the Directive, the plaintiff would have to give credit for the extent to which he was responsible for his own injuries'.

Geoghegan J. apportioned the fault as to 75% on the plaintiff and 25% on the Council. His analysis is worth quoting *in extenso*:

> It has been argued on behalf of the plaintiff that in apportioning liability, I should have regard to the fact that the absence of the under-run

safety barrier caused the really serious injuries and that, if there had been such a barrier, the injuries would have been relatively minor. The argument then runs that, that being so, by far the greater proportion of liability should fall on Waterford County Council. I cannot accept this submission. The exercise which I have to do under the Civil Liability Act, 1961 is to apportion fault or, in other words, blameworthiness. This accident was primarily caused by the unfortunate plaintiff not keeping a proper look-out. On the other hand, in apportioning liability on Waterford County Council, I think that I must treat the County Council as though it was the State itself. On that basis, I consider that the fault should be apportioned as to 75% on the plaintiff and 25% on Waterford County Council.

One aspect of Geoghegan J.'s observations that may be noted is the emphasis on the respective *causal* contributions of the parties: the accident was 'primarily caused' by the plaintiff's failure to keep a proper look-out. Some earlier decisions in Ireland (in contrast to other common law jurisdictions) have emphasised that the court should contrast the respective degrees of blameworthiness of the parties rather than their respective causal contributions: see McMahon & Binchy, *op. cit.*, 362. Frankly, it is not possible to unravel moral and causal attribution so easily. Such concepts as *novus actus interveniens* involve a healthy mixture of both: cf. McMahon & Binchy, *op. cit.*

PASSING OFF

In *R. Griggs Group Ltd. v. Dunnes Stores Ireland Co.*, High Court, October 4, 1996, McCracken J. declined to grant an interlocutory injunction restraining the defendant from passing off a range of boots sold by it as those of the plaintiffs. The plaintiffs were the manufacturers of Dr. Martens boots. These had a series of distinctive features, including a two-toned, grooved sole edge and a distinctive sole and overall configuration. The plaintiffs claimed that these characterisations were unique to them. The defendant had purchased the boots sold in their shops from a British manufacturer and an Italian manufacturer.

It was 'quite clear' to McCracken J. that the proceedings were 'but part of a world-wide claim by the plaintiffs to a monopoly in boots of a particular design, or even class of designs'. It appeared that no court in any jurisdiction had yet finally determined the issue.

Applying Lord Diplock's definition of passing off, in *Erven Warnink B.V. v. J. Townsend & Sons (Hull) Ltd.* [1979] A.C. 731 and the principles set out by the Supreme Court in *Adidas Sportschuhfubriken Adi DasslerKa v. Charles O'Neill & Co. Ltd.* [1983] I.L.R.M. 112, McCracken J. accepted that the plaintiffs had 'just about done enough to establish an arguable case', though it was 'certainly not a very strong one.' He refused to grant an interlocutory injunction, however, stating:

> What influences me more is that this is part of world-wide campaign by the plaintiffs to establish a monopoly in a certain design of footwear. While the outcome of the action eventually will depend only on the reputation of the plaintiffs in this jurisdiction, nevertheless I am entitled to take into account the fact that this is a small battlefield in a world war, and that the attack in this battle is against what I call a secondary target – namely a retailer – while no real attack is mounted against the primary target, namely, the manufacturers.

The granting of an injunction is an equitable remedy, and the concept of balance of convenience is an equitable concept. It seems to me inherently inequitable in this case that the proceedings should be brought against the retailer which, on the evidence before me, bona fide purchased these goods from two manufacturers, which goods were offered to the defendants as being goods which they were entitled to sell, while no action is taken against the manufacturers.

If it were ultimately held that the defendant was guilty of passing off, the basic misrepresentation would have been that of the manufacturer. While this would not relieve the defendant from liability, it was certainly a factor to be considered in granting or refusing an equitable remedy. The damage likely to be suffered by the plaintiffs, in the context of their world-wide sales and world-wide campaign, was minimal. On the other hand, the defendant would be deprived of the sales of a complete range of a very popular style of footwear, which, taken in context, would be much more serious for it. The apparent weakness of the plaintiffs' case was also a factor to be taken into account.

PRIVACY

In a comprehensive *Consultation Paper on Privacy: Surveillance and the Interception of Communications*, published in September 1996 the Law Reform Commission tentatively recommends the creation of a statutory tort affording a range of civil remedies to a person whose privacy has been infringed by surveillance. It also recommends the creation of a statutory tort of disclosure or publication of information or material obtained by means of privacy-invasive surveillance. In the event that these recommendations are not accepted, if proposes tentatively, as a 'much less preferred option' (para. 9.22), the imposition of civil liability on range of activity which, elsewhere in the Consultation Paper, it recommends should be criminalised.

At present tort law, equity, contract and copyright go some way towards affording protection to privacy interests but there are clear *lacunae*: cf. McMahon & Binchy, *op. cit.*, ch. 23 and the Consultation Paper, ch. 4.

The Commission helpfully includes heads of draft legislation which clarify the nature of the torts it proposes. It should by tortious and actionable for a person intentionally:

(i) to invade the privacy of another person by means of surveillance;

or

(ii) to disclose or publish the purport or substance of information or material obtained by means of privacy-invasive surveillance.

The Commission make it plain that it is the protection of privacy which these torts are designed to protect even though unwanted surveillance is also well capable of infringing interests other than privacy, such as the legitimate commercial interests of a trading company. The Commission disdains any definition, or even specific indicative or exemplary criteria, of the notion of privacy:

> The courts of many countries have been asked, in interpreting a right of privacy, to decide whether or not particular interests pertain to privacy and have not found the task to lie outside the judicial function. The scope of the concept in general has been defined somewhat differently in different jurisdictions, and in general we think it should be left to the courts, at lest in the first instance, to identify the matters properly to be regarded as matters of privacy. We have considered whether a general definition in line with the language used in some of the international treaties to which Ireland is party might be helpful to the courts but have concluded that it would not. For example, Article 8 of the European Convention on Human Rights refers to respect for 'private life, family life, home and correspondence'; but, in our view, not all observation of a person's home constitutes an invasion of a person's privacy. We therefore prefer to leave the question of definition entirely to the courts for the time being. Para. 9.25 (footnote reference omitted).

It may well be true that the language of Article 8 would not afford the best model for the establishment of a statutory tort of invasion of privacy through surveillance but this would not be because certain acts, such as observation in some circumstances of a person's home, would not constitute an invasion of that person's privacy. Homes represent a particular zone of enhanced privacy, as Article 40.5 of the Constitution recognises: cf. J. Kelly, *The Irish Constitution*, 914-920 (3rd ed., by G. Hogan & G. Whyte, 1994).

The Commission sees merit in having the legislation provide that surveillance *includes* certain conduct, without this conduct being regarded as exhaustive of the forms surveillances may take. This enables the courts to take account of future developments in surveillance technology. The draft legislation provides that 'surveillance' includes aural and visual surveillance, irrespective of the means employed, and the interception of communications.

On the important particular issue of whether recording a conversation to which one is a party should come within the meaning of the term 'surveillance', the Commission takes no view, preferring to welcome submissions. It debates the merits as follows:

> There are legitimate reasons for recording such conversations, e.g. to ensure the accuracy of information conveyed or as evidence of the details of an agreement. Moreover, where the fact of the recording is known to the other person, that person has the option not to enter into the conversation or to tailor what she or he says so that nothing is recorded which the person wished to keep secret. Where a recording is made without the knowledge of the other person, although this may be reprehensible, the person whose voice is recorded intended to engage in conversation either with the person making the recording or in the presence of that person. The former was therefore aware that the latter would hear what was said. On the other hand, engaging in a conversation is different from consenting to being recorded. Consent to being recorded implies acceptance that not only one's words but also the way in which they were spoken are on permanent record in the hands of another person. Para. 9.30.

Turning to *defences*, the Commission, in the draft legislation, that it should be a defence to either of the two torts to show that:

(i)   the plaintiff, or some other person legally entitled to give consent on behalf of the plaintiff, consented, either expressly or impliedly to the invasion, disclosure or publication, as the case may be;

or

(ii) the defendant was fulfilling a legal duty or exercising a legal power or right *and* the impact of the surveillance, disclosure or publication on the privacy of the plaintiff was not disproportionate to the legal interest pursued having regard to the values of a sovereign, independent, democratic state.

It would also be a defence to an action for disclosure of information obtained by means of privacy-invasive surveillance that the defendant did not believe and had no reasonable grounds to believe that the information had been obtained by means of privacy-invasive surveillance. All of these defences would be without prejudice to any constitutional rights of the defendant.

The notion of express consent is unproblematic. Implied consent is understandably more troublesome. The Commission appears to envisage that, if a person 'ha[s]' no objection' to publication (para. 9.35), this amounts to implied consent, but at what point does a person's failure to object warrant the conclusion that he or she has no objection?

The Commission rightly acknowledges that the courts interpreting the Constitution, as well as the international treaties to which Ireland is party, have employed a criterion of proportionality. Nevertheless, the scope of this defence, however theoretically justifiable in its definition, is entirely uncertain in its practical application. The nature of the statutory torts cannot be assessed until one has some idea of the scope of the defences. One should not criticise the Commission for this lack of specificity: the defence of qualified privilege in defamation actions, used every day by juries, with what understanding we can only guess, is scarcely much less opaque.

The Commission rejects the argument that the legislation should include a specific defence that a violation of privacy was reasonable in the circumstances and necessary for or incidental to ordinary news-gathering activities. It considers that this would not 'draw the proper balance between the privacy of the individual and the public interest in news [n]or . . . satisfy the international criteria to which Ireland subscribes (para. 9.41). It took the view that journalists and broadcasters should not have any special privileges in the gathering of information and that the general criteria it proposes should afford responsible journalists a sufficient defence, 'while protecting the privacy of the individual from the irresponsible': *id.*

In one respect the Commission favours protection for publishers. It proposes that there should be a defence to the tort of disclosure or publication that the defendant did not believe and had no reasonable grounds to believe that the information had been obtained by means of privacy – invasive surveillance: para. 9.48. Finally, the Commission notes, and its draft legislation provides, that the defences it proposes should be without prejudice to any defence available under the Constitution, in particular any constitutional rights which the defendant may enjoy.

While the elements of the two torts, and of their defences, are eminently defensible form a conceptual standpoint, it must be acknowledged that what emerges are shadows rather than substance, giving credibility to Gray's view of statutes as potential law. Until the courts flesh out these torts, the Commission's recommendations can give us no real sense of their parameters.

The Commission proposes a broad range of civil remedies for privacy-invasive surveillance. These naturally include damages but also a privacy order, in effect an injunction prohibiting privacy invasion or disclosure where the court is of opinion that there are reasonable grounds for believing that one of the two torts is being or is about to be committed.

Turning to criminal sanctions, the Commission proposes that photographing or videoing a person in such a way as to infringe his or her integrity should be an offence, provided the defendant acted intentionally or recklessly and the person in question had not expressly or impliedly consented. The Commission considers that the reference to a person's integrity 'rather than to privacy as such' (para. 10.42) will confer '[a] greater degree of specificity' (*id.*) It envisages that such conduct as surveillance by a private detective or climbing onto a boundary wall to ogle at sunbathers would not fall within the scope of its proposed offence. One must seriously doubt, however, whether the parameters of the offence have any such specificity. A team of philosophers could earn substantial fees as expert witnesses in debating the notion of infringement of another's integrity. The shadow of *King v. Attorney General* [1981] I.R. 223 falls over this recommendation.

The Commission does envisage specific defences of this offence, including the defence that the surveillance was intended to protect a person's life or that it occurred in the exercise of lawful authority. It regards as 'somewhat anomalous' (para. 10.56) the distinction between the interception of postal packets and telecommunications messages for the purposes of investigating crime or in the interest of national security and visual surveillance by the State for similar purposes. The former category of interception is extensively regulated by legislation; the latter not at all. It notes that the historical explanation is simply that the post and telegraph have long been used as methods of communication whereas it is only in recent years that sophisticated aural and visual devices have been developed. It does not regard this as providing a sufficient justification for the difference in legal regulation, which it proposes should be abandoned by requiring is essence the regime that exists under the Interception of Postal Packets and Telecommunications Messages (Regulation) Act 1993 to be extended, analogically to the newer modes of surveillance.

The Commission goes on to recommend that bugging should be an offence where it infringes a person's private life, as should be the disclosure of the purport or substance of what was thus obtained. Again there would be defences, including consent, the investigation of serious crime and the interests of State security, subject to regulations on the lines of the 1993 Act. The Commission is undecided as to whether to go further and recommend a general defence relating to the prevention or exposure of crime. It does, however, consider that there should be a defence that the defendant had acted solely to protect his or her person or property or another person and that the material was destroyed once the reason for its retention had ceased to exist.

Finally, we may note that, in a detailed series of recommendations designed to fine-tune the 1993 legislation and the Postal and Telecommunications Service Act 1983, the Commission proposes the creation of a new offence embracing the wrongful interception of electronic mail. Naturally the 1983 legislation could not have anticipated the development of e-mail, though several of the provisions of that Act, the 1993 Act and the Criminal Damage Act 1991 are capable of being interpreted to include it within their scope.

TRESPASS TO LAND

Trespass to airspace The Irish courts have yet to give a comprehensive analysis of the contours of the tort of trespass to airspace. There is old English judicial authority (e.g. *Pickering v. Rudd* (1815) 4 Camp. 219, at 220-1) against imposing liability in the absence of damage. Since McNair J.'s judgment in *Kelsen v. Imperial Tobacco Co.* [1957] 2 Q.B. 334, it has been accepted that such trespass is actionable even in the absence of damage. Nonetheless, the English courts have taken the view that a person in possession of land has a right to airspace over it only to the height that is necessary for the ordinary use and enjoyment of the land and the structures on it: *Bernstein v. Skyviews & General Ltd.* [1978] Q.B. 479. This introduces some sense of realism and fair play, preventing unmeritorious and opportunistic claims.

In the context of urban building development, the problem has arisen starkly. To erect houses and offices, it is frequently necessary to use tall cranes whose jibs intrude into neighbouring airspace in circumstances where they fall within the scope of the *Bernstein* test. If the person in possession of land over which these jibs will travel seeks an injunction, should one be granted?

In *Wooleerton & Wilson Ltd. v. Richard Costain Ltd.* [1970] 1 W.L.R. 411, Stamp J., conscious of the fact that the plaintiff had, before seeking the injunction, unsuccessfully sought to sell the entitlement to use the airspace to the defendant at a relatively high price, granted the injunction but suspended it for a period that was long enough to enable the defendant to complete the building operation. There is, perhaps, a certain poetry in using the formal instruments of judicial remedies in a way that is designed to achieve substantive justice but subsequent decisions in England have not approved of this approach *Charrington v. Simons & Co. Ltd.* [1971] 1 W.L.R. 598, *John Trenberth Ltd. v. National Westminster Bank Ltd.* (1979) 39 P. & C.R. 104. The position in England today is that the plaintiff will normally be entitled to an injunction against the incursion into his airspace by cranes 'even thought this state of the law allows him to take a "dog in the manger" attitude and force the defendant to pay him a sum in excess of any damage he has suffered': *Winfield & Jolovicz on Tort*, 388 (14th ed. by WVH Rogers, 1994).

In *Keating & Co. Ltd. v. Jervis Shopping Centre Ltd. and Pierse Contracting Ltd.*, High Court, March 1, 1996, Keane J. declined to grant an interlocutory injunction against crane incursion during building operations. One reason was that the developers and builders were asserting a right to act as they had done on the basis of an agreement with the plaintiff. Since this raised a serious question to be tried, and the plaintiff had not established that damages would not be an adequate remedy, an interlocutory injunction was not forthcoming: cf. *Patel v. W.H. Smith (Eziot) Ltd.* [1987] 2 All E.R. 569.

Keane J. went on to state that, apart from these considerations he would in any event have refused the injunction, having regard to the behaviour to the parties. He expressly adopted the same approach as Stamp J. had taken in the *Woollerton* case. He made no mention of the later English decisions in which *Woollerton* had fallen into disfavour.

The *Six Carpenters* case   In *Richards v. Dublin Corporation and Motor Insurance Bureau*, Supreme Court, June 12, 1996, the plaintiff had been knocked down and injured by a motorcyclist in a public park who had 'disappeared without a trace'. The Motor Insurance Bureau contended that the location of the accident was not a public place and that it therefore had no liability to compensate the plaintiff. O'Hanlon J. rejected this contention and the Supreme Curt affirmed. The Supreme Court was of the view that, once the place was permitted to be accessible to persons using bicycles, it was a 'public place' with the definition of the Road Traffic Act 1961 and accordingly motorcyclists fell within its scope. The fact that the Superintendent of the park had sought to chase away motorcyclists from time to time did not alter the position. Motorcyclists, said O'Flaherty J., did seem to have ready access to the park and did use it frequently. The point about that was not so much whether the implied permission could be inferred from the ineffectiveness of the Superintendent's efforts of stop them as much as the failure by the Corporation to pass bye-laws, or at least to put up a notice to say that motorcyclists were prohibited. The Corporation had admittedly not taken these steps. O'Flaherty J. observed that:

> [i]n these circumstances, I would uphold [the trial judge]'s findings that one could reach the conclusion that indeed there was a form of implied permission allowing motorcyclists to have access to the park though with a somewhat different emphasis to the trial judge.

Keane J. observed that the *Six Carpenters* case (1610) 8 Co. Rep. 146a did not assist the contention that an entrant to the park, when challenged, would lose the entitlement to be there as a right or by permission. That old decision meant that 'if the trespasser was a person entering the property legally who then proceeds to commit a tortious act, whatever it be, be it assaulting somebody, or something else, then he becomes a trespasser *ab initio*. . . .' On this ancient doctrine, see further McMahon & Binchy, *op. cit.*, 434-5.

NUISANCE

In the 1995 Review, 533, 544, we discussed *Convery v. Dublin County Council*, Supreme Court, November 12, 1996, where the Supreme Court, reversing Carroll J., held that the defendant council was guilty of neither nuisance nor negligence in relation to the large volumes of traffic using the road where the plaintiff resided as a 'rat run'.

Keane J. (O'Flaherty and Barron JJ. concurring) rejected the action for public nuisance on the basis that 'the traffic did not originate in any premises owned or occupied by the County Council and was not generated as a result of any activities caused by them on land in the area.' Kelly J.'s decision in *Kelly v. Dublin County Council*, High Court, February 21, 1981 was thus clearly distinguishable. The fact that the traffic reached a volume which caused significant inconvenience and discomfort for the residents was the result of a combination of factors: 'the development of large scale residential and commercial projects by private interests, the decisions of thousands of individual drivers to use this particular route, and the failure of central government to allocate funds for the provision of the necessary roads infrastructure, to mention the most obvious.' The decisions of the county council to which objection was taken represented only one of a number of factors which had resulted in the position of which the plaintiff complained. To treat the county council, in these circumstances, as being the legal author of a public nuisance 'would be entirely contrary to principle and wholly unsupported by authority.'

As to the claim founded on negligence, it was clear that the plaintiff had failed to establish that there was a relationship between her and the county council which created a duty to take reasonable care arising from its public duty under any statute.

The powers and duties of the county council as planning authority and roads authority are vested in them in order to ensure the proper planning and development of their area and the provision and maintenance of an appropriate road network in that area. While their existence of those powers and duties can be regulated by the High Court by means of the judicial review process so as to ensure that they are exercised only in accordance with law, the plaintiff does not belong to any category of persons to whom the council, in the exercise of those powers, owed a duty of care at common law.

The result in this case is not perhaps surprising. There is little to be gained by the courts' scapegoating local authorities for the social problems that result from rapid urbanisation and the irrevocable commitment, excluding all passengers, that so many drivers make to their cars. Nonetheless, there are less difficulties in principle about imposing liability in public nuisance or negligence than the Supreme Court envisaged.

Let us alter the facts somewhat to make the point clearer. If, for example, a local authority exercised its statutory functions in such a way that vermin-infested vehicles were thronging the highway, carrying diseases to neighbouring householders, it could scarcely avoid liability for nuisance on the basis that this pestiferous traffic did not originate in its premises and was not generated as a result of any activities carried on by it on land in the area. Strategic decisions taken from afar by a local authority are capable of generating liability for public nuisance, just as a telephoned hoax bomb warning which causes the streets in a locality to become thronged with frightened office-workers and residents.

So also, it is quite possible to envisage liability in negligence attaching to a County Council in its capacity as road authority if, as a result of its unreasonable decision, traffic on the roads caused injury or damage to householders nearby. If, for example, a Council constructed a road in such a way that traffic driving on it with due care was nonetheless likely to leave the highway and crash into a house, the issue of liability would be beyond argument.

Finally, we may note with some relief that the maverick decision of the Supreme Court in *Weir v. Dun Laoghaire Corporation* [1983] I.R. 242 received *its quietus* in *Convery*. Keane J. noted that it seemed that the Court's attention had not been drawn to section 26(11) of the Local Government (Planning and Development) Act 1963. While *Weir* had been cited in *Sunderland v. McGreavey*, it had not been referred to in McCarthy J.'s judgment. It was 'clearly irreconcilable' with the decision in *Sunderland* and had to be regarded as having been reversed *sub silentio*.

DEFAMATION

Qualified privilege   In *Bell v. Pedersen*, High Court, May 14, 1996, Morris J. was called on to determine whether, at the close of the plaintiff's case, he should withdraw it from the jury. The proceedings involved an admittedly privileged occasion. The crucial issue was whether the defendants' malice destroyed their putative defence of qualified privilege.

Morris J. quoted at length from passages of three judgments in *Hynes O'Sullivan v. O'Driscoll* [1988] I.R. 436 and drew from them a rule of law that:

> the onus being on the plaintiff to establish malice, if the case is to go to the jury, I must be satisfied that on the balance of probabilities a jury would find malice.

He formed the view, 'with great reluctance', that the plaintiff had failed to satisfy him 'that *on the balance of probabilities* the jury would, at this stage of the case, come to the conclusion that the defendants or either of them was guilty of malice'. (Emphasis supplied by Morris J.) Accordingly Morris J.

withdrew the case from the jury in favour of the defendants.

One may question whether the judgments in *Hynes v. O'Sullivan* place quite such a formidable obstacle in the plaintiff's path.

Henchy J. (in a passage quoted by Morris J.) stated that:

> it is for the Judge to decide whether the evidence is *such as would reasonably entitle the jury to hold* as a matter of probability that the publication was actuated by malice, in the legal sense, on the part of the defendant. (Emphasis added).

Similarly, McCarthy J. (also quoted by Morris J.) stated that:

> the learned trial Judge has to determine whether or not *it was open to the jury to conclude* that the evidence was more consistent with the existence of an improper or ulterior motive than otherwise. (Emphasis added.)

Finlay C.J.'s analysis is admittedly confusing, since it appears to set two separate tests, presented as though they were identical:

> . . . [The] trial Judge should leave an issue of malice to the jury only if he is satisfied that the evidence given was more consistent with the existence of malice than with its absence or to put the matter in another but identical way, that the existence of malice, as a matter of probability, was an inference which the jury would be entitled to draw from the evidence given.

A trial judge who concludes that the jury would be entitled to draw the inference of the existence of malice does not necessarily also have to conclude that the jury would in fact draw such an inference.

Criminal law   Geoghegan J in *Conway v. Independent Newspapers (Ireland) Ltd.*, High Court, October 23, 1996, refused to give leave under section 8 of the Defamation Act 1961 for the institution of proceedings for blasphemous libel against the respondent newspaper company.

DAMAGES

Assault   In *McCarthy v. Dunne*, High Court, December 5, 1996 (Circuit Appeal), Barr J. awarded £22,000 general damages against the first and second defendants, who had engaged in 'a grievously vicious' physical and psychological attack on their neighbour, a women aged fort-five. Their animus appears to have centred upon the plaintiff's family's appeal to An Bord Pleanála against the defendants' family's planning application. The plaintiff suffered from post-traumatic stress syndrome. She had panic attacks and was concerned about being in confined or crowded areas.

An unusual feature of the case was Barr J.'s decision to grant an injunction against the defendants ordering them not to abuse, intimidate, assault or threaten the plaintiff or any member of family, even though the plaintiff had not apparently sought injunctive relief.

Loss of consortium   In the 1992 Review, 613-18, we analysed the Supreme Court decision of *McKinley v. Minister for Defence* [1992] 2 I.R. 333, holding, on the basis of the constitutional mandate of equality, that the common law action for loss of *consortium* should be available for wives as well as husbands. In *Coppinger v. Waterford County Council* [1996] 2 I.L.R.M. 427, Geoghegan J. had to determine two issues: whether a husband's contributory negligence should reduce his wife's claim for loss of consortium and what principles should govern the computation of damages in these actions. The plaintiff's husband had been very severely injured in a traffic accident. He had obtained damages for his injuries in an action against the defendant, reduced by 75% to take account of his contributory negligence. (We discuss an aspect of the husband's action, so far as it relates to his damages, above, 601)

Section 35(2)(b) of the Civil Liability Act 1961 provides that, in an action 'for the loss of the consortium or services of a wife or for the loss of the services of a child or servant', the contributory negligence of the wife, child or servant is not to reduce the claim of the husband, parent or employer, as the case may be. This provision was, of course, premised on the assumption (reinforced by the House of Lords decision in *Best v. Fox* [1952] A.C. 716) that wives had no right of action for loss of consortium. The Oireachtas did not foresee the activism of the " Dálaigh – Walsh years, just about to unfold.

Geoghegan J. did not descend to a narrow textual analysis of the limitations of section 35(2)(b). Instead he reasoned that, since the statutory provision had done no more than reflect the common law position in most jurisdictions, including England (cf. *Mallett v. Dunn* [1949] 2 K.B. 180), that a reduction should not be made for the spouse's contributory negligence, 'it would be completely contrary to th[e] principle [of equality] if a wife was to suffer reduction by reason of her husband's contributory negligence when, in the reverse situation, that would not happen.' This is surely a correct conclusion. There would be no purpose in holding the provision unconstitutional or in refusing to heed the equality point on the basis that the constitutional issue had not been pleaded. Either of these courses would appeal only to a narrow and formalistic judicial mind.

The question of how to compute damages in actions for loss of *consor-*

tium presented Geoghegan J. with somewhat greater difficulty, since he was clearly discomforted by O'Flaherty J.'s *obiter dictum* on the issue in *McKinley*, in the following terms:

> When the matter proceeds in the High Court the judge will be venturing on largely unchartered territory, and he is entitled, I believe, to some guidance on the question of the quantum of damages, in respect of this cause of action. Kingsmill Moore J. in *Spaight v. Dundon* [1961] I.R. 201 was of the opinion that such damages should not be 'too generous' (at p. 215). That precept, of course, applies to any award of damages. However, I think a benchmark might be sought and found in the level of damages that are awarded for mental distress under the Civil Liability Acts in the case of the death of a spouse. It would seem clear in principle that damages for loss of consortium should be related to those recoverable for the death of spouse.

Geoghegan J. thought it necessary, in particular, to note what O'Flaherty J. had *not* said. He had not been suggesting that mental distress for which damages were recoverable for the death of a spouse was 'in any way a similar kind of injury to loss of consortium'. O'Flaherty J.'s use of the word 'benchmark' indicated to Geoghegan J. that he 'was not in any way suggesting that because there was a particular ceiling under the Civil Liability Acts for damages for mental distress, the same ceiling should also apply to damages for loss of consortium.'

With respect, while O'Flaherty J. did not seek to make the ceiling for damages in wrongful death actions identical to that in actions for loss of *consortium*, he was indeed trying to bring them close together. His reference to 'a benchmark' and his view that damages in the two actions should be 'related' to each other indicates this fairly clearly. Why else enter into an *obiter dictum*? It is hard to interpret O'Flaherty J.'s remarks as amounting to no more than a requirement simply to note the ceiling for mental distress in the wrongful death actions, but not be significantly influenced by it when assessing damages in an action for loss of *consortium*.

Geoghegan J. went on to make two further observations. The first was that the court, in actions for loss of consortium, should allow for the devaluation of monetary value in the fifteen years since the Oireachtas in 1981 had fixed the ceiling for mental distress in wrongful death actions. He considered it 'illogical' that a wife such as Mrs. Coppinger who took her action in 1981, should be awarded the same as Mrs. Coppinger fifteen years later, 'simply because of the fact that the Oireachtas has never brought that figure up to date.' But is it not equally unjust that a plaintiff in a wrongful death action in 1996 should be held to the figure of £7,500? There is something formalistic about the argument that the court, in a wrongful death action, is bound by the statutory figure but not in an action for loss of *consortium* which, on O'Flaherty J.'s approach, should have damages determined by reference to the level of damages awarded in the former action?

Geoghegan J. found the earlier Supreme Court decision of *O'Haran v. Devine* (1964) 100 I.L.T.R. 53 'extremely helpful' on the question of assessment of damages. There, the plaintiff had suffered forty-two weeks' loss of his wife's consortium. The Supreme Court held that a jury award of £350 had not been unduly high. The figure of £350 would translate into £4000 on the 1996 values. Geoghegan J. noted that Mrs. Coppinger had already suffered total loss of *consortium* for ten years and would probably do so for a further sixteen or seventeen years. Her loss was 'infinitely worse' than the mental distress which she would have suffered if her husband had died in the accident. Had he done so,

> she would have been very upset but I think it likely that she would have rebuilt her life. She was and still is an attractive, intelligent woman and there is no reason to believe that she would not have found another husband if she had wished to remarry. Although account must be taken of the fact that she is still able to communicate with her husband, he is not the man she married and I think that she has suffered real agony in her loss of *consortium*.

Accordingly he awarded the plaintiff £60,000.

The decision provokes a couple of comments. First, Geoghegan J. is surely right in concluding that some cases of loss of *consortium* can involve more suffering for the plaintiff than cases of wrongful death. There is simply no necessary relationship between the two actions and nothing is to be gained by seeking to find a bridge between them, unless there is some good policy argument, not mentioned by O'Flaherty J. in his *obiter dictum*, for the courts to introduce an *artificial* ceiling on damages for loss of *consortium* as the Oireachtas did in respect of what in 1961 was an entirely new head of damages. The courts, prior to *McKinley*, had shown no propensity to be extravagant in their awards for loss of *consortium*. They had doubted whether it was possible to award *any* damages for partial loss of consortium and, in cases of a total loss, there was a judicial prescription that the quantum should be moderate: see McMahon & Binchy, *op. cit.*, 597-8.

It is worth noting in this context that, when awarding damages for mental distress in wrongful death cases, the courts proceed on the basis, initially, that there is *no* statutory ceiling, decide how much should be awarded and, only then, if the figure is in excess of the level of the ceiling: *McCarthy v. Walsh* [1965] I.R. 246. This means, of course, that, if the Supreme Court were in the future to decline to follow O'Flaherty J.'s proposal to link this statutory ceiling with the amount to be awarded for loss of *consortium*, the sum of £60,000 for damages such as Mrs Coppinger suffered could be revised upwards substantially.

Geoghegan J.'s reference to the attractiveness and hypothetical remarital prospects of the plaintiff may cause some controversy. Presumably it would be possible also to speculate on similar prospects of a male plaintiff but one can wonder whether this would ease the sensitivities of those who perceive the investigation of remarriage prospects as *inherently* sexist. In Britain, concerns of this type led to the legislature to introduce a statutory provision requiring the courts not to take into account the remarriage prospects of women, but not men, thus replacing one form of sexism by another. When we recall that *McKinley* was inspired by the principle of sex equality, perhaps this aspect of Geoghegan J.'s judgment may be revisited by a court in future years.

In *Reid v. The Minister for Finance*, High Court, July 29, 1996, in an application under the Garda Síochána Compensation Acts 1941 and 1945, Budd J. quoted at length from Geoghegan J.'s judgment in *Coppinger*. He observed that,

> [i]n assessing compensation in respect of the death of a policeman, judges over the recent years have frequently glanced over the fence at comparatives in the area of loss of *consortium*. Accordingly, I bear in mind Geoghegan J.'s remarks with regard to loss of *consortium* at times being infinitely worse than the mental distress suffered by reason of a husband's death.

Failure by trial judge to give reasons for rejecting evidence of an expert witness In *O'Sullivan v. Sherry*, Supreme Court, February 2, 1996, where the quantum of damages awarded by Carroll J. was upheld by the Supreme Court, counsel for the defendants contended that Carroll J.'s failure to give reasons why she rejected the evidence of a defence witness should be a ground for overturning her judgment. The Supreme Court rejected this argument. Hamilton C.J. (O'Flaherty and Blayney JJ. concurring) denied:

> that there is any obligation on a trial judge to give any reasons why she accepted the evidence of one witness rather than the other, be they expert or otherwise, because in many cases it might be particularly invidious if she were to criticise the evidence of expert witness and give reasons why she rejected it.

It is hard to see why the sensitivities of expert witness should be given such protection. Even though non-expert witnesses are apparently to be given similar respect, this does not appear to accord with judicial practice. Justice is surely occluded if the weakness of a particular witness's evidence, which affected the judge's determination of the case, is not identified in the judgment. This need not be done harshly: it is relatively easy to use tactful and unhurtful language to accomplish the goal.

Expenses relating to plaintiff's disability   In *Jeffers v. Cahill*, High Court, May 21, 1996, Costello P. was called on to answer questions which one suspects he might not wish he had been asked to resolve in relation to the compensation of the plaintiff's damages. The plaintiff, a young woman, was seriously injured in a car accident. Among her several injuries, she lost the sight of one eye, and had a seriously disabling injury to her left thigh and knee, as well as a disability in her right foot. Her left lower limb was significantly shortened, though the medical evidence was to the effect that, while she was at the time of trial unable to bear any weight on that leg, bone grafting procedures had removed the difference in length between the two lower limbs.

An occupational therapy consultant prepared a report on the plaintiff's likely future needs, including extra equipment, support, housing and assistance. It estimated her loss under these headings at £346,397. This was completed at a time when the plaintiff's condition indicated that her future expenses 'would be close to those which a paraplegic might have met'. In the light of medical evidence not available to the consultant, Costello P. concluded that the expenses which the plaintiff would have to meet were 'much less' than those itemised in the report, because the level of her future disability would be much lower than could then have been predicted.

Costello P. noted also that:

> disabled plaintiffs are entitled to damages not only for future pain and suffering but also for loss of enjoyment of life resulting from the disability. Whilst expenses to meet the physical consequences of the disability can reasonably be ascertained and with some precision, this is not the case when considering what specific expenses may be incurred for the rest of the plaintiffs life to attempt to mitigate the loss of enjoyment of life the plaintiff as suffered from. Generally speaking, therefore, the damages are awarded under this heading as part of the figure for general damages to which a disabled plaintiff is entitled.

Accordingly, Costello P. was obliged to refuse compensation, under the heading of expenses, for the provision of an electrical wheelchair, photocromatic glasses, membership of the Automobile Association, a mobile phone, a personal alarm, a portable television and video recorder, extra jumpers and tapestry materials (with a capitalised assessed value of £11,800). As to the latter, Costello P thought it unlikely that the plaintiff would have much need for them as she was 'by nature an active and go ahead type of person.'

'CARER'-COSTS

The law relating to compensation for having to have a carer is easy to state in theory. If the plaintiff has been put to such an expense, has received such a service for which he or she has not yet paid or will in the future need such a service, it is a straightforward matter to put a value on the amount that is due.

When one moves into the area of personal relationships, notably marriage, the issue becomes far more difficult. It is a natural human instinct, where one spouse has been injured, for the other spouse to come to his or her aid. The work involved may involve hundreds of hours' hard labour, every year, at the most unsociable times. Society has only recently woken up to the intensity of these demands, which can of course arise not only in accident cases but also in relation to the development of particular physical or mental conditions, such as Alzheimer's Disease.

If the 'carer' spouse has appropriate qualifications, such as where he or she is a nurse, the question arises as to whether *any* compensation for the service should be awarded and, if so, *to whom*? In favour of no compensation, it could be asserted that such loyal commitment is part of the marriage undertaking to love one's spouse 'in sickness and in health'. Yet it may seem harsh to the plaintiff and his or her spouse that the wrongdoer should be entitled to benefit from the magnanimity of the 'carer' spouse.

If, therefore, compensation should be ordered, who should be the beneficiary? One's natural inclination might be in favour of the 'carer' spouse who provided the work now given a legal value. But if this is so, what is the juridical basis? The traditional action for loss of *servituim* and *consortium*, modernised by *McKinley v. Minister for Defence* [1992] 2 I.R. 333, would go some way towards providing that basis but in truth it would be necessary to subject it to a legislative recast, as proposed by the Law Reform Commission in its *Report on Family Law* (LRC No. 1-1981). Another strategy would be characterise the 'carer' spouse's action as one in negligence based on a duty to him or her as foreseeable plaintiff. If we consider that a spouse may recover damages as foreseeable rescuer (*Philips v. Durgan* [1991] I.L.R.M. 321), as foreseeable victim of 'nervous shock' relating to injuries inflicted on his or her spouse (*Kelly v. Hennessey* [1995] 3 I.R. 253; *Mullally v. Bus Éireann* [1992] I.L.R.M. 722), it seems entirely reasonable for a 'carer' spouse to proceed under the banner of negligence.

The other approach, now apparently the preference of the Irish courts, is to award the *plaintiff* compensation for the 'carer' spouse's work. On the face of it, this is quite misconceived, unless the plaintiff is impressed with a trust in favour of the 'carer' spouse; but why should such an elaborate legal fiction be created?

In *Donnelly v. Joyce* [1974] Q.B. 454, at 462, the English Court of Appeal sought to justify giving the plaintiff the compensation as follows:

> The plaintiff's loss . . . is not the expenditure of money to . . . pay for the
> nursing attention. His loss is the existence of the need for . . . those
> missing services, the value of which for the purposes of damages – for
> the purpose of ascertainment of the amount of his loss – is the proper
> and reasonable cost of supplying those needs. . . . So far as the defend-
> ant is concerned, the loss is not someone else's loss. It is the plaintiff's
> loss.

It must frankly be acknowledged that this rationale is not fully satisfactory.

The Irish courts have yet to provide an elaborate conceptual analysis of
the issue. Instead they usually simply award the compensation to the plaintiff, without comment, or, more rarely, to the 'carer' spouse, again without
comment.

In *Hughes v. O'Flaherty*, High Court, January 19, 1996, the plaintiff sustained devastating injuries in a car accident. His wife, a professionally qualified nurse, tended to his needs. Carney J. awarded the plaintiff £35,000 to
compensate him for this service, even though he was satisfied that payment
was not in the wife's mind when she devoted herself to nursing him. He 'balanced' her role as a professional in respect of which she was 'in the absence
of any express contractual agreement entitled to payment on a *quantum meruit*
basis' and 'her role as a loving and devoted wife in respect of which she is
not under our social and legal system entitled to payment? Carney J. rejected
a similar claim by the plaintiff's son, who took a year off work to mind his
father because he was 'acting primarily as a devoted son', without the professional qualification that his mother had.

In *Coppinger v. Waterford County Council*, High Court, March 22, 1996,
Geoghegan J., under the heading 'Care Costs' awarded the plaintiff £10,000
'past costs', as 'a reasonable sum to attribute to the therapeutic as distinct
from merely social effect of [his wife]'s visits to the hospital' where the plaintiff
was receiving treatment.

In *Smith v. Ireland*, High Court, August 16, 1996 Flood J. apparently
awarded *the wife* of the plaintiff over £15,000 for the nursing services she
had provided for her husband who was severely injured in an accident. It
does not seem from the judgment that this was a separate claim by the wife in
her own right.

GENERAL DAMAGES

The *Sinnott* test   In *Connolly v. Bus Éireann/Irish Bus*, High Court, January 29, 1996, where a teenage girl, injured in a road accident, received serious brain injuries which reduced her intellectual capacity and made her
incapable of managing her own affairs, Barr J. awarded her £200,000, repre-

senting the 'true value' of the cap of £150,000 set down by the Supreme Court over eleven years previously in *Sinnott v. Quinnsworth Ltd.* [1984] I.L.R.M. 523. He stated:

> The Supreme Court has not laid down in *Sinnott* that a cap on general damages of £150,000 (subject to adjustment in the light of changing monetary values) should be regarded as a pinnacle to be awarded only where the injuries and the consequences thereof are appallingly catastrophic as they were in that case. O'Higgins C.J. referred to such a cap for general damages 'in a case of this nature'. I interpret that phrase as meaning in all cases where major permanent personal injuries have been sustained which render the injured party dependent of others to maintain a viable way of life and where he/she has suffered a grievous permanent change in pre-accident capacity to lead a normal existence and to enjoy the normal range of pleasures in life which he/she might reasonably have expected to enjoy but for the injuries sustained. There is no doubt that Nicola's grievous permanent injuries put her within that category. It is now over eleven years since the *Sinnott* cap was fixed at £150,000. It seems to me that its true value now is £200,000.

This approach, interpreting the phrase 'in a case of this nature' as being of generic rather than ultra-specific import, is surely sensible. Another possible interpretation of O'Higgins C.J.'s observations is that the 'cap' should represent an artificial limit beyond which awards should not venture, without any requirement that a proportionate reduction be made with regard to injuries of a somewhat less devastating intensity. A parallel here is the statutory cap on damages for mental distress in wrongful death actions, where it is clear that the courts are not required to make proportionate reductions in cases where the distress is less than the worst that can be envisaged.

In *Coppinger v. Waterford County Council*, High Court, March 22, 1996, where the plaintiff sustained 'quite appalling' injuries, exacerbated by his full awareness of them, Geoghegan J. followed the approach favoured by Barr J. in *Connolly* and awarded £200,000 general damages (discounted substantially on account of the plaintiff's contributory negligence). The plaintiff suffered total paralysis of his right limbs and of his speech function. He was fed by means of gastrostomy tube. He was depressed and resentful of his condition for a very long period, though his family and friends detected a distinct improvement in his mental condition as time went by. (We discuss Geoghegan J.'s judgment in the claim of Mrs Coppinger for damages for loss of *consortium* resulting from the accident, earlier in this Chapter, above 600.)

Evidence on lack of awareness of injury In *Hughes v. O'Flaherty*, High

Court, January 19, 1996, a case involving tragic facts, Carney J. had to determine whether the plaintiff's lack of awareness of his injuries was such as to
require the court to reduce the compensation under the head of general damages to little or nothing. The Supreme Court has so ordained in *Cooke v.
Walsh* [1984] I.L.R.M. 208. In *Hughes* the plaintiff had suffered devastating
injuries in a traffic accident. These injuries included very severe damage to
the brain. Carney J., who visited the plaintiff at the National Rehabilitation
Centre, found that he had a general apprehension of his situation because he
volunteered the words that he was prepared to suffer if that was God's will
for him. Accordingly, the diminution principle did not apply. Carney J. awarded
£225,000 for general damages.

Increase in award *Forde v. Forde*, Supreme Court, May 20, 1996 was a
rare instance of the damages awarded at trial being increased on appeal.
Costello J. had awarded the plaintiff £15,000 general damages for the injuries he had sustained up to the trial and £15,000 for future loss. The Supreme
Court increased the award for general damages to £50,000. The plaintiff,
who had been badly bitten by a dog, had sustained facial injuries, including
an injury to his hip. On appeal, O'Flaherty J. (Barrington and Murphy JJ.
concurring) was satisfied that, taking the two figures of £15,000 up to and
after trial separately or adding them together, the total was "too low for the
case". In adopting this approach, he was adhering the requirement, expressed
by the Supreme Court in *Reddy v. Bates* [1984] I.L.R.M. 197 that the fact-
finder at trial and the Supreme Court on appeal should take a second look at
the global amount of the award in order to see whether it represents fair compensation. See McMahon & Binchy, *op. cit.*, 784-5. There is, of course, much
to be said for maintaining a sense of realism in the process of awarding damages, but one has to criticise an approach which would encourage or require
a court to bring in a verdict based on the principle that the whole may be less
or greater than its parts. It is sensible that the fact-finder, having confronted
the global sum, should review the constituent elements of the award, but it is
quite another thing that he or she should substitute an amount which 'feels'
proper where the constituent elements of the award do not present difficulties.

Multiple injuries In *Murphy v. Cork County Council*, Supreme Court,
November 18, 1996, (*ex tempore*), the Supreme Court, affirmed an awarded
£55,000 general damages by McCracken J. The plaintiff had sustained injuries to her next, leg, arm and lower back. These greatly disrupted her social
life and her ability to play badminton. In affirming the award O'Flaherty J.
(Barrington and Keane JJ. concurring) observed that:

the impression that a plaintiff and his or her witnesses make on the trial judge is critical. In those cases where there is not something palpable such as a loss of a limb or loss of the sight of an eye and so forth, when one is dealing with subjective matters, then one must rely on the trial judge and the cold pages of the transcript, not to speak of medical reports, are often a very poor substitute for what the trial judge has before him in the way of oral testimony.

In *Moran v. Murphy*, High Court, June 21, 1996, Flood J. awarded £20,000 general damages for injuries sustained before trial and a further £25,000 for future general damages where the plaintiff sustained injuries to his head, neck, shoulder, lumbar spine, elbow, wrist and hand, as well as suffering from a depressive reaction.

Transport

AIR TRANSPORT

Aerodrome standards   The Irish Aviation Authority (Aerodrome Standards) Order 1996 (SI No. 323 of 1996) requires that Irish aerodromes comply with the standards in Annexes 4 and 14 of the Chicago Convention referred to in the Irish Aviation Authority Act 1993 (1993 Review, 584-5).

Airworthiness of aircraft   The Irish Aviation Authority (Airworthiness of Aircraft) Order 1996 (SI No. 324 of 1996) revises and replaces the Air Navigation (Airworthiness of Aircraft) Order 1964, with effect from March 1, 1997. It lays down detailed maintenance standards required in order to have an aircraft certified as being airworthy in accordance with the Irish Aviation Authority Act 1993 (1993 Review, 584-5).

Nationality of aircraft   The Irish Aviation Authority (Nationality and Registration Of Aircraft) Order 1996 (SI No. 322 of 1996), also made under the Irish Aviation Authority Act 1993 (1993 Review, 584-5), revoked and replaced the Air Navigation (Nationality and Registration of Aircraft) Order 1963. It also took account of changes effect by the Chicago Convention and came into effect on March 1, 1997.

Air navigation: fees   The Air Navigation (Fees) (Amendment) Order 1996 (SI No. 49 of 1996) amended the Air Navigation (Fees) Order 1995 (1995 Review, 547) by providing for the remission or reduction of fees where the Irish Aviation Authority is satisfied it is reasonable to do so.

Air navigation: personnel licensing   The Air Navigation (Personnel Licensing) (Amendment) Order 1996 (SI No. 50 of 1996) and the Air Navigation (Personnel Licensing) (Amendment) (No. 2) Order 1996 (SI No. 321 of 1996) amended the Air Navigation (Personnel Licensing) Order 1966 by clarifying the technical requirements for the grant and renewal of various licences described in the Order, for logging and crediting flight time, abolishing the senior commercial pilot licence, adding certain definitions in respect of avionics equipment and including references to the Chicago Convention. SI No. 50 of 1996 also revoked the Air Navigation (Personnel Licensing) (Amendment) Order 1995 (1995 Review, 547).

Air traffic management and air-navigation equipment The European Communities (Air Traffic Management Equipment and Systems) (Standards) Regulations 1996 (SI No. 221 of 1996) gave effect to Directive 93/65/EEC and provide that the Eurocontrol standards shall be specified in any contract for the purchase of air traffic management equipment and systems and air-navigation equipment. The came into effect on July 18, 1996.

Warsaw Convention: liability of air carrier In *Burke v. Aer Lingus plc.* [1997] 1 I.L.R.M. 148 (H.C.), the plaintiff had arrived in Dublin airport in August 1989 as a passenger on board a flight operated by the defendant. A shuttle bus was provided by the defendant to convey the passengers to the airport terminal. The plaintiff claimed that she suffered personal injuries during the shuttle bus journey when the bus braked suddenly and that this was due to the defendant's negligence and breach of duty. Proceedings were commenced in December 1991. The defendant submitted, *inter alia,* that the plaintiff's proceedings were barred by virtue of the Air Navigation and Transport Act 1936, which incorporated the Warsaw Convention into Irish law by the 1936 Act, as the action had been commenced more than two years after the date of arrival of the flight in question. The plaintiff argued that her action was not statute barred since it did not fall within the Warsaw Convention, so that the three year limitation period for personal injuries actions applied. The question for the High Court was whether the accident on the shuttle bus was within the ambit of Article 17 of the Warsaw Convention, which provides that the carrier is liable for damage sustained in the event of bodily injury suffered by a passenger if the accident which caused the damage took place on board the aircraft 'or in the course of any of the operations of embarking or disembarking.' Article 29(1) provides that the right to damages shall be barred if an action is not brought within two years from the date of arrival at the destination. Barr J held that the shuttle bus journey fell within Article 29. He referred to the extensive case law on Article 29 and quoted a number of lengthy extracts from the leading text, Shawcross and Beaumont on *Air Law*, 4th ed, Chapter VII. These included *Ricotta v. Iberia Lineas Areas de Espana* (1979) 15 Avi. Cas. 17, *Adatia v. Air Canada* (1992) 2 S. & B. Av. R. VII/63 and *McCarthy v. Northwest Airlines Inc.* (1995) 25 Avi. Cas. 17. Having reviewed these, he considered that the use of the phrase 'any of the operations of embarking or disembarking' in Article 17 of the Convention suggested that it was not confined solely to the act of embarking or disembarking from an aircraft, but that it had a wider meaning, including some activity by the passenger prior to entering or after leaving the aircraft. He concluded that, where airline passengers were discharged from the aircraft at a significant distance from the terminal building and it was necessary to convey them by bus to the terminal, the bus ride across the apron, or from some other point within the airport was part of the passenger's journey to the destination. While using the shuttle bus the passenger remained in the exclusive control of the airline or its agent as the passenger was while on board the aircraft, and the bus ride was an air-related risk having regard to the nature and purpose of that part of the airport where it took place. accordingly, the plaintiff's claim was dismissed on the ground that it was statute-barred.

MARITIME TRANSPORT

Liability Conventions The Merchant Shipping (Liability of Shipowners and Others) Act 1996 was enacted with a view to implementing in Irish law a number of international Conventions which provide for the extent of liability of shipowners and carriers. The Act will give effect to: the London Convention on Limitation of Liability for Maritime Claims (1976); the Athens Convention Relating to the Carriage of Passengers and their Luggage by Sea (1974) as amended by the London Protocol thereto (1976); the Brussels International Convention for the Unification of Certain Rules of Law Relating to Bills of Lading (1924), as amended by the 1968 and 1979 Protocols thereto. The Act consolidates and updates previous legislation in this area. These will be repealed when the 1996 Act comes into effect. At the time of writing (July 1997), the necessary Commencement Order had not been made. The 1996 Act should be seen in the context of other legislation which implements international transport obligations, such as those dealing with air, road and rail transport. In particular, in the context of the limitation of liability provided for under such legislation, it is to be noted that 'domestic' legislation on limitation for supply of services contracts, such the Sale of Goods and Supply of Services Act 1980 and the European Communities (Unfair Terms in Consumer Contracts) Regulations 1995 (1995 Review, 40) provide that they do not extend to these transport-related contracts.

London Convention on Limitation of Liability Part II of the Act (ss.6 to 17) concern the London Convention on Limitation of Liability for Maritime Claims 1976. Section 10 provides for the right to limit liability under the Convention to extend to non-seagoing ships. Section 11 provides for the non-application of the right to limit liability to claims in respect of the raising, removal, destruction or the rendering harmless of a ship which is sunk, wrecked, stranded or abandoned. Section 12 provides for the definition 'nuclear ship' to include non-nuclear powered ships carrying nuclear material. Section13 provides for the conversion of the limits of liability specified in Articles 6 and 7 of the Convention into the currency of the State.

Athens Convention on Passengers and Luggage Part III of the Act (sections18 to 29) concern the Athens Convention on Carriage of Passengers and their Luggage by Sea (1974). Section 21 provides for the mandatory application in the State of those parts of the Convention relating to carriage by sea which do not have force of mandatory application in the Convention itself in certain cases. Section 22 provides that in the application of Article 6 of the Convention reference to the law of the court shall be construed as a reference to the Civil Liability Act 1961. Section 23 provides for the Minister for the Marine by Order to increase, in relation to a carrier whose principal place of business is in the State, the limit of liability specified in the Convention. Section 24 provides for the conversion of the amount of damages that may be awarded pursuant to the Convention into the currency of the State. Section 26 provides for exclusion of contracts of carriage which are not for reward from the provisions of the Convention. Section 28 provides for an action for damages under the Convention to be deemed to be an action founded on tort.

International Convention on Bills of Lading Part IV of the Act (sections 30 to 37) concern the Brussels International Convention for the Unification of Certain Rules of Law Relating to Bills of Lading. Section 33 provides for application of the Convention Rules in respect of bills of lading. Section 34 provides for the application of the Rules where the port of shipment is a port in the State, whether or not the Convention provides for their application. Section 35 provides that an absolute warranty of seaworthiness is not to be implied in contracts to which the Rules apply. Section 36 provides for the conversion of limits of liability into the currency of the State. Finally, s.38 provides for exclusion of liability in certain cases.

RAIL TRANSPORT

Access to infrastructure The European Communities (Access to Railway Infrastructure) Regulations 1996 (SI No. 204 of 1996) gave effect to Articles 2 and 10 of Directive 91/440/EEC. They set out the conditions under which international groupings and railway undertakings shall be granted access to Ireland's railway infrastructure for the purposes of operating international services, including combined transport services. The provision of solely urban, suburban or regional services are excluded. The Regulations came into effect on July 1, 1996.

Dublin light rail system The Transport (Dublin Light Rail) Act 1996 is an enabling Act intended to empower the Minister for Transport, Energy and Communications to authorise by Order the construction, operation and maintenance by Córas Iompair Éireann, the State transport company, of a light railway system serving the Greater Dublin Area. The provisional title for the light rail system is Luas. Section 3 of the Act provides that CIE may apply to the Minister for a Light Railway Order and specifies the documentation to accompany such application, including a draft of the Order, a plan of the proposed light rail works, a book of reference to the plan and an environmental impact statement. Section 4 provides that the carrying out of works authorised by the Minister by Order consisting of the construction, maintenance, improvement or repair of a light railway shall be exempted development for the purposes of the Local Government (Planning and Development) Acts 1963 to 1992. Section 8 provides that there must be a public inquiry into the application for a Light Railway Order. It also provides for the appointment of an Inspector after consultation with An Bord Pleanála, the Planning Board, to hold the inquiry and for the appointment of a person or persons to act as assessor(s) to assist the Inspector in carrying out his/her functions under the Act. Section 9 provides, *inter alia*, that if the Minister is of the opinion that the application for an Order should be granted that the Minister will make an Order authorising the construction, maintenance and improvement of the light railway, the use of the works authorised by the Order for the purposes of the operation of a light railway and the operation, maintenance and improvement of a light railway, subject to such conditions and restrictions as he or she thinks proper and specifies in the Order.

The Act also contains various other incidental and supplemental provisions. Thus, section 19 provides that trespass on a light railway or on any land, machinery or equipment used for purposes of a light railway will be an offence and, while section 24 provides that CIE may make bye-laws for the management, control, operation and regulation of a light railway. Under both sections, a person who is in breach will be guilty of an offence and liable to a fine not exceeding £1,500 and/or imprisonment for a term not exceeding six months. Section 26 of the 1996 Act generally applies the Railways Acts 1840 to 1889 and any other Act relating to railways, to any light railway under the Act.

It was estimated during the debate on the Act in the Oireachtas that the financial costs associated with the consultancy and inquiry costs associated with the light rail project would be in the region of £500,000 per annum for 1997 and 1998. The costs of actual construction of the light rail project authorised under the Act would be met from a combination of national and European Union funds (largely the latter). The urgency in the process was underlined by the need to secure EU funding, and a starting date of 1999 for the construction itself was mentioned during the Act's passage. While it appears that some light rail project will proceed, its exact extent remained unclear at the time of writing (July 1997).

ROAD TRANSPORT

Carriage of dangerous substances The Dangerous Substances (Conveyance of Scheduled Substances by Road) (Trade Or Business) (Amendment) Regulations 1996 (SI No. 389 of 1996), made under the Dangerous Substances Act 1972, further amended the Dangerous Substances (Conveyance of Scheduled Substances by Road) (Trade or Business) Regulations 1980 in order to take into account amendments to the European Agreement Concerning the International Carriage of Dangerous Goods By Road, the ADR Agreement. The Dangerous Substances Act 1972 (Part IV Declaration) Order 1996 (SI No. 387 of 1996) declared certain classes of goods to be dangerous substances for the purposes of the 1972 Act and replaced the list contained in the Dangerous Substances Act 1972 (Part IV Declaration) Order 1986, which was revoked. The Dangerous Substances (European Agreement Concerning the International Carriage of Dangerous Goods By Road (ADR)) Regulations 1996 (SI No. 388 of 1996) provide that in any proceedings under the Dangerous Substances Act 1972, the ADR Agreement may be proved by producing a copy of the Agreement and revoked the Dangerous Substances (European Agreement Concerning the International Carriage of Dangerous Goods By Road (ADR)) Regulations 1986. All three statutory instruments came into effect on 19 December 1996. The Dangerous Substances (Conveyance of Petroleum by Road) (Amendment) Regulations 1996 (SI No. 386 of 1996), also made under the Dangerous Substances Act 1972, amended the Dangerous Substances (Conveyance of Petroleum by Road) Regulations 1979 in order to introduce an amended form of examination of tankers for a leakproofness test.

Construction Standards The European Communities (Motor Vehicles Type Approval) Regulations 1996 (SI No. 314 of 1996), which came into effect on October 22, 1996, further amended the European Communities (Motor Vehicles Type Approval) Regulations 1978 to take account of a number of Directives, all of which lay down technical specifications for the construction of motor vehicles. The 1996 Regulations now contain the most updated listing of the Directives to which manufacturers must comply. The result is that the list of Directives in the European Communities (Motor Vehicles Type Approval) (Amendment) Regulations 1995 (1995 Review, 550) became obsolete.

Emission levels The European Communities (Mechanically Propelled Vehicle Emission Control) Regulations 1996 (SI No. 318 of 1996) prohibit the issue of first licences for certain new vehicles from January 1, 1997, unless they comply with the air pollutant emission control requirements specified in Directive 96/1/EC. Certain limited exemptions are specified for end of series vehicles as well as penalties for non-compliance. The Regulations came into effect on 23 October 1996. The European Communities (Mechanically Propelled Vehicle Emission Control) (Amendment) Regulations 1996 (SI No. 382 of 1996) amended the European Communities (Mechanically Propelled Vehicle Emission Control) Regulations 1995 (1995 Review, 441) by altering the transitional arrangements for establishing compliance with Directive 94/12/EC.

Hackney licences: statutory restrictions   In *Mintola Ltd. and Ors. v. Minister for the Environment and Ors.*, High Court, April 18, 1996, Costello P. rejected a claim that the Road Traffic (Public Service Vehicles) Regulations 1963 and the Road Traffic (Public Service Vehicles) (Amendment) Regulations 1983 were *ultra vires* the Road Traffic Act 1961. The plaintiff companies held hackney cab licences. They applied for an interlocutory injunction in an action in which they claimed that the 1963 and 1983 Regulations were *ultra vires* the powers of the Minister. The impugned Regulations concerned the use of radio and telephonic equipment in the hackney vehicles in taximeter areas, and the use of advertising signs on hackney vehicles. The effect of the 1983 Regulations was that a hiring for a hackney vehicle could not be initiated or facilitated by means of a radio or telephone communication while the vehicle was in a public place. Section 82 of the 1961 Act empowered the Minister to make Regulations for the control and operation of public service vehicles, including the conditions subject to which vehicles may be operated as public service vehicles. The Wireless Telegraphy Act 1926 provided that a licence was required for an apparatus for wireless telegraphy. The plaintiffs had obtained licences under the 1926 Act making it lawful for them to have radios in their vehicles. They contended that the 1963 and 1983 Regulations amounted to an amendment of the 1926 Act and the licences granted under it. As indicated, Costello P refused the interlocutory relief sought, and also cast grave doubt over the substantive action.

He held that it was quite clear that since the 1963 and 1983 Regulations laid down conditions for the use of hackney vehicles, *prima facie* they were *intra vires*. What was therefore to be considered was whether there were other factors which established invalidity. Costello P. was satisfied that the Minister had not amended the 1926 Act; rather the Regulations had restricted the use of radios which were lawfully in the possession of the plaintiffs and in that respect the plaintiffs had not raised a fair issue for trial at the hearing of the action. Neither did he consider that the suggestion that the 1983 Regulations were arbitrary, unjust or illogical and as such *ultra vires* had been made out. The plaintiffs' objections that their financial interests were affected by the operation of the 1963 and 1983 Regulations was very different from establishing invalidity on the ground of injustice.

International carriage of goods: Czech Republic The Road Transport (International Carriage Of Goods By Road) Order 1996 (SI No. 52 of 1996), made under the Road Transport Act 1971, allows the Czech transport authorities to issue permits on the State's behalf for access by Czech hauliers to Ireland. Correspondingly, the Road Transport Act 1978 (Section 5) Order 1996 (SI No. 53 of 1996), made under the Road Transport Act 1978, exempts certain types of road transport operations performed in Ireland by Czech hauliers from the requirements to be authorised by permit. Both Orders came into effect on February 16, 1996.

Licensing: photograph In *Coughlan v. Dublin Corporation*, Supreme Court, March 28, 1996, the Supreme Court confirmed that an applicant for a driving licence must provide a photograph with such application. The applicant had submitted photocopies of his photograph with his application to renew his licence, stating that he had particular difficulty with the flash when his photograph was taken. The application was rejected by the respondent Corporation on the basis that an original photograph was required under the Road Traffic (Licensing of Drivers) Regulations 1989. The applicant sought an order of *mandamus* directing the Council to grant him a licence. The High Court refused the relief sought and this was upheld by the Supreme Court. The Court noted that the stipulation as to photographs was a mandatory requirement under the 1989 Regulations; it also pointed out that the applicant could have his photograph taken in the open air without a flash. Finally, the Court noted that since the remedies of *mandamus* and *certiorari* were discretionary, there was no case in law or on the facts requiring the High Court to engage in such an enquiry. These latter comments must, of course, be read subject to the well-established case law, including *The State (Vozza) v. Ó Floinn* [1957] I.R. 227, that in certain circumstances *certiorari* will issue *ex debito justitiae*. Clearly, the Court felt that the instant case did not come within this category.

Licensing: provisional licence The Road Traffic (Licensing of Drivers) (Amendment) Regulations 1996 (SI No. 328 of 1996), made under the Road Traffic Act 1961, amended the Road Traffic (Licensing of Drivers) Regulations 1989 to provide that a person who fails to comply with the requirement to undergo a driving test in order to obtain a third or subsequent provisional driving licence may be issued with a provisional licence which will be valid for one year only and that, if a driving test is not undertaken within that year, no further licence will be issued.

Local authority: duty to maintain roads In *Brady v. Cavan County Council* [1997] 1 I.L.R.M. 390 (H.C.), Carroll J. granted the applicants an order of *mandamus* to compel the respondent local authority comply with its statutory duty under section 13 of the Roads Act 1993 (1993 Review, 588-9): see the discussion of the case in the Local Government chapter, 465, above.

'On-the-spot' offences   The Road Traffic Act 1961 (Section 103) (Offences) Regulations 1996 (SI No. 319 of 1996) list those road traffic offences to which section 103 of the Road Traffic Act 1961 applies, which provides for 'on-the-spot' fines to be imposed for certain offences, for example parking a vehicle in a prohibited area such as a clearway. The Regulations also prescribe the form of notice to be affixed to vehicles, to be given to persons alleging offences to have been committed and the amount of the 'on-the-spot' fine which a person may pay as an alternative to the institution of a prosecution. The 1996 Regulations, which came into effect on December 1, 1996, revoked and replaced the Road Traffic Act 1961 (Section 103) (Offences) Regulations 1995 (1995 Review, 552).

Testing centre appointment   In *Navan Tanker Services Ltd. v. Meath County Council*, High Court, December 13, 1996, Carroll J. granted the applicant judicial review of the respondent Council's refusal to be appointed as an authorised tester of vehicles pursuant to the European Communities (Vehicle Testing) Regulations 1991 (1991 Review, 464). The Council refused the application 'having regard to the small number of goods vehicles in the County and to the presence of the existing test centres which are of relative convenience for vehicle owners.' The manager of the applicant gave evidence that he had been told by an official of the Council in 1993 that one licence as a vehicle tester was still available and that, with the encouragement and advise of the official, it had invested £50,000 in adapting its premises for use as a vehicle testing centre. The Council referred to Guidelines issued in 1992 by the Department of the Environment stating that issuing authorities 'should bear in mind the consequences of appointing too many testers – individual testers have greater difficulty recovering their outlay on test equipment, test standards tend to slip as testers compete for business and a greater burden of supervision falls on both the authority and the department.' The Guidelines also stated that issuing authorities should strike a balance between the numbers appointed, equity between applicants and the relative convenience of locations for vehicle owners. There were five vehicle testing centres in County Meath, that four of these had objected to the appointment of the applicant but that this had not been disclosed to the applicant.

She referred with approval to the decision of Murphy J. in *Jennings Truck Centre (Tullamore) Ltd. v. Offaly County Council*, High Court, June 14, 1990 (1992 Review, 631), in which he had held that the provisions of the European Communities (Vehicle Testing) Regulations 1983, which had preceded the 1991 Regulations, and under which a local authority 'may' appoint authorised testers, clearly imposed a discretion on the local authority. Carroll J. accepted that the use of the word 'may' in Article 5 of the 1991 Regulations also conferred a discretion on the Council to refuse to appoint a vehicle tester even where the applicant had complied with the requirements set out in Article 5. She went on to state that the object of Directives 77/143/EEC and 88/449/ EEC (implemented by the 1983 and 1991 Regulations, respectively) was to provide for an adequate number of test centres which could be supervised by the State. In this context, she stated that it was reasonable to consider all the matters set out in the Department of Environment Guidelines in deciding whether to make an appointment Accordingly, the number of test centres was a matter which it was proper to consider in deciding whether to make an appointment and was *intra vires* the residual discretion conferred by Article 5.1 of the 1991 Regulations.

Nonetheless, Carroll J. held that the Council had been in breach of natural justice in refusing the applicant' application on the grounds that there were sufficient vehicle testing centres when the applicant had not been informed that this was a matter which would be taken into account in considering its application. As a result the applicant had been deprived of an opportunity to make submissions on this issue. Referring to the decision in *Tara Prospecting Ltd. v. Minister for Energy* [1993] I.L.R.M. 771 (1993 Review, 23-5), she also considered that the applicant had a legitimate expectation that it would be treated fairly and, in particular, would be heard on the issue of the sufficiency of the existing vehicle testing centres before the Council refused its application.

Vehicle side guards The Road Traffic (Construction, Equipment and Use of Vehicles) (Amendment) Regulations 1996 (SI No. 26 of 1996) provide that the area to be protected by side guards on goods vehicles and trailers with extendible chassis is to be determined when the chassis is at its minimum length. The Regulations came into effect on February 5, 1996.

Vehicle height limit The Road Traffic (Construction, Equipment and Use of Vehicles) (Amendment) (No. 2) Regulations 1996 (SI No. 27 of 1996) made under the Road Traffic Act 1961 extended by five years the transitional period for older vehicles and trailers to comply with the maximum height limit laid down under the principal Regulations of 1978. They came into effect on February 5, 1996.

Vehicle lighting The Road Traffic (Lighting Of Vehicles) (Amendment) Regulations 1996 (SI No. 137 of 1996) consolidated provisions in relation to the use of flashing blue or amber warning lights on certain emergency vehicles. They complement the provisions of the Road Traffic (Construction, Equipment and Use of Vehicles) (Amendment) (No. 3) Regulations 1996 (SI No. 138 of 1996), which also consolidate the provisions in relation to the use of sirens on such vehicles. Both Regulations came into effect on May 23, 1996.

Vehicle weight   The Road Traffic (Construction, Equipment and use of Vehicles) (Amendment) (No. 4) Regulations 1996 (SI No. 139 of 1996) allow for the use of vehicles not exceeding 4,000 tonnes laden weight on certain journeys to and from the State. They came into effect on May 23, 1996.

Index